Global Dawn

Global Dawn

THE CULTURAL FOUNDATION OF
AMERICAN INTERNATIONALISM,
1865–1890

Frank Ninkovich

HARVARD UNIVERSITY PRESS

Cambridge, Massachusetts, and London, England · 2009

Library of Congress Cataloging-in-Publication Data

Ninkovich, Frank A., 1944–
    Global dawn : the cultural foundation of American internationalism, 1865–1890 /
Frank Ninkovich.
        p. cm.
    Includes bibliographical references and index.
    ISBN 978-0-674-03504-1
    1. United States—Foreign relations—1865–1898. 2. Internationalism—History—
19th century. 3. United States—Civilization—1865–1918. 4. National characteristics,
American—History—19th century. 5. United States—Race relations—History—
19th century. I. Title.
E661.7.N56 2009
973.7—dc22   2008054851

To Marina and Francesca

Contents

Acknowledgments

I would like to thank various individuals who have helped me along the way. As always, my wife, Carol, has tolerated my idiosyncratic work habits and provided quiet encouragement. The graduate colloquium in history at Ohio State University allowed me to present some very preliminary ideas and research, while the faculty seminar of Dalhousie University provided a stimulating group interrogation of an early draft of Chapter 1. Kathleen Burk of University College, London, generously allowed me to read her draft chapter on Anglo-American relations in the late nineteenth century. Dolores Augustine of St. John's University read and painstakingly corrected Chapters 5 and 6 while alerting me to the different ways in which race and social Darwinism were construed in Europe. Michael Latham of Fordham University was kind enough to read the entire manuscript and to provide a detailed and quite useful critique. Anders Stephanson of Columbia University also read the piece, even though I informed him that I was interested chiefly in disqualifying him from becoming a postpublication reviewer. David Ekbladh of Tufts University helpfully brought his knowledge of modernization and foreign relations to bear in his reading of the manuscript. Akira Iriye and Ernest May provided early thematic inspiration and, later on, some timely assistance. I am especially grateful to Kathleen McDermott, senior editor at Harvard University Press, for sticking with the manuscript through some tough times. My appreciation also extends to the anonymous readers whose evaluations—some favorable, some not—forced me to sharpen my views and saved me from some blunders. Special thanks go to my copy editor, Betty Pessagno, for doing what I should have done, only much better. Still, errors are bound to occur, responsibility for which rests on my shoulders alone.

The book is dedicated to my granddaughters and next-door neighbors, the best arguments that I know of for the extended family.

Global Dawn

Introduction

Culture and Causality

This is a book about Gilded Age America's understanding of the world. At first glance, this topic would seem better suited to the internationalist twentieth century than to an era celebrated for its isolationist temper, but it is my belief that the post–Civil War years hold answers to some important questions about the course of history in the twentieth century and beyond. I am not alone in finding enduring significance in the more distant past. Charles Taylor, for example, has pointed out in a notable work that the modern sensibility was formed in the high Victorian years of the nineteenth century. "We still instinctively reach for the old vocabularies, the ones we owe to Enlightenment and Romanticism," he writes. "What is remarkable is that the basic moral and political standards by which we congratulate ourselves were themselves powerful in the last century."[1] Although Taylor had other concerns in mind, his argument about the lasting influence of nineteenth-century mindsets also applies to the way that Americans think about foreign relations. For it was during these years that many Americans came to picture their country as existing within a global economic, political, and cultural environment, and it was at this time that the cultural foundation was laid for America's turn to empire and world power.

But what do I mean by "cultural foundation"? Culture is a contentious word whose mere mention, according to the apocryphal tale, prompted Hermann Göring to reach for his pistol.[2] More plausible, if only a little, is the story of the scholar who reportedly reaches for his dictionary upon hearing its mention.[3] My own inclination, if I owned a gun, would be to shoot the dictionary. Over the years, I have become more and more skeptical of the anthropological meaning(s) of culture, to the point that I wonder whether it exists at all except as a term that stands for ensembles of behaviors that can be called, in shorthand, a "culture."[4] I am in good company, apparently, judging by the many anthropologists who have long been puzzled, tortured even, by the idea of culture.[5] Given their notorious inability to agree upon their discipline's foundational concept, I am not sure what, exactly, cultural anthropologists have to offer to historians of foreign relations. Consequently, although this study is about culture, it does not rely on any established anthropological idiom.

It had occurred to me to describe this book as being about an ideology that was establishing itself in American culture, and it may well be possible to view its subject-matter from this interpretive angle. But if one defines a political ideology as an organized collection of ideas, normative and descriptive, that also includes a felt necessity for purposive action, the liberal internationalism of the late nineteenth century, with its one-sided emphasis on globalizing processes, suffered from a combination of conceptual and practical immaturity that made it pre-ideological. Its views on world politics, though often quite acute, were politically undeveloped, embryonic, a diffuse nebula of ideas swirling about in the larger culture that had yet to collapse into the stellar plasma of ideology. Its economic and cultural concepts, though somewhat more advanced, also suffered from the lack of a coherent political framework that could be applied to global conditions. Even if the ideas had been more fully formed, they lacked the political weight needed to put them into effect. Thus, even though the volcano that was the international system was already starting to rumble, neither the political consequences of its eruption nor an appropriate course of action was clear at the time. For the time being, anxious hand-wringing would have to do.

Apart from finding ideology a poor fit, I had some positive reasons for choosing to frame this work as an exercise in cultural history, the most obvious being that it does look at culture in a number of ways. At bottom, it is based on a reading of nineteenth-century American magazines whose content reflected a "high culture" shared by a relatively small group of people—the educated middle and upper classes—whose ideas as writers and readers are the focus of the book. As we shall see, these journals were amazingly broad in their intellectual scope and ambitious in the kinds of subject matter that they tackled. Indeed, they dealt with an incongruous mixture of subject matter that would seem strange to contemporary readers. They were tuned to a fairly high pitch of intelligence, in contrast to which many of today's most successful and best-known magazines are mass market publications aimed at a less demanding public. The quality of thought on display in these journals was high enough that, had the nation chosen to abandon isolationism and become a world power in, say, 1880, it would have been able to tap the social intelligence of a cosmopolitan group that commanded the knowledge needed to manage a widely expanded agenda of foreign affairs.

Some of the issues and views that I follow have been associated with a small group of liberal republicans known as "Mugwumps," but because my intellectual stage and cast of characters are much larger, this study should not be confused with intellectual history.[6] While intellectual history can provide in-depth coverage of seminal thinkers, the trade-off for this focus on individuals entails a sacrifice of cultural breadth. Besides covering a broader range of themes, I would hope that my approach has some depth of its own to offer, without doing violence to the journalistic context from which the ideas were lifted. It is in any case not an either/or question of depth versus breadth, for the pattern of ideas covered herein itself constituted a discursive network of no little complexity.

Exactly how many people made up this web of writers and readers is unknown, but available circulation figures make clear that it counted for only a modest fraction of the American population.[7] The body of opinion represented by this group was not cultural in a holistic sense, for it constituted only one segment of a larger culture. Nor was it culturally hegemonic.[8] But one justification for looking at this relatively small number of people is that foreign affairs in the United States have always been shaped by elites, and if we want to look for the sources of thinking on important international issues it is usually among the elites that we will find them. Besides, prior to the twentieth century, it was people of the type found in this study, and not America's diplomats, who were the chief repositories of knowledge about the world.[9]

The thematic content of their ideas was also cultural. As the text should make clear, they were fully alive to the importance of mass culture, to problems having to do with the shaping of cultural values, and to the historical centrality of intercultural relations. In pondering the mysteries of the modern era, liberals turned to culture—which also happens to be "the central conservative truth"[10]—as the key to explaining progress toward civilization, or lack thereof, in societies at every level of development (including their own). In their view, international relations were grounded in contacts between peoples and societies, not between states, and the most promising development of international relations was the emergence of what today is called, rather mis-leadingly, a global culture. Cultural metamorphoses that resulted from eco-nomic and intellectual contacts with outside societies were believed to be even more consequential in the long run than changes produced by politics and war.

    This does not mean that power was at odds with culture or that global pro-cesses were independent of the political and military practices of states—far from it, for in their view power could, on occasion, be both positive and nec-essary. The intimate connection between power and culture was most clearly evident in relations with nonindustrial peoples, in which power was to cul-tural relations what corporal punishment was to education. To those on the receiving end, the use of force was a reminder to pay attention, a notification that there were things that one couldn't get away with, and a powerful in-ducement to learning from one's teacher. In other words, it was a necessary means to the tutelary end of deracination, even though it was understood that the resort to such harsh means could well compromise that end. In contrast, in relations between developed nations, the resort to force as the *ultima ratio* was thought to be a highly dangerous cultural pathology. But here, too, cul-tural development—that is, the evolution of more mature civil societies with democratic forms—was seen as the royal road to progressive historical change. Although power could be beneficially necessary or historically harmful, "hard" power alone could never transform the world. From a long-term perspective, ideas about cultural relations and cultural transformation were foundational to how Americans conceived of their nation's global role.[11]

    Although these ideas were a minority crosscurrent of the cultural main-stream during the years covered in this work, they made themselves felt in the political debates of the day by wielding political influence at times on various issues and by serving as a counterpoint to opposing viewpoints, if only as an intellectual anvil upon which political elites could hammer out their posi-tions. This surprisingly rich body of internationalist thought is worthy of in-terest in its own right and because in many ways it prefigured the globalist thinking of the twentieth century. However, its larger significance has to do with its effect on the future, for nineteenth-century liberal internationalists were carriers of a living body of ideas that would, over time, evolve and flour-ish in the larger culture and take political form in American globalism. Those ideas and the policies that they made possible, I would submit, offer deeper insights into the history of U.S. foreign relations than accounts that seek to portray that history as a tale of commercial acquisitiveness and empire or, alternatively, as a story of exceptionalism run amok.

The long-term impact of these ideas brings me back to my opening point about culture as foundation, for in addition to the cultural elements just enumerated, this book makes a case for culture as an essential element of historical explanation. Of late, more and more diplomatic historians have begun to investigate cultural themes in the history of U.S. foreign relations, and I happily count myself among their number. Sad to say, however, despite an efflorescence of innovative work on cultural themes, little progress has been made in relating this work to power and causality, which remain the chief concerns of traditional diplomatic history. Doubters have understandably been heard to wonder: What good is a cultural approach to history if it deals only in meaning and not in cause-and-effect relationships, that is, in the kinds of explanations offered by science? The culture concept, groused one critic, "has about as much concrete definition as a snowflake in June." Judged by a rigorous explanatory standard, the skeptics are saying, culture is of little interest because it has nothing substantial to contribute to our understanding. Not only is its importance disparaged, the cultural approach is also considered to be dangerous and thus unworthy of toleration, since the admission of culture into the club of intellectual respectability runs the risk of unleashing a potentially lethal contagion among diplomatic historians. If enough scholars were convinced that culture truly did matter, the fear is that the widespread acceptance of the postmodernist insistence on treating the past as a text could well lead to a disciplinary sex-change in which history, a form of knowledge that once prided itself on its connection to the sciences, became a mere branch of literary studies.[12]

The standard comeback to this kind of objection is that cultural meaning is itself a part of the historical record because history is populated by people for whom the world is meaningful. This world of meaning is most commonly accessed through texts that can best be understood by using the interpretive and analytical tools developed by disciplines devoted to textual studies. This is only another way of saying that history is, of necessity, a humanistic discipline—at least in part. This kind of defense is nothing to be ashamed about, for it is based on how things are, but it does not try to turn the tables on the tough-minded by pointing out some cognitive embarrassments that befell science, the gold standard of explanation, over the course of the twentieth century. Although knowledge compounded at an astounding rate during this period, it was also a time in which more and more scientists came to believe in indeterminacy, randomness, and discontinuity, in the inherent incompleteness of modes of explanation, and in the fundamental inability of human beings to explain reality in ways that transcend the terms of their experience. *Tu quoque.*

These are valid arguments, but to insist on placing culture side by side with what appears at first sight to be an incompatible, if not hostile, mode of explanation is uncomfortably akin to a shotgun marriage that promises to satisfy neither partner. The fact remains that historians of foreign relations tend to handle culture and power discretely and often in mutually exclusive ways. Is it conceivable, then, to arrange nuptials that do not require a surrender of individuality or a demand for subordination? If love is not a prerequisite, the answer is yes. Convenience could substitute for affection as the decisive consideration, leaving open the possibility of an arranged match in which love might emerge over time. Stranger things have happened. If physicists have come to reject thinking about matter, energy, space, and time as unrelated phenomena, why not at least allow for the possibility of important connections between culture and causality? Making a go of that kind of discordant marriage would substantially help overcome the incompleteness of explanation that comes when each party leads the single life.

What makes such a union possible is the powerful common bond that transforms members of each clan into historians: all rely on the same standards of gathering and presenting evidence. The very idea of evidence raises the question of what kinds of data are sufficient to present a credible historical explanation in any particular instance, but this question cannot be answered in advance. There is no way of effecting this kind of reconciliation simply by doing theory because, for most practitioners, the problem does not exist at that level and can only be solved in practice.[13] As long as the data are collected and presented in a professionally acceptable manner, the possibility remains that we will find new information with a practical bearing on our understanding of events whose importance would not have been apparent beforehand. In the chapters that follow, I shall use the canons of evidence devised by our profession (for that is the way we manage to continue talking

with one another) to make my case. If I do my job, it should become plain
how culture mattered. In essence, then, this study is empirical, an attempt to
harvest grapes that, for one reason or another, other toilers in the vineyard
have not yet seen fit to pick. It is a late harvest, but perhaps the grapes are all
the sweeter for that.

Of course, a theoretical case can be made for the indispensability of cultural forms of explanation, but that argument is better reserved for the conclusion of this work where, one hopes, the force of accumulated data will
lend it more substance. For the time being, I will limit myself to asserting
that culture does indeed have a causal dimension, but only if we are willing to
reconsider what we commonly understand by causality. If this argument is accepted, culture's relevance can be understood in relation to a sizable number
of other explanatory variables. Regardless of how those arguments are received, my primary concern is to show that the cultural soil of the Gilded Age
was favorable to the growth of internationalism; it is hoped that this will be
sufficient to establish the importance of cultural phenomena in an intuitive
way.

For my purposes, since the period at issue immediately preceded America's
emergence as an empire and a world power, it is enough to show that public discussions provided a discursive context for understanding subsequent
events. At the very least, since this quarter century preceded the explosive
events of the fin-de-siècle, we can assume that they had *something* to do with
what followed them. I would think they had a good deal of influence, for in
the absence of this body of opinion, it is hard to see how twentieth-century
internationalism could have emerged, much less flourish. My wish is that
others will see this as well. If not, I would hope that reasoned disagreement
inspires skeptics to construct a more plausible story about the emergence of
internationalism. It may happen, but I won't be holding my breath in anticipation.

Those for whom theory triggers big yawns are more likely to be interested in
the empirical content of this book. In other words, what's the book *really* about?
For readers who intend to strip-mine this book (a wholly defensible scholarly
approach), its main points can be stated with ease. First and foremost, the
book explores a complex world of ideas populated by ideas of the world that

flourished in a period when political isolationism was in its prime. Thus far, this cultural domain remains largely unexplored by historians. Those ideas were suffused with a global sensibility that would seem quite familiar a century later. Take, for example, the attempt by Harvard geologist Nathaniel Shaler to express this sense of an encompassing globality. "It is impossible to depict in an adequate way the measure of dependence of our modern civilized man upon the world about him," he wrote. "The functions of his body and mind depend curiously on objects from the end of the earth."[14] Shaler's understanding of what would come to be called interdependence is but one example—and I shall cite many more—of how Americans talked about the world in ways that would continue to characterize their conversations about international relations to the end of the second millennium and beyond. Far from being captives of a parochial mentality, educated Americans of the Gilded Age displayed an extraordinary degree of interest in events abroad. Indeed, many Americans took more than an academic interest in international relations by seeking to define the nation from a global perspective in which the United States was an active and important participant.[15]

What kinds of things, specifically, did they discuss? They talked about anything and everything, but the central theme was "civilization," or what we today know as globalization, around which much else revolved and to which everything else was seemingly connected. Within this context, the European balance of power was analyzed in impressive detail, as was the internal political situation on the continent and the relationship of war to international order and industrial progress. Americans also paid attention to developments in other areas of the world—the Middle East, Africa, Asia, and, to a lesser extent, Latin America—thanks to the broad geographic coverage provided by the journals. Educated Americans were also quite attentive to Europe's imperial expansion and methods of colonial administration long before imperialism became a political issue in the late 1890s. To my surprise, social Darwinism figured hardly at all in analyses of international relations, and, to the extent that it did, comment was overwhelmingly negative. Cultural relations, on the other hand, *were* viewed in Darwinian terms, but the implications of this outlook for how race was understood differed radically from what I had been conditioned to expect. Although Americans understood the world in racial terms, they did so in complex ways that left open the possibility of progressive development for nonwhite peoples.

The liberal internationalism of this period had a number of distinctive features that are worth pointing out in advance. Economically, it imagined a global economy organized ideally by free trade, galvanized by new technologies of communication and transport, undergirded by market practices and property rights, and validated by economic science. In terms of social structure, it assumed that global linkages were intensive as well as extensive; that is, the process of civilization was inevitably modernizing nonindustrial societies in a convergent way that would over time reduce differences among formerly incommensurable ways of life. Beneficiaries or victims of civilization (or both, simultaneously) would not simply be placed in limited contact with the rest of humankind; they would become residents of a new world that had the power to transmute traditional folkways into a modern way of life.

Culturally, liberal internationalism assumed the unity of humankind and was hostile to the idea of permanent racial inequality, which stands to reason, for without this supposition of fundamental human equality internationalism would have been an incoherent outlook. This issue is a bit tricky, for this body of belief was basically anticultural; that is, it was hostile to the very idea of culture as a repository of blind tradition even as it admired national genius, and it was, to boot, quite hierarchical in its judgments of cultures, which gives it the surface appearance of racism. Socially, internationalism was elitist; the prevailing belief was that a cosmopolitan outlook required "cultivation" that would enable one to judge cultures by an international standard in which, depending on the particular cultural commodity, some cultures were demonstrably superior to others.[16] Politically, it assumed the eventual triumph of liberal democracy within states and the emergence of a peaceful international order of sovereign states, even as it displayed a strong suspicion of mass democracy whose low cultural level made it prey to demagogues and repackaged aristocrats.

Historically, liberalism rested on the belief that progress was global and that continued advance depended on the expansion of liberal commercial and cultural processes on a global scale, among and within societies. And yet this body of beliefs exhibited a surprising degree of skepticism and self-doubt that was fed by the illiberal trends of the late nineteenth century. Some may not find this to be surprising, but the connection between liberalism and progress was far more problematic than I had supposed it to be. Although liberalism is inherently optimistic, I now understand that it has always been an embattled creed, and that was quite clearly the case in these years. All of this was quite consistent with political isolationism, as long as the process of civilization appeared to be securely on course.

. Much of what passed for global knowledge then may strike some observers today as rather primitive, self-contradictory, and Eurocentric, and they would not be wrong to think so. But while our present-day generation has benefited from enormous advances in the theoretical and factual understanding of foreign lands and international relations, it would be a serious mistake to look down on Gilded Age types as cultural knuckle-scrapers. If there is anything to Charles Taylor's argument, we need to recognize that in many important respects our contemporary grasp of the globalization process is not all that much further advanced than their understanding; that in some ways their discussions of important issues such as race and culture were far more holistic, and more candid, than corresponding discussions tend to be today. Americans, at least those Americans who wanted to know, were often surprisingly well informed and, where they were not, showed a willingness and eagerness to learn. The academic study of international relations did not emerge until the early twentieth century, but the intelligent appreciation of global affairs began long before then.[17]

A brief survey of the hilltops will be given, then, for the strip miners. The opening chapter establishes that Americans had a firm conceptual grasp of the central themes of globalization and, using world fairs and travel as examples, shows that they were intent on understanding the United States in relation to new global facts of life. Chapter 2 looks at three issues—the quest for international copyright, the free trade polemic, and civil service reform—in order to show the extraordinary degree to which liberals relied on internationalist arguments in their reform rhetoric. Chapters 3 and 4 shift the focus to American views of Europe in order to take a reading of how the continent was thought to fit into a global future. Although a fair number of monographs have been written on American perceptions of this or that country, missing from such accounts has been a sense of the European scene as a whole. Viewed synoptically, the future of republicanism on the continent seemed quite problematic. Worrisome democratic deficits were evident even in Great Britain and France, two countries that would seem on the surface to have been natural ideological partners of the United States. In the case of Britain, the idea of Anglo-Saxonism, which was supposed to be the core of a newfound unity between the two peoples, was itself a significant source of misunderstanding.

Chapters 5 and 6 return to the United States to look at American views of race. The point of the exercise was to find out if racial attitudes allowed, conceptually, for a logically consistent universalism, and if they did, to determine if this was just talk. To my surprise, the idea of human equality was alive, if not exactly well, and appears to have been quite genuine, though it was understood within an evolutionary framework of intercultural relations that many liberals today would find impossible to endorse. Chapter 6 surveys the politics of race in the United States in the Gilded Age and makes two chief points. First, as is shown by the varying views displayed toward African Americans, Chinese immigrants, and Native Americans, there was no one-size-fits-all view of race. Second, the politics of race was not altogether bleak even during these years of racial reaction.

These two chapters sail against the prevailing winds of historical interpretation, I realize, but they address some serious problems in explaining the history of race in the United States and in weighing the claim of American ideas to universality. Unless we believe in spontaneous generation, any attempt to figure out how we got from there to here needs to consider the possibility that the vision of a nonracially ordered society, far from being limited to a few isolated and eccentric reformers, was firmly established in American political culture. For unless there was something deeply organic about the civil rights revolution, it is hard to understand how the United States should suddenly in the mid-twentieth century have retreated from an outlook that was so apparently deep-seated as racism. There would have been little point to the long struggle for racial reform unless there was a sense that success was possible. Outside the nation's borders, too, American universalism would have been perceived as a hollow creed lacking in genuine commitment to human equality. In sum, the view presented in these chapters fits the facts at the time, is consistent with the globalization hypothesis, and helps explain subsequent developments. As it now stands, we have a Whiggish history without Whigs, an ongoing overemphasis of the negative on race that is top-heavy with bad guys.[18]

The remaining chapters return to the international scene. Chapter 7, following an examination of American views of non-Western peoples along an east–west axis, ends with the conclusion, based on a comparison of how Americans viewed Islamic societies vis-à-vis Japan and China, that religion was a far more important barrier to modernization than was race. To put it somewhat differently, orientalism did not apply to most Orientals. Although the inertial drag of a non-Christian religion such as Islam could impede modernization, Christianity itself was not necessarily the answer. In fact, during these years the much-ballyhooed role of Protestant evangelism as an indispensable agent for modernization appears to have been viewed with growing skepticism. Chapter 8 looks at a sizable body of periodical literature on imperialism before 1890 and shows that Americans were exposed to a good deal of writing about the European empires, particularly about India, and that they were divided on the subject of colonization. On the one hand, they were resigned to its historical necessity as a carrier of civilization, while on the other, they were sensitive to its dehumanizing and exploitative features.

The concluding chapters consider the international politics of the period. The penultimate chapter shows that Americans looked at international politics from both a power and a progressive historical perspective, which made for some ambivalence, conceptual tensions, and conflicting points of view. They had their prejudices and half-baked notions, to be sure, but they also had a solid grasp of the issues and a sophisticated global sense of the ways in which political rivalries were linked together in a geographic chain that stretched from Europe to Asia. The final chapter is about American views of the future of international relations. A sizable body of writing on the deeply entrenched politics of war in Europe led to the conclusion that the only avenue of escape from militarism appeared to lie in a global future—conveniently so, as this appeared to be America's destiny in any case—which would also lead Europe to abandon its system of power politics. Although this point of view remained politically isolationist, the emphasis placed on the centrality of a liberal global environment made it possible in future to entertain a more activist posture when that environment was threatened. Using the political implications of this understanding of the world as a point of departure, the conclusion returns to a more specific analysis of some of the theoretical matters raised in this introduction by arguing that culture deserves a seat at the table in the causal accounts of international relations.

Inasmuch as this work is empirical, the question arises: How accurate is my transcription? Alas, history is not like shorthand, nor do historians command the equivalent of the compression algorithms that squeeze musical data into incredibly small files while retaining an impressive fidelity to the huge body of information stored in the original. To undertake this study at all, giving free rein to my internationalist hunch—prejudice, if you will—meant that I selected for certain kinds of data in the process of research and, in the process of refinement and writing, excluded much information that another writer would eagerly have incorporated. More could have been said, for instance, about gender, or about regions like Africa and South America, or about international socialism. But these were peripheral concerns in the periodical literature, and I had my hands full with what I saw as the central themes. Much of interest has been left out in the process of selection, though that is to be expected. Unlike scientists who expect to be able to replicate their results, two historians looking at the same data will never write the same book.

It would also have been possible to look more closely at some of the people whose words are cited in the text, with a particular view to investigating the degree to which they set words to action, but that would have made for a completely different and much longer book, with probably not much to show for the effort since we already know the practical outcomes of their collective efforts during these years. For better or for worse, this is a study of a historical body of thought and not of a historical process. Yet it is not strictly speaking synchronic, for I have tried wherever possible to note changing ideas in relation to new developments. Exploring the interior of that outlook was all that I could handle because I already had too much material to work with. Notwithstanding all these caveats and disclaimers, I would maintain that my account is empirically grounded—as Casey Stengel used to say, "you could look it up." Admittedly, when dealing with complex phenomena, the data are never univocal, but, on balance, the views found in the journal literature are solidly and coherently "liberal," and not just in a nineteenth-century sense. At the same time, as will become obvious in due course, this is also a "strong" reading, but one that was prompted less by ideological predisposition (I hope) than by the necessity of making sense of what I found.[19]

My ideal way of writing this book would have been to capture the quality that Thomas Hobbes observed in Thucydides' historical style: "that the narration itself doth secretly instruct the reader, and more effectually than can possibly be done by precept."[20] Unfortunately, it was not possible for me to meet that standard, for a tension existed between reporting my findings and making sense of them. Sad to say, I lost my authorial voice, which is a writer's equivalent of tripping over his own feet. Instead of writing with a flowing style that carries the reader along in a smooth current of fact and interpretation, the oversupply of material led to a plenitude of quotations that created something of an unsightly logjam. I realized after a few drafts that, for reasons of both space and readability, the manuscript would need to be drastically pruned—and it was. But the conviction remained that I ought to allow the voices to speak for themselves as much as possible. Because so many voices needed to be heard the manuscript does not read as fluidly as I would have liked. What it loses in readability, however, I hope is made up in substance.

Still, to name and identify each author would have made the text completely unreadable. Thus I have named only those writers who contributed substantially to the discussion of the issues taken up in this book. In many cases, where articles were unattributed, the identity of the author could have been ferreted out easily enough. For *The Nation*, the most important journal of the time, many of the anonymous contributions by E. L. Godkin and his stable of writers have been indexed by Daniel C. Haskell.[21] In other cases, even though one could easily attribute the authorship of certain editorial pieces—George William Curtis, for example, as the author of the "Editor's Easy Chair" in *Harper's*—I have chosen to quote them under the anonymous journal feature heading in which they appeared. For a host of more obscure authors, it has been possible to unearth basic information through use of biographical dictionaries such as *Appleton's Cyclopaedia*, Scribner's *Cyclopaedia of American Literature*, and *American National Biography Online*. I should also mention Google's valuable book search, which made it possible to come across the mention of people who could not have been identified through traditional research methods. In many instances, however, I have chosen not to name them in the text for reasons of style. In most cases, too, I have not called attention to what today would be glaring misspellings.

1

A Global Civilization

As a chapter in the history of U.S. foreign relations, the Gilded Age remains the golden age of isolationism. It was a time when a self-absorbed United States, plunging headlong into industrialization, coped with incidental foreign policy problems while maintaining only a shallow involvement with the world across the oceans. Over time, this story has been modified in some respects, most notably by historians who have pointed to the fateful incubation of expansionist economic impulses during these years. Economically, it is clear that the United States was far from isolated, for the extraordinary expansion of the American economy was related to revolutionary changes taking place elsewhere. Riding atop the "first wave" of globalization that washed over the world in these years, the United States was rapidly internationalizing its foreign trade and investment to the point that by some measures the American economy was more "international" during this period than it would be a century later.[1] But these economic developments had little effect on foreign policy. Despite the economy's growing entanglement in the thickening web of global finance and commerce, a highly protectionist trade policy had the effect of reinforcing, even glorifying, the nation's self-absorption and political isolation.

When viewed culturally, however, this period looks very different. These were years in which the cultural soil was prepared and planted with internationalist ideas that would germinate and eventually blossom in the 1890s and beyond.[2] Although much of the American mass public remained oblivious to events abroad, the educated middle and upper classes displayed an extraordinary degree of intellectual curiosity about trends in the world at large. For those with money, education, leisure, and the desire for self-cultivation and travel, the insularity of America's raw democratic culture was a serious flaw in the national character that needed to be overcome by brutally honest intro-spection, unrelenting self-education, and an imaginative construction of the nation's global future. Convinced that there was a universal historical mean-ing to the national experience and that the nation's future was global, Amer-ica's educated elite engaged in an ongoing, wide-ranging, and sophisticated public discussion of international developments that seemed destined to have profound effects on the future of their country.

Curiosity about the world was expressed in many places—in private con-versations, letters, speeches and lectures, newspapers, clubs, political gather-ings, and reform associations—but nowhere were international developments considered in greater depth and breadth than in the magazines of the period.[3] Following upon the success of *Harper's*, the post–Civil War years saw an ex-plosive increase in the birth rate of new magazines, often underwritten by book publishers hoping to use these periodicals to promote their books. Al-though the Civil War had made national distribution a possibility, the market for these new journals was modest, far smaller than the eye-popping circula-tion numbers that the new mass-circulation magazines would rack up at the end of the century. Prominent among these new journals was what one author has called "the quality group." Quality had a graphic component, with maga-zines such as *Harper's Monthly* and *Scribner's* featuring "high-class illustra-tions" that relied on new engraving techniques. However, it was primarily the high quality of the written word that connected these magazines to their au-diences. Although the magazines mixed popular and elite forms to varying degrees, they decidedly spoke to a relatively small cultural elite rather than to vernacular culture. As the editor of *Appletons'* pledged: "The public who can appreciate pure literature and correct taste may be small, but the JOURNAL will continue to be published solely for this class, whatever may be the pecu-niary temptation to cater for any other."[4]

A relatively small readership should not be equated with modest influence. In the case of E. L. Godkin's *The Nation*, whose first number appeared in 1865, the journal was read by many newspaper editors and public intellectu-als of the day and therefore shaped opinion to a far greater degree than its modest circulation would suggest. *The Atlantic Monthly*, *Harper's*, and *The North American Review* featured an all-star cast of editors like Charles Eliot Norton, James Russell Lowell, Henry Adams, George William Curtis, William Dean Howells, Charles Dudley Warner, and many others. Taken as a group, these magazines provide a good entree into the thinking of the nation's educated elites, who at the very least framed issues for discussion even if they did not necessarily decide them. But the journals were important, too, in advancing an internationalist outlook. Reminiscing in his memoirs about the long-term impact of periodicals, Henry Holt remarked that, thanks to the constant influx of information from Asia, Africa, and elsewhere, "a man is to-day more thoroughly a citizen of the world than, thirty years ago, he could be of his own country."[5]

The self-described stance of these magazines was uncompromisingly cosmopolitan. As *The Century* declared after concluding its first year in print, "to be American does not imply that one must be provincial, or that the only subjects with which an American magazine must deal, and the only writers it must employ, are American subjects and American writers: otherwise Americans (of all men!) must care nothing for 'abroad'." In its first issue, *The Nation*, which was second to none in the catholicity of its intellectual interests or in the pitiless logic of its fierce critiques, informed its readers of its planetary concerns: "nothing that concerns man anywhere is foreign to the rest of mankind." Although the journal endorsed the Monroe Doctrine as a canonical text for political isolationism, that did not mean "that we should so shut ourselves up in hemisphere as to be ignorant of what is passing in other countries of the civilized world." Similarly, *Scribner's*, in its first number, struck a cosmopolitan pose by declaring: "The nations of the earth are constantly approaching a solidarity of interests in government and religion, art, literature, and science; and we propose to scan these fields abroad, and gather such sheaves of intelligence as can most interest our readers on this side of the water." *Appletons'* also vowed to omit "all ordinary news" and instead to take on "all subjects in the wide range of literature, science, art, and education," relying on "all resources, original and selected, domestic and foreign, which could give interest and variety to its pages." As for the formidable *Atlantic Monthly*, William Dean Howells recalled that it was "characterized by what was more national, what was more universal, in the New England temperament." Even a nationalist journal like *Putnam's Monthly*, which refused on principle to publish foreign authors, nevertheless cultivated an air of cosmopolitanism in its discussions.[6]

Cosmopolitanism has a long history, of course, but its emergence as a broad cultural phenomenon during this period comes across unmistakably in the surprising range and depth of international coverage provided by these journals. Often described as literary quarterlies, they were much broader in orientation and far less specialized than periodicals today. Typically, they offered combinations of reportage, accounts of travel and exploration, original fiction, political analysis, discussions of developments in science and technology, book reviews, editorial commentary, and, for titillation, gossip about the doings of royalty in Europe. The reporting and analysis of foreign political developments could be quite detailed and at a high level. Book reviews covered volumes published abroad, not only in English but in French, German, Italian, Russian, and occasionally in other languages, without waiting for English-language translations. Although these reviews often served as summaries for busy readers who were unlikely to read the books for themselves, they nevertheless provided exposure to expert knowledge about the wider world, as well as to critiques thereof. Europe received the lion's share of attention, but there was also an enormous quantity of writing on Asia, with less space accorded to Africa and Latin America. At a time when specialized academic journals had not yet appeared, these periodicals also opened their pages to academics who were capable of writing prose readily understood by educated lay readers. All in all, they were remarkably ecumenical in character and did an extraordinary job of instructing their public on virtually all the major developments then taking place on the international scene.

Fathoming the Global

Happenings abroad were almost invariably discussed in connection with "civilization"; this buzzword, encountered at every turn, was understood as the encompassing historical reality of the time. In many ways, civilization was the functional equivalent of what, more than a century later, would come to be called globalization, but it was also more diffuse. In keeping with its global conceptual sweep, civilization appeared to contain a world of meanings. Civilization was, *inter alia*, a universalizing historical process, a geographic designation, an anthropological category, a value-laden binary distinction usually paired in opposition to "barbarism," a term connoting evolutionary differences in social structure and the life of the mind, a word that could carry class and regional meanings, as in descriptions of workers and southerners as uncivilized, and much more besides. Depending on the context, its purport could be hierarchical or egalitarian, pacific or belligerent, Euro-American or global, faux-cosmopolitan or genuinely ecumenical. Despite this apparent surfeit of meaning, civilization exercised a powerful gravitational pull in discussions of international developments because, however inadequately, it referred in a meaningful way to a new and vitally important emergent reality in history: the formation of a global society.

Because civilization was an exasperatingly inexact concept, there were inevitable—and much ridiculed—attempts to give it a mathematical precision. One writer, for example, insisted "that the intensity of civilization at any time is proportional to the square of the cosine of the latitude multiplied by a power of its sine" (which was simply an arcane way of making north-south and east-west distinctions). Less opaquely, and perhaps more accurately, another author argued that "the average consumption of soap gave the scale of civilization" and went on to suggest that "the competition for cotton and linen rags denotes a still better index, because it is a measure of the distribution of education and love for literature." Better still, as *The Atlantic Monthly* suggested, tongue not altogether in cheek, a nation with superior indexes and finding aids "is the country in which the play of intellect is the freest and most active; it is the country in which there is the highest civilization." But no definition succeeded in capturing the concept in all its baffling complexity. After venturing a lengthy, though admittedly inadequate, definition of his own, one editor confessed that "What is still wanting, is some standard by which to measure civilization in any particular case."[7]

Notwithstanding a tendency to overuse that threatened to empty it of all meaning, the term *civilization* continued to command a good deal of analytical power thanks to a rich vein of ideas that would become the conceptual currency of first modernization theorists and then scholars of globalization a century later. Among other things, civilization clearly referred to the figurative shrinkage of the world made possible by new communications and transportation technologies; to dazzlingly rapid technological change; to the "disembedding" of institutions by virtue of their being lifted out from local contexts and linked functionally to distant places; to structural interdependence born of linkage; to the thoroughgoing makeover of societies that were plugged into the global grid; to the emergence of what today is somewhat misleadingly called "global culture"; and to the reformatting of basic appreciations of time and space. Later staples of sociological jargon like space-time distantiation and time-space compression first appeared in simpler dress in the ordinary discourse of late nineteenth-century middle-class Americans. In fact, the literature of the day is filled with unadorned matter-of-fact remarks whose meaning social scientists would later reclothe as full-dress theory.[8]

The most abstract feature of civilization, spatiotemporal unification, was not lost on contemporaries who were endlessly fascinated by "man's conquest over time and space." Take, for example, the observation that "by mechanical suppression of time, the planet is ever being made smaller for us." The delocalization of space and time was given particularly striking expression in a piece by the Boston writer and artist T. G. Appleton, in which he imagined that "the world is spread out like a map before us, and time and space are annihilated as we bend in sympathetic curiosity above it." An epochal event in the history of internationalism, the adoption of a global standard for time— "cosmopolitan time" as one essay called it—was the result of the 1884 International Meridian Conference in Washington, which chose the longitudinal line running through Greenwich, England as the prime meridian for plotting a universal day. The symbolic importance of this delocalization of time received relatively little notice at that moment because it was intended as a practical remedy for some vexatious problems then plaguing the railway "system." Railway schedules based on idiosyncratic local times were so incongruous and discordant that, according to one critic, "studying a map of the system is like tracing the intricacies of a labyrinth." Although some nationalist opposition emerged to the idea at the conference (France proved to be the chief obstacle), "petty, school-boyish patriotism," as one letter-writer described it, was easily enough brushed aside. The result was that culturally singular and often incommensurable times were now subordinated to a universal temporal rhythm.[9]

Time has always been among the most baffling of topics, but the unification of global space, often described in terms of compression and connectedness, was more readily understandable and, indeed, quickly became a cliché. As one writer put it, "the more we know of the earth the smaller it seems." People formerly awed by the vastness of the planet now had to deal with "the new sensation of annihilating spaces." Making possible this conquest of distance were the new industrial machines, which, if one were to believe the effusive rhetoric of technological utopians, were imbued with the power to transform both primitive societies and the civilized world. Typical was the

Virginia scholar Maximilian Schele de Vere's description of the modern age as one in which "trade and commerce have extended over oceans and continents which were heretofore strangers to their civilizing effects; and the intercourse between man and man, and nation and nation, has been marvellously facilitated by the new instruments, telegraphs, steamers, and railways." "Steam has wrought more wonders than all the dragons," wrote William Eliot Griffis, a leading expert on Japan. "The ocean has become a pathway, [and] steppes and defiles can he made into roads by ties and rails." More concisely, another writer concluded that "Modern inventions have 'shrivelled' our globe." In combination, technology and commerce had globalizing implications that were impossible to miss.[10]

Although metaphors of shrinkage and contraction tended to dominate the rhetoric, expansion better conveys a sense of the degree to which the horizons of modern societies had opened out in every respect. The contraction of space was only an illusion made possible by the revolution in transport and communication; but it was equally the product of a parallel but related process, the cultural expansion of the west. "Every fresh year seems to bring the nations into more cosmopolitan relations," noted Appleton. After the preliminary genuflections to technology and trade, most commentators quickly turned their attention to the cultural impact of global contraction. According to E. L Godkin, the "growing community of manners" associated with modern life was "producing a sameness of type in many ways of thinking and of acting all over the world." In other words, a narrowing of cultural distance was taking place on a global scale. This process of convergence made it possible for people from different cultures to more easily understand one another, but the growth of intercultural communication also made possible the quickened transmission of the Word of God. Missionaries were on the whole quite alert to the connection between globalization and the potential for spread of the Gospel. "The most distant nations are brought, as it were, to our very doors," wrote one man of the cloth. "Our neighbors are no longer the men of the next town or state, or, those who use a common speech, but the human race."[11]

The inevitable consequence, it appeared, would be the unification of the world, the creation of a global ecumene. Applying the then widespread belief that history moved according to knowable laws, one interpreter wrote that "Whatever is homogeneous is combining all the world over in obedience to an irresistible law. It is the law of gravitation applied to human affairs." "What is known as 'the business world' exists everywhere," said the *Atlantic*. "It forms one community of mankind." Another writer maintained that the universality of capitalism or "the competitive system" was "sufficient proof of its being an expression of some natural law." For others, the law lay within. Wherever one looked—science, trade, migration, even the transnational spread of freemasonry—everything testified to the historical irrepressibility of "the cosmopolitan bias in human nature." Rome and other empires in their hey-days had been quite impressive, but any comparisons with the past were inex-act, for the universalizing thrust of modern civilization was now operating on a global scale. After discussing the homogenizing impact of railroad travel, an anonymous article in *The North American Review* ended with a rhetorical question that was typical of the times: "Judging from accomplished results, how can the whole world avoid being cosmopolized?" All this was happening, in short, because it had to happen.[12]

Amazing as modern technologies were, still they were only tools, hardware in need of human software to give them life. They were globalizing only inso-far as they extended the geographical reach of modern commercial cultures and ideologies. The breakdown of cultural insularity was dramatically evi-dent in the rapid disintegration of age-old language barriers. Constructed in-ternational languages like Esperanto and Volapük attracted a few devotees, but these were esoteric and trivial hobbies in comparison to the workaday function that English was expected to play as the world's lingua franca. This prospect was so pleasing and uncontroversial that it made its way into Ulysses S. Grant's second inaugural address, where the president announced that "the Great Maker is preparing the . . . world to become one nation, speaking one language." Already, it was noted, English was "heard in every quarter of the globe, and everywhere recognized more and more as the language of the highest civilization." Writing from Egypt, the poet and travel writer Bayard Taylor remarked on "the astonishing spread of the English language within the last twenty years." Taylor attributed the change largely to the influence of burgeoning swarms of English and American tourists, but English was be-coming the lingua franca of commerce in general. Some Americans were even under the impression, for a time, that the Japanese were seriously contemplat-ing the adoption of English as their national tongue. But even if the Japanese did not so decide, commerce and contact would compel the Japanese to learn

English as a second language. Senator Charles Sumner, taking stock of John Adams's prediction in 1780 that English would become a global language, concluded that "this prophecy is already accomplished" and that the further spread of the mother tongue seemed assured.[13]

English as an international language seemed the natural counterpart to the gold standard that governed international exchange. One day, it was predicted, English would be "received everywhere as legal currency for common purposes, the others surviving only in the precarious condition of dialects." Although the resort to English was increasingly a matter of convenience, it owed its initial impetus to the combined geopolitical weight of the Anglo-Saxon powers. Not surprisingly, then, explanations of its global spread were often colored by politically charged language. One writer, for instance, declared that "at this moment it takes hold of the balance of power among the tongues. Whatever there is in it, of good and bad, tends to overspread the earth." Sometimes the process of linguistic unification was described in a Darwinian idiom. "The doctrine of the Survival of the Fittest," suggested a piece in *Harper's,* "points to the ultimate unification of language." In these shorthand ways, the globalization of language could be attributed to the complex workings of underlying commercial, power political, financial, and biocultural processes without having to actually explain how they worked.[14]

The delocalization of experience, the separation of space from place, was accompanied by an unparalleled acceleration of history that quickly and sometimes disconcertingly estranged humans from their remembered pasts. Ironically, this experiential discontinuity was emerging at the same time that historians, for the first time, were creating a broad and unified panorama of the human adventure. Karl Marx, among many others, had long since declared that the industrial revolution was transforming the world, but his insight from *The Communist Manifesto* that "all that is solid melts into air" was hardly alien to liberal thinkers. In 1866, at the beginning of the new year, *The Nation* paused to take inventory of some of the recent changes that had overtaken the world:

> The material progress made within the present century is, to be sure, a trite subject, but, then, we doubt whether, in spite of all that has been said upon it, many people have sufficient acquaintance with its details not to be startled by seeing them grouped together. A man need not be

very old to remember the time when there were no railroads, no locomotives, no steamships, and no telegraph wires—no gaslights, no petroleum, no California gold, no india-rubber shoes or coats, no percussion caps or revolvers, no friction matches, no city aqueduct, no steam printing-presses, no sewing-machines, no reaping machines, and no postage stamps or envelopes or pens of steel or gold.

The essay went on in this fashion for a lengthy paragraph, adding that only a generation ago "a voyage to Europe was like a departure to the next world."[15] Subsequent generations would also be awed by this dizzying rate of change, but their experience would lack the contrasting first-hand knowledge of premodern life that informed these observations.

The quickening of history was taking place in a way that made the present appear increasingly eventful in comparison to the relatively inert past. Consider the summary by C. C. Hazewell, a Boston political journalist, of the whirl-wind 1860s:

There is hardly any thing that can move the sympathies of men, or excite their wonder, that has not occurred since the beginning of the year 1861. Mighty empires have been overthrown, old dynasties have fallen, great interests have been uprooted, the most ancient of temporal polities has ceased to exist, new nations have been created, wars of unparalleled proportions have been waged with new weapons and on new military principles, continental railways have been laid down, obstacles to maritime commerce have been cut through or removed, remote nations have been brought into daily intercourse through telegraphic cables that lie at the bottom of seas over which men once were afraid to sail, and great discoveries and inventions in science and in art have added vastly to the means at man's command to reclaim that earth over which he has the promise of dominion on condition that his exertions shall show him worthy of such supremacy.

Things were moving so much more rapidly, according to the southern politician Wade Hampton, that "more progress is now made in human civilization in one year, than in a century then." Looking back from the vantage point of 1890, one observer concluded that "the application of invention, the progress of scientific discovery, the industrial conquests of the earth, and the liberalizing of religious and political thought, have virtually made for us a new world."[16] In this sense, the New World had itself been superannuated.

For many, it seemed evident that history had entered a wholly new era in which discontinuity would rule the future. With the past quickly losing its grip on the present, N. C. Meeker, reporter and founder of the utopian community of Greeley, Colorado, suggested that "we may now expect the events before us to be wholly unlike any hitherto known." Despite the inherent uncertainties of the topic, the editor of *Appletons'* believed there was at least a consensus on this point: "That development is the vital principle, so to speak, of civilization is universally admitted." According to John Fiske, the Harvard historian, essayist, and prominent disciple of the theorist of evolution Herbert Spencer, progress was "on the whole the most prominent feature of the history of a considerable and important portion of mankind." Reviewing a book of the century's celebrities, *The Nation* maintained that "no one can turn its pages and observe the splendid names which it celebrates without being impressed with the exalted rank of the present century in any comparison with those that have gone before—material, moral, intellectual. Music, poetry, philanthropy, statesmanship, the art of war, the triumphs of man over nature, the progress of discovery and invention, have all been illustrated by names on Fame's eternal bead-roll worthy to be filed."[17]

Even more stunning changes were expected in the future. The Statue of Liberty, the Eiffel Tower (which replaced the great pyramids as the highest structure in the world), the Brooklyn Bridge, and other monumental architecture instantiated "the power of thought over the refractory materials of the earth." The opening of the Suez Canal in 1869, the completion of the transcontinental railroad in the same year, and the cutting of the Mont Cenis tunnel in Switzerland promised even more daring triumphs of science and engineering. *Appletons'* predicted an Adriatic-to-Mediterranean canal through Italy, an interoceanic canal at the Isthmus of Panama, the massive use of artesian wells to irrigate the Sahara, and a suspension bridge spanning the Straits of Dover. In 1879, there were reports that English and French engineers were developing a scheme to flood the Sahara desert with waters from the Mediterranean and "transform its waste into a watery highway for the commerce of the nations." Projects that were "visionary and impracticable" to the layperson were merely reputation-making challenges to scientists and engineers, and, once completed, they quickly became "commonplace fact—a matter taken for granted." So pronounced was the emphasis on novelty that inventions proliferated with little understanding of their utility apart from the presumption that inventiveness was useful in itself. For example, in 1878 the practical applications of the telephone, phonograph, and microphone remained unclear to a puzzled editor, who wrote that "the imagination wanders excitably through a vast field of conjecture as to what uses these latest marvels of our time are destined to serve."[18]

There was no denying the quantitative revolution in production and consumption wrought by global capitalism. But for all the buoyant effusions about the benefits of civilization, internationalist thought during this period was not made up of unalloyed optimism. Utopian declarations were part of the mix, but thoughtful liberals more typically agonized over the imperfections and shortcomings of modern life. As we shall see in much greater detail in subsequent chapters, American internationalists were only too well aware that progress was a tension-laden process that contained some deep and worrisome contradictions. Although they did not harbor the apocalyptic fears of civilizational collapse that would become common in the late twentieth and early twenty-first centuries, present in their thought at all times was a powerful rhetorical crosscurrent of nostalgia as well as a deep practical concern about the negative features of these worldwide transformations. Taking note of its many contradictions, the historian Francis Parkman predicted that the nineteenth century would become "the riddle of history."[19]

From the standpoint of 1889, it seemed only yesterday that the American west had been wild country, which in the blink of an eye had become "one huge stock ranch covered with cattlemen and settlers," increasingly devoid of big game. *The Overland Monthly,* in a rumination on the meaning of its corporate symbol (a bear wandering across the tracks of the Pacific railroad, which it described as "the symbol of local primitive barbarism"), advised its readers to "Look at him well, for he is passing away. Fifty years, and he will be as extinct as the dodo." The same perception applied to once-remote attractions in the cultural wilderness. E. L. Godkin, in contemplating the larger implications of the British presence in Egypt, predicted the "speedy disappearance from the observation of the ordinary tourist of a civilization which, with all its moral and material imperfections, had certain charms in which ours is more and more wanting, and for which we yearn the richer and more powerful we become." Even if civilization marked an improvement over previous ways of life, its very generality was bleeding particular cultures of their trademark uniqueness and distinctiveness. Given the ferocity of the onslaught, it came as something of a surprise that cultural uniqueness managed to survive even in denatured form. "Is it not wonderful," reflected *The Nation*, "that, with such a mixture of the fluids in this great vessel of the world, there is any national flavor left?"[20]

Unable to offer a real alternative to civilization, romantic critiques took the form of elegiac laments about the encroachment of the modern world upon nature and cultures. Here and there one encounters sad, sometimes bitter, and by-now familiar commentaries on the downside of modernity. One editor, for example, bemoaned the detritus of this universal civilization: "The march of civilization is marked not more clearly by lines of railroad and the wires of the telegraph than by the empty cans, boxes, and bottles which the all-pervading unrest of the age has scattered broadcast over the face of the earth—here, there, and everywhere . . . for if the white man has not made the wilderness to blossom as the rose, he has caused it to be well seeded with the rejectamenta of picnics and wayside camps, and a harvest of tin cans and junk bottles can be gathered anywhere. The face of nature is defaced, the trail of the pale face is over it all." Tourism, in particular, had a built-in propensity to defile the very objects that had called it into being. The following jeremiad tells it all: "The steam-whistle shrieks where Demosthenes harangued; the electric wire winds along Judean paths which the feet of prophets trod; five lines of omnibuses will soon take you 'right away now, all the way up!' from the Bosporus on the Asia Minor side; Cook's excursionists picnic on potted meats among the Pyramids; steamers thread the Red Sea which Moses—pshaw! the story grows stale as I tell it." Not everyone agreed that civilization was an improvement, even when compared to barbarism. Theodore Child, the Parisian agent for *Harper's*, noted that while "so-called barbarism" was vanishing, so too were "the splendors of a world which was more concerned with beauty than with convenience."[21]

As a result of modern civilization's homogenizing effects, the likelihood that travelers would encounter something genuinely different abroad was becoming remote. One review spoke of the inevitable disappointment of tourists in search of the exotic who found themselves jostling with other vacationers in what not long ago had been secluded, all-but-inaccessible destinations. Thus it was, Godkin lamented, that the magical had been demystified: "With European danglers and flirts picnicking in the Vale of Cashmere, English beer-bottles strewing the streets of Herat, and members of the Holy Orthodox Church swarming in Samarcand and Kaschgar, the great Oriental spell by which the imagination of the Western world has so long been bound is broken." By this time, unspoiled destinations were already in short supply. Tibet, noted the *Nation,* "is as yet one of the few Indian countries which have not been overrun either by English troops or English tourists." *Harper's* was almost rueful in recalling the not-too-distant past when "there were once countries in which it was a capital crime to be a stranger." A more authentic travel experience, it seemed, was to be had in the good old days of the antebellum period. "Since then," the complaint ran, "Europe has become Americanized and America has become Europeanized, and travelling has become so common that there is, comparatively speaking, little novelty in it." Those who recognized the despoiling side of modernity produced some advice to see the world while it was still there for the seeing. "Arcadia cannot always remain Arcadia," warned W. T. Brigham, an ethnologist and a leading student of the Hawaiian Islands, for it would not be long before Eden was "modernized, civilized, and spoiled."[22]

The propensity of modernity to effortlessly appropriate the new provoked many pained reflections. The privileging of new ideas caused one conservative to grumble (in a fashion that postmodernists might appreciate) that "novelty now gives a favorable presumption, as it gave an adverse presumption in the days of our fathers. The truth is more in danger in our day from the prejudice that accepts without question the new, than from that which unreasonably holds to the old." That this was being done in the name of an unrelenting demystification of the world did not make it any easier to accept for those who viewed as cause for regret the passing of the strangely different, the mysterious, and the traditional. Edmund Quincy, novelist and former abolitionist, anticipating Max Weber's view of modern life as a process of disenchantment, noted that travel to out-of-the-way places was no longer unusual enough to evoke interest or envy among friends and acquaintances. "All that is long since gone," he wrote. "Steam and the electric telegraph have disenchanted the world and left the imagination small room to run riot in." Another writer regretted that "the magic and the marvels that filled our childish souls with adventurous longing are fading away in the change." For a certain type, globalization bred world-weariness because the world had become too small and, as a result, had "lost its mysterious charm of indefiniteness." Even relatively pristine locales no longer seemed exotic because, even if not visited personally, they had most likely been described by someone who had passed through; hence one knew beforehand what to expect.[23]

There was a decidedly non-Marxist class dimension to this issue as cultural elites came to realize that the privileged delectation and appreciation of the extraordinary was being replaced by mass consumption. As *The Nation* acknowledged: "The wonders of the world have become almost commonplaces of popular knowledge." Before long, there would be "no privileged places any more than privileged persons." While recognizing that there was "something grand" about this demystification of the world, an editorial added that "there is also something which everybody must, in his secret heart, find appalling. There is no place on the globe now to which a weary man can go for rest; no 'boundless contiguity of shade' to which the terms that shake the busy world cannot find an entrance." But even if there had been a place to stop and get away from it all, the very act of stopping seemed increasingly difficult to pull off as modernity—a world in which everything was in motion: raw materials, goods, peoples, and ideas—came to resemble a runaway train. Speed itself, abstracted from its social embodiments, became a cause of complaint. For one editor, "the velocity and headlong rush of modern existence" associated with "rail and telegraph, ocean steamers and extreme-bred horses" was "a melancholy product of high civilization." Developments like the craze for archaeology only underscored the radical incompatibility of the old and the new. What remained true was that "the faster the modern world lives the quicker the remains of the ancient world disappear."[24]

The suspicion that civilization depended in some fundamental way on the continued existence of something antithetical to itself led to reflections about what would happen to the civilizers once there remained nothing left to civilize. In one particularly insightful essay, the popular writer and editor Charles Dudley Warner, co-author with Mark Twain of *The Gilded Age*, speculated about a future in which the earth had been thoroughly civilized and subdued. "Are not barbarism and vast regions of uncultivated land a necessity of healthful life on this globe?" he asked. "In a word, if the world were actually all civilized, wouldn't it be too weak even to ripen?" Globalization had just begun, but already some were voicing the strong feeling that it had gone too far,

resulting in an "overcivilization" that was "making the educated classes de-
spondent and melancholy. Weariness of life is eating, it is said, into the heart
of society."[25]

This draining of mystery from the world could be worrisome even to those
who were enthralled by civilization's triumphs. For them, the problem resided
in the possibility that the process of disenchantment might be slowing down
or coming to a close. By 1881, the growing expense at the margins of finding
and penetrating new frontiers prompted John Fiske to declare, with an air of
disappointment, the approaching end of the era of exploration: "The surface
of our globe is now so well known that no room is left for mystery, and most
of the savage portions of it have been appropriated," he wrote. "We can never
again expect to see anything like the wonders of that heroic age of adventure."
But for the majority of those who thought about such things, what mattered
most was neither what was left behind, nor the excitement of the journey, but
the destination. Alluring termini of civilization's voyage such as democracy,
peace, and global development, albeit not manifestly imminent, could at least
be seen clearly in the mind's eye.[26]

Romantic nostalgia was complemented by a sociological awareness of the
negative systems effects produced by global networks. An appreciation of
global interconnectedness and interdependence, the sense that faraway events
could seriously impact affairs close to home, was well entrenched, even commonplace, in the nineteenth century. Here is the editor of *Appletons'*, in one
of many such declarations: "The world is getting to be so small, and all parts
of it are growing so near to each other by reason of steam and electricity, that
the bonds between nations become of more practical importance every day."
In 1864, *The Atlantic Monthly* noted the global impact of once-local events:
"what depresses or exalts one nation is felt by its effects in all nations. There
cannot be a Russian war, or a Sepoy mutiny, or an Anglo-French invasion of
China, or an emancipation of the serfs of Russia, without the effect thereof
being sensibly experienced on the shores of Superior or on the banks of the
Sacramento." For the same reason, the American Civil War was thought to be
a global event. John Fiske, a leading prophet of globalization, pointed out that
"in these days scarcely anything can happen in one part of our planet which
does not speedily affect every other part."[27]

Economic perturbations, in particular, were known to generate global
shock waves. Stock markets tumbled in unison, and economies rose and sank

as one. The growing tendency to international market stampedes was dutifully noted. One college professor described the contagion effects of interdependence as follows: "Infinite mutually dependent interests unite us with Europe and with the very antipodes. Every pulsation in the financial system is felt alike on each side of the Atlantic. A crisis in London has its instant counterpart here, and the great revulsions which periodically sweep over the commercial world may begin, almost as chance may dictate, in New York or in Vienna." According to the English economist James E. Thorold Rogers, a rise in interest rates in London, wars, pestilence, epidemics, bad harvests (or superabundant yields), the scarcity or abundance of products or commodities, shifting currency values, the emergence of new industries, technological innovations—any or all of these, and more, could cause disturbances elsewhere in the world. Formerly, the economies of the globe had resembled "landlocked lakes," relatively immune to storms elsewhere, but the world had since become "more and more like an open ocean, and a storm which gathers on a continent thousands of miles away may steadily, surely, and irresistibly come on a region which might be thought far too remote for its influence. Industry and its forces have become cosmic." Thus the dangers resulting from the close coupling of societies were recognized to be every bit as far-reaching as the benefits. "Calamities, and especially great calamities," noted *The Nation,* "are fast ceasing to be what is called local—they are all now general."[28]

One therefore had to keep one's eyes open to developments abroad. An interest in the issue of poverty in England, for example, was not simply a matter of moral concern. Already anticipating an economic race to the bottom, one essayist argued that "Whatever threatens or injures the moral advance and material prosperity of one of the leading nations of the world threatens and injures those of all others in a greater or less degree." No one, "from the hod-carrier to the millionaire," was exempt from the system's reaches. Any person could "any morning read in the paper news from the uttermost ends of the earth depriving him of his fortune or his daily bread." The minister Henry Ward Beecher advised people to take out life insurance, for "the man that is rich to-day, by causes beyond his reach is poor to-morrow. A war in China, a revolution in Europe, a rebellion in America, overrule ten thousand fortunes in every commercial community."[29]

The changes were partly structural, having to do with mechanical exchanges of goods, but partly they were the result of the accelerated flow of information and ideas, which was itself the consequence of a global economy of cultural transmission in which thoughts were "communicated with the rapidity, and even by the power of lightning." In a McLuhanesque observation *avant la lettre, The Atlantic Monthly* pointed out the revolutionary impact of the new media technology: "By the telegraph the senses of sight and hearing are to be extended around the globe." Up-to-date access to news of fast-developing events abroad was quickly accepted as a commonplace. Another journal marveled at the quantity and variety of information being transmitted: "Daily the nerves of civilization, the post and telegraph, convey the thoughts and interests of one-half the globe to the other half. The speech in the French Chambers, the English Parliament, or the western legislature, the new dancer or singer at St. Petersburg, the fossils upturned in the Nevada prison-yard, the operations of some village benevolent society in western Massachusetts, have each and all a vital interest for denizens of the rest of the world." The whole world had literally become a stage and the public inveterate theatergoers, now that the expectation that every modern person needed to stay abreast of breaking news had already become part of the cultural environment.[30]

This mass movement of information had a vast cultural impact. The good news was that markets would become more transparent and hence more competitive once privileged access to information was eliminated. But if political opinion was now susceptible to rapid change from foreign stimuli, all bets for political stability were off. Thanks to the telegraph and the modern press, according to *The Nation*, "we often now witness in a single year revolutions in sentiment, and above all in political sentiment, which in the last century it would have taken twenty years to bring about." The flow of information, carelessly reported and uncritically digested, could also cause great confusion among those eager to keep up with events abroad. At a time when the cable monopoly reported events as it chose, *The Nation* complained continually of "the gentleman who bamboozles the American public with European 'news.'" Even fresh facts in the absence of intelligent contextual commentary made the cable "a misfortune to persons in this country who wish to study and keep the run of European politics." Poor reporting was one thing, but the press's susceptibility to sensationalism was more serious. It could lead to significant political distortions as events which in the past would have caused barely a ripple of concern were amplified into *causes célèbres*.[31]

It seemed that every credit associated with modern civilization had a corresponding debit. Indeed, civilization had its trade-offs, "its inconveniences not less than its manifold comfort and advantages." For example, cheap, reliable transport shortened distances and made available low-cost goods, but it also provided convenient conduits for the spread of epidemics and the importation of new pests and plant weed species. Railways connected peoples to their mutual benefit, but they could also "bind distant nations together in affliction, and make them partakers of calamity." "Pestilence travels by steam nowadays," said the *Galaxy;* "cholera takes to the rail." Thus an outbreak of plague in eastern Russia in 1879 briefly stimulated fears that it might spread rapidly throughout the globe. Agricultural science was providing humankind with food in unparalleled quantities, but Malthusians worried that science was "hastening the time when the whole world will be over-populated." Abundant harvests abroad made for cheap food, but crop failures or shortages could also cause great distress in faraway places. Better diets, coupled with improvements in hygiene and public health, were dramatically extending life expectancy, but the problem of suicide, which would engage the attention of Durkheim a generation later, was already making itself felt. In an essay on suicide, one author asserted that "Self-killing is emphatically the crime of intellectual peoples. Almost unknown to savages, rare among Mohammedans, it rages among the nations most advanced in culture and refinement with a fierceness exactly proportional to their mental development."[32]

The same inventions that produced new benefits also created new hazards of all kinds: "railway and steamer accidents, the crush of vehicles in crowded streets, the grip of swiftly running machinery on the careless workman, the dangling electric wire, the treacherous bobtail car, and the like." For all the conveniences introduced by technology, it was already a cause for serious concern as to whether the end of slavery made possible in part by machinery—"our iron-boned, coal-eating slave"—would be replaced by an enslavement to machinery. Some were pessimistic. In *Appletons'* view, humans had "already lost power over it" and could only ask, "What will it do to us and with us?" As we shall see, many also worried that technological advances might unleash hitherto unimaginable powers of destruction. Moreover, just beginning to appear on the horizon was the international counterpart of the "social question" that increasingly agitated modern societies. Despite the universality of modern civilization, its "most serious difficulty," for Charles Dudley Warner, was "the fact that all nations do not make progress at the same time or in the same ratio." Warner was clearly putting a charitable face on the matter, for many peoples were failing to progress at all.[33]

While change destabilized and produced its share of anxieties, it also contributed to a greater sense of control and predictability inasmuch as interconnectivity had stabilized and strengthened modern society. Scientific engineering offered once unimaginable material conveniences, but social engineering in the form of new business techniques such as insurance brought unprecedented security in people's lives by attenuating and even eliminating catastrophic risk. The calamities of the past had become the manageable upsets of the present. With its capacity to harness contingency, insurance was seen as "one of the most wonderful phenomena of this wonderful age." In principle, as fate gave way to statistical certainty, and as accidents became "normal," nearly everything seemed insurable. Given the potential of insurance, some wondered why it had not extended its compass to "the occurrence of every event of an unpleasant nature which it is not in our own power to prevent." In due course, insurance companies would exploit this realization. Put differently, life insurance was a way of cultivating risk—"colonizing the future," in Anthony Giddens's phrase—one of the many tools now available for the rational planning of one's life. But far from being an exceptional development, insurance was "the natural outgrowth of a state of civilization and . . . an essential part of it." Modern society was still far removed from the "production of risk" that later theorists would see as its defining characteristic.[34]

If calamities were being globalized, so too were humane responses, as a result of a reflexive mechanism that was one of the core features built into modernity. As Adam Smith had noted a century earlier, a famine in Persia or in India could never elicit the same degree of compassion and concern as disasters closer to home, but the news could nonetheless elicit sympathy and speculation about the problem and suggestions for possible solutions. Gratified by English generosity in the wake of the Charleston earthquake of 1886, *The Nation* pointed to "a circulation of charity going on all over the world with scarcely a pause in its healing influence. Its quality is not strained by the boundary-lines of nations. It is a messenger of fraternal love and a proclamation of the brotherhood of man." In another essay on this theme, the same journal concluded that "the effect of the possibility of relieving distress at great distances in stimulating the feeling of the unity of the human race, and diminishing the dividing force of political boundaries, can hardly be over-rated." Not only natural disasters, but also man-made moral outrages could mobilize world opinion and collective action on behalf of the victims. In discussing why people ought to be concerned about Russia's persecution of the Jews, *The Century* suggested that "no part of humanity can be hurt without pain to the whole body." In this area, as in others, global modernity cut two ways. It had "enormously increased the area over which any great calamity is felt, at the same time that it has increased the area from which succor and sympathy are drawn."[35]

On balance, audits of the assets and liabilities of civilization tended to end on a positive note. Certainly by nearly every quantitative measure, it was agreed that life had improved, and not only for the few. Merely to list the achievements was to clinch the argument: "The growth of wealth, the improvements in agriculture, the advance in the mechanic arts, the increase of comforts, the amelioration of personal, domestic, and social habits, the general culture, the diffusion of education, the elevation of morals, the refinement of manners." The top-down diffusion of culture, which in the past occurred slowly, if at all, had been accelerated almost beyond belief. Even the meaning of deprivation had been changed for the better: "Now the rich are separated in the style (not of course in the material) of dress and furniture by only a few years, sometimes by only a few months. Formerly they were centuries apart." Suicide could be brushed off as an acceptable statistical and moral aberration. "We really have almost a right," insisted one letter to an editor, "when a man dies before eighty, to ask why he killed himself."[36]

Complaints about modern life, concluded one writer, "are due to the ignorance of the spirit of the age." Despite all the inevitable annoyances and aggravations, one editor, obviously exasperated by faultfinders, asked: "Where is the harm, and where the wear and tear?" "What has industry done for mankind?" asked John Hittel, who was known chiefly for his writing about California and the Pacific Coast. His response was to ask: "what has it not done?" And while progress had not yet spread throughout the world, it showed signs of doing so sooner rather than later. Despite the widely recognized existence of serious problems and for all its unevenness, the consensus held that "the general progress has been onward and upward in all civilized nations; for it has gone on side by side with civilization." Interdependence and the global division of labor assuredly had disadvantages, but, as Fiske insisted, "That the rapid and permanent character of modern progress is in great measure due to this circumstance will be denied by no one." There was no last word on this issue, but if there had been, it could well have been decreed by the editor of *Appletons'*: "Progress is the law; and the gloomy gentlemen cannot stay it with their lamentations."[37]

American Unexceptionalism

What part would the United States play in this global drama? The answer to that question was not clear, but the belief that Americans needed to stay abreast of global developments with a view to answering it was manifest in discussions of international expositions and travel. Exhibitions and tourism were first-hand experiences that involved growing numbers of people, but their influence was multiplied many times over by expository accounts. Explicitly stated in nearly all the writing about these exhibitions and about travel was the need for Americans to understand the rest of the world, to measure themselves against it, to face up to shortcomings where necessary, and to adopt superior foreign practices as the case required. "Let us admit that there is moral progress," wrote the radical cleric O. B. Frothingham in 1883, "but let us admit, at the same time, that the progress is a result of civilization in the world, not in the Western Hemisphere especially." Many other Americans were eager to learn about, and from, the rest of the world at this time.[38]

Following the success of the Crystal Palace exhibition in London in 1851, international exhibitions became an increasingly popular way for industrializing nations to celebrate, promote, and monitor their relative progress. An exhibition, according to Senator Joseph R. Hawley (R-Conn.), was "mostly a collection of what civilization has to show for itseif to-day . . . it is a flash photograph of civilization on the run." Describing the 1867 fair in Paris, one of a long string of such French productions, one writer said: "An English poet said all the world's a stage; but it was necessarily left to the French to actually put the world upon the stage, and set the nations to acting their several parts." The editor of *Appletons'* gave his readers a sense of what to expect from the forthcoming Centennial Exhibition in Philadelphia: "Here, within a few acres, the world is to be epitomized. . . . Here, Orient and Occident, the equator and the poles, the zones from the frigid to the tropical, are to show their products and their industries; here the nations are to meet cheek by jowl." By the 1870s, these fairs had become so common that one editor described the compulsion to host them as "permanent facts in modern civilization." One writer, struck by how regular and fixed these celebrations of industrial civilization had become, noted ironically that "already there are curious signs of a sort of industry of international exhibitions."[39]

Although these exhibitions relied on national pride for much of their spectator appeal, they were self-consciously internationalist in design and in intended outcome. In discussing the Centennial Exposition in Philadelphia, an occasion par excellence for nationalist self-celebration, one writer believed that it was "possibly an odd fancy to select for the main feature of our national jubilee an international show." But it was not at all odd, for it would have been pointless to extol the achievements of the United States without having some sense of where the nation stood in relation to other countries. As the art critic Earl Shinn pointed out, "an International Exhibition in which foreigners do not exhibit is, ex termini, a failure." The exhibits needed to include "in great profusion and variety, the products of industry of every civilized country." In his 1889 reflections on the value of international fairs, Hawley insisted that a purely national show was "practically an impossibility." Even if one could be pulled off, it would be self-defeating, for "the profit lies in comparisons with the works of peoples of older, or otherwise different, civilizations, of various climates, soils, traditions, habits, and processes." By design, then, the exhibitions underscored the fact of globalization.[40]

For Americans, these fairs were occasions for appreciation, comparison, and self-evaluation. In the words of an *Atlantic* essayist, they offered an "unprecedented opportunity for studying and comparing" the cultural and technological achievements of other nations. A serious study of the exhibits could teach many things, the editor of *Appletons'* agreed. "An exhibition that simply gives opportunity for self-glorification has altogether insufficient reasons for its being," he wrote. "The important thing for us to do is to learn to watch for and search out all that is superior, instructive, and suggestive, in the products of our foreign friends." The exhibition needed to be viewed as "a great school" from which Americans might "hope to see as a consequence vast improvement in the taste and in the execution of our home manufactures." In this way celebrating the success of the republican experiment was turned simultaneously into an occasion for national humility. Americans were right to take pride in their political institutions, agreed *Appletons'*, but it was quick to add that "we should sadly delude ourselves if we assumed that material progress, intellectual development, or popular education, are things that we have in any measure whatsoever exhibited more notably than some of the peoples of Europe." This humility was in some ways uncharacteristic—it extended neither to all aspects of relations with Europe nor to dealings with noncivilized peoples, as we shall see—but it was prevalent enough to suggest that Americans who thought about such things knew better than to confuse the part for the whole. "Philadelphia will not be likely to think herself a smaller place for all this," wrote the *Atlantic's* essayist. "The point is that she shall know how much larger the world is."[41]

By this time, Americans already knew that their unrelenting introduction of the mechanical inventions that symbolized the new industrial era of civilization meant that they had nothing to be ashamed of; the nationalist promotion of America's technology had always been one of the chief rationales for American participation in the world fairs. The stunning Corliss engine at Philadelphia, all 680 tons of it, symbolized America's worship of the new god of machinery. But even in the mechanical sphere, U.S. achievements did not stand alone. "We are doubtless an industrious and practical people," said one observer. "But are we distinctively so? Are not the French and the Germans equally industrious, and the English and Swiss equally practical? In most civilized States laziness is the exception, not the rule." Fifteen years later, the Cincinnati journalist Murat Halstead issued the same warning about "national conceits." "A conceit that should be removed from the American mind," he wrote, "is that these United States constitute the only country where there has been during the latest generation marked advancement. The truth is that all countries have improved in the era of railways and telegraphs, of steam and steel." As a number of pieces pointed out, in many ways great and small, the United States was becoming "more and more like other countries," caught up in a transnational process of development that was "running, in parallel lines and with nearly equal rapidity, in many countries and in many races."[42]

Americans brought the world to their doorstep, but they also brought themselves to the world. Exhibitions were artificial worlds in which artifacts were often incongruously displayed; by contrast, travel forced people to confront the world on its own terms. The emergence of modern mass tourism in the Victorian era, the transformation of travel from an onerous necessity of one's trade to a commodified means of pleasurably fulfilling desire, was made feasible by technologies that made travel less arduous: reliable steamship service that shortened the transit to Europe, railway networks, the invention of postal money orders in the 1860s, and, particularly in Europe, the creation of a tourist industry, most notably the Thomas Cook agency, that catered to foreign visitors. "How easy travelling has become in our days!" exclaimed one correspondent. "Distance now is a bagatelle," maintained Richard J. Hinton, a popular writer and frequent Republican placeman. "The question beginning to be asked of all proposed travel is, not how many miles is it to the desired destination, but how long does it take to reach there?" The voyage, formerly part ordeal and part adventure, was becoming a pleasurable experience as the destination came to eclipse the journey.[43]

British tourists had shown the way—50,000 annually after the Napoleonic Wars—but Americans were not far behind. The number of Americans going abroad increased from about 35,000 in 1870 to more than 100,000 in 1885. "The English have been called the greatest of travelers, but of recent years the Americans have outstripped them, particularly on the continent of Europe," reported J. D. Phelan, the future mayor of San Francisco and U.S. senator. To some extent, travel was assumed to be a national trait. Americans traveled well, it was thought, whereas other peoples, like the French, seemed more inclined to stay at home. Reports from abroad that Americans were "the keenest and most pertinacious sight-seers in the world" were noted with some pride. By the 1860s, retired politicians like William Seward and President Grant took tours of the world, though Godkin suggested cattily that the political wisdom acquired from such journeys, if any, ought to have been acquired much earlier. The California writer and horticulturalist Edward Berwick reported that "the Yankee tourist, armed with a valise, successfully invades Europe, Asia, Africa, or Australia, and occupies where he lists." A dramatic drop in the cost of travel led to predictions of mass tourism in the near future, but until the 1890s, when the middle classes began to travel in larger numbers, tourism as a leisure activity remained largely "a pleasure of the wealthy."[44]

Although modern means of transportation and communication made possible the first-hand acquisition of knowledge that previously could only be imagined through books, travel did not replace travel literature. Only the most intrepid and tireless traveler could get a sense of things at the global level.

Instead, the rapid growth of tourism created a demand for information about remote places and peoples that was satisfied by an explosion of travel literature. Before 1850, 323 travel books had been published; between 1850 and 1900, this figure had risen to more than 1,400. The novelty soon began to wear off, however, and by 1870 the journals were already complaining that the genre had grown stale. According to *The Galaxy,* "Within the past ten or twenty years the reading public have become critical about books of travels, and demand either new and important facts or unusual felicity of description." *The Nation* underscored this sentiment by quoting Dr. Johnson's comment to Boswell: "The world is now not contented to be merely entertained by a traveller's narrative; it wants to learn something." By the 1880s, the same journal noted that library shelves were filled with redundant travelogues. "To write now of an ordinary tour abroad would be very much like describing a trip from New York to Philadelphia," it concluded.[45]

In addition to covering the minutiae of travel such as sightseeing attractions, accommodations, and local customs, the journals devoted much space to the meaning of travel. People obviously traveled for many reasons—business, health, recreation, escape, personal liberation and self-discovery, or pilgrimage. Travel was also an expression of class, a way to acquire cultural capital, to experience dissipated pleasures, to travel through time, or to confirm the superiority of the American experiment—to name a few possibilities. For cosmopolitan liberals, however, the awareness of the outside world entailed the corresponding obligation to learn something about it. Despite its ease and growing affordability, travel was not about amusement. The purpose of travel was to cultivate "the bird's-eye view of the intellect," as one author aptly phrased it. For one reviewer, Charles Sumner's arduous tour of Europe had been a model of edifying travel, an exemplification of Thoreau's grim remark that "true and sincere" travel was "as serious as the grave, or any other part of the human journey." In a deep sense, tourism was supposed to be a voyage of self-discovery and learning. Even the early travel handbooks of the day assumed that the hard work of cultural self-improvement, not pleasure as such, was one of the chief motives behind tourism.[46]

Comparing ways of life had its practical uses. The discoveries that the French sent out their washing, that they did not bake their own bread, that foreign cities had pleasant courtyards and parks, that food abroad could be better, that high-rise living had its advantages, that public administration could be vastly more efficient, that life in many ways could be more civil, generally—all these could be copied at home. According to S. G. Young: "we ignore whatever is really convenient and agreeable in continental ways of living; and this we do partly from ignorance and partly from the idea that all New World customs in regard to the manner of life are preferable to the ways of an older and more artificial society." *Appletons'* argued that the attentive American tourist was forced to confront the fact that his country was "deficient in some of the most elementary necessities of civilization," and then the editor proceeded to go into chapter and verse, particularly on the shortcomings of American cities. The net effect of having their eyes thus opened, *Appletons'* maintained on another occasion, was that Americans returning from abroad "come home rather in a subdued than a puffed-up state of mind." The observations extended to civic government, educational institutions, tipping, corruption, governmental methods, the arts and sciences, and much more. European societies had addressed and resolved many kinds of problems, while Americans were "still floundering in tedious and costly experiments." But if humility was the watchword in many discussions of Europe, hauteur was the most pronounced element of appraisals of the underdeveloped world, where Western ways had only recently begun to penetrate and globalization was still an unwelcome intrusion.[47]

The flip side of this willingness to appreciate and praise the foreign was a relentless ridicule of American provincialism. Travel for purely chauvinistic reasons, as a form of cultural missionary activity, was generally frowned upon. One guidebook declared: "It is scarcely worth while to go to Europe for the purpose of proclaiming all the time that America is in every way better." Thus *The Nation,* in discussing travel to Switzerland, asked: "why not take the further pains to improve his opportunity by gaining some knowledge of the nature of the country, the habits of the people, and the peculiarities of the language which they speak?" Arguing that "self-idolatry" was the source of China's failure to come to terms with the modern world, an essay in *Scribner's* insisted that "there is no cure for this overweening national vanity but travel." Mark Twain might burlesque the difficulties of the German language, but it was more common for American readers to encounter ridicule of the linguistic incompetence of their fellow countrymen in everyday situations abroad. Notwithstanding the spread of English, knowledge of French and German was still indispensable to becoming a bona fide cosmopolitan. "Without a knowledge of these two languages," insisted Harvard president Charles W. Eliot, "it is impossible to get at the experience of the world upon any modern industrial, social, or financial question, or to master any profession which depends upon applications of modern science."[48]

The antiparochial objectives of travel were also highlighted by frequent jibes at the shallower forms of tourism that all too often translated into unmannerly behavior abroad of "gaudy and ill-behaved Americans." "Vulgar, vulgar, vulgar," sniffed Henry James. "Why is it that Americans," one article asked, "who are the most charming people at home, are the most disagreeable people abroad?" Too many returned with no cultural capital to show for it, "with hardly anything more than a list of their breakfasts, and especially of the breakfasts they did not eat." Clearly, many were simply going through the motions, traveling because it was the thing to do; they were traveling for travel's sake, in order to satisfy "the invincible craving of nearly every one to be considered persons of taste." *The Nation,* in passing on the comments of a London paper, provided a description of what would later become an all-too-familiar scene with tourists from other nations: "They pass over the European Continent no longer as single spies, but in heavy battalions, sometimes 'personally conducted,' in squadrons of 50 or 100, by one of Cook's captains, but oftener still in helpless little family or neighborhood groups, going they know not where to see they know not what . . . but they swarm everywhere." They knew only what their English-speaking guides or guidebooks told them, and they went from place to place in such haste! "The speed at which our countrymen get across Europe is proverbial," noted George Pond, a *Galaxy* editor, with evident disapproval. For some, the speed of the journey became literally more important than the destination, as the title of one work, *"A Race with the Sun,"* suggests. For this kind of tourist, European travel amounted to little more than "a change of air and scene and a heavy expenditure of cash." Already visible in such comments is the germ of what would become a long-running debate on high culture versus mass culture as instruments of cultural change.[49]

A question asked then, as well as later, was how many people were culturally "broadened" by tourism? In some cases, especially when confronted by technological backwardness and an apparently irrational worship of tradition in other lands, travel clearly had the provincializing effect of hardening prejudices and confirming the superiority of American ways. One article, for example, scorned "the ten thousand shams that are worshiped because of their antiquity." But was such a stance appropriate? The editor of *Harper's* doubted "whether the true spirit of Americanism consists in sneering at the intelligence and advancement of other lands." No people pretending to greatness could afford "to present itself to mankind as a testy, bragging, boisterous bully, the youngest and most remote of powerful nations, but too experienced to care to learn and too wise not to know more than the whole world." Such behavior was indicative of a lack of culture, that is, a cosmopolitan sensibility. It was culture that bestowed meaning on tourism by creating the genuine desire to travel, and it was cultural growth, in the form of insightful appreciation of the sights and societies encountered abroad, that constituted the payoff to travel.[50]

Some doubters and critics pointed to the dangers of travel and complained about the money that was being spent abroad, when so much of value could be discovered at home. Some expressions of cultural isolationism were even heard in reaction to the growing Europeanization of some Americans. Phelan preferred that Americans keep their distance from Europe, lest "a fickle and perverse generation might become enamored of a condemned civilization, and fall away from their own." For Phelan, travel was "one of the principal de-Americanizing forces at work" and "every shipload of returning tourists of this sort [was] a Trojan horse of danger." Even *The Nation*, easily the most ecumenical of journals, realized that cosmopolitanism could be taken too far. By the 1870s, it noted that growing numbers of Americans were leading bicontinental lives, "their hearts and affections being wholly in neither." *The Atlantic* reported fears that the current generation of American travelers had "no trace of republican simplicity." But, as a matter of principle nineteenth century liberals saw no conflict between nationalism and internationalism. There was nothing un-American about an appreciation of other ways of life.[51]

The journals gave counsel and provided meaning to Americans who traveled abroad, primarily to Europe, but for those who pined for more exotic climes they made available first-hand narrative accounts and reviews of books describing out-of-the-way locales that few would ever experience directly. The prolific travel writer Thomas W. Knox observed that only a few years earlier Americans would have thought his journey through China and Mongolia as likely as a voyage to the South Pole. A wonder like the Great Wall of China was a matter of schoolbook knowledge, "but its location and character were little better defined than those of the Mountains of the Moon." In this way, the textual mediation of experience continued to outrun direct exposure, to the point that travel itself was no longer considered *de rigueur*. For a cultural nationalist like Phelan, this was all to the good. Rather than make the actual journey, one could "sit down in his library and read accurate accounts of distant places with perfect confidence." Even internationally minded types sometimes agreed that some places were too remote, too dangerous, and perhaps too disturbing to visit. Mexico, by one account, was best encountered in books, whereas Europe deserved to be visited in the flesh.[52]

It was also understood that tourism was only one of many kinds of cultural interchange that produced knowledge of the world. Those who championed high culture believed that an extended sojourn abroad was indispensable to personal formation. "At no time in our history has a year or two in Europe, for study and travel, been regarded as a more indispensable part of a young gentleman's education than in this year of grace, 1882," noted *The Century*. For the American lucky enough to spend a year abroad, *Scribner's* insisted that he had "got more pleasure for his money, more priceless memories, more useful knowledge, more culture in language, and manners, and art, than it would be possible for him to get at home in fifty years. This may be 'treason' and, if it is, we hope it will be 'made the most of.'" The value of popular travel was small compared to the blessings that flowed from intellectual exchange and sustained study abroad, preferably in one of the world-leading German universities, even though only about 2,000 students were enrolled overseas in any given year. According to *The Nation*, "the interchange of benefits takes place through books and the intercourse of quiet students." Yet, whatever its complexities and limitations, few would have disagreed with *Harper's* contention that "travel is worth doing. It is education, and a very great part of education."[53]

As Americans sought to get a conceptual grip on global civilization, it was clear that the United States was playing an important part in this great process. It was already the acknowledged leader of technology. An 1888 essay in *Scribner's* pointed out what had long since become obvious: "Nearly all of the mechanical inventions, now so indispensable, such as railroads, iron ships, telegraphs, agricultural implements, labor-saving machinery of all kinds, have come into use within less than two generations, but in no part of the world have such changes taken place as in the United States." The United States' technological dominance had become obvious to Europeans, too. As early as the 1867 exposition in Paris, "Americanization" had made its first (already unflattering) appearance as an image of the nation's prowess in commerce and industry. In some quarters America-bashing had already set in, as Americans were well aware. Noting this widespread acknowledgment of America's material superiority, *The Nation* complained of "the fashion just now for thoughtful Europeans who take up the evil tendencies of the time to attribute them en masse to the influence of the United States."[54]

But to place the United States in control of a process it was only beginning to understand is to get far ahead of things. At this point Americans were more concerned with learning how to think about global developments and their nation's place in history. In the absence of such concern, the incremental changes introduced by modernity could easily have been normalized, unthinkingly taken for granted by being assimilated into everyday culture. Not only would the extraordinary character of the transition to a global civilization have been lost to reflection through such a process of familiarization, so too would the extraordinary problems that attended this historical sea change. Resisting this tendency to divest the new of its strangeness, the journals continued to focus on globality as a subject of discussion, evaluation, and national action.[55]

The understanding that the United States was not a world unto itself and that it was being swept up into a broad historical current that was only to a small degree under its control posed many challenging and disturbing questions. One set of questions was evaluative: How should the United States imagine itself politically, racially, and culturally in a world in which unification appeared to be the inexorable fate of humankind? Was it even possible to imagine the United States existing outside of such a context? What was the country's relationship to other centers of modern civilization from which there was much to learn but which, in other ways, seemed incorrigibly retrograde? How should one think about nonindustrial societies and cultures, some of which were once the seats of flourishing civilizations? On a more practical level, awaiting American responses were some challenging international problems: the future of democracy in Europe, the relationship of race and culture to global progress, power politics and imperialism, and the prospects for world peace. The question underlying all others was: How could the United States best contribute to global civilization? It is to the examination of such topics that the succeeding chapters are devoted.

2

Creating an International Identity

Culture, Commerce, and Diplomacy

In the wake of the Civil War, the establishment of a viable national identity was understandably of great concern to Gilded Age Americans. But while nationalism was the dominant theme of the day, liberals also believed that this new national personality should have a cosmopolitan face, that it be both sovereign and global. As a reflection of their desire to create a cosmopolitan culture, liberal writers wove internationalist themes into nearly every debate about culture, economics, and government administration. This tendency to use civilization as a referential totality or normative frame of reference was evident in the struggle to create an international copyright regime; to enact a tariff that embraced universal free trade principles; and to create a civil service and diplomatic corps that could meet international standards of competence. Although they often struggled to make themselves heard in parochial Washington, liberal internationalists did on occasion achieve a measure of political success.[1]

Copyright Law and Internationalism

After 1865, the hope of internationally minded Americans that the United States would join the ranks of the world's leading nations was frustrated by the stubborn perception among continental thinkers of their country as a degraded or inferior copy of Europe. With only slight exaggeration, one annoyed writer scoffed at the stereotype of "a semi-civilized nation of fourth-rate importance, who all carried bowie-knives down their backs, picked their teeth with a fork, and were constantly fighting Indians and flogging negroes." Despite the astonishing pace of modernization in American society, luminaries like Oliver Wendell Holmes felt obliged to combat eighteenth-century biological notions, originally propagated by the Abbé Raynal and Buffon, that the New World

climate caused physical degeneration. The issue, Holmes complained mock-
ingly, was "whether or not we are on the wrong half of the planet." For the noted
neurologist William Alexander Hammond, this was plainly "false science,"
though he was forced to agree that degenerationism still held appeal for some
European intellectuals. More galling still, he confessed, the notion was "entertained with a lingering dread by some of our own people."[2]

However preposterous, degenerationist biology was taken seriously by
Americans because the cultural indictment that gave it force struck home.
They knew that European scholars like Friedrich Rätzel commonly characterized the United States as a cultural colony of the continent. Respected savants
like Alexander Von Humboldt described the United States as "a dead level of
mediocrities," a critique that had powerful domestic echoes. The nation's
most glaring shortcoming, and one that nearly everyone conceded, was cultural provincialism, together with its feeble-minded offspring, intellectual
philistinism. Even international successes, such as the enthusiastic reception
given to Buffalo Bill's Wild West extravaganza in Europe, underscored the
absence of a high culture in the United States capable of generating overseas
interest. James Bryce, in explaining the distaste of educated Americans for their
home-grown literature, noted that they "occupy themselves with European
books, watching the presses of England, France, and Germany more carefully
than almost anyone does in England." The disproportionately high consumption
of European culture was just one more indicator of American provincialism.[3]

At a point in time when nationalism was the reigning ideology and when
nations were widely believed to be embodiments of unique national spirits, the
suggestion that the United States lacked such a spirit had serious implications
about the country's ability to keep pace with the rest of the world. Even in a
gelded Hegelianism excised of its guiding World Spirit, the absence of a Burck-
hardtian high culture implied that the country lacked the spiritual rudder necessary to achieve national greatness. The coarse politics and corruption of the
Gilded Age only made matters worse. "What is the name of America now in
Europe?" asked a writer in *The Atlantic.* The answer: "A synonym for low ras-
cality." The United States was "a country without solidarity, without a soul; an
accidental conglomerate of uncongenial particles, a population of immigrants,
a base mart." As late as the 1870s, American intellectuals were still responding
to European contentions that their country did not possess a national character. "Have We a National Character?" asked one piece. Perhaps there was something in the air after all.[4]

In a landmark essay that appeared in *The Atlantic* in 1869, an aggrieved James Russell Lowell was willing to stipulate that American culture "had certainly been provincial, one might almost say local, to a very unpleasant extent," but he insisted gamely that the situation was changing and that discussion was now taking "a broader scope and a higher tone." Few people appeared to believe Lowell, however, for the most visible sign of the nation's extraordinary economic success was an epidemic of materialism. Culture-vultures felt the lash of John Stuart Mill's description of America as a nation in which "the life of the whole of one sex is devoted to dollar-hunting, and of the other to breeding dollar-hunters." Charles Dudley Warner worried that materialism was so powerful in America that it was "more likely to get the mastery over the spiritual and the intellectual here than elsewhere." On this score, Thoreau as usual gave no quarter in delivering a tongue-lashing to his countrymen. Americans, he claimed, were "warped and narrowed by an exclusive devotion to trade and commerce and manufactures and agriculture and the like, which are but means, and not the end." Twenty years later, Walt Whitman would make much the same case. He pronounced the nation "an almost complete failure in its social aspects and in really grand religious, moral, literary, and aesthetic results."[5]

To cosmopolitan intellectuals, a major cause of the nation's cultural inferiority was the absence of international copyright protection for American authors. For twenty-five years after the war, the intelligentsia, publishers, politicians, and, at times, diplomats all debated the issue of copyright. Copyright was a multifaceted problem: it was a business matter that involved profits for publishers and jobs for workers; it raised moral and philosophical questions having to do with the rights of authors; and it was a cultural issue that touched on American cultural development and its relation to ideas emanating from abroad. But it was also a matter in which practical issues of culture, commerce, and national pride were linked to the creation of an international identity. What was, on its face, a nationalist yearning for a self-constituted culture was moved, beneath the surface, by an internationalist spirit and the assertion of the pecuniary interests of a rather small group of people, authors, who asserted universal human rights. And in a twist that could be supplied only by a political ending, in the end the problem was resolved only by bowing to the interests that had long blocked its solution.

The United States did have national copyright legislation. Following British practice, the copyright act passed in 1790 granted privileges for fourteen years to American authors (extended to twenty in an 1831 revision), with renewal rights of another fourteen. But protection of intellectual property by national means alone proved impossible in the context of a growing international cultural marketplace in which works circulated with few legal hindrances. British authors, in particular, fell victim to large-scale piracy in the United States as American publishers, taking full advantage of the golden age of the English novel, scrambled to reprint recently released manuscripts of proven British writers. "Publishing in America was a queer business then," recalled Henry Holt, often less a matter of publishing than of reprinting. Another publisher's memoir recalled that the works of Darwin, Huxley, Spencer, and other greats were "stolen with perfect impunity." The United States' dependence on Great Britain's literary production was also evident in the large numbers of reprints from British journals and reviews. The result was a strange form of cultural imperialism in which the British exercised a cultural hegemony without receiving the corresponding economic benefits normally enjoyed by imperial powers.[6]

Unsurprisingly, British publishers who complained noisily about American practices lost no time in hoisting the black flag of piracy when popular American authors emerged. "To steal English books is piracy," complained *Scribner's* of this double standard in 1872, "to take American, a matter of course." The situation was further complicated by the fact that not all American publishers were "highwaymen." Over the years, there had emerged gentlemanly understandings in which many of the better known British writers attached themselves to particular publishers and were paid nonobligatory royalties in what was called the "courtesy of the trade," a practice that was, as one prominent publisher described it, "an act of grace and not of legal obligation." Because many foreign authors habitually sold advance sheets of their most recent books to American publishers, their financial situation was not as bad as it first appeared. For a privileged few, the payoff was greater than it would have been under copyright protected royalties.[7]

Although publishers and the reading public benefited economically from the absence of international copyright, the literary community perceived that the net effect of this massive reliance on cheap British literary products was, as Noah Webster had warned, disastrous to American letters. A generation of great American authors did emerge by midcentury, but after the Civil War the charge of mediocrity became credible again as the brief golden age ended.

One essay, written in 1886, complained that "already a decadence in our literature is apparent; most of our brilliant writers of the last generation are passing away, and where will we find others to fill their places?" In 1888, the editor at *Harper's* concluded: "We have something worse than a literary past: we have a second-hand literary past, the literary past of a rich relation." For some the old question posed by Sydney Smith in 1818 in the *Edinburgh Review*, "Who reads an American book?" was threatening to turn into the question "Who writes an American book?" Although one editorial described the state of American authorship as "depressing to the last degree," by the 1880s calls were increasingly heard for someone to produce "the great American novel."[8]

International copyright advocates claimed that American writers, handicapped by their inability to break into the market for novels, were being forced to write for the magazines to put food on their table. A sizable number of novels did appear on a serial basis, many of them, ironically, in magazines published by the very same houses that took so little notice of home-grown writers in the book trade. It was better than nothing, but authors who serialized their work usually did so for a straight fee in which they abandoned copyright privileges. Those authors who had been successful, it was maintained, had independent incomes that afforded them the time to write, a situation that ill befitted a republic. Politicians were partly to blame for this situation. They had not hesitated to defend special industrial interests through high tariffs that harmed consumers, but their solicitude did not extend to literature. "In all schemes and appeals for the protection of native industry that we have ever seen," complained the novelist and editor William Dean Howells, "the claims of one section of national workers, the authors and artists, have been entirely overlooked." To be sure, some rather Byzantine ways could be used to secure copyright abroad, but these expedients probably made more money for lawyers than for authors and did not make the need for copyright reform any the less urgent.[9]

Why did it matter where novels came from? Those who gave serious thought to the question of why culture mattered were convinced that it was not simply an adornment, pleasing only to aesthetes and high society types, but rather a prerequisite of healthy national status. In a speech given to the Yale Political Science Club, Henry Holt described literature as "a foundation stone of a nation's greatness and permanence. It first awakens the patriotism of the child, and it informs the patriotism of the man. To a nation at war, poetry is almost as essential as powder." The hoary culture–materialism dichotomy was misleading, for it made culture appear to be solely a matter of art and aesthetic appreciation, when in fact it permeated every aspect of social life. When culture was construed more broadly as social intelligence, it was of enormous practical relevance to solving urgent problems of politics and economics. *The Nation* made the case that "civilization is the result of culture, and high culture; and it is based on the old and impregnable truth that reason ought to rule; and the better trained it is, the better it rules." *Appletons'* argued that the American people deserved a literature "that implants ideas connected with their best development, and strengthens intellectual growth in those directions favorable to national character." If culture was essential to national character, America, as the author Maurice Thompson argued, could "ill afford to have her children's characters formed in any large degree by direct alien forces."[10]

Nationalism was thus the chosen insignia of those who advocated international copyright and they were not shy about displaying it as prominently as possible. The absence of an international copyright accord "amounts to self-stultification and self-condemnation" declared *Scribner's*, in one of its many articles devoted to this issue. Finding it humiliating that an advanced nation of forty million could not generate its own literature, another of its editorials played to lingering anti-British sentiment. "Are we to be children always, living upon the wealth of the British mother that bore us?" it asked. Literary independence was, of course, a matter of national pride, but the good of the people was also at stake. "The literature which is the outgrowth of their own life, country, and institutions, is the best for them," it was argued. *The Century*, another journal that was much concerned about this issue, also took a nationalist tack. "By reason of this injustice," it claimed, "the literary production of our own country has been cramped and well-nigh crushed."[11]

A second line of argument, one that was very much contrary to the inclination of the courts, held that intellectual property, as a matter of natural right, deserved the same protection as real property. It was frequently pointed out that the United States, though eager to provide patent protection for inventors, was not nearly as interested in safeguarding the literary inventions of writers. According to one editorial, "A creator and inventor has a natural right to the product of his brain." In a talk reprinted in *Scribner's*, the British academic and editor Charles Edward Appleton insisted that "the primary, vital value of every book is given to it by its author, and this in equity he never alienates," regardless of where in the world the book was purchased. If literary production was truly property; if, as advocates maintained, "property is simply the absolute right of individual enjoyment and disposition of the thing owned," then the absence of comprehensive copyright protection amounted to government toleration of theft. A few extremists suggested that the ideal solution lay in *eliminating* copyright legislation altogether and in placing intellectual property on the same footing as other forms of property.[12]

Because the natural right position was, by definition, a universalist outlook, attempts were made to set it in a global context in which the rights of authors were coming to be more broadly recognized. "The idea of property is a product of civilization," noted Arthur G. Sedgwick, a New York lawyer and frequent contributor to *The Nation*. "In copyright, however, we have a sort of property which is even now, under our very eyes, freeing itself from the early communistic fetters, and establishing for itself a footing," in part by gaining "an almost universal recognition." *The Century* argued that "the logic of civilization is inevitable—either the rule of property in what a man makes is universal, or it should be wholly abolished. . . . If a book does not belong to him who wrote it, then a horse does not belong to him who bred him, or a ship to him who built it. The question is not between the author and publisher, but between civilization and barbarism." This argument from the universal natural right and justice perspective made it easier to point out something that tended to get lost in the confusion: that the immediate victims of the existing system were British authors, who continued to lobby their government on behalf of a copyright arrangement with the United States. A few writers, like Oliver Wendell Holmes, did emphasize this side of things, but for obvious reasons it was not politic to show undue sympathy for British grievances.[13]

By this standard, the toleration of literary piracy was "a most undignified and disgraceful," even barbaric, practice in which the United States lagged far behind more enlightened nations who were actively addressing the problem. In 1884 the European nations took steps to negotiate a multilateral international copyright convention. The U.S. State Department did send a delegate to the 1886 conference in Berne but showed no interest in pursuing American membership. As the decade dragged on, the continued delay in enacting legislation was depicted by Thorvald Solberg, who would later head the Copyright Office, as an "eternal national disgrace." The United States and Russia, it was unhappily noted, were the only two civilized nations standing outside the copyright union. Worse still, by 1889, even the South American states had formed a copyright union of their own, which in some respects was even more liberal than that of the Berne convention. Embarrassed by his country's retrograde position, George Parsons Lathrop—poet, novelist, and founder of the American Copyright League—complained that "we are at a lower stage than nations which we are glad to look on as less moral and more backward."[14]

Internationalists had to tread lightly for fear of being labeled un-American, but the cultural nationalism of the copyright reformers was not a sham. Identifying with a global literary community was every bit as necessary to identity formation as negating and rejecting foreign works, for American highbrows of the day saw culture as a universal phenomenon. In Matthew Arnold's influential definition, it was "the best that has been thought and known in the world"; a definition that stands in contrast to today's view of culture as something unique and incommensurable. The cosmopolitans were less interested in national self-assertion than in the degree to which the nation was participating in the universal, supracultural drama being played out through globalization. "We cannot step out of the world's current," said *The Atlantic Monthly,* ". . . because there is a spiritual demand in us which cries louder than the thin voice of a self-conscious national life." How could one judge a nation's literature except by reference to the whole? There should be a willingness, argued *The Nation,* "to submit to a universal standard of criticism." For its part, *The Century* argued that "the classics of every nation should be read by every nation." For a very few, the ultimate goal was an international literature. In his "plea for culture," Thomas Wentworth Higginson envisioned a vibrant global marketplace of ideas in which America's participation would assure the nation's cultural greatness. In time, through talent and not chicanery, American authors would enjoy the same degree of international esteem as that achieved by English writers. By this logic, promoting American authors was also a way of promoting an international literature—and vice versa, of course.[15]

The argument on behalf of international copyright was presented with passion, sophistication, and much rhetorical skill. But whether a problem did indeed exist, and, if so, whether anything needed to be done about it, remained open questions. As one writer observed, the absence of international copyright, though a symptom of provincialism, also had given Americans "greater facilities for an acquaintance with European literature than the Europeans themselves enjoy. And cultural inferiority would not last forever." If not in the production of culture, then at least in its consumption Americans ranked high. "We learn easily and civilize quickly," said the *Atlantic*. Americans had been preoccupied with practical affairs, but that situation would surely change in the natural course of things. The prevailing view of American cultural backwardness was that it was due to growing pains, as in Emerson's description of the country "passing through a crisis in its history as necessary as lactition or dentition, or puberty." Taking the long—and optimistic—view, John Fiske saw the nation "traversing what may properly be called the barbarous epoch of our history." This phase would in due course be outgrown, as there was no lack of talent. "Our possible Titians and Leonardos have invented machinery, or made enormous fortunes in newly discovered ways of their own," explained *The North American Review*. In any case, the situation was not as bleak as advocates of international copyright suggested. Any dispassionate observer would have to grant that American literature was not entirely a blank page and that some progress was being made in the arts and music. In point of fact, some American authors were being read abroad.[16]

Moreover, those who criticized the nation for materialism could be criticized in turn, either for outright hostility to modernity or for failure to understand its spirit. "Their eyes are turned backward, not forward," said John Hittell. Anyway, without a supporting foundation, culture was of little value. First things first, suggested the editor of *Appletons'*, who complained that "art is continually discussed as if it were the fabric rather than the embroidery of existence its object rather than an incidental feature." One had only to consider the sad example of Italy to conclude that "instead of art necessarily elevating a people, it may lend itself with fatal facility to their decline." In short: more matter, less art. Given the overwhelming need to apply intellect to "the problems of Nature and of life," an excessive concern for art and literature was "an absolute injury to the common weal." America, in its "peculiar genius," had much to be proud of.[17]

In addition, a powerful theoretical case could be made for inaction on copyright. The high priest of protectionist theory of the day, Henry C. Carey, argued that the existing system well served American culture and the national interest. Carey attacked copyright reformers in their philosophical citadel when he rejected the natural right argument rooted in property by arguing that copyright was an unnatural monopoly. Nearly a century before Roland

Barthes declared the death of the author, Carey insisted that novelists like Dickens, Scott, and Irving had not really created anything. Instead, they "drew largely upon the common stock of ideas, and dressed them up in a new, and what has proved to be most attractive form." "The man who makes a book uses the common property of mankind," Carey claimed, while the author's contribution was limited to "workmanship." Far from suffering, American authors were flourishing and were likely to do even better in the future. The United States was, in his view, "the paradise of the author." After all, publishers, he claimed, were being inundated by poor and unpublishable manuscripts, which suggested that writers did not lack for incentives.

In any event, Carey insisted that international copyright would not bring the marvelous results being predicted by the reformers. Rather, its chief beneficiaries would be established British authors. Because of lower production costs, international copyright would only accelerate U.S. demand for their books and would result in "increasing our dependence on foreigners for the means of amusement and instruction." Copyright reformers, Carey believed with some justification, were using nationalism only as a smokescreen. The entire copyright movement smacked of being a front for his bugbear, British economic imperialism, which as usual was cloaked in universal principles of free trade. Industrial independence preceded literary or political independence, and by virtue of its growing industrial might the United States was well on its way to erecting "a great literary and scientific edifice." Because the industrial foundation was "already broad, deep, and well laid," Carey concluded that nothing should be done.[18]

By the 1880s, the situation had reached a stalemate. Decade after decade, bills had been introduced, only to languish in committee, leading some frustrated reformers to suggest the adoption of a diplomatic approach. But neither congressional legislation nor treaty negotiations with Great Britain went anywhere because publishers in each country pursued one-sided agendas. Writers began to organize themselves more effectively in the 1880s by forming the American Authors' League, and prominent English authors such as Tennyson and Matthew Arnold joined the battle. The magazines tried to make the issue a cause célèbre. Most notably *The Century* invited open letters from distinguished authors in a special issue. But the real impetus for change came from domestic competition, in the form of more efficient pirates who beat the established publishers at their own game by publishing cheap, mass market editions at prices that the well-known presses could not match. *The Nation* could not resist rubbing it in, praising the work of "an ingenious system of piracy within piracy" in which the new buccaneers had succeeded in "ruining the once profitable business of respectable piracy." *Homo homini lupus.* More embarrassing still, no shortage of legitimating ideological support was to be found for this new plague of thievery. For those who cared to look, noted Sedgwick, for more than a generation the popular press and congressional documents had offered numerous arguments that justified literary piracy as "one of the main bulwarks of national progress."[19]

Another source of concern among established publishers was the decline in readership. Insiders talked about "the decadence' of the book trade," especially outside of the cities, where bookshops were declining in number. Henry Holt complained of the "sudden and tremendous falling off in the demand for books of all kinds." Earlier questions about audiences for American books and the future of American authors were in danger of being replaced by an even more alarming query, one that was raised in a popular novel by an English visitor to the United States: "Do Americans read?" To counter this threat to their business model, the publishers mobilized to break the long deadlock. When they and their trade unions—an estimated 60,000 members—decided to protect their interests, the gridlock in Congress began to break up. When it came to political influence, it was said of the influential publishing firm of Harper and brothers that "the little finger of Mr. Harper is thicker than the loins of all the literary and scientific men in the United States put together."[20]

Once the publishers were on board, the outline of a deal acceptable to all became clearly visible. After many false starts, a bill finally passed Congress in 1891 that allowed for international copyright by bilateral treaty, provided that the works of foreign authors were reprinted in the United States. The publishers were pleased, as were the unions, and the authors got what they wanted. Henry Holt looked forward to "a new race of Irvings and Hawthornes and Longfellows and Emersons to bring us back from Anglomania . . . to a sober working out of our own free ways." But, as is usual with legislation, the connection between intentions and outcomes was murky. The New York *Tribune* wrongheadedly interpreted the bill's passage as evidence that "the provincial spirit . . . happily grows less prevalent and obtrusive in this country year by year," even though the rationale underlying the legislation was frankly nationalist and the property rights of authors were an afterthought in what, everyone agreed, was primarily a publisher's bill. For those who believed in natural rights, the authors' right to sell their property to any publisher they desired was being violated because they were in effect being forced to sell to American houses. And while the United States no longer flew the skull and crossbones, it was hardly a model citizen of the international republic of letters. It refused to join the Berne copyright convention, and it would not accept international norms until well into the twentieth century.[21]

The copyright solution also did nothing to moderate a tight protectionist regime in other cultural matters, particularly with respect to importing books and works of art, which continued to be taxed at high rates—and English-language works were taxed at the highest. Imported foreign books, for example, continued to carry stiff tariffs. Following the imposition of a 35 percent duty on British books in 1867, *The Nation* complained that "in all that regards the acquisition and diffusion of knowledge, the legislation of the last two Congresses has been little better than might be expected from an assemblage of Goths or Huns." The book trade, led by Henry Houghton and supported by some authors as well, continued to back the tariff in the face of proposals for repeal of import duties, which began to appear in 1877. Because American authors came under tariff protection, many more writers favored tariffs than the old copyright system. In this case, the publishers, fearful of competing with British publishers who enjoyed lower production costs, shunned the populist robes they had donned in the copyright debate. Their once-ballyhooed desire to provide American readers with cheap books was blithely disregarded, as the high tariff wall blocked the flow of low-priced English reprints of American authors.[22]

The copyright debate was more confusing than it should have been because it was difficult to read the true convictions of the various parties. Internationalists used nationalist justifications; monopolists argued in favor of educating the masses through cheap literature; and self-interested authors cloaked their desire to pad their incomes by resort to internationalist reasoning. Yet all this rhetorical cloaking of motives did not mean that the debate was devoid of principled ideological beliefs. As Henry Holt pointed out, "Our most active agitators against international copyright include the most active agitators against international trade and against an honest dollar." For internationalists, the ultimate goal was to create a global marketplace in which the natural property rights of authors were universally recognized, in which the physical circulation of texts was allowed to proceed without impediment, and in which Americans would participate as equals in a global traffic of ideas, art, and literary productions.[23] That kind of ideology could not be unclothed to reveal naked self-interest.

Internationalizing the Tariff Debate

For many liberals, the solicitude for corporate interests that lay behind the copyright dispute was indicative of a deeper problem: a wrongheaded philosophy of protection that gave ideological cover to special interests. With the rise of the Republican Party and the defeat of the Confederacy, a trend toward lower tariffs in the antebellum years gave way to an era of high protectionism that was not definitively reversed until after World War II. The Morrill Tariff of 1861, one of whose intellectual architects was Henry C. Carey, inaugurated a rise in rates, with some ups and downs, from about 17 percent in 1857 to an average rate of 49.5 percent in the McKinley Tariff of 1890 (a moderate tariff was considered to be in the 30s). The tariff was extraordinarily cumbersome, too, for instead of charging uniform ad valorem rates, duties were determined separately for individual items or classes of items. With time, the tariff turned into a fixed feature of the political landscape—so immovable that Godkin denounced it as "a sort of American fetish." But protectionism was never naturalized to the point of being unchallenged dogma. By the late 1880s, it had once again become the most contentious issue in American politics. Although tariff debate could be extraordinarily dreary stuff, no other issue so clearly revealed the underlying conflict between nationalist and internationalist assumptions about the modern world.[24]

Free trade is intrinsically an internationalist doctrine, as can be seen by looking at the international and global arguments deployed by liberals. First and foremost, they believed that free trade was rooted in economic science and was therefore true everywhere and at all times, in which case the protectionist pursuit of self-interest was the negation of self-interest correctly understood. "The question whether free-trade or protection is the best policy is a scientific question," insisted *The Nation*, which took the lead in the never-ending quest for tariff reform. Protection, suggested Godkin, was "as much of a chimera as trying to make mountains of water in mid-ocean. When everybody is protected, nobody is protected." For the sociologist William Graham

Sumner, protectionist logic was implanted in the belief that there was "no universal science of wealth, but only a national science of wealth." Hence, to deny economic internationalism was to deny the universality of science. But such unmindful ignorance could not last forever. The idea of free trade would win the struggle in the end, insisted Godkin, "just as the Copernican system and religious toleration won it, and Darwinism is winning it."[25]

Unfortunately, what constituted scientific knowledge in this area was still hotly contested. Liberal polemicists attributed the failure of free trade doctrines to take root to parochialism and to a lack of theoretical interest in political economy. Writing in *The North American Review* in January 1876, one academic lamented the sad fact that "the United States have thus far done nothing towards developing the theory of political economy." This was true if one defined theory narrowly in free trade terms, but as Paul Bairoch has pointed out, "the modern protectionist school of thought, the one connected with the 'post-industrial revolution' was actually born in the United States." Alexander Hamilton was an early patron saint of protectionism. Another founder of the school, the German Friedrich List, spent a decade in the United States. But more influential at the time was "the Philadelphia school of political economy" and its high priest, Henry C. Carey, whose idiosyncratic but impressive outpouring of writings spanned the middle third of the century. Although Carey championed an optimistic version of domestic laissez-faire, he fiercely rejected the arguments of what he called the "cosmopolitan school" of political economy on various grounds. Free trade was an instrument of British imperialism, he believed, and in addition was likely to embroil the United States in foreign wars and lead to governmental centralization. Carey objected to the internationalist approach because it overlooked the basic fact that humankind was an abstraction built atop the underlying reality of discrete national units. Largely forgotten today, Carey's ideas were influential enough to be taught side-by-side with free trade doctrine in many colleges in the last half of the nineteenth century, much as a century later creationist views would be presented in tandem with Darwinian thought in American high schools.[26]

The absence of a scientific consensus allowed the conflict to be fought on a variety of other intellectual battlegrounds, especially political philosophy. As with international copyright, the attempt was made to base free trade in the universal natural right of property. In one notable polemic, David A. Wells, widely respected for his work as special commissioner of the revenue and one of the most formidable defenders of free trade, argued that freedom of exchange was "the highest right of property," without which "civilization would obviously be impossible." He concluded that "free exchange between man and man—or, what is the same thing, free trade—is therefore action in accordance with the teachings of nature." In a disingenuous variation on this theme, Godkin went so far as to suggest that protection, by virtue of the way in which it transferred property into the hands of the undeserving, contained within itself "the germ of communism"—the ultimate violation of natural right—because it provided socialists with a precedent for schemes to redistribute property. If "it is right to use the ballot for taking, by law, the property of the consumer and giving it over to the manufacturer and his workmen, it is equally right for the poor to use their ballot to take from the rich and give to the needy," his editorial reasoned.[27]

History and the lessons of the past were also brought into play. Protectionist contentions that free trade doctrine consisted of empty theories that had no basis in experience elicited the liberal rejoinder that all history demonstrated its truth. "The history of civilization is in reality the history of the liberation of the race from a variety of arbitrary interferences with men's industrial activity," claimed Godkin. Protectionism ignored a discredited past in which rulers had repeatedly and clearly frustrated the workings of economic law. Liberals maintained that protectionism was, at a minimum, "as old as feudalism," having originated in the archaic tradition of bestowing monopolies. It was therefore something of a mystery why protectionists, living in a society that claimed to be antifeudal to the core, would refer to this medieval practice with pride as "American political economy." According to Wells, mercantilist notions, "which had come down from the Middle Ages," seemed "very strange and most absurd" when viewed in the light of late nineteenth-century knowledge. Dubious etymology, too, was conscripted by liberals who suggested that the word "tariff" had disreputable origins, stemming presumably from the Moors of Tarifa who demanded extortionate payments to permit goods to cross the straits of Gibraltar. But the point was clear enough: To the extent that history could be construed as the history of freedom—which was "the prime moral principle in the civilization of today," according to one statistician—laissez-faire and free trade were among its principal contemporary agents. On the other hand, tariffs and trade restrictions were a "relic of past times, when nations were held to be the natural enemies of each other."[28]

The argument for civilization in making the case against protection was used time and again. Writing to *The North American Review*, the British M. P. John Bright, a liberal idol, attempted to embarrass Americans into free trade. Its absence, he wrote, "seems now your one great humiliation." As a cautionary example of the dangers of a self-enclosed national economy, critics often highlighted China's alleged insularity over thousands of years. In measuring a nation's vitality, it was argued, it was "unrestricted intercourse . . . which saves it from stagnation or decline." Chinese methods were medieval not only externally but also internally, "based on the logical assumption of hostile interests between different parts of the same country as well as between foreign Countries." All of the evils in China that Westerners condemned—infanticide, slavery, abysmally low pay for laborers—could be traced back to this self-enclosure. "Protectionists make a great fuss about introducing English Free Trade," said Abbott Kinney, an early conservationist. "What then? Is it the doctrines of the Flowery Kingdom they prefer?"[29]

Free traders stepped onto more treacherous terrain when the argument shifted to American history. Since the American Revolution was caused in part by the British desire to inhibit manufacturing by passage of the mercantilist Navigation Acts, it could be argued that protectionism was, in a foundational sense, un-American. The subsequent experience of the American union and its economic success demonstrated the utility of free trade domestically, hence warranting the inference that the system deserved universal application. Given American resources and know-how, it was suggested, there was little to fear from foreign competition. When protectionists countered that America's economic expansion under protection was proof positive that they were right, free traders were compelled to offer evidence from abroad. Great Britain's experience provided the most dramatic historical example, though one that was readily turned against them. "If there ever was a principle the soundness of which seems proved by experience, it is the free-trade principle in England," argued Godkin. Since the abolition of the Corn Laws, it was said, Britain had prospered in every conceivable way: production, consumption, wages, and government revenues were up, pauperism was down, and trade had "pushed into remote regions of the globe as never before."[30]

Although free trade advocates were internationalists, they were at the same time true believers in nationalism and hence unwilling to allow protectionists to wrap themselves in the flag of patriotism. The Philadelphia industrialist

Joseph Wharton believed he was playing his trump card when he identified protection with nationalism. "The doctrine of protection to home industry, no matter by what means, grows directly and inevitably from the idea of nationality," he said. "The nation exists of itself and for itself, not by the grace or for the benefit of any beyond its boundaries." But free traders who resented the insinuation that purchasing foreign products was unpatriotic responded that it was not the nation that benefited from the tariff, but rather special interests at the expense of the great mass of consumers. "It is the consumer who pays, whoever he is," said one anonymous author. Nationalism, the author stated, was merely a flimsy euphemism that sought to cloak the "perversion of the functions of the State as the agent of all to the exclusive benefit of a few." If the object was to benefit specific businesses at the expense of foreigners, direct subsidies, justified by appeals to the national interest, would have been a more honest policy. Moreover, there was nothing particularly American about the constant readjustment of tariff schedules with a view to accommodating parochial manufacturing interests. Whatever the faults of free trade, at least it would not cater to subnational interest groups, nor would it tolerate the perennial tariff donnybrooks in Congress that were "a positive curse to everybody." On this issue, therefore, no distinction could be drawn between nationalism and internationalism, for the economic interests of a country were, "when rightly understood, the true interest of the whole world."[31]

Another international theme emphasized by free trade writers was world peace. "Free trade in its fullest development tends to make men friends rather than strangers," wrote Wells, "[and] does more to maintain amicable relations between them than all the ships of war that ever were built or all the armies that ever were organized." In contrast, protectionism bred war, as evidenced by the long period of mercantilist conflict in Europe. According to one writer, mercantilism had "deluged the earth in blood." At the extreme, the refusal to trade could itself be considered an act of hostility. This argument was applied, with not a little casuistry, in the course of "opening" Japan and China. According to Yale professor D. Cady Eaton, "A nation which withdraws itself from commercial relations with other nations withdraws itself from the brotherhood of nations and from the brotherhood of mankind." On the other hand, if peace was the natural inclination of humankind and if economic relations were rooted in natural law, then it made sense to assume, as the British reformer Richard Cobden had argued, that all foreign relations "ought to conform to and be ruled by the laws of political economy." Statesmanship, from this viewpoint, "was to be looked upon as a branch of economics." By this standard, all the shibboleths of traditional diplomacy, above all the mantra of "balance of power," were "little better than empty phrases."[32]

The protectionists, swinging the still powerful ideological club of Anglophobia, responded that free trade was the surest route to imperialism. As one writer in *The North American Review* put it, free trade meant "the unflinching march forward in the conquest by British arms of Africa and the entire Mohammedan world and ultimately of China and Japan." Free trade thus promised only "the career of unending foreign war." In the words of Van Buren Denslow, a Careyite, Great Britain's remarkable expansion was the direct result of the search for foreign markets. "Every sunrise is announced by the reveille of English drums, awakening English soldiers to back with the bayonet some new intrusion on the rights of barbarian races," he wrote. Competition in world markets was already so fierce, it was pointed out, that only imperialist methods of forceful entry like those employed by the European powers could assure an American place at the table. Moreover, in reality free trade meant unequal terms of trade. It was simply a British imperialist trick that would "keep every agricultural community chained hand and foot to the car of Imperial Britain." By this reckoning, it was easy to conclude that free traders were dupes of the British. According to one letter writer, the American free trader "delivers the messages and does the errands of the English Cobden Club."[33]

Despite their arguments, the political tide turned dramatically against the free traders. Economic depression in the 1870s led protectionists to argue that any opening of the home market at this moment of weakness would have calamitous consequences. Although politicians began increasingly to talk about overproduction and the need to export the surplus manufactures through increased trade, free trade prescriptions were even less palatable than before. Instead, protectionists developed the idea that the nation's problems were due to the fact that tariffs were not high enough; the problems of protection could be solved only with more protection, by putting in place prohibitive tariffs. The protectionists also identified the weak merchant marine as both consequence and cause of hard times and proposed bounties that would make American shipping competitive. A merchant marine, it was claimed, might also prove useful in time of war. Adherents of the so-called Manchester School of free trade pointed out the flaws in each of these arguments and were quick to respond that protection had caused the problem in the first place, but to little effect.[34]

Developments abroad also turned against the free traders. In the 1860s, it could still be argued that the United States was out of step with the rest of the world. For example, in 1869, *The Nation* declared confidently that "the tendency of opinion the world over is towards the recognition of the free-trade doctrine as the natural law of human intercourse." But only a decade later free trade had given way to a protectionist trend as Italy in 1878, Germany and Canada in 1879, and France in 1881 imposed high tariffs. "Protectionism is running mad on the continent of Europe," reported *The Nation*. "It would seem as though the civilized world, with the exception of England and Sweden, were going back to the mercantile system of the seventeenth century." Although European protection was moderate in comparison to American levels, the future looked grim. There even began to emerge ominous rumbles in Great Britain about "fair trade." When viewed on the bright side, these developments could be attributed to political zigzagging rather than to a principled reversal of course. In explaining the attraction of protectionism to Bismarck, for example, *The Nation* noted that he was "not a theoretician." The German tariff was thought to be the product of political maneuvering pure and simple, dominated by "the landed interest," which was true enough, but this explanation failed to point out the extent to which Bismarck had drawn inspiration from the results achieved by American protectionism.[35]

But intellectual currents were shifting, too, as continental scholars, particularly in Germany, began to develop a "historical school" of political economy. In 1867 many observers had argued that Americans were far behind Europeans in their understanding of economics, but fifteen years later it was the teachers who had abandoned their faith. "The Manchester School may be considered as practically an obsolete affair-*ein überwundener Standpunkt*-in that country," announced the up-and-coming economist Richard T. Ely. The new historicists, who at times styled themselves "realists," eschewed abstraction in favor of studies of historical development. Consistent with the rise of nationalism as the central feature of historical writing in the late nineteenth century, they insisted that national peculiarities had to be taken into account to the point that "every country is hereafter to have 'a political economy of its own.'" This sea change was affecting American economic thought as well.

"The younger men in America are clearly abandoning the dry bones of orthodox English political economy for the live methods of the German school,"
said Ely, who himself was Heidelberg-educated. The situation was so grave,
warned Cornell historian Herbert Tuttle, that American students who studied
political economy in Germany were bound to return not only as protectionists,
but as "scientific protectionists [who] believe that protective duties can be defended by something better than the selfish argument of special industries."
The cosmopolitans' appeal to trends in other civilized countries had clearly
backfired.[36]

By the early 1880s, some of the free traders' predictions about foreign retaliation started coming true as Germany, France, and other countries imposed
prohibitions on the importation of American pork, prompting some discussion
of retaliation against French wine. More than a whiff of *Schadenfreude* was
discernible in the analyses of free traders. Adopting a we-told-you so tone, *The
Nation* harped on the simple point that it was impossible to sell unless one also
bought: "The absolute prohibition of imports means the absolute absence of
exports," it chided. "One-sided commerce can by no possibility continue."
Finally, in the election of 1888, with the embarrassingly large revenue sur-
pluses being piled up by the government, the tariff became the central issue of
the national political campaign. Inasmuch as revenue had been a major justification for higher tariffs during the Civil War, the budget surplus provided an
opportunity for reformers to push for downward revision. Corruption provided another talking point. As Wells pointed out, excess revenue provided "a
constant incentive for needless and corrupt expenditures, the multiplication of
offices, and the enlargement of the sphere of influence of the federal government." The system, Wells fumed, was "a disgrace to our civilization."[37]

Over the next two years a wide-ranging debate on the future of the tariff
took place. One of its more revealing moments came when *The North American Review* asked William Gladstone, the avatar of international liberalism, to
state the case for free trade. Ten years earlier, *The Nation* had argued that the
first principle of protectionism was "that each nation should think of itself as
alone in the world." It was this nationalist conceit that Gladstone sought to
challenge. After reciting the standard litany of the evils associated with protection, he ended on a global note by asking how the United States, which was
"about to become the largest and most powerful [nation] on the stage of the
world's history," would make use of its power. He acknowledged that its

continental scale made the United States "not so much a country as in herself a world, and not a very little world." He had no doubt that the United States would have an enormous impact on the rest of the globe, but he wondered how that influence would be exercised. "Will it make us, the children of the senior races, who will have to come under its action, better or worse?" he asked. American power in the world could prove either "a blessing or a curse." Would the United States have the vision to act for the good of the global whole?[38]

A gaggle of protectionists enthusiastically engaged Gladstone's internationalist arguments. Secretary of State James G. Blaine noted that the most "remarkable feature" of Gladstone's case was "the universality of application which he demands for his theory." American protectionists were more pluralistic, hence broad-minded and tolerant than British free traders, he suggested, because "no intelligent protectionist in the United States pretends that every country would alike realize advantage from the adoption of the protective system." Seizing on Gladstone's reference to the United States as a world in itself, Blaine found it odd that "a policy which is essential to an island in the northern ocean should be adopted as the policy of a country which even to his own vision is 'a world within itself.'" Thus, in Blaine's view, economic nationalism was a reflection of particular and contingent historical realities. The nationalist view of free trade as a noble end but a dangerous means was stated with even greater starkness by Justin Morrill, senator from Vermont and author of the landmark 1861 tariff bill: "If the whole world were one vast Utopia of communistic brethren, and swords were to be beaten into ploughshares and spears into pruning-hooks, free trade might be the accepted gospel of all international intercourse, and the glories of patriotism shunned as a reproach." Unfortunately, however, the world that Americans faced was far from approaching that ideal condition. The world was in reality "a conglomerate of different races of men."[39]

If anything, the protectionists argued, the historical trend was away from free trade. It made no sense, said Iowa's David B. Henderson, for the United States to open its ports when the rest of the world was shutting its commercial doors. It would be irresponsible under these circumstances, according to then-Senator William McKinley, for Americans to allow other peoples "to enjoy with our own citizens equal benefits of trade in the United States." Summing up the anti–free trade argument, Andrew Carnegie, though liberal in so many other respects, declared that "the case against free trade as being of universal application is closed, for, after twenty-five years of struggle, it is to-day in full retreat all over the field." Carnegie also questioned Gladstone's invocation of "the consensus of the civilized world." It was silly, he said, to equate civilization with the policy of Great Britain and to suggest that high tariff nations like France, Germany, Canada, and the United States were barbarians.[40]

The practical outcome of the debate was the McKinley Tariff of 1890, which sought to diminish revenue by making tariffs nearly prohibitive and by expanding its reach to encompass taxation of raw materials. Some of the revenue surplus would be dissipated by spending for naval construction and by a bounty for domestic sugar producers. "Have the Secretary of the Treasury and Mr. McKinley gone mad over protective taxes?" asked *The Nation*. This was, in its view, a "monstrous" bill. It would have been more logical to go all the way and prohibit international trade altogether. This last comment suggested that tariff reformers, though continuing to rely on reasoned arguments, increasingly sensed that things would have to get worse before they got better, that only a catastrophe would finally bring the people to their senses. The problem was that protection had been introduced and expanded in relatively flush times. Only when the lean years came would people begin to question the de facto subsidies awarded to protected interests. That day could not be too far distant, the free traders believed. With the system already "feeding on its own vitals," they claimed to see "the beginning of the end, the twilight of a high tariff." The United States, they predicted, was entering the "ultimate stage of high-tariff history."[41] But though the system would receive occasional freshening over the course of the next half century, the mechanicals of the protectionist model remained intact.

For reformers the failure of free trade to catch on was attributed to the failure of people, lured by the song of high tariff sirens, to properly appreciate their own interests. "Protection is something which people understand," said one politician, and free trade was presumably beyond their ability to grasp. Although *The Nation* agreed that protectionism was "emphatically the remedy of the 'plain people,'" it felt compelled to add that these were people "who do not carry their enquiries very far or remember very long." Public opinion, said one essayist, was the product of credulity, of "ignorant good nature." Protectionism, liberals believed, was also the product of a corrupt political system. Even the tariff reformers occasionally recognized that no amount of argumentation, no matter how elegant or deductively persuasive, could overturn so deeply vested a system of special interests. The basic problem, *The Nation* complained, was "the enormous difficulty that always attends the removal of an artificial stimulus under which special industries have been unnaturally inflated." In the end, only the double catastrophe of depression and world war would generate the political force needed to dislodge the huge inertial mass of the protective system. Until that time, no alternative scheme could get around the overwhelming fact that protection had worked. Ideological arguments cannot be settled by arguing ideologically.[42]

Catching up to the World in Civil Service Reform

Although the campaign for free trade provided little cause for optimism, high hopes existed for success on another front: civil service reform. For liberals of the period, "the single great end," the reform of reforms, was to end political corruption by creating a professional civil service. Civil service reform was the Holy Grail because nearly every evil of the day appeared to be founded in the spoils system. "This question of the reform of the civil service really includes all the other questions of the day," said *The Nation.*" On one occasion it spelled out the areas in which rational governmental administration would transform policy for the better. Such an administration would reshape "foreign relations, Indian policy, prison reform, provide the basis for a scientific approach to the tariff, and the bringing of competent educated men to the public service thanks to an improved system of higher education." In short, civil service reform was the *sine qua non* of national progress.[43]

Ending corruption meant attracting the right kind of man to politics and government service to replace the horde of "loafers and drunkards, and ignorant and incompetent men in the highest offices as well as the lowest." The entire system was "vicious, root and branch." Again and again, reformers stressed the need for new blood selected from "the truly self-educated and self-cultured men of the country," "the better portion of the people," "our best men," "able men of ideas." Since the educated were confined to the social elite, this proposal was very much one designed to restore rule to the upper classes. Henry Cabot Lodge said as much on one occasion when he spoke of the desirability of creating "an aristocratic republic." That the people could not be relied upon was in part a consequence of their having been repelled and/or debauched by the spoils system, a cancer that had eaten away at the entire body politic. Its malignant influence was so extensive, argued *The North American Review*, that "beyond the limit of political activity the evil extends ultimately to the relations of man to man, degrading and corrupting society itself."[44]

In this area as in many others, reformers attempted to connect their cause to modernity by arguing from world history. Alluding to the broad fund of foreign experience from which the nation could draw lessons, F. H. Morse asked: "may we not yet learn something from countries which have had many centuries of experience in civil government?" The general approach was to argue that patronage was a primitive practice whereas civil service reform was a product of modernity. In response to the common contention that patronage was rooted in Jacksonian democracy, attempts were made to identify it with the evils of traditional monarchist practices. Typical were the conclusions of Dorman B. Eaton's widely praised history of civil service reform, which argued that "the spoils system was born at the opposite pole to free government. It sprang from the king's will." Eaton saw little to distinguish the use of patronage as a tool of aristocracy from its contemporary factional uses, each being antidemocratic at heart. Plumbing even deeper into the past, Richard T. Ely noted that "a fair exterior covered a mass of corruption and immorality which were slowly but surely preparing the way for the downfall of Rome." Yet another way of discrediting patronage was to point out that the personal bonds of fidelity at the core of the spoils system were feudal in nature. Thus it was not uncommon for political appointees to be derided as "pretorian guards" and "janissaries."[45]

The universalization of the reformist position was also accomplished by ranging across the global space of modern civilization. An essayist in *Harper's* claimed that "the relative importance of the civil service has constantly increased with the spread of civilization and national intercourse, and the developing variety of modern life." For E. L. Godkin, choosing an administrative system was like choosing the best literature or the best of anything, for that matter. The modern approach was guided by superior quality, without regard to national origin. Progress required "conscious assimilation," the effort by a nation "to adopt for its own use whatever seems to it good in the customs and legislation of other countries." This comparative sensibility, it was believed, marked a major dividing line between the modern and the medieval/ancient world. By this standard, the United States came off poorly, for as *The Nation* pointed out, "the modern scientific method" was "in use in all other first-class Christian states." Civil service exams had been "pretty thoroughly tested abroad," it said, and the more positive effects could be "easily be transplanted into our own system."[46]

The reformers derived much of their inspiration from Great Britain's example. "In England a man earns his position," the *Atlantic* pointed out, whereas "in America he begs it or is a political parasite." Starting with a Parliamentary Commission appointed in 1853, the House of Commons in 1856 and 1857 approved the principle of competitive examinations; shortly thereafter, it was extended to the government of India and by 1860 to the home service. In 1870, an order in council provided for open competitive examinations for most positions, the chief exceptions being the foreign office and the diplomatic service. In the 1860s and 1870s, Canada, Australia, and New Zealand followed suit. Great Britain's ability to overcome its notorious history of institutionalized corruption augured well for America's ability to do the same. But reformers did not rely slavishly on a British model. Notwithstanding Prussia's autocratic ways, modern Germany was generally considered to be "the best governed country in the world." If one discounted the inevitable human failings, the Prussian system was, by one account, "almost perfect." Even France and Italy were said to have better systems of administering the public business. If monarchical states could appoint officials for their efficiency and honesty, why could not a republic do the same? How could a nation so politically advanced be so backward in this respect? "Shall it be said that a democracy is unequal to the same task?" asked *Appletons'*.[47]

Reformers well understood that learning from England was a hard sell, so when they put forward their cosmopolitan arguments they typically did so with an American twist. The proof of the new methods' efficiency purportedly lay in the fact that modern businesses were adopting examinations as a way of staffing their offices, and business methods were "gradually taking possession of government business all over the world." Why, then, should not Americans, who were naturally business-minded, conduct their government on the basis of commercial principles of efficiency? More broadly, Theodore Roosevelt was one of many who described merit selection for officeholders as a system "of fair play, of common sense, and of common honesty," which, therefore, was "essentially American and essentially democratic." The other side of the coin was to play on anti-British sentiment by portraying patronage as a British import. In response to neo-Jacksonians who portrayed patronage as "a pure product of the American mind," Godkin noted the resemblance not only to past British abuses, but also to the way in which they had been defended. Lodge stressed the undesirable British provenance of patronage. "Patronage in office is no more a peculiarly American institution than the common law," he said. "We brought the patronage system with us from the Old World, as we brought many things, good and bad."[48]

Comparison with the best also merited measurement against the worst. *The Nation,* in particular, took great relish in setting American practices against those of noxious regimes abroad. When it came to administration, it suggested, "we have retrograded towards barbarism, and are gradually getting back to a level with Turkey and Afghanistan." In its predilection for "appointment through caprice or favor," the United States had much in common with such nations. Even the Koran, according to one professor of constitutional law, was more enlightened on this issue. China, normally a synonym for ossified backwardness, also became a witness for the prosecution. In this instance, maintained an editorial in *Harper's,* the "youthful contempt" that many Americans displayed toward China was wholly inappropriate. If the West had already borrowed from China the compass, gunpowder, and printing, among other innovations, why not the idea of a governmental meritocracy? Lodge, who had numerous differences with cosmopolitan liberals, sided with them on this issue. "There is only one thing more contemptible than a feeble imitation of other people," he wrote, "and that is an equally feeble refusal to adopt something intrinsically good because some-body else has tried something like it and found it beneficial. We are hardly likely to abandon gunpowder or printing because the Chinese are said to have been the first inventors of both."[49]

Civil Service and Diplomacy: Conflicted Feelings

The adoption of international standards was also a central theme of reform efforts in the area of diplomacy, though it featured much more ambivalence. In view of the country's general lack of concern with foreign policy, the flaws in the United States' diplomatic representation attracted a surprising amount of criticism. Instances of "wanton removal," just as much as unwarranted appointments in the first place, drew much fire for violating the bureaucratic principle of tenure of office. John Lothrop Motley's ouster as minister to Austria in 1867 generated a flurry of irate commentary, as did the replacement of the urbane George Bancroft in Berlin in 1874. The best that could be said of Bancroft's successor, given his complete lack of diplomatic experience and linguistic qualifications, was that he would bring "a thoroughly fresh and unbiassed mind" to his post." (One joke making the rounds was that the U.S. representative to England was the only American abroad who could speak the language of the country to which he was assigned.) The situation was getting so bad, it was claimed, that men of high quality would no longer agree to serve abroad. Constant congressional meddling in appointments and frequent shuffling of representatives, said *The Century,* served only to "to disgust and demoralize other members of the service, and to lower our Government in our own eyes and in those of the world." Whatever the merits of spoilsmanship in domestic affairs, partisanship needed to stop at the water's edge because diplomats served the nation, not a party.[50]

Notwithstanding its relative unimportance in the hierarchy of government agencies, the State Department was regularly indicted for causing embarrassment to the country. "Favoritism, partisanship, ignorance of diplomatic usage," noted *The Atlantic,* "and indifference to international courtesy have been often and arrogantly displayed by it, and upon it must rest the blame for the extraordinary folly which has too frequently marked the selection of envoys." Some critics went so far as to suggest that jettisoning the entire diplomatic corps might be a net plus, given the discredit that the existing collection of incompetents was bringing to the country's reputation. The problem was reciprocal, however, as other nations rewarded American behavior by appointing nonentities of their own. Instead of being complimented by the appointment of illustrious representatives, the United States was still being treated "as if she still were a small English colony, instead of being the most powerful nation of Christendom."[51]

Unfortunately, pointing to the virtues of foreign models in diplomacy was a hard sell for reformers because Americans had always seen statecraft as an aristocratic profession, an adjunct to the warlike system of power politics that still dominated European practice. In this area, it had long been a matter of republican pride that American representatives abroad not fit the international mold. Populist sensitivities on this score flared from time to time, as in Congress's attempt in 1867 to prevent American representatives abroad from appearing in court dress. A toned-down resolution mandated simplicity of attire, which was evaded by having many ministers wear their former military uniforms. Yet liberal cosmopolitans, too, harbored plenty of reservations about adopting international standards of diplomatic practice. Court costumes, according to *The Nation,* "would suit a harlequin better than the ambassador of a republic." Albert Rhodes, writer and sometime U.S. consul, detected "a degree of humbug in the exercise of diplomatic functions which cannot but excite commiseration in a true republican."[52]

There was yet another complication. In an era of rapidly developing technologies of communication, internationalists were questioning the need for any professional diplomats at all. *The Nation* saw the system of diplomacy as "an antiquated absurdity," an Old World tradition that was "designed to bring together two things which cannot be brought together—a thoroughly democratic society and an aristocratic one." After ridiculing "the pompous old padded figures which prescription has surrounded with awe," *Appletons'* asked: "What is the use, in these days, of ambassadors and envoys extraordinary, of ministers resident and charges d'affaires?" Representatives abroad were "little more than the mouth-pieces of the home government," delivery boys who conveyed messages. In fifty years, Rhodes predicted, all diplomatic missions would be abolished. Apart from their usefulness as sinecures for faithful party hacks, there was no good reason to keep them. On the few occasions when serious diplomacy was called for, the country had done quite well by appointing men of competence and stature, and it could do so again. All things considered, *The Nation* argued, abolishing the entire diplomatic service "would entail no inconvenience whatever."[53]

Whatever need for representation remained, it was proposed, could be met by strengthening the consular machinery. Consuls could convey news when necessary, but even here the newspapers had largely taken over the reporting function. Small problems could be settled by telegraphic communication, and negotiating positions could easily be transmitted by cable. Because the real business of the nation abroad was business, in an era of intensifying commercial competition abroad the primary need was to create "a first-rate consular service." It was in this area that the principles of civil service reform were most clearly applicable. The principles were identical—payment of a decent living wage as a deterrent to corruption, tenure in office on good behavior, appointment and promotion for merit. Meager salaries, in particular, were a matter of concern. It was pointed out that the reliance of American consuls on paperwork fees to supplement their incomes was an outright inducement to corruption.[54]

Unlike diplomacy, international comparisons of consular systems were entirely appropriate. "The American people," argued *The Atlantic*, "ought to understand how and why their consular system is the shabbiest in the whole world." Great Britain's consular establishment, though similar in size to that of the United States, cost much more to maintain. The internationalist dimension of consular reform was evident, too, in the demands for a more cosmopolitan type of representative. Criticisms abounded of American consuls who were ignorant of the local language, of French (which then was the language of diplomacy), and of international law and local conditions, leading to excessive dependence on native vice-consuls and clerks. Examples of corruption, incompetence, and general buffoonery were legion. George M. Towle, who served as a consular official before becoming a successful writer and editor, pointed to the singular lack of proficiency in foreign languages among American representatives when compared to their continental counterparts. "Europeans regard the fact with astonishment in the representative of a nation boasting to possess a leadership in civilization," he noted."[55]

The issue of abolishing the diplomatic service altogether was kept alive as a matter of hypothetical discussion throughout the 1880s, but it was never really a live option. Diplomacy was a fixed feature of international relations that no regime, however revolutionary, could afford to ignore. Despite their occasional grumbling, even critics of elite diplomacy could not gainsay the necessity of diplomacy itself. Here was one argument in which the nationalists clearly held the advantage. As one senator pointed out in *Harper's*, this was an area in which the United States had no choice but to adapt to international norms: "If we are to maintain diplomatic relations with the great powers of the world, we must maintain them after the manner in which they are universally maintained." But if diplomats were a necessary evil, it followed that only the most capable men should be selected for foreign service.[56]

What would count as qualifications for these diplomatic posts? Making the best of a bad situation, liberal internationalists hit on the idea that American diplomats should function more as cultural than as political representatives, in contrast to the current crowd of envoys "whose narrow vision and lack of cosmopolitan ideas peculiarly disqualify them for efficiently representing this Government in a foreign land." American representatives abroad should not simply reflect the power and prestige of the country, but the best of its culture as well. "Society looks to him to typify the best phase of American education and refinement," said Towle. According to *The Galaxy,* in the absence of a professional school of diplomacy, "highly cultivated literary men" seemed the best choice for such positions. They were the only types in a democratic society with "the intellectual culture, and very often the knowledge of society, and the breeding, which are of the first importance in diplomacy, and which are absolutely necessary to the creditable performance of the mere routine duty of a minister." The Japan expert Edward Sylvester Morse argued that England set an example worth emulating here, by sending "scholars and gentlemen to represent her abroad and not political adventurers." "The social representation of the country should only be attempted by what is best in it," agreed *The Nation.*[57]

Of the three controversies surveyed in this chapter, civil service reform was the most successful, though hardly because its arguments carried the day. In the short run, contingency mattered enormously. For the reformers, the tragedy of President Garfield's assassination in 1881 was "a modern miracle" that made possible passage of the Pendleton bill in 1883. Thereafter reform of the federal bureaucracy would proceed slowly and piecemeal, often accompanied by expressions of disappointment. Over time, however, thanks to presidents like Theodore Roosevelt who had a personal political investment in the civil service system, fundamental change did take place in incremental fashion. In the case of diplomatic reform, change would have to wait until the 1920s. In a decade better known for its commercial and cultural internationalism than for political interventionism abroad, the passage of the Rogers Act in 1924 depended heavily on the kinds of modernizing business arguments that had been emphasized in the Gilded Age, while the simultaneous creation of the professional Foreign Service within the State Department was heavily dependent for its original staffing on the nation's cultural elite.[58]

Attempts to frame discussion of domestic issues in an international context were not restricted to the three areas just discussed. Across a spectrum of issues, liberal reformers sought to fashion a supranational identity for the United States. In the drive to create a modern university system and a modern currency, as well as in social reforms of all kinds, some Americans looked abroad for a model. Although the internationally minded were a politically outgunned minority, they were influential in at least three ways in the short run. First, they forced their opponents, for purposes of debate if nothing else, to formulate principled nationalist arguments in response to a broad range of issues such as the universality of science, the importation of international innovations to the United States, and the desirability of employing a global frame of reference. Second, the internationally minded enjoyed a modest degree of success in copyright and civil service reform despite an unfavorable political climate. Finally, even where success eluded them, they managed to lay a discursive foundation on which new generations of reformers could build in the changed circumstances of the twentieth century.

The long-running debate between nationalists and internationalists was about many things—science and knowledge, theories of property, politics, morality, corruption and the role of special interests, and the role of government in promoting industry—but it was also a clash of world views. The free traders clearly situated the United States within a modern global civilization that was united, ideally, by the free flow of goods and ideas, whereas protectionists saw the United States as a world unto itself that owed little regard for "the alien and the stranger," in McKinley's words.

Notwithstanding this profound difference of perspective, it would be a mistake to describe the struggle in terms of wholly opposed ideologies. Even the arch-free trader Godkin was compelled to concede, on a rare occasion, that "the protectionist theory is not wholly irrational." For their part, high tariff advocates were far from committed to isolating the country from the world economy, as they welcomed immigration from Europe, encouraged direct investment of foreign capital inside the country, and subscribed to the gold standard. Nor was it fair to describe protectionists as cultural know-nothings who reveled in a blissful ignorance of "abroad." By 1911, the Taft administration was able to articulate a high tariff policy with a global program of "dollar diplomacy" that embraced many of the themes of Manchester liberalism, without being noticeably bothered by any contradictions. For their part, internationalists, for all their attempts to place history and foreign examples on their side, were helpless before the nationalism that they themselves encouraged as one of the chief tendencies of modernity. *The Nation* admitted as much when it noted the failure of free trade theory to anticipate that nationalism, along with socialism, would be the strongest influences in modern European history.[59]

For reform liberals, civilization began at home, but it did not end there. An understanding of international developments was necessary not only for purposes of fighting partisan battles on narrowly American issues, but also for understanding the broader geographical and historical context of American development. Seeking to expand the nation's horizons, the journals provided abundant coverage, factual and analytical, of events in the rest of the world. The criteria of judgment, however, differed from those employed in domestic political debate, where the tendency was to cite superior foreign models as examples to be emulated. Happenings abroad, especially the course of politics, were measured by the benchmark of American republicanism, which resulted in discussions that were much darker and more critical in tone than the many admiring assessments of overseas social and cultural developments. Notwithstanding the overall image of global progress, there was much to dislike, and much to worry about, in Europe as well as the rest of the globe. The next two chapters will look at Europe.

3

Europe I

The Mirage of Republicanism

American journals after 1865 closely followed social, cultural, and political trends in Europe, taking pains to compare American and continental ways of life in nearly every respect. Food, clothing, architecture, manners, education, the beauty of women, home life, wealth and poverty, politics, and much more went under the microscope. This satisfaction of curiosity, though edifying, was not particularly reassuring. Being universally acknowledged as culturally inferior, Americans could not point to a single area of preeminence by way of compensation. Wherever the spotlight was aimed—at social reform, higher education, civic administration, or the quality of political leadership—Europe appeared to be clearly in the lead. Even the nation's strong suit, its leadership in "material development and mechanical contrivance," offered surprisingly little opportunity for vainglory because the fruits of industrialization had not fallen into American laps alone. As the editor of *Appletons'* reminded his readers, "Every other civilized people have also made great strides in the things of which we boast." In 1892, the New Orleans writer Sally Rhett Roman suggested that a general comparison of the progress of the arts, sciences, and commerce in Europe and the United States could lead to only one conclusion: "the chauvinism of the American is ill-placed."[1]

However unexceptional the Americans' other achievements, they continued to take pride in the republican civic creed as their distinctive contribution to civilization. Only frivolous Americans, of whom there were far too many according to economist Henry Carter Adams, would make the "mistake of accepting numbers and wealth as the criterion of national greatness." The true test of a nation's advancement, asserted one meditation on the meaning of civilization, was emancipation. "Not the census, nor the size of cities, nor the crops,—no, but the kind of man the country turns out" lay at the heart of the matter. Despite many parallel developments, the gap in ideology and its political expression between the two sides of the Atlantic remained enormous. *The Nation* in 1865 put the issue most starkly. "The American idea was "strikingly opposed to the European one," it said. Because European civilization had been founded on force and the American on freedom, it followed that "practically, in fact, our institutions are an exact inversion of theirs."[2]

Whereas Europeans associated "Americanization" with mechanization and the adulteration of elite values and standards, Americans equated it with the global spread of republican ideology and democratic institutions. It was this meaning that the historian and diplomat John Lothrop Motley had in mind in 1868 when he declared that "the hope of the world lies in the Americanization of the world." Antebellum republicanism, crippled by the fratricidal politics of slavery, had curbed American idealism while severely tarnishing its legitimacy, but the civil war had finally put the nation on the map ideologically by creating a great nation committed to an ideal. Lincoln's wartime description of the national republic as "the last, best hope of earth" had left open the possibility of failure, but the Union triumph appeared to mark a decisive reversal of the tide of reaction that had flooded Europe following the revolutions of 1848. "A democracy that could fight for an abstraction," warned James Russell Lowell, "was the nightmare of the Old World taking upon itself flesh and blood, turning out to be substance and not dream." This was a world-historical development that, according to Oliver Wendell Holmes, would have a shattering impact on Europe. "Out of the hive of nations," he predicted, "no Saracens sweeping from their deserts to plant the Crescent over the symbol of Christendom, were more terrible to the principalities and powers that stood in their way, than the Great Republic, by the bare fact of its existence, will become to every government which does not hold its authority from the people." The expectation was that a world "wretchedly misgoverned" by kings and aristocrats would soon have governments that were "not sacerdotal, nor monarchical, nor aristocratic, but national," that is to say, controlled by the sovereign will of the people. It was in this ideological sense that the Civil War was widely considered to be an epoch-making event.[3]

Americans had good reason to believe that the idea of political freedom was steadily approaching realization. In 1872, Emilio Castelar, a liberal who would serve briefly as prime minister in the short-lived Spanish republic, asserted that, notwithstanding royal armies and continued papal pretensions, "modern civilization is democratic." Twelve years later, he restated his faith in human liberation in more qualified language by describing the preceding century as a passage from monarchy to mixed democracy; pure democracy, however, would have to wait until the following century. Although monarchies were still visible, Castelar likened them to "distant stars which the astronomers tell us are apparent to our retina long after they have become extinct and all trace of them in the heavens is lost." With the future thus written in the stars, it seemed a safe prediction shortly after the Civil War that in a half century aristocracies would go the way of serfdom. One writer, pointing to advances in education and growing concessions to the principle of representation, predicted that "the reign of Absolutism, whether in church or state, is nearing its end, and that the rule of the People is fast approaching." All in all, there seemed every reason to take seriously Victor Hugo's description of liberty as "the climate of civilization." It was in the air, contended Adams, "an element in the general life of the present age."[4]

These appraisals seemed plausible enough when viewed from a cosmological vantage point, but the political quanta of everyday life provided less cause for certainty, for the closer Americans looked, the less reason for optimism there seemed. With a few exceptions, American-style constitutionalism, though widely studied abroad for its useful features, particularly in Latin America, had not been widely copied. On rare occasions, candor required the admission that the mixed British form of government had been far more successful in spawning imitators. True, absolutist monarchy had pretty much disappeared in Western Europe, but still the republican heavenly kingdom was nowhere in sight. Liberal elements were present in each state, but the chemistry of politics tended to relegate them to minor ingredients of predominantly conservative compounds. The stubborn resiliency of monarchism and conservatism in Europe led to the disappointedly cynical conclusion that "the republic of a great many European radicals resembles the kingdom of God in not being of this world." The old countries of Europe, *The Nation* reported in 1882, had "settled down into a not wholly uncomfortable belief that things will be one hundred years hence very much what they are to-day." Even after taking into account trends toward the expansion and liberalization of the suffrage, by 1890 it was questionable whether the political climate had become more liberal after the Civil War. By this time, even Castelar had tempered his previously millenarian expectations. The most he could bring himself to say was that democracy had "passed from revolution to evolution." Castelar was putting the best face on things, but others were frank to acknowledge that conservatism and traditional were more than holding their own.[5]

Explanations of the causes of Europe's political inertia were not reassuring. Typical of the evaluations was a *Scribner's* editorial that attributed the problem not only to the quite predictable "interests and prejudices of the educated and powerful classes," but also to "the low intelligence and low morals of the masses." This was a little like saying that everything was chemically in place for the making of water except for the H_2 and the O. One could understand the tenacious desire of aristocratic elites to cling to privilege, but the conservatism of European mass publics and their continued willingness to support the old elites was more difficult to fathom. What if European politics was fixed not in arbitrary rule and the suppression of the popular will, but instead in deeply ingrained traditions to which people readily, if irrationally, assented? What if differences were not merely a matter of political ideology but of custom? To emphasize culture over political rationality was to stress the endurance of the particular over the inevitability of the universal and the misty spell of irrational tradition over the clear light of reason. Seen in the light of experience, American-style democracy, far from being the harbinger of a universal form of government, might be "a very exceptional phenomenon," itself the product of peculiar cultural and historical circumstances.[6]

Although such glum reflections did not signal a retreat to conservatism, they made unavoidable the disturbing conclusion that progress and civilization were somehow compatible with political backwardness and reaction. If this period showed anything, it was that the liberal failures of 1848, far from being reversed, had been followed by a reaction in which popular approval was used to bolster the ongoing rule of traditional elites. The continued hold of the Tories and social traditionalism in England; the emergence of a plebiscitary authoritarian regime in France and the unsteadiness of its republican successor; the astounding success of a conservative regime in Germany that managed to appropriate elements of both liberalism and social democracy; and the stubborn hold of the czarist autocracy in Russia demonstrated that the conservative backlash was still in progress. Thus, while the cosmopolitan view of Europe was colored by hope, it was also tinctured by the knowledge that a republican future was not yet in sight among the other leading nations of the world. Despite the overall air of optimism about historical trends, then,

Americans developed a contradictory view of Europe in which progressive conviction was obscured by a thickening fog of evidence to the contrary. In 1867, *The Nation* had consoled itself with the thought that if things did not work out for the best, Americans at least had "the consolation of knowing that the world can hardly be worse governed in the future than it has been in the past."[7] By 1890, that assessment was open to question, as the bright light that formerly suggested the way out of Plato's cave had given way to sepulchral overcast, making uncertain the possibility of an exit.

Great Britain and the Mirage of Anglo-Saxonism

Of all the Old World nations, Great Britain most resembled the United States—in its market-driven economic prosperity, its political openness, and its culture. The combination of shared heritage, language, literary culture, and charged political relationship had created a complicated mixture of attraction and repulsion that was not present in America's relationship with any other nation. As one book reviewer observed, Americans could know themselves only by understanding how they differed from the British—the greater the similarity, the more meaningful the differences, apparently. Thus joined at the hip culturally, it seems natural that the relationship between the two, despite some heavy tensions during the Civil War, entered smoother waters and became so close that historians have discerned the beginnings of a "special relationship" during these years. And yet, when seen in the context of global aspirations for republicanism, the story of Anglo-American reconciliation was a disappointing tale. After a period of bullish hope that a republican future was in store for Great Britain, it became apparent that the cultural distance between the two peoples, including their political cultures, was widening at the very moment that contentious political issues began to fade away. Even the newly popular racial doctrine of Anglo-Saxonism proved to be a cultural mirage.[8]

In 1865 the two nations were politically so estranged that the odds for convergence must have seemed very small. *The Atlantic*, noting that "England in her heart hates us as profoundly as ever she did," had predicted correctly in 1861 that postwar relations would be very rough going. The depth of the animosity was expressed by the remark, reportedly uttered by Charles Frances Adams, the wartime minister to London, that "the American people cherish an undying hatred toward England." As late as 1870, one writer predicted that the war would be "for long years, a favorite skirmishing ground between the word-warriors of the two nations." The normally sedate Theodore Dwight Woolsey, a pioneering scholar of international law and president of Yale until 1871, put the British on notice that "the memory among us of what they felt and allowed in the late rebellion will not soon sleep." In his famous reaffirmation of American nationalism, James Russell Lowell went so far as to say that "we are worth nothing except so far as we have disinfected ourselves of Anglicism." The bad blood ran freely on both sides. One British lord believed that had such a degree of ill feeling existed between two European states, the outcome surely would have been a war.[9]

But this hostility was directed more toward Tory Britain than toward Britain as a whole. One lesson to be drawn from English behavior, said a letter to the editor, was that "this republic can count upon friends only among the peoples, not the governments and 'governing classes,' of Europe." A number of British advocates of Anglo-American reconciliation were at pains to emphasize that, in contrast to the ruling conservatives, the hearts of the British public had been with the North during the war. They also signed on to the widely held perception that the war was part of a global drama by noting that it was being played out in their land as well. According to Goldwin Smith, a liberal radical and strong supporter of the Union cause, the Civil War was "a vast episode in the same irrepressible conflict between Aristocracy and Democracy; and the heirs of the Cavalier in England sympathize with your enemies, the heirs of the Puritan with you." Whatever problems remained between the two countries would be settled by the ideological commonality that would follow the triumph of liberal, popular forces in Britain.[10]

American journals followed English politics quite closely in anticipation of the predestined liberal ascendancy. The political rivalry between Tories and Liberals was generally placed in the context of a larger struggle in Europe between "two mighty antagonistic forces," in the course of which the aristocracy had managed to cling to power. Though a small, shrunken minority, the aristocratic caste nevertheless exercised a striking cultural hegemony, a continuing dominance that was attributed to the refractoriness of British culture and the irrational but powerful hold of tradition. *The Nation,* speaking of the Americans' little notice of habit and tradition, pointed out that "few influences in England are more powerful." *De Bow's* European correspondent,

Percy Roberts, agreed that "the spirit of conservatism deeply imbues the national character." For Adam Badeau, diplomat, journalist, and confidant of President Grant, it was a marvel that "this relic of barbarism should still survive, wrought into the very nature of the people." In the end, only cultural inertia could account for the enduring sway of the lords and the Anglican establishment.[11]

Reporting on British politics took on a clear black and white aspect, with the great leaders William Gladstone and Benjamin Disraeli serving as the foci of good and evil. Disraeli, the leader of the Tories, typically wore the black hat, despite securing passage of the second reform bill and bucking his party by supporting the North during the Civil War. He was perceived as a conservative wolf dressed in a liberal sheep's clothing, a British fellow-traveler of Napoleon III who had engineered the partial democratization of British politics for the cynical purpose of maintaining aristocratic rule. In assessing his career during the parliamentary turnover of 1880, *The Nation* described him as "a foreign adventurer, who has made the best use of the passions and prejudices of the people with whom accident has thrown him to obtain power, distinction, and place." He was a man without ideas "except those suggested by the necessity of the moment." His foreign policy adventures, in particular, were seen as calculated efforts to stir up jingoist emotion on which the Tories could capitalize. *The Nation* was happy to pass on the Gladstonian quip that his foreign policies, far from deserving the monument then being proposed, "almost merited the penitentiary." The aristocratic Tories were virtuous in one vital respect, however: in their adaptability to the democratic temper of the times. For all their defects, the Tories had thus far given way to liberal reforms with admirable grace.[12]

By contrast, the progress of British liberalism under Gladstone's leadership excited an enormous amount of admiration. Just as American revolutionaries in the eighteenth century had borrowed the rhetoric of the country Whigs, so too American liberals of the Gilded Aged tended to take their ideological cues from their opposite numbers. British political economy, particularly the pioneering support for free trade, provided instruction for like-minded Americans, while notable liberal leaders such as John Bright, William Cobden, John Stuart Mill, and Gladstone were virtually idolized in some quarters. As Godkin recalled later in life, "John Stuart Mill was our prophet, and [historian George] Grote and Bentham were our daily food." The noted political theorist

Walter Bagehot was well respected in the United States, while the high priest of evolutionary theory, Herbert Spencer, was lionized by Americans. But Gladstone, with his breadth of knowledge, human sympathy, and superb oratorical skills, was clearly the most admired of the lot, enjoying an esteem that amounted, in some cases, to "Gladstone worship." Despite running into some rough patches, particularly on foreign policy during his second ministry, Gladstone's role as prime minister in expanding the suffrage was enough to qualify him as "by far the greatest England has ever had." Taken as a group, *The Century* described these liberal leaders as "a body of able teachers." For a generation of civil service reformers, these men, forged of more noble metal than base American politicians, were the kinds of leaders that American politics so desperately needed. British liberals happily reciprocated the attention as they discovered sympathetic counterparts across the Atlantic.[13]

It was clear that Great Britain was in the forefront of reform in Europe. As Dimbleby and Reynolds note, reform politicians had succeeded in making Britain "a strikingly liberal country by European standards." Vast change had already taken place. "All the roads, whether material or mental, by which mankind travels to its ultimate purpose, have been graded, widened, solidly equipped and built," said one report. The adoption of the paper ballot in Great Britain in place of public *viva voce* voting, claimed *Appletons'*, would "shake the foundations of the British aristocratic caste." The extension of the suffrage in the second reform bill only whetted American appetites for its further expansion to poor peasants in the rural districts, which, it was expected, would produce a veritable "social revolution." With the passage of the third reform act of 1884, writers looked forward to still more change: the anticipation was that the House of Lords—the last redoubt of "the party of pleasure" dominated by the idle rich—would be the next victim of liberal ideas. Other fortresses of privilege—the Church of England and the university system, both "aristocratic and conservative in every sense"—were lined up in radical cross hairs as talk of disestablishment increased. By 1885, Emilio Castelar, in one of his periodic reviews of republican prospects in Europe, sounded more optimistic than ever about the imminent creation of a "great democracy." Americans took heart from statements by luminaries like Mill that two of the most important nations were being "irresistibly driven to adopt republican forms of government."[14]

For two decades after the Civil War, journal articles anticipated that England would become republican, though it was granted that the shift would take place slowly, as was the habit in British politics. "Republicanism is gaining ground," declared *Appletons'* in 1874. According to Adam Badeau—diplomat, journalist, and confidant of President Grant—the real revolution of sentiment, a "ceaseless but silent revolution," had already occurred and merely awaited institutional embodiment. Noting that London working men had cheered the formation of the French republic in 1871, Justin McCarthy, an Irish-born journalist who spent a number of years in the United States before moving on to a career in Parliament in the 1880s, described them as "earnest republicans—republicans by conviction and by sympathy." In 1873, *The Nation* stated boldly that "the Americanization of England, of which we used to hear so much a few years ago, is already an accomplished fact." A decade later, in discussing the "American invasion of Great Britain," *The Nation* predicted that that "the ultimate conquest of this little island is only a question of time." Various essayists also looked for signs of a weakening of "the monarchical superstition in England." This was not too difficult a task, it seemed, inasmuch as the periodic follies of the royal family arguably made it "the worst enemy of royalty in England."[15]

This fervent expectation was based on the assumption that Britain, even though it boasted a corps of ideological all-stars, lagged politically behind the United States. Allen Thorndike Rice, editor of the influential *North American Review*, pointed out that "in the science of government the United Kingdom has no title to exult." In the words of one editorial, the English were "struggling desperately, almost hopelessly, with problems which were solved in the United States decades since." Nevertheless, the reforms enacted in Great Britain over the course of two decades provided welcome confirmation that history was following the republican path for which the United States had blazed the trail. In 1866, George M. Towle urged readers to "rejoice in the approach of the mother country to the end we have already reached." The expectation, then, was that British institutions, as Andrew Carnegie later impolitely suggested, "will be rapidly colonialized and Americanized."[16]

But this was not the way things were viewed from London. Ironically, it was Gladstone, the liberal's liberal, who poured cold water on the dream of an American-style republican future in Great Britain. In an 1878 fence-mending essay in *The North American Review,* he announced with brutal directness that friendship would have to be based on something other than the congruence of political systems, ideologies, or culture. He made it clear that "neither nation prefers (and it would be an ill sign if either did prefer) the institutions of the other." The English did not believe in equality or that all men were created equal. "They hold rather the reverse of that proposition" he said, being "determined inequalitarians" in practice. Although the worst evils of inequality would be eliminated in due course, inequality in the United Kingdom lay "imbedded in the very base of the social structure." Moreover, he saw no future for the American constitutional model in Europe, where instead "the practice and idea of constitutional kingship" would be the wave of the future. The passage of another fifty years would see Europe adopting this institution "and peaceably sailing in the wake of England." Instead of America republicanizing his country, he preferred to believe that "in some respects, British politics [would] provide a model for liberal Americans." The same held true on a global scale, where Great Britain, with its history of spreading democratic institutions abroad, constituted "a kind of universal church in politics."[17]

As the era of liberal ascendancy gave way to a period of protracted conservative rule beginning in 1885, speculation about a republican future dried up quickly. In accounting for Gladstone's defeat, the London correspondent of *The Nation* speculated that the English constitution had "been growing far more democratic than the average sentiment of educated Englishmen." But the problem was less the ascendancy of the mass public than the Tories' recently discovered ability to turn the new electoral realities to their advantage by playing upon the naiveté of the people. If properly handled, Toryism, as *The Nation* reported, could be "just as vigorous and popular among the poor as among the rich." The British reverence for tradition was played upon particularly well, culminating in the orgy of patriotism surrounding Queen Victoria's diamond jubilee celebration in 1897. By that time, the U.S. minister to England, John Hay, noted that "the monarchical religion has grown day by day, till the Queen is worshipped as more than mortal." The conservative revival was followed by the emergence of social democracy as a successor to liberalism. As a new generation of English reformers and radicals gravitated toward socialism, it was the Americans, from their perspective, who appeared to be stuck in the past. By 1901, Thomas Wentworth Higginson, on a visit to England, could "get no glimpse anywhere, even in the newspapers, of that strong republican minority of which one caught sight thirty years ago."[18]

In retrospect, the expectation of a republican Britain was an ideological bubble that contradicted commonly understood facts, for even during the high point of optimism about political convergence Americans were self-conscious about the vast social differences between the two countries and aware of numerous peculiarities of their national characters. Economically, Great Britain was the workshop of the world, but Allen Thorndike Rice saw no reason for the United States to shrink from a comparison. By whatever quantitative measure—population, cities, immigration; number of post offices; number of periodicals; wealth; railroads; increase in houses; value of land, cattle, furniture; manufactures; inventions—America came out on top or would soon do so. British high society had its attractions for some, but America had it all over the mother country when it came to the life of the masses. The contrasts of wealth and poverty were not as pronounced in the United States, something that stood out in the American complaints about the large numbers of beggars, some of them well-dressed, that one encountered in London. For all the loose talk about the Americanization of Great Britain, Americanization seemed to work only when Britons became naturalized Americans. Once that happened to an Englishman, said one condescending essayist, "It gradually dawns upon his medieval intellect that there is some reason in the belief that nine-tenths of the world were not created to be patronized by the other tenth."[19]

Culturally, too, the differences were striking. Americans were better educated, more religious, more self-reliant, and, all in all, better mannered. British travel reports had long delighted in belittling Americans for their vulgarity, but articles about British visitors to the United States complained of "English gaucherie, English stupidity, English barbarity, English rudeness." *Appletons'* could not help remarking on the irony of "how it is that a people so censorious of our shortcomings, and so assured of their own superiority, should so frequently exhibit absolute boorishness." There was, insisted Albert Rhodes, "a higher social and moral tone throughout the Union than in the best parts of the Old Country." On other occasions, British rowdyism, wife-beating ("a crime almost unknown among Americans"), public drunkenness, crime, and English philistinism offered provocative topics for tongue-clucking. Anticipating the lament of George Bernard Shaw's Professor Henry Higgins, there were numerous complaints about the unintelligibility of the spoken language in Britain. The vernacular in England, according to one indictment, was "uncouth and barbaric," while Emerson insisted that "more people speak English correctly in the United States than in Britain." Some even felt it necessary to impugn the notion that English women were the fairest in the world.[20]

In some circles, admittedly, there was a growing fondness for things British. The British gentleman was admired in some quarters as "a dignified embodiment of manliness and truth," and when compared to the nouveaux riches of America the British peerage seemed less vulgar than the aristocracy of wealth. As in literature, British fashions in clothing were followed closely by "Anglomaniacs." By the 1880s, the Anglophilia of a few high-mugwumps had progressed to the point of expatriation. But the very genuflection of these types before British culture and politics suggested that they had given up on the idea of cultural convergence. And morganatic marriages between down-at-the-heels aristocrats and American heiresses were hardly representative. In truth, as *The Nation* noted, "the class of Americans who like to be mistaken for 'Britishers' is a small one, and is eyed with some jealousy and distrust by their fellow-citizens." For Henry Cabot Lodge and the young Theodore Roosevelt, Americans who put on English airs were appropriate objects of ridicule. Lodge believed that excessive concern for things British was a "morbid . . . characteristic of provincial, colonial or dependent states." And, of course, Anglophobia continued to be an important force in American politics, as was evident in the continued pandering after the Irish vote and in the anti-British diatribes of protectionists. Taking stock of the situation in 1882, *The Nation* concluded that the idea of cultural convergence had been taken too far, in overreaction perhaps to Americans' earlier tendency to exaggerate the cultural differences. [21]

Although a prima facie case can be made that politically, socially, and culturally the two English-speaking nations had grown apart and were continuing to diverge, a rapprochement did take place, converging on the increasingly popular idea of Anglo-Saxonism. But here, too, there was less than met the eye, for the rise of the Anglo-Saxonist discourse had less to do with acculturation than with a common understanding of the global future (of which much more will be said in Chapter 10). The issue was not the Americanization of England or the Anglicization of America, but rather the globalization of both. As *The Atlantic* put it, "For better or for worse, the English race has become cosmopolitan, and cosmopolitan powers cannot indulge themselves in provincial emotions."[22]

The resolution of the *Alabama* claims controversy—a dispute over the damages caused by Confederate commerce raiders that had been built in British ports—illustrates the internationalist thrust of the rapprochement. Before the issue was settled by arbitration in 1871, American politicians played to the galleries of nationalist opinion by arguing that, because the Confederate warships had in effect prolonged the war, Britain should pay a far greater amount (the cession of Canada, perhaps) than the "direct" damages that had been inflicted on Union shipping. This demand so inflamed nationalist feeling that for a time negotiations were in danger of breaking down. But there was no chance that the United States would seriously press a demand for indirect damages or that Britain would actively consider the demand. The only true function of the claims, as *The Galaxy* correctly noted, was "to act as a lever upon English acknowledgment of the direct claim."[23]

From a global standpoint, the worst-case outcome would have been a British acknowledgment of the extreme nationalist demand for indirect damages. Although some observers interpreted the limited award in triumphal terms, it was more readily bathed in an internationalist light. Philip Quilibet [G. E. Pond's nom de plume] of *The Galaxy* more nearly caught the larger significance of the outcome when he described the Treaty of Washington as a great triumph for America," but more importantly, as "a victory for modern civilization, . . . of good sense over bad blood, and of the pen over the sword." Similarly, *The Nation* applauded "the adoption by the two greatest nations of the world of the only civilized and Christian mode of settling disputes." Bad feelings were washed away in the solvent of civilized cooperation as the *Alabama* dispute became, for Americans, a prime test of the future of arbitration and a precedent for the peaceful settlement of international disputes. Not adhering to the terms of the bargain, said Theodore Dwight Woolsey, risked incurring "the moral disapprobation of mankind."[24]

Once the *Alabama* claims were finally laid to rest, by the late 1880s war, a hypothetical possibility not all that long ago, was being talked about only by "fanatics." Looking back to earlier disputes, in 1881 a reviewer remarked: "It is all so far away now, that it is difficult to believe that we ever could have been so puffed up with our own conceit, and so absurdly aggressive toward Englishmen." By 1890, when *The North American Review* ran a series of essays on the theme, "Do Americans Hate England?," the question had become rhetorical.

Thomas Wentworth Higginson concluded that the disputes were not unlike those between cousins, "where the essential kinship makes the trivial variations more exasperating." Similarly, Andrew Carnegie spoke of "our little family jars." But the relationship had immense importance far beyond the immediate bilateral confines of the family. Since the end of the Civil War, commentators had been warning of the disastrous global implications for freedom and progress if a war were to be fought between the two nations. An 1873 musing in *The Atlantic* struggled to articulate this sense of the significance of both Anglo-Saxon parts to a larger global whole. England, it said, was "bringing itself under the influence of the spirit which it was the fashion a generation ago to call "American," but which now really belongs to no one country, but is the common spirit which animates civilized society at large." But "the effect on the interests of the civilized world at large" of a falling out only came to be generally recognized in the 1880s. For Murat Halstead, what remained when all the bygones had been left behind was "a community of interests world-wide between us that we shall stand by forever."[25]

But this global dimension of Anglo-Saxonism had different meanings for each side. Influential Britons like Cecil Rhodes and Joseph Chamberlain tended to emphasize the ideal of imperial federation, with Britain at the center, whereas Americans were more interested in the broader process of globalization in which America would have the starring role. A typical statement of the continued centrality of Britain came from George R. Parkin, a leading Canadian advocate of closer imperial ties. "The development of the Anglo-Saxon race, as we rather loosely call the people which has its home in the British Isles," he wrote, "has become, within the last century, the chief factor and central feature in human history." For Americans, however, Anglo-Saxonism took on a rather different aspect in which, as one might expect, the United States was at the center of the process. In contrast to Gladstone's view of continuing British leadership, the Reverend Josiah Strong, who took a back seat to no one in his stress on Anglo-Saxon world dominance, saw the relationship rather differently. In his best-selling *Our Country*, he took a dim view of British claims to primacy. "England can hardly hope to maintain her relative importance among Anglo-Saxon peoples where her 'pretty island' is the home of only one-twentieth of that race," he wrote. The Anglo-American relationship paired the two nations in the performance of a new global dance step in which the British would follow their American partner's lead. [26]

Thus, even when measured with a global yardstick, the British, for all their virtues, tended to come up short. On this score, one finds repeated references to British cultural parochialism that contrasted incongruously with the empire's global reach. It was a "well-observed fact," according to one author, "that insularity is a characteristic of the general British or English mind." *The Atlantic* charged that "No nation [was] so straitened, illiberal, and hard of hearing as England, except, perhaps, China." If it was true, as was commonly complained, that the English failed to understand even their American kinsmen, how then could they be expected to understand the world? Americans may have had less practical experience and knowledge of the world, but they possessed "greater sympathy and imagination," as well as less capacity for "mischief."[27]

For all the talk of kinship, this global Anglo-Saxon relationship was not really founded in blood ties. One essayist in *The North American Review* took strong exception to the idea of a special relationship rooted in common ethnicity. This notion, whose origin he traced to a group of British chauvinists, was "received with enthusiasm by some here in America, with indifference by others, but by a large section of our people with dislike, because it is false and because it is offensive." Anglo-Saxonism was a misleading rallying cry for an America that was ethnically far more diverse. "When, overpowered by his emotions, the average Fourth-of-July orator eulogizes the Anglo-Saxon," the essayist wrote, "he does not pause to consider that the Celts and Germans among his audience may inquire of one another if there is any room on this continent for them." Allen Thorndike Rice also saw a broader heritage for the United States. "It is true now, and a century hence will be still more widely true," he wrote in an 1887 piece, "that Europe, not England, is the mother country of America." Europe's strong claim to patrimonial status could also be argued in the realm of culture. According to Herbert Tuttle, Americans were "engaged in a struggle between the surviving traditions of our English ancestors and the influence of different ideas acquired by travel and study on the continent." For politician-publisher J. D. Phelan, it was "nearer true to indicate Europe and not England alone as the source of America's intellectual subsistence."[28]

Although an Anglo-Saxon sentiment was undeniably emerging (what Richard Olney would later call "a patriotism of race as well as of country"), the importance of these kinds of differences about each nation's place in the world would become manifest in the next century in a relationship that was highly uneven and full of ups and downs. Investing in the informal alliance would pay political dividends for both nations after 1895, but the "special relationship" had a firmer grip on the thinking of Britons than of Americans, and it was from the beginning largely one-sided in favor of the Yankee cousins, who were quick to take advantage of Britain's proliferating strategic vulnerabilities. If in American minds the relationship was more American than Anglo, it was also much broader. The Anglo-American duet was understood as part of an oratorio of modernization that featured a global ensemble of voices.[29]

The Oxymoron of French Republicanism

Most prominent among the continental nations followed by Americans in the postwar period was France. As Henry James explained, "There are no people of any pretensions to liberal culture, of whatever nationality to whom the destiny of the most brilliant nation in the world is a matter of indifference." But although the Anglo-American relationship was, on balance, headed in a positive direction, fitting France into an optimistic global narrative of progress was far more difficult. On the face of it, France should have been viewed as a success story, but it continued to be plagued by a serious image problem with Americans long after the Second Empire had been succeeded by a republican regime. The major reason for this empathy gap was that French history and culture seemed in many ways even more resistant to the spread of the republican ideal than Britain's, despite the fact that France more nearly met the republican expectations of Americans than any other major nation. Unfortunately for American onlookers, however, it met those expectations in a deeply unsatisfying way.[30]

France's role in the Civil War gained it even lower esteem in American eyes than Britain's. Whereas a sizable chorus of British voices had spoken up for the Union, the French had actually flirted with the Confederacy. Moreover, Napoleon III had made an ill-considered use of French troops in an attempt to place the hapless Maximilian on the Mexican throne, an action that had put Americans in an unforgiving mood. "The most restless, ambitious, and warlike nation in Europe our neighbor!" sputtered *The Atlantic Monthly.* Following the removal of French forces in 1866, America directed its hostility at the person of Napoleon III—the "Prince of Darkness," John Lothrop Motley called him—the perfect embodiment of "imperialism," a word that, at the time, connoted popular dictatorship.[31]

What most concerned Americans was the broader danger posed by imperialism as an ideology rather than the man Napoleon III himself, for France was widely seen as a test case of the viability of this new model for organizing sovereignty. After 1848, imperialism looked for a time as if it were destined to become "the ultimate destination of the whole of the civilized world." Basing itself in popular, plebiscitarian approval that took advantage of mass ignorance, the system seemed to be a plausible substitute for liberal democracy. This "Napoleonic system"—autocracy with a veneer of popular consent—was "a political monstrosity," but it was certainly popular. It was too widely known to be a dirty secret, but the underlying problem with imperialism was that it reflected the general will with such accuracy. "The people submit to monarchical and despotic rule because it meets with their approval," wrote the economist Edward Stanwood. Napoleon III's rule "was not distasteful to the French people." Indeed, *Scribner's* doubted "whether the sentiment of French nationality had ever a more perfect expression than under the leadership of the two Napoleons." Consequently, discussions of the imminent collapse of the Napoleonic regime seldom emphasized unpopularity as a cause of its demise.[32]

Part of imperialism's appeal lay in the ruler's ability to bypass the cumbersome, all-too-often tawdry, legislative processes of democracy. In a retrospective report card, *Appletons'* allowed that "Napoleon III, to do him justice, had the greatness and prosperity of his country sincerely at heart." Eliciting an admiration for authoritarian rule that can always be found in some segments of American opinion, Napoleon was complimented for introducing a "wonderful harmony and singleness of purpose" to French domestic policy, which, despite its authoritarian features, was "progressive, active, and surprisingly successful." One editor quoted Balzac to the effect that "Despotism illegally performs great things, while liberty will not take the trouble to legally perform very small things." Louis Napoleon's reconstruction of the center of Paris and his willingness to entertain other grand projects such as a channel tunnel were much admired. Combined with the liberalization of his rule during the 1860s, he was, in some respects, "by no means a bad Caesar."[33]

Despite imperialism's inherent advantages in getting some things done, it was not efficient enough to successfully govern a highly complex society.

Developed nations, whose commercial life thrived on predictability and regularity, could not be governed on horseback by the whims of a single individual for whom personal glory was of the essence. "Imperialism," declared *The
Nation*, "so far from being the government of the future, has been proved totally unsuited to modern society." By the late 1860s, the regime was widely believed to be living on borrowed time, given the steady coalescence of liberal
and radical opposition in the once-docile legislative assembly and the growth
of labor unrest. Not unlike the crisis of 1788, the options appeared to narrow
down to two: a surrender of power or a descent into political chaos. American
commentators impatiently awaited the emperor's inevitable departure in the
hope that this authoritarian interlude, like that of the Greek tyrants, had prepared the ground for democracy.[34]

When the Napoleonic regime did collapse following the outbreak of the
Franco-Prussian War in 1870, the event was greeted with considerable satisfaction and 1870 was instantly hailed as a great year in human history. As *The
Nation* saw it, "if we judge the dead year by the importance of its contributions to the work of human progress, it would perhaps be difficult to find one
to match it." The collapse of Bonapartism was interpreted as an epochal blow
against aristocracy generally. Speaking hopefully of aristocratic decline, *The
Atlantic* predicted that in fifty years this institution would seem as remote
historically as serfdom. Although public opinion appeared to be weighted
heavily against France in the war itself, the U.S. minister in Paris, Elihu B.
Washburne, was the first to extend recognition to the Third Republic, which
had been declared in September. The rationale, as President Grant explained
in his annual message, was that "we cannot be indifferent to the spread of
American political ideas in a great and highly civilized country like France."[35]

The fall of Napoleon was one thing, but the formation of the French republic was not perceived as a millennial event, ideological affinity notwithstanding.
It was undeniably a genuine republic as well as the only other major republic
in the world, but it was a *French* republic, which made people uneasy. Regret-
tably, as one editor concluded, France was "a calamity to herself" as well as "a
standing cause of unrest in Europe." If the past was a reliable guide, the unhappy history of the First Republic suggested the possibility of another round
of revolutionary and expansionist warfare in Europe. Well aware that the fall of
this particular Bonaparte did not mean the end of Bonapartism, *The Galaxy*
repeated Lamartine's *bon mot* to the effect that "when the Creator wishes to set

the world on fire he kindles the blaze in the breast of a Frenchman." It was for this reason that *The Nation* urged its readers to suspend judgment, arguing that "no French republic is worthy of confidence, support, or respect which keeps up the standing army, as French republics have hitherto done." For Godkin and his journal, the best government the French had ever known was the two decades-long rule of Louis Philippe, the bourgeois king.[36]

For a nation to simply call itself a republic was not enough. *Appletons'* warned that "we should not be deluded by the name of republic, nor suppose too hastily that, by a mere change of names, or change of forms, despotism is overthrown and liberty installed." There was an enormous difference between true republicanism and its superficial expressions. In the preconditionalist opinion of *Scribner's* editors, a republic "can only be permanent in a country where intelligence is universal, where thought is free from priestly domination, and where men have faith in God and in each other"—all these characteristics presumably being absent in France. A republic could not be willed into being by the fiat by a few political leaders, no matter how well intentioned. An 1870 editorial maintained that "France, even if her leading men were sincere republicans, is entirely unable to maintain a republic."[37]

The oft-predicted (and much feared) outbreak of revolutionary unrest in Paris in March 1871 under the Commune validated the view of France as a turbulent society and reinforced the long-held skepticism about the prospects for French liberalism. In a one-sided account that ignored the government's butchery in quelling the rebellion, Minister Washburne accused the insurrectionary communards of committing "crimes which shall never die." "We must needs have the brush that painted the Apocalypse to portray these scenes," said another horrified commentator. "Reason is staggered before them." Only in one way, and a quite chilling one at that, could it be said that France was showing the way to the future, insofar as the socialist ideas behind the commune were a bloody portent of things to come. For *The Nation*, the commune was "the most extraordinary episode of modern times" because it showed that "the barbarians whose ravages the modern world has to dread, live not in forests, but in the heart of our large cities." Thus the overall effect of the insurrection was to confirm "the French incapacity for self government," a judgment that would persist well into the next century.[38]

The overarching explanation for French political instability was a widespread belief in "the decadence of France"—"sloth, ignorance, and want of political sense"—which a republic in name alone could not cure. If it was true that government was a reflection of a society, then over time it seemed clear that the French had gotten the kinds of regimes they deserved. "Providence does not rain tyrants or peculators on any people," said *The Nation*. "He lets them earn them through vices of their own." According to another journal, France's social system was "rotten to the core." Other observers, like George Towle, best known as the translator of Jules Verne's *Around the World in Eighty Days,* saw the disastrous outcome of the war as a consequence of cultural decay, which suggested the need for a thoroughgoing cultural reconstruction above and beyond the incessant political remodeling to which France was addicted. Unfortunately, held the consensus, the great majority of the French people did not have the right stuff of modern liberal politics. "So gifted and accomplished a people," mused *Appletons',* "but with respect to political sagacity . . . they have yet to learn their A B C."[39] A few believers in France, like Walt Whitman, viewed the nation's low state, its "dim, smitten star," as only temporary, but skepticism about culturally rooted French political pathologies was the norm.[40]

This cultural deficit was attributed to a host of causes: lack of popular education, an irresponsible press, militaristic propensities, and a decadent high culture. However popular, heavy military spending perpetuated "that curse of popular ignorance," particularly among the superstitious and easily manipulated peasantry. The French press, which was assigned a good deal of blame for starting the war, tended to be unrepresentative of the French people and was so appallingly parochial that they formed "a Chinese wall between the French people and its neighbors." American and English newspapers concentrated on reporting the news, Brander Matthews noted in 1887, but "the primary quality of a good French paper is not news, but criticism." French news, then, was an oxymoron. "The newspaper can hardly be said to exist in France," said Albert Rhodes, which left the people "ignorant of what transpires outside of their own country, and of much that is inside of it." An American-style newspaper in Paris, it was suggested, would go a long way toward making possible a more mature republic.[41]

Also culpable was French literature. French novels, according to Herbert Tuttle (an expert on Germany), were on the whole "clever, fascinating, shallow, egotistic, and dangerous." Though stylistically refined and cultivated, they were too racy for the more squeamish and conventional American moral sensibility. One reviewer described French fiction as "a sort of synonym for flimsy sentiment, frivolous thought, doubtful morality, and prurient peerings into the morbid anatomy of the human mind." Not all French novels were guilty of moral debasement, of course, but everyone could point to examples that justified the caricature. Cynicism was another flaw. Works by popular authors like Dumas, *fils,* were held to be "full of the venom which saps the morals and encourages propensities which are all the worse because they are cynical." Typical was the critic in *The Nation* who referred to "the filth of M. Zola." One redeeming feature of the French book industry, however, was that it made available for the first time, in French translation, the works of Russian novelists like Dostoyevsky.[42]

More broadly still, it was the French way of life that was at fault, as social looseness tended to correspond with what formerly had been called political licentiousness. This line of analysis was tricky, for France was being condemned for what many Americans found most attractive about the land and people. "Good Americans, when they die, go to Paris," went the saying (attributed to T. G. Appleton). But the city did not need dead Americans, for it already contained sizable numbers of the living kind, about 5,000 residents in 1870 with an additional 8,000 or so tourists. Five years later the American colony in Paris was larger than ever, up to 30,000 strong by some estimates, though no one knew for sure how many. Despite some initial fears that the Franco-Prussian war had sapped the city's vitality, Paris soon regained its preeminence as a modern urban Mecca. By the end of the century it had some 20,000 cafes and bistros and approximately 4,000 hotels. The artist Eugene Benson, who wrote frequently on France, could not contain his enthusiasm: "WHAT a city! Gayety, brightness, movement, largeness, magnificence! City of bridges, palaces, monuments, banners and women! City of pleasures and sins; city of sirens and idlers; city to admire and detest. . . . It is like a million-petalled flower, with each petal exquisitely adapted to touch the senses and warm the imagination of man in the full pride of life." Paris was "exhilarating," "electric," and a source of endless fascination. American journals went into extraordinary detail in exploring the social life and byways of the city, with apparently no detail too small or unworthy of micro-description. For example, in 1869 *Appletons'* ran a series of pieces by Towle describing the markets, vendors, bootblacks, gamins and street urchins, peddlers, and chestnuts. Even the city's blemishes appeared to add to its beauty, as articles discussed the ragpickers and foundling children.[43]

Expressions of delight in Parisian pleasures were offset by periodic censorious outbursts as the decadence that had evoked so much criticism in the waning years of the Empire appeared to have carried over into the Third Republic. France was still the roué of nations, occasionally amusing perhaps, but not to be relied upon in fundamental matters. What kind of society was it, wondered Rhodes, in which social ostracism was more likely to result from bankruptcy than from marital infidelity? The problem was that American men might prove susceptible to degeneration through overexposure to French culture. Too much time in Paris, suggested Rhodes, would lead to a loss of "that industrious and aggressive nature which is an American characteristic." Lucy Hooper, for a time the Paris correspondent for *Appletons'*, complained about the loose behavior of "spotted peaches"—women from the "fast set" in American cities, who made spectacles of themselves by receiving men in their bedrooms. This topic was seldom encountered in high-tone American journals. Americans of this "dissipated set" played too hard in this "vast moral whirlpool into whose vortex is drawn all the floating evil of a world." Hooper inverted the standard quip by saying that "If anybody wishes to be or has been particularly bad, he or she goes to Paris."[44]

Too materialistic and pagan on the one hand, France was condemned for being too religious and too Catholic on the other. Some essayists maintained that France's chief flaw, common to all Latin nations, was the enduring grip of a Roman Catholicism that befuddled the French mind with "the great awe of superstition." It was "largely due to the absence of a pure and reasonable faith," according to one writer, "that French society has been so unstable, unreliable, and difficult to govern." American readers, long accustomed to seeing the Vatican described as a reactionary force, were doubtless pleased to read that what little Protestantism there was in France was "an element of light, of progress, of religious life, very salutary for the present and very important for the future." The decline in France's population was also duly noted, anticipating what in the fin-de-siècle would become a broader concern with "race suicide." If current population trends were not reversed, it was predicted that "France must in the end, be invaded and overflowed, like an island sunk below the level of the sea."[45]

Especially galling, in light of these many shortcomings, was "the absurd vanity" of France's inflated self-image. Herbert Tuttle offered the following summary of French conceits: "They thoroughly believe that France is the greatest nation in the world; that she stands at the head of civilization; that she has produced the greatest men in every department of life; that she alone has a language, a literature, and an art; that her soldiers are the best in the world, and in the late war were defeated only by treachery." The idea that such a narcissistic society could conceive of itself as the most cosmopolitan of nations was fiercely attacked. "They are the Chinese of the West," said Rhodes. And if the French were on the whole insular, Parisians were even more so. According to *The Atlantic*, "Humanity outside of France—one might almost say outside of Paris—is a sealed book to the generality of Frenchmen."[46]

As late as 1888, *The Nation* accused the French of being "famous for their lack of curiosity with regard to other peoples." This problem began early and could be traced to the absence of international education in the elementary schools. With regard to geography and history, *Harper's* claimed that "the ignorance of the French, as a people, upon these latter subjects is as surprising as their want of interest in everything occurring abroad." The French reluctance to learn foreign languages on the assumption that everyone else should speak French was another indicator of the country's provincialism. Although the French intelligentsia showed some indications of broadening horizons following the establishment of the republic, even at the elite level the ethnocentric narrowness and ignorance of the world remained all too common. The French Academy with its so-called immortals (mostly "nobodies" and "mediocrities," according to Rhodes) was seen as an institution for the promotion of intellectual stultification.[47]

For all its imperfections, the superiority of certain features of French culture was incontrovertible. "Whatever sins the French may be guilty of, they never sin against art and good taste (except when in the frenzy of revolution)," said the naturalist John Burroughs. French fashion ruled the women's world, though not always to the liking of those Americans who still adhered to the ideal of republican simplicity and resented the dictatorship of fashion. Americans were more enthusiastic about French art. The sizable number of aspiring artists who studied in Paris was evidence that Americans recognized good taste, but it also suggested that American art could look forward to a splendid future once the lessons of the French masters had been assimilated. The preeminence of French cuisine was also unquestioned, though resident Americans under-standably tended to miss their home cooking after a time. The French stage, too, was an object of attraction for those who had learned the language. It was, said *The Nation*, "excellent because the French audience has a cultivated taste; the French are born artists and critics." By contrast, the American the-ater was thoroughly coarse. In all these areas, the French were intolerant of the mediocrity that Americans meekly accepted.[48]

France was not without defenders who argued that Americans were being blinded by the "injustice and falsity" of British prejudices and clichés. Accord-ing to one editor, French family life, which was based on a "very powerful" instinct for domesticity, was quite solid. A "roving American" insisted that "neither in England nor in America is the marriage-vow kept more inviolate." By the end of the 1880s, a series of essays by W. C. Brownell in *Scribner's* on "French Traits," later collected and published as a book, had scarcely a negative thing to say about the French and even suggested that American criticisms of French politics were the product of "some other touchstone for discovering truth, of which we are ignorant, or perhaps some substitute for truth itself." In addition, there were occasional remonstrances against facile generalizations about the French national character. *Appletons'* observed that the "French character is about as multiform and many-sided as we can possibly conceive: and yet such is the force of prejudice that among the English-speaking nations French character is but another term for frivolity and irreligion." Interestingly, such cautionary comments were sometimes made by editors of the very jour-nals who were most guilty of cultural character assassination. In this inconsis-tent spirit, *The Nation*, a leading violator, scored critics who were "more ready to remember the points of difference between different nations than to remem-ber the points of likeness between two communities of human beings." Even so, Francophile comments swam weakly against a powerful tide of negative evaluations of French national character.[49]

Given the prevailing assumption of cultural decay, postmortems on the events of 1870–1871 offered little hope for survival of the republic. "There is nothing in the present condition of France, or in its history during the last twenty years," said *The Nation* in 1872, "which is not calculated to create de-spondency about the future of free government." The republic seemed des-tined to be an interim regime only. With the National Assembly dominated by Orleanists and Bourbon legitimists, the new regime was "a republic without republicans," incapable of commanding the allegiance of the public. In the absence of a stable core, the greatest need for France was for a period of parliamentary and social stability without the kind of revolutionary unrest that seemed always to accompany popular dissatisfaction, but that seemed unlikely in a country in which a constitution had a shorter life span than "a very moderate farm-lease." Given the sorry history of French republics, the forecasts were understandably quite pessimistic. "Those who know France well will be surprised if she remain a republic for a year," *Scribner's* predicted.[50]

The French lacked the humdrum civic-mindedness and public spirit that allowed political questions to be settled through regular elections, hence their fateful proclivity to despotism. For the historically inclined, the ideological source of French political shortcomings could be traced to the baneful traditions established by the French Revolution. The tendency to cast its protagonists in superhuman terms had given rise to a "legendary romance" that one reviewer found absolutely ridiculous. The result, said *The Nation*, was that "Jacobins whose policy was, in its stupidity no less than in its cruelty, the policy of savages, have been credited with high statesmanship." Contrary to what people on the Continent thought, the importance of the French Revolution as a landmark in the history of human liberty had been vastly overestimated. The revolution needed to be viewed in a broader light, "to be considered a mere portion of the European Revolution." Liberty, equality, and fraternity were sound doctrines, but for France itself it had been a case of too much, too soon, as the revolution had created a standard of freedom that French society was unable to meet and infected the country with a political disease from which it had yet to recover. Given the unsettled history of republicanism in France, the best outcome that many could imagine was a restoration of a constitutional monarchy under the Orleanist Comte de Paris that might re-create "the peaceful and happy years" under Louis Philippe. The Bourbons were too hidebound, the imperialists too ridiculous, and the republicans too few and feckless.[51]

Still in all, France was indeed a republic—and as the *only* republic among the great nations apart from the United States, it mattered immensely as a marker of historical progress. As one author observed, "there is a magic in the word republic for us Americans." Because they could not help themselves, most everyone agreed with Emilio Castelar's judgment that "In the republic, and only in the republic, is the salvation of France." And so American interpretations of the perils of the Third Republic in France over the course of the next two decades took on the character of a compulsively watchable soap opera, full of emotion, drama, and one false climax after another, in which most of the themes adumbrated shortly after the Civil War found repeated expression. American opinion of the Third Republic did improve over time, but only slowly and with guarded expressions of confidence about its long-term prospects. Danger lurked around every corner, for France was, after all, "a land of coups d'état [where] kings, emperors, republics, conventions, and mobs, have equally availed themselves of a favorable opportunity to overturn the political organism, and substitute a new one."[52]

The constitution of 1875 got off to a shaky start with President MacMahon's pro-monarchist maneuverings, but a republican backlash produced majorities in both chambers and the election of conservative republicans with Jules Grévy as president. The plain-living Grévy, a leader with "no pictorial effect," was blandly though refreshingly reassuring. The monarchists, meanwhile, had missed their chance to regain power when the Bourbon pretender, the Comte de Chambord, refused to accept the revolutionary tricoleur as the national flag. By the time of his death in 1883, public sentiment had shifted away from the royalists. As the republic stabilized, ministerial crises now appeared to be taken in stride. Commenting on Gambetta's fall in 1882, a *Nation* editorial took heart at the peaceful denouement. "Every time Frenchmen get over an internal difficulty without the aid of troops they make an immense gain," it said. French politics seemed to be settling down to a mundane concern for "peace, a quiet life, and good markets." Even the Bonaparte name appeared to have lost its magical appeal, leading to the hope that France had finally kicked the imperial habit. "The public is getting used to be governed by plain men in black coats," said *The Nation*.[53] As if to absolve France of unique responsibility, some observers, notably Godkin and Henry James, were willing to entertain the notion that the susceptibility to demagogues was "common to civilization in general."[54]

The republic's peaceable demeanor also came as a pleasant surprise. "The transformation of France from the most bellicose to the most pacific of nations has been commented upon by all the journalists with astonishment and in some cases, one fancies, with a slight feeling of disappointment," it was noted. In the blink of an eye, France had created "the reputation of being the least warlike and most pacific people in Europe." Although the republic remained vulnerable to attacks from the revanchist right, there was much less talk of revenge than in the immediate aftermath of the war of 1870–1871. In the more sober climate of the early 1880s, the call for revenge was "apt to draw some cheap applause from popular meetings in the capital," but to little practical effect.[55]

In 1882, E. F. Noyes, who had served as minister to France in the Hayes presidency, concluded in a fit of optimism that France's success had finally provided republicanism with the critical mass necessary to set off a global chain reaction. "The example of two great Republics, like France and the United States, cannot be lost to the world," he wrote. "Their prosperity, beyond all comparison with that of other nations, cannot fail to commend democratic institutions to the people of all lands." It was at this point in time, when the republic appeared to have been successfully institutionalized, that the Statue of Liberty was dedicated (in 1886) as a symbol of Franco-American friendship and of a common devotion to freedom. But lingering antagonisms prevented a Franco-American project of liberty from getting on track. The less than gracious *New York Times* description of the unveiling described the statue as "a perpetual reminder of the realization in America of political ideas of which the origin may be fairly claimed for France, but of which the realization in France seems more precarious and less complete." Americans, after all, were "a race less theoretic, less excitable, and less impatient than the French people." Instead of memorializing the Franco-American relationship, the statue soon became exclusively a symbol of American openness to immigration. As the historian Jacques Portes has noted, the rocky relationship between the two nations goes a long way toward explaining this dissociation.[56]

Despite the republic's achievements, then, not everyone believed that monarchy was finished. "The Republic has just reached the period in its life when all French Governments find the ground under their feet become unsteady," warned *The Nation* in 1883. "That sooner or later the monarchy will be reestablished, even many who are antagonistic to the principle feel to be more than a probability," said Anna Bicknell, formerly a governess in the Tuileries Palace. The deeper problem, however, was that French republicanism did not seem to marry well with peace. There remained always the danger of Caesarism—the possibility that the French would fall in love with a man on horseback. One vital measure of a republic's stability was the ability of civil society to deter coups and military takeovers, which, notwithstanding a predilection for electing military heroes to the presidency, were virtually inconceivable eventualities in the United States. Few could imagine that France had achieved that kind of ingrained stability. France's large army continued to be a concern, as much for its domestic implications as for its impact on European power politics. And the decision to take up colonial expansion in Indochina and elsewhere—"crazy colonial enterprises" in one view—raised further questions about the depth of the republic's commitment to peace.[57]

American suspicions, never fully laid to rest, were revived in the late 1880s when the French public, apparently bored by peace and prosperity, were on the verge of being seduced by the martial charms of General Georges Boulanger, the minister of war in the Freycinet ministry. Boulanger's meteoric rise, fueled by dissatisfaction with the social legislation of the republic, his popularity within the army, and the desire for a war of *révanche* against Germany, quickly resurrected all the old fears of Napoleonic adventurism. At first the *Nation* dismissed Boulanger as "a fool as well as a charlatan." Still, if this "politicomilitary adventurer" were successful in gaining power, he could well shake Europe to its foundations. The expatriate 48er, Karl Blind, worried that "until this would-be revival of a demagogic Caesarism is finally put down and really rooted out, Europe will continue . . . darkly to resound with the threatening clangor of arms." Even though the general's political star plummeted in the wake of his failure to pull off a coup early in 1889, the Boulangist flirtation was "very disappointing to those who think the French Republic can be made permanent."[58]

The Boulanger affair rekindled all the nagging uncertainties about France in American minds about the Third Republic's long-term prospects. Perhaps it was true that all democracies were susceptible to the kind of missteps taken by France, but this adventure had all the earmarks of being a peculiarly French *faux pas.* Giving vent to underlying doubts that had been suppressed for much of the decade, *The Nation* categorized the Boulanger affair as a "proclamation of the imbecility and failure of the Government of his own country based on universal suffrage." The journal's earlier prediction that twenty years of political stability were necessary to consolidate republicanism was now revised upward by a decade. "Until something turns up which lasts at least thirty [years]—that is, lasts so long that the younger generation of voters remembers nothing else and thinks of nothing else as possible—French politics will continue to be the seething cauldron we now see it." Boulanger's rise according to Godkin, was "a striking illustration of the great difficulty of working Republican institutions in the presence of a large standing army—and of glorifying the soldier's trade on all public occasions."[59]

The Paris exposition of 1889 was a good time to take stock. The great powers of Europe refused to participate in the event and even temporarily withdrew their ambassadors in order not to have to listen to the recently adopted revolutionary anthem, the *Marseillaise.* But in most other respects, the exposition was a big hit. The newly constructed Eiffel Tower, the tallest structure in the world, advertised the progressivism and modernism of republican France. According to *The Century,* "once again the capital of France was un-questionably the capital of Western civilization." One correspondent described French successes in industry, art, and science as "a better "revenge" than could have been gained on a battlefield." That was the good news, but as the Fabian writer William Clarke pointed out, fundamental political questions had not been answered and the political situation remained unsettled, as monarchists, democrats, imperialists, and republicans continued to vie for power. "No one seems to believe that the present regime will be permanent," Clarke concluded. Indicative of the lingering skepticism was an essay entitled "Are the French Capable of Self-Government?" Obviously, the historical verdict was not yet in.[60]

As with Great Britain, the assertion that the post–Civil War years built the foundation for a Franco-American rapprochement is, in a general sense, true. But twentieth-century unease about the French national character was also a lineal descendant of nineteenth-century skepticism about French culture and politics. The troubled, conflicted commentary about France during these years would have a familiar ring to succeeding generations of Americans simultaneously attracted to and repelled by the French. The misgivings were reciprocated in the 1880s by French intellectuals on the left and right who found little in American politics or culture worth emulating.[61] Instead of being an occasion for rejoicing, France's admission into the family of republics illustrated the truth of Tolstoy's aphorism that every unhappy family is unhappy in its own way. But if nothing else the French republic was still recognizably part of the family, something that could not be said for the rest of Europe.

4

Europe II

Premodern Survivals

The pioneering political scientist Francis Lieber once imagined the leading nations of the world "draw[ing] the chariot of civilization abreast, as the ancient steeds drew the car of victory." Notwithstanding some worrisome developments, underlying cultural and political affinities at least furnished grounds for optimism about the ability of the United States to work in harness with Great Britain and France, the two other members of this global troika, even though in their common march through history, as one essayist archly put it, "they have marched back to back rather than side by side." When Americans contemplated the future of the rest of Europe, however, the prospect of finding additional partners seemed dismal. In the heart of the continent, economic successes were offset by political backwardness, while to the east and south cultural immaturity made the adoption of democracy unlikely in the near term. With countries where premodern survivals were still in the ascendant, teamwork was difficult to imagine.[1]

The Rise and Decline of German Preeminence in Civilization

Although Anglo-Saxonism was a common expression of America's cultural affinities in a global civilization, other ways of categorizing ethnocultural groupings yielded a broader spectrum of societies with which Americans could identify. For example, when John Hittel asserted that "modern civilization is predominantly Teutonic," he was opening membership in the civilized core to a broad arc of societies in northwest and central Europe, most notably to Germany, whose renown for cultural achievement briefly placed it at the apex of modern civilization. But Germany's top ranking was brief, as its political progress failed to match its stellar achievements in the arts and sciences.

Between 1871 and 1890, the country underwent a dramatic turnaround in American eyes: once Europe's best hope, it now became its principal danger. Whereas Great Britain and France evoked mixed feelings, Germany's historical trajectory was highly disappointing by comparison.[2]

Admiring Americans viewed the creation of a German nation state during the Franco-Prussian War as a world-historical event, the culminating act of many hundreds of years of European history. That German unity had been achieved by an autocratic regime was an inconvenient fact, but this unpleasantness was generally explained away by depicting Otto von Bismarck, the new chancellor, as an embodiment of Hegel's world-historical great man unwittingly doing the work of the Idea via the Cunning of Reason. By this reckoning, it was not the man, nor the Hohenzollern dynasty, but the larger historical process that mattered; hence Bismarck's successes were less personal or dynastic than "national, popular, natural achievements." It was "the German national spirit, as opposed to a crafty, self-seeking, dynastic policy," that had triumphed. Unwittingly, Prussia had achieved unification only through "the agency of forces which she herself constantly repudiated and ignored."[3]

At some point in the near future, this line of thinking went, Bismarck would suffer a domestic political reversal and the way would finally be open to a bona fide democratic government. As one reviewer predicted: "Not even Bismarck can long maintain against the progress of the age the feudalism of which he is the most distinguished representative." Because his successors were likely to be less skillful in suppressing the irrepressible desire for freedom, many liberals believed that a Prussian-dominated Germany was the prelude to the formation of a modern constitutional state modeled on the United States. Without knowing it, argued the German-born journalist and railroad entrepreneur Henry Villard, Bismarck had reinvigorated the spirit of 1848 and "expedited not a little the final collapse of monarchy." Not unlike the depictions of Louis Napoleon as freedom's unintentional forerunner, these rationales suggested that more than a few American liberals were comfortable with the idea of an authoritarian transition to democracy.[4]

If France's shortcomings were traceable to the underlying instability of the nation's cultural foundation, Prussia's successes were thought to be grounded in the bedrock of cultural virtue. Power, said one editor, had been "transferred to a more cultivated and substantial people—to educated, enlightened, and peaceful Germany." According to John Fiske in 1874, "The country of our time where the general culture is unquestionably the highest is Prussia." The "giant in the spiked helmet" was the product not only of military training, but of a system of universal education that turned out intelligent soldiers and provided a source of power far more lethal than the peasant cannon fodder of traditional armies. German achievement also owed much to a brilliantly effective bureaucracy, whose extraordinary administrative skills were greatly admired by civil service reformers. Richard T. Ely and others extolled the efficient and honest Prussian civil service as "the most admirable of which we have any knowledge." Here, too, the secret was culture. "The necessity of a moral foundation for social and political life cannot be enforced too often," said Ely. Although Germany was a far from perfect society, fault-finding extended only to trivialities. Minor blemishes here and there only underscored the overall beauty of the system. "There is no state more modern," concluded *The Nation*, "in the best sense of the word, than Prussia."[5]

The lopsided German triumph in the Franco-Prussian War was widely portrayed as a triumph not only for *Kultur* and for the principle of nationhood, but for Europe and for civilization as Americans happily crowned the new German empire as Europe's, and perhaps the world's, leading nation. "The political supremacy of Germany over France will inevitably carry with it the intellectual supremacy also," wrote H. W. Hemans, a British consul, in the pages of *The North American Review*, "and by that intellectual supremacy we do not doubt that civilization will, on the whole, largely profit." "No greater conquest of ideas has been seen in modern Europe," *Appletons'* concurred. The German writer Karl Hillebrand, a frequent contributor to English-language journals, proudly announced "the intellectual supremacy of Germany." For the journalist C. C. Hazewell, primacy in Europe was "the same thing as the first place in Christendom, or the world—meaning by the world that portion of mankind which has power and influence and leadership, because of its knowledge, culture, and wealth." The noted historian John Lothrop Motley, a college friend of Bismarck's and U.S envoy to Austria during 1861–1867, was positively ecstatic. "Intellect, science, nationality, popular enthusiasm, are embodied in the German movement," he rhapsodized. "They must unquestionably lead to liberty and a higher civilization."[6]

German superiority was often expressed in the racial idiom of Teuton versus Latin. In *Scribner's* caustic assessment, Germany's triumph over France was far more than a military success. It was, in addition, an epochal racial event,

> the triumph of the Teuton over the Latin, of Protestantism over Roman-
> ism, of the new civilization over the old. The Latin races, with their in-
> triguing priesthood; their ignorant, poor, and superstitious peoples, their
> monkeries and nunneries, and relics and shams, are sinking to decay. . . .
> The Teuton blood, with its affiliations, is the blood of the future. The
> Teutonic languages are the languages of the future; and Protestant civi-
> lization, under various forms and phases—moving through various
> modes of progress—is the civilization of the future.

T. G. Appleton agreed, writing that "the Latin races are now being weighed in the balance and found wanting."[7]

The key to Germany's cultural superiority lay in its universities, which were generally considered to be without peer in the world. By defining scholarship as the creation of new knowledge rather than the stewardship of the old, Germany had become "the land of advanced ideas." German devotion to painstaking, precise research was "something almost incredible to our Western haste and superficiality," according to *The Nation.* German scholars were without question the best of the best and showed the competitive system in its most flattering light: only the fittest made it to the top in the universities, while lesser lights were relegated to the second rank. Every aspect of the system, from the preparation of students, the rigors of their studies, and the awe-inspiring scholarship of the professoriat, was far superior to the rudimentary American system of higher education. Small wonder then that as late as 1890, a time when the modern American university system was only in its formative stages, large numbers of American students continued to go to Germany for their studies, especially in the sciences. From time to time, Americans poked fun at German academics who made more obscure what many considered to be an already difficult language. But despite the penchant for "heavy, dull, and awkward" prose, frequent descents into obscurantism, and an inability to communicate findings to nonacademic audiences, German scholarship was unmatched. In addition to its superiority in pure scholarship, Germany was also much farther advanced in technical education.[8]

Impressed by the triumph of nationalism, culture, and the promise of democracy to come, in the aftermath of the war Americans gave themselves up to hero worship. Most strikingly, Bismarck's image as a reactionary roué— one writer had described him as "a daring, unscrupulous adventurer"— underwent a remarkable transformation as he was suddenly promoted to the rank of historical genius. One correspondent penned the following worshipful report: "It is as if half-a-dozen intellects had served to compose his head. Physical and moral courage, shrewdness and an indomitable will, wit and humor, sagacity and recklessness, a certain intuitive comprehension of men's characters and calm steadiness, I do not know which of these qualities is most wonderfully developed in this modern Proteus, this personification-to finish the Greek simile-of both Ulysses and Ajax." There were many more depictions in this vein. The new emperor, William, and military leaders like Helmuth von Moltke were also awarded the status of demigods. William I, for example, was "a stalwart monarch of a stalwart race."[9]

No one doubted that Bismarck was an authoritarian whose ideas belonged to the past. But he was seen as a transitional figure who, as one author put it, had been necessary "to sweep away the accumulated obstructions of centuries, and prepare the way for a truly popular government by the people." In the immediate aftermath of unification, liberals like the lawyer and writer Friedrich Kapp, who returned to Germany after a twenty-year sojourn in the United States, looked forward to "a commonwealth in the heart of Europe, founded on nationalism in place of Caesarism, parliamentary institutions instead of personal government, peaceful development under constitutional laws rather than military glory." Instead of "Prussian despotism," the more likely result was predicted to be "the curtailment of Prussia's power, and the enlargement of true German liberty." Ideally, a republic or federation of republics would be the eventual outcome. The new Germany's federal structure, which at first glance resembled that of the United States in broad outline, was a hopeful sign, as was Bismarck's declaration that Germany was a *Rechtstaat,* a state governed by rule of law. [10]

For a time, Bismarck's domestic policies met with acclaim. The *Kulturkampf* was, in general, greeted with approval by mainstream antipapists, who saw the Roman church as an impediment to liberal modernity. "How richly they need the discipline they are receiving," said *The Nation,* referring to the ultramontanists. "Christians like these will be none the worse of an occasional visit from the police." However, Bismarck's war against the papacy soon prompted second thoughts, not least because it backfired among German Catholics. The traditional Hohenzollern policy of religious toleration came to seem far more enlightened, especially in light of the perceptible rise of anti-Semitism. Bismarck's often high-handed parliamentary maneuvering, his intolerance of dissent, and the resort to press censorship also soured opinion on his domestic achievements. In particular, the absence of parliamentary responsibility—"simply monstrous," according to the liberal reformer Carl Schurz—suggested that Germans, for all their progressive qualities, had "not yet secured the essence of a parliamentary government." Passage of the antisocialist laws also raised some eyebrows, as they seemed more designed to prevent the expression of opinion than to safeguard property. More shocking still was the social security legislation pushed through by the chancellor, which was widely viewed as "socialistic" and taken as further proof of Bismarck's ignorance of "economic science." Bismarck's lurch toward protectionism also elicited heavy criticism as an act of "fanatical impetuosity . . . utterly deaf to the voice of either reason or caution"[11]

By the mid-1880s, Germany's cultural virtues were no longer sufficient to compensate for its political shortcomings. The once-ballyhooed political resemblances between the United States and Germany no longer merited serious discussion. Germany was not Prussia writ large, but it was clear that the crown's authority was rooted in Prussia's preeminence in the state structure. For all the democratic trappings, it was still, at base, a dynastic system managed by the Hohenzollerns. While all eyes were turned on Bismarck, Bismarck's adoring gaze was fixed on the emperor. By all indications, the country was not being prepared for liberal democracy, for which the prospects appeared to grow more remote with every passing year. The original hope that Bismarck, like Louis Philippe, would govern with and for the middle classes, "with the brains of the country," was replaced in the late 1870s by the recognition that Bismarck's was "the government of one man of commanding talent," who was at heart a "parliamentary bully." His insistence on controlling all legislation meant that following his departure there would be no parliamentary force to pick up the reins. Democratic forces were not completely absent, but on the whole the Bismarckian system was creating a situation "almost calculated to make representative government ridiculous and impossible."[12]

Unfortunately, one writer complained, the only creed that seemed to have triumphed was "the cult of the nation," whose chief expression was German militarism. "Does Prussia Love War?" became a common theme for editorial columns. Although some pointed out that militarism was hardly unique to Germany, the charge stuck. The paradox of a nation so highly developed in so many ways and so backward in this one important respect was cause for both puzzlement and alarm. In the view of the translator and prolific author Helen Zimmern, who was a notable conveyor of German and Italian culture to Anglo-American readers, Germany was a nation "educated, yet combative, advanced in many directions of thought, yet left far behind in one of the most essentially civilizing." By this time, the idea of the ennobling functions of military service had been supplanted by the view that conscription was dehumanizing. German military institutions were "steadily annihilating individual selfhood." [13]

The infatuation with Germany and Bismarck was clearly over. But while Bismarck's domestic leadership was widely judged to be a failure, the undisputed brilliance of his foreign policy preserved his aura of greatness. In the opinion of the level-headed John Kasson, who served as U.S. minister in Berlin in the mid-1880s, Bismarck was "the most illustrious figure of the nineteenth century." For all his shortcomings, Bismarck remained the indispensable man, though for reasons quite different from those offered at the beginning of his career. By the late 1870s, there emerged a torrent of speculation about the chaos that might follow upon Bismarck's retirement from office. The "great man" theory was inverted as Bismarck's indispensability, once thought to presage a democratic future, was now seen as "an ominous sign for Germany and for Europe." His historical task was re-envisioned as staving off a relapse into authoritarianism and political chaos. Contemplating the disappearance of this "colossal figure," *Appletons'* predicted that "his absence will create a void larger and harder to fill than any other political character of this century.[14]

The disappearance of the great man was bad enough, but worse still was the realization that there was no Bismarckism to survive Bismarck. "The secret of his power will be buried with him in the grave," lamented Professor Herbert Tuttle. There would be no institutionalization of his charisma, nor would there be a replication of his genius because, in *The Nation's* view, Bismarcks were "among the rarest products of this world." Thus the commanding genius who produced so many German successes would also be the source of grave tribulations that would certainly bedevil Germany following his departure from the scene. Bismarck's greatest mistake in an otherwise brilliant career, Schurz opined, was "his failure to train a new generation of leaders to succeed him." Some people continued to hope that Bismarck would pave the way for a liberal succession, but few thought this likely. Another possibility was that Germany would muddle through, unhappily but harmlessly, with a succession of mediocrities.[15] But Bismarck's Germany was too firmly in the grip of authoritarianism, with its propensity for making disastrous decisions, for this to be a likely outcome.

The Bismarck problem, however, was not the sole worry of the day. Astute observers recognized that the Bismarckian system also required a sympathetic emperor. To function effectively, a Bismarckian Germany needed, as one essay put it, "not only a succession of Bismarcks, but a succession of Williams." The unlikelihood of such a double transition became apparent following William's death in 1888 at age 91. His well-regarded successor, Frederick III, was known to be terminally ill with cancer of the larynx. Frederick, a man of liberal sympathies, was described as "a Prussian Prince, of the best type, with all the good qualities of his house and none of the bad ones." His son William, however, was another story. Following Frederick's death in June after a reign of only ninety-nine days, the first reports on the young emperor, William II, were the cause of considerable apprehension abroad. *The Nation* quickly pegged him as "a young man of the military type, who has little sympathy with or comprehension of constitutional liberty or the parliamentary system." It was generally accepted that Bismarck's foreign policy, though hardly pacifist, had at least been peaceful and nonexpansionist. With the impetuous young emperor at the helm, talk turned quickly to the possibility of "a real calamity for European politics."[16]

It was not long before the young emperor's comments and behavior led to open questioning of his sanity. "His mental as well as bodily activity is exciting alarm all over Europe," reported *The Nation*, "and is increasing the apprehension of some brain trouble which the family history would seem to justify." His mania for things military and his eagerness to inculcate in his young son a military mind-set seemed "sadly out of place in an industrial age." In a repetition of the criticism that had been leveled at Napoleon III, it was pointed out that monarchs had caused trouble enough in the preindustrial age, but their capacity to wreak havoc was multiplied many times over in a modern society. After all, what qualifications did William have to run a great state, wondered Godkin? Intelligent though he was, he certainly would have been unable to attain a professorship. Without the accident of birth, the best that he could have aspired to would have been a minor position as a functionary in the army or the business world. Without the emperor's clothes people would have felt no need to hang on his every word.[17]

The other shoe dropped with Bismarck's forced departure in 1890. Although the iron chancellor's retirement had been anticipated, his dismissal by William still came as a great shock. In *The Nation*'s estimation, it was the greatest event in Europe since 1870. The journal duly noted "the passage from the stage of the greatest figure—this is hardly too strong a phrase—in German history. Frederick the Great and Luther were certainly his only competitors." For some, Bismarck had been responsible for keeping in check a German society that was not yet ready for democracy when he arrived on the scene, for by this time the formerly adoring view of German culture had been turned upside down. The Germans were "like inexperienced children who needed a strong taskmaster to lead them up to vigorous manhood," wrote George Moritz Wahl, a professor of German literature at Williams College. In some ways they were much like the French in that "an overdose of political freedom would have led to their national destruction." Even the French appeared to feel sympathy for the sudden departure of their old antagonist, who had prided himself on being predictable. It was, in all, a somber turn of events. The *New York Times* correspondent feared that "the future may be stormy and discolored by fire and blood." *The Nation* predicted that the German people now had before them "a fair prospect of what are called 'lively times.'"[18]

Russia's Explosive Future

If a politically mature culture was the precondition of progress, Russia, culturally backward and absolutely absolutist, was clearly ineligible for serious consideration as a civilized power. Even so, Americans showed a surprising degree of optimism, at least at first, when searching for signs of liberal development in Russia. It was a long shot, but if the seeds of liberalism already were beginning to germinate, then the long-predicted future clash between two expanding continental empires need not take place. Instead, the Bering Strait that separated the recently acquired Alaska from Siberia could just as well become "a commercial thoroughfare" in the future. In any event, Russia's importance to Asia, Europe, and the world was too great to ignore. "No country has attracted so much of the attention of the world during the past few years as Russia," said William L. Kingsley, publisher-owner of *The New Englander*.[19]

On the surface, following the U.S. Civil War, Russia had a much better image among Americans than either England or France. Russia's emancipation of the serfs at the expense of a "haughty aristocracy" was seen as a parallel to the liberation of slaves in the American South and appeared to put the two nations on the same historical track of human liberation. Moreover, the sale of Alaska in 1867 and the good-will visit of Grand Duke Alexis to the United States in 1871 suggested closer geopolitical ties to come. Most commentators, however, believed that Russophilia was baseless. As *The Atlantic* pointed out, favorable comparisons tended to emphasize "a few accidental, and no doubt transitory, similarities, with omission of the deep and characteristic diversities." *The Nation* also dismissed Russomania as pure fantasy, for no thoughtful person believed "that there is anything in common between the two countries but size." America's infatuation with Russia, the piece concluded, was "based on little or nothing, and can have no endurance." Apart from the two nations' obvious political contrasts, Russia and America had fundamental cultural differences. Russia had no middle class to speak of and, unlike Britain, France, and Germany, had few tourist or cultural attractions. All in all, cultural connections with Russia were quite meager.[20]

Until the 1870s, Russia was pretty much a terra incognita. Only with the recognition of Russian literature, the works of Dostoyevsky, Turgenev, and Tolstoy in particular, and the emergence of serious analysts like Eugene Schuyler, did Russia enter into the national consciousness in more than a glancing way. *The Nation* welcomed this newfound interest, noting that previous knowledge was "fragmentary, superficial, and untrustworthy." The exceptional quality of Russian literature came as a pleasant surprise. Besides opening a window on Russian culture, it proved the Russians' capacity for high culture and progress in other areas. For Emilio Castelar, it demonstrated that Russia "was not to remain a monstrous exception in the earth; that it could not much longer drag the weight of its chains after so many peoples had broken them." At the same time, Russian literature, world class though it might be, also tended to reinforce the country's image of medieval darkness. One reviewer, for example, wondered "why Russian novelists seem to bend all their energies towards increasing the gloomy tendency of the Russian nation under its present gloomy conditions."[21]

The aura of bleakness was somewhat relieved by a travel literature that described exotic sections of Russia. After spending a few weeks with the Don Cossacks, Frank D. Millet, the illustrator and writer, described with pleasant surprise his admiration for people who, often stigmatized as barbarians, more closely resembled American frontiersmen. "Independent in spirit, self-reliant, and full of resource," they were a welcome contrast to the typical Russian peasants who formed "an inferior order of human beings." A traveler to the Caucasus described "scenes of Arcadian enchantment" where he was struck by "the grandeur of the mountains, and the beauty of the women." But travel into the south was very much an adventure into an "unknown world," as the region was well off the beaten tourist track. Even more exotic were reports of travel to the ethnographically diverse territory between the Caspian and the Pacific. Readers of travel reports from these regions were often delighted by reports of the bizarre customs encountered there. One essayist, for example, cheerfully described a Kirghiz custom in which the dinner host would politely "take a handful of pieces of meat and stuff them into the mouth of an inferior guest."[22]

There were, by most descriptions, two Russias, only one of which was real. The genteel opulence and cosmopolitanism of St. Petersburg and Moscow was inauthentic, a fake. It was, according to George Carey Eggleston, a journalist and prolific writer of books for young people, "an artificial Russia, so to speak, a sort of French veneer, which misrepresents the real fabric that it conceals, and unluckily it is only this unreal thing that travelers in the Muscovite dominions commonly have opportunity to become familiar with." In another review, Eggleston, speaking of all the changes introduced by the czars, insisted that these reforms had brought Russia into Europe but without Europeanizing the Russians, who remained "Russians still, of the old, semi-Oriental sort" with "the old, semi-Oriental way of thinking which belonged to their forefathers." The notion that the entire country was a Potemkin village was repeated time and again, but the fact that it was a cliché was not held against it. Take, for example, *The Nation*'s defense of hackneyed thinking: "The saying about scratching Russians and finding Tartars is something more than merely 'smart,' for it expresses in a terse form the fact which every writer on Russia, from Mr. Mackenzie Wallace downwards, brings out, that the Russians, with all their external polish, are in some respects still in a condition of comparative barbarism."[23]

Despite some modern features, Russia on the whole seemed scarcely civilized. According to the widely read newspaper writer and student of comparative civilizations George Townsend, Russia's power had outstripped Russian culture. Russians remained a people who had "created nothing and discovered nothing," having borrowed the military technologies of the West for their expansionist purposes. Most telling of all was the brutish, superstitious condition of a degraded Russian peasantry that existed in a "state of total ignorance." This was not a permanently fated condition, for many saw possibilities in the *muzhiks*. General George McClellan, for example, insisted that they were "not of an inferior race, but were capable of improvement and civilization." They needed to be, for the Russian aristocracy was incapable of mastering the new world, which was governed "by steam, electricity, and, though last not least, by dynamite and other explosives." One of the most fateful shortcomings of the czarist system was that it denied to Russia the services of talented men who in other circumstances would be the natural leaders of the country.[24]

Consequently, those who sensed that Russia was on the doorstep of modernity tended to place their hopes in a modernizing autocracy, thereby again illustrating the recurring liberal flirtation with authoritarianism. If modern society had grown in the surrogate womb of monarchy elsewhere, why not then in Russia? During the reign of Alexander II in particular, writers put an optimistic spin on Russian internal developments. Serfdom had been abolished, and it seemed that the barbaric practice of corporal punishment with knout and stick would soon follow. Reforms in other areas suggested even more change to come, perhaps even the end of that Russian scourge, chronic drunkenness. Writing in *Scribner's*, Thomas Knox saw Russia treading the clearly marked road to democratic progress. "The feeling is almost universal that there is much good in store for Russia," he wrote. "She is yet in her developing stage. Time, patience, and energy will accomplish all that her ardent friends can wish." More rhapsodic than most, Edna Dean Proctor, poet and author of *A Russian Journey*, also expressed optimism. "Under the Emperor Alexander II, him of the firm will and the tender, generous heart," she wrote, "Russia has begun a new existence, with sublime possibilities of greatness yet to be." Once the process of top-down reform had run its course, explained the enthusiastic clergyman-educator Robert L. Stanton, Russia would abandon absolutism "and the power of the people will thenceforth be everywhere recognized." Alexander alone was not enough, but a succession of Alexanders, McClellan believed, would produce a democratic soft landing, "without convulsion." For optimists, even the Mongol conquest, the famous Tatar Yoke, could not check Russia's inevitable progress. In the words of John Fiske, "The most the greasy Mongol could accomplish was to check for a few generations the growth of a national life among the Slavic tribes of Russia."[25]

This optimism evaporated quickly when discussion turned to Russian foreign policy. Lurking in the background of American analyses was Herbert Spencer's famous linkage of militarism and barbarism. *The Nation*, for example, quoted James Bryce to the effect that Russia was backward because "uncivilized states have always confounded success in war and extension of territory with real increase of greatness and power." Despite an amazing career of territorial expansion, many observers considered militarism to be Russia's Achilles' heel because its foreign policy dynamism was based on, and reinforced, a domestic status quo that was ultimately unsustainable. Michael Heilprin, a polyglot émigré from Poland who wrote extensively on Eastern Europe for *The Nation*, believed that pan-slavist adventurism was a way of deflecting Russia from its internal troubles, a way "of giving a new direction to the aspirations and wild yearnings of the Russian people." External successes would serve to distract the people from the allure of the revolutionaries. But by using its very inferiority as a way of validating moral superiority, Russia was cutting itself off from values essential to internal reform. It was in some ways a deeply embedded cultural problem. For Eugene Schuyler, who as chargé of the Petersburg legation had played a role in publicizing the "Bulgarian horrors," the atrocities perpetrated by the Ottomans in 1876, the country had been put on the wrong track long ago by Peter the Great. If only Peter had emphasized the civil aspects of civilization, he mused, "what real and lasting benefits might he not have conferred upon his country!" By seeking to prop up its rule through foreign adventurism, czardom was only digging its own grave and hastening its destruction.[26]

As in the rest of Europe, the emergence of public opinion in Russia was cause for grave concern, for the Russian people seemed at times to be more conservative than the czar. *Appletons'* complained that "the liberation of the

Russian masses only swells the multitude of zealots, who, with a fiery, religious zeal, look forward to the coming to pass of the dream of the "Father of Russia." *The Nation*, as usual, was skeptical about the radical contention that eliminating czardom alone would end Russia's problems. If the history of Jacobinism and its Napoleonic aftermath was any indication, the problem had a source far deeper than the Romanovs. The czar was captive to too many domestic interests that looked to expansion, including army officers interested in promotion and pan-Slavist ideologues. One could not absolve the czars of blame, of course, but the regime was in actuality "a many-headed hydra, drawing its lifeblood from yet unsubdued native barbarism and intellectual and moral sloth."[27]

Thus when nihilism and anarchist terrorism erupted in the 1870s, most observers treated them as a logical outgrowth of Russian history. In Godkin's view, nihilism was cultural, "the display in a very striking form of some of the peculiarities of temperament of the Slav race." Nihilism and reaction were two sides of the same cultural coin or, better yet, structurally necessary opposites. As Heilprin put it, "each of the two seems to call for the other, to justify the other." For Karl Blind, the government's "Mongol cruelty" was combined with "all the deleterious subtleness of a culture that was rotten before it had become ripe." However hateful their deeds, the nihilists were at least credited with a powerful idealism. They had displayed "a self-abnegation so admirable and a devotion so fervid that they cannot be said to be without a religion." *The North American Review* even opened its pages to a nihilist, who placed blame for Russia's misery squarely on the shoulders of the czarist regime, "that cancer which has for centuries sucked the life's blood out of the Russian people." Unfortunately, the consensus was that the nihilists were only making things worse. According to Albert F. Heard, who had served as a consular official for Russia in Shanghai, they had destroyed for the foreseeable future any possibility of continued top-down reform. In retrospect, Alexander II's innovations were misconceived half-measures that had succeeded only in whetting popular desires, thus inaugurating a period of revolutionary unrest and reaction. Alexander II would eventually pay with his life at the hands of bomb-throwing assassins in 1881.[28]

After a false dawn of Alexandrine reform, Russia began to slip into a dark cycle of reaction and radicalism that pushed the possible emergence of liberalism into the realm of pure fantasy. "The dreary reign of undiluted despotism has been resumed," said *Appletons'* in 1875. A few voices continued to hold out the hope that the czar would see the light by granting Russia a constitution, which would deny nihilism its raison d'être. But for Albert Heard in *Harper's,* top-down reform was impossible, owing to the unbridled corruption of the bureaucratic regime. The only possible solution lay in long-term education of the masses, during which time despotic rule would remain in place until Russians were prepared for "the final revolution" that would inaugurate the reign of the people. Others agreed that the system was rotten at the top. *The Nation* insisted that the nihilist contagion had penetrated the upper classes, the army, and even the secret police. By the end of 1884, a midterm report card on Alexander III's reign gave little cause for optimism: "Not a single important measure of reform has been enacted," said *The Nation,* "not a single step in the direction of freedom taken. By the late 1880s, Russia appeared to be locked into a pattern of violence and reactionary repression, with no end in sight. Unfortunately, this was not Russia's problem alone. As *The Century* believed, the revolutionaries were "setting an example of violent and lawless methods to political agitators everywhere."[29]

It was in this context that George Kennan's sensational exposes of the brutish Siberian penal system entered public consciousness. The exile system had actually been discussed earlier in the decade, in reviews of Dostoyevsky's *Buried Alive* and in a general examination of Romanov dynastic practices, at which time it had been described as "the greatest injustice of all." But Kennan's writings, which went far beyond former travel accounts or second-hand descriptions, struck a nerve, perhaps because they confirmed the irredeemability of the regime. As *The Century* noted, Kennan proved that the system was "a natural result of the absence of civil liberty." For *The Nation,* his writings underscored "the incurable barbarism" of the system. Commenting on a petition on behalf of the Siberian prisoners, *The Nation,* which not long before had designated Russia as the agent of civilization in the Balkans, ruled out of bounds any statement of previous friendship between the United States and Russia. "Any one who in our time permits, or connives at, or orders such atrocities," it declared, "is considered throughout Christendom an enemy of the human race."[30]

Kennan himself despaired of change in the foreseeable future; he was confident only that the exile system would "remain, for many years, one of the darkest blots upon the civilization of the nineteenth century." The only change possible seemed a revolutionary explosion. Karl Blind wrote of "the inevitable thunder clouds of a necessary storm destined to purify the air, to drive away the foul mists of tyranny, and to confer upon long-suffering Russia the blessings of Light and Right." Already present was the awareness of an historical irony that would become a commonplace of the twentieth century. Modern socialism and radicalism, though theoretically rooted in industrial societies, appeared to have their greatest practical influence "in the most rigidly governed and least intelligent population in Europe." This was puzzling, for as *Appletons'* had earlier noted, Russia should have been least threatened by socialism and communism. Ironically, too, Russia appeared to possess the police resources to deal with such a threat, for the time being at least. Few other European states could boast of such a vast, ruthless, and effective apparatus.[31]

This ominous situation led to fascinated ruminations about the brittleness of absolute despotisms. "Certainly, if the throne of Peter the Great is not secure from the iconoclasm of the Commune, where is to be found a throne in Europe that is?" asked one editorial. *The Nation* could only shake its head at a government whose chief preoccupation was "keeping the Czar and his family from being blown up"; this was hardly a position from which to contemplate reform or change of any kind. One year into the reign of Alexander III, one his few visible achievements was self-preservation, and the only kind of visible progress was the advance of nihilism. By the end of the 1880s, though a modicum of political calm had returned to Russia, Americans remained convinced that the autocracy was doomed. [32]

Ordinarily, the impending collapse of a despotic monarchy would have been cause for exultation, but in this case a republican happy ending was not even remotely in sight. The general opinion was that change would most likely be explosive, cataclysmic, and radical. The Russian Empire, most understood, was "little different from a slumbering volcano." Would there be, wondered one editorial, a Russian Sédan, followed by a brief republic, and then a Moscow commune? In the same vein, General George McClellan, like many others, feared that change would come only through violence "and the horrible upheavals of socialism and communism." Henry James, in reviewing Wallace's book on Russia, found Russia to be a country so deeply mired in the past that it was especially susceptible to the allure of "a road that looks like a short cut into the unknown future."[33] Tragically, this upheaval was not likely to bring much improvement in its wake. Whatever the exact sequence of events, it was likely to play out much worse than the French story. If Russia was, like the United States, the only other nation with a future, it was a worrisome, perhaps nightmarish future for Russians and outsiders alike. American observers' dim view of Russia's prospects was uncannily accurate in their presentiment of grave crises to come.

Spain and Creeping Progress

Besides classifying European peoples along an axis that ran from west to east, Americans also perceived a north-south divide in which "Latin" peoples were juxtaposed unfavorably with the Teutonic. Spain was perhaps the most dramatic example of how culture defined a nation's place in civilization. After France, the most interesting experiment in republicanism—though one that received far less coverage in American media—was taking place in Spain precisely at the moment that the prospect of war loomed between the United States and Spain over Cuba in the 1873 *Virginius* affair, in which an American-flagged vessel loaded with arms and Cuban rebels was seized and taken to Cuba, where some American citizens were executed. Whereas France at least held out some hope for the future of republicanism, Americans tended always to belittle Spain's prospects on the assumption that republicanism required a cultural base that was foreign to Spanish experience. Unwilling to invest much emotional capital in the Spanish republican experiment in the first place, Americans consequently showed little disappointment at its failure and were willing to countenance authoritarian solutions for republican troubles.

Following a revolution in 1869 in which Spain's queen, Isabella II, fled the country, the constituent Cortes voted to continue constitutional monarchy. After an unhappy period of rule by Ammadeo I, the son of Victor Emmanuel of Italy, a republic was declared in 1873, but continued political turmoil resulted in a military coup in 1874 and the establishment of another monarchy in the constitution of 1876. This sequence of events, with its brief republican interlude, did little to alter fundamental views of Spain: it merely confirmed that time had passed Spain by and that it was but a minor actor on the global stage. Charles Gates amply conveyed the picture of a people who had succumbed to historical lethargy: "A time of stately stepping on the shore, A time of glorious triumph on the main, And centuries of nothingness—what more is in the book of Spain?"[34]

Given the low expectations, when revolution broke out in Spain in 1868 Spanish republicanism seemed doomed in advance to defeat. Reacting with wariness to the news of political unrest, the editor of *The Galaxy*, with memories of the short-lived Second French Republic still fresh in mind, anticipated the republic's overthrow before it was even created. "It is with great apprehension that one perceives the prospect of a Republic in Spain," he wrote. Whatever the cultural prerequisites for popular rule, "the Spanish mind probably does not yet possess them," he concluded. Similarly, one detects little enthusiasm in *The Nation*'s comments upon receiving news of the revolution. "In calculating the political and social prospects of the kingdom," a Godkin editorial said, "we have to bear in mind that it stands in the very lowest scale of civilization, and has nearly as much to do to get abreast with France or Germany, or even Italy, as Turkey herself." When a republic was established a few years later, Godkin took little pleasure at a less than historic victory that was destined to be soon reversed. "There are no countries in Europe in which the seeds of anarchy and social desolation are so deeply sown as Spain and France, none in which the work of government is beset by such awful difficulties," he wrote. The problem was that the radicals who were most opposed to the monarchy tended to be suspicious of the kind of middle-class republicanism that was the American norm. Citing a comment by Tocqueville, Godkin declared that Spain "would never give the true friends of freedom any cause for rejoicing; that the country seemed made to disgust people with liberty."[35]

Shaky though it might be, a republic was a republic, making it hard for Americans to bottle up their hopes entirely, no matter how deeply skeptical they might be of Spanish shortcomings. For a brief moment in the 1860s and 1870s there seemed a slim chance that Spain might, against all odds, be claimed for republicanism. Perhaps, the speculation went, modern times could accelerate the emergence of a temperate public opinion, even in Spain. "Popular spirit, too, works with velocity in these times; a nation is born, as a dynasty dies, in a day" said *Galaxy* editor George E. Pond. Why not, then, hope for the best? "We Americans are free to descry whatever courageous and friendly omens we may, even amidst our strong misgivings," he concluded. And even if Spain did not go forward, there was no possibility that it would turn the clock back. As the progressive clergyman and editor Lyman Abbott stated: "It is hardly conceivable that it will ever return to the prison-house from which it has emerged;

that the extinguished fires of the Inquisition will ever be relighted, or the broken sceptre of the Bourbons mended." Despite its likely failure, the republican experiment was worth attempting, and Spain stood to learn a thing or two from it.[36]

Contributing to this burst of optimism was the incessant propagandizing and journalistic skill of Emilio Castelar, a former professor of history at Madrid, who for a few fruitless months in late 1873 sought to fulfill his dream of a Spanish republic. A brilliant orator and fervent republican, Castelar wrote not only about Spain, but more broadly about the prospects of republicanism in all of Europe and became a well-known contributor to American journals. Although his political acumen was sometimes questioned, he received rave notices from Americans who knew him as a friend of republicanism everywhere; as a man who was "as conspicuous for his probity as for his earnestness and genius." Alvee Adee, a State Department official, described Castelar as "the embodiment of the republican idea, in a land where traditional religious faith and ingrained obedience to the extremest tenets of absolutism offered an unpromising soil for the development of democracy." A brief pen portrait in John Hay's *Castilian Days* was especially laudatory. For a fleeting moment, Castelar and his desired federal republic seemed to be exactly the solution to Spain's political instability.[37]

But American enthusiasm was halfhearted at best, and it was not long before political chaos and the desire for stability in Spain elicited calls for an authoritarian, law-and-order solution. As the republic struggled to survive in the midst of a Bourbon rising, *The Nation* commented that "no such spectacle of moral and political disorder has, we think, been witnessed since the fall of the roman empire." One year later, troubled by reports of atrocities on all sides, it called for an abandonment of the republic by the European powers that had recognized it. "The interests of humanity and civilization demand that the country should not be entirely free to give itself up to rapine and murder," it concluded. Even a protectorate might not be a bad idea for, whatever its ideological shortcomings, it was a solution that at least would produce order. As the chaos subsided early in 1875 with the generals rallying to the cause of Alfonso, son of Isabella, *The Nation* looked back with disgust at "a somewhat ludicrous picture of the conversion of a republic into a monarchy." "Indeed," it summed up, "there is something farcical in all Spanish revolutions."[38]

Embarrassed by this outcome, some Americans wondered why they continued to hope when everything they knew about Spanish history, especially the Moorish background and heavy influence of Catholicism, had argued against success. *The Nation* tried to imagine how silly Americans would look for having supposed that a country like Spain could become a republic simply by declaring itself to be one. It was "one of those things which will before many years amuse people as much as attempts to foretell future events by examining the entrails of a hen." At the same time, the new constitutional regime's denial of rights to Protestant confessions led some to question Spain's right to be considered a civilized state. Even Castelar was disgusted with his people, attributing the reaction to "Moorish blood." Now that the priests were back in power, the best-case scenario for the future was the prospect of imperceptible change offered by John Hay in his *Castilian Days:* "The shadow will go forward on the dial, though so slowly that only the sharpest eyes can see it move."[39] Thus, in an era of otherwise blindingly fast progress, Americans imagined Spain as slouching listlessly into the future. But in comparison to the halting progress and even retrogressive tendencies of ostensibly more advanced nations whose behavior worried Americans, Spain was by no means an unusual object of criticism.

Contradictory Italy

To its everlasting glory, Italy was the ideological cradle of modern liberal nationalism under the leadership of Mazzini and Garibaldi. Although Garibaldi's republic never came to pass, Americans applauded the constitutional monarchy for its leadership in the ongoing struggle against an iniquitous papacy. At the same time, as the source of Latin civilization, Italy was cursed with a severe cultural handicap: corrupt and ineffectual liberal politics and swollen and unrealistic Italian pretensions to great power status. Worrisome, too, was the state's inability to settle its all-important relationship with the Vatican. Further confusing the picture was Italy's status as a Mecca for art and architecture and as a site for tourism, sun, and excellent cuisine, a combination that elicited conflicting opinions from Americans about Italy's chances for modernization. The balance sheet was complicated, but the bottom line simple: notwithstanding all its contributions to civilization, Italy's capacity for full modernity was open to question.

The news of Mazzini's death in 1872 prompted numerous recollections of how Italy had taken the lead in restoring the momentum of liberalism at a time when the rest of Europe was mired in reaction. Throughout its history, Italy had produced a long line of great men, and Mazzini, because of his ability to nurture the common consciousness that made Italy possible, was perhaps the greatest of all. Prior to his time, said *The Nation's* tribute, Italy had been only a geographical expression that had been treated by tourists "as an old curiosity-shop." Like Germany, Italy was also fortunate in having a monarch skilled in selecting competent men and giving them power to lead. Cavour was singled out for brilliant statesmanship that faced and overcame far more roadblocks on the path to unification than had Bismarck. But it was Mazzini's ideas when considered as a whole—anticlericalism, republicanism, nationalism, and economic liberalism, all contained within a worldwide perspective—that formed a "sublime scheme."[40]

Italian unification had placed the nation in the vanguard of history, but Italy continued to be weighed down by a burdensome past that was given concrete form in the national character. One writer referred to "a certain historicism (if such a term may be used) of the Italian mind, which loves historic continuity and is lo[a]th to break with the past." Whereas Americans might fairly be characterized by their inventiveness, for Italians, with their artistic heritage, "their underlying unity may be found in the fact that every Italian will sing and make verses." Even the Renaissance, which was commonly seen as a watershed of modernity, was criticized as a backward-looking era that looked to the re-creation of classical city-based life rather than the cultivation of a modern national identity. One had only to experience its cities to know that Italy was far from being a modern nation. Lyman Abbott caustically noted: "As to modern Rome, the less one sees—and smells—of that the better."[41]

Creating a nation-state was one thing; making a success of it was quite another. Many thought that, like Spain, Italy was incapable of sustained progress, and for the same reason: The cultural level of the Italian masses was too low. Typically, one writer wondered whether the Italian people were "quite competent for their newly-acquired institutions." Ernst Gryzanovski—a German-born scholar, a friend to Henry Adams and William James, and a frequent contributor to *The Nation* and *North American Review*—complained that Italy contained "seventeen millions of illiterate savages." "If all we now see in Italy were permanently or essentially Italian," he continued, "we should have to despair of Italy: her future could be nothing but chaos and moral death." But he was optimistic about the power of education to "eliminate from the Italian character many of those traits which we are wont to consider as essentially Italian." The relatively uncultivated and unemancipated condition of Italian women was also cited, though few were willing to advocate female suffrage. Education was more important than political emancipation, anyway, since far too many Italian women continued to be educated in convents, where they picked up "that narrow, intolerant, superstitious, and retrograding spirit" that acted as a drag on development.[42]

This cultural retardation meant that the Italian people, though reared in a land of art and antiquity, were unpardonably guilty of being unable to appreciate or build on their magnificent heritage. For all their antiquity, "they are a childish race," said Thomas Bailey Aldrich, a popular writer who would edit *The Atlantic Monthly* from 1881 to 1890. Henry James, writing of the decline in artistic talent, lamented the fact that "the people who but three hundred years ago had the best taste in the world should now have the worst; that having produced the noblest, loveliest, and costliest works they should now be given up to the manufacture of objects at once ugly and flimsy." As proof of the loss of artistic taste, the Victor Emmanuel monument became the object of a critical scorn that continues to this day. The aesthetic elitism that lay behind such comments was even more evident in scalding descriptions of the boorish tourists who had overrun the country and prompted a repulsive commodification of culture. A typical complaint about Rome was that "the city of the soul has become for the time a monstrous mixture of the watering-place and the curiosity-shop." Still, it was clear that the tourist trade kept many towns alive that otherwise would have disappeared.[43]

The new Italian state's track record was correspondingly poor. Its first mistake had been the adoption of a centralized state on the French model, which seemed to fit neither Italian history nor character. Critics felt that a decentralized polity should have been put in place either on the German or the American pattern, but though it was hardly ideal, centralization was at least understandable in light of the fear that Italy's anarchic municipal traditions might otherwise reassert themselves. Corruption and ineptitude plagued the new state, though writers were quick to note that it was no more corrupt than the United States. In addition, a series of statist measures undertaken in the

1880s—protection, state ownership of railways, and subsidies for the creation of a sizeable merchant marine—was expected to have harmful economic consequences. There were worries, too, that Italy was making a grave mistake in its attempt to become one of the great powers of Europe by building a steel navy and pursuing an irredentist policy when, above all, the nation needed peace and internal reform. Taking stock after ten years of full unification, the journalist Jessie W. Mario concluded that "in the opinion of all impartial men, the representative system has proved an entire failure."[44]

But the most troubling question for American observers was the Italian state's inability to resolve the standoff with the Vatican consequent to the annexation of Rome and the papal states. This issue, more than any other, was the benchmark of Italy's progress. With the obvious exception of the Catholic journals, American views of the Roman church were thoroughly saturated with a traditional Protestant hostility that viewed monarchies as quite progressive institutions in comparison to the papacy and its universalist pretensions. For some, it was the church, not "blood," that enervated Latin civilization. According to the recent Harvard graduate, future president of the American Historical Association, and lifelong Italophile William R. Thayer, Italy had been cursed by a debilitating birth defect, "that most slippery and embarrassing of enemies, the Papacy, in her very heart." Much was excused the Italian state for having to labor under this handicap. The granting of civil rights to the Jews of the Roman ghetto and the erection of a statue of Giordano Bruno in 1889 were signs that the government's heart was on the right side of the (imagined) reason–religion divide. Hence, various anticlerical measures taken by the state were easily enough explained away. "What Italy has done, she has done because absolutely compelled to do it," explained one sympathetic essayist. No state pretending to modern status could afford to do less. "An infallible church has so sucked the life and manhood out of the other States," argued a *Scribner's* editorial, "that they all sink into second and third rate powers."[45]

Still, American disappointment was palpable: following the evacuation of French forces from Rome, the expectation had been that the temporal power of the papacy was doomed. "The Pope must come down off his now bloody throne and that before long," *The Nation* predicted in 1867. The simultaneous end of papal sovereignty in 1870 and collapse of Napoleon III's regime was seen as an epochal defeat for the principle of caesarism. No one would have predicted, *The Nation* remarked, that in the course of a year following the declaration of infallibility that the pope would lose his temporal sovereignty with so little fuss. But 1870 proved to be a false start, as the fledgling state began an uneasy cohabitation with the church that came as an unpleasant surprise to American onlookers. To some, the situation was perversely working to the papacy's advantage, as the image of the pope (self)-imprisoned in the Vatican appeared to be generating some sympathy.[46]

The antiliberal, antimodern papacy of Pius IX (1846–1878) provided the occasion for some scathing denunciations of the Vatican. Pius was described as "a very simple-minded and somewhat fanatical old monk," whose dubious claim to distinction was to elevate Catholicism's apologia for backwardness to an article of faith. His various pronouncements were, as the unremittingly antagonistic *Nation* put it, "one long wolfish howl against the scientific and social progress, the civilized and enlightened Christianity, the spirit of charitable association, and the disinterested philanthropy of modern times." Pius IX was depicted as determined to turn back the clock to the repressive Middle Ages, a period of intolerance and arbitrary power. The basic problem—and here Pius no doubt would have agreed—was his antipathy to modernity and to liberalism. The convening of the Vatican council at which the doctrine of papal infallibility was decreed was described as "an uncalled-for, inopportune, and dangerous step." How far could the church go, wondered Godkin, before its resistance became positively ludicrous? That stage, he believed, had been reached in Pius's pontificate. Yet the church continued to make pronouncements on matters such as currency policy, about which it knew nothing.[47]

The hope was that with the death of Pius, the church would change by putting an end to "the present monstrous mixture of things sacred and profane." The accession of Leo XIII did bring some rhetorical cooling off, but fundamental differences seemed fated to remain well into the future. The pope continued what *The Nation* called a "sham captivity" in the Vatican. Although restoration of the church's temporal power was extremely unlikely, the journal argued that no pope was willing to go down in history as having given up on the principle. Only time would demonstrate the absurdity of a position that had become "ridiculous even to the most pious believers." As for doctrinal matters, *Scribner's* at one point predicted the kind of liberalization that would be adopted at Vatican II in the 1960s: "Some future pontiff of a liberal spirit and a courageous temper, hearing the cry of the people for some lightening of their load of dogmas and ceremonies, and knowing that the time is at hand, may rise up and wield that supreme and unquestionable power which the Vatican Council has conferred upon him, in the reformation of many abuses, and in the great enlargement of the liberties of the Roman Catholic people." It was quick to add, however, that this day would be long in coming.[48]

In time, with the decisive battle fought and won, the church came to seem less of a threat. The Vatican continued to try to play a role in politics, in Italy and elsewhere, but in a self-defeating manner that further weakened its religious authority. Even the benighted monarchical powers of Europe refused to accept the doctrine of papal infallibility. The church, it appeared, no longer had the ability to intimidate rulers. "The Pope's curses in Rome die on the empty air" was the smug claim. Dissidents, said *The Nation*, "simply stay at home on Sundays, or take a walk in the country, and smile when infallibility is mentioned." Instances of public dissent were no longer matters of life and death. Besides, a politically neutered papacy had its uses to the Italians, serving as a source of profit just like "any venerable ruin or work of art."[49]

Perhaps, some essayists suggested, the real story lay not in the papacy, but in the faith itself—in "the decline of its spiritual power." How religious, after all, were the Italians? Infidelity and anticlericalism seemed to be equally widespread among the Italian people. Some more thoughtful evaluations advanced the thesis that Protestant–Catholic differences needed to be seen from a broader perspective. "It is not Protestantism, nor the Papacy, nor Calvinism, nor Trinitarianism, nor any other secondary Christian dogma that is now on trial; it is the main question whether there is any such thing as religion," said *The Century*. It was the existence of God and the capacity of *any* religion to speak authoritatively on His behalf in human affairs that was in question. "Upon these issues Protestants and Roman Catholics stand together," the editorial concluded, "and their agreement, so far as it goes, ought to be recognized and emphasized." In any case, it was not as if Protestantism stood to gain from the church's failures, for it had made few converts over the past centuries among educated Europeans who had been born and bred in the church.[50]

Upon revisiting Italy in 1878, Henry James concluded that in many respects the country was undeniably modern; or, as he put it with typical circumspection, it would do "no real harm to think of her, for a while, as modern." It was widely agreed that Italy was in the throes of momentous change and had progressed immensely since 1848. In *Scribner's* description, "the trowel of the mason fills the air with the sound of growth and industry, and reform, moral and material, is the order of the day." William Kingsley described the changes since Victor Emmanuel's accession in 1849 as "one of the most marvellous which this age of wonders has witnessed" and predicted that Italy's best days lay ahead. Trade was on the increase; wealth was being created; brigandage and secret societies were being suppressed; schools were being created; newspapers were flourishing. According to one expatriate resident of Rome, people who refused to recognize such improvements were guilty of willful misunderstanding out of "a determination to see no merit in anything not American and English." As for the alleged lull in cultural creativity, the lack of artistic progress was excused, as it was in the United States, by Italy's single-minded determination to become an industrial power. For those who were bullish on Italy, other features of the national character spoke well of the people. Italians appeared to make good colonizers, better than the French, anyway, and the success of Italian emigrants in Argentina testified to the strength and vitality of Italian culture, even as massive emigration was an indictment of government policies.[51]

In an extended comparison of Italian and American history over the thirty-year period that began in 1860, Italy did not come off that badly. Many of the problems that afflicted the new state had yet to be resolved successfully by the United States as well. Commenting on the shortage of great leaders in Italy following the passing of the heroic founding generation, *The Nation* concluded with what seemed a backhanded reference to the post–Civil War situation in the United States. "It seems to be the law of the ebb-and-flow of national life," said an editorial, "that, after the high tide when great deeds are launched, the waters must recede, leaving bare slime, and ooze, and stagnant pools." Italy did not have the makings of a great power and had made many mistakes, but at least it had not "been forced to blush, as honest Americans have been, at the general corruption of her public men." In sum, when it came to American evaluations of Italy, little was expected and much forgiven.[52]

European Backwaters

American journals took the rest of Europe far less seriously. The vast Hapsburg domains received little attention, but the coverage given tended to be surprisingly sympathetic and sensitive to the complexities of keeping alive a multiethnic state in an era of nationalism. At first, memories of 1848 and Austria's resistance to the creation of Germany tended to dominate appraisals of the empire. Austria was, in Godkin's uncharitable view, "a decayed trickster and bully . . . built up in the Middle Ages and projected into the modern world, rather as a relic of things long passed away than as a living political organization." Culturally, it was seen as something of a desert. "The house of Hapsburg," said *The Nation*, "has done nothing for literature, nothing for science, little for art, and has probably inflicted more misery on the world than any race with which it hath pleased God to curse it." With nationalism in the ascendant, it seemed only a matter of time before the empire's collapse. A writer in *The Galaxy* described the empire's life in four phases: "The first was a mission, the second an illusion, and the third a crime. It is now entering its fourth phase—its doom." The best that could be said on its behalf was that it had contributed more than its share to preserving Europe from the Ottoman threat. [53]

In this area of Europe, however, nationalism was perceived as a problem rather than a solution. Thus it was not long before analyses became more nuanced and even sympathetic as the *Ausgleich,* the power-sharing arrangement between German-speakers and Hungarians that sought to better balance nationalities within the empire, came to be better understood. The sympathy for the empire was no doubt grounded in a sense that its "feeble nationalities" were unprepared for self-rule. As *Appletons'* put it, the collapse of Austria, though seemingly impossible to avoid as the idea of national self-determination took hold, "cannot be regarded without regret." The sheer magnitude of the task of creating nation-states and redrawing the map of Central and Eastern Europe would entail huge disruption, probably through war. Perhaps, it was hoped, the empire might yet find a way to hang together with the help of some new political architecture. One possibility was a federal solution to replace the dualism put in place in 1867. *The Nation* took refuge in paradox, noting that "he would be rash who should conclude from so much internal friction and threatening collision that disruption must ensue." To the logical observer, the empire seemed doomed, but its editors preferred to believe that "there is safety in the very multiplicity of its problems." [54]

Occasional articles appeared on Poland, Belgium, and Norway, but they did not receive the ongoing coverage accorded to the major nations. As for southeastern Europe, Americans had abandoned the romantic philhellenic enthusiasm of the 1820s. Now, fifty years later, Greece was more notable for its glorious past than its doubtful future. The past had become deadweight for a people who, according to philologist and Yale professor of Greek Thomas Seymour, were "more ready to boast of their ancestors than to emulate them." Greece was independent but far from civilized, a nation still in transition "from the enforced barbarism of Turkish slavery to the civilization of freedom." As Seymour stated: "The kingdom of Greece is known to modern statesmen as an insignificant country, important only as a disturbing element in European politics."[55] Romania fared even worse in American eyes, for it seemed scarcely civilized at all. Although the country was well endowed by nature, living conditions in its countryside were primitive. The Romanian peasant, picturesque and affable, was still "one of the most inferior and progressless types in Europe," having been isolated from the rest of European civilization. As for the other Balkan nations, these were usually dealt with in connection with the Eastern Question, which shall be treated in a coming chapter.

By 1890, it was clear that Europe had failed to meet the sunny republican expectations that were so prominent a generation earlier. In a review of a book that summarized thirty years of recent European history, *The Nation* concluded glumly that "the world has suffered much from that gradual apostasy from faith in individual liberty which grew up between 1848 and 1878." To the editor of *Harper's*, the persistence of inherited authority and privilege was "an unexplained thing in human affairs" and "a philosophical anomaly." Cumulatively, developments in Europe since 1865 pointed inescapably to the big question: How civilized was the civilization that American liberals liked to invoke as a universal standard? If Europe was indeed the core, then a global civilization was being constructed around a rather unstable nucleus—a problem that shall be explored in Chapter 10.[56]

Not all was bleakness, as strong expressions of confidence in the growth of republicanism and human freedom continued to flourish. George Towle, for one, reaffirmed his faith by quoting from Victor Hugo's collection of poems, "Les Châtiments," in which Hugo imagined people of the late twentieth century looking back in amazement at the nineteenth. Americans "would exclaim, in wonder, 'What! I had slaves!' Europe would, with a shudder, retort, 'What! I had kings!' " But while the progressive view of history remained an article of faith, it struggled to find empirical justification in the history of these years. Belying all the talk of the acceleration of history in modern times, political progress, if progress it was, had become invisible, moving at best by imperceptible evolutionary advances, as if the Spanish example had become the universal model. In the words of one essayist, "The world improves, but it improves as the tree grows, without observation."[57] In certain important countries, moreover, progress may have suffered serious reverses. Liberal modernization, far from being inevitable, appeared to be entering a period of challenge, if not crisis. The sense of doubt and uncertainty about the fate of European democracy would remain well into the second half of the twentieth century, while the self-image of liberalism as an embattled creed persists to this day.

The economically determinist view that industrial development would produce democracy in its wake found few supporters in an intellectual milieu that entertained a more complex understanding of how societies evolved. After all, democracy in the United States had preceded industrialization, which suggested the folly of relying on economic transformation as the principal agent of democratization. Technology and the market had indeed performed miracles, but the stubborn persistence of traditional forms showed "the irregular, hesitating, sometimes retrogressive character of all progress." Custom was "still the tyrant of humanity." Not surprisingly, then, explanations of the failure of democracy to catch on in European societies typically pointed to cultural shortcomings, deep-seated cultural traits that frustrated the progressive development of societies. This is the way these people were, after all.[58]

Because civilization presupposed a diminution of cultural differences, the failure to close the gap between the political cultures of the United States and Europe posed a serious problem. It was not insurmountable, however, because Europe was only a part of a more significant whole. Of greater importance was a continuing process of integration and narrowing of cultural distance on a global level. But if so much depended on culture, and if culture could be so resistant to change, how did Americans conceptualize culture and how did processes of culture change merge together into a global liberal pattern? What culture was thought to be, and how it was connected to conceptions of race and of civilization, will be the subject of the next three chapters.

5

The One and the Many

Race, Culture, and Civilization

One of the most striking characteristics of liberal ideology was its universality. In Walt Whitman's words, liberalism was a creed that "seeks both to universalize as well as individualize." This universalizing predisposition received frequent expression in the magazine literature from editors and writers who assumed that history was tending toward the social and cultural unification of the world. Writing about the effects of travel by railway, an unidentified author in *The North American Review* noted that "already the whole Caucasian race looks alike and talks alike, and is rapidly growing to live alike and to think alike. We mix and mingle, until there is no strangeness left." Cross-cultural similarities were more readily apparent in the Euro-Atlantic region than elsewhere, but it seemed inevitable that the rest of the world would in due course be drawn into this homogenization of experience, an assumption that would later become a mainstay of modernization theory. According to George Munro Grant, the Canadian educator and one of the chief advocates of a global time standard, the technological conquest of space meant that "everything that interferes with the full recognition of the unity and solidarity of the race must be shaken and disappear."[1]

Yet for all the talk of global unification as a necessary consequence of the annihilation of distance, everywhere that Americans looked they saw differences. One especially perceptive writer insisted that "it would be more correct now to speak of differences than of distances. The difference between one country and another is all that now makes the distance between them." Even for a convinced internationalist like the west coast theologian George Mooar, it would likely be a long time, if ever, before particularism was overcome. "Although the modern believes himself to be easily cosmopolitan," he warned, "it is nevertheless hard for him to escape the limitations and prejudice of class, and race, and sect." But the problem of difference was deeper than that. If viewed on a horizontal plane, differences were functionally essential to a thriving global network, for by definition only different musical notes—the diverse needs and capabilities of peoples—could produce a melodious harmony of interests. But differences were also vertical. The nineteenth century, in many ways a century of global integration, was also an epoch in which flourishing doctrines of nationality, race, and imperialism divided peoples into higher and lower sorts. In this spirit, George Cary Eggleston observed that the world "is filled chiefly with inferior people."[2]

For most people, it was race, above all, that explained backwardness and inferiority. "Race is all, there is no other truth," said the hero of Benjamin Disraeli's novel *Tancred*, echoing the mantra of the British racial theorist Robert Knox. This fixation on race makes for something of a problem, for as the historian George Fredrickson has noted, "What makes Western racism so autonomous and conspicuous in world history has been that it developed in a context that presumed human equality of some kind." One can understand how contradictory doctrines might exist side by side in a state of antagonism within a society, but how was it that liberals could be simultaneously racist and universalist without fatally compromising their beliefs and their self-integrity? Ideologically, the stakes were quite high, for hard racialist doctrines flew in the face of the civic religion of republicanism, the core beliefs of Christianity, and the tenets of Enlightenment universalism. The belief in racial superiority, explained the editor of *Appletons'*, was "anti democratic, and originates in the most stationary civilizations of the far East, and is a part of the hateful doctrine of caste." It was hardly a secret that racism and its fellow-traveler, caste consciousness, had potentially devastating implications for American political beliefs.[3]

Doctrines of racial superiority, by throwing into question the claim that Christianity was a universal faith, had the potential for provoking a much more explosive struggle between religion and science than the one that actually took place. Although the Bible was ambiguous about the moral status of slavery, it was outspokenly egalitarian in its position on the essential unity of humankind. For those who believed in the historically close connection between Protestantism and political liberty, caste and Christianity were, prima facie, "utterly irreconcilable." Caste might make religious sense in India, said one missionary, but Christians who believed in caste dishonored their God.

"Are we all one?" asked Tayler Lewis, the noted classicist. "The negative cannot be maintained unless we close our Bibles, and come to the sad conclusion to consult that oracle no more." "Take away our faith in the common parentage of the human race," argued a defense of the biblical account of creation, "and we have left so much community of nature as exists among different tribes of horses or monkeys, and about as much possibility of civilized society." Moreover, as another minister pointed out, the doctrine of universal brotherhood, a horizontal relationship, was "the foundation of all efforts to civilize barbarian peoples." Given the conceptual marriage between Christianity and civilization, how could one justify the civilizing mission in a permanently hierarchical world or, for that matter, realistically expect other peoples to accept willingly a creed that consigned them to a permanently inferior status?[4]

Many historians have assumed that Americans neither could resolve this contradiction between equality and hierarchy nor were much interested in doing so; that the optimistic universalism of the time was simply an ideological mask that concealed a racist face in which equality, as in Greece and Rome, was a privilege that applied only to a superior minority. "The nineteenth century was obsessed," says one, "with the idea that it was race which explained the character of peoples." In this view, egalitarian and Christian creeds had been trumped by the higher authority of science. "Both hierarchy and bigotry were not only culturally approved but also encouraged by science," say the scholars. The mood was so pessimistic that "before World War I few in Europe or North America developed a conception of global internationalism, embracing different races and peoples." But if racial inequality was understood to be a biological fact, and if social life was intrinsically a struggle for survival among races, then the unification of the world would necessarily be a grim process with a nasty outcome: competitive warfare among the conquering races; conquest, permanent exploitation, colonization, and perhaps even extinction of the weaker. In multiracial societies, ethnic struggle would become the norm, necessitating the creation of caste systems or the expulsion and/or forcible extinction of inferior groups. In these kinds of circumstances, globalization might still be possible, but the result would be an illiberal world, the product of imperial unification devoid of universal moral authority. The fact that few Americans envisioned that kind of world, a "civilization of force" divided permanently between hierarchs and subalterns, requires some explanation.[5]

Discussions of racial attitudes during these years typically pay little attention to science because, for the many Americans who took racial inferiority
for granted, there was no need for scientific justification. But racism, unlike
prejudice, is an articulated belief, and to the extent that arguments could be
shaped by reasoned debate, science mattered. If the magazine literature is any
indication, liberals tended by and large to reject the evidence and conclusions
of scientific racism, and they did so in large part from a scientific point of
view. Science, as they understood it, told them that racial inequality was an
unavoidable fact of life, but only as a temporary condition that looked toward
the eventual attainment of civilized status by all peoples. However, the fee for
entry into a universal civilization was quite steep, for it would require either
the voluntary abandonment or forced destruction of traditional ways of life,
the erasing of racial distinctions through a ruthless process of acculturation.
This understanding of globalization as a process of deracination owed less to
biological science than to new disciplines like anthropology and history in
which race was understood largely in terms of culture. From this point of
view, the long transit from common human origins, then to difference and
inequality, and finally to global unification and individual equality was explained in a nonbiological idiom of competitive struggle and survival of the
fittest, a cultural Darwinism that presupposed a rejection of cultural relativism and all its works.[6]

Race and Hard Science

How then were racial differences fitted into a liberal and egalitarian scheme
of global understanding? The hurdles were formidable, for there was indeed a
scientific racism in the late nineteenth century that sought to lend the legitimacy of science to the view that not all races were created equal. This was the
heyday of physical anthropology, in which scientists adduced evidence from
craniology, from the measurement of facial angles, from brain configurations,
and other indices in attempts to prove the natural inferiority of some peoples.
It was not uncommon to see racial differences explained in apparently matter-
of-fact terms, such as: "Predominance of white blood increases cerebral development, while the presence of one-quarter, one-eighth, or one-sixteenth
produces a brain capacity decidedly inferior to that of the pure negro." And
yet, notwithstanding the many scientific explanations of human inequality in

the marketplace of ideas, in reading the periodical literature one is struck by how many of the writers continued to reject biological ideas of rigid racial hierarchy. Christianity and universalist political doctrines of equality undoubtedly had something to do with this, but so too did a suspicion of a so-called science of race that had failed to establish the kind of claim to authority that one associates with scientific knowledge.[7]

One of the problems with racial science was the absence of anything remotely approaching a standard definition of race during this period. The term *race* as used in the nineteenth century, besides referring to biologically distinct groups of humans, could also encompass culture, gender, class, religion, occupational and functional groups, dynasties, ethnic groups, tribes, nationalities, species of animals, and much more. Thus one finds references to "the Christian race," "the hereditary race of officeholders," the "contemporary races of mammals," "the race of geologists," politicians as a "race of savages," "the Anglican race," the "Bourbon race," and "the races of plants and animals." Moroccan rulers were described as "the most hopeless race on earth," American women as "a race of invalids," and certain intellectually minded clergymen as "a race of thinkers." Races and species were often mixed up in locutions like" the "domestic races of the dog," or "a race of monkeys or elephants." Darwin's *Origin of Species,* part of whose subtitle was "on the preservation of favoured races in the struggle for life," barely mentioned human beings in the text. Even a widely used term like "the Anglo-Saxon race" was shot through with inconsistencies and contradictory usages. In short, there was no "discourse" of race in any precise sense. Race was a commonplace and impossibly vague term for conveying a sense of difference.[8]

Even if one were to concede that race as used in scientific discussion was understood to mean the inherited characteristics of biologically discrete groups of humans, the would-be science of race labored under some serious handicaps. According to Robert K. Merton, who pioneered the sociology of science, in science "an idea becomes a truth only when a vast majority of scientists accept it without question." But within the scientific community of the late nineteenth century, racial science was pre-paradigmatic; that is, there was nothing resembling the kind of consensus that Thomas Kuhn has called "normal science," a state of affairs in which scientists work under the influence of a taken-for-granted paradigm by engaging in the kind of research that he described as a mere "mopping up operation." What was there to mop up? There could be no such productive consensus in a racial science in which basic questions of what was being measured, the mechanism by which it was transmitted, and the end effects thereof remained utterly mysterious, in which the most fundamental issues were hotly contested, and whose leading ideas differed significantly from country to country. For all the advances in quantification techniques, the state of knowledge about what was being measured remained so meager that Franz Boas, in an 1899 review of a work on physical anthropology, felt obliged to remind his readers of "our ignorance of the conditions which influence modification of inherited form." In Foucauldian terms, there was no "regime of truth."[9]

Yes, race was "a respectable scientific category" to the extent that the idea generated claims and conclusions backed by research, but the protoscience of race, such as it was, did not enjoy the kind of authority exercised by other scientific fields that offered convincing explanations and exercised demonstrable powers of prediction and control. Reflecting on the utility of racial measurement as a way of generating knowledge in this area, one reviewer concluded that, compared to other techniques, "none seems to promise more definite results, and yet none oftener disappoints the promise." Thus a leading historian of anthropology has noted the unwillingness of many in the late nineteenth century "to accept the physical determinism which the very idea of physical anthropology seemed to imply. Within the social sciences, the dominant tradition was clearly environmentalist."[10] Racial science then was very much what some postmodernists now accuse all science of being—a transparent social construction. And many educated people knew it to be such. In the words of the French historian Ernest Renan, race was "something that makes and unmakes itself."[11]

Although the body of scientific knowledge of the day was rather primitive in comparison to that of a century later, the understanding of what constituted a science was quite well developed. Well embedded as part of the spirit of the age were a solid Baconian appreciation of science as a communal enterprise and a post-Baconian realization that science did not proceed through pure induction. In the face of questionable theorizing and inconclusive evidence on matters racial, scientific uncertainty was the default condition. That was not entirely a handicap, for uncertainty did not mean ignorance. It was well understood that perplexity, albeit of a rather sophisticated kind, was essential to science. In a piece in *The Overland Monthly*, for example, the geologist G. Frederick Wright attempted to dispel the notion that science meant absolute truth. "On the contrary," he insisted, "the so-called science of the present day, so far as it relates to the actual facts and laws of nature, is almost wholly devoid of certainty, and scientific men themselves are the first to disclaim infallibility for their views. Scientific men pride themselves on always being ready to learn." The same point was made by the philosopher Josiah Royce, who articulated a view of science that would later be called organized skepticism. Royce pointed out that "The territory of all the sciences is a more or less disputed territory. The exact sciences themselves are no exceptions to the rule. Their fundamental concepts are disputed problems." As would be the case more than a century later in matters pertaining to diet and nutrition, as orthodoxies came and went with the swiftness of fashion, there was a good deal of confusion about the idea of race.[12]

The historicity of scientific knowledge was also taken as a given. One writer, stressing the provisional nature of knowledge, was certain only "that everything is shifting incessantly, and that the truth of to-day may be the error of to-morrow." Moreover, the realm of the unknown was understood to be vast. Thus the editor of *Harper's* was prompted by a recent work to muse on the lacunae and unknowns confronting science. "One is reminded how much of science is still conjectural," he wrote. "The atomic theory is still a theory, the nebular hypothesis still a hypothesis; the missing link in the Darwinian chain is missing still." Scientists were, for the most part, modest about what they really knew, and the more philosophically inclined among them possessed a deep appreciation of the tensions that existed among axioms, empirically based understanding, and truth with a capital "T," a combination that could be puzzling to the scientifically illiterate. Nevertheless, science had a high standard of proof, which when met provided it with extraordinary explanatory power. This sophisticated understanding of the nature of scientific knowledge helps to explain why much of what purported to pass as a science of race at the time was rejected, by scholars and educated laypeople alike, for its failure to meet the standards of verification and falsifiability that were essential to the successful functioning of science as an institution.[13]

To speak of "scientific" racism in the nineteenth century, then, is merely to assert that some scientists argued on behalf of hierarchical inherited characteristics and some people believed them—how many, exactly, and to what effect is difficult to say. Even when science was able to speak with a single and more credible voice on race in the next century, the gap between knowledge and power remained enormous. In any event, because the science of race was a "soft" science based on conjecture and the absence of conclusive evidence, many educated people, alert to what Lewis Menand has called "the use and abuse of science" in matters racial, remained skeptical enough to publicly articulate their doubts. In one of the many discussions of race found in *The Nation*'s pages, William James warned: "we in America all know too well how often 'science' has been appealed to in the least calm of public assemblies to bear evidence in favor of one view or another of the way which we ought to treat the inferior races that live with us." The marvel, he concluded, "notwithstanding the vast mass of bad anatomy, worse psychology, and statistics worst of all," was that science was somehow still being furthered.[14]

The idea of evolution, an epochal intellectual achievement which by the 1870s scientists had accepted as the paradigm of biological development, was as unhelpful as the experimental branches of science in providing hard answers to questions surrounding race. The Darwinian theory of evolution could explain, in a general though still suggestive way, humankind's evolution from other animal species, but this was secondary to the more basic idea of biological evolution through natural selection. Darwin, quite mindful of the potential for controversy in the idea of human evolution, had chosen to steer clear of this incendiary topic when he published *On the Origin of Species* in 1859. Only with *The Descent of Man (1871)* did the legendarily cautious Darwin finally take up human evolution and the connected problem of race. In this work, he explicitly made the case for human beings having developed from common progenitors "in a series of forms graduating insensibly from some ape-like creature to man as he now exists." Although the tension between religion and evolutionary science had opened one of the widest cultural fissures of the day, religion and Darwinian science were largely united on the issue of human oneness.[15]

If Darwin was correct, the advocates of polygenesis or separate racial origins were wrong, which was itself a hugely important point. But biological evolution—assuming a long enough timescale (and time remained a huge problem for the theory)—still left open the possibility of significant differentiation and divergence following monogenesis, or so argued the degenerationists. After considering the arguments, Darwin dismissed degenerationism for its "pitiably low view of human nature." There were, admittedly, many obvious differences among races, but a goodly proportion of these were superficial. "We are clearly much influenced in our judgment," he noted, "by the mere colour of the skin and hair, by slight differences in the features, and by expression." Hard-and-fast distinctions between races were almost impossible to make because the single most distinctive feature was similarity rather than difference. While races could in principle be similar yet distinct, racial boundaries were in fact ill-defined because races tended to "graduate into each other, independently in many cases, as far as we can judge, of their having intercrossed." The evidence also suggested that different races possessed "similar inventive or mental powers." As a result, it was "hardly possible to discover clear distinctive characters between them." Almost despairingly, he concluded that "man has been studied more carefully than any other animal, and yet there is the greatest possible diversity amongst capable judges whether he should be classed as a single species or race." This was, in any event, not a problem to be obsessed over, since for Darwin it was individual organisms and not species that counted as the fundamental biological reality.[16]

That is one reading of Darwin, and an arguable one at that. Less disputable is Darwin's understanding that the explanatory power of the biology of race left much to be desired. Darwin was the kind of scientist who knew what he did not know. Moreover, he was not a reductionist; he understood that purely biological factors alone failed to explain everything, and he was careful to acknowledge the role played by acquired characteristics, that is, the products of experience and learning, and he allowed freely that the most important moral qualities of human beings, as well as the causes of human difference, might have little to do with biology. These traits, he admitted, were "advanced, either directly or indirectly, much more through the effects of habit, the reasoning powers, instruction, religion, etc., than through natural selection." Already in *The Origin of Species* and in a more pronounced manner in subsequent works, Darwin genuflected before the competing Lamarckian theory of exercise by conceding that "great weight must be attributed to the inherited effects of use and disuse, with respect both to the body and mind." It would seem, at first sight," wrote the Cambridge philosopher Chauncey Wright, "that Mr. Darwin has won a victory, not for himself, but for Lamarck."[17]

If biology pointed to human unity, the explanation for difference had to lie elsewhere, in culturally acquired behaviors, which by virtue of their contribution to societal reproductive success could also be subject to evolutionary selection pressures. Lamarckism was a hybrid theory of race-culture that assumed the voluntarist ability of humans to improve themselves and to pass on these learned traits via biological descent. Darwin was not alone in taking this approach. The Lamarckian drift of evolutionary theory away from the theory of natural selection in the late nineteenth century contributed to a greater emphasis on acquired characteristics, which helps to explain why, in the journal literature, ascriptions of hard-wired racial differences were distinctly a minority view. For that matter, the Lamarckian model made it almost impossible to draw a clear line between race and culture. It should be added that Lamarckism was not entirely wrong. Although it flubbed the biology, it got the cultural part right, for cultural transmission is Lamarckian in nature.[18]

Cultural change is also a historical process, about which Darwinian evolution had little or nothing useful to say. "Darwinianism in history is a nuisance," said the mining engineer and author R. W. Raymond. "The time is not ripe for it, if, indeed, it ever will be." Organic evolution was no doubt always at work, but in his opinion history could more readily be explained by the operation of "that unDarwinian agent, the human will." Chauncey Wright made pretty much the same point in an essay on "the limits of natural selection." Physiological explanations were superfluous, he maintained, "since the race has come to depend mainly on its mental qualities, and since it is on these, and not on its bodily powers, that Natural Selection must act." According to John Fiske, "the chief differences between civilized man and the other members of the order to which he belongs are psychological differences, and the immense series of psychical changes to which they are due has been all along determined by social conditions." To the extent that one could talk about racial differences, then, they would have to be treated as the product of historical development. For all practical purposes, biology ended where culture and history began.[19]

The biological unity of the human race was hardly a settled point, and in the absence of hard scientific evidence or even criteria with which to judge the evidence, no one was in a position to deliver a conclusive judgment.[20] But in his disclaimers about the limits of biological determinism, Darwin left open the door to competing forms of explanation. Through this door would walk a variety of disciplines that asserted the unity of humankind, each with a sizable following and claim to equal scientific status. In retrospect, the new social sciences of anthropology and history proved to be no more scientific than the scientific racism that they contested. For the time being, however, they attracted many adherents who believed in their potential as scientific disciplines in the making. In this hothouse atmosphere of disciplinary innovation, claims of scientific authority for assertions of racial difference could be and often were often greeted with skepticism.

Race as Cultural Evolution

Despite Darwin's enormous importance, one should not overstate his influence on the science or social thought of his day. Evolution was a central concept of the time that was commonly used to explain a much broader range of phenomena than organic development. The "cosmic philosophy" of the British thinker, Herbert Spencer, in particular, provided an all-embracing and powerfully attractive evolutionary theory that combined universalism with a quest for scientific uniformities. Spencer was lauded at the time for his attempt to "to obliterate this provincial spirit in the realm of knowledge, and reach universal principles which shall represent the unity and truth of nature." Such was his reputation that John Fiske, his chief American disciple, characterized the master's contributions in idolatrous terms as "comparable to those of Newton both in scope and in importance." Within Spencer's capacious (Lamarckian) scheme, according to E. L. Youmans, founder of *Popular Science Monthly* and tireless booster of Spencerian evolution, Darwinism was "but a subordinate part . . . a principle superadded to a previously existing body of thought."[21]

Whereas Darwinism tended to stammer when attempting to explaining social phenomena—and, as one historian writes, "for most Victorians Darwinism as a theory was restricted to evolution in the animal kingdom"—Spencerian evolution spoke fluently an interdisciplinary language that addressed matters of economy, society, politics, culture, biology, physics, and more. According to *The Century*, Spencer focused on "the natural history of society—every fact which can help us to an understanding of the way in which nations grow, and the conditions under which they prosper or languish." Although Spencer was not immune to attack from skeptics who detected more ideology than science behind his system, his speculative synthesis expressed more satisfactorily than any other thinker of the day the faith that evolution was a progressive phenomenon whose secrets would be revealed to scientific understanding.[22]

If there was any single discipline that established the common origins of humankind and came up with a superior explanation of the source of human differences, it was the new "science" of cultural anthropology (proto-anthropology in today's idiom) which at the time was quite fresh "science born, so to speak, yesterday," as one review described its emergence. The craze for archaeology also bespoke a concern for origins, although some writers detected, particularly with reference to Greece, a powerful streak of romanticism behind public interest in Heinrich Schliemann's well-publicized excavation of ancient Troy. Like everyone else, nineteenth-century anthropologists used the word "race," but the nearest twenty-first century approximation to race as it was ordinarily used then would be "culture." Some anthropologists believed in hard-wired racial differences, so deeply, according to one historian, "that no amount of failure could convince them that it might be an illusion." But for many others, including some of its leading figures, biological explanations had little to contribute in explaining differences among peoples. For the founding fathers of the discipline, these differences had emerged historically and could be traced back in world-historical time, but the developmental gaps that had opened up in the process could also be closed through continuing social and cultural evolution.[23]

The antiquity of humankind had been established at around the same time that Darwin's *Origin* first appeared. As the origins of human beings receded into the mists of a prebiblical and prehistoric past, it was hoped that cultural anthropology or ethnology could shed light on the beginning and nature of humankind. According to the editor of *Harper's*, "The origin of things appears now to have a greater interest to the student than almost any other problem." Though it was no easy task, by "tracking the wilderness of primeval speculation" the ethnographers of the late nineteenth century were able to discover an underlying humanity in peoples whose customs and behaviors were usually thought to be quite repulsive by contemporary lights. Somehow, in this extreme jumble of differences, they could identify with strange peoples by finding basic connections and affinities. These were, after all, "races with which we have almost nothing in common except . . . the elementary feeling that we should eat when hungry, and sleep when sleepy." However pronounced the dissimilarities between prehistoric and civilized humans, the principle of scientific regularity held sway for all. For this new science, it was axiomatic "that like ends are attained by like means, and that the human mind has for

the same purposes worked and developed in every country in the some direction, up to a certain stage."[24]

The preeminent anthropologist of the era was E. B. Tylor, who would eventually hold the first chair of anthropology at Oxford. Tylor's pathbreaking
Primitive Culture was widely acclaimed in the United States; it was greeted by
John Fiske as "one of the few erudite works which are at once truly great and
thoroughly entertaining." In one assessment, Tylor was even placed on Darwin's level. The central theme of Tylor's work, according to a review in *The
Atlantic Monthly*, was human progress from "comparatively rude beginnings." Tylor's skillful treatment of irrational cultural survivals seemed to
provide incontrovertible proof of civilized humankind's brutish and superstitious origins. Although human beings everywhere had been subject to superstition, modern man had simply developed his powers of reason (though far
from completely, which was why anthropology was "a reformer's science") at
the expense of folk belief. The continued appeal of spiritualism in the modern
era therefore had quite profound implications. "In a word, a modern medium
is a red Indian or a Tartar shaman in a dress-coat," concluded a reviewer for
Appletons'. The history of all humankind, then, was a journey from ignorance
and superstition to scientific awareness.[25]

In a later work, Tylor concluded that "the wide differences in the civilization
and mental state of the various races of mankind are rather differences of development than of origin, rather of degree than of kind." The journals widely
echoed this view. In criticizing one author for his "ignorance of modern science," *The Nation* virtually adopted Tylor's views in their entirety. "It is now
generally agreed," it asserted, "that conclusions once founded on assumed
hereditary varieties of races must be greatly modified, and that mankind
should be treated as of homogeneous nature though found in different degree
of civilization, the progress toward which is still everywhere in regular operation." As Tylor wrote in *Primitive Culture*, "All the world is one country." Human beings everywhere were united by their potential for rationality and by
their common enslavement, in varying degrees, to irrational custom. In all, Tylor's work was a powerful confirmation of the Enlightenment view that an innate rationality was a common possession of humankind whose potential
would, in time, be universally realized. This insight capped the conclusion to
his general introduction to anthropology, where he asserted that "it is a law of
human progress that thought tends to work itself clear." He later referred to

physical differences between civilized (white) and uncivilized (dark-skinned) peoples, but whether these differences were the cause or the consequence of development was unclear. Most likely they were thought to be both.[26]

The widely respected work of Lewis Henry Morgan added another important anthropological voice on behalf of a common human identity. Morgan, an armchair anthropologist from Buffalo, is best known for devising a taxonomy of human development that still appears in world civilization textbooks. His evolutionary trichotomy of savagery, barbarism, and civilization (itself of Scottish Enlightenment origin) is still used as a rule-of-thumb formula for demarcating historical milestones, though the preferred convention today is to speak of the transitions between Paleolithic, Neolithic, and civilized eras. As Morgan explained it, the purpose of his magnum opus, *Ancient Society,* was to demonstrate that "the history of the human race is one in source, one in experience, and one in progress." Civilized and uncivilized societies merely represented "different points along a common line of progress." Like Tylor's view of the psychological oneness of humankind, this was an a priori assumption, but then so too was the conviction of fundamental inequality that lay behind racialist science.[27]

Anthropology was a scientific time machine in which modern societies could travel backwards to reexperience their long-forgotten childhoods. The belief in a common human ancestry made it possible, by studying apparently strange peoples, to understand how modern civilization had developed without having to compile an encyclopedic knowledge of human history. Thus one author, passing through the Sudan in Africa, could not resist the feeling that this was what life must have been like in prehistoric Gaul. Differences in what were conceived as comparative stages of development were often described in orthogenetic metaphors of maturation from childhood to adult status, which presupposed that all societies evolved in the same order by taking the same steps, as in Shakespeare's seven stages of man. In looking at primitive peoples, modern men were looking at themselves as the children they used to be: "an adult mind in an infantile state . . . savage reason trying to illumine the darkness." Australian bushmen were described as "children, and bad children, with no lovable traits . . . cruel and filthy in their ignorance." The psychologist G. Stanley Hall's term, the "anthropology of childhood," in which young people were believed to be recapitulating civilization's rise from savagery, was a clever if misleading appropriation of the evolutionary model.[28]

Other disciplines offered support and corroboration. Philology, or historical linguistics, in its investigations into the evolution of language developed a branching tree of life that began with common descent or linguistic monogenesis that suggested a primordial "language of Paradise." History, too, contributed. It was, as Tylor said, "an agent powerful and becoming more powerful, in shaping men's minds." Although the point would often be obscured by the tendency of anthropologists to focus on particular societies in a timeless "anthropological present," ethnological insights made sense only if one appreciated the historical process of human differentiation. Even though the nineteenth century was the golden age of nationalist history, there existed at least the understanding in principle of its inherently global nature. On the threshold of institutionalization as a profession in the United States, history was viewed as no less scientific than any other discipline. "Social changes, as well as physical changes, are within the sphere of immutable law," insisted Fiske. The transcendentalist Frederick Hedge argued that enough law was discoverable "that a science of history is possible," a view that would be widely held through at least the middle of the next century. However obscure the beginnings and however complex the events, *Appletons' Journal* reported that "The historic [*sic*] method rests on the doctrine that the successive phases of society are linked together by the chain of cause and effect."[29]

If history was in fact a science, certain consequences followed. For one thing, the understanding of history could not become the monopoly of cultural insiders. Science, said *The Galaxy*, "affords a common ground upon which men of all races, tongues, faiths, and nationalities may work together in harmony." Because the same laws operated everywhere, history was of necessity a unitary process capable of producing a common understanding of human experience. Take for example, the English historian Edward A. Freeman, who, though Eurocentric in his own work and racist in personal outlook, propounded the thesis of the unity of history. "As man is the same in all ages, the history of man is one in all ages," he wrote. "The scientific student of language, the student of primitive culture, will refuse any limits to their [*sic*] pursuits which cut them off from any portion of the earth's surface, from any moment of man's history since he first walked upon it." This universal history was also thought to be progressive. Pondering the mystery of globalization, William E. Gladstone, in the pages of *The North American Review*, argued that history was not just one damned thing after another. It "is not a mere congeries of disjointed occurrences," he maintained, "but is the evolution of a purpose steadfastly maintained, and advancing towards some consummation, greater probably than what the world has yet beheld."[30]

The anthropological-historical position attracted an impressive number of subscribers. A bevy of British intellectuals who enjoyed wide readership in the United States—writers such as John Lubbock (inventor of the terms Paleolithic and Neolithic), Sir Henry Maine, John Moreley, and the historian W. E. H. Lecky—won renown for investigating the emergence of rationality, the law, and languages from an evolutionary perspective that provided corroborating evidence for the view that human differences were cultural in origin. For example, a review of Maine's work reported that "differences of race are, in general, far overrated." Differences among Aryan peoples, it concluded, were "differences merely in degree of development." As for non-Aryan races, they were "after all human beings, and further investigation may perhaps diminish our opinion of the difference between even the larger divisions of mankind." Works that claimed the opposite were duly taken to task. A critic for *The Nation*, reviewing Hippolyte Taine's *History of English Literature*, remarked with disapproval that "there is always a tendency to push the doctrine of race too far."[31]

In the context of this broader understanding of what constituted science, it is not surprising that many liberals, regardless of what some scientists said, preferred to think about race as "race prejudice." Christian missionaries and a few civil rights reformers could be expected to take the position that "all talk about race prejudice is nonsense," but that is hardly the end of the story, for there was a larger discursive community of educated readers and writers who tended to take the same view. *The Nation*, reviewing a book entitled *The Human Race*, was critical of the racial conception of the author, which was based on skin color, as "a basis long since abandoned as untenable." "All the principles, beliefs, and sentiments in which we are educated tend to impress upon us the unity of the human race," insisted another reviewer. Although this journal grew noticeably more conservative about the politics of race over time, in 1889 it could still laud the work of the French zoologist-anthropologist Jean Louis Armand de Quatrefages, whose environmentalism had already been promoted in the pages of *The Popular Science Monthly* for helping "to dispel the unscientific prejudice which holds that all barbarous races are proved by the mere fact of their barbarism to be inferior in capacity to civilized races."[32]

Numerous other expressions of this type can be found sprinkled liberally throughout the literature. Typical was the lesson that the editor of *Harper's* took away from a reading of *The Autobiography of a Japanese Boy*. The book, he contended, would "help to clear away the delusion that the quality, the essence of human nature is varied by condition, or creed, or climate, or color; and to teach the truth of our solidarity which we are so long a-learning." Commenting on the widespread use of race as an explanation of group differences, the southern writer George W. Cable called it "pure twaddle." "It may be there is such a thing," he granted, but was quick to add that "we do not know. It is not proved." For James Bryce, the much-admired British observer of American ways, racism was the very opposite of knowledge. It was "the contemptible resource of indolent prejudice . . . a confession of ignorance." There is also some question as to how widely this racist "knowledge" was circulated—not very far, by some accounts. These universalist views would eventually be enshrined in the 1911 *Encyclopedia Britannica* article on "civilization."[33]

But it was easier to assert the unity of the process than to explain its particular variations. What had made peoples so different? The "local peculiarities" that one found everywhere were evident, but their causes were not. "How deep do these provincialisms go?" asked one writer. "Are they born with the children? Can not all men who choose, by persistently cutting off these habits at the top, finally kill them at the root?" It was a confusing business. Thomas Wentworth Higginson's biographer suggests that, for his protagonist, "'race' was confused with religious, national, and ethnic groups." James Parton, best known for his biographies, suggested that class was the key, part of a broad historical pattern of treating others as inferiors: "These antipathies, we repeat, are all very much alike—Whig and Tory, Federalist and Democrat, Brahman and pariah, Spaniard and Moor, Mohammedan and Christian, Christian and Jew, Protestant and Catholic, Church-man and Dissenter, noblesse and peasant, Indian and squatter, white man and black man." The Lamarckian paleontologist Nathaniel Shaler, though he believed in polygenesis and the inferiority of the Negro, attributed much race prejudice to simple in-group, out-group dynamics. Some authors who thought they were making the case for the centrality of "blood" wound up arguing something altogether different when they emphasized the transforming potential of education or Christianity. Moreover, intelligent people could take inconsistent lines of argument.

John Fiske, for instance, at one point advanced the hypothesis that smaller brain size prevented certain peoples from becoming fully civilized, but that did not prevent him from devoting the bulk of his career to showing how processes of cultural diffusion and acculturation, working "through long ages of social evolution," had made their mark in history.[34]

A common past in which all humans had been gifted with common capabilities, when viewed in the light of globalizing trends, implied a common future. Differentiation had emerged from unity; and now unity was reemerging from differentiation. True, some forms of savagery were likened to "perpetual infancy, an incurable atrophy of the noble faculties which are the privilege of our species." Yet it was obvious that there had been significant turnabouts and reversals in the past. The idea of permanent inferiority, it was noted, was "a prejudice which, twenty centuries ago, would have ranked Germans and Gauls in natural intelligence below Egyptians and Chinese." Even if hereditary gaps had opened up, the increasingly popular Lamarckian version of evolution suggested that "races" could play catch-up. Thus *The Nation* rejected one scientific hypothesis which suggested that whites had permanently left non-whites far to the rear. "The question is not of the formation but of the transference of a civilization," it argued, "and to imply even, in the examination of such a subject, that this physical basis of life cannot be built up rapidly in lower races by the tutelage of the higher, is as yet gratuitous."[35]

Revolutionary departures were often the product of long processes of cultural development, but, once in place, the innovations were there for all to copy. In culture as in technology, the wheel did not have to be reinvented. Take the following analogy offered by a contributor to *Appletons' Journal:*

In the human race, puberty is analogous to flowering in the plant. The child develops slowly from year to year, showing no special change except in size of body and an imperceptible increase of mental strength, until a certain age is reached, differing in different races and under different social conditions. Then comes a marvellous change, and in a few months the whole being is transformed as by magic. Functions, undreamed of by the child, commence an irresistible play; old attractions die, new ones are born, and childhood becomes a simple memory of the past. These comparatively sudden transformations are common, in some form, in the evolution of all organized existence.[36]

As an example of especially rapid cultural turnabout, one author pointed to the Maoris of New Zealand. "Not only fierce savages, but cannibals" a generation earlier, wrote John Manning, "they have now a native literature, can read and write their own language, and are, almost all of them, Christianized." And then, of course, there was the hugely important example of modernizing Japan, and the potential of China and India, of which more will be said later. The lesson appeared to be that divergence could be reversed, for if differences had emerged historically, then human unity would surely reemerge as a consequence of the global process of civilization.[37]

Cultural Darwinism: Assimilation, Race-Mixing, and Extinction

For those who thought about race in cultural terms, the unification of the world would not produce cultural equality. Instead, relations between individuals and societies were governed by a form of cultural Darwinism that, in today's context, would more properly be called evolutionary culture theory. Phrases like "the struggle for existence" and "the survival of the fittest" have often been attributed to a social Darwinian worldview that, for later generations, stood for a dog-eat-dog individualism domestically and racism, imperialism, and war internationally. But if we scrape away that modern layer of interpretation, with its imputation of racialism and international warfare, and focus more intently on what Americans were saying, one sees a liberal outlook, universalistic and egalitarian, in which cultural change operated much like Joseph Schumpeter's famous description of economic development as a process of "creative destruction." For liberal egalitarians, cultural Darwinism provided a mechanism for narrowing racial and cultural distances by allowing less developed cultures the opportunity to transform themselves. But egalitarianism in principle did not mean social equality in practice, for not all cultures were created equal, nor did they possess a right to cultural survival.[38]

Like race, the "struggle for existence" was a catchphrase used promiscuously, and its meaning was correspondingly loose. Strictly speaking, it had little to do with Darwinian thought, a shortcoming that later led Lester Frank Ward to complain that he had "never seen any distinctively Darwinian principle appealed to in the discussion of social darwinism." The notion of a struggle for existence was applied in a wide variety of contexts: in discussions of economics, war and conquest, assimilation or race-mixing, and even in matters of personal hygiene. But the most common connection was between natural selection and economic laws—unsurprisingly so, as the idea had first occurred to Darwin when he was reading Malthus. At a time when biologists were shunning natural selection, the idea was gaining ground in the dismal science. "Whatever may be true of biology, the law of natural selection seems to rule in commerce," observed *The Century*. Similarly, Chauncey Wright noted that "at least for the purposes of illustration, we may compare the principle of Natural Selection to the fundamental laws of political economy, demonstrated and actually at work in the production of the values and the prices in the market of the wealth which human needs and efforts demand and supply."[39] Since commercial and cultural relations were often mentioned in the same breath, it seemed a matter of common sense that, in relations between cultures, the survival of the fittest would hold true in that realm as well.

Arguments to that effect could be found everywhere. Tylor, for one, maintained that history and ethnography "combine to show that the institutions which can best hold their own in the world generally supersede the less fit ones, and that this incessant conflict determines the general resultant course of culture." According to George Ripley, founder of Brook Farm and co-editor of the *New American Cyclopaedia*, societies with superior traits and technologies enjoyed a competitive advantage that would enable them to conquer or overtake those less well endowed. "Thus," he explained, "the social and moral qualities, which now form the chief distinction of the race, would tend slowly to advance and be diffused throughout the world." George Cary Eggleston, after acknowledging some of the more controversial features of Darwinism as biological science, saw it vindicated in the study of society. "No thinking person now doubts that the Darwinian theory, as applied to the improvement of species already existing, is true," he wrote. "We see around us every day the effects of the struggle for existence, and we know that in the end the fittest survive, while the unfit fall silently out of the ranks." Egalitarianism and social Darwinism were reconcilable in the same way that equality of opportunity and inequality of outcomes are compatible. Competition made possible the overcoming of inequality at the same time that inequality was a necessary product of competition. This grand process of cultural evolution, as John Fiske sought to show in many of his essays, was the very stuff of history.[40]

How exactly did the process of racial and cultural survival work? What happened when races and cultures came into contact? Societal interactions ranged from mixing to almost complete assimilation of one by another, to the complete physical disappearance of people and culture alike at the other extreme. At its most lurid, mixing meant miscegenation. Speculation about "the outcome of the amalgamation of the numerous languages, races, colors, customs, and conditions of life in America" was a common topic in the periodical literature of the day. It was common knowledge that much race-mixing was taking place. Summing up the changing color chart, one writer foresaw what in the twenty-first century would be called the browning of America. "In brief," concluded the free-lance journalist William Hosea Ballou, "it may be said that the tendency of color of southern races in the United States has been toward the white, and of the white races toward the red, or copper-color, of the aborigines." In 1887, Ballou was confident that "species of the same family invariably interbreed with the best of results, often producing a higher type of an animal." Others, however, believed that miscegenation resulted in inferior types. Sociology professor E. W. Gilliam of Charleston, an advocate of colonization as a solution to the race question, thought that the blending of white stocks made for a stronger race, but that "every instance of blending between white and black has proven adverse, creating, in the end, a half-breed race below the pure African ancestry." T. T. Munger, a Congregational clergyman, though acknowledging that racial amalgamation was once seen as a plus, claimed that science now proved otherwise. Miscegenation produced "disastrous physical and moral results," and theology, the law, and sociology would have to deal with this reality. It was on the basis of this kind of reasoning that southern mulattoes were reportedly inferior, both physically and mentally, to pure black field hands. The growing number of states that outlawed mixed marriage testified to this antimiscegenationist tide.[41]

But the miscegenation–mongrelization nexus was hardly canonical for the many nonracialists to whom the science of the matter seemed muddy and unpersuasive. If mongrelization was the rule, *The Nation* wondered, why was it such a point of pride to avow that Indian blood ran through one's veins? "Why do a large number of very respectable families throughout the country mention this as one of their genealogical claims to respect?" it asked. As usual, the journal's views were tempered by an awareness of the limitations of knowledge on the issue. Thus Godkin complained a few years later that "stuff of this sort would have more value if anything certain was known of the effect of any intermixture of races on character." Godkin's view cannot be dismissed as mere idiosyncrasy, for it drew on a reputable body of opinion that dismissed the mongrelization hypothesis in favor of a more positive view of hybridization. In 1870, *Appletons'* reported the views of the pioneering German ethnologist Adolf Bastian. Supporting Quatrefages and arguing against theories of degeneration as "profound confusion," he insisted that "wherever civilized peoples appear in history, they are but the highest product out of an infinite number of mixtures." To the explorer and ethnographer John Wesley Powell, racial conflict was metaphorical. "Civilization overwhelms Savagery," he wrote, "not so much by spilling blood as by mixing blood, but whether spilled or mixed, a greater homogeneity is secured." Others argued the exact opposite of mongrelization. Thinking through the implications of race mixing for the United States, N. C. Meeker predicted: "America beholds on her soil the meeting of all the races of men, and it is foretold that what is good in each shall be preserved, and what is bad gradually shall perish." Canon George Rawlinson, the Camden professor of ancient history at Oxford, whose essays appeared from time to time in American journals, pointed to "a general rule, now almost universally admitted by ethnologists, that the mixed races of mankind are superior to the pure ones."[42]

Debasement was a legitimate concern in matters of coinage, but, from this point of view, the desire to maintain racial purity and cultural isolation was far more threatening than race-mixing. Ballou, in pointing to the sad fate of societies that had sought to maintain their distinctiveness, called this "proof presumptive that an intermixture of races by intermarriage, and in customs and languages, must endure forever." Rawlinson pointedly drew policy conclusions for Americans from this lesson of history. "Their aim," he argued, "should be to absorb and assimilate the inferior races with which they are brought into contact, to fuse the different bloods into one, and become as soon as possible a united, homogeneous people." One essay in *Appletons'* propounded a late-nineteenth century vision of multicultural hybridism: "By means of immigration . . . the amalgamation of the Anglo-Saxon, Celtic, Teutonic, Scandinavian, and Mongolian, will result in a new and distinctively American race—more vigorous, more enterprising and cosmopolitan, than our boasted Anglo-Saxon." So much mixing had already taken place that some questioned whether the United States was any longer an Anglo-Saxon nation. Skepticism about amalgamation was, for this group, a betrayal of the very idea of America.[43]

This pro-assimilationist view of race presupposed a confidence in the United States' ability to maintain its identity by cultural means. To this point, history appeared to back up the optimistic view that American society possessed a nearly unlimited absorptive capacity. One of the nation's most powerful attributes had been its ability to assimilate peoples from different lands and cultures. But as the source of new immigrants shifted to Eastern Europe, worries about the nation's ability to digest such alien peoples began to emerge. George Mooar noted an ominous change, "a growing feeling that the assimilating potencies are nearly spent." Those who opposed a continued influx of immigrant blood were often frightened sorts who saw themselves as potential victims of social Darwinism, for assimilation, to be effective, required "a race-stock sufficiently positive and vigorous to assimilate all foreign elements into its own individuality." This pessimism was confusing, to say the least, for it coexisted jarringly with other Anglo-Saxonist scenarios that foresaw the English-speaking peoples crowding out all the others, with the exception perhaps of Chinese and Russians.[44]

For some assimilationists, ideology and not culture was a more congenial frame of reference because it set a less demanding standard of inclusion. An adult first-generation immigrant could not be wholly uprooted, but a full transfer of ideological allegiance could readily be made. Mooar, for example, defined assimilation in ideological terms as "the determined affirmation by the majority of the voters of those fundamental ideas and policies that are the axioms of our form of government." If the American creed was thoroughly internalized, what difference did culture make? As J. D. Phelan put it: "the essence of American nationality must be sought and found in the republican form of government and all that flows from it; for the distinguishing characteristics of the people are not in the color of their skins, but in the color of their minds; not in the words they adopt to express their ideas, but in the ideas themselves." The Democratic politician Horatio Seymour, speaking to fears about the impact of immigration from Eastern Europe, predicted that "this mingling of European races on this continent will give us higher civilization, greater power and prosperity, than have yet been seen in the history of the world."[45]

For the optimists, hard racial usages were open to challenge. The editor of *Harper's* maintained that "the ideal America, which is the only real America, is not in the keeping of any one race; her destinies are too large for that custody;

the English race is only one of many races with which her future rests." Mooar, for one, was not worried about the racial character of the new immigrants. Contrary to the fears of restrictionists, he found it "extremely doubtful whether, on the whole, the later immigration is socially or morally inferior to what came over thirty or forty years ago." As one might expect, some missionary groups paid no heed whatever to scientific racism. The American Missionary Association, dedicated to the uplift of Negroes, Chinese, and Indians within the United States, saw the solution "in the fusing of these various races into one grand new race, we might call it certainly one grand new nationality." One of their number claimed that science supported the idea that in the future "the last man, then, is to be a white man, a negro and a Chinaman." This would not happen quickly, however. Even among so racially liberal a group as this, the Lamarckian language of race could be used to warn of the difficulty of the task: "It will take generations to accomplish the work. Habits are not changed in an hour. Superstitions get into the blood."[46]

The obverse of assimilation was cultural extinction. Cultures, like species, were known to come and go. In "the great adventure of humanity," as one essayist put it, "We behold, perhaps, but the survivors of the mighty armada." As N. C. Meeker put it, "races sweep over races, and one race obliterates another." Although many had started the journey, it seemed clear that not all peoples were equally endowed with the skills needed to succeed as voyagers. One writer imagined waves of humanity washing over one another, "inferiority never being permitted to cohabit amicably with superiority, but perishing under its inimical contact, to make room for higher organizations." For weaker peoples, culture contact could result in physical displacement or, at the extreme, biological extinction. Thus *The Nation* in 1879 anticipated that in another half century, the Sioux and the Zulus would be gone. Similarly, an author who had spent years living with the Australian bushmen was convinced that "their complete extinction is only a question of time." Population crashes and cultural decay in Polynesia were widely remarked upon as object lessons of the high stakes of cultural contact. The common assumption of the time, as expressed by John Hittel in 1888, was that "as a general rule, savages die out when they come in contact with civilization. . . . The wider the gap between the savagism and the civilization brought together, the more fatal the contact to the lower race." Darwin had duly noted this tendency to disappearance in *The*

Descent of Man, where he cited the causes as the introduction of new diseases, vices, and declining fertility. In contacts between civilized and barbarian societies, the struggle was short, save for areas that were climatically inhospitable to the advanced civilization. Degeneration, or complete disappearance, was "the dark side of progress."[47]

Physical extinction could be a product of genocidal practices—as in the "the only good Indian is a dead Indian" variety—but it was more often viewed as the ill-understood but inevitable product of objective natural causes rather than as an outcome of policy desiderata. For *The Nation,* the decay of the Polynesians in Hawaii was a matter of both scientific and sentimental interest. "If one is impressed by the extinction of a plant or a bird, how much more noticeable is the passing away of a finely-endowed race," it noted. Among the more frequently mentioned causes were tight clothing, drugs and liquor, loose morals, female infertility, and epidemic diseases. For others, like the political science professor D. McGregor Means, the historical record suggested that a disparity of power was always the ultimate cause. "The possession of the earth has been decided by force," he said. "Stronger races have destroyed or expelled the weaker; rae victis has been the rule of invaders." But power was hardly a satisfactory explanation in all cases, for while some races disappeared upon contact with advancing white civilization, others did not. As John Fiske pointedly noted, England was "civilizing, not exterminating, the Hindoo."[48]

The ironic nature of anthropology as a discipline that belonged to a civilization that was systematically destroying its object of study in one way or another—a practice that later came to be called "salvage ethnography"—was even then unavoidably clear. Anthropological study at the time sought only to preserve the memory of societies, not the cultures themselves. Perhaps, E. B. Tylor mused, anthropology was dependent in a ghoulish way on the destruction of the societies it studied. "Perhaps it is not quite so familiar a thought that knowledge of savage life has actually gained in the course of its destruction," he wrote, for knowledge of these kinds of societies was being "collected in the process of improving them off the face of the earth." In a review, *The Nation* noted that "It was only as the extinction of the Polynesian race hastened toward completeness that its origin began to be adequately studied." Traveling backward in time was thus also a race against the forgetfulness of time. It was in this sense that writer and painter T. B. Thorpe, in advocating the further study of Amerindian societies, defended such inquiry as "a contribution to that history which will soon be all that is preserved of our native races."[49]

For premodern peoples, continued biological existence required a willingness to die culturally. In cultural terms the effect of cultural interaction would be the same as extermination or disappearance before the superior race. "Nothing can save the inferior race but a ready and pliant assimilation," said the minister Josiah Strong, an important herald of Anglo-Saxonism, in *Our Country*. For those who valued the emerging global civilization, the disappearance of traditional ways of life was cause for rejoicing. Quite provocative, and ruthlessly truthful, was Rawlinson's description of cultural assimilation as a kind of reincarnation without karma. "The process may be described as extinction, as ceasing to be," he wrote. "But it is at any rate a euthanasia. It is a death out of which life springs." Thus put, there was no need for prolonged mourning, since the potential for true equality could be realized only if inferior cultures adopted the values of civilized societies. In any event, liberal Americans tended naturally to assume that humanity was rooted in individuals, not in cultures; culture should exist for individuals and not vice versa. As Thoreau said: "It is individuals that populate the world." Culture was not the constitutive mediating form between the individual and the universal; it was something that got in the way of both.[50]

Rawlinson's provocative way of putting the issue was exceptional. It was more common to discuss the acculturation of weaker peoples under the less incendiary heading of education, which for liberals remained "the first article of the humanitarian creed." According to one preacher, "it is the lack of education; it is the lack of developed intelligence, not of native ability" that lay at the root of backwardness. Viewed from this angle, inferiority was a product of ignorance rather than blood. On the other side of the coin, *The Nation* argued that "civilization is the result of culture, and high culture," that is, the product of a culture that allowed people to emancipate themselves from traditional culture. For Tylor, the difference between advanced and noncivilized peoples boiled down to relative degrees of rationality, for progress was essentially "the emancipation of the human spirit from the thraldom of ignorance." At its most efficient, education could carry an individual "at lightning speed over the ground toilsomely traversed by those who came before him, to raise him in a

few years to the height which it has cost them scores of centuries to attain."
This was commonly called "culture" at the time, but its acquisition implied education in it most radical sense: deracination, the inculcation of ideas so radically foreign as to force the recipient to leave her culture behind.[51]

This unquestioned belief in the material and moral superiority of Western
societies was not based on ideas of fixed inheritance. Thus, when making the
case for the superiority of the Teutonic races, John Hittel was quick to add this
qualifier: "It is not my purpose to assert or to suggest that the Teutons have
superior mental or moral capacities, or that less is to be expected of a man because he is of Latin, Celtic, Slavonian, or even of a dark-skinned stock." Differences, he believed, were attributable "more to the influence of training than of
blood; and the training was the result of circumstances." In 1870, *Appletons'* argued the case against success in war as the ultimate test of a people's superiority. "All history is against the pretensions of a superior race," it insisted, "and, in
truth, no people is virtuous enough to be invested with the power that would be
in the hands of an all-conquering race."[52]

To apply a biological conception of race to American thought in the late nineteenth century is to guarantee a confusing and misleading account of how
Americans thought about human group differences—their thinking was
complicated enough without the superimposition of our own confusions.
Considered as a high-cultural concept, racial biology explains very little about
discussions of differences among groups of human beings during the Gilded
Age. Racism was neither ideologically hegemonic in culture, (i.e., so taken for
granted that it was neither discussed nor questioned), nor was it paradigmati-
cally triumphant in science during these years.[53] Although it is commonplace
today to observe that race and difference are culturally constructed, this would
not have come as a revelation to liberals of the time for whom race meant primarily culture.[54]

This homology between race and culture affirmed the possibility of the creation of a global civilization, but only if cultural difference was dethroned and
the immanent rationality of individual human beings was allowed to unfold in
its stead. Although egalitarian in its affirmation of a common human identity,
liberal thought was not pluralistic or tolerant in its judgment of cultures.
When measured against the universal standard of civilization, there could be

no cultural relativism. Cultures were not primordially sacred; on the contrary, as John Stuart Mill noted, the "magical influence of custom" as second nature was attributable to its being mistaken for the first. In the Enlightenment view, tradition was the enemy. Civilization and culture were binaries. Civilization was culture with a capital C, a global culture that could only be achieved by the elimination of culture understood as blind adherence to tradition. Civilization thus stood for a process of ecological simplification whereby the number of vital cultures would be reduced drastically through radical acculturation. The loss of cultural identity, whether through mixing, assimilation, or extinction, might be regrettable, but it was a historical fact of life whose unblinking acceptance was the price of progress. It happened to everyone, even to the civilized peoples, who had recently experienced an enormous cultural upheaval in their transition to modernity. To the extent that it was understood historically and anthropologically, race/culture was not an unexamined prejudice or arbitrary scheme of classification. It was, rather, a concept that captured the creative destruction entailed in the emergence and disappearance of human forms of life.[55]

Once the nineteenth-century language of race is translated into the twentieth-century language of culture, it is more readily understandable to contemporary sensibilities. Many of the ideas held at that time about race and culture continue to have a powerful resonance in today's world, where inequality tends to be explained in cultural terms. If, for instance, we consider the dominant explanations for why Japan and South Korea have modernized and most of Africa has not, once we go beyond superficial answers that emphasize the effects of imperialism, we are likely to encounter cultural explanations that in the nineteenth century would have been expressed in the idiom of race. The chief difference between then and now is that many contemporary liberals are willing to make allowances for behaviors and values that do not conform to Western standards and accept the need for institutionalized racial preferences as a way of removing inequalities deeply embedded in the social structure.

At first sight, these might appear to be huge differences, but my sense is that they are outweighed by the continuities in liberal thought. Modern multiculturalism, despite its principled toleration of difference, is not pluralist in a fundamental sense. Thus it's okay to introduce one's ethnic cuisine and to wear colorful native dress on certain holidays, but it is not permissible to raise and slaughter goats in one's back yard, hold cock fights in the basement, or per-form genital cutting on the young females in one's family as a cultural rite of passage. In other words, cultural difference is welcomed as long as it does not tread on our basic values. Multiculturalism is to globalization what anthropol-ogy was to civilization: an ersatz form of preservation that fails to deflect or slow down the anticultural juggernaut of linguistic and cultural extinction. For its part, affirmative action, which was controversial from its inception, was never meant to be permanent and would at some point have to be phased out, after which individuals would presumably be judged on their merits. Given the performance ethic that is built into the still-powerful idea of equality of opportunity, an ethic in which it is the duty of the laggard to come from be-hind, it does not require an anthropological sensibility to understand the nineteenth-century liberal posture toward race because, in its essentials, it would persist over time as the fundamental stance.

One can see how it might make sense to characterize as racist the numer-ous depictions of non-Western cultures as inferior, since all of the deficiencies associated with hereditary racial inferiority can also be transposed to a cul-tural key. Because culture may, in the right circumstances, absorb the same facts, attribute the same disabilities to other peoples, and harbor the same hatreds, the acceptance of culture as the basis of human difference does not confer interracial sainthood. If all this suggests a certain confusion about the use of such terms, that should come as no surprise. If people of the Gilded Age did not know what race was, the same holds true for the many uncertain-ties that surround the meaning of culture in our day.

But the skeptical-minded reader may ask, if at any point in time cultural and racial inferiority can come to the same thing, is this not, functionally speaking, a distinction without a difference? Why spend so much time belaboring the question? Well, it matters because the difference between nature and nurture, far from being trivial, encompasses the enormously important difference be-tween whether and how. Only after the question of whether other races could modernize was settled could one move on to the issue of how they might do so. The "how" question, which takes into account the historically inherited re-sources that societies can bring to bear in their quest for modernization, will be addressed in a later chapter.

Still, it might be objected that this abstract view of race and culture, even if one grants its logical coherence and its theoretical potential for egalitarian globalism, neglects the all-important distinction between theory and practice. Surely, in this view, the politically institutionalized racism of this period reveals the bad faith behind the expressed willingness of Americans to accept an equality abroad that they found unacceptable within their own borders, for without at least the possibility of universalism at home the global pursuit of human equality was hopelessly flawed at its core. If true, that would be a devastating indictment. But as the next chapter will show, the domestic politics of race was quite complicated and left room in practice for the eventual achievement of racial equality. More surprisingly, perhaps, the idea of equality discussed in this chapter even enjoyed a modicum of success during these years.

6

The Promise of Local Equality

Assimilating African Americans, Chinese, and Native Americans

America's double standard on race relations would become most strikingly apparent after World War II, when the U.S. desire to win allies in the Third World was undermined by embarrassing publicity about discriminatory practices at home. But the incongruity between internal enforcement of caste and the promotion of universalism abroad was already obvious to some thinkers in the late nineteenth century, for whom it would have been pointless to think about a global civilization if racial equality was being denied within the United States. To these thinkers, globalism entailed a primacy of the local. According to one domestic missionary, "The battle against caste must be fought, and the victory won, in America." This perspective involved more than moral consistency or a belief in American exceptionalism. If modern history was about the overcoming of time and space, it was precisely at the local level that formidable barriers of this kind had to be encountered and overcome.[1]

On its face, the dismal record of American racial policy in the Gilded Age seems to offer little room to argue that liberals were serious about the possibility of racial equality. The political abandonment of African Americans to the hands of white southerners following the failure of Reconstruction, coupled with a tightening of the color line in social relations, a ban on Chinese immigration, and the relegation of Native Americans to permanent squalor within the reservation system, all make a strong case for an across-the-board indictment. But without minimizing the social, economic, and psychic damage inflicted by racist outlooks and behaviors, there was also an egalitarian side to race relations during these years, without which it would be difficult to explain subsequent progress toward equality.[2]

As reflected in the journal literature, there were some strong antiracist countercurrents in liberal thinking about the politics of race in the late nineteenth century. The complexity of racial discourse during this period should give us pause about leveling a categorical accusation of racism against nineteenth-century Americans, for instead of a single race problem, it would be more accurate to speak of overlapping and intersecting fields of problems. Discussions of the status of blacks, Chinese, and Native Americans evinced enormous conceptual variation, and, at the level of practice, substantial differences in political outcomes. This diversity of opinion was apparent to the Yale sociologist William Graham Sumner; writing in 1881, he remarked on "the strange difference of our attitude at this moment towards black men, red men, and yellow men." That is, the problem of difference was addressed quite differently for each of the different racial groups.[3]

The Negro Question: Capitulating to the Future

America's treatment of the Negro Question displayed the greatest gap between entrenched commitments to racial hierarchy and the universalizing pretensions of civilization. By 1890, any hopes white Americans had entertained for the quick integration of the former slaves into American society as free and equal citizens had been abandoned. Disgust in the North with the excesses of Reconstruction, combined with a sink-or-swim approach to racial advancement, disappointment at the slowness of Negro progress, and a desire for reconciliation with the South, meant that the fate of blacks was once again placed in the hands of southern whites. But while racial sentiment as a whole turned sharply in an antiblack direction, it is simply not true, as one historian has asserted, that "American thought of the period 1880–1920 generally lacks any perception of the Negro as a human being with potentialities for improvement." Even Nathaniel Shaler—a scientist who took racial inferiority for granted—believed that improvement was possible. Many others, meanwhile, maintained a faith in racial justice: the social gospel movement was still alive, and the ideological descendants of the abolitionists continued the struggle for equality. In the face of widespread pessimism about the immediate future, the majority point of view in the journals was that inequalities could be redressed over the long term through education and cultural change.[4]

In the 1870s, some hoped that the problem would solve itself on the Australian or Polynesian pattern through the natural disappearance of the Negro. "Is the Negro Dying Out?" asked one typical essay. Following the 1880 census, however, those who had been hoping for "the providential riddance of the negro" through autogenetic extinction suffered a rude shock when the figures reported a 34 percent increase in the black population. The rate of population growth was so high and the black population so concentrated that a few alarmists feared for the future of the southern white population. In a symposium on "The Future of the Negro" in the *North American Review,* Professor Charles A. Gardiner, in what today seems a cockeyed analysis, concluded that "the whites must either amalgamate with negroes, or they must migrate from the South, or they must remain an inferior element and submit to negro supremacy." The migration of desperate blacks to Kansas in the late 1870s and the creation of the Congo Free State as part of the partition of Africa in the mid-1880s temporarily revived hopes, even among religious groups, that colonization might resolve the problem—but only temporarily. Given the newly revealed statistics, the prevailing view was that "the negro is here to stay."[5]

Black southern votes had been indispensable to the Republican Party shortly after the Civil War, but as Reconstruction wore on, the Negro connection became a liability to the party in its quest for ongoing national dominance. Increasingly, northerners, southerners, and foreign observers agreed that Negro suffrage, combined with white disenfranchisement, had debased the political process. "It is not good," said Daniel H. Chamberlain, the former carpetbag governor of South Carolina, "for the black race, not good probably for any race, to exercise power or to stand in places of responsibility for which they are unfitted and unequal." The end of Reconstruction was thus rationalized as a political blessing for blacks and for the party system because it presumably broke down the race line in politics. Indeed, those who had formerly been among the strongest advocates of universal suffrage were now condemning it. By 1890, Godkin reported "a rapidly growing sympathy at the North with Southern perplexity over the negro problem." The exercise of power by unprepared southern Negroes had been rooted in a debased form of equality. Instead of being valued as men, under the terms of the postwar arrangement blacks had been treated "simply as the property of the Republican party." The truth, according to the liberal editor Henry Watterson, was that neither party had a stake in the Negro: "Each would enslave him to its uses."[6]

The widespread belief was that any further federal intervention on behalf of the Negro would violate the liberal principle of self-help. Even during the most radical phase of Reconstruction, liberal objections to proposals for early versions of affirmative action were quick to be raised. Thus Wendell Phillips's proposal to elevate a black to the vice presidency was likened to "regulating the temperature by forcing the mercury up and down in a thermometrical tube." To continue federal paternalism, Godkin observed, would be "to adapt a political structure, specially created for the benefit of valor, foresight, industry, and intelligence, to the special needs of the ignorant, the weak, the lazy, and incompetent." Even to a clergyman sympathetic to Negro equality, there seemed something fraudulent and distasteful about a political process in which militarily protected voting "would represent the musket and not the man." The entire business, *The Nation* came to conclude, was an attempt to provide, "by means of legal chicane and military interference," a status that ought to have been earned. Initially a backer of federal activism, by 1890 the journal was advocating "a resolute and peremptory resistance to any further political sacrifices for the negro's benefit," going so far as to deny that racial wrongs could be righted by any form of political action.[7]

A broad variety of writers agreed that well-intentioned government intervention would only discourage the development of the self-reliance that alone could bring equality. Even the American Missionary Association, which was probably as egalitarian and color blind as any organization could be in those days, agreed that further protective legislation on behalf of the Negro would be counterproductive. "The race must show itself equal to the race with which it has to cope, or go under," said one of its members. The only sphere in which philanthropy seemed justified, duly emphasized in President Benjamin Harrison's 1889 inaugural address, was in education, which would provide the indispensable means to self-uplift. "Education and the chance of a fair opportunity," argued a review in *Harper's*, would produce a change of opinion among whites skeptical of black abilities. Black leaders like Frederick Douglass and Booker T. Washington agreed, though they were quick to add that education of the whites was equally necessary. Withal, education, broadly conceived, was seen as an alternative to political solutions. That, too, is how the feminist writer Gail Hamilton viewed the Negro's prospects: "If he is ever to be raised it is to be by education of himself; not by a crusade at the North against race prejudice at the South." The apparent cruelty of leaving the Negro to fend for himself was regarded as a form of tough love that would force blacks to understand that self-reliance was the only route to racial equality.[8]

Earlier generations of liberals had favored property holding as a qualification for the right to vote; now blacks were judged unfit for equality because they lacked the necessary cultural capital. The rude condition of former slaves meant that their relative cultural level remained, by every measure, depressingly low. The problem, *The Nation* had earlier insisted, was "not with the man's color or party, but with the man himself—with his ignorance, his degradation and his facility in being used as the tool of designing men." To avoid the imputation that racial bias was at work, the growing resort to proscriptive measures such as literacy tests for voting was defended as a color-blind approach because it would apply also to whites. With respect to political privileges, Joel Chandler Harris stated that Negroes "must be tested by the same rules that are applied to white men." The corollary of equality of opportunity was equal exposure to the penalties for failure. This attitude was not far removed from the free soil ideology of the 1950s, which had been less antislavery than pro-opportunity.[9]

Unlike Native Americans, whose aversion to labor was widely noted, the former slaves were willing to work and improve themselves. This embrace of the work ethic opened the door to cultural redemption, societal acceptance, and political inclusion. "Change the [economic] condition and the color is of no consequence," said one reformer. "Colored millionaires will not suffer much from prejudice," predicted Samuel Chapman Armstrong, a founder of Hampton Institute. "Train the negro to do skillful work, and you will make of him a good citizen," the journalist Edmund Kirke assured his readers. Performance was the bottom line, insisted *The Nation*. Until Negroes succeeded in business, science, the professions, and academia, no amount of antiracist evangelism could produce social equality. To expect otherwise would be to hope for suspension of "the laws of the moral universe." Some, like the sociology professor E. W. Gilliam, saw a profound social threat in the prospect of Negro advances, but they were the exception in the journal literature. The argument for abandonment was spoken in the liberal tongue of self-empowerment, the *Ursprache* of the republican creed.[10]

Advocates of separation and ultimate equality could both agree on economic progress as a key to advancement of race relations. Yet economic progress alone, however indispensable, seemed unlikely to lead to complete brotherhood. By 1890 defenders of human equality had shifted to a position that stressed the distinction between civil and social equality. Even the more daring critics of the discriminatory drift of racial policy stopped short of advocating social equality. Episcopal Bishop T. U. Dudley drew the line against racial mixing at the front door: "my taking away the pariah badge which caste has affixed to the negro is by no means the presentation to him of a card of invitation to the soiree in my parlor." George Washington Cable, one of the South's most outspoken critics of his region's racial mores, distinguished sharply between civil and social spheres in arguing for voluntary separation. "The one is all of right, it makes no difference who we are; the other is all of choice, and it makes all the difference who we are," he wrote. He concluded that "national unity need not demand unification of race." Gail Hamilton, though an advocate of "absolute political equality and civil rights for all," insisted that the U.S. government had "no right whatever" to interfere in the South's social relations. This emphasis on social separation, liberals believed, was not dictated solely by white preferences, for even the achievement of economic success was not likely to change the blacks' desire to associate almost exclusively with their own kind. Only the most radical egalitarians foresaw a future of racial amalgamation. According to the Virginia educator W. H. Ruffner, "Some of the most cultivated Caucasians have declared their preference for a mottled society—or as an eloquent orator expressed it, for 'a rainbow of colors on the social sky.'" Perhaps, but they were few and far between.[11]

But even a future of civil equality and social separation was abandoned as liberals gave way to southern demands for inequality. As a matter of ideological principle, the decision to leave the South to its own devices was consistent with the voluntarist beliefs of nineteenth-century liberalism. But as they played out in practice, the arguments were clearly rationalizations for a refusal to pursue solutions that were true to fundamental liberal values. Instead of acknowledging the simple fact that the rights of Negroes as citizens were being taken away, liberals chose instead to act as if the granting of special privileges was at issue. In doing so, they chose to ignore the imposition of a de jure caste system in which special status of another kind was imposed on African Americans. In concluding that they had done too much to promote equality of condition, liberals succumbed to a de facto denial of the equality of opportunity that lay at the core of their creed. It was a two-faced approach in which one face spoke of the possibility of advance while the other denied access to the political, economic, and educational opportunities that would have made such advance possible. This was less a solution than a guarantee of future trouble. Cable, most notably, pointed to the ominous implications—"the red fruits of revolution"—of burying the issue of racial justice beneath "the silence and concealment of the covered furrow." [12]

On the positive side, throughout this period of reaction, few asserted that racial inferiority was a permanent condition. Indeed, numerous writers continued to maintain that Negro shortcomings were the product of their habits and harsh circumstances, not their organic nature. "The negro, in his essential being," wrote the editor Oliver Johnson, was "a legitimate member of the great human family, endowed with the same attributes and capacities as his Anglo-Saxon brother." Negroes had already produced sufficient proof of exemplary achievement to disprove blanket assertions of white superiority. This positive evidence, complemented by a paucity of negative data, led the Chicago lawyer, educator, and writer William Mathews to argue that the case for innate inferiority was lacking. "Granting the present inferiority of the negro, we affirm that it has never been proved," he insisted, "nor is there any good reason to suppose that he is doomed forever to maintain his present relative position, or that he is inferior to the white man in any other sense than as some white races are inferior to others." Col. J. T. L. Preston, a former aide to Stonewall Jackson and a professor at Virginia Military Institute, applied the same counterargument against ascribed inequality for negroes that John Stuart Mill had used in defense of women's rights: until they were given a fair chance, who was in a position to say with certainty that they were innately unequal? A few even held that if their social and historical positions had been reversed, the white race would have been equally degraded. [13]

There remained hope for a liberal future in which education and economic uplift would do their profound transformative work, while predictions of a future of permanent inequality were remarkably few. The biggest problem, in Chamberlain's view, was to combat the natural impatience that accompanied reform and not expect too much too soon. Despite the rapidity of change in the modern world, nearly everyone agreed that the Negro problem was not amenable to rapid adjustment. Advocating a wait-and-see approach, one writer argued that "if in time the race shows equal power of intellect with the white, among whom they exist, in time that equality will be acknowledged and accepted," thereby affirming American society's deep respect for talent and hard work. "The truth is," said *The Nation*, exuding a sense of weary resignation, "that there is no possible off-hand solution of the negro problem at the South." "To overcome this prejudice," it wrote on another occasion, "must be the work of time, and a long time at the shortest." For William Mathews, the route to acceptance could only be a slow journey. "How could it be otherwise?" he asked. Changes of this kind, according to *The Century*, were "silent and gradual," but they were every bit as revolutionary as new inventions or scientific discoveries. "A generation passes," it wrote, "and the people suddenly discover that a revolution has occurred, and that the world they are living in is a wholly different world from the one in which they were living but a few years before."[14]

Here liberals were forced to apply to themselves and their nation the same kind of analysis that they had directed at European and other societies. If cultural problems required cultural remedies, it was equally true that there were cultural limits to the amount of cultural change that was possible at any given time. Given the deep-rooted impediments to achieving equality, the only practical way to solve the Negro Question was to leave it alone and trust in cultural laissez-faire. This simultaneous acknowledgment of failure and unwillingness to admit lasting defeat proved to be, in some respects, an uncannily prescient formula: time, education, and changing circumstances at home and abroad did eventually make possible political solutions to some racial problems. It would require the passage of another three generations, but liberals would eventually reclaim the ground of civic equality that they had surrendered in 1890, though even at the height of the civil rights revolution it would be difficult to conquer and hold the new terrain of affirmative action. By its insistence on bleeding the patient, liberal ideology was part of the problem, but it would also be a major factor in making possible an eventual cure.[15]

Race, Culture, and Chinese Immigration

The passage of the Chinese Exclusion Act of 1882 was yet another landmark of race relations during this period. Chinese immigration had become a contentious political issue in the 1870s as a result of the rapid influx of Chinese into California, where they soon numbered about 100,000, or roughly 20 percent of the state's population. Although race figured prominently in the debate, the debate about the future of the Chinese in America took a very different form, intellectually and politically, from that of the fate of the Negro. First, pronounced sectional differences between east and west, class antagonisms among whites, and broader apprehensions about undesirable immigration from Eastern

Europe were themes unique to this discussion. Second, and more importantly, many of the arguments applied to blacks could not be used credibly against the Chinese. Whereas Negroes were often compared to savages low on the scale of civilization, the Chinese were viewed as serious competitors to white Americans. Because it was the Chinese who enjoyed a competitive advantage according to social Darwinian reasoning, exclusionists were forced to frame their arguments in terms of cultural incompatibility in which the fear of Chinese superiority loomed large, with the result that color and blood were forced into a subordinate position. The political outcome was one-sided, but the debate highlighted "so many limiting and qualifying circumstances" surrounding the issue of immigration that it was difficult, as *The Nation* recognized, to come to any clear conclusion.[16] To call immigration restriction the product of racism would be to oversimplify a very complicated debate about, among other things, the meaning of culture.

To begin with, it was generally conceded that the Chinese, unlike American blacks or Native Americans, belonged to an ancient, highly developed civilization. At the height of the anti-Chinese agitation, one writer felt obliged to remind his readers that "indiscriminate invective" was uncalled for in dealing with "a race that has produced sages, scholars, inventors, patriots, among the greatest the world has known." It was understood that the Chinese had benefited from a powerful tradition of reverence for education and literacy. As a result, insisted people like George Seward, a former consul in China, many of the Chinese in America were "well qualified by education and intelligence to vote." For all the cultural differences, the explorer and geologist Raphael Pumpelly reminded his readers that the Chinese possessed many of the characteristics most valued by Americans: energetic hard work, a flair for commerce, a capacity for organization, a love of education, and a democratic sensibility. All these characteristics, claimed Pumpelly, were "in harmony with the spirit of the present age." Overall, Chinese virtues compared favorably to those of the average American. "We think it demonstrable," asserted *Appletons'*, "that the average Mongolian will not suffer in comparison, either in morals or in manners, with the mixed population of most of our large cities, particularly in the far West."[17]

There was also a high degree of fascination with Chinese culture. In *The Overland Monthly*, whose offices were located in San Francisco, the mining engineer and author R. W. Raymond argued that "the first imperative necessity for us, having to deal with these people, is to understand them." In the late 1860s, the Reverend R. W. Loomis wrote a series of pieces about the Chinese in California for the magazine, which sought to correct "many incorrect notions" and "groundless assertions." Loomis pointed to "the natural docility of their character," and their "respect for superiors and for all those who occupy positions of honor and power." They had a great reverence for education and honored their great philosophers and sages. Their only deficiency, Loomis found, was their religious beliefs, which were "foolish in the extreme!"[18]

The urge to know more about Chinese culture was reflected in numerous descriptions of their opera and theatrical productions. Generally, these articles suggested that Chinese opera, music, and theater were at best an acquired taste. "The costumes were very magnificent, but the music was fearfully Chinesey," went one typical review. "The confused sound of that awful orchestra still rings in the ears," said another, "and its barbaric strains tyrannize over one's dreams." As for the stage, one theatergoer reported leaving the performance "with a confused idea of the plot, with the blare of the trumpet and the strident wail of the fiddle in your ears, with the smell of all Chinatown in your nostrils, with a head-ache, perhaps, but with little added to your stock of information." Still in all, the Chinese passion for theatergoing, which appeared to be "more or less developed among all nations not absolutely barbarous," was a sign of a developed civilization.[19]

But the Chinese peasants from Guangdong province who composed the bulk of the arrivals to the United States were far removed from their civilization's high culture. It was their humble folkways that evoked descriptions of the Chinese as "a degraded race, ignorant of civilized life." Popular amusements like gambling provided cause for alarm, and negative portrayals of Chinatowns as cesspools of vice and iniquity quickly became media stereotypes. Such negative images were more than counteracted by descriptions of the virtues of the common Chinese. They were excellent agriculturalists and made quite docile and desirable laborers. As *Appletons'* explained: "They make no eight-hour protests; they have no strikes; they cannot understand what a trade-union means. . . . They have no barrooms; they drink no strong drink; they do not fight, or curse, or break things." They were by common agreement "steady and trustworthy." Besides, noted Arthur G. Sedgwick, critics of alien lifestyles too often demanded behavior of a higher standard than they were willing to apply to themselves.[20]

But that was the problem: the Chinese were too good at what they did. Unlike blacks and Indians, they were an economic threat. M. J. Dee, author of a book on Chinese immigration, viewed the problem in comparative terms. "The negro is as far behind us in the art of sustaining life as we are behind the Mongol," he wrote. One writer, watching a shipload of Chinese immigrants being unloaded in 1869, wrote ominously that the issue of Chinese labor was "destined within the next ten years—five years, perhaps—to become what the slavery question was a few years since." There seemed no limit to the kinds of tasks the Chinese laborer could perform. As Loomis put it, "the inventive genius of Americans is constantly finding out new ways by which to accumulate wealth by means of Asiatic skill and muscle." For many residents of the east coast, the Chinese influx was a blessing. An "American housewife" looked forward to the "cleanliness and order" that Chinese domestics could bring to well-to-do-households. Chinese servants, not yet infected by democratic prejudices against class, might well "contribute a satisfactory solution to the 'servant-gal' question."[21]

In the course of working its way through these contradictory arguments, *The Nation* suggested that nativist objections to their presence must be a source of puzzlement to the Chinese: "On one day they hear that they must 'go' because they are so barbarous and uncivilized; on the next, because they are so skilful and intelligent." "Which are we to believe," asked *Appletons'*, "that the Chinese are a foul, dangerous, pestilence-threatening, demoralizing element, or a valuable addition to our productive labor?" For liberals, the choice was clear: economic rationality, in particular global market processes that would permit labor to flow to where it was needed, argued strongly on behalf of continued openness to immigration. "There should be nothing freer than labor," argued the journalist Frank H. Norton. "Our market should be open to the world, since only by that means can the natural laws which regulate it gain opportunity for their working." Readers were reminded that the Chinese were willing to do work that Americans found beneath their dignity, which was itself the mark of an advanced society. The market forces demanding their labor were in any event too powerful to be rolled back, argued Godkin, "in spite of any amount of popular prejudice." Given the size of the United States, worries about too many Chinese laborers flooding the country were dismissed. "We have an immense territory to develop, and new fields for labor are continually opening," said *Appletons'*[22]

The potent ideological argument on behalf of free labor was also applied in defense of the willingness of Chinese to work for low wages. To deny them the competitive advantage that they had gained through the sweat of their brow was wrong as a matter of economic principle. "Will any capitalist or intelligent laborer be willing to make a general application of this theory?" asked Edward R. Burlingame, the negotiator of the 1869 treaty that allowed unrestricted Chinese immigration into the country. Besides, as "a shoemaker" pointed out, quite logically, in a global marketplace cheap labor in China could be just as injurious to American workers as Chinese in San Francisco. Preventing the Chinese from entering the country seemed alien to the global temper of the times. "We might as well expect to retard the motion of the heavenly bodies as to arrest this progress of civilization," argued one essayist.[23]

There was, in addition, an unmistakable whiff of elitism in criticisms aimed at the restrictionists. In 1879, President Grant, while on his world tour, explained to a group of indignant Chinese merchants that anti-Chinese sentiment was "the work of demagogues." And so it was widely perceived. Dennis Kearney, the leader of the anti-Chinese movement in California, was described as "profane, vulgar, and violent in his harangues. . . . The spectacle of such a man controlling the politics of a State would be a monstrous mockery of free institutions." From this perspective, the Chinese were being made scapegoats for the failings of unsavory whites who were venting their irrational economic resentments. "There is hardly a lazy vagabond or tramp in the United States," claimed *The Nation*, "who does not try to believe that the Chinaman is keeping him out of work." The Chinese were industrious, "which is more than can be said of a good many Christian laborers whom we have around us," *Scribner's* remarked acidly. Many of the poor conditions in San Francisco for which the Chinese were being blamed were traceable to inefficient and corrupt city government and to "hoodlums." Reports of murders and mistreatment of Chinese were routinely greeted with disgust and calls for enforcing the law against depraved cutthroats.[24]

Some defenders of the Chinese sought to turn the tables by questioning the American bona fides of the restrictionists. According to *The Nation*, the 1885 massacre of twenty-eight Chinese coal miners in Rock Springs, Wyoming, appeared to have been caused by nonnaturalized foreign workers from Europe. "The man who is loudest in crying that somebody else "must go" from the country," it editorialized, "is pretty sure to be a man who has only recently come to it himself." Other journals were not above using anti-Irish prejudices to counter anti-Chinese sentiment. One speech at the annual American Missionary Association gathering accused "Patrick" of disliking the frugality of the Chinese, "so he flourishes his ballot over the head of the politician, and his shillalah over that of Ah Sin." As this suggested, the arguments against the Chinese could easily have been applied to other ethnic groups as part of a larger debate over immigration: many of the same fears of mongrelization and unassimilability applied to immigrants from Eastern Europe. But while those who believed that the United States had become "a dumping-ground for the human garbage of Europe" would have welcomed the opportunity to limit immigration in general, this was, for the moment, a far more difficult proposition politically.[25]

The most ferocious battles were fought on racial and cultural terrain. Principled opponents of immigration condemned the cowardly attacks on the Chinese but insisted that this did not invalidate their larger concerns. Although the restrictionists granted that the problem was for the moment a western problem, they predicted that it would inevitably become national as soon as the Chinese began to move eastward. It would be a different story once easterners became "exposed to an immigration of masses of men of an alien and unassimilable race." In an essay in *The North American Review*, M. J. Dee granted the economic rationality of immigration but wondered about its cultural impact. "Where and how are we to ascertain what the effects of unrestricted Asiatic immigration will be upon the growth and distribution of the human race upon this continent?" he asked. This, agreed *The Nation*, was the core issue to which economic arguments must cede priority. "A state is after all not a manufacturing company simply," it said. "It is an association for moral and social ends." Thus, too much virtuous behavior could add up to a cultural threat. As one west coast writer put it: "Individually, John Chinaman is a clean human; collectively, he is a beast."[26]

The debate did not lack for scaremongers who sought to link miscegenation and mongrelization by raising the specter of "the debasing effects of amalgamation across color lines." But in contrast to the oft-voiced fear of racial mingling between whites and African Americans, the chief objection against the Chinese was that they could not and would not assimilate. In the words of A. A. Sergeant, a former Republican senator from California, Chinese immigration was of a totally different kind from the European. The Europeans "soon sink into the body politic, and their children are not distinguishable from other native born," he argued, but not so with the Chinese, who had no intention of assimilating. Another California senator, John Franklin Miller, saw the Chinese as unchangeable, "as immutable in form, feature, and character as if they had been moulded like iron statues when made." This cultural invariability, attested to by six thousand years of history, made it impossible for the Chinese to adopt republican ideas. Hence immigration needed to be reconsidered "when its operation threatens the destruction of our democratic society and the dissolution of our republican institutions."[27]

Chinese ethnocentrism was taken as confirmation of a natural tendency for races to stick to their own kind. Taking a particularly alarmist view, Theodore Dwight Woolsey described the Chinese as "invading armies rather than men seeking for homes and for quiet." In the worst case, some Cassandras envisioned an eventual Chinese majority that would Sinify American culture, society, and politics. "These yellow people," warned E. W. Gilliam, "are an alien and distinct race, that will not mingle with the whites, and threaten, through numbers, to Mongolianize the Pacific slope." Fearing the political problems caused by growing numbers and cultural separatism, Professor Henry R. Day bemoaned the emergence of Chinese ghettoes in the major cities. Taking an alarmist view of the Chinese diaspora that would have great resonance in Asian societies, the burgeoning Chinatown in San Francisco was seen less as an ethnic neighborhood than "an Asiatic colony."[28]

The ironic effect of these arguments was to turn survival-of-the-fittest reasoning on its head. Pondering the prospect of a race to the bottom caused by the willingness of Chinese to work harder for less pay, John F. Miller foresaw defeat for the white man. "The mind shrinks from the contemplation of the possibility of such a fate for the Anglo-Saxon race on this continent," he worried. Noting the growing resistance in white Australia and New Zealand to Chinese immigration, *The Nation* saw the same fears of being outcompeted at work: "the ready reception of them apparently is likely to result in their extirpating all rivals in such callings as they follow." The degradation of American labor by Chinese competition threatened to produce the kind of immiseration that Karl Marx had predicted. One writer foresaw a society divided "into a class of wealthy owners of land and manufactories with the professional classes they would sustain, on the one hand; and on the other, side by side with the class of Chinese laborers, a class of wretched whites doomed to labor for a pittance." "It is really, therefore, those characteristics of the Chinaman which we most despise," said M. J. Dee, that "make him a most formidable rival for ultimate survival as the fittest, not only in America, but wherever he may find a footing." Even Gilliam, who believed that race-mixing produced inferior offspring, opposed Chinese immigration because of Chinese virtues. They were, he conceded, "a vast, ancient, stoical, and, in many respects, singularly gifted race."[29]

This hatred of the Chinese for being successful in areas in which other races were deficient did not escape the notice of the intelligentsia, who took the occasion to demonstrate the absurdity of social Darwinist arguments by turning them on their head. William James argued that the decision to restrict immigration "would seem to be a proof that they are the best race." If force became the criterion for deciding issues of racial superiority, James wondered what would happen if the Chinese became Darwinian and applied their superiority by extorting an unequal treaty from the United States. "Might not a cosmopolitan and unprejudiced follower of Darwin well hesitate which side to espouse, for might not either prevail?" he asked. Tongue firmly in cheek, Raphael Pumpelly twitted those racialists who foresaw an Anglo-Saxonization of the world. "If the probabilities of the case bear any proximate relation to the possibilities," he predicted, "the teeming population of our hemisphere two or three centuries hence may have more Chings and Changs in their genealogical trees than Smiths and Browns." *The Nation* could not resist rubbing the noses of the restrictionists in the incoherence of their arguments. "It is natural that those who desire to expel the Chinese both because they are barbarous and because they are civilized, and who desire to expel them because they refuse to be naturalized or 'assimilated,' should also desire to forbid their being naturalized or assimilated if they wished it," said an editorial. It concluded that "everything about this Chinese agitation is characterized by the most delightful absurdity."[30]

The ideological appeal to republicanism cut both ways. Senator George Hoar, for one, mocked the allegiance of restrictionists to republican principles. For all the talk of republicanism spreading, it was now said to be under threat in its homeland. "Lo and behold," jeered Hoar, "75,000 Chinamen landed on our shores and the great republic has struck its flag! Men are not free and equal any longer! God has not made of one blood all the nations of the earth any more!" Godkin was palpably shocked by what the Republican

Party had come to only fifteen years following the end of the Civil War as it began to treat race as a disqualification not only for voting but also for residence in the country. Professor Henry N. Day reminded his readers that the Civil War had been fought to establish on a national basis "the principle of the equality before the law of the races of men." Others went back to the Declaration of Independence to point out that the American polity had been founded upon the inalienable rights of man—"not excluding even the Chinaman." The debate began to hit its stride just as the Statue of Liberty was being installed. A poem by Ella Wheeler Wilcox, a "plea" to Columbia, struck a critically ironic tone: "Your children rise up and demand That you bring us no more foster brothers To breed discontent in the land." The entire exclusionist business was "undemocratic and hostile to the spirit of our institutions," concluded *The Nation*.[31]

Liberal optimists also responded with a vigorous reaffirmation of America's power of assimilation. Acknowledging the enormous difference between the Chinese and Americans, one writer insisted that "the people of the two nations are very wide apart, not because they are of different races, but because of the great difference in their civilizations and their religions." Viewing differences as a matter of culture, they saw no reason to doubt that the Chinese could be assimilated or Americanized. Early in the debate, Raphael Pumpelly argued that Americanization, not restriction, should become the focus of attention. "Place these China-men on the same footing with other immigrants," he said, "and the result will be that, while many will return to the home of their forefathers, a large portion will make this the home of their descendants." An essayist in *Scribner's* also struck an optimistic tone. "So long as they love the school and its associations, are open to kindly Christian influences, are temperate and industrious," he wrote, "we see no reason why our broad territory, a haven for the oppressed of every clime, should be denied to the Celestials." Immigrants, argued George Mooar, were not colonists; they were a self-selecting population who were ripe for deracination. "The assimilation had set in long before the emigrant took ship," he maintained. "The republic had begun its transforming work upon him when he was dreaming of the far-away land."[32]

Granted, assimilation would not happen right away, but that was to be expected. Previous experience with Irish and German immigrants had shown that the first generation always remained outsiders. Besides, a look at other countries suggested that assimilation of the Chinese was decidedly possible.

Using Australia as an example, one writer, in an otherwise unsympathetic audit of Chinese virtues and vices, claimed that "in dress, manners, methods of thought, and customs of life, the second generation, though never ceasing to be Mongolian, is marvellously metamorphosing into Caucasian." A review of a book on Australia noted that the Chinese there "have made steady and good citizens, become Europeanized in dress, and attained to a considerable prosperity." The influential clergyman Lyman Abbott described the process of acculturation in relatively simple terms: "It involves bringing them into our schools and into our churches; teaching them that which we teach ourselves and our children." Once education and Christianization had done their work, said the American Missionary Association, "you will make them to be Chinese no longer, but Americans." Given the many fine qualities of the Chinese, Seward predicted that "they would become a valuable accession to our society if we would allow them."[33]

As they had with copyright legislation, opponents of immigration restriction argued that the issue needed to be considered from a global historical perspective. In its largest aspect, Chinese immigration was a major event in international history. The meeting of east and west, according to Professor Henry R. Day, "marks an epoch in the history of the world, as well as of our own country." When viewed in that context, restriction was clearly a historical throwback to medieval parochialism; it echoed precisely the frame of mind— "the old barbarous spirit of seclusion"—that the West had been seeking to eradicate in China. In addition, the immigration bill was quite illegal under international law, as it explicitly contravened a treaty signed in 1869. Although this legal embarrassment would eventually be papered over, the treaty revision of 1888 made up in insults what it recovered in legality. The inability and unwillingness of the federal government to protect Chinese within U.S. territory was also scored. "Making treaties when it has not power to compel its own citizens to observe them!" exclaimed *The American Missionary.* "What a farce." By 1885, when some Californians were beginning to demand deportation of the Chinese, *The Nation* judged the anti-Chinese agitation to have "reached its limit of insane folly." It made one wonder whether the United States was in point of fact a nation.[34]

Finally, some critics warned, China was on the verge of becoming a power. It was easy to pick on the Chinese, "a meek and unresisting race," on American turf, but the foreign policy of a rising China would not necessarily be pacific. The Chinese, as part of their self-strengthening program, were amassing a considerable naval force in their home waters and would not be as susceptible to easy intimidation from gunboat diplomacy as in the past. George Seward suggested that, in Chinese waters at any rate, the U.S. Navy could not match China's gunboats. Restrictionists tended to forget that the relationship was a two-way street, the other side of which was the modernization and Christianization of China. What about the future of the trade relationship? How would American missionaries be treated in the aftermath of this discriminatory legislation? Members of missionary boards were already expressing concern about the possibility of retaliation against Americans in China. "Our strength has been in our moral position, and that we seem determined to abandon," wrote Seward. "To be neither feared nor loved by an Asiatic state is to be despised, and that is, what we are coming to, apparently, in China."[35]

Despite the passage of the Chinese Exclusion Act in 1882, advocates of continuing immigration from China had mounted a vigorous and many-faceted defense of the virtues of the Chinese and the benefits they would bring to the United States. Importantly, acculturation rather than race proved to be the central theme in the debate, probably because a reliance on hard racial arguments would have worked to the disadvantage of both sides, albeit in different ways. Pushing acculturation to the forefront was a significant rhetorical step backward for advocates of restriction because it implied a willingness in principle to accept the Chinese into American society if only they could have found it within themselves to abandon ancestral ways. Culturally, the dislike of the Chinese was not as deeply embedded historically as the antagonism toward African Americans. But the move to cultural terrain as a site of debate, while it made for a stronger argument, could not overcome the superior logical consistency and intellectual force of the arguments deployed by opponents of restriction. In the absence of compelling racial and cultural explanations, other rationales probably carried more weight as motivators of political action. Economic causes, in particular, jumped to the front of the line in a period of depression when jobs were at stake, just as economic interests would work to powerful effect against cultural arguments for restricting Mexican immigration a century later.[36]

Whereas the debate on the Negro Question was tinctured with despair at the lack of political remedies, the issue of Chinese immigration was amenable to simple legislative resolution. For the time being, restrictionists were content simply to slam the door shut. For opponents of restriction, success would have required only that the government continue to do what it was already doing in order to achieve a satisfactory outcome without contemplating a fundamental restructuring of American society. Either way, the problem was easily solvable. By contrast, effective political action on the Negro Question would have entailed rebuilding the entire house to accommodate those who had formerly occupied the servants' quarters. Convincing the white population rather than reshaping the Chinese, whose Americanization would take care of itself, was the issue, one that could be revisited in future. Like a lost battle in a protracted war, a political setback over immigration restriction was a long way from being a decisive defeat for liberal ideas of race.

Assimilating the Native American

In the case of Native Americans, liberal ideas would not have to wait to achieve political success. The relationship between Americans and Native Americans was an extreme example of cultural Darwinism at work; yet of the three racial tragedies taken up in this chapter, it was also the least racist and most assimilationist. Politically, Americans in the 1870s and 1880s showed a greater willingness to accept the American Indian into American society than they did African Americans or even Chinese immigrants. Disturbed by the imminent prospect of the biological extinction of Native Americans and embarrassed by the intractability of the problem, reformers seized upon the solution of cultural deracination or complete Americanization of the Indian. The debate over the future of the Indian illustrated both the plasticity of race in liberal thought and an anticultural ruthlessness whose spirit, though 180 degrees removed from twentieth-century liberal multiculturalism and its "genuine acceptance of difference," would remain very much a part of the modern liberal outlook.[37]

After the Civil War, the Indian problem appeared to be entering its final phase. Though sporadic military skirmishes and police actions continued in what were called "Indian wars," these were more akin to mopping-up actions. As one journal noted, "It is absurd to call such chases and skirmishes by so dignified a name." The Indian population, meanwhile, was declining so quickly that biological extinction seemed a near certainty. From an objective point of view, the Indian problem was well on the way to being permanently "solved."

Despite this trend, dissatisfaction reached a crescendo in the 1880s as critics castigated the government for numerous failures and demanded a drastic
change of course in Indian policy.[38]

The critiques expressed no outrage at the displacement of Indian populations
by whites, a development that seemed inevitable and desirable even to those
who sympathized with the Indians' plight. *The Nation* was brutally frank in discussing the situation. "One need not shed many tears," it said, over the thought
that "by the process of natural selection, the earth is being given over to the
races best qualified to make use of it, of which the Indian race is not one."
A happy pluralism of live-and-let-live seemed impossible of achievement.
"There does not seem to be any possible modus vivendi between them and the
whites," concluded another editorial, for there was no practical way of stopping the process of physical and cultural displacement made inevitable by this
lopsided techno-environmental mismatch. "Civilization cannot be brought to
a halt on its march because savages choose to get in the way and cry 'No thoroughfare,'" said another essay. In a review of a history of the Indian wars,
the journal concluded that the story "is not flattering to our wisdom or our
humanity; but the history is one which cannot be greatly varied in any case of
conflict between civilized and uncivilized man." Even Herbert Welsh, the secretary of the Indian Rights Association, believed that from the start the situation was "hopeless." It was, from the very beginnings of white settlement,
"an irrepressible conflict." Modern times had simply accelerated the inexorable process of crowding out hunter-gatherer societies and agrarian chief-
doms that had been going on since the start of the Neolithic era.[39]

But while the inevitability and desirability of displacement were universally
conceded, the cruel and deceitful methods by which it was accomplished generated a good deal of soul-searching and breast-beating. In 1881, Carl Schurz,
having just completed a stint as a reformist secretary of the interior in the
Hayes administration, described the history of U.S.-Indian relations as "in
great part, a record of broken treaties, of unjust wars, and of cruel spoliation."
Helen Hunt Jackson's electrifying exposé, *A Century of Dishonor,* was unspar-
ing in its critique of government bad faith through repeated treaty violations.
Security against the Indians was widely understood to be a ruse used by land-
hungry settlers and commercial interests who pushed forward the frontiers of
white settlement and then called for the government to rescue them from the
wars that they had instigated. As in the case of the outrages perpetrated upon

Chinese and blacks in the South, the assumption was that this was the work of riff-raff—"the most ruffianly population in the world," a population of "white savages," to quote but a few descriptions. Even government reports noted the unfairness of analyses that typically highlighted Indian outrages while omitting to mention the white misdeeds that had prompted them. One attempt at a two-sided view described the relationship this way: "On our part, it is a history of cupidity, injustice and bad faith; on his—the defense of the weak—treachery; revenge, cruelty." After running through its various elements, *The Nation* concluded: "The Indian question is nothing but one of horror, however viewed."[40]

The gross mismanagement and corruption in the Indian Bureau fit nicely into liberal campaigns for civil service. But it was policy rather than administration that generated the most criticism as it became increasingly clear that the government was pursuing de facto a genocidal course. G. E. Pond put bluntly an argument that was increasingly voiced in public: "We have tacitly accepted the theory of extermination, while we have made public profession of the desire to protect and improve the races which were not readily assimilated or which refused the role of a servile class." To this point in time, said Herbert Welsh, the priority given to warfare had forced the objectives of civilization and Christianization into the background. According to the *American Missionary*, there had been "two Indian policies" since the time of settlement, "the one represented by the word civilization, and the other by the word extermination." But theory and practice were out of kilter, as the civilizing mission in theory was being ignored in favor of extermination in practice. They were so far out of line, according to one writer, that Indian policy was "really a policy of extermination, and if not speedily changed for something better, the whole Indian race of our country will become extinct within the next half century."[41]

Clearly, some Americans, politicians included, unashamedly favored extermination as a matter of policy, and the issue was definitely in the air. "Shall the Red Men Be Exterminated?" asked one provocatively titled article. In 1886, the Carlisle Indian Industrial School staged a debate: "Resolved, That the Indian Should Be Exterminated." Though rhetorically intended to titillate, such titles were echoes of ideas that were circulating in the culture. *The Nation* in 1870 noted that the widely expressed wish among whites to see all Indians "dead and buried" was, unfortunately, "not far from the truth." One official in the Bureau of Indian Affairs (BIA) reported hearing almost daily expressions such as "'I wish all the Indians were swept off the face of the earth; or, 'Why don't the Government kill them all?'" But active exterminationism would have been superfluous when all signs pointed to biological extinction as a consequence of letting nature take its course. In 1873 a writer in *The Nation* concluded: "That the red men are doomed to disappear seems tolerably plain." This seemed to be the obvious fact of the matter to many. John Hittel, in imagining the future of the California Indian, seemed to be predicting the future of Native Americans in general: "A few shell mounds, a few arrowheads and mortars, a few names of counties, valleys, rivers and towns, a few drops of dark blood mixed with the white—these will be all that will remain of its aboriginal population in the California of the twenty-first century."[42]

The demographic methodologies were suspect and inconsistent, and the figures varied wildly, but by the 1880s, the growing view was that reports of the death of the Indian were greatly exaggerated. Various statisticians began to argue that the Indian population was not decreasing, and that, in any case, government policy could reverse any further decline. With pacification nearly complete, the possibility that the Indian was not dying out helped to shift attention to the neglected option of civilization, but the chorus of arguments on behalf of reform had begun to swell even before the new numbers became available. If the survival of the Indian was a powerful argument for action, more powerful still was the prospect of extinction. Schurz portrayed the choice in stark terms that had been used to describe the Indian question at least since the eighteenth century, but now with a sense of highest urgency. In a speech to the American Missionary Association, Schurz declared that "the alternative of civilization or extermination is immediately before them." If policy, however well administered, hewed to the existing course, he was convinced that extinction was "only a question of time." This was, as we have seen, hardly a blockbuster revelation. Jacob D. Cox, who had served as Grant's secretary of the interior, had arrived at the same conclusion. Citing Tocqueville as his authority, Cox suggested that, given the alternatives of separation or amalgamation, separation usually meant "extermination of a weaker race."[43]

Thus the argument for taking seriously the civilizing mission gained ground for quite contradictory reasons. The survival of the Indian meant that the problem of civilization would have to be given more than lip service. But the prospect of his disappearance with little serious attempt at a workable alternative was already generating a huge burden of guilt. "What a logic of infamy!" said one writer to *Scribner's*. "Because we have had one century of dishonor, must we have two?" That the government could and should do better became a central conviction of liberal reformers. The alternative was to do nothing and then try to erase the sordid business from the national memory. After toting up the by-now finely itemized inventory of white misdeeds, *The Nation* offered, for shock value, precisely that option: "Nothing could happen at this moment that would seal up such a fountain of white iniquity so well as the death of the last Indian." But reformers refused to take this route.[44]

Before anything could be done, the Indian had first to be humanized, but that presupposed reliable knowledge of Indian ways of life that was quite hard to obtain. In addition, most Americans simply did not care to learn, according to the writer and editor J. C. Cremony. *The Galaxy* complained that Americans knew more about "the insignificant Tasmanians" than about tribes with which they had been in close contact for centuries. For all that, by the 1880s, the humanization of the Indian was well under way. In the absence of actual contact, imaginative empathy increasingly closed the gap between ignorance and an understanding of the Indian and his culture. Helen Hunt Jackson's next book, the novel *Ramona,* went so far as to feature a mixed-race romance at the heart of its story. As quasi-ethnographic portrayals emerged, reviewers pointed to family life, friendship, honor, tribal loyalties, capacity for grief, and belief in a Great Spirit and an afterlife as indicators of a common humanity. Many saw Indian behavior as quite understandable and even justifiable, given the circumstances. For example, one L. Edwin Dudley asked: "Would the people of New York abandon their homes, and retire before the advance of another people, no matter how high their claim to superior civilization, without a struggle? I am glad to believe not." This ethnographic narrowing of distance was accompanied by a growing ability to identify with Native Americans in the context of the grand historical-evolutionary narrative. "We must look upon the North American Indians as representing our own ancestors of the Stone Age," cautioned *The Nation,* "and as well able to emerge in time from savagery and barbarism as were the pristine men of Asia and Europe, whom they strongly resemble in their customs and mythology."[45]

However, to liberal reformers humanity reposed not in culture, which was perceived as the enemy of civilization, but in the individual. Although Indians as individuals were increasingly conceded to have the basic human qualities, few believed that Indian cultures, whatever their virtues—and many continued to see them as barbaric abominations—could or ought to survive. By the 1880s, humanitarian reformers and liberals, supported by the work of social scientists like Lewis Henry Morgan who held that private property was the key to civilization, came to the conclusion that the chief obstacle to assimilation was a reservation system that separated Indians from the general population. The root of the problem was a treaty-making process that had treated the tribes as sovereign powers with original rights to the land, which in retrospect struck many as ludicrous because the treaties granted Indians a form of sovereignty at the same time that it made them dependent wards of the United States. In any event, although an end had been declared to treaty-making, the United States was now stuck with an anachronistic system of forced dependency.[46]

Whatever cultural virtues the Indians had possessed (there had long existed a respect and even admiration for the Indian's fighting qualities and spirit of resistance) were being inexorably sapped by reservation life, if they had not already disappeared. As the prolific writer on Indian affairs Elaine Goodale complained, "this race of involuntary prisoners and paupers . . . has lost to a great degree its pristine courage, patriotism, independence, and honor." "Wardship tends to emasculate him," said General S. C. Armstrong, a founder of the Hampton Institute, which began admitting Indians in 1878. The reservation system, which had done nothing to create new virtues or improve the Indian's condition, came to be viewed with the same disdain that would be directed toward the welfare system in the late twentieth century: as an arrangement that contributed to ongoing self-debilitation and a squalid, degraded form of existence. This critique, then, focused on the effect of paternalism on character rather than on racial handicaps. Eugene Smalley, in trying to imagine how white people in similar circumstances would fare, concluded that "they or their descendants would become about as lazy and barbarous as the Indians in a short time." This system was remarkably improbable for a democratic republic that believed in individual self-help. "The most ardent communist," noted the Indian reformer Anna Dawes, "could hardly want more than this: land held perpetually for him, as much as he desires, and every public want supplied." With what result? The creation of "a great unprogressive animal class."[47]

For the great majority of reformers, the reservation system was at best an interim solution. Hampton's Armstrong described reservations as "merely places for herding Indians; temporary, necessary experiments, that, after a given time, may become growing evils." The guardianship metaphor was deeply flawed, for the current system was designed, as *Scribner's* put it, so that "the Indian 'ward' never comes of age." Because by definition tribes could not attain civilized status, Godkin felt justified in describing the reservation system as "simply a clumsy machine for the perpetuation of barbarism." Even if successful, the best case being the Cherokees, it too closely resembled the Chinese and Japanese attempts at seclusion from the world, which were contrary to the universalizing tendency of the times. At the same time, tribalism was contrary to individualism and republicanism. "If Indians be men, why all this exceptional sentimentalism in their governmental relations, which tends only to keep all their manly faculties undeveloped?" asked a California writer. It was remarkable, noted the *New York Tribune,* that the Indian, from whom the land was taken in order that America could become the bastion of freedom and human equality, was "the only man in it who is not recognized as entitled to the rights of a human being." As an afterthought, the paper noted that a woman in the tribal system was "almost literally a slave."[48]

Although the desire to civilize the Indian can be traced back to the seventeenth century, its clearest ideological articulation came in the discussions that preceded the passage of the Dawes Act in 1887. National politicians had been pointing to a definitive assimilationist answer to the Indian question for two decades. In his first inaugural address, Ulysses S. Grant had outlined the general solution: "civilization, Christianization and ultimate citizenship." Confessing the failure of Indian policy, Chester Alan Arthur proposed "gradually to absorb them into the mass of our citizens." Reformers who attended a conference at Lake Mohonk in 1884 agreed that the reservations should be eliminated, relations with the tribes ended, and government aid cut off. Not everyone went along with this program. Some advocated the maintenance of the reservation system as a form of apartheid, under military supervision and with strict controls on white depredations. This, the dissidents believed, would avoid the perils of race-mixing. But most advocates of change held that "the Indians should not be taken from, but rather toward, civilization."[49]

The decision on behalf of radical assimilation was widely viewed as a belated recognition of the Indian's humanity. As one rancher put it: "The simple thing to do is just to treat them as men, and that will be all there is to it. That will settle it, and there will be no such thing as an Indian question." The writer Benson J. Lossing similarly saw radical Americanization as a way of affirming the Indian's humanity: "Make the Indian a citizen of the republic, wherever he may be, and treat him as a man and a brother. Give him all the privileges of citizenship, on terms of equality with other citizens, and exact from him all the duties of a citizen." Hewing to these guidelines would make it simple enough to Americanize the Indian. In an uncharacteristic outburst of optimism, *The Nation* suggested that "we only need to treat Indians like men, treat them as we do ourselves: putting on them the same responsibilities, letting them sue and be sued, and taxing them as fast as they settle down and have anything to tax."[50]

But Americanization meant, as Francis Prucha has noted, doing away with "anything that deviated from the norms of civilization." Or, as one divine observed, "exterminate the savage, but save the man." Army Captain E. L. Huggins, writing in *The Overland Monthly*, put the choice starkly between biological and cultural extinction. "There are but two possible final solutions of the Indian question," he wrote. "The Indians may be exterminated by war, famine, whisky, and disease, or they may undergo the euthanasy of merging into and being absorbed by the 'superior race.'" To survive, "they must learn to live like white men," Schurz insisted. That is, they needed to be assimilated and Americanized. *The Nation* had already announced its support of phasing out the reservations and tribal system in favor of "a fusion of the Indians, under proper safeguards, with the great body of citizens, black and white."[51]

This willingness to pursue a combined course of deracination and miscegenation encountered surprisingly little resistance from scientists. Even though some experts held that racial intermarriage produced inferior mongrel offspring, more than a few, like the French anthropologist Quatrefages, believed that the mixing of races was "of the greatest importance in developing new and desirable types of mankind." One finds numerous expressions, general and specific, of the desirability of miscegenation. Given that Indians comprised only about 1 percent of the population, even those who had qualms about intermarriage saw little danger from it. Philip C. Garrett of the Indian Rights Association, professing not to fear race-mixing, used a homeopathic metaphor that inverted the one-drop rule: "it is quite conceivable that while ten grains of Indian to one hundred of white man might be injurious to the quality of the white race, [but] half a grain to one hundred might supply exactly the element needed to improve it." In one review, the ethnologist Garrick Mallery declared that "in the absence of race prejudice regarding intermarriage, amalgamation will assist in absorption."[52]

Considerable miscegenation would in due course occur, but it was thought that education was the key to abolition of the reservations in the interest of "transforming savages into citizens." Here, too, there were doubters. Could Indians be educated? Anticipating this skepticism, an article on education at Carlisle and Hampton noted wryly that many readers would "smile at the title of this article, much as if it had read, 'Education for Buffaloes and Wild Turkeys.'" But reformers argued that the record of individual educational successes proved that civilizing the Indian was not a fool's errand. There was also enough testimony to refute "the revolting suggestion" that past failures were attributable to natural deficiencies among Indians. The prolific writer and social reformer Hamilton Wright Mabie, in response to some impressionistic essays written by Frederic Remington, insisted that "the results at Hampton and Carlisle have settled the question of the capacity of the Indian for education." The history of the so-called five civilized tribes in particular left no doubt that Indians could learn the white man's ways. According to Schurz, the only people who continued to voice skepticism were those who, for selfish reasons of their own, did not want to educate the Indian.[53]

The key to transforming the Indian, as is true of all cultural programs, was to concentrate on the young, to place them in an environment free of the pull of tribal culture. "Our hope is in the rescue of the rising generation," said Goodale. The reliance was on the same forces of acculturation that were at work on the second generation of immigrants. If done correctly, predicted University of California professor Sherman Day, "the savage tribal relations, superstitions, barbarous and cruel games, and 'medicine' humbugs of the adults will vanish spontaneously." Inevitably, debates broke out over the best form of education. Would bilingual education do the trick? Should missionaries read the Bible in the vernacular? Should there be free common schools or boarding schools? Shock treatment or gradualism? Industrial education or education in the arts and sciences? Should different approaches be adopted for different tribes?[54]

But many doubters remained. How great an instrument of acculturation was the school, anyway? It was open to question whether the common school had achieved significant results for the white race. In a reflection on "race education," James C. Welling, president of Columbian University (later the George Washington University), argued that acculturation was a more complex process in which everything was related to everything else in an intricate equilibrium. "The education of a few Indians at Hampton and Carlisle," he predicted, would be "a waste of new cloth and new wine." George S. Wilson, an army officer, illustrated the difficulty of a program of forced acculturation through this imaginative parable:

> Suppose some superior race should come from another planet, and find us as inferior and barbarous, according to their standard, as we consider the Indians, when measured by our standard. And suppose they should conquer and put us on reservations. Could we at once quit the life which is the outgrowth of all these thousands of years? Changing everything but our color,—giving up our philosophy, religion, code of morals, customs, clothes, and means of obtaining food—could we at once adopt a mode of existence so different from anything we ever heard of that we could not form the least conception of it?[55]

For those who took this skeptical line, the school could only be an effective institution when it worked from within a society. Schooling was completely ineffectual in the end, argued Remington, for once returned to the reservations the former students would "go back to the blanket, let their hair grow, and forget their English." Instead, he advocated putting them into the army, like the Cossacks had been, where their skills could be put to good use and where they could more effectively be acculturated. Optimistic believers in the melting pot argued, on the other hand, that the process was already well advanced. Explorer-anthropologist John Wesley Powell, for example, praised "the presence of civilization, which, under the laws of "acculturation," has irresistibly improved their culture by substituting new and civilized for old and savage arts—new for old customs—in short, transforming savage into civilized life."[56]

But if such forces were not undergird by land reform, they could only be partially effective, at best. The Archimedean lever that would complement education and broader acculturating processes was the dissolution of communal tribal landholding. The holding of land in common was a defining characteristic of barbarism and was recognized as "one of the strongest bonds of their tribal cohesion." The stated intent of the Dawes Bill was to break up the reservations into individual holdings, turn Indians into property owners, and propel them into industrious pursuits. It would end the era of wars of Indian removal and open the door to American citizenship and its legal protection of civil rights. "The passage of the Dawes Land in Severalty Bill was, indeed, a great day for the Indian," said a report of the American Missionary Association. As *The Atlantic Monthly* concluded, it was a "far-reaching, and beneficent law relating to the Indians."[57]

The Dawes Bill was, in part, a triumph of liberal ideas whose deracinating logic was fully in keeping with the universalistic spirit of the time. It is hard to see how the legislation could have passed without the enthusiastic support of the reformers. But as subsequent events would show, it was in equal measure a land grab. The political consensus forged in the 1880s combined elements of guilt, reformism, a relatively small and shrinking number of Indians, and those who were unscrupulously attracted by the allure of acquiring still more reservation land. Far from resolving the problem of Native Americans, the legislation made a bad situation worse and contributed to its indefinite prolongation when events failed to follow the reformers' script.

The most notable result of the Dawes Bill was to expedite the alienation of land into the hands of whites and to increase the dependence of Indians on the federal government. It also quite unintentionally contributed to miscegenation, as land-hungry whites sought to cash in on the allotments by marrying Indians.[58] It was not long before "disgraceful scenes" of "legalized trespassing" were being replayed in the Oklahoma territory. By 1934, 90 million acres, approximately two-thirds of Indian reservation land, had changed hands before the government reversed course and returned to paternalist protection. In the end, the United States wound up pursuing two logically incompatible strategies, each in a half-hearted fashion: civilizing the Indians and protecting them on the reservations in a way of life that bore little relation to a self-sufficient tribal existence. The overall policy was neither ruthless enough to break up tribal culture and assimilate the Indians, generous enough to maintain tribal societies in good health, or trusting enough to see the Indians lead a meaningfully sovereign separate existence on reservations.[59]

In summary, post–Civil War discussions of race and culture in the periodical literature reflected the liberal belief in universality, albeit in complicated ways that played out quite differently for blacks, Chinese, and Indians. The Negro Question ended in exhaustion and a willingness to shelve indefinitely the pursuit of civic equality. The possibility of a future of civic equality in which African Americans had raised themselves by their bootstraps was indentured to a hierarchical present. The dispute over Chinese immigration, by contrast, though it ended in a political defeat, featured a more vigorous and wide-ranging defense of liberal values (including some classic Thomas Nast cartoons) that betrayed little of the defensiveness and weariness found in discussions of the fate of the Negro. In the case of Native Americans, liberal universalism registered a political triumph, at least in principle, with the passage of the Dawes Act, only to be followed by failure in practice.[60]

Differences of tone with regard to the prospects of race-mixing and assimilation were evident, too, ranging from optimism in the case of the Indians to thinly concealed pessimism for the immediate future of African Americans, for whom things would have to get worse before they could get better. In these debates the meaning of race was defined not only by skin color, but by the perceived level of civilization, work habits and education, cultural survivability, religious belief, ideology, scientific opinion, population numbers, and geographic location. In each case, a unique configuration of political interests had as much to do with final outcomes as did racial motives. "Racist thought does not necessarily produce racist action," writes one historian in arguing the case for a political explanation of the exclusion act. Politics deals with particular issues in uniquely different ways that are difficult to describe in terms of pure rationality, ideological consistency, or even the triumph of majority opinion.

I would only add that the attribution of racist thought can itself be quite problematic. In each case, deracination—the nearly total reformatting of cultural identities—was the objective. This was a harsh approach: brutally honest in the way that the issues were discussed and brutal, too, in its resort to hierarchical judgments that today would be considered unpardonably offensive. Yet in the case of Native Americans it was also suffused with the kind of guilt that is most difficult to bear, the kind that accompanies the conviction that a tragic result is inevitable from one's behavior. The admission of helplessness in resolving the Negro Question was also testimony to the limited ability of good intentions and political behavior to produce the desired consequences. The failure of egalitarianism was due less to political cowardice or tactical ineptitude than to the limits imposed by the temper of the times on what it was possible to achieve.

Whatever we may think of these debates and their outcomes, American liberals mounted intellectual challenges to racist opinions and policies of the day in a way that at least left open the door for equality at home and abroad. With regard to the domestic and foreign implications of liberal egalitarianism, the domestic would appear to have greater weight, for the possibility of a genuine universalism has long been challenged by the cynical observation that idealism in international affairs is directly proportional to distance. The racial corollary of this perspective would suggest that the farther away the nonwhite people, the easier it is to be nonracist. That is, sweeping pieties about global brotherhood are not to be taken seriously because nothing of consequence is likely to be done about them. But this is the kind of cliché that needs closer examination, just as does Adam Smith's oft-misinterpreted observation in his *Theory of Moral Sentiments* that a man would more likely be put out by the loss of a finger than by news of a catastrophic earthquake in China.[61]

For a number of reasons egalitarianism had a more open field of action abroad than at home. Liberals operating in a foreign environment did not have to face the kinds of domestic political roadblocks erected by interest groups who felt threatened by the presence of blacks, Chinese, and Native Americans. In the absence of such political pressures, they enjoyed relatively uncontested freedom to voice their view that race was not a fundamental factor in international relations. Abroad, missionary voices were louder, workers were less fearful for their jobs, and travelers and intellectuals were more concerned with knowledge and progress from a universal perspective. In the international context, moreover, there was no effective ideology with which to counter universalism. American racists, unlike some in Europe, did not have an ideology or worldview with which to conceptualize the race issue abroad in a fundamentally hierarchical fashion. Instead, the kinds of people who were interested in the wide world tended, both theoretically and practically, to have a broader perspective in which egalitarian racial views harmonized with globalization.

All of which is to say the external world was the natural habitat for universalism as both a matter of principle and as a practical political matter. If globalization began at home, it ended abroad. The following two chapters discuss the ways in which racial and cultural views were applied to an understanding of problems overseas. But that same view also left room for accepting imperialism as a necessary part of a global civilizing mission.

7

Beyond Orientalism

Explaining Other Worlds

Despite its spectacular achievements, civilization fell far short of living up to its global pretensions. In 1869, John Fiske pointed out that civilized communities, chiefly Euro-American societies, constituted only "a numerical minority of mankind." Another writer reminded his readers that civilization "does not embrace all the nations of the earth; nor does it carry onward and upward with equal steps all that are within its area." This numerical asymmetry prompted a wide-ranging discussion in the periodical literature about the future of the world's nonindustrialized populations that differed in some fundamental respects from the debate about the future of non-Caucasian minorities at home. Although assimilation was the dominant theme domestically, it was not possible to think about non-Western societies in the same way. Some peoples would undoubtedly be inundated by the tidal wave of globalization, but only a few "superficial thinkers" were counting on the rapid dissolution of age-old Islamic and Asian societies. For the foreseeable future, the emerging global civilization would have to contend with the survivability, resistance, and capacity for learning and adaptation of many long-lived societal groupings with deep civilizational roots of their own. Expectations of how these other worlds would fare in the encounter among civilizations, and the reasons for their likely success or failure, varied enormously.[1]

The Problem of Islamic Antimodernism

America's modest commercial, cultural, and political ties with Muslim lands did not prevent American journals from displaying a high degree of curiosity about Islamic civilization. The Eastern Question, the future of Egypt and Africa, the relationship between Hindus and Muslims in India, the Great

Game in Asia, pilgrimages to the Holy Land, and the competition between Christianity and Islam in Africa served as thematic points of departure for exploring the relationship between Muslim societies and the modern world. "When, as in these our days, aggressive civilization is brought into so close and so frequent contact with Mahometans," wrote the orientalist and philologist Fitzedward Hall, "it is only natural that curiosity about their religion and its founder should be more than usually active." There was much to be curious about, given the relative strangeness of the Islamic world. General George McClellan, who for a time contributed occasional reflections on the Middle East, suggested that a colony of invaders from Jupiter or Saturn would seem no less strange than the peoples of Islamic lands. Still, he believed that Muslim societies were not so alien as to be beyond comprehension on their own terms.[2]

Anticipating the approach that would be taken in countless Western civilization courses in the following century, some writers were quick to affirm the positive historical "contributions" of Islam during its golden age. It was, after all, a monotheistic faith that had played a huge role in preserving and transmitting the classical heritage of the West during Europe's Middle Ages. Islam had also made some notable additions of its own to civilization. In one account, the Arab conquests were likened to a thunderstorm: "They fertilized while they destroyed; and from one end of the then known world to the other, with their religion they sowed seeds of literature, of commerce, and of civilization." If Charles Martel had not turned back the raiding party at Tours, the absorption of Europe into the magnificent Moorish culture would have been " 'the least of our evils," according to a noted historian of Islamic Spain. Another point in favor of Islam was that Muslim societies had been relatively tolerant of religious strangers in their midst, more so than the Christian societies of Europe had been when the shoe was on the other foot. Charles Dudley Warner urged his readers "not to forget that they have set some portions of Christendom a lesson of religious toleration." When instances of present-day Islamic extremism were brought up, most notably the "Bulgarian horrors" sensationalized by Gladstone, defenders were quick to point out that such behavior was a violation of basic Islamic principles. An inflammatory writer like John W. Draper could even maintain that Islam was far friendlier to science than his bête noir, Roman Catholicism.[3]

But for every author who praised Islam's positive impact on civilization there were many others who belittled it. "There was no Arabian Plato or Aristotle," insisted one clerical writer. To detractors, the caliphates shone only by comparison with the then-wretched state of a barbarous medieval Europe, while the Ottoman Turks had excelled solely in military organization and armament. Tear away the romantic veil, and the much-praised Haroun al-Raschid was revealed as "a representative Oriental despot." Even those who were willing to credit Moorish achievements agreed that it had been all downhill since the *reconquista*. "What have the Moors done since they left Granada?" asked the normally generous Charles Dudley Warner. "What have the Moors ever done since, anywhere, that has been of the least service to the world?" Islam had done very little of late, it seemed, except to dwell on its extraordinary past. "Its work is done," concluded the Harvard theologian and social reformer James Freeman Clarke. "It is a hard, cold, cruel, empty faith, which should give way to the purer forms of a higher civilization."[4]

Islam's important affinities with Christianity and its status as a universal religion unbound by race or place won more than a few admiring comments, as did the faith's austere beauty, inner consistency, and ability to translate orthodoxy into orthopraxy. But while "an ideal Islam" had its attractions, real-world Islamic civilization seemed unquestionably inferior in nearly every respect. Time and again, reports from travelers to the Arab world overflowed with revulsion at what had been witnessed. Passing through the Holy Land, Jacob R. Freese, a commissioner to the Paris Exposition of 1867, shared the following impression: "Cursed in the past and doubly cursed in the present, Jerusalem sits like a widow in her weeds," a view shared to varying degrees by the likes of Melville and Mark Twain. Travelers to Alexandria reported never before having encountered "so much nakedness, filth, and dirt, so much poverty, and such enjoyment of it, or at least indifference to it." The people in Morocco, a traveler noted, were "uniformly repulsive." A portrayal of the Bedouins indicted them for being deceitful, treacherous, and filthy, for thievery, licentiousness, and indolence, and, before the days of fast food, for eating with their hands. Arabs possessed "a disposition to treachery requiring perpetual vigilance on the part of the traveler." They also had "filthy and licentious habits." Particularly repulsive—and titillating—was the sequestration of women in the harem and the mistreatment of women generally. This kind of existence, according to the well-published clergyman Charles S. Robinson, was "inconceivable to our enlightened minds." *The Nation* described Orientals as "essentially childish," reminiscent of "precocious children," and more like girls than boys. And, oh yes, they were cruel to animals.[5]

Islamic government? It was an oxymoron. "Of all rottenness and dead men's bones that the world ever saw, the Mohammedan state contains the worst and the most," said a review in *The Atlantic*. Clarke, in a piece on the place of Mohammed in universal history, concluded that Islam's absolute authority meant that "the worst Christian government, be it that of the Pope or the Czar, is infinitely better than the best Mohammedan government." As a faith, "It has made social life lower. Its governments are not governments. Its virtues are stoical. It makes life barren and empty. It encourages a savage pride and cruelty. It makes men tyrants or slaves, women puppets, religion the submission to an infinite despotism." *The Nation* pronounced Ottoman rule to be "a tyranny more blighting than any ever known in Europe."[6]

Although Americans tended to be disgusted by what they saw, Islamic hatred of Christian societies was thought to run even deeper. "It is scarcely possible for the ordinary Christian to realize the contempt which a Mahometan feels for him from a moral point of view," wrote an essayist in *The North American Review*. Although a few writers suggested that mutual understanding was possible, most saw Islam as a faith of uncompromising fanaticism and intolerance. "With the true son of Islam there can be nothing but absolute hatred and contempt for unbelievers," wrote McClellan, "no servitude more galling than Christian rule; no triumph more rapturous than that which enables him to grind his heel into the Christian's face." Protestant missionaries, in particular, vehemently denied the idea that Islam was a tolerant creed. Whatever success it enjoyed was attributed, erroneously, to *jihad*. When a Turkish *effendi*(an educated gentleman) was given space to make his case in *Appletons'*, he only reinforced the idea of a struggle of civilizations by contrasting the West's technological and material foundation to Islam's unpolluted spiritual base. There seemed little reason to humor a civilization that was at its core irredeemably hostile to others.[7]

The big question for most observers, with the exception of missionary types who would have answered near unanimously in the negative, was whether Islamic civilization was capable of modernization. The major test case of Islam's regenerative possibilities was the tottering Ottoman Empire, perceived as a

historical "anachronism," decadent and "sinking into barbarism." Six hundred years of Ottoman rule, exclaimed Godkin, had "converted so many of the
fairest lands on the globe into wastes which no civilized man ever traverses
without shame and indignation." Painfully aware of their weakness vis-à-vis
Europe, from 1839 to 1876 the Ottoman sultans had embarked on a program
of self-strengthening, the *Tanzimat* or "reorganization" reforms, that created
more than a few believers in the possibility of self-directed westernization.
S. G. W. Benjamin, who would serve as the first U.S. minister to Persia in the
1880s, thought that the Ottomans had made great strides since the 1820s.
Warner, in reflecting on the impact of American-founded Robert College in Istanbul, observed that Western-style education was the solution to the Eastern
Question. The next generation, he believed, might bring "a stalwart and intelligent people, who would not only be able to grasp Constantinople but to ad-
minister upon the decaying Turkish empire as the Osmanli administered upon
the Greek." With a good government, there was no reason why Constantinople
could not return to commercial greatness. Signs of change were already visible
in the growing prevalence of Western fashions and manners in Istanbul, and
even the sequestration of women might be ended with a few more decades of
progress.[8]

But to most American onlookers, these efforts were destined to fail; even if
good intentions were granted, it was felt, the problems were too deep-rooted to
be addressed through reforms. Most writers would have agreed with *Harper's*
editor, A. H. Guernsey, that only incurable optimists believed in the possibility
of Ottoman reform. The very idea was a "hallucination," insisted *The Nation*.
Henry O. Dwight, the Constantinople correspondent for the *New York Tribune*
between 1876 and 1879 and author of *Turkish Life in Time of War*, suggested
that Western education would do little good. Scratch a seemingly westernized
Turk, he wrote, and "if he is subjected to analysis he will be found entirely
unchanged, and still a Turk in feeling, to the very backbone . . . a blood-thirsty
fanatic fiend, who is ready to take arms against the world." "Powerful to destroy,
they have ever been powerless to construct," said *Appletons'*. "Industry and art
are foreign to them. They know no pleasure more delicate than the grimaces of
buffoons, lascivious dances, and spectacles of revolting obscenities."[9]

Although the Ottomans appeared to welcome Western forms, the changes
were dismissed as being only skin deep. "All this affectation of dress and manner before Europeans is but a masquerade," concluded the "roving American"

in *Appletons'*. "The fire of the militant faith still burns," agreed its editor, "a savage spirit lurks beneath the apparent submission of the Turk to the necessities of Western civilization." It was true that Muslims respected Western power and were quick to adopt the latest military technology, but they had little use otherwise for Western civilization and its ideas. The novelist and essayist John William De Forest was astounded at how little impact the West had made on the Islamic world after centuries of living together cheek by jowl in southeastern Europe. To some eyes, the East appeared to be as resistant to assimilation as it had been in Roman times.[10]

More unremittingly Islamophobic than any other journal, Godkin's *Nation* was unimpressed by superficial indicators of modernity, insisting that "there is not as yet any sign that a single Western idea has made the slightest impression on any Turkish brain." Although occasional reforms were all well and good, Godkin insisted that they could not begin to compensate for "the absence of courts of justice, or for the want of police, or for the lawlessness and violence of the police, or for constant exposure to spoliation and outrage at the hands of an armed caste, raised by custom and tradition above the law." Convinced that the royal family was suffering from sexual exhaustion, Godkin attributed Ottoman decline to a creeping sensualist suicide in which the harem and female slaves had bred an increasingly enfeebled dynastic elite. It was pointless to count on top-down reform from men raised in the corrupting environment of the harem, "that most beastly institution." "All the sultans," ranted one editorial," like all the Asiatic despots, seem insane to the Western world in our day, owing to their habit of gratifying every whim the moment it seizes them, and recognizing no artificial bounds to the power of their will." While top-down political reform drew much attention, scarcely any attention was given to the role of westernizing intellectuals within these societies.[11]

The journal's anti-Ottoman views were seconded many times over by other commentators on the empire who dwelt on "the obstinate stupidity of its rulers, in refusing to recognize and to conform to the spirit of the age." In addition to pathologies at the very head of society, a gangrene of corruption had spread well throughout the body politic to the point that reform-minded Turks were unlikely to be able to push through meaningful reforms. Even the best-intentioned sultans were therefore powerless to bring to heel subordinates who felt free to disregard commands from the center. The net result, concluded Edwin De Leon, a versatile southern writer who had served as consul in

Alexandria in the 1850s, was that "the Turkish administration and policy are as traditional and immutable as the religion of Mohammed, and can be altered just as readily." *The Galaxy* suggested that if human ingenuity had been given free rein to create the worst possible polity, "the system could not have been worse than that which exists in European Turkey."[12]

What was the source of this cultural immobility? Race, conceived of as a biological handicap, was not a problem, nor was Ottoman misrule the taproot of this listlessness. Rather, the first cause, the unmoved mover, was Islam. For Godkin, writing under a byline in *The North American Review*, Islam was a faith "wholly out of harmony with the needs and aspirations of modem society," an antimodern creed that was "simply an obstacle to be set aside, if not destroyed, with as little ceremony as possible." Some of the more striking contrasts with the West—militancy, polygamy, and the slave trade—were, according to *Harper's Weekly*, "not accidental bad habits," but rather "the legitimate outward expression of an inner inferiority in ethnical, mental, and moral traits." Was Islam really a beautiful and noble creed? If so, said one reviewer, "only an ironical Providence can have ordained that it should bring forth so foul and fetid fruit." On another occasion, a reviewer quoted approvingly the words of an author who, after pointing to the absurdities of Islam's sacred texts, was surprised "not that Moslems should be steeped in ignorance, vice, and superstition, but that their moral and intellectual capacities have not been more completely crushed beneath this weight of rubbish." Following this line of reasoning, the achievements of Islamic civilization had been won in spite of Islam rather than because of it. "In short," said *The Nation*, "it is the religion which has worked the mischief and which has created what seems an almost impassable moral social, and intellectual barrier between the Mussulman world . . . and all the active, moving portion of the race."[13]

Unfortunately, the impulse to fanatical revivalism that roiled the Islamic world seemed far more powerful than desires for reform. In 1869, Richard Hinton reported the spread of "religious enthusiasm" throughout Asia. More than a decade later, in the course of recounting a visit to see the "Howling Dervishes," one missionary noted uneasily that "there has been a great revival of Mohammedanism lately and fanaticism." Explanations of this religious enthusiasm were usually presented in a secular register. Fanaticism and revivalism, far from pointing to a revival of Islamic greatness, were widely perceived as symptoms of Islam's continued backwardness. All the failures in the here and now, General McClellan suggested, made martyrdom more attractive. "The masses of the Orientals have little but life to lose in this world," he wrote, "and much to gain in the other by entering it direct from a conflict with the unbeliever." Clearly, argued Professor Edward S. Salisbury, impending political collapse dictated the shoring up of religious foundations, including tightened restrictions on missionary activity that elicited predictable howls of outrage. These attempts at religious renewal evoked numerous comparisons with the beleaguered papacy, whose antimodern biases had prompted a zealous defense of the very creed that had been the source of failure. But the more rabidly Muslims sought redemption through their faith, the more irredeemably decadent they became. This fusion of faith and power, once a source of strength and durability for Islamic societies, was now the cause of their inability to modernize.[14]

But Islamic revivalism was less a threat than an inconvenience. Muslim armies could no longer traverse large distances to strike terror into the hearts of Christian populations. To be sure, an aroused Islam remained capable of causing difficulties to infidels who were unfortunate enough to get caught exposed in the occasional local squall. But *The Nation* dismissed out of hand the possibility that an Islamist revival would have major political repercussions:

> The notion that there is enough Mussulman fanaticism left anywhere in the East to produce a formidable movement is a chimera. Whenever during the last forty years this fanaticism has been tested for warlike purposes it has been found all but dead. It is undoubtedly useful in giving glow and animation to editorial articles, but for little else.

A formerly desperate struggle of civilizations was now essentially all over except for the cheering, the contest having been decided in favor of the West. A conflict of civilizations implied ongoing contested contact, but the only response to the continuing challenge of the West was "the rapid moral decay of Islam." Islam still had its zeal, Godkin thought, but because science was on the side of the infidels, the West's victory was irreversible.[15]

For many missionaries, a modernizing Christianity seemed to be the only solution to Islamic stasis. Give Christianity a chance, with adequate governmental support and protection, and then one would find, as one such plea argued, "that even Arab Moslems were, in the main, very much like all other races of mankind." On such grounds, Samuel Wells Williams, the pioneering scholar of China and Japan, argued on behalf of a strong governmental commitment to a religious civilizing mission in the Middle East, lest the region remain "degraded and turbulent." But others were not so sure of Christianity's ability to turn the situation around. So meager was the harvest of converts to date that *The Nation* was openly suspicious of "missionary slang" and questioned the usefulness of efforts to date in the Middle East, which seemed to have focused largely on proselytizing communicants of other Christian sects. "In any other branch of life," it editorialized , such behavior "would be considered false pretences, malversation, and a breach of trust." In this view, Christendom, which had internal problems of its own, had too little power to become a catalyst for modernity. Arguing that the truth of a creed was judged by its "fitness to succeed," one reviewer went so far as to wonder what the failure to uproot Islam meant for Christianity's claim to be a universal religion.[16]

One irony of the American view of Islam was the belief that, despite its historical and doctrinal connections to Christianity, of all the world's great civilizations it seemed the least capable of adapting to global modernity. On the whole, Islamic civilization was seen as irredeemably antimodern because it was a faith that, in Godkin's view, caused "a sort of paralysis, deadening the faculties." Taking care to deny he harbored any religious bigotry, Dwight insisted that "the fact needs no proof that the Mohammedan religion is opposed to the spirit of Western civilization." With all avenues of progress apparently closed, the best possible solution would have been for Islamic civilization providentially to disappear altogether. Freese, for one, gave voice to such a wish when he exclaimed: "Oh ! that we had the power to wipe this people from off the land which they so much disgrace and pollute by their presence!"

But this was clearly a fantasy. In the absence of compelling commercial or strategic interests that would bring a weightier Western presence, the only realistic prospect for the region was to become a living museum of cultural backwardness. For example, after taking a tour of the Nile, one traveler was convinced that the spell cast by tradition was so powerful that even the distant future would show little improvement. He foresaw that "many seasons will yet show to the traveler the same Arab village, with its gray-headed sheik, its indolent men, coy women, and naked young beggars." Or, as a review in *The Atlantic Monthly* put it: "Islam, common enemy of civilization and Christianity, has been our friend in this one thing, that it has kept for our time and a future time a preserve of voyage and adventure, where tourists will not swarm, and where there will, for a long time yet, be something to explore and discover." The Middle East appeared destined to remain a remote backwater where Islam, formerly a carrier of civilization, would reign only as a chronically enfeebled opponent.[17]

China: New Wine in Old Cultural Bottles

In contrast to this gloomy view of Islamic civilization, American images of East Asia were far more optimistic. To the extent that the cosmic belief systems of East Asia qualified as religions in a Western sense, religion was far less a barrier to modernization in East Asia than it was in the Middle East. Although race might seem to have been the logical stand-in for religion, it was instead culture, in the form of seemingly timeless traditions, that was commonly identified as the chief impediment to progress. But even the fortress-like cultural walls of Asia could be reduced by means of cultural revitalization. Had the verdict been otherwise, it is difficult to see how confidence in a global civilization could have been sustained, inasmuch as the fate of China, Japan, and the Pacific touched Americans more directly than did the future of Islam. The sizable immigration from China and the commercial attractiveness of East Asia introduced important practical considerations that were present scarcely at all in discussions of the Middle East.[18]

Americans were more embarrassed by their lack of knowledge of China than of perhaps any other country. In 1887, the western writer A. A. Hayes complained of the nation's "crass ignorance" about China. By that time, the shortfall in learning was beginning to be addressed by an outpouring of books about the Middle Kingdom, but the situation was still far from satisfactory. John Bonner, best known for his children's histories, noted "whole libraries of works on China by residents and travelers" that conveyed "no information." A large part of the problem was the sheer difficulty of penetrating Chinese culture. The formidable barriers to learning the Chinese written and spoken languages were beginning to be successfully assaulted, but Sinology remained an amateur discipline acutely self-conscious of its shortcomings. Every culture was different, of course, but China's was "peculiarly dense and puzzling," according to one reviewer of S. Wells Williams's pioneering *Middle Kingdom*. China was a "riddle" to Westerners. It was difficult to penetrate the Chinese mind, to enter into the spirit of Chinese literature in the same way that was possible with classical Greek and Roman works. The abstract philosophical problem of radical translation became acutely concrete when one was faced with the need to render cultural meanings between Chinese and English. Trying to explain the difficulty of translating the U.S. Constitution into Chinese, one author noted the absence of corresponding words such as liberty or the judiciary, or terms such as "we, the people." How could the meaning of liberalism be rendered when there were no liberals or liberal ideas in China?[19]

Once the glimmerings of understanding did start to emerge, it was the differences that leaped to the eye. As the journalist John Addison Porter put it, "one begins to realize the vast differences separating their race from our own— differences extending not merely to manners and customs, but, apparently, to the very structure of the brain and texture of the heart." "We find in China, to some extent, what we might expect to find if we could get across to a neighboring planet," said Bonner, using the same analogy that McClellan had employed to convey Islam's strangeness. It quickly became trite to describe Chinese culture as an antipodal inversion of the West in nearly every respect. This fascination with differences could be instructive, in its own way, in improving one's understanding by emphasizing the relativity of cultural viewpoints. Thus one writer suggested that by juxtaposing Chinese and Western worldviews, the two combined would result in a cultural equivalent of stereoscopic vision. For others, China's uniqueness offered unparalleled opportunities for historical and anthropological study. According to an essay devoted to Chinese music, China was "a picture of marvelous antiquity, not dead and embalmed, but living . . . a beautiful case of arrested development" made to order for in-depth scholarly investigation.[20]

All this would seem to suggest that China was the paradigm of the unfathomable "other," but it was widely understood that this kind of thinking could be taken too far. Assertions of the uniqueness and oddity of China were, according to the California ethnologist Stephen Powers, but "the shallow objection to the theory of the common origin of mankind." First contacts always brought with them impressions of strangeness, but ongoing interaction produced familiarity that in time generated the kind of effective communication that confirmed the common humanity underlying each culture. The emphasis on identity comes across in one reviewer's glowing appraisal of a book that was particularly sensitive to China. The author invited the reader to view the Chinese "as men and women with like feelings as ourselves, and not, as has often been the case, as curiosities, if not monstrosities, with whom it is needless to cultivate sympathy." Before long, a growing number of writers were capable of explaining how the world looked from the Chinese point of view. After reading such culturally informed works, said a review in *Harper's,* it was easy to see how the Chinese could see Christian foreigners as barbarians or how they might chafe at the inferior status assigned to them in the Western-ordered system of international relations.[21]

Improved understanding even brought with it a degree of cultural relativism, a disposition, as *The Nation* noted, "to exalt, or at least to justify, Oriental thought and practice as something different, but not worse, in comparison with our own." Perhaps the editors were speaking from experience, for the journal was itself a main source of China worship in its appreciation of Chinese customs and refinement. It was highly impressed by China's unmatched record of continuity, which suggested that it had done more than a few things right. "We have much to learn from the Chinese," wrote Godkin in 1869. His journal was also quick to excuse China's barbaric punishments by pointing out that until quite recently Western legal codes had been equally harsh. Despite its reliance on an archaic literary canon, the examination system that regulated China's governance by an educated elite struck a favorable chord, particularly among civil service reformers. Chinese cuisine also had its pioneering defenders. If Americans did not understand Chinese tastes, wrote one Walter A. Rose, that was their loss. "How prone man is to despise that which is beyond his comprehension!" he chided. A few writers even challenged the stereotype of China's cultural stasis. Professor J. S. Sewall of Bowdoin College, who had sailed with Admiral Matthew C. Perry to Japan, added a Viconian twist to the usual view of the metronomic oscillation of Chinese history by insisting that "the progress of national life has made each century broader and richer than the last in the appliances of oriental comfort and art."[22]

Although China had its charms and glories, when measured by modern standards it was generally acknowledged to be in a state of decay. "As far as soap and water furnish a test," noted one observer, "Peking is in a very primitive state." Beijing was "an epitome of decay," wrote one traveler, "a skeleton dropping into dust." From a distance, it was a beautiful metropolis, but once inside one was met "on every side by ruins, poverty, dust, dirt, and bad odors." "No sewers, no closets, no drains!" complained one report. "Streets uncleaned for centuries, save by the hogs and vultures!" Decay and dirt were simply material instantiations of inner atrophy. That most iconic structure of all, the crumbling Great Wall, was emblematic not only of cultural rot but of China's long isolation from enriching contact with the rest of the world. According to *The Nation,* China had lost "that mysterious something . . . which gives nationality its vigor, its self-reliance, and without which the finest body of philosophy in existence has but little more influence on national life than the sighing of the idle wind."[23]

Why had China fallen so far behind? The question, and its competing answers, anticipated debates that would take place a century later between those who blamed the culture and those who pointed to structural causes of paralysis. On the one hand, China was nearly everyone's outstanding example of how cultural inertia could produce backwardness and decay. Every Chinese, according to this argument, was "an inveterate hater of innovation in any thing that has become time-honored and venerable from thousands of years' usage." China's immobility and the seeming paralysis of its institutions were explained by a slavish "veneration for antiquity." China's high culture had fallen prey to the cultural equivalent of foot-binding, in which the finest minds of each generation were permanently hobbled. "We could not help but regret that, in China, men's brains, like women's feet, must be so cramped," said one author of a piece on the examination system. Education, which should have been a progressive and intellectually liberating experience, "really promoted ignorance by arresting intellectual development, and forbidding the spirit of inquiry." For others, the root cause lay in vested interests, the system of oriental despotism that formerly had served the Chinese well but which now repressed the individual freedoms essential to cultural advance. It was as if the West continued to be ruled by Tory squires hostile to all modern improvements. But inertia was no longer an option. The choice, according to Raphael Pumpelly, was between reorganization and progress or disintegration.[24]

For all the complaints about China's attachment to tradition, only a few skeptics doubted its capacity to modernize. Numerous statements attested to the native intelligence of the Chinese people. Former Secretary of State William H. Seward, following a stopover in China during his round-the-world tour, asserted that "the Chinese, though not of the Caucasian race, have all its political, moral, and social capabilities." Despite ethnocentric conceits and other shortcomings, General James Harrison Wilson, the author of a book on commercial possibilities in China, contended that "the Chinaman's natural intelligence . . . is quite as great as that of other races." He went on to predict that he "may be expected to play his full part in the future of the world." China's culture was both its greatest weakness and its greatest strength, for the virtues of the Chinese people, particularly their undiminished vitality and commercial acumen, it was widely agreed, provided a solid cultural platform for modernization. One reviewer predicted that "the regeneration of China will be accomplished, like the operation of leaven in meal, without shattering the vessel."[25]

The inability of China's intellectuals to understand natural science was a poor predictor of future performance. "In such knowledge he is a child," said one essay, "but in mental force he may at the same time be a giant." Institutions like the examination system, the capacity for hard work and deferred gratification, and the high seriousness of state functionaries could, if suitably redirected, become immense advantages. As for Confucianism, the fact that it was not a Western-style religion suggested that it could be more easily overcome or adapted to the requirements of the modern world. Not surprisingly, then, many were quick to detect signs of a reinvigoration of national spirit. "A mental awakening is taking place among the people of China, by which the Chinese mind will be brought proportionally nearer to our own," declared the Rev. W. A. P. Martin. Richard J. Hinton wrote that the Chinese had already "crossed the Rubicon" and were "breaking through the reserve and isolation of centuries." The progress already made, according to *The Nation*, was enough "to convince the most sceptical as to the possibility of her advance in everything which makes a nation great."[26]

Unfortunately, it was equally apparent to most Americans that China would not modernize without external stimulus. Either the Chinese did not want to modernize at all, or, what came to the same thing, they wanted the fruits of modernity without paying the steep cultural cost of acquiring them. According to Porter, change would not take place in the absence of "some extraordinary and constant friction." That friction could take a number of forms. Missionaries and their allies tended to view Christianity as the key to China's spiritual and secular salvation. Writing of "the missionary invasion of China," W. L. Kingsley asserted that "the revolution of thought has begun." But many doubted the ability of Christianity alone to effect China's rejuvenation. Porter gave pride of place to commerce, as did many others. Christianity, he argued, was "far more likely to be reinforced or preceded by the advances of commerce and science, than to lead in the regeneration of that country." Observers in China in the 1880s were already noting that the impact of the missionaries was felt chiefly through their schools and hospitals rather than through the Gospel.[27]

Ultimately, religion, commerce, and science could help to realize China's cultural potential only through the "friction" applied by the application of military power. Partially civilized nations, asserted one treatise on international law, "yield only to superior force and cunning." Even those who sympathized with Chinese complaints about foreign imperialism tended to believe that the use of force was unavoidable in order to shake China out of its deep ethnocentrism. "It is useless to say we must not exercise any pressure upon her," argued *The Nation.* "If we really allowed her to do as she pleased, not a foreigner would be found on her soil within three months." It was possible to write humorously about the Chinese detestation of foreign barbarians. "The feeling pervades all classes of the people, and not only the people, but the lower animals," noted the prolific travel writer Thomas Knox. "Chinese ponies snort and start when you come near them, the dogs bark at you, the cats snarl and flee with enlarged tails and elevated back hair, and even the meek and ruminant cow takes a shy at you with her horns." But it was no laughing matter. Equality of potential was one thing, but the navel-gazing of the Chinese produced only "absurd pretensions of superiority."[28]

It was also unclear how rapidly the transformation of China would take place. Given the immensity of the required change, some believed that the transition to modernity would be a protracted affair. *The Nation,* responding to complaints of fitful progress, suggested that "the most far-seeing policy, after all, consists in the slow, gradual, but steady development of powers which centuries of stagnation have paralyzed." President Grant, on his own round-the-world tour, resorted to an alpine metaphor. While progress in America occurred with the speed of an avalanche, he said, "in the valley of the Yangtze it could only be that of the glacier." But others envisioned a faster pace. *Appletons'* was betting that the introduction of railways would have explosive consequences. With the railroad leading the way, it predicted that "the Chinese will span twenty centuries at a leap." Whatever the scenario, current velocity was an unreliable indicator of the potential for explosive growth in the future.[29]

Although the direction and speed of the process were unclear, and although it was easy to foresee a turbulent stretch of diplomacy down the road (see

Chapter 9), what stands out in retrospect is the general conviction that China could and would modernize. The only questions that remained were when and how. China's weakness was due not to race, but to a stagnant way of life that contained within itself the resources indispensable to revitalization once the rudiments of Western ideology were assimilated. Most striking is the contrast between the upbeat prognoses of China's future and the dismal prospects of Islamic civilization. Americans clearly believed that a non-Christian, nonmonotheistic country had a greater potential for modernization than Islamic or even Roman Catholic lands whose cultural traditions and religions were much closer to those of the West. In this comparison, religion loomed larger than both race and culture as an obstacle on the road to modernity.

The De-Orientalization of Japan

The dramatic metamorphosis of Japan in these years proved beyond a doubt—to West and East alike—that a tradition-laden culture could find the inner resources and the will to modernize itself. As with China, writing about Japan tended initially to emphasize its other-worldly strangeness. Until Perry's arrival, according to one account in 1868, Japan was viewed "as a kind of dreamland, or as belonging to another world." Like other oriental societies, Japan seemed at first "as remote from human knowledge and interest as though the empire were shut up in another planet." It was, one early appraisal said in 1872, "a mere terra incognita . . . of particulars we know next to nothing." The following year, E. H. House, an early Japan hand, complained of "the universal ignorance upon the subject of Japan." But that changed soon enough. After some bizarre initial speculations, the quantity of writing about Japan exploded to the point that *The Nation*'s reviewer was complaining of yet another addition to "the overburdened shelves in the library of works on Japan." As information continued to accumulate and improve in quality, it was not long before Japan was fitted into a global narrative as one of its most strikingly optimistic chapters. By 1889, *The Nation* declared flatly that Japan compared favorably with any Western nation "in everything that makes a country happy, prosperous, and contented."[30]

Even before the scope and pace of Japan's changeover became apparent, the land received rave reviews for its physical and cultural charm. To begin with, writers gushed over its physical beauty, the transparency of the atmosphere, the brilliance of the sky, and the purity of the air. Japan was "the most beautiful country in the world," said one traveler. The elegance of Japanese art—bronzes, lacquer ware, porcelain, and painting—also made an extraordinary impression on American visitors. "What has really astounded me more, perhaps, than any thing here, is art," said James Brooks, former congressman and world traveler. Whatever the benefit to Japan of contact with the West, said the painter Theodore Wores, "the benefit we have derived through contact with their art is inestimable." True, critics were quick to point out that the Japanese were deficient in the rendering of perspective and depiction of human forms, but their way with nature was amazing, and as the reporter Noah Brooks noted, "everything is drawn with a nice firmness of touch which reveals the hand of the true artist." Certain themes, according to *The Nation*, were drawn "without formality, with absolute freedom, and with almost absolute truth." On its own terms, Japanese art was "a wonder to all European artists and critics."[31]

The aesthetic sense, a "richness of symbolism," was, moreover, deeply suffused in the popular consciousness and, if transferable, suggested possibilities for the creation of a genuinely democratic art in the United States, "free from snobbery and vulgar standards." Summing up the artistic exhibits at one world's fair, one observer declared that "after the Japanese collection everything looks in a measure commonplace, almost vulgar." The Japanese garden was widely praised as "a marvelously beautiful artificial landscape." Although the country's architecture had yet to be fully appreciated, Japanese homes were admired for their airiness, cleanliness, and simplicity. Japanese music and literature were not highly regarded in most estimations, though Japanese poetry had its supporters, but the overall aesthetic balance sheet was overwhelmingly favorable nonetheless.[32]

Japanese society and people were similarly extolled. In contrast to the dirt and disorder that assaulted the senses in so many other non-Western lands, Japan was a peerlessly clean, orderly, industrious, well-regulated society. The Japanese themselves possessed a long list of virtues. They were, according to one report, "an enterprising, energetic, ambitious, and capable people, but amiable, sunny-tempered, courteous to each other and to strangers." Their politeness to strangers surpassed anything seen in the West, "even among the high-bred nations of civilized Europe." Lyman Abbott described them as "brave, noble, true . . . a nation of heroes." The beauty of Japanese females was also remarked upon—with the exception of the married women who by custom colored their teeth black. One writer found it a marvelous harmonious society, apparently unplagued by poverty. "It would seem easier to realize Plato's Republic than to find such conditions actually combined," he said. The few unsparingly critical works on Japan that did appear were themselves criticized by reviewers for "unfairness and onesidedness."[33]

At first, Japan, like China, was cast in the mold of Asiatic immutability as a "living Pompeii." But as Americans became familiar with the full extent of the modernizing initiatives that followed the Meiji Restoration of 1868, it became apparent that "the curse of stationariness" was being overcome with a vengeance. Since 1854, reported Thomas Knox, Japan had "undergone a change little short of miraculous." The Japanese *Wirtschaftswunder* dispelled the idea, still quite commonplace, that all orientals were alike. On the contrary, China seemed in so many ways to be the polar opposite of Japan. "What a strange contrast do we see here to the lethargy of the bigoted and conceited Chinese!" said one review of an early sojourner's account The pioneering Japanologist William E. Griffis noted that the Japanese had not "reached that depth of disease, to have suffered with that delirium tremens of superstition, such as enthralls and paralyzes the Chinese, and prevents all modern progress." China and India were continually looking backward, "like Lot's wife," but for the Japanese, as one scholar put it, "the future is theirs." This divergence from the China narrative generated a split between American Sinophiles and Japanophiles that would resonate well into the twentieth century, but the immediate effect was to steal attention away from China to "its worthier neighbor."[34]

Although the narrative trope of the China story remained unsettled, the story line of Japan quickly took the form of a "romance." The changes, nearly everyone agreed, were "unparalleled in history." Unlike China, Japan was "just entering on the international rivalry of progress with the other great nations of the world." In just about every area of life, its traditional ways were "fast disappearing before the reasonableness of European practice." Writers groped for metaphors to describe the change. One writer compared the Japanese to "the snake that has cast its skin, or the deer that has shed its horns." Griffis, like many others, fell back on the hermitry-sociability analogy when he wrote that "the hermits have chosen the world's society." The upheaval had yet to run its course, for Western ways were still limited to the cities and to travel into the interior was to take a journey backwards in time—a universal time that reminded many of feudal Europe. But it would not be long before railroads crisscrossed the land and a fully modern commercial and industrial society emerged. There was, of course, the language barrier, a result of "the punitory miracle at Babel," but the commercial necessities of globalization would take care of the communication problem.[35]

There was very little discussion of racial disabilities in the case of the Japanese. The process of deracination through education, much talked about in theory, was being successfully implemented by a culture that appreciated the strategic importance of Western knowledge. For that reason, the Japanese embassy to the United States in 1872 was "one of the most remarkable occurrences of the day." Japanese students were described as "among the quickest and brightest in the world," which helped to explain the rapidity of the nation's progress. Those students burned with "a zeal in study that has brought many of them to the grave." Americans expected that these students would carry back with them not only their knowledge, but, of equal importance, "also liberal notions concerning the relations between the government and the people." Japanese success would in turn reverberate farther afield, particularly on the mainland of Asia. If Western pressure alone could not force China to turn around, a modernized Japan would be "the most efficient helper in breaking down the Chinese exclusiveness and altering the decay of the Flowery Kingdom." And for all the talk linking Christianization and modernization, it was undeniable that Japan was advancing without relying on Christianity. Despite its indifference to Western religion, the hope remained that Christianity would henceforth make rapid inroads, by piggybacking on Japan's modernization rather than leading it.[36]

Could the best of the old be blended with the new to produce uniform change for the better? Not everyone thought so. For Americans of romantic disposition entranced by Japan's beauty, the prospect of modernization evoked an antistrophe of loss and melancholy. "We shall miss the old picturesqueness," said Noah Brooks, adding that "possibly Japan may seem to be less happy in the new order of things." He suspected, moreover, that much loss and sorrow would result from "this pathetic spectacle of the rude awakening of a great nation." An essay on Japanese theater considered it "an open question" whether the people would be happier or wealthier. *Appletons'*, suggesting that westernization would be traumatic to the Japanese way of life, hoped that "this cup, at least, may pass from them in their present universal passion for Western civilization." A few romantics were out-and-out pessimistic. The modernization of

Japan, in one striking analogy, was "like an oyster, the opening of which killed it." For romantic antimodernists, it was sadly ironic that one of the world's most beautiful cultures should also be so intent on destroying that beauty.[37]

A simple-minded conceit that proved irresistible to many writers attributed the momentous changes to the Americanization of Japan. Perry's arrival at Edo in 1853 was seen as a world-historical event, suitable for inclusion in Fourth of July orations. Noah Brooks saw Japan's "awakening" as a product of America's westward movement: "Western thrift, western civilization, and western enterprise, crossing the American continent in successive waves, have swept at last into the sea-girt empire which peacefully slumbered by the gates of the Orient." This may have been the dominant view at first, but more serious analysts well knew that American actions alone could hardly begin to explain the amazing response that followed. Already in 1872, *The Nation* chided one essayist for failing to explain the complex causes of the revolutionary ferment in Japan. A decade later, it cautioned readers not to give too much credence to the influence of outside forces. That was "only half the truth . . . and what lay upon the other hemisphere of this political moon the average gazer saw not." The Meiji Restoration, it argued, was the product of subterranean pressures that had been building for more than a hundred years. "Commodore Perry did in reality but approach a volcano," it suggested. "Literary, political, and religious forces were at work in the core and coming to vent with a rapidity frightful to Tycoons and their followers as early as 1853." In addition, other nations had played a very significant part in Japan's rebirth, so that it was an outright falsehood to describe it as predominantly the product of American influence.[38]

By 1890, after an eventful quarter century, the key question was no longer whether Japan would modernize. Rather, it was, as *The Nation* put it: "How shall the nation take its place in the midst of modern civilization as a factor deserving consideration?" This "how" was the source of considerable apprehension. Mixed in with the superlatives was a sense of foreboding about the dangers to civilization posed by the modernization process: more than a few doubts were expressed about the degree to which the Japanese had incorporated Western values. Normally a big booster of Japan, *The Nation* would from time to time air these worries. The Japanese, it said on one occasion, "can possess only in a weak form that sense of the human brotherhood, that sympathy and imagination, which are the sources and supports of the humane spirit among us; democratic sentiments and power of imagination do not characterize that race." The powerful sense of Japanese exceptionalism and superiority, it was feared, prevented Japan from adopting more than a cosmetic cosmopolitanism.[39]

Cropping up again and again was the suspicion that all the marvelous changes were merely superficial, a veneer. The Japanophile Griffis was himself not immune to this kind of thinking. "The Japanese have made themselves such a reputation as varnishers," he wrote, "that many suspect that their adoption of Western civilization is not thorough, but is merely a thin lacquer." Because he believed modernization to be an all-or-nothing affair, unless reform was literally root and branch Japan would have "but a glittering veneer of material civilization." But Japan showed no signs of going this far. There existed "a strong tendency to conserve the national type, pride, feelings, religion, and equality with, if not superiority to all the nations of the world." In Griffis's eyes, the Japanese had not modernized. They had merely cast off feudalism, and had "returned to ancient ideas reinforced by whatever foreign elements seem best fitted to aid them in national progress." Others, in varying degrees, expressed similar concerns.[40]

In practical terms, Americans worried that, as in some European lands, Japanese modernization was proceeding without democratization as a result of being imposed from the top down. In the late 1870s *The Nation* described Japan as "a typical autocracy, in which the paternal benevolence of the Mikado becomes perverted and polluted in passing through the channels of an intricate bureaucracy." The emperor's status as priest-king was also troublesome. It presaged a potentially violent crisis on the inevitable day when his sacred status came into question, for the emperor institution rested atop "the tortoise of mythology and not on the solid earth of fact." By the late 1880s, the journal viewed the near-term prospects of a popular rule that was more than skin-deep as "exceedingly remote." Already the Japanese government showed a worrisome tendency to control opinion, and if this authoritarian behavior continued, the outside world would eventually understand "the real character of Japan's much-boasted 'civilization.'" These kinds of short-term anxieties were balanced by a need to view Japan's future in long-term perspective, from which there was "every reason for hope, of success." These things took time, after all, and the progress to date was undeniable. In comparative terms, moreover, Japan came off quite well. It already bore a close resemblance to Bismarckian Germany and was far in advance of Russia, which remained mired in oriental despotism.[41]

Overall, American writing expressed a cautious optimism that was characteristic of the liberalism of the period. On the one hand, it was too soon to predict outcomes with finality. As one author colorfully expressed it, "the new skin is yet very thin, and the new horns still 'in the velvet." But while a turn to reaction was possible, a return to "the old-time seclusion" was out of the question. "Japan is destined to remain among the accessible nations of the world," said Knox. Despite the many cautions and warnings about excessive optimism, even the skeptical Griffis saw hope in a more distant future. "A people mainly agricultural cannot be thoroughly transformed in a day," he noted. Although originally he had hoped for the Christianization of Japan, he ultimately turned to education as the answer, which he thought would slowly dissolve "the old fictions, dogmas, and mystery-plays which awed the people into obedience." Over the long term, E. H. House foresaw a period of turbulence before Japan settled down. He predicted "for a time overstrained effort and forced vitality, then a period of prolonged depression and anxiety, and subsequently a laborious but certain rise to a respectable, perhaps a prominent, position among the civilized countries of the world." But it was the early thoughts of Noah Brooks that remained the dominant view. "We know," he wrote in 1872, "whatever may be the destiny in store for Japan, that its admission into the great brotherhood of nations must ultimately advance the great interests of our common humanity." Such ideas would have a powerful effect on American perspectives on Japan in the coming century and beyond. Henceforth, Japan would constitute a key element of America's world picture.[42]

Pacific Destruction

The Pacific islands and Australasia evoked rather different racial and cultural views than those for Asia and the Middle East. In the worst case scenario, contact with the West was threatening the biological extinction of peoples who were perceived to be less developed than those in Asia or the Middle East. In the best case, racial amalgamation was rapidly eroding traditional ways of life and was offering few prospects for successfully blending modernity and tradition. In this portion of the globe, modern civilization was at its most destructive and least regenerative.

Because the experience of Australia seemed in so many ways to mirror the American story, the continent was a subject of considerable fascination.

Among the resemblances were an English-speaking population, a vast land mass, the fluidity of frontier conditions, the civilizing process, racial problems, and a problematic relationship to the mother country, all of which prompted the thought that perhaps the United States was not so unique after all. Australia demonstrated that strangeness was not the result solely of encountering difference but of discovering the existence of similarities that had been ignored. "Perhaps no part of the modern world is really less known to us, in general, than Australia," noted a *Nation* editorial.[43]

Writers took an uncommon degree of comfort in comparing Australia's racial problems with those of the United States. One writer described the aborigines as "perhaps, the most ignorant and degraded people in the world." They were "even uglier than the Negro," according to John Hayes, and "almost incapable of improvement." In this vein, *Appletons'* published a long excerpt from Anthony Trollope's journals in which the renowned novelist described the aboriginal population of Australia as "savages of the lowest kind." Although Trollope was not especially keen on Australia's white population either, he came away convinced that "the negro cannot live on equal terms with the white man." Some writers disagreed with Trollope's low opinion of the Bushmen, but few held out hope for their survival. It would be surprising if they had, since American views of the Bushmen closely resembled the extinctionist expectations that characterized thinking about Native Americans in the 1870s. For the more sympathetic, their hopeless condition was explained by "atrocious injustice" at the hands of the whites.[44]

Writings about New Zealand and the fate of the native Maoris were the exception that proved the rule. In contrast to the Bushmen, the Maoris were, according to one writer, "a fine, stalwart race, very warlike, and quick in acquiring the arts of civilization." Some found them attractive as a physical type and, in one instance at least, praised the outcome of miscegenation with their women. "Few women in any part of the world, not excepting even the Andalusian damsels, possess greater natural attractions than the half-breeds of this warlike race," said the smitten writer. Formidable as enemies and faithful as friends, they were in many respects like Native Americans, with the notable exceptions of their temperance with alcohol and their ability to adopt white ways. Sir Julius Vogel, a former premier of the New Zealand government, optimistically predicted a happy outcome for this people. They would, he foresaw, "become thoroughly civilized and incorporated with the English race. The ancient Briton presented a much less hopeful object to the Roman colonists than did the Maori to the English colonists." Unlike the Australian Bushmen, who refused to be improved, the Maoris were blessed with "intelligence and capacity of the highest order."[45]

Reports from the South Pacific and Hawaii were decidedly less sanguine, for in these regions the chief theme was cultural extermination, with an unmistakable counterpoint of melancholy. Many of the islands were described as human paradises whose ways of life were so appealing that even some of the more ghastly activities of the locals—head-hunting and poisoning in New Guinea, for example—could be seen in a surprisingly positive light. Much of the writing about the region took care to note the attractiveness of the women and the hospitality with which foreigners were received. "If the islands are lovely," said one description of Tonga, "the Islanders are more so." Of Samoa, said one writer, "the heart that can pass through Samoa unscathed must be one of flint." The first impression of this smitten traveler was that he had "fallen among the most hospitable people on earth." A socially frictionless kindness and politeness seemed to be the norm in which local life revolved around "dancing, feasting, swimming," disturbed only by occasional inter-island war-making.[46]

Obviously, the Polynesian way of life exercised a powerful attraction on many Western visitors, notwithstanding the conventional wisdom that tropical languor and sensuality were dangerously seductive. *Appletons'* wondered whether these islands "bestow their loveliness on others to the enervation of their souls and the overthrow of their energies?" The anarchic lure of easily available interracial sex was usually a part of the story. One account featured a Fijian version of the story of Cio-Cio San and Pinkerton, in which a besotted sailor, smitten by the beauty of the women and seduced by the attractions of life without work, takes a native bride, only to become "disgusted with the listless ennui of the island life." After leaving her behind to resume his peripatetic career, the wife is inevitably reduced to prostitution "and another victim of the white man's civilization is added to the already long list." It was as if the Westerners who visited these islands were traveling so far back in time as to get a real-life glimpse of paradise and to see repeated before their eyes the story of The Fall.[47]

One naval lieutenant who passed through Tahiti was led to a bitter reflection. "In the century to come Tahiti will be a meaningless name," he predicted, "and from among the people of this pushing world will have passed away a race that might have been led to no mean place in the estimation of those who read a nation's influence at its purest and truest worth." A traveler to Bora Bora described "a happy little kingdom" and hoped earnestly that the people might be "spared from French protection, civilization, and misrule." Normally unsentimental about such matters, *The Nation,* permitted itself "a tender touch of regret" before concluding that these cultures "must soon fade away entirely before the combined influence of the foreign trader and Christian missionary." With survival seemingly out of the question, the next best resort was to make use of salvage ethnography, whereby, at least, languages and customs might be preserved by western anthropology.[48]

Ironically, it was the missionaries who were often blamed for offering the forbidden fruit of a civilization that offered a problematic improvement in return. Because of the commanding American commercial and missionary presence in Hawaii, the fate of the kingdom generated a large amount of discussion. By 1881, more than three hundred books had been published on Hawaii, not to mention an imposing journal literature. In this case, however, the powerful missionary presence on the islands was reflected in one-sided evaluations of traditional Hawaiian culture in which what passed for attractions elsewhere were depicted as forbidden fruit. Hawaiian feasts were criticized for "scenes of unbridled debauchery and drunkenness." Poi, the staple dish made from mashed taro leaves, "was more fit for swine's food than for any other use." For all the poetic invocations of "dusky maids" and "feather-cinctured chiefs," argued Rev. William Thompson Bacon, the Hawaiians "were degraded and miserable creatures . . . actually living in the stone age" when Captain Cook first encountered them in 1778. They lived in "abject fear and servitude," in the grip of "an iron tyranny," said George B. Merrill, a colleague of Bret Harte, in a lengthy article. They were "a nation of thieves, and murderers, and fighters," susceptible to the "vilest intoxication" and "all the excesses of human degradation." The chiefs treated their men as slaves, and the men in turn tyrannized the women. "Stupendous revelry," said Merrill, "was the glory and the consummation of the barbaric life." High on the list of degraded native mores was an unbounded sexual promiscuity. Before discovery, the Hawaiians were "just about as bad as human nature is capable of becoming," he claimed. It was no accident that they had been called the cannibal islands.[49]

Even so, disgust with the native way of life tended to mix polyphonically with guilt and confusion over the extent of white responsibility for the rapid decline in the native Hawaiian population. A catastrophic population crash forced Americans to confront anew the tragic aspect of civilization contact. "The only real good civilization seems to have done them is to lessen their number," said an 1868 essay in *The Overland Monthly*. "The Hawaiian is being peaceably extinguished," announced *The Nation* in 1879. Sadly, by 1860 more than half the original population had been "civilized and Christianized out of existence." When the effects of racial mixing were added to the equation, it would not be long before no pure-blood Hawaiians remained. In another essay, the editors, treating the phenomenon in a clinical, matter-of-fact manner, noted that the islands were being quickly repopulated by Asians and Caucasians. In a few years, they predicted that "there will be no more Sandwich Islanders, but only a number of rich foreigners with their Chinese proletariat."[50]

Much of the decline was attributed to sexually transmitted diseases. "The Hawaiians have acquired scarcely more fame as a civilized than as a syphilized race," said *The Nation* in a particularly cruel play on words. War and infanticide were believed to have contributed to the population crash, but a more important cause was the notorious promiscuity of the natives, first among themselves and later with ardent sailors. "In the prodigious dissoluteness of all ranks and the brutish promiscuousness of intercourse, a few years were enough to poison the blood of the entire people," said Bacon. Because no one really knew the causes behind the decline, one explanation seemed as plausible as another. "The deleterious habit of wearing clothes has, I do not doubt, done much to kill off the Hawaiian people," suggested a contributor to *Harper's*. But while the specifics were murky, the general cause was crystal clear. According to *The Nation*: "It is before civilization and Christianity itself that the Polynesian is passing away."[51]

The role of the missionaries in the near-extinction was an issue that occasioned more than a little irritability. Theologically, the benefits of eternal salvation may have seemed a reasonable trade-off for temporal annihilation, but the missionaries in Hawaii did not live up to expectations of how the missionary enterprise ought to function, nor did they provide a fitting example of missionaries as benign agents of civilization. The missionaries were on the spot. Unlike the case of the Native American population decline, one could not blame the population collapse in Hawaii on rapacious settlers and warfare. *The Nation* simply accepted the missionaries' responsibility as a fact. "Doubtless the main result of missionary labor upon the Polynesians has been to hasten the destruction of the race," it insisted. But while the arrival of the missionaries had been a regrettable "race-destroying blunder," the journal was quick to absolve individual missionaries of guilt. "It was one of the fatalities of philanthropy that the Hawaiians should perish," it concluded."[52]

Apologists for the missionaries were unwilling to go this far, maintaining to the contrary that the missionary presence had checked population decline, since it was common knowledge that civilization generally increased the life span and led to denser populations. If it had not been for the missionaries and their introduction of Christian civilization, insisted Rufus Anderson, secretary of the American Board for Foreign Missions, "the Hawaiians would be already, like the dodo, an extinct race." The dominant motif was a direct statement of the theme of civilization triumphant. The large view credited the missionaries with having "completely transformed the national character, and displaced a degraded savagery with the order and much of the culture, of the Christian state." Ultimately, dwelling on the past was fruitless and the discussion of the islands turned from human to natural endowments. Their resources, climate, and strategic location remained. Agriculture, trade, and tourism—prosperity—beckoned.[53]

Doubts, Countercurrents, and Second Thoughts

Civilization did not always sweep everything before it nor did it always work as advertised. Prior to visiting the Middle East, Charles Dudley Warner had believed that "modern civilization had more or less transformed the East to its own likeness." To his relief, however, once there he changed his mind. "There is still an Orient," he said, "and I believe there would be if it were all canaled and railwayed and converted; for I have great faith in habits that have withstood the influence of six or seven thousand years of changing dynasties and religions." Some, like Theodore Child of *Harper's*, took open delight in Turkish resistance to westernization. "They at least, among all the nations of the earth, have not bowed the knee before the idol of progress," he wrote. "Firm in the faith of their fathers, they calmly ignore Western civilization; and if they do recognize the existence of the Occidental, it is only to despise him, and not to ape him, and thereby lose their own personality, which has been the fate of so many nations who have become the victims of Western propagandism and Western ideas." For better or worse, Istanbul remained magnificently "unimproved and unexpurgated, in all its splendor of color, its brilliant sunlight, its primitiveness, its dirt, and its perfidy."[54]

Observers could not help noticing, too, that universal progress was at best highly uneven and a mixed blessing to boot. Writing for *The Atlantic,* the psychiatrist and statistician Edward Jarvis described pure civilization as an "unmixed good," but because it was never found in its pure state it was "sometimes accompanied with evil." The social gospel minister George Washington Gladden doubted whether economic progress was quite as universal as advertised. "We said that the world is growing rich," he noted in an early version of the-rich-get-richer critique, "but it is our world—the world with which we are brought into closest political and commercial relations—of which this is true." Neither was civilization producing homogeneity. Moncure D. Conway, the expatriate antislave minister and author, reflecting on the Paris Exhibition of 1867, wondered whether it made sense to equate progress with westernization. In his eyes, he saw "a large section of the world, comprising a half of its inhabitants, which is making definite progress toward an entirely different kind of civilization." A correspondent for *The Nation,* reporting on the Paris Exposition of 1889, with its spectacular re-creation of a Cairo street, derived little sense of humanity from the spectacle. "These races brought together from all parts of the world seem to have nothing in common except blind and brutal instincts," he noted.[55]

Globalization also prompted second thoughts and doubts on the subject of the ideological bedrock of Western expansionism. One of the grand shibboleths of the period held that Christianity was the spearhead of civilization and that civilization followed the spread of the Word of God, a piece of received wisdom encapsulated in David Livingstone's trinity of Christianity, commerce, and civilization. According to this view, Christianity was the principal causal force behind global modernization. In Rev. L. L. Paine's description, Christianity was "the great leavening power in the world, gradually moulding and transforming by its own inherent virtue human governments, institutions, societies, customs, beliefs." "Conversion from barbarism to Christ is conversion from barbarism to civilization," was one way of putting it, and many more such statements could be cited. Even Gladden argued that Christianity was "the one grand cause of the production of wealth in modern times." One implication of such comments was that the proof of Christianity's fitness to be

a universal religion would lie in the secular results, not in the number of converts it attracted. So: Was Christianity the indispensable force propelling globalization, or was it merely riding in the sidecar?[56]

The role of Christianity was a matter of some debate. This was an important question because it was no secret that proselytization carried with it an
overweening air of presumption. The author Gail Hamilton delivered a blister-
ing critique of the propensity to consign heathens to "damnation without representation," complaining that "we consign them to perdition without even
hearing their side of the case." A letter writer, inspired by Hamilton's attack,
excoriated the "theological crusaders who mistake themselves for the Good
Shepherd's meek and gentle lambs." The low opinion of meddling missionaries
expressed by the travel author Henry Field also received wide play. One chapter of his popular book, *From Egypt to Japan,* asked: "Do missionaries do any
good?" His answer, in the case of India, was "yes," though not for religious reasons. Even though proselytizing was a great offense "against that mutual concession of perfect freedom which is the first law of all human intercourse," it
was acceptable in this instance only because conversion to Christianity offered
relief from the appalling social consequences of Hindu beliefs. For Field, the
religious message continued to carry modernizing social consequences. But
others, even some men of the cloth, expressed doubt about Christianity's ability to serve as an effective agent of modernization. The Rev. W. A. P. Martin,
author of a well-received introduction to China, inverted the usual relationship between the sacred and the secular by arguing that the Word of God was
not enough, for Christianity alone did not possess this kind of transforming
power. "We are required to prove our commission to teach men spiritual things
by showing our ability to instruct them in worldly matters," he insisted. One
can see why, shorn of their modernizing cover, the Hawaii missionaries were
so defensive about their role in the population crash.[57]

For others, all the question marks pointed to a need to separate missionary work from the civilizing mission. Being so heavily dependent on secular
justification made some missionary supporters nervous, and the tensions
in the missionary communities occasionally reached the boiling point. In
1889, *The Nation* reported on a "hot discussion" in England on the question
of whether the missionary enterprise had been successful. The occasion was
an address delivered by Canon Thomas Taylor entitled "The Great Missionary
Failure." Statistically, he pointed out that missionaries were failing to keep

pace with a powerful historical tide of population growth. If the fruition of global civilization was dependent on worldwide Christianization, such numbers suggested that it would never be achieved. But Taylor also objected to the idea that missionaries should go abroad as representatives of "a superior race." To Taylor, and to a growing number of critics, the emphasis on westernization resulted in the missionary becoming "an efficient schoolmaster instead of a proselytizer." Christianity's civilizing function, according to this point of view, ought to be secondary to its theological mission. It was not only the quantity but the quality of conversions that needed to be considered. Because of the material inducements offered by missionaries, the suspicion was that superficial conversions were commonplace. A Hindu convert, according to *The Nation*, "becomes a convert but not a Christian." But if one were to rely on the unadulterated Christian message alone, what would be the ultimate effect of disappointing numbers on the belief in Christianity as a universal religion?[58]

Christianity was itself not immune to modification in what was, despite its unbalanced character, still a reciprocal process of cultural exchange. "Christianity is invading the world," said the Rev. M. E. Dwight, but he was quick to add that "the World is also invading Christianity." At the very least, the Rev. Noah Porter suggested, "stiff abstractions" were bound to generate unexpected questions and responses from intended converts, which would require some recasting of the creed. James Field had no doubt of this reciprocal impact. "Surely it is not Japan alone that has been 'opened' by trans-Pacific intercourse," he wrote, "but Puritanism as well." At the extreme, some foresaw a trend to religious eclecticism, in which bits and pieces of the various religions would be "selected and combined in that Church of the Future now in the process of formation." One even detects the emergence of ecumenicalism, a recognition, as Charles Loring Brace put it, that the religious impulse common to all humans meant that "all the great religions are at one, however much human passion and folly have degraded them from their purpose." Those who gave the matter some thought could not help but notice the many resemblances between Christianity and Buddhism. "Are these remarkable analogies only casual resemblances, or are they real affinities?" wondered one reviewer." Once launched down this anthropological road, it seemed clear that the source of religion was not revelation, but "the common and universal needs and nature of man, which repeat themselves again and again in like positions and like circumstances." Western universalism could be blind to its own particularity, but it was also capable of stimulating a self-awareness of the relativity of one's own culture. This sensibility would become much more pronounced in the next century, but it was definitely present, if only *in ovo*, in the nineteenth.[59]

An unsettling example of the bidirectional thrust of cultural flows was the growing enthusiasm felt in some quarters, particularly in Boston, for Buddhism. For those discontented with modern materialism—and journals were filled with complaints about "the moral dry-rot which is so marked a modern characteristic"—the ascetic features of eastern religions were bound to appear attractive. To traditional Christians, the warm reception provided to Edwin Arnold's *Light of Asia*, a verse exposition of Buddhist doctrine, was particularly alarming, especially its suggestion that Christianity had borrowed certain basic ideas from Buddhism. The counterattack from scandalized traditionalists was multipronged, but, significantly, much of it came from a nondoctrinal and this-worldly direction. Were societies in which Buddhism prevailed more moral than Western societies, asked an alarmed cleric? Definitely not, he insisted, for Buddhism promoted "a view of life which makes it a tomb." Christianity, it was argued, was "synonymous with a progressive civilization," whereas Buddhism was "everywhere connected with one which is arrested and stationary." Whatever its moral virtues, critics stated, historically Buddhism's best days were behind it. It was a pre-progressive creed, a religion of despair, "as compared with the hopefulness of Christianity." For Fannie Roper Feudge, author of a history of India and frequent contributor to journals on eastern topics, what remained of Buddhism was "but the putrid carcass, meet for destruction." In short, Christianity met the civilizational test; Buddhism did not.[60]

These discussions of the connection between religion and global civilization were both interesting and surprising. When one combines the doubts expressed about Christianity's civilizing role in Asia and its meager results in Islamic lands, the oft-expressed belief in religion as a vehicle of modernization appears to have been a rhetorical bromide. Certainly, there was scant empirical evidence to support the idea. In countries like Japan and China, the native culture and not Christianity provided the platform for modernization. There modernity could and did proceed independently of large-scale conversions to

Christ, with Western power in the background to provide motivation as necessary. The grumblings about the disastrous impact of Christianity in the Hawaiian Islands and its disappointing performance in the Middle East indicated that, in practical terms, many had doubts about the civilizing impact of the faith. When American missionaries began to invest considerable sums in educational and charitable activities, they themselves would realize that a reliance on proselytizing was insufficient even to spread the Word of God, let alone take on the huge task of civilizing alien peoples. Clearly, the missionaries played a significant role in modernization, but religion possessed far less power to civilize than it had in the past.[61]

If religion's positive role in the spread of global civilization was more fanciful than factual, it continued to matter, more negatively, as a handicap that could be more crippling than race. The principal case in point was Islam, whose self-crippling doctrinal tenets were perceived to be so deeply ingrained as to constitute an insuperable roadblock to development. In China, discussions of obstacles to modernization rarely mentioned race as a major consideration. Instead, the biggest barrier to the Middle Kingdom's joining the emerging global civilization was the crushing weight of tradition, absent the burden of a crippling religious orthodoxy. But if culture was the problem, China and Japan suggested that it could at times also be a part of the solution by providing resources indispensable to grappling with contemporary challenges. Owing to Islam's tenacious hold, these cultural resources appeared to be more readily available in Asia than in Muslim lands.

It is sometimes assumed that in the American outlook the non-Western world was consigned to a racial outer darkness, representing a fundamentally different "Other." But American thinking was more complex than that. In fact, it made room for a gamut of possible outcomes—ranging from disappearance to stasis, to death, and to rebirth—that did not fit within a rigidly stratified view of the world. American thought was without doubt powerfully ethnocentric, but it was also extremely flexible in leaving open the possibility of cultural advance to civilized levels while not excluding the possibility of doomed outcomes. Negative judgments of societal capabilities were part of a broader worldview in which non-European peoples in general were presumed to have the potential to modernize. And this outlook was not wedded to ignorance. Whereas modernity at the individual level has tended to produce impersonality and anonymity, at the cultural level American "orientalism" promoted a more intimate knowledge that contributed to a deeper appreciation of the oneness of humankind.[62]

These civilizational encounters were not conceived solely in terms of culture, religion, and race. Their outcomes were also understood politically as the consequence of disparities in power between modern and nonmodern societies, of which the chief political expression at this time was imperialism. On this topic, as with so many others related to global developments, Americans had much to say.

8

Empire and Civilization

When the issue of empire came up for debate in 1898, Americans already knew a good deal about it. The possibility of U.S. overseas expansion had been the subject of political discussion on several occasions after 1865, especially in connection with Santo Domingo and Samoa, but America's familiarity with imperialism owed more to written accounts of European colonialism than to direct experience. In these reports, imperialism was seen partly as a feature of the international politics of the period, a theme that will be addressed in the next chapter, but more attention was typically paid to issues of race, culture, and civilization that had been taken up so intently in a domestic context.[1]

In the liberal view, imperialism was a product of modern civilization, not its motive force. Writing of "the passion for colonization" that had swept up the European powers, *The Nation* matter of factly categorized imperialism as "one of the incidents of the modern industrial development and competition." In keeping with the Spencerian emphasis on the peaceable character of modern industrial society, some commentators sought to distinguish modern imperialism from empires of the past that relied principally on conquest and forcible extraction of tribute and labor. In this spirit, the orientalist Samuel Wells Williams argued that whereas Rome's expansion had been driven by war, modern civilization sought "to establish one civilization among peoples of different modes of government by means of mechanical appliances and commercial regulations." This emphasis on the underlying importance of technology and trade was enthusiastically echoed by the University of Virginia philologist Maximilian Schele de Vere. "Wherever steam has established its rule," he wrote, "there new life is infused, trade and commerce assume gigantic proportions, industry prospers, civilization spreads abroad, and liberty, in state and church, replaces the rule of old prejudices and arbitrary power." As such comments suggest, it was widely supposed that economic forces would work their global-izing magic among uncivilized peoples, "awakening men from the slumber of ages, and the stupor of a mere animal existence," by emancipating a common human identity from the shackles of tradition.[2]

But liberation was no stranger to power. While Williams and de Vere mini-mized or ignored the role played by military conquest, others were quick to point out that European dominion was manifestly the product of force. As Thomas Knox observed, "The musket, the sabre, and the cannon, were potent civilizers, and introduced European principles more rapidly than any other agency." The progressive implications of trade and technology, many under-stood, were lost on those who happened to be on the receiving end of Euro-pean weaponry, for whom power and inequality appeared to be the primary ingredients of Western expansion. In Richard J. Hinton's opinion, "Europe, to all Asiatic peoples, represents conquest." This conceptual rift over the causes and consequences of empire, between those who understood global processes in terms of liberating commercial and cultural processes and those who per-ceived international relations as driven by hierarchical exercises of power, would divide theorists and political practitioners to the end of the colonial era and beyond.[3]

In general, American evaluations of colonial rule followed the views of John Stuart Mill, whose thinking typified the broad turn among liberal thinkers away from Enlightenment anti-imperialism. But this liberal imperialism was conditional, for it presupposed the primacy of social and cultural desiderata. Mill held that imperialism, or a "vigorous despotism," was justifiable only if the subject peoples could not progress on their own and if outside rule was exer-cised for the benefit of the subjugated. Absent these conditions, the foreign rulers were "guilty of a dereliction of the highest moral trust which can devolve upon a nation." Mill doubted that a high-minded approach would be easy be-cause European settlers, who considered dependant peoples to be "mere dirt under their feet," would inevitably enjoy the attentive ear of the government when proposing schemes that would further their interests at the expense of the colonized. Nevertheless, Americans hewed to this high standard, an imperialist analog of just war theory, as they weighed the cultural characteristics of the local population against the sense of justice displayed by the conquerors and the overall effectiveness of the civilizing mission. Although they had difficulty in making up their minds about the larger historical meaning of Europe's colonial outburst in the 1880s, they did come down eventually on the side of empire, but in an ambivalent way that would characterize discussions of imperialism well into the future [4]

Evaluating British Rule in India

Of all the areas under European control, British India generated the greatest amount of commentary and interest. "The terms magnificence, grandeur, and splendor do not reach the limit of hyperbole without the pre-fix 'Oriental,' and India is the country, of all countries, which has given this adjective to the vocabulary," said a writer in *Scribner's*. George M. Towle observed in 1876 that India, more than any other country in the world, was worth studying because of its large population of 200 million, its huge cities, wealth, history, art, and architecture, and cultural peculiarities. India was important in countless ways, not least as a source for providing a better understanding of the Western past via civilizational connections that extended into antiquity. The subcontinent had made notable contributions to Western languages, literature, religion, and mathematical and astronomical learning, though many would have agreed with Macaulay's crack that "a single shelf of a good European library was worth the whole native literature of India and Arabia." The long history of trade between East and West, *The Nation* concluded, appeared to be prima facie evidence of "the unity of history." India scholarship, which got seriously under way in the late eighteenth century, had already stimulated a new understanding of religion and provided enormous impetus to the emergence of philology, which was perhaps the queen of humanistic disciplines in the nineteenth century.[5]

But much scholarly work remained to be done, as India remained an exotic and mysterious land to Americans. James Freeman Clarke complained that "it has no history, for history belongs to time. No one knows when its sacred books were written, when its civilization began, what caused its progress, what its decline." In one striking analogy, the mystifying complexities of Indian mythology were compared to the Indian jungle, "which harbors in its tangled depths every monstrous and uncouth shape." An enterprising scholar in this field would be assured, according to one writer, "of contributing his share toward the solution of the vast and many-sided problem of human development." In the event, the written output of various genres grew so large that complaints were soon being made about the number of works written about India, a "vast, dreary, and increasing mountain of Anglo-Indian literature."[6]

Using Mill's standard, Americans found much to criticize about British rule, enough at least to prompt Goldwin Smith to complain in 1890 that "the Indian Empire is the regular theme of Anglophobists. They never mention it without giving utterance to burning words about the oppression of the Hindoo." This was unfair, for criticisms of British rule were quite common even among Anglophiles. Henry Field, for example, confessed to feeling proud of English rule but was quick to add that "this pride of empire will not extinguish in any fair mind the sense of justice and humanity." Thus J. R. Seeley's *Expansion of England*, though well received on the whole, was nevertheless attacked for "a curious unwillingness to contemplate the darker aspect of that marvellous history." At any rate, more often than not, American writers relied on descriptions provided by numerous British critics, as in one striking description of India as "a gigantic model prison."[7]

Although Mill himself had good things to say about the British presence—he worked for the East India Company for thirty-five years—much Anglo-Indian behavior came under fire for failing to pass the test of ruling in the interest of the natives. Great Britain's trade and investment in India were of "enormous scale," and so too were the profits. Whereas Australia was a refuse heap of convicts, India was seen as "a dumping-ground for Manchester goods and missionaries." In addition, many agreed with Cobden's quip that the British Empire was a vast system of outdoor relief for the nobility, an export market for "surplus men of the upper class." Although there were many able administrators, at the same time, as Knox noted, there was "a large proportion of drones, who waste their substance in riotous living," perpetually in debt from living beyond their means. The cost of supporting these wastrels was "a crushing incubus on the country."[8]

The coddling of these special interest groups went hand in hand with a cultural obtuseness that prevented the British from connecting empathetically with the native population—a charge that American imperialists of the twentieth century would have done well to remember. Writing for *The Nation*, R. D. Osborn, who had served in the British military in India, suggested that the problem began at the moment of debarkation. Not knowing the local languages, the English were reduced to keeping company with their own kind, forming "no attachments; no friendships, with the people of the country." Describing one Briton who did mix with the people, he suggested that there were probably fewer than a dozen individuals like him in all of India. This seemed to be part of a larger problem, a general "incapacity of the English mind for entering into the state of feeling of men of different origin, or manners, or order of thought." What passed for British governance took place "in the midst of a saturnalia of balls, picnics, lawn-tennis tournaments, social scandals, and a ceaseless babel of gossip." Otherwise, members of the transplanted governing elite appeared to spend much of their time in complaining about their situations. "Speaking generally," said one account, "we may say with very little exaggeration that all Anglo-Indians hate the country, hate the climate, and dislike the people. The one great object of their lives is to get out of the country as soon as they possibly can." And heaven help the poor British Isles when these blue-blooded incompetents finally returned home![9]

The core problem appeared to be "a sense of unquestionable superiority, originating in the fact of conquest." According to Osborn, the British were "too absolutely confident . . . that everything British must be immeasurably superior to all things that are not British—to possess the insight of sympathy for the character of those among whom his life was passed." The central feeling of the British rulers, claimed A. H. Guernsey, was "contempt for the people over whom they were placed." Knox noted that "the meanest tramp among them considers himself of more importance and better by blood and birth than the highest native prince." All this had its ironies, for the British had blinded themselves to native discontent and failed to notice that they were considered in many ways to be cultural inferiors. "Your servant who will not touch, through fear of pollution, the food you eat, can not hold you in great respect," noted Knox. Small wonder, given their cultural isolation, that the British had been so ill-prepared for the eruption of 1857, the great Sepoy Mutiny. This inability to know the minds of subject peoples was, by one account, "the greatest of the many dangers which threaten the stability of the Empire." Ignorance of popular feeling was a matter of huge practical importance because it condemned the Raj to legislating in the dark.[10]

The British were commonly applauded for introducing law and order, but it was questionable whether the rule of law was being put to good developmental use. Prefiguring what would later become a staple of historical scholarship, the well-known writer Edward Everett Hale went against liberal orthodoxy by criticizing the devastation of India's textile industry under the pretext of introducing free trade. In addition, the reform of the land tenure system in which legal titles were established on the British models was said to have resulted in "havoc and devastation." As problematic as it was, progressive change did not come cheaply. In an impressive review of Wheeler's *Short History of India,* the British legal scholar and journalist A. V. Dicey noted that "civilized government further means expensive government"—paid for by the locals, of course. Some even suggested that their imperial predecessors, the Muslim Moghuls, had done far better at governing than this modernity-minded and progressive nation.[11]

Gainsaying the ritual claims of the beneficence of British rule in India was an almost unimaginable poverty in the country that haunted most Americans who saw it. Knox, who wished never again to return, recalled that "want in all its forms stares you constantly in the face, and the only way for a traveler in India to escape the sight of it is to sail away to some other land." An early piece in *The Atlantic Monthly* had described India as a land "where dirty little fakirs and yogees hold their dirty little arms above their dirty little heads, until their dirty little muscles are shrunk to dirty little rags, and their dirty little fingernails grow through the backs of their dirty little hands, . . . ; where plucky little widows perform their little suttees for defunct little husbands, grilling on little funeral piles; where mangy little Pariah dogs defile the little dinners of little high-caste folks, by stealing hungry little sniffs from sacred little pots." Despite all the government's efforts, by the late 1880s the typical peasant remained "a wretched, unclothed, insufficiently nourished, and hopelessly indebted creature."[12]

The most distressing problem in India was famine, which was a recurring phenomenon in the second half of the nineteenth century. One essay on the great famine of the late 1870s marveled at the likelihood that "a population nearly as large as the whole population of Scotland will be swept away in the course of a few months by the cruelest of all deaths." Defenders of British rule offered the counterintuitive argument that these intermittent disasters were the product of good government. Typical was Goldwin Smith's Malthusian defense, according to which the introduction of law and order had encouraged population growth, which in turn led to famine. The pressure of numbers, he argued, "not British extortion—is the main cause of the ryot's poverty," the implication, of course, being that nothing could be done for the peasantry. For the most part, however, American readers got the impression from a chorus of critics that these disasters were largely man-made and were hardly inevitable. Although the British were not above floating huge public loans and eventually adopting a battery of measures in attempts to ameliorate the country's distress, the desire to help did not translate into administrative competence. There was little agreement, however, on precisely what the British were doing wrong. One writer blamed the famine of the 1870s on the Raj's misconceived administrative and public works schemes, which resulted in the perverse export of food in time of famine. For Charles Dudley Warner, the fault lay in the widespread cultivation of opium poppies; while Henry George, in *Poverty and Progress*, attributed British misrule in India to "the rapacity of man, not the niggardliness of nature." But if Great Britain, the world's wealthiest and most powerful nation, could not deal effectively with the basic food problem, as one editorial suggested, the position of the Raj in India would be seriously, perhaps fatally, undermined.[13] Although the various diagnoses of causes tended to overlook British-imposed changes in land tenure, taxation, and the marketization of agriculture, the enormous cultural distance between the British and their subjects provided reason enough to establish autocracy as the root cause of famine.

Quite understandably, then, Americans rarely fell over themselves to praise the British performance in India. In response to the orthodox British insistence that their rule in India was "a marvellous and beneficent success," a cynical reviewer suggested that, were this true, it would be "a perennial miracle—as direct a violation of the laws of nature as if water should flow up a hill." Goldwin Smith, in an earlier essay, had conceded that Britain was guided not by "equity, humanity, or respect for human life, but British interest and the requirements of British policy." For those who looked at British conduct from a broader geographical perspective, it was hard to take seriously the professions of devotion to the civilizing mission. Although the British maintained their grip on India in the name of civilization, at the same time they supported the Ottomans against the Russians with little regard for delivering the Armenians and Bulgarians from their tyranny. When compared to Ottoman misgovernment, one essayist argued that "almost equal misery is being inflicted over a far wider area, under the best-meaning of governments and through the most scientific of systems." For Knox, "the British gush about 'our noble mission in the East' must be taken with a good many pinches of salt, or rejected altogether." To such critics, the empire was principally about profit and power.[14]

But . . . what would happen if the British should suddenly depart? The consensus was that India, if left to its own devices, could not possibly rule itself to the benefit of its many peoples. It was not a question of native incapacity to do so. Although some writers wondered whether it was possible "to graft upon Oriental minds the practical capacities of the West," Americans expressed few doubts on this score. "If we take an average Englishman and contrast him with an average Indian, there is no such difference between the two as to account for their relative positions," wrote Rollo Ogden, who would later cap his career as editor of *The New York Times.* "The Indian possesses, perhaps, the quicker and more agile intellect of the two. He is, man for man, not less brave, not less diligent in his vocation, not less quick in the acquisition of knowledge." In some respects, notably the regard for personal cleanliness, articles stressed that the peoples of India were far in advance of the laboring classes in the West. Impressed by the many positive traits that he found among the Hindus, one writer concluded that India "has, I believe, great future possibilities before it." Another essay in *The North American Review* argued that the peoples of India were "Aryan relations—since the people of India proper are really very nearly akin to our Anglo-Saxon blood; much more closely, indeed, than, say, the Hungarians, the southern Italians, or the Russians."[15]

Unfortunately, these naturally gifted people were being held back by a timeless and irrational culture whose supreme expression was the caste system. In Ogden's view, caste meant "perfect submission to whatever is customary, no matter how gross, monstrous, and irrational it may be." As Goldwin Smith was quick to remind Americans, "there is no exclusiveness of race like the exclusiveness of Hindoo caste." Hindu religion, typically viewed with a combination of wonderment and disgust, was condemned for "the complete crushing out of the desires and affections that make up the best parts of man's nature." Its fatalism was the negation of the Western ideal of life as the pursuit of happiness and it was, to boot, incompatible with modern science. Whereas the universe was governed by natural law, for Hindus, in contrast, it appeared to be guided by "unpredictable caprice." The respect for reason, which went a long way toward explaining Western power, was "wholly absent from the moral and intellectual conceptions of the native of India." A broad assortment of atavistic cultural traits resulted in a "moral and intellectual helplessness which caused them to succumb, and keeps them in subjection to a handful of alien conquerors." This deference to irrational hidebound tradition, according to George Towle, was responsible for the "want of manliness" and "slavish constitution" that helped to explain the relative ease with which fewer than 100,000 Englishmen could rule a population of 200 million. There was, in short, an enormous gap between the prevailing culture and human potential.[16]

The sensationally bizarre aspects of India's cultures tended to attract the greatest attention. The practice of suttee, or ritual widow-burning, which had been banned by the British, never failed to elicit wonderment and speculation as to its origins. Widow-burning was generally seen as an infallible indicator of the backwardness of Hindu society and was symptomatic of the larger problem of the denial of female individuality. One essay which cited Sir Henry Maine argued that the recognition of individuality in a society could not be complete "until it has fully and finally assimilated the legal position of women to that of men." Infant marriage was seen as another barbaric practice that contributed heavily both to India's overpopulation and to cultural infantilization. "The offspring of children remain children all their lives," insisted *The Nation*. It was this childish quality that the British played to in their growing reliance on ostentatious ceremony as a way of impressing the locals, "a race whose imagination is greatly stimulated by external pomp and high-flown language." Such comments make it clear that criticisms of British lack of cultural empathy did not originate from a relativist sympathy for India's ways of life.[17]

Although the British often failed to meet Mill's criterion of ruling in the interest of the natives, their faults were weighed against a long list of achievements. Law and order provided domestic peace under a growing body of Anglo-Hindu law; English was becoming the lingua franca; widow-burning had been outlawed; female infanticide was now proscribed; and thuggism, a semi-religious criminal cult, had been successfully suppressed. Other changes, most notably an epochal loosening of the caste system, were also thought to be in progress. In 1867 *The Nation* predicted hopefully that "the old framework of Hindoo society is in a fair way of being broken up through the agency of material progress." In 1885, Knox, who a few years earlier had written quite critically of British rule, allowed that some things, most notably a more open commercial environment, had changed for the better since the East India Company had given way to the Raj. The building of railroads, which forced castes to intermingle, had, according to Knox, "shaken the faith of the Hindoo more than centuries of Christian teaching, and brought confusion and perplexity to the heart of the native priest." Overall, Knox believed that the changes of the preceding twenty-five years had surpassed the changes experienced during any full century of India's past.[18]

Most consequential of all were accomplishments in education, a "daring political experiment" that marked a giant step forward toward equality and independence. George M. Towle wrote with admiration of how the Hindu and Bengali elites were receiving British educations and occupying increasingly important positions in the civil administration, which had been promised to them by the queen following the Mutiny. They were "assimilating their characters and customs to English ideas," he wrote, "and setting the example which the English would fain see followed by all the vast population of the empire." But education was not something solely for the elites. "The passion for reading has struck every part of India," noted one essay in the course of explaining the explosion of books and newspapers being printed throughout the subcontinent. A measure introduced by the Viceroy Lord Ripon that made possible the trial of Europeans before Hindu judges was viewed as a step in the direction of equality before the law. Noted *The Nation:* "A great many of the upper class are becoming Anglicized, they are educated in England, and practice at the English bar, occasionally try to get into Parliament, and distinguish themselves frequently as speakers on the stump."[19]

For all that, it remained unclear how serious the British were about cultural conversionism. Despite achievements in education and access to the professions, Godkin had early pointed to deeply rooted prejudices that blocked the road to civic equality. "The contempt with which the average Englishman regards the Hindoo," he suggested, "can hardly be surpassed by anything which the negro has in this country to undergo from the most besotted Democrat." Time did not prove him wrong. Lord Salisbury's reference to an Indian as a "black man," which was widely taken to mean "nigger," had set off a brouhaha and the evidence from India appeared to indicate that racial sentiments among the Anglo-Indian elite were hardening. Despite the British pose of racial benevolence, *The Nation*'s London correspondent was "startled at discovering the social and moral gulf which still yawns between English and natives in India." Some suspected that efforts to cement the loyalties of Indians were cynically prompted solely by fear of Russian encroachment from the north.[20]

Even when the results of westernization were not in doubt, an acculturation that was too complete was disconcerting and raised questions about the efficacy of the educational strategy. A review of a book on travel through India written by a Hindu expressed unpleasant surprise at its European flavor and tone. "His political sentiments are wholly English," complained the reader. "He does not protest against, or even apparently deplore, the rule of the Westerner." This sort of deracinated individual seemed altogether too representative of the growing number of educated Hindus who had been made aliens in their own land, "almost as much an exotic in the land of their birth as the British themselves." Whether or not they could survive the downfall of the British power that had created them was doubtful. "The manufacture of these people is beyond all question the most productive industry carried on in the empire, but it cannot in our judgment be regarded as either healthy or promising," concluded *The Nation*. These kinds of Brahmin nationalists were described by one Indian "as trousered patriots, tittle-tattling in English." Even Goldwin Smith predicted that such educated Hindus "would be crushed like egg-shells" in the chaos that was bound to follow decolonization. This suggested that none of Britain's remarkable achievements had been able to touch "the deeper springs of thought and conviction." Yet, on balance, the creation of an educated native elite was considered to be beneficial.[21]

Ultimately, when forced to make the hard choice, American assessments of British rule in India, despite its long list of imperfections, were almost always positive. In 1857 *The Atlantic* had declared that "English rule in India has been, with all its defects, an enlightened and beneficent rule." That view remained constant throughout this period. "The general judgment of the American people," said the journalist Murat Halstead in 1890, "is that the British do the world a service in holding India." Yes, there were irresponsible officials aplenty, but one also found a new breed of administrators, particularly after the mutiny, "who thoroughly feel the responsibility laid upon them as custodians of the happiness of a vast nation." The Chicago social worker Graham Taylor claimed that the Indian service had "that element of heroism . . . which has attracted the very best brain and brawn of the English race to India." One administrator, Sir George Bowen, was described as an embodiment of "the heroic work of colonization." For all its faults, British rule was "the best India has ever had."[22]

The ironic consequences of British rule were subjects of repeated reflection in *The Nation*. In advancing the civilizing mission, the British had created the conditions for a national feeling, which found political expression in the formation of the Indian National Congress in 1885. The British, it was noted, had "themselves kindled a new spirit in India which no earthly power can now re-strain." Some deracinated types aside, the better the education, the greater was the discontent among "cultivated natives" with foreign rule and inequality. The combination of growing education and continuing mass poverty was a com-bustible mixture. Even if British India was a benevolent despotism, it was inherently unstable, for its very merits created the social forces that would challenge it and perhaps the empire as a whole, thus pointing up the necessity of allowing some form of home rule. If the British did nothing to promote local autonomy, then it seemed clear that it would "certainly, sooner or later, be applied after a very destructive fashion by the people of India." Unfortunately, the Raj, seemingly oblivious to the problem and wholly unwilling to entertain the idea of a devolution of its authority, put off independence to "some uncon-jecturable period of time." For the moment, the desire for self-rule appeared to be offset by mutual hatreds among Hindus, Muslims, Dravidians, and Parsis that continued to make divide and rule a viable strategy. But this did not bode well for national unity in the wake of a British withdrawal.[23]

Only on rare occasions were the subalterns given leave to speak, but in those few instances the gulf between rulers and ruled stood out with stark clarity. In 1885, *The North American Review* took the unusual step of publishing an essay on British rule in India by Amrita Lal Roy, a Calcutta-born, Edinburgh-educated physician and independence advocate who briefly associated with Henry George. Roy argued that all the talk of the British "genius" for coloniza-tion had been "stereotyped into a cant." Despite the alleged benefits of civiliza-tion, Roy insisted that it came down to this: "India has given to England wealth and fame; England has brought upon India penury and shame." The civilizing mission was simply an ideological smokescreen hiding the work of "three interested industries—the military, mercantile, and missionary, aided by co-operative journalism—in behalf of privilege and power." For Roy, it was not the benevolent aspect of British rule, but its harsher Darwinian side—"the ed-ucation of circumstances"—that would prove most instructive in the end. One also finds the occasional rejoinder from a Hindu defending his faith and re-jecting the Christian view that Hinduism was "an immeasurable curse." On one occasion, *The North American Review* printed a defense of child marriage from the local point of view.[24]

For Americans, achieving an understanding of India required drawing up a complex balance sheet in which sympathy with the aims of the British was offset with criticism of the imperial means used to promote them. Appreciation of native abilities and the belief that effective rule required almost an anthropological appreciation of local ways was balanced, perhaps even contradicted, by the belief that India's culture needed to be drastically modernized. Given the small European population in India, however, it seemed unlikely that the natives of India would long continue to allow this beneficence to be perpetrated upon them. "The British domination in India," concluded A. H. Guernsey, "rests upon a thin shell overlying a bottomless quicksand; and this shell is liable at any moment to give way." There was a sense that in the final analysis the parting of the British and the peoples of India would not be a sweet sorrow.[25]

The Egyptian Phoenix Turns to Ashes

For a brief moment in the decade following the Civil War, standing out as a shining exception to the host of gloomy commentaries on the decay of Islamic civilization was Egypt, which appeared to be on the doorstep of a remarkable rebirth. With the opening of the Suez Canal in 1869, one essay predicted that Egypt "will, within the lifetime of this generation, be covered with towns and villages, possessing all the accessories of modern civilization." Five years later, the editor of *Appletons'* speculated about the likely revival of Egyptian greatness. "It seems as if civilization, having passed around the world, and reached its limits on the American shores of the Pacific, had begun to return again to its ancient seats in the Orient, to the localities of its remote infancy." He saw "no reason why Egypt should not in a very few years take high and independent rank among the powers," for the Egyptians were "really a deft and capable people." Many others agreed. Schele de Vere declared Egypt to be "in the process of regeneration through European influence," while a piece in the *Princeton Review* described Egypt as "the Phoenix of history."[26]

What made this all the more remarkable was that Egypt had long been the epitome of timeless constancy. "Immutability," Eliot Warburton had written in the 1830s, "is the most striking characteristic of the East." The pleasure of traveling back in time on a voyage up the Nile—an "unadulterated, dreamy, Oriental pleasure tour"—was precisely what made it such an attractive tourist destination. In addition to revisiting the ancient past, one could encounter the best of the orient in Egypt. "Here Oriental life finds its highest expression," said

Albert Rhodes, former consul turned travel writer, in describing Cairo. But those who cherished this enchanting picture were rudely informed that "the 'march of civilization' is breaking and destroying the most lovely picture on the face of the globe." To go from Alexandria to Port Said was to pass "from the mystic past of the land of the Pharaohs to the commercial future of Egypt and the world." [27]

There were no racial bars to modernization because Egyptians were perceived to be Caucasians. "The ruling race in Egypt comes from the pure Caucasian stock," reported the "roving gentleman," who described the Egyptian gentleman as "a white man in blood and breed, as well as in physical conformation and structure of skull." General McClellan described Egyptians as a "kindly, intelligent, and industrious race, who, under good government, would soon acquire wealth and prosperity," a people whose talents had too long been bottled up by oriental despotism. They had fallen far since the glorious epoch of the pyramids, but they could be reinvigorated through education. Impressed with the Khedive's institution of compulsory education, the travel writer and novelist Edwin De Leon lauded this effort "to educate an entire people all at once—to drag them up from utter ignorance into the light of culture and civilization through the instrumentality of absolute power." If successful in this project of cultural reclamation, the Egyptian would compare favorably with the rural population of England, who were accused of being "scarcely more intelligent than the oxen they drive." Another feather in the Khedive's cap was that polygamy and slavery appeared to be reeling from his reforms, though it was clear that such deeply embedded practices could not be rooted out overnight. [28]

Much of the change was attributed to the pioneering reformer Muhammed Ali, who was sometimes compared to Peter the Great, Russia's modernizing czar. For a time, the mantle of modernizer from above descended to the shoulders of his son, Ismail, who embodied "the progressive spirit of the nineteenth century." Given this succession of reformist rulers, the process of rejuvenation had been ongoing, at an accelerated pace, for the better part of a half century "and with increasing hopefulness." Although the idea of authoritarian modernization was always greeted with some suspicion, it usually received grudging justification under the heading of extenuating circumstances. "It is scarcely just to judge Egypt, with a population sunk in decrepitude, indolence, and corruption, from the point of view of a European nation," argued *Appletons'*. But all of this work was understood as preliminary, "the extirpation of the rank weeds of centuries rather than planting seed and gathering a harvest."[29]

The grand experiment eventually soured when Ismail's government began to encounter serious difficulties stemming from the financing of the Suez Canal. Following the construction of the new waterway, it became increasingly clear that the Europeans were unduly prospering at the expense of the Egyptians. Although the canal was unquestionably a stupendous engineering achievement, its financial engineering struck some as being "the greatest scheme of plunder that was ever conceived." But the Egyptian government was far from blameless for its growing troubles, as excessive borrowing by the Khedive had already given rise to speculation about impending bankruptcy. The combination of debt, heavy taxation, and improvident expenditure had led to corruption and waste (which, fair-minded liberals were quick to point out, was not unknown in the United States). [30]

When everything was taken into account, the intrusion of Europe had "contributed to Egyptian decadence in morals and manners." The net effect of this reversion to Islamic type was to sour American observers on the possibility of native development in Egypt. Thus when Great Britain purchased a majority share in the Suez Canal in 1875, it was seen as a historic milestone: here was yet another pushing back of the frontiers of Islam, with the likelihood of greater control to come. Henry Mitchell, who had been sent to Egypt by the U.S. Coast Survey in 1868 to monitor progress on the canal, predicted that the canal "will never be secure from interruption till the territory is neutralized or otherwise wrested from Mohammedan misrule." Some observers, like Mc-Clellan, saw this as only the beginning of an even greater assertion of British power. In his view, it was justifiably so, for he seriously doubted "whether really good government is possible under Mohammedan rule." If progress was the desideratum, then "it surely [was] desirable that Egypt should come under the dominion of Great Britain." As events headed toward the crisis of 1882, *The Nation* described Egypt's government as a "crew of swindling debauchees and eunuchs," all the more loathsome because it was to some degree the concubine of a European concert.[31]

By the time the nationalist revolt led by the army officer Arabi Pasha in 1882 prompted the British attack on Alexandria, American opinion was on the whole quite favorable to a British takeover, though explanations of the source of the problem were rather wobbly. One view held that it was about corruption, pure and simple. Pro-Arab British experts who attempted to generate sympathy for Arabi's cause as entrenched in nationality and religion were dismissed for having "'Islam' on the brain." Instead of being viewed as nationalist reformers or religious zealots, *The Nation* depicted Ismail and Arabi as Egyptian versions of Boss Tweed's Tammany clubhouse in New York. They were merely the latest in "the gang of Turkish and Arabic official scoundrels who have for centuries lived off the earnings of the peasantry." The Arabi movement, despite some justifiable grievances, was "from the beginning an immense imposture." Nationalism was only a subterfuge to fool the naïve, "the wandering European philanthropists, jurists, and travelers." McClellan described the revolt as "simply a scramble for office." Subsequent reports of massacres of Christians, the flight of foreigners, abandonment by faithless servants, and other disorders tended to validate these anti-Arabi interpretations. But there was still ample room for a religiocultural explanation of the familiar sort. On one occasion, in dismissing nationalism as a red herring, *The Nation* described Arabi and his followers as "good Mussulmans, to whom reform and equality are detestable and impious. . . . They have only one country, which is Islam."[32]

But this anti-Egyptian animus could not conceal the embarrassment that American liberals felt over the invasion, much like the chagrin that Gladstone's ostensibly anti-imperialist Liberal government had shown. Whatever the evils of the old regime and the shortcomings of Arabi, rescuing the British and European bondholders seemed an illegitimate excuse for intervention. "A war in the interest of the bondholders would, every impartial person admits, have been a crime," said *The Nation*. Taking charge of Egyptian finances in the interests of the bondholders was "if not monstrous, very injudicious." Nevertheless, the British move seemed proper. There were only two acceptable justifications for intervention—security and civilization—and the prospect of a disorderly Egypt provided ample reason for concern about defense. Murat Halstead suggested that if the United States had been in England's position with a canal as "one of its most precious possessions," the United States would have behaved in precisely the same way. But, as Gladstone described it, control of the canal was important not only to Great Britain; it was a vital interest of all Europe and "the whole civilized world." To round out the list of beneficiaries, Gladstone rationalized his action as necessary to rescuing the Egyptian population "from the oppression of military tyranny" while instilling the

blessings of liberty and prosperity. Godkin agreed with all this, but he charac-
teristically added an anti-Muslim justification by portraying British action as
a civilizational milestone in which Europe had begun "to roll back the tide of
Mussulman barbarism." Still, Gladstone's insistence that the occupation was
only temporary did little to discourage the suspicion that Egypt was now being treated as British property, a view that *The Nation* described as "the brute-
force theory."[33]

In the years that followed, with the signal exception of *The Nation*, American journals lost interest in Egyptian modernization. Godkin's journal had
been equivocal about the invasion and occupation, but had accepted it as a
fait accompli from which there was no turning back. England "may have had
no right to go to Egypt," wrote Michael Heilprin, "but she has now the duty to
stay there until she performs what she undertook to do." Once ensconced, the
British had no other choice than to "govern the country decently, soberly, and
economically." Initially, it was hoped that the installation of principled British
bureaucrats would transform the corruption-ridden Egyptian administration. It soon became apparent, however, that the British were re-creating their
experience in India. By 1890, it was difficult to see how the early optimism
about Egypt could have arisen. There had been change, but little progress, and
the people continued to be "steeped in the degradation of a truly miserable
existence." As for the British, the quest for security had created further complications in the diplomacy of imperialism, a theme that will be taken up in
the next chapter.[34]

One-and-a-half Cheers for French Imperialism

While British imperialism received its fair share of criticism at American
hands, French imperialism came under withering fire. For starters, the French
were widely believed to be poor travelers and mediocre colonizers. "An impression prevails, and has found frequent expression," said one account, "that
the French are not a colonizing people." The French were, for whatever reason, "a home-keeping race," perhaps, some speculated, because they felt at sea
when at sea. "Nothing beyond the seas touches the French popular imagination," declared Godkin, playing up the alleged French ignorance of geography. "The world for it contains France and two or three adjacent countries, all
flat, and beyond them there is the ocean stream and American darkness." The

Boston journalist C. C. Hazewell, one of many who called French coloniza-tion an oxymoron, suggested that there was "something eminently ridiculous about French colonization." Despite a promising beginning, France's control of far-flung colonies had nearly always given way to "Anglo-Saxon backbone and force." According to Heilprin, from start to finish French colonial policy was "a failure-complete, disastrous, merited, and ignominious." Compared to Anglo-Saxon settlements, French overseas establishments were little more than "operatic villages." Given this long string of "either failures or sterile suc-cesses," it was all the more amazing that so many French believed their coun-try to be "the apostle of civilization." If the British effort was questionable, the French version of the civilizing mission seemed an outright fraud.[35]

France's "colonial fever" appeared to be caused less by belief in the civilizing mission than by a need to vent national frustrations. Following Louis Napoleon's downfall, French expansion in Africa was a way of salving some badly bruised national pride that could not be relieved by a suicidal war against Germany in Europe. "Certain it is that since 1870," explained Rollo Ogden, ". . . France has sought in Algeria and China that military glory which was denied her on Euro-pean battlefields." In the aftermath of the catastrophic defeat at Sédan and Bis-marck's extraordinary success in isolating France on the continent, the quest for empire was also seen as a way for France to regain a measure of international prestige. "A great nation like France cannot always drink the cup of humilia-tion," said Godkin in one of his more charitable moments. If Spain, Portugal, and the Netherlands were worthy of colonies, and overseas expansion was oc-curring all about her, why not then France as well? If Bonapartism had pros-pered by feeding the beast of expansionism, the Third Republic needed to show that it, too, was capable of satisfying the French appetite for "republican adven-tures."[36]

A secondary motive was the desire to find a use for the French army lest in-activity should breed atrophy in the military. Thus Algeria was described as a school for French officers "where they would learn to shoot a little, massacre a little; in short, practice their trade upon the Arabs and half-breeds in order to be better able afterward to operate upon the Parisians and the Lyonese." Similarly, the French invasion of Tunisia seemed to have been prompted by the need to find "a little work for soldiers to do, so as to keep alive the national pride in the army as a great institution," even though nothing important was being gained. But these expansionist thrusts were described as "a trap" into which the French had fallen under the impression that they would be cheap and easy, the kind of miscalculation that had already produced disasters for the British in Afghanistan. This "foolish aggression" also had the misfortune of making an enemy of Great Britain, whose own imperialist Cassandras had begun to perceive a strategic threat to British interests. How beneficial, then, was all this to France? "Bismarck alone applauds," concluded *The Nation*.[37]

Algeria was an exception. As a settler colony, it served as a safety valve for France, "giving active employment to the idle, the discontented, and the revolutionary." The domination of North Africa meant that France could "find work for her soldiers, engineers, colonists, and speculators during the next half-century." *The Nation* believed that Algeria's amalgamation with France was possible and saw "no reason why this colony should not at last resume its ancient place as the granary of the Old World." Moreover, French administration, by comparison with the Muslim rule it replaced, was "excellence itself." As for the native peoples, the Berbers and Kabyles were thought to be assimilable, while the Arabs—"wild, untameable and incapable of civilization"—were said to be "melting away." Yet for all its advantages, the integration of Algeria came at a very high military cost, and commentaries continued to show little faith in the French capacity for combining empire and civilization. Nothing that the French did was sufficient to change an early judgment handed down by *The Nation* that "they know nothing of colonization in the Anglo-Saxon sense of the word.[38]

French expansion in Asia also prompted mixed feelings. The conquest of Indochina was portrayed as "an immense mistake" prompted by the conceit that the prestige lost in Europe could be recovered in Southeast Asia. "There is literally nothing in French experience to support this notion," insisted *The Nation*. Commercial motives were loftier. but hardly weighty enough to justify a military embroilment that appeared to have the makings of a debacle. Complaining of "the monstrous character of this war," *The Nation* described the French presence in Tonkin as "a story of gross cruelty and fraud." But, as usual, the civilized struggle against barbarism had some traction among those who believed that France was ridding the region of pirates. "Clear out all these robbers, protect the people, establish a firm, just rule, and population will flow in to enjoy the security of the foreign flag," argued Augustine Heard (a leading figure in the China trade). "France," he insisted, "is pursuing no common or unworthy object." Still, suspicions of hypocrisy abounded. How exactly, wondered Rollo Ogden, did the republic's anticlericalism mesh with France's pose as "the great champion and protector of Catholic missions abroad"?[39]

Russia in the Valley of the Blind

By consensus, Russia was viewed as backward relative to Europe, but just as uncontested was the perception that it was a modernizing force in Asia. Discussion of Russian imperialism began in the 1870s when a spate of books appeared on the topic of Central Asia. Many of these works draped the area in a gauzy romanticism that made it appear as "a kind of wonder-land, which more than any other region has impressed the imagination of the modern world" as a fertile source of "great swarms of men" who had pulled off some of history's greatest conquests. Although the region possessed little commercial attractiveness, a few writers saw in it an object of historical and cultural interest. According to Selah Merrill, the noted Holy Land archaeologist, Central Asia was "the true cradle of the race," the source of "many of the things which modern civilization claims as peculiarly its own." Thanks to steady Russian expansion to the south and east, the once mysterious heartland of Genghis Khan and Tamerlane was "almost within reach of Cook's tourists."[40]

Describing the slow but steady Russian advance in that region, *The Nation* in 1870 judged it to be "unquestionably to the great advantage of civilization." This expansion, though accompanied by "amazing rapacity and unscrupulousness," was nevertheless the vehicle of a greater historical movement of which people generally approved. Praising the skill behind Russian military successes, Godkin extolled Russian expansion in Central Asia as "one of the most exciting and romantic episodes in the history of war." Russian achievements, claimed Merrill, "call forth the admiration of the enemies of Russia, as well as the praise of her friends." A review of one of James Bryce's travel books compared Russia favorably as an empire and colonizer not merely with archaic empires like the Ottoman, "but with any other country that is stretching out its hand over weaker races." "Russia seems to have a genius for colonization," said an essay in *The Atlantic*. Russians had a "wonderful faculty for absorbing and assimilating the various Asiatic races and peoples, and for transforming them into loyal and contented units of the empire—in fine, for Russianizing them." One author noted how quickly conquered peoples assumed the roles of Russian subjects and were accepted into the military and civil service. Unlike the British, there seemed little danger that the Russians would be evicted by popular revolts "even if supported by foreign intrigue and money." Although the amalgamation process could be "very slow, and in many places imperceptible," nationalities like the Georgians and Armenians were nevertheless "sharing some of the advantages of the foreign civilization which is thrusting itself upon them."[41]

As with French colonization, favorable reviews owed more to the backwardness of the peoples being absorbed than to any progressive features of Russian rule. Because commercial prospects in Central Asia seemed meager, the emphasis was on the cultural benefits of expansion. To Samuel Wells Williams, the peoples of Central Asia were "more like Apache Indians than organized nations and their reduction is a mercy to themselves as well as their neighbors." The British artist William Simpson described this section of Asia as "a den of thieves and murderers . . . all but separated from the rest of the world." Given the low cultural level, then, a little civilization went a long way. Thus while acknowledging that Russian administration left much to be desired, Eugene Schuyler, the nation's leading Russian expert of the day, managed nevertheless to conclude that Russian rule was "on the whole beneficial to the natives." At a minimum, Russian administration brought with it law and order, peace, and a bit of commerce. For his part, Godkin smiled on Russian expansion to the east and south because it checked a revivalist Islam among peoples who were "carrying their religious fanaticism to an insane pitch of excessiveness."[42]

But there were limits to the praise. This was, after all, autocratic Russia, the oriental despot par excellence, so it could only be portrayed as a backward modernizer. Attenuating the admiration for Russia's achievement was the conviction that it was precisely the cultural retardation of the Russians vis-à-vis Europeans and their hybrid semi-oriental character that made them such good civilizers in Asia. Taking this line, George McClellan attributed the success of the Russians to their "Asiatic characteristics," which gave them "a peculiar facility for conquering and assimilating to themselves the purely Asiatic countries." "It is the primitive simplicity of their style and manner of life," argued *The Nation*, "that enables them to elevate the Mongol"—from which one might infer that too much cultural distance between civilization and barbarism could be a handicap in the application of the civilizing mission. In practice, this perspective signaled approval of a more brutal style in ruling populations who were accustomed to cruelty as a basic feature of political life. In the valley of the blind, the one-eyed were the colonizers.[43]

There were other caveats. Although the Russians introduced law and order, it was stability czarist style—heavily militarized, oppressive, and burdensome in its exaction of taxes. Moreover, any fair cost-benefit analysis could only conclude that the conquests had weakened Russia. Schuyler's popular book, *Turkistan*, argued that the agricultural, mineral, or commercial resources extractable from Central Asia could not repay the expense of conquering it. Given Islam's powerful hold on the region's inhabitants—it was "a stronghold of Mohammedanism"—it seemed likely that expensive armies of occupation would be necessary for the foreseeable future. Moreover, this incessant process of expansion, though good for civilization, was also politically mindless and ultimately very dangerous, as the security of each new possession seemed to require the annexation of yet another. This situation spelled trouble—big trouble—in the form of a looming confrontation with Britain to the south. Thus far, Russia's advance had taken place in the absence of geopolitical resistance, but any future progress would encounter the complexities and dangers of the diplomacy of imperialism.[44]

An American Empire?

Where did the United States belong in this picture? Nowhere, seemingly. In contrast to the large amount of ink spilled on European imperialism and the civilizing mission, little was written about the possibility of the United States joining the club. In the two instances in which colonial expansion did become a live political issue—the debates over the Dominican Republic and Samoa in the early 70s and late 80s—the discussions were surprisingly parochial. The lack of general interest was evident from the fact that *The Nation* was the only journal to follow these debates in any detail. The occasional arguments on behalf of colonial expansion in the Western Hemisphere tended to follow a principle of contiguity in which expansion was made to appear a natural development—territories would fall to the United States through natural gravitation, as the result of a need to build a canal or defend the Monroe Doctrine, or perhaps as a result of the accumulation of sediment deposited by the Mississippi. But little was said about conquest or about the global imperatives of the civilizing mission.[45]

On the assumption that any new territories would follow the pattern of republican expansion established earlier in the century, race and culture were powerful arguments against annexation. The chief concern in this issue was a perceived lack of cultural compatibility with American society. Thus a retrospective on Seward's expansionist diplomacy argued vigorously that it would be "a mistake to reach for regions not preoccupied with peoples of kindred habits and or similar progressive spirit." *The Nation* was particularly scathing in offering racial/cultural reasons against expansion, referring to the Dominican Republic's "120,000 barbarians" and "200,000 ignorant Catholic Spanish negroes." Expanding on the climatological theories that were then in vogue, the journal insisted that the lands to the south were "incapable of self-government" thanks to a population that was "grossly ignorant, poor, superstitious, and indolent." Once the civilizing mission was accepted as a legitimate rationale, there would be no end to the process, argued Godkin, for many other countries in the Caribbean region suffered from "ignorance and turbulence and weariness of their own management of their own affairs." At a time when the United States had corruption enough to deal with at home, the nation would be absorbing, according to Representative Jacob Cox, "all the tumultuous, corruptible and corrupting elements which have made the so-called Spanish republics a burlesque of self-government."[46]

If annexation of the Dominican Republic was out of the question, the acquisition of Samoa did not even appear to be within the realm of possibility, notwithstanding a near miss confrontation with German warships in Apia harbor in 1889. For the jingoists, Samoa (like Grenada would be in the 1980s) was important because it was so unimportant. The discussion was about abstractions, not about Samoa itself; specifically, the debate centered on what the loss of Samoa would mean to national honor rather than on what Samoa would bring to the national purse. As one historian has said, "Samoa, as Samoa, did not matter at all; it might have been anywhere in the world." The annexation of Santo Domingo, which at least lay close to home in an area of growing commercial interest, seemed almost rational by comparison to acquiring Samoa. On the assumption that they needed no reasoned rebuttal, annexationist pleas were shrugged off with ridicule as infantile jingoism. In its evaluation of the documents released over the Samoan affair, *The Nation* said that "nobody could do justice to them in a summary but Gilbert and Sullivan or Offenbach. The condition of affairs in Samoa, as a basis for the warlike utterances of our bellicose contemporaries, is very good bouffe." The entire business was waved off as the product of "bumptious editors."[47]

In both the Dominican and the Samoan cases, the concern was less with what the United States could do for them than with their likely impact on the United States. Apart from objections to the insider dealing that plagued the Grant administration, *The Nation* wanted nothing to do with such "semi-civilized additions, whose absorption may exercise a serious influence on our polity." Anticipating the causal analysis of imperialism that John Hobson would offer, the root of colonial schemes was perceived to lie in special interests and speculators. To concede the issue to such people would only increase their rapacity and further degrade the tone of American political life. For the civil service reformers, colonialism was a thinly disguised system of outdoor relief for spoilsmen. "What a splendid field will be thrown open by the purchase to all unemployed collectors, assessors, appraisers, postmasters, consuls, and district attorneys," predicted Arthur G. Sedgwick. The whole project would be an even more disastrous replay of reconstruction, "a wretched farce" in which "the political machinery would inevitably be worked by white sharpers and adventurers and speculators from the North."[48]

Nevertheless, the debates did introduce many of the constitutional and ideological rationales that would reappear in 1898. An important argument against assuming foreign responsibilities was the nation's inability to take care of similar problems at home. The problem was not a lack of territory but an inability to govern adequately the existing national domain. "The first duty of the American Union is to its own people," insisted Godkin. "As long as there is ignorance, poverty, and corruption within its own borders, it owes it not less to civilization than to its own influence and home not to saddle itself with fresh loads of responsibility." Even in cases of peaceful purchase, there were better uses for the money. Why purchase a foreign territory when the money could be used to purchase the public good of education for the freedmen? In response to some proposals for expansion in the Caroline Islands for the purpose of protecting American missionaries, *The Nation* scoffed at the idea, pointing out that the United States had shown an inability to safeguard people residing within its borders. "When we are able to protect innocent foreigners at home like the Chinese from massacre and pillage," it might consider the idea, but not before. Civilization, in this view, began at home. [49]

If republican assimilation was not the objective, then serious constitutional issues and values came into play. "For the government of such communities as these are, either for their good or for ours, the Constitution supplies no machinery," concluded Godkin. *The Atlantic Monthly* insisted that "a republic is not like an empire; the law of its being forbids it to annex anything which it cannot thoroughly incorporate." Similarly, a *Century* editorial declared that "this republic does not want any people who are not capable of autonomy under our federal system." Charles Sumner's belief that forcible annexation was inherently unrepublican because it ignored the sacred principle of seeking the consent of the governed still held a strategically important place in American views of empire. Imperialism ran counter to the self-image of the United States as the exemplar republic whose global role, according to *The Nation,* depended "no more on the extent of its territory than on the color of the people's hair or the length of their noses." Anticipating Schumpeter, one essayist described annexationism as "a survival" for which there was no necessity in the modern world.[50]

Thus, although peaceful acquisition was merely unpalatable, a premeditated policy of forcible annexation was unthinkable, European even. "We cannot follow in the footsteps of our European cousins," insisted Richard Hinton. "Our triumphs are to be peaceful; commerce will be the reawakener." Noting the "immense cruelties" inflicted by the British upon India, a naval officer urged that America's commercial supremacy in the East Indies would not be "by rapine or murder, but by the energy of the American people." The civilizing mission might be a good thing, but these were also Spencerian liberals, and Herbert Spencer, as was well known, was a little Englander with no love of conquest. "Might, in his eyes, would hardly seem to be right," it was noted, "even when evolution is carried on by its means." Although William James had little sympathy for Spencer's "almost Quakerish humanitarianism and regard for peace," he agreed with his critique of imperial expansion through force.[51]

Nevertheless, the American attitude toward empire was more complicated than this outright dismissal would seem to suggest, for it took into account different varieties of colonialism. Although editors and essayists were fundamentally sympathetic to the civilizing mission of imperial powers, they were more enthusiastic about the possibilities of transformation through acculturation in the British Empire's white settler colonies. According to one reviewer, there were two kinds of colonialism: "quasi-colonization" and "actual colonization" (colonies of exploitation or conquest and settler colonies, in later usage). "Actual colonization" tended to take place in "all the outlying lands," whereas "quasi-colonization" consisted of "influencing the ideas and habits of less developed nations." Each type of colonialism highlighted different kinds of problems. Great Britain's treatment of the settler colonies raised questions of democracy, imperial federation, and global Anglo-Saxonism, whereas "quasi-colonization" raised issues of power, domination, and social justice. Each type also raised different kinds of problems with the native inhabitants. In settler colonies such as Australia and Canada, the problem of extermination of indigenous peoples came to the fore, whereas in the more recently acquired colonies of conquest acculturation was a more pressing concern. Moreover, it was possible to be in favor of one kind of colonialism while opposing the other. [52]

In the 1880s, American readers were exposed to a fair amount of ballyhoo from British promoters of empire. For example, the Canadian educator George R. Parkin told his American audience that the survival of Great Britain and its empire as a political unit would be the chief world-historical issue of the future. The key to Britain's survival would be imperial federation, without which British preeminence would go by the board. There was even some talk of enticing Americans into participating in a grand Anglo-American imperial confederation that would be composed of self-governing settler colonies and administered possessions. Trying to summon up the kind of enthusiasm for empire that was becoming commonplace in Britain, J. E. Chamberlain (an American) imagined the "gorgeous pageant" that an Anglo-Saxon confederation would produce on celebratory occasions: "What a triumphal procession of subject races: Indians of the East by thousands, their rajahs, richly apparelled, mounted up-on elephants; tribes of red Indians from the Western plains, tamed for the nonce; Nubians, Egyptians, picturesque Arabs from the Barbary deserts; dark masses of Ethiopians, piratical Malays, dragon-bearing Chinese from Hong Kong and San Francisco."[53]

Americans did bask in the reflected glory of the Anglo-Saxon civilizing mission as expressed in the success of the settler colonies, which were perceived as a progressive force for civilization. Among the most vocal supporters of Anglo-Saxon empire building was the Harvard historian John Fiske. "Of all the modern nations which have sought to reproduce and perpetuate their social and political institutions by colonizing the savage regions of the earth, England is the only one which has achieved signal and lasting success," he wrote in 1882. But this was only the beginning. Godkin, though he granted that "the dream seems in places a wild one," nevertheless contemplated with satisfaction the continued worldwide spread of the English-speaking races.

"The settlement in this fashion of vast continents will, indeed, be a moral renewal of the face of the earth," said one of his journal's reviews. Among other writers, the role of the "English race" as the dominant factor in the forging of a global civilization was treated as a matter of fact.[54]

But pride in the spread of common institutions on a global scale failed to translate into endorsement of schemes for imperial federation, with or without the United States as a member. The insistence of J. R. Seeley, in his book *The Expansion of England,* that Great Britain was supremely fitted to govern a large empire ran afoul of the American preference for the breaking of imperial ties. Federation was viewed as an unsatisfactory British response to the growing demand for democracy, which, according to *The Century,* if not heeded "might otherwise force a second break-up of the Empire." The colonies could not develop "higher moral qualities" without the responsibilities of independence, whereas the British threatened to become overburdened by imperial cares and fears at the expense of crying domestic needs. Equally important was the fact that England remained tied to Europe, whereas its colonies belonged naturally to different political systems. An imperial federation would simply connect them with "an old-world power in whose ever-increasing complications they would be inextricably involved." To maintain these European ties would be to sacrifice the interests of these proto-nations for the specious benefits of the imperial connection.[55]

James Anthony Froude's book, *Oceana,* another tract that sought to peddle the idea of imperial federation, had some nice things to say about American democracy but stirred up angry reviews because it justified centralized rule from London on the basis of an alleged "mental superiority" of the British elite. The British, the complaint went, "seem[ed] to regard the concession to colonists of power to manage their own affairs as in some way an infraction of their own excellency." It was only a matter of time, anyway, before the colonies lost their attachment to the mother country. In a review of Charles Wentworth Dilke's *Problems of Greater Britain* (1890), *The Nation* pointed out that the younger generation in Australia had "no personal knowledge of or sentiment for the old country." In the absence of the continuing bond of sentiment, the survival of the English language and British political traditions was all that Britain could rightfully expect. Like all parents, these legacies would have to do as "her reward for rearing a family of apparently ungrateful children." However painful the inevitable breakup, by letting nature take its course Great

Britain could achieve more acclaim and self-satisfaction as "the mother of free nations . . . than as the ruler of unwilling dependencies." Fiske, for all his admiration of British prowess in creating settler colonies, viewed the process as one that culminated rightly in independence. Only then would Protestantism and self-government "become forever the undisputed possession of all mankind." Discussions of imperial federation were merely "dreams," useful primarily for didactic purposes because they threw light on "the tendencies of history," according to a writer for *The Atlantic*.[56]

Although the idea of imperial federation was one possible gateway to a global future, it opened no new political doors for Americans who were already beginning to think in postimperial terms of integrating *all* former colonial possessions into a liberal world system. Whereas the role of the settler colonies was taken for granted, the effective tutelage of colonies of occupation/exploitation would be crucial to the formation of a global civilization. The British version of an Anglo-Saxon global civilization was too heavily anglicized to appeal to those whose preference ran to an Americanized world in which empire had been left behind. Among the most articulate and influential proponents of global Americanization as the wave of the future were Fiske and Josiah Strong. Although the final chapter of Strong's best-seller of the 1880s, *Our Country*, has often been depicted as a powerful clarion call to imperialism, it was no such thing. This much-discussed chapter makes no mention of conquest, empire, or colonies. Instead, Strong, a Protestant clergyman, was concerned with the spread of Christianity and civil liberty throughout the world, tasks for which history appeared to have chosen the Anglo-Saxon peoples. Strong began this chapter by defining Anglo-Saxons as "all English-speaking peoples," but before long the emphasis (the title is *Our Country*, after all) shifted to demonstrating that Americans were the crème de la crème.[57]

Strong went to some lengths to establish the superiority of American Anglo-Saxons over the British variety. The core principles of civil liberty and Protestant Christianity, he argued, were "more effective here than in the mother country." Religiously, there was no union of church and state in the United States, while economically, Americans had demonstrated a superior "money-making power." Strong also laid great emphasis on population growth outside of Europe (the revised 1891 edition would be "based on the census of 1890"). In terms of numbers alone, England, a "small island," could not hope to keep up. In addition, the restless energy of the North American people coupled with an unprecedented degree of social mobility ensured that North America would become "the great home of the Anglo-Saxon, the principal seat of his power, the center of his life and influence." Citing Darwin in support of his contention that the progress of the United States was due to natural selection, Strong saw the marked superiority of this race as being due "in large measure, to its highly mixed origin." Following Rawlinson, Strong believed that mixed races were "superior to the pure ones," and it was this new mixture that would become the core of "a growing world consciousness." In asserting "the marked superiority" of the race in the United States, Strong, who was a vocal advocate of racial equality, was speaking almost entirely in a cultural sense. Unlike some pessimists who considered open immigration to be a eugenic disaster in the making, Strong viewed it as a test that, once passed, would "add value to the amalgam which will constitute the new Anglo-Saxon race of the New World."[58]

Anglo-Saxons, he agreed, did possess "an instinct or genius for colonizing" what was often called the "waste spaces of the world." But the fact was that there were no more waste spaces, "no more new worlds." Heretofore, the spread of English-speaking peoples had taken place at the expense of peoples who could be easily shoved aside or, at the extreme, driven to extinction, but the coming era would be different. In Strong's opinion, the world was entering upon "a new stage of its history—the final competition of races, for which the Anglo-Saxon is being schooled." With places like Hawaii perhaps in mind, Strong admitted that "the extinction of inferior races before the advancing Anglo-Saxon," however sad, "certainly appears probable." But other "stronger races" would be able to "preserve their integrity." To hold their own against the Anglo-Saxon, however, they would "probably be forced to adopt his methods and instruments, his civilization and his religion." Indeed, Strong noted that among these peoples there was already taking place "a widespread revolt against traditional beliefs" in which "old superstitions [were] loosening their grasp."

In a much-quoted phrase, Strong predicted that the Anglo-Saxon race, "having developed peculiarly aggressive traits calculated to impress its institutions upon mankind," would "spread itself over the earth." However, this expansion would not take place through the agency of imperialism, but as the result of cultural superiority that would enable the Anglo-Saxon to "dispossess many weaker races, assimilate others, and mold the remainder, until, in a very true and important sense, it has Anglo-Saxonized mankind." But the contest (and contest it was, for he definitely did speak in terms of the survival of the fittest) was "no war of extermination." The struggle was "not one of arms, but of vitality and civilization," in which Anglo-Saxonism would be spread by "travel, commerce, the missionary." Lastly, Strong equated the advance of civilization with the growth of peace. "As civilization advances," Strong argued, "it will learn less of war, and concern itself more with the arts of peace, and for these the massive battle-ax must be wrought into tools of finer temper." The triumph of Anglo-Saxonism would be "but the consummation of a movement as old as civilization—a result to which men have looked forward for centuries."[59]

When translated into a more modern idiom, it is clear that Strong was making a case for the Americanization of the world. He was a globalist, a believer in racial equality and miscegenation who was firmly committed to the spread of a global culture grounded in the American version of Anglo-Saxon values. But it would be a mistake to reduce Strong's message to secular terms, for he was also a missionary enthusiast who believed that the United States was "first and foremost the instrument for the world's conversion." But clearly his religious perspective had secular implications. Strong would have doubts about empire in the future, but he would never recant his enthusiasm for globalization.[60] He was among the first of the social gospel school to preach global responsibilities for the nation—"not America for America's sake, but America for the world's sake"—and he would later go so far as to elevate world interests above the national interest.[61] Fittingly, he ended his chapter by repeating Jacob Grimm's prediction that the English language seemed "chosen, like its people, to rule in future times in a still greater degree in all the corners of the earth." Strong's was an audacious, even hubristic, vision of an Americanized globalization, but it was not a brief for empire. As we shall see in the concluding chapter, John Fiske shared a similar vision of America's leading role in a process of global acculturation, but with special emphasis on the transmutation of Europe.

Readers of the journals that contained these reflections on imperialism were treated to a nuanced and complex body of ideas that examined imperialism in the light of globalization. American liberals were generally unsympathetic to empires as exercises in exploitation or as outlets for national glory, and, as we shall see in the next chapter, they took a jaundiced view of colonies as pawns in a global diplomacy of imperialism. But while they believed that power alone failed to justify conquest or to confer à certificate of superiority upon imperial rulers, their criticism of imperialism was conditional, not fundamental. Imperialism was a necessary evil, which, however flawed they found some of its particulars, was also an inescapable feature of modernity. Most writers therefore tended to be sympathetic to the civilizing mission as a justification for colonial rule, even to the extent of excusing much unsavory behavior, which at least was preferable to policies of "indirect rule" that left the locals to themselves. Indeed, in the case of Great Britain, it is safe to say that the American faith in the future of globalization presupposed the existence of the British Empire as a necessary condition—at least for the time being. Notwithstanding this sympathy, there was as yet no visible enthusiasm for an American empire. The preference instead was that the United States play a leading American role in the larger process of which imperialism was but one expression.

9

International Politics

Americans who followed international politics after the Civil War soon learned that the foreign policy behavior of states fell embarrassingly short of the liberal vision of nationalism and internationalism marching smartly abreast; if anything, global processes of civilization and international relations were increasingly at odds. Already in 1865 *The Nation*'s Paris correspondent, Auguste Laugel, was complaining that "in this Europe of the nineteenth century, which prides itself on its liberalism, the axioms and dogmas of Hobbes, of Machiavelli, of Julius Caesar, are reviving like forgotten phantoms." Over the course of the next quarter century, cosmopolitan Americans looked in vain for any signs of improvement in international relations, only to conclude repeatedly that the outbreak of a massive new conflict in Europe was inevitable and imminent. A remark excerpted from Talleyrand's memoirs well summarized the course of international politics during these years. According to the master diplomat, the sad moral of human history was that "the spirit of strife rushes to every spot on earth to which communication is opened."[1]

The failure of peaceful liberal diplomacy to take root was worldwide. No doubt European politics lay at the heart of the world's problems, but reports of wars and explosive tensions covered a broad arc that stretched from the Balkans across the Middle East and through Asia. As a result of this global coverage, Americans were treated to a panoramic view of international relations in diverse regions as parts of a larger whole in which events in one area were linked to events in another. In evaluations of conflicts across the globe, two concepts appeared again and again: civilization and what William Seward had called "the crazy balance of power in Europe." The greater the distance from the Old World, the greater the weight given to civilizational issues, but whatever the geographic locus of conflict, the balance of power and civilization were the x and y axes of the discursive matrix that Americans used to analyze international politics.[2]

Civilization and the Balance of Power in Europe

In principle, war in Europe was considered undesirable, but in practice exceptions were made in the name of progress. Thus it was common for a time after 1865 to distinguish between national and dynastic wars in the belief that hostilities that advanced the great historical principle of nationalism were acceptable, even necessary, because they rendered a service to humanity. The wars of national unification were accordingly explained away as transitional spasms of violence following which "pacific influences" would "gain strength in a geometrical ratio." When seen in this light, Prussia's swift victory in the Seven Weeks' War against Austria, was interpreted as a victory for modern civilization. While Prussia was a cultured nation whose armies were filled with literate conscripts, the decrepit Hapsburg realm, in Godkin's view, was by comparison not a modern polity, but "a relic of things long passed away," with "not a single claim on the sympathy of any human being." To this way of thinking, the war's outcome was less a victory of the Hohenzollerns over the Hapsburgs than a triumph of "the invincible forces of modern society."[3]

Although the Seven Weeks' War had settled some momentous intra-German issues, its successful outcome for Prussia soon pointed to the historical necessity of yet another, even more momentous conflict. "The adjustment of the Continent on its new political basis of popular sovereignty, instead of royal or imperial arrangement, cannot be completed without a fresh trial of material strength," predicted *The Nation* in 1869. Looked at from the standpoint of power and traditional national interests, French nervousness at the imminent emergence of a new German nation was quite justifiable, but for Americans that kind of old thinking ignored the central point: France was on the wrong side of history. For Napoleon III, a war with Prussia and the new North German Confederation would be dynastic, pure and simple, its purpose being to firm up his grip on the French imperial throne. By comparison, Germany's national existence had much the greater claim to historical legitimacy.[4]

By an overwhelming margin, Germany also seemed a desirable center of power on the continent. With the stunning defeat of France in the Franco-Prussian War, the reins of European power, reasoned one editor, had been "transferred to a more cultivated and substantial people—to educated, enlightened, and peaceful Germany, in whose steady hands that power may undoubtedly be more safely trusted than in those of the ambitious and war-loving French." No tears needed to be shed at the end of France's political and cultural dominance in Europe, for her ascendancy had been based on an "artificial equipoise." "The naked truth of the matter," wrote Godkin, was that France had been on top for so long that Frenchmen had convinced themselves that they had "some sort of divine right to regulate the affairs of all her neighbors." France's displacement by Germany was "one of the greatest gains humanity has made." Whatever the fate of the fragile Third Republic, at least the world would be spared another outbreak of the plague of Bonapartist militarism. The war's outcome, wrote the émigré historian Hermann Von Holst, sounded "the death knell of war-like Gaul."[5]

The war had paid a huge historical bonus by ending the papacy's temporal sovereignty in Italy following the withdrawal of French troops from Rome. Godkin rejoiced that "so deep a stain on the Christian name has at last been removed." Papal absolutism, which was just another form of Caesarism in American eyes, had been reduced to a matter of hollow principle in the declaration of papal infallibility. *Appletons'* went so far as to suggest that divine retribution had been at work as a punishment for "supremely wicked acts." This rosy view of the war's wider ramifications was stretched to include even the tensions between Russia and England over Russia's denunciation of the Black Sea clauses of the Treaty of Paris of 1857. Should Anglo-Russian hostility culminate in war as a consequence, this would be a good thing for civilization, went this line of reasoning. Such a conflict, according to the editors of *Scribner's,* "would probably drive the Turk out of Europe and liberalize the whole political system of the Old World." Thus, for a moment, the war's end seemed to make possible a bright and open-ended new era of international relations. Now that the balance of power had been overturned, George E. Pond of *The Galaxy* wondered "what new law will guide the map-making of the future." His nominee for the newly ascendant idea was "the 'solidarity of nations'—that oneness wrought by language and race which has been so coveted and also so largely accomplished of late." To this way of thinking, then, the Franco-Prussian War had been the storm before the calm.[6]

As the euphoria subsided, sober second thoughts began to be expressed about the implications of the stunning German victory. It soon became clear that the triumph of the national principle had created more problems than it had resolved. As Pond recognized, "Dazzling at first, the ethnic theory of political sway soon presents difficulties—presents them in all border lands inhabited by mixed peoples, and elsewhere too." Although American liberals wanted to believe that the new Germany was peaceably inclined, war clouds were clearly visible on the horizon. French revanchism was a powerful motive in its own right, but in addition Germany's imprudent annexation of Alsace-Lorraine had given France "a respectable and powerful reason" for a war. And despite some premature speculation about its permanent decline, France was far from washed-up. The *Catholic World* was in the minority when it argued the need for France's survival as a way of preserving the balance of power, but most other commentators believed that the national principle itself ensured a French revival. "Great nations do not fall irreparably under a single disaster," said *The Galaxy*. "The Gallic cock will soon crow more lustily than ever." The possibility of French decline also provoked some disquieting reflections about a world civilization that possessed no counterweight to Germanic culture. Even as it sympathized with Germany against a "decadent" France, *Appletons'* had its doubts. "This may be the best, as it is clearly the strongest branch, of the human stock," wrote the editor, "but still a branch with no right and no capacity to supersede humanity."[7]

If anything, the emphasis on power was greater than ever. The tone of speculation about the war's implications changed so quickly that the ink on the peace treaty was barely dry before predictions of a new war filled the air. By the mid-1870s, there was already talk of a Franco-Russian alliance and German trepidation about the possibility of a two-front war, which was described as "the cloud which hangs over the German future." German power began to take on a more menacing aspect, too. With the balance of power as a continuing feature of the European landscape, the only change was that Germany had replaced France as the power most likely to pursue hegemony. As Pond noted, the balance of power was "still alive in European politics" and perhaps even "the master force." As standing reminders of the danger, it was "a plain lesson" even before the Franco-Prussian War had ended that new standing armies would "far exceed in numbers the armies of other days."[8]

This was gloomy speculation, but Americans needed to understand the workings of European power politics, no matter how alien or distasteful to the national sensibility. As *The Nation* explained, "There are certain political ideals which have a powerful hold on the European imagination which can hardly be successfully described to an American audience, so far have we drifted away from them in thought and deed." On the bright side, Germany's desire for peace was still taken for granted, and it was possible that the French craving for vengeance would ebb over time. But while the future might conceivably bring peace, it was more plausible to anticipate tempestuous times ahead. By the mid-1870s, reporting on events in Europe typically announced the sighting of "war clouds" or "storm clouds." The war scare of 1875, in particular, provided a foretaste "of alarms for many years to come." Franco-German enmity was the immediate low-pressure center disturbing European tranquility, but Americans realized that the thunderheads were drifting in from another direction, in the form of the "Eastern Question." From the mid-1870s onward, the eyes of Europeans and Americans alike shifted toward the darkening southeastern horizon.[9]

The Eastern Question: Civilization or Russian Autocracy?

The tension between civilization and power was also present in the Eastern Question, but in complicated ways that made choosing a favorite more difficult than it had been in continental politics. The basic divide was between those who welcomed a collapse of the Ottoman state and those who feared that the price of its disappearance would be a disastrous expansion of Russian power in Europe and in the Near East. One group saw the issue as the last stage of the age-old struggle between Islam and Christendom, whereas the other foresaw a general European war, accompanied perhaps by a turn to reaction, as the consequence of a Russian triumph. Either way, some fundamental issues were at stake. As Pond put it, the struggle between Moscow and Constantinople revealed at work "those vast underlying forces of popular sentiment, those mighty tendencies of modern civilization, which work so powerfully in shaping events, and aid in casting the horoscope of the future."[10]

The illness was protracted, but there seemed little question in American minds that the "sick man of Europe," the term famously coined by Stratford Canning, the British ambassador to the Porte, was on his deathbed. Financial disarray, corruption, xenophobia, and a profound commitment to Islam, among other failings, signaled the imminent end of the Ottoman state. The clergyman and popular historical writer J. S. C. Abbott predicted that "wherever our sympathies may be, the doom of the Ottoman Porte is apparently sealed. The lazy Turk, stupefied with tobacco and opium, knowing no joys but those of a mere animal existence, with a religion whose doctrines deaden the intellect and paralyze the energies, can never keep pace with the nations of Christendom." Although he compared Turkish rule favorably to that of the Byzantines, Charles Dudley Warner also regarded the Turks as irredeemably decadent. "Enfeebled by luxury and sensuality," they had lost "those virile qualities which gave to their ancestors the dominion of so many kingdoms in Asia, Africa and Europe." Especially after the insurrection of 1875, the handwriting was on the wall. "The Turkish empire is near its end," pronounced *The Nation.* "No one now pretends that it has any future."[11]

More than anything else, it was the empire's treatment of awakening nationalities in southeastern Europe that provoked calls for its complete expulsion from Europe. The Turks were criticized at every turn for being either too listless or too repressive in their handling of this problem. On the one hand, as George F. Herrick, a long-time missionary in Turkey, insisted, "the very supineness of the Turk is—more than he is aware—inviting the Christian races to awake to the assertion of a manly energy long dormant." This was a wholesome development, he felt, in the direction of the "recovery of long lost human rights." However, when the Ottomans acted energetically to stamp out these nationalist stirrings, their responses were condemned as barbaric, the product of a "medieval state of mind which sees in wholesale massacre a possible political expedient."[12]

For many, the issue was settled by the revelations of atrocities committed by Turkish irregulars against rebellious Christian populations. To Godkin, these "Bulgarian horrors," which were made famous by Gladstone's incendiary essay, demonstrated the "Turk's ignorance of the essential conditions of his political existence, and, one may say, of his incapacity for civilization." The issue stirred emotions to the point that even a women's magazine, ordinarily little given to discussion of international affairs, pleaded for intervention: "the cries and struggles of eleven millions of Christians against the wicked and cruel tyranny of Turkish fanaticism, and against a Government that is too wretchedly helpless to protect them, can not much longer be disregarded."[13]

In larger terms, the events were seen as a struggle between civilizations in Asia and Europe. An anonymous contributor to *The Atlantic Monthly* in 1878 put the case in extreme form when he wrote that "there seems to be no possibility of good-will, or even tolerance, between the races of the two continents, when brought into a state of co-inhabitation [sic]." A year earlier, John Fiske, reviewing Europe's historical relationship with invaders from the East, concluded that "in every case the stake has been the continuance of the higher civilization," though he was quick to add that in recent centuries the risk to Europe had become "very slight." Citing "the unquestionable verdict of all history," the educator Daniel S. Gregory described the Ottomans as "from the beginning the enemy not only of Christianity but of all true civilization as well." Combining culture and religion, Gregory defined the Eastern Question as "not a question of Mohammedanism, pure and simple, but of . . . the worst form of Mohammedanism compounded with the peculiar character of a very bad race." For *The Nation*, meanwhile, continued Ottoman rule was simply "a blot on civilization."[14]

What would follow an Ottoman collapse? Godkin foresaw a rosy future in which a fertile region, once freed from Islamic rule, would experience a commercial and cultural rebirth. Constantinople in Western hands would become "one of the most attractive resorts of the globe—a superb city, in which the frivolous and restless elegance of the West would be sobered and chastened by contact with eastern repose." For those who adopted this view, a Russian victory would signal the final triumph of the long frustrated crusading impulse. Inasmuch as the myth of military invincibility was thought to be essential to maintaining Islam's exceptionalist self-image, the fall of Constantinople, in conjunction with European advances in the Mediterranean and the Middle East, was bound to produce profound demoralization and distress among Muslim believers. Thenceforth, it was suggested, "the creed of the prophet would enter on a new and very interesting phase in its history." The death of Pius IX in 1878, which followed on the heels of the Ottoman defeat in the Russo-Turkish War, appeared almost providentially to sweep aside the two major religious obstacles to progress in Europe.[15]

Unfortunately, it was not that simple. Because the principal opponent of the Porte was czarist Russia, forming an opinion on the Eastern Question required choosing between two evils. Those who sympathized with Russia believed that the struggle between civilizations was far weightier than internecine disputes within Europe. For this group, the Turkish pot was demonstrably blacker than the Russian kettle, a perception that *The Nation* tried to sell as historical truth. "We are not admirers of Russia, nor of the Russian government, nor of the Russian political system," it argued in one piece, "but surely it is impossible to overlook the fact that for two hundred years she has been a civilizing agent of extraordinary effectiveness. While she has been doing this Turkey has been reducing the fairest portions of the earth's surface to degradation which the most careful observers begin to call hopeless." The struggle, another editorial argued, was a coda to the Civil War, a continuation of the battle for human emancipation. The Russians were "doing the last and greatest work of deliverance now left for Christendom to do." For Godkin, however crude and backward the Russians might be at the moment, they at least possessed the germ of progressive potential, whereas the Ottomans had "inflicted more moral and material damage on manhood than any slavery which the modern world has witnessed." William L. Kingsley, editor of *The New Englander and Yale Review*, agreed, comparing the Russians to the barbarian Franks in the fifth century: "They believe that they are to have a future; that great things are in store for them; that the progress of civilization in Asia is to depend in great measure upon their efforts to propagate it."[16]

Still, a sizable body of opinion thought otherwise. Although the massacres could not be ignored, it seemed equally evident that Russian meddling in the region had upset the relative tolerance of the Ottomans toward ethnic and religious minorities in the Balkans. Moreover, Ottoman military performance gainsaid all the talk of decadence. The courage and tenacity of Turkish resistance in the face of superior Russian resources forced even their harshest critics to acknowledge that the Turks had admirable qualities that could not be fully explained by the large number of British officers in the employ of the Sultan. For example, the surprisingly stout Turkish military performance caused the Turkophobic J. W. DeForest to have second thoughts. At the very least, descriptions of the Turks as "decadent and effeminated [*sic*]" were wide of the mark. "We have not read their history thoroughly and with discrimination," he concluded. There were even some apologists for Ottoman rule. Edson L. Clark's *The Races of European Turkey* praised the subject peoples of European Turkey to such an extent that it led a reviewer to wonder wryly if the American, English, or German peoples "might be considerably improved by a century or two of Turkish bondage." In some cases, it was possible to hold contradictory views of the Turks, as sensual and lazy in normal circumstances, but also as capable on occasion of considerable heroism.[17]

These forgiving views of the Ottomans were usually accompanied by warnings that the extension of Russian power, far from advancing civilization, would only install another form of Asiatic despotism. *Appletons'*, for one, found it impossible to see Russia as a liberator or champion of Christian civilization in southeastern Europe. "It is very clear," said the editor, "that her paramount object is dominion, and that the Bulgarian oppressions are but a cloak and an excuse." Some of *The Nation's* writer's took issue with Godkin's pro-Russian stance. "The Russians are a conquering nation," Heilprin maintained, and a backward one at that. Apart from the recent emancipation of the serfs, Russia's history was "a dreary narrative of tyrannies numerous and remorseless, of systematic cruelty to the races subject to her rule, and a haughty adherence to old despotic ways of governing by force." Why should Russia be expected to govern Bulgaria any more justly than it did Poland? How would the substitution of one oppressive master for another benefit the European Christians? Whichever side won, "the cause of civilization [would] not be advanced one iota." The British traveler and writer, Laurence Oliphant, concluded that all talk of civilization, humanitarianism, and Christianity in the Middle East was mere cant, a sordid spectacle of "the nations of Christendom endeavoring to forget the feelings of jealousy, hatred, and distrust by which they are usually animated, in the effort to unite upon a common basis of race prejudice and of religious intolerance."[18]

Worse still, not only the Balkan peoples, but also the rest of Europe, stood to suffer from a Russian triumph. Constantinople may have represented civilization to some, but for others it stood as a symbol of *realpolitik* at its worst. As early as 1868, Heilprin had described the consequences of Russian success: "it would replace the crescent by the Greek cross on the dome of St. Sophia, would convert the Euxine [i.e., the Black Sea] into a Russian lake, and make the Czar . . . the most powerful ruler that ever wielded a scepter." The Franco-Prussian War had already altered the political balance of Europe by pushing Russian expansion southward, thereby giving impetus to what many believed was the program of Peter the Great, a desire to control the Bosporus and the Dardanelles so deep and persistent that it was thought to be culturally ingrained. In the words of an anonymous writer, this impulse to southward expansion was "a deep, ineradicable, and most formidable instinct in the character of the Russian people." If one were to believe *The Atlantic*, the Russian gaze had been fastened on Constantinople for a thousand years.[19]

Although Godkin and those of like mind were willing to take their chances with this outcome, others feared that so powerful a Russia would be able to impose its style of autocracy on the continent. The only proven way to avoid this calamity was to rely on the balance of power, which was like building a house on a foundation of dynamite. Even those who detested the Porte understood that a decisive Russian victory would have explosive implications for the European equilibrium. According to J. S. C. Abbott, it was "manifestly for the interest of the other leading nations in Europe, in view of what is called the balance of power, to check the growth of a nation thus threatening to overshadow all Europe." It was, in some ways, a very strange situation, for without this concern for the balance of power Turkish rule in Europe would most likely have collapsed long ago. As a result of conflicting concerns, as one reviewer put it a few years later, "the Turk is now dependent on the protection of the countries which he formerly threatened."[20]

American views on the war and the peace settlement also cast doubt on Great Britain's commitment to promoting civilization. How serious could the British be when Disraeli was so intent on pursuing a balance of power that enabled the British elite to turn a blind eye to Turkish cruelty and misgovernment? "Whatever danger to England there may be in the appearance of Russia on the shores of the Mediterranean," complained Godkin, "there has been something monstrous and ignoble in trying to guard against it by upholding an organization so rotten as the Turkish Empire." Disraeli's policy was "complete folly," according to Herbert Tuttle, because Russians had no designs against the British, being much more worried about nations closer to their frontiers. Some writers even dragged anti-Semitism out of the closet by advancing the idea that Disraeli's policies, far from reflecting Great Britain's interests, were being driven by Russia's mistreatment of Jews. Others went so far as to suggest that reports of revolutionary unrest in Russia prompted by an overbearing autocracy were simply British propaganda. E. W. Stoughton, freshly returned from a tour as minister to Russia, claimed that this propagandist literature was "in the main of English origin," the product of long-standing Russophobia.[21]

After overcoming determined Turkish resistance at Plevna, the Russians imposed a harsh peace on the Ottomans in the Treaty of San Stefano in 1878. Despite the hope of some Americans, former President Grant among them, that Turkey would be evicted from Europe, the Russians were unable to win Constantinople, but they did manage to create a greater Bulgaria, a pawn through which they hoped to dominate the Balkans. With an Ottoman collapse now a forgone conclusion, essayists voiced a growing uneasiness about the consequences of Russia's enhanced position in the region. For one writer, the less desirable alternative in Napoleon's prophecy about Europe eventually becoming either republican or Cossack was on the verge of being realized. Providing a small measure of consolation, the reverses suffered by the czar's armies suggested that the Russians had exhausted themselves for the foreseeable future. Russia's military potential had evoked an "almost superstitious dread" through the first half of the century, but the failure to finish off the Turks raised doubts about Russia's capacity to exercise a decisive influence in Europe. Kingsley predicted that "it will not be in our day that Russia will be strong enough to attempt anything to the disadvantage of the western nations." Still, Russian weakness would not last forever.[22]

Structurally, the old Eastern Question had become the even more combustible new Eastern Question, as Herbert Tuttle put it. By most accounts, the Congress of Berlin, convened hastily in 1878 because the European powers were alarmed by the extent of Russian gains, had accomplished little except to put off the various explosive problems such as the future of the Ottoman Empire, the fate of the South Slavs, and the European balance of power. Meanwhile, the underlying causes of the Eastern Question—the "manifold diversities of race, language, and religion"—had been touched scarcely at all. The Ottomans were still in Europe, the nationalities question continued to smolder, and the Russian presence had grown even more ominous. For a few optimists, the Congress had at least bought some time during which modernizing processes might take hold in southeastern Europe. According to this best-case scenario for the Balkans, Austria-Hungary would successfully fulfill the civilizing mission implicit in its mandate in Bosnia and Herzegovina, thereby blunting the appeal of Pan-Slavism. But for a cynical "old diplomatist," writing in *The North American Review*, the treaty had only made a bad situation worse. Austria, he predicted, had "placed herself politically in a position which must, sooner or later, lead to her complete disintegration." The treaty was Austria's "death-warrant." The effect of the treaty was "precisely that of throwing a fire-brand into a powder-magazine." Opinion was near unanimous on this score. Even before the congress met, *The Catholic World* was predicting that the great powers would sooner or later stumble into a general war that would "determine the destinies of the world for the next ensuing age." In taking this pessimistic line, Americans were only reporting the expectations of Europeans themselves about the inevitability of a great war.[23]

A positive outcome seemed to depend on all kinds of improbable developments: Ottoman reform, Russian liberalization, successful foster care by the Austro-Hungarian Empire, and a diminution of tensions within Europe. Which of these developments was least likely to occur was a matter of some discussion. At first, most American commentators got it wrong by predicting Ottoman collapse rather than Balkan nationalism and the weakness of the Austrian state as the source of future trouble. Over the course of the 1880s, however, more and more observers looked to European difficulties, especially to an Austro-Russian showdown, as the most likely source of future trouble. It was just a matter of time—when, as opposed to whether—before the Berlin system came crashing down, taking the European balance down with it. In 1885, *The Nation* was writing of "the great European war, the necessary war, which everybody expects, hopes for, and dreads." "Sooner or later," it predicted, "some untoward event will force Russia or Austria-Hungary to intervene and begin the great irrepressible conflict in the east of Europe," a war that far too many groups seemed eager to launch. Michael Heilprin, having just received a handsome new German atlas, noted that the map of the Balkans needed to be understood "as a war-map of the future."[24]

The only mechanism holding Europe together appeared to be Bismarck's alliance system, whose combined power was "so colossal that no one of the hostile neighbors will, single-handed, dare to defy it." Militarist institutions notwithstanding, Germany had the saving grace of being a status quo power. Thus when Moltke said "the whole world knows that we do not contemplate conquest," he was taken at his word. Nevertheless, the warning signs continued to pile up. Russia and Germany continued to have interests in common, most notably a dislike of radicalism, but there were many anticipations of a falling out in the near future. As early as 1880, *The Nation*, recalling the public glee in Germany at news of the Russian defeat at Plevna, predicted that "the time cannot be far distant when the rulers, like the statesmen and the people, of the two countries will be arrayed in open hostility, making an armed conflict inevitable." On another occasion, it concluded that "the great conflict between the Slavic East of Europe and its Germanic centre, however, must one day take place." From the Bulgarian crisis of 1885 onward, reports of war scares were the order of the day. Crises in southeastern Europe, the rise of Pan-Slavism in

Russia, the emergence of Boulangism in France, the increasingly irresponsible behavior of the Balkan nationalities, and the prospect of Bismarck's departure all pointed to big trouble ahead.[25]

At the same time it was difficult to know how seriously to take all this talk of "a great blaze of war." Few Europeans really desired war, and much of the talk could not be taken at face value. More often than not, scare stories appeared to be prompted by partisan politics aimed at securing larger budgetary appropriations for the military. By the late 1880s, war-scare weariness had set in, by which time *The Nation* had begun to discount reports of an impending conflict. It attributed the "war scare" (in scare quotes) to semiofficial newspapers eager to pump up distribution. "A war scare is the best mode of running up 'sales' known to them," it wrote, "because, as long as the armaments are so large, war will always seem a not improbable contingency." In 1889, commenting on "the usual annual war alarm," it concluded cynically that "when the time comes for a war scare, every event of the day is made to support it."[26]

The final element in the equation was the emergence of the Franco-Russian alliance and the creation of opposing alliance systems. In 1888, *The Nation* foresaw "the lineaments of another constellation formed by France, Russia, and perhaps even a third power." Only a few years earlier, the French had been ridiculed for their courtship of Russia, for their willingness to "burn cheap incense to Russophilism." At that time the dispatch of representatives to attend the funeral of the Pan-Slavist Mikhail Katkov was described as having "made the French Republic ridiculous before liberal Europe." But it did not take long for people to realize the weakness of ideological repulsion in relation to the powerful forces of attraction generated by *realpolitik*. In 1889, *The Nation* reported that common opinion in France held that no treaty was really necessary, "that the interests of France and Russia are common, and that the two countries must be found together in the next European struggle."[27]

Through all of these troubling uncertainties and developments, Bismarck was believed to be the aging Atlas holding up the European world. Although the course of German foreign policy in the 1870s had dashed the hopes of liberal admirers, who now recoiled from "the despotic temper of the new masters of Europe," Heilprin was forced to admit that Bismarck's combination of preparation and prudence had been "uncontestably and brilliantly successful." John Kasson was one of many to speculate about what Bismarck's departure might mean for Europe. "What demons of war shall be unchained by his death we do not know," he wrote. Not everyone was pessimistic, but the course of events had given no reason to change the widely held view that war was only a matter of time. "Should this contest come, it will be the colossal war of the century," *Appletons'* had predicted in 1875. They were right, although they got the century wrong.[28]

Making Sport of the "Great Game"

The Eastern Question was connected in journalistic accounts to another Russo-British conflict, the contest for domination in Central Asia that came to be known as "the great game." For Heilprin and *The Nation*, the competition in Afghanistan was but "one phase of the vast Eastern question." Similarly, George M. Towle saw Russian expansion in Asia as having "a not very remote connection with what is called "the Eastern question in Europe." Although most observers continued to see the Balkans as the source of the next war, some believed that the fuse to the powder keg was much longer. It was in Asia, opined *Appletons'*, "that the seeds of what must sooner or later be an obstinate European conflict are being sown." By the late 1870s, as the Russians were reported to be nearing Afghanistan, this remote, undeveloped, and landlocked country threatened to become an Asian version of the Balkan tinderbox. Beginning with the Second Afghan War of 1878–1880, the alarm bells continued to peal throughout the 1880s.[29]

As with the Balkans, there was no agreement over exactly what was at issue. Some observers insisted that highly important national interests were in play, while others viewed the stakes as largely imaginary. American confusion reflected British opinion of the day, which was fiercely divided on the Afghan question. One body of thought held that Russian expansion in Asia was a ploy aimed at diverting British attention from the Balkans and stretching British resources. According to this interpretation, Russia's southward thrust into Afghanistan was a payback for having been rebuffed in the Balkans. Thus, speculated *The Nation*, Russian movement in the direction of India "was a natural outcome of the extreme hostility which England had then manifested toward Russia," a development that a reviewer at the *Atlantic* called a "counterplot." The wish to divert England's attention away from Europe, Godkin suggested, "was the mainspring of her Central Asian policy." When combined with Russian expansion to the Pacific, some sensed a broader threat to British interests, while others perceived a more general ideological menace in the making. In this view, it was not Russian aggression but Russian absolutism that threatened Europe and Asia. Pulling out all the stops in *The North American Review,* Sir Edwin Arnold warned that a Russian triumph in this region "would be the triumph of the Slav over the Saxon, and would set back the development of Asia, and the advancement of the human race generally, at least a thousand years."[30]

But a sizable body of opinion downplayed these kinds of fears, dismissing them as products of overheated imaginations and fanciful strategizing. For these skeptics, Russia had always been less concerned with Europe than with Asia and the Middle East. Russia's eastward expansion was already centuries old, Selah Merrill reminded readers, and went forward independently of developments in the Black Sea region. Moreover, from the standpoint of civilization, the Russian advance was clearly beneficent and to be applauded. "Considering what she has done and suffered," said Merrill, "a careful and just historian might say with truth that she deserved to succeed." Some of these febrile imaginings were attributed to blinkered Russophobia. As Godkin pointed out in an assessment of Russian expansion in Central Asia: "it would puzzle the acutest moralist to point out in what it differed, either as to motive or means, from the construction of the British Empire in India, the story of which no Englishman reads without justifiable pride." For the skeptics, the British were on the wrong side of history in Central Asia as well as in the Balkans.[31]

Probably the most influential view was represented by Russian expert Eugene Schuyler. He was convinced that there was no threat to India, nor did he see any necessary connection to European politics in Russia's Central Asian policy. If one looked at the facts on the ground, there was no "magnificent scheme," as one review of Schuyler's book explained, to "flank and thus finally take Constantinople; to gradually draw near to, and on an opportune occasion to invade, India; and to obtain the full control and monopoly of Oriental commerce." On the contrary, Russian conquests in Central Asia were the product of "what yearly and almost daily changing circumstances dictate." Schuyler believed that Russia was advancing in Turkistan without knowing how impoverished the area was, but it felt compelled to stay for reasons of prestige. Once securely established, it was easy to use newly acquired territories as platforms for renewed rounds of expansion. Far from augmenting the power of the czarist regime, *The Nation* argued that the unceasing Russian conquests had resulted in a net weakening. "Even with a wise and economical government," it reasoned, "the country must form a drain on the imperial treasury as long as it is necessary to maintain an army of occupation."[32]

In other words, because Russia was only doing what Russia habitually did in Asia by taking the course of least resistance, the threat to India was nothing more than "an idle fear." William Kingsley saw the threat to India as chimerical because it was Central Asia that comprised "the destined field of her operations." By the time Russia was actually capable of moving on India, the subcontinent would likely be independent. Thomas Knox, too, doubted that the Russians had any designs on India, and added that whatever conflicting interests there were in the region could be settled readily enough by diplomacy—there was no irrepressible conflict. But whatever Russia's intentions, the threat to India was laden with potential for war, for India was unquestionably a vital interest for which Great Britain was willing to fight. As *Appletons'* put it, "even the modern commercial spirit could not resist the thought of losing a treasure won with such difficulty." Especially since the revolt of 1857, the British were well aware of native dissatisfaction with their rule and sensed that some Hindus were curious about the arrival of the Russians in the expectation that "things will be different." But here too, skeptics like Merrill were convinced of "the absurdity of the fear that Russia has any serious designs on India."[33]

Critics of the great game could only shake their heads in amazement at the cultural and geographical ignorance of those who saw Afghanistan as a prize worth fighting for. Samuel Wells Williams wondered, after analyzing the people and the geography, "why either of these powerful rivals wants it, or what practical use it will be to the one who gets it." The tribal and ethnic conflicts in the country had "little more influence on the rest of mankind than the quarrels of African negroes." Afghanistan ought to have been anything but alluring, if one could believe *Harper's* reference to "its constant tumults of all the passions, its reckless indifference to life and to death, its total ignorance of the sentiment or principle of honor (as we understand it), its delight in brutal exploit, its headlong obedience to its own crude and violent emotions." Rugged terrain coupled with a history of formidable Afghan resistance made rule by outsiders virtually impossible. If past experience was any guide, argued Godkin, "the Afghans themselves constitute one of the best frontiers the Empire can have, far better than any mountains or passes." It would be impossible for the Russians to make any headway in that land. The military disaster of the First

Afghan War, in which the entire British Kabul garrison had been wiped out in 1842, ought to have provided a salutary lesson to the British against going into that country once more, which would be "from first to last a crazy adventure." Because the conquest and subjugation of Afghanistan exceeded the capability of any of the great powers, the best policy for the British was to get out. Despite all the warnings and past experience, the British entangled themselves in a costly, though eventually successful, Second Afghan War.[34]

For all that, by the 1880s "the great game" had taken on a life of its own based on a house-of-cards logic. One example was the panic that developed following the news that the Russians were advancing upon the oasis at Merv, which had suddenly become a strategic point—"Mervousness," it was called. For some reason, it was feared that Russian capture of this oasis, "this mysterious geographical expression," would mean that "the British Empire in India is as good as overthrown." If so, if it were unquestionably the gateway to India, why had it not been occupied earlier? By this logic, any Russian advance anywhere was cause for alarm. The tendency to see every Russian success, no matter how small in itself, as a strategic defeat gave force to arguments on behalf of a forward defense by expansion outward from India. This, too, nonplussed the critics. Instead of taking advantage of Afghanistan as a natural barrier that would frustrate the Russians, the British were only causing themselves grief in attempting to subdue it. This expansive definition of defense threatened to promote the very confrontation that British policy so dreaded.[35]

Brought into question, too, was the perceptual dimension of the great game, in which defeat at the hands of the Russians might provoke a drastic deflation of Britain's reputation among its subjects elsewhere, the sort of puncturing of the myth of invincibility that was thought to have been partly responsible for the Indian rebellion of 1857. By this logic, even events far removed from Central Asia might have an important subjective bearing on the British position in India. In strategic terms, it was well understood that Egypt was, as one analysis put it, "now more than ever, an appendage of the Indian Empire." In psychological terms, this meant that the disaster in the Sudan might contribute to the unraveling of British prestige in the subcontinent, while a defeat in Asia might lead to disaster in Egypt. This kind of thinking was too much for Godkin, who attributed it to the "half-crazed condition of the English mind." This fear was "probably the most absurd of the Jingo bugbears." According to this critique,

British foreign policy had been uprooted from the soil of reality and was being nourished only by delirious imagination.[36]

The Perilous Diplomacy of Imperialism

The Great Game, apart from its connection to India and the European balance, was also understood as part of a larger phenomenon that has since come to be called the diplomacy of imperialism. For Americans who sought to understand the motivation behind Europe's scramble for colonies in the 1880s, mimicry of Britain rather than any desire or need for colonization appeared to be the guiding motivation. British power had evolved through "the force of circumstances," but the continental powers decided parrot-like to create those circumstances for themselves. Making this point, an essay in *The Atlantic* described "French diplomacy in the far East [as] simply a reflection of English diplomacy." Considered coldly, this struck some people as a futile effort, for there was no way of catching up to the British at this point. If Germany were to annex all areas still open to colonial annexation, it was pointed out, "she would still be as far inferior to her rival in this sort of distinction as New Guinea is inferior to Australia." Thus interpreted, the scramble for empire was a free-for-all for the remaining crumbs on the table, the anticlimax to an all-but-completed grand narrative.[37]

When coupled to the civilizing process, imperialism could seem salutary, but the implications of intramural imperialist foreign polices were quite dangerous. The diplomacy of imperialism was tainted by the polluted domestic sources from which it sprang, by the stimulus it gave to great-power competition, and by the dragon's teeth that colonial injustices were sowing for the future. In the British case, imperialism was associated with the corruption of democracy in the form of "Jingo excitement," for in empire the Tories had discovered an issue that resonated positively with the working classes. To Godkin, imperialism was the product of "the intellectual degeneracy of a party which had ceased to have anything behind it but wealth." The wars of empire, it was suggested, were connived at by small but powerful groups within the government, "by secret and irresponsible departments—a Foreign Office, an India Office, a Colonial Office, and the like." The British public, it was alleged, had become "the dupes and tools of their own administrative agents." Of course, the Tories could not help it if the masses thrilled to empire. "The ear of the

English workman still loves, full as well as, and even better than the ear of the lord, to hear the roll of the imperial drum following the course of the sun round the globe," noted one editorial. Unfortunately, there was little evidence that popular opinion was becoming any the wiser. On the contrary, the belief in British superiority made "the English people the most aggressive and encroaching people whom the world has ever seen."[38]

The British invasion of the Sudan in 1885 and its aftermath demonstrated how a trumped-up threat of Islamic revivalism could be used to conceal the ugly face of jingoism. *The Nation* blamed the war on "the blind, unreasoning, sentimental jingoism of the British public of all parties, which really forced the Ministry into the wild and criminal attempt to rescue Gordon." Simple vengeance was the desire, masked by "this bugbear of a Mussulman revival." Anyone who actually believed in the revival of Islam as a conquering faith was "the victim of a hallucination," a case of "Mahomet on the brain," in Godkin's view. Although Egypt was in no real danger, the eccentric general "Chinese" Gordon had nevertheless been turned into a hero. Despite his many martial virtues, Gordon was a "fanatic," it was claimed, whereas the Sudanese slaughtered in his memory were engaged "in as good a cause as any in which men have ever drawn the sword." And who was to say that another Mahdi would not appear as a result of this mass martyrdom? Largely for reasons of this kind, a follow-up punitive expedition of 1890 was characterized as a "tremendous mistake." But this strong dislike of imperial adventurism was offset by a powerful anti-Muslim current of desire to see the Islamic infidels chastised, the effect of which was to temper and perhaps even negate the critique of British adventurism.[39]

Once in power, the liberals fared no better than the Tories, as Gladstone's second ministry became the occasion for an extraordinary spasm of imperial expansion. Normally revered by the liberal media in the United States, Gladstone suffered criticism from his American friends for having compiled "one long record of war, conquest, annexation, and huge expenditure." Notwithstanding the greatness of Gladstone's career in other respects, *The Nation*, was deeply disappointed by his willingness "to preach the gospel from behind Martini-Henri rifles and Gatling guns." There appeared to be three ways to break the imperializing habit: disaster, a reality check, and true democratization. It was hoped that the second Anglo-Afghan War might shock the British public into withdrawing its support for military adventures, but the favorable military outcome this time only reinforced imperialist sentiment.

There was also speculation that the European balance of power would force the British to make cutbacks in their colonial policy. Last, but not least, a few believed that the coming of true democracy would quell the imperialist impulse. "The role of the conquering philanthropist is one which is in our time forbidden to a democracy," insisted *The Nation*. After criticizing the British penchant for engaging in an endless series of colonial wars, Andrew Carnegie blithely predicted that "all this will change, however, when the Democracy rules their country."[40]

To some extent, the success of the Bismarckian coalition in creating stability in Europe had the effect of displacing the pressure for expansion to other regions of the globe. In Heilprin's opinion, Bismarck understood this quite well, for by deliberately encouraging French and Russian imperialism in Africa and Asia, he hoped to "secure peace and Austro-German predominance in the centre and the peninsulas of Europe." While that was good for Europe, on the whole, the creation of a geopolitical stage led to a more complicated and problematic relationship between Europe and the periphery, for as Europe expanded so too did the European system of politics. Thus *The Nation* described the "scramble for Africa" of the mid-1880s as "one of the most striking incidents in European politics." The colonial contestation in North Africa was "looming up on the horizon" and was likely to "set Europe by the ears." In the Pacific region, too, the system was spreading. By 1890 it seemed clear that the Pacific Ocean was "fast becoming the focus of international politics." Problems avoided in Europe only created problems elsewhere, which in turn complicated European affairs.[41]

In some cases, the imperialist game seemed almost comically senseless. Italian expansion in Africa was ridiculed as the waste of "more men and more money to pursue, in a deadly climate and through trackless wastes, an enemy who can never be conquered, and victory over whom has no result but the slaughter of so many men." Theodore Dwight Woolsey argued that colonies generally had little impact on the power equilibrium and were more likely to be strategic liabilities. As he put it: "A nation with colonies on every continent has points of attack which use up its resources, while one which is compact and can unite its strength against its enemies at a few points is more likely to come unscathed out of a struggle." The conceptual opposite of this scattershot mentality was embodied by Bismarck, who viewed colonizing projects as expensive diversions from the main task at hand. Although imperialism was not considered to be a fundamental problem of international politics, it did threaten to bring the powers to blows over minor issues. For Godkin, the "colonial fever" was a pathology of modern times that threatened on occasion to bring European politics to "the boiling point" of war."[42]

Another problem with the diplomacy of imperialism was the way empire was acquired. It was true that the emergence of colonial relationships between civilized and uncivilized peoples fit the social Darwinian scheme of explanation. National power, said *The Nation* on one occasion, was "the product of industry, order, forethought, love of country, determination, and persistence. It is these things which make nations able to thrash the weak; it is the absence of them which prepares the weak for the thrashing. The fittest survive, even more surely among nations than among individuals." But that was true only in a general sense, for power without civilizing purpose, power militarized and placed in the one-way service of profit, was obscene. According to Thomas Knox, the blessings of commerce as defined by the British meant "putting money into John's pocket and taking it away from those whom he seeks to benefit." The Opium War in China was a classic, much-criticized instance of how imperial conquest could be undertaken in the service of narrow commercial interests. The British had taken advantage of their progressive image to pull off a caper which, had it been any other nation, would have been convicted in the court of public opinion of "incredible folly and impossible crime." The entire opium business was "an immense disgrace," while the war, fought in the name of free trade, was "a scandalous blot on English morality."[43]

But while Americans felt free to criticize Europe's competitive colonial conquests from a position of detachment, they also appreciated that the United States fully merited inclusion among the overbearing nations of the earth. Reviewing a book about Perry's much vaunted "opening" of Japan, *The Nation* compared his mission to the invasion and conquest of Mexico. Both episodes, it said, "were concocted by a strong Power against a weak" and "were not justifiable in the forum of morals." The United States was deeply implicated in the diplomacy of imperialism in East Asia by virtue of its active participation in the treaty regimes that severely restricted the sovereignty of Qing China and Meiji Japan. America's extortion of one-sided treaty rights from China had been made possible by piggybacking on the military successes of the French and British and by cooperating with them. With respect to Japan, William Elliot Griffis accused the United States of having "long been mixed up in one of the most disgraceful as well as most entangling European alliances." Perspicacious observers realized that from a Chinese perspective the United States was at best the smallest of all evils, "the least conspicuous of the principal aggressors." One essayist, upset by the way the United States had chosen to profit from British aggression, argued that "from the very first we have taken a course which is humiliating, hypocritical, and Pharisaical."[44]

Given the moral difficulties that accompanied it, imperialism could be justified in the liberal mind only as a provisional instrument of civilization. European in origin, the legal rationale behind the opening of backward nations was, in theory, an egalitarian one based on the idea of civilization. Once civilized status had been achieved, unequal treaty privileges would be relinquished. However, Americans had doubts about whether the system of extraterritorial rights and the competition among powers for spheres of influence were substantively promoting civilization and independence for nations under imperial control. In their view, the horizontal dimension of imperialism required a tempering of great-power competition with cooperation and, in its hierarchical aspect, demanded more than mere lip service to principles of justice and equality. But this was not the way things were playing out. The policy of cooperation among the great powers in East Asia, which was intended to avert conflict among the imperial powers, seemed designed for purposes of exploitation rather than civilization.[45]

This dissatisfaction with the European way of empire found practical expression in a major change in America's China policy. The immediate cause was the concern that the chaotic Taiping rebellion (1851–1864) was making China the "sick man of Asia." *The Nation* predicted that continued Western interference in China might lead to imperial collapse and "a state of awful anarchy—such anarchy as the world has not seen since Rome fell." A lapse into chaos "would probably extinguish every spark of civilization amongst a third of the population of the globe." Internal dissolution raised the specter of external absorption. Should China fall victim to centrifugal forces, there seemed little doubt that the European powers would quickly move in. Because no single-power domination of China on the Indian pattern seemed likely, partition seemed entirely plausible. If "the foreign vulture comes in and claims his share of the carcass," asked John Bonner in 1890, "can we afford to sit by quietly, and see the partition of China between three or four European powers?" Chinese resources and manpower, some predicted, would quickly be conscripted for selfish European uses.[46]

The shift from cooperating against China to a policy that sought to preserve China as a political unit was detectable as early as 1863. According to W. A. P. Martin, who variously served as missionary, diplomat, and foreign adviser to China, "China's greatest danger is from the great Powers of the West." As Martin saw things, "The doctrine of the balance of power, formerly limited in its application to the map of Europe, is now transferred to Eastern Asia; and it is under the shield of this principle alone, that either China or Japan can hope to maintain her independence." It was the need to avoid a "Polandlike partition" that gave the United States its role. With no territorial interests but a significant cultural role and potentially a huge economic stake, the United States was "directly interested in preserving the integrity of the Chinese empire." Martin envisioned "a grand position for the United States . . . to be a key-stone among the great nations of the earth; which, instead of crushing China, combine to extend over her the arch of their power, and to protect her in the career of improvement, on which she has so happily entered."[47]

The new cooperative policy was an important development that, it was hoped, would buy time for China's transition to modernization and equality. In contrast to the cloud of pessimism that hung over the future of the Ottoman Empire, there was significant optimism that the metamorphosis of China could be accomplished, even though it was certain to be "a painfully slow and uncertain process." Maintaining harmonious relations among the great powers was only one element of the new strategy, however, the other being a changed relationship with China itself. Anson Burlingame, author of the 1868 treaty that bore his name, advocated treating China with respect, as a sovereign equal like any other country, in the hope that the Chinese could live up to civilized expectations. Richard J. Hinton, following a conversation with Burlingame, explained that the treaty was intended to put a stop to "the policy of absorption." Once "the energizing influences of modern and material civilization" took hold, China would be able "stay the progress of Russia on the one side and of England on the other."[48]

Thus the Burlingame Treaty was initially interpreted as a way for the United States to break away from the harsh pattern established by the European powers in China. As *The Nation* hopefully suggested, although civilization had failed to be introduced from the West, it would "finally succeed in penetrating by way of the eastern coast." The key point for the United States was to stop taking its cues on China from the Europeans, "from writers under monarchical influence—from those of England, which has brutally drugged her that she might rob her, or from French and Italian priests, who flattered and lauded her rulers that they might aggrandize themselves and their work." The missionary William Speer, writing in *Harper's*, argued strongly that America was in a position to make good China's two greatest deficits, the absence of democracy and Christianity. Speer imagined the process as being akin to a transfusion of blood: " 'The youth and health of Christian America could be poured out in no nobler cause than in the rejuvenation of a nation so interesting and so great." Occasionally, an ironic account would appear that mocked American altruism, but on the whole those with an interest in China took this rejuvenating mission seriously, whether from motives of profit or of spiritual uplift. At the time of the Burlingame Treaty, many were predicting a huge trade "of more importance to us than the trade we now carry on with the nations of Europe."[49]

At some point, if imperialism was indeed a self-liquidating project, imperialist practices would have to be reconsidered as a nation began to approach a civilized level of development. This became clear in the case of Japan, whose rapid industrialization made the policy of diplomatic solidarity and cooperation, in which the United States was tied to the European powers, come to appear increasingly "anomalous and anti-American." By the late 1880s, numerous writers in the journals were beginning to call for treaty revision. *The New Englander and Yale Review* published an essay by a Japanese national advocating the granting of the sovereign rights that had been "unjustly taken away from her by the Christian nations of the world." The justice of the Japanese claim had long been clear to *The Nation*, which agreed that releasing Japan from "political and moral enslavement" was called for "by all the sound traditions of American policy, and by the convictions of our people." The journal demanded "withdrawal from the European league and 'cooperative policy' " because binding the United States to the collective judgment of the European powers was "anomalous and anti-American." Besides, it was doubtful that the powers were any longer prepared to take action against Japan, should it abrogate the treaties unilaterally.[50]

While Japan was clearly ready for emancipation, treating China as an equal at this time was premature. *The Nation*, though it approved of the objective, was wary of "extravagant expectations." The modern state system, it pointed out, was "based on a common stock of religious and moral ideas, which really influence life and manners, and which the Chinese do not as yet share." The cultural distance was so great that China could not be talked into liberalism. Were true sovereign equality granted at once, the Chinese would be sure to revert very quickly to their traditional ways of treating foreigners as barbarians. If given a free hand, they would certainly subject Americans "to every ignominious restraint they might fancy, under pain of expulsion." Following a massacre of Westerners in a French orphanage in Tientsin in 1870, the journal's position hardened significantly. The assumption behind the Burlingame Treaty—that it was possible to treat the Chinese as sovereign equals—had been proved false, as had the expectation that differences could be worked out through diplomacy. "There should be no weak hesitation in the use of force," John Norton Pomeroy, the noted international lawyer, now concluded. However disagreeable, continued extraterritorial jurisdiction was a necessity. "We do not now discuss the morality of this procedure, but only state the historical fact," explained *The Nation*.[51]

This hard line was far from ideal, for continued enforcement of extraterritoriality gave to American riff-raff in China, of whom there were more than a few, "almost insured impunity for every kind of crime" while it also stimulated "hatred of the foreigner." In short, the failure of the well-intentioned Burlingame policy meant that the United States would have to maintain the cooperative policy both for and against China. Too little cooperation with the European treaty powers would feed the forces of dissolution, whereas too much would retard development. Too little force would encourage Chinese contempt for foreigners, whereas too much could be disastrous if China were to disappear altogether as a political unit. The problem was "bringing [China] back without killing the patient." However dissected, the situation in China was rife with tensions and contradictions: dislike of power could not obviate the resort to power; removal of the system of oppression meant becoming a more active participant in it; the pursuit of international equality meant treating other peoples as inferiors.[52]

In general, the liberal party line was that China's modernization would resolve all important problems. But when the implications of China's economic development were more fully thought through, the results were not necessarily reassuring. At the very least, China seemed likely to become a formidable economic competitor; for with its seemingly unlimited supply of cheap labor, abundant natural resources, and enterprising population, its economic impact was bound to be immense. One writer foresaw stiff economic competition down the road: "We have never looked for competition from that quarter of the world. Yet the last hundred years have taught the people of those two empires something, and they are applying their newly acquired knowledge with a vigor and ingenuity worthy of Europeans." The Chinese capacity for hard work, the commercial acumen of the people, their respect for education, and, of course, their great numbers, as Raphael Pumpelly later recalled, created "potentialities that must seem threatening to the industrial civilizations of the West." Perhaps the worst and certainly the most ironic eventuality was broached in General Irvin McDowell's vision of how China's great economic potential would play out. "What is there in the nature of the case," McDowell asked, "to prevent China if all protective laws are to be abandoned, and the world thrown open to free trade from doing the work and producing all the manufactures which the world requires?"[53]

More somber types foresaw the possibility that China might adopt some less enlightened Western practices and principles, especially those relating to warfare. After all, what was China really learning from the West? For all the rhetoric of imparting civilization, the chief exports to China were opium and firearms. "Can it be that the rifle and the shell are the only solvents?" wondered *The Nation*. In 1890, the former minister to China, John Young, used heavy sarcasm to suggest why the Chinese were so resistant to the adoption of Christian virtues: "They have not, because of the dense ignorance of their heathenism, awakened to the dignity of that beautiful thought, which will come to them with the Beatitudes and Psalms of David, that man's chief end is to cut the throat of man; that the consummation of our noblest civilization is to be found in armaments; the burden of stupendous debts; a geography strewn with battlefields; a history little more than chronicles of desolation and rapine." No matter how noble the ideas on whose behalf conquest was carried out, the humiliating fact of conquest was certain to generate powerful resentment.[54]

The military possibilities were certainly disturbing. On one occasion, *Appletons'* reprinted a selection from the *London Spectator*, which wondered "whether the strange spectacle of a handful of [European] aliens holding half the population of the world in subjection is likely to be a permanent one." What would happen following the inevitable day when a Western power suffered a convincing defeat at the hands of Japan or China? Although many considered that possibility a fantasy, at a minimum Western victories would grow progressively more difficult to pull off in that part of the world. *The Nation* expected that, properly organized, the Chinese could produce "a very formidable army." In 1883, it speculated about a future Chinese war with a European power as "anything but frivolous." On another occasion it pondered the significance of China's emergence as "an aggressive, militant power, with all the appliances of modern military art, and with a population of 300,000,000 endowed with a vitality and persistence which puzzles both ethnologists and physiologists." The result, it forecast, would be "a phenomenon for which the wildest political speculator is still unprepared."[55]

China's interest in westernization for purposes of self-strengthening pointed to a possible showdown with the West, in the form of "a possible furious fanatical movement to extirpate the actual foreign settlements." A review of a book on China concluded that "all that China wants from the western world is its implements of war and destruction, the more effectually to protect itself against the encroachments of the European trader." Military modernization was to modernization what military music was to music, a far cry from the real thing. As "one of the cheapest and easiest features of modern civilization," it was obvious that this kind of modernization could easily veer in an anti-Western direction. "But does not all this wear rather an aspect of hostility?" asked Martin. Having been soundly defeated by the West, were the Chinese not preparing to regain the upper hand? Martin consoled himself with the thought that the Chinese were antimilitarist at heart and that their peaceful commercial impulses would prevail.[56]

The prospect of Asia's modernization prompted some gloomy reflections that if China were to achieve great-power status the United States would suffer retribution for its misbehavior, notably, its extraterritorial abuses, its immigration restriction policies, and its failure to protect Chinese nationals against outrages committed on American soil. "The galling principle of extraterritoriality," as Samuel Wells Williams called it, was understood as "a potent engine of repression," and the system of consular courts was "little else than a shield for crime." Referring to the operation of extraterritoriality in Japan, E. H. House noted that an American "might cheat or rob his native partner to any extent, and redress could be sought nowhere but from a judge who would almost certainly be ignorant of law, who would probably be swayed by partiality, and might very possibly have a direct interest in defeating justice." William Elliott Griffis, commenting on its one-sided nature, pointed out that "there is little chance of a native Japanese getting justice as against a foreign brute."[57]

America's immigration restriction policies and its failure to deal with the outrages committed against Chinese nationals were also known to be sore points with the Chinese. "It is only the Barbary States of North Africa which have in our day ever treated a friendly Government as Congress proposed to treat China," said one editorial. A. A. Hayes, Jr., who had spent some time in China in the 1860s, warned that Chinese "memories are long, and time is fleeting. Some day they will collect their bill—and it will be made up with compound interest." Comparing the Chinese position to that of the United States in the *Alabama* claims issue, *The Nation* predicted that "the Chinese officials and Government will not lose sight of the claims which are being created on the Pacific side." Eventually, the United States would have to pay, predicted Godkin, "as England paid the *Alabama* claims, making merit in our own eyes for the act of justice to which the Orientals have constrained us." American misbehavior was hardly unique, but that was small consolation. "The shameful truth," insisted the reverend J. H. Twichell, was that the United States shone only by comparison with the other powers, a mere difference of degree that was nothing to be proud of. Bishop Charles Henry Fowler, just returned from China in 1889, reported that the Chinese were "preparing for war to vindicate the citizenship of their countrymen in all parts of the world, and particularly with the United States, against whom they have a bitter grievance."[58]

Whatever the scenario, China's destined rise to world power was something that succeeding generations would have to face. The journalist John Addison Porter saw China as "the great vantage-ground of the future." "One hundred, two hundred, three hundred or more years hence," he wrote, "when California and Australia teem with population, great race-problems will surely have been solved on Chinese soil, and our civilization and our religion will have been tested, to their higher glory or their deeper shame, by the sternest yet truest of all earthly judges, Time." Thomas Knox floated the idea that the next quarter century would bring "another Genghis Khan, or another Tamerlane, who will roll the Orient upon the Occident over the route that was followed centuries ago by the great conquerors." An offhand comment in *The Nation* in 1885 professed to see at least one good result from China's resurgence: the unification of Europe, "federated not from any philanthropic motive, but driven to it by terror of the Mongols." It was a long way from these early premonitions to the Yellow Peril thinking of the 1950s and 1960s or the many predictions fifty years later of imminent Chinese supremacy, but the anticipations were certainly there.[59]

As the survey in this chapter suggests, isolationist America was well informed about the issues and trends of international politics that extended across a broad arc from Europe through Asia. Whatever the regional issue—the balance of power in Europe, the contest in the Balkans, the Great Game in Asia, or the diplomacy of imperialism in East Asia—the correlation between civilization and power lay at the center of analysis. The global pieces were connected, not in a hub and spoke pattern, but serially in a *leg bone connected to the foot bone* manner that inserted the United States into the global political narrative at the far end of the series. Geographic distance and a moderate level of involvement allowed the United States to participate as a lesser power in East Asia without being involved in European politics and to engage in the diplomacy of imperialism without competing in the game of colonial expansion. In this way, the nation could, apparently, enjoy world power status without becoming embroiled in European politics—but only apparently, for the connection between imperialism and the European political system was plain to see. It was clear, too, that by being linked to the tail end of the geopolitical chain the United States, despite the prevailing isolationist consensus, was thereby implicated in world politics. In contrast to the worldview held in the early days of the republic, when Alexander Hamilton in *Federalist* 11 had conceived of the globe as separated into four mutually exclusive political spheres, "each having a distinct set of interests," the conceptual boundaries between regions were becoming much more porous. They may not have known it, but Americans living in the paradise of isolationism were already sampling the forbidden fruit.

Still, this did not mean that American conceptions of foreign policy were becoming Europeanized. The interest taken in the politics of East Asia suggested that the farther away from Europe that Americans looked, the closer they came to the core issues that dominated their thinking about international relations. By situating relations with China and Japan in a global frame of reference, and, conversely, by seeing European issues in civilizational terms, nineteenth-century Americans laid the conceptual groundwork for two important developments. First, they developed a tendency to look at European issues in a global framework. Second, the propensity to evaluate issues from the ideological standpoint of civilization as well as in terms of power signaled a shift in the relative importance assigned to different regions. As a factor in the balance of power or as an object of narrow national interest, Asia was of little consequence, but its civilizational significance was another matter entirely. Once the future of globalization became a central concern, one can see how Americans could manage to link Asian problems with Europe's crises and, on occasion, to pay far more attention to Asia than Europeans thought reasonable. Asia's global importance would not become fully evident for another half century, when it became first the gateway to American involvement in World War II and then a hot spot in the cold war, but it was already clear by 1890 that the American presence in East Asia was not being pictured solely in regional terms.

Although the analyses were quite good at dissecting the contradictions of the international scene, they originated from a perspective that was itself filled with tensions and ambivalence. The civilization-power schema suggested that problems originated in a lack of development—that is, the solution to civilization's problems lay in more civilization—but civilization itself could be problematic. If global civilization possessed a universal potential for good, it also made possible evil on a new order of magnitude. As if out of structuralist necessity, benefits and perils were paired in such a way that their very existence depended on their opposite. But instead of negating or offsetting one another, the perils were gaining the upper hand as prospects for a more peaceful world grew ever more distant as the century's end approached. This disheartening state of affairs forced Americans to some deeper reflections about the connection between war and human progress in the modern era. Those ideas will be explored in the next and final chapter.

10

The Future of International Relations

To liberals who believed in progress, modernizing forces at work in the late nineteenth century were revolutionizing the time-honored structures of international relations in ways commensurate to the immense internal upheavals wrought by industrialization and nationalism. Future generations would find it hard to muster the enthusiasm to write rhapsodic poetry on the order of Francis Lieber's "Ode on the Sub-Atlantic Telegraph," but at that time new technologies of communication and transport were often described ecstatically as possessing an immanent globalizing power, an almost magical ability to "bind nations together in a closer friendship than they have ever yet known." A leading characteristic of modern civilization was that it not only made possible, but demanded, cooperation over great distances. Although it would take some time, it seemed inevitable that economic integration, followed by ideological liberalization and increased cross-cultural understanding, would lead to political unity—in Tennyson's famous phrase, "the federation of the world." Utopian declarations were rare, but even measured assessments almost always exuded optimism about the end result.[1]

But expectations of a sunny global future were in very short supply when the focus shifted to contemplation of the contemporary world scene, where prescriptive optimism was matched by descriptive pessimism. The most glaring challenge to liberal predictions was the escalating arms race, which seemed certain to lead to war. In the aftermath of the Franco-Prussian War, large and lavishly equipped standing armies came to dominate the political landscape of Europe. By 1880, Europe had over three million men under arms, with more than twice that number as reserves. Taking stock of developments over the past century, in 1890 *The Atlantic Monthly* listed the growth of arms and armies as a major feature of the era since 1789, in addition to the end of monarchical despotism, the rise of nationalism, and the triumph of science. Given this "unparalleled expansion of militarism," war had become almost "the natural condition" and peace "but a temporary armistice." The situation seemed so dire that one essay, trying to imagine how extraterrestrial aliens might respond following a first encounter with the deeply entrenched war system, suggested that the visitors could not help but be repelled by the "grotesque horror" of the international scene. Clearly, Herbert Spencer's clean distinction between the militant and industrial phases of social evolution failed to do justice to an era that somehow exaggerated both kinds of societal impulse.[2]

This martial turn of events came as a surprise, for the period of relative calm in European foreign relations following the Napoleonic Wars had nourished expectations of even more peaceful times ahead. During those years, recalled Arthur G. Sedgwick, who wrote frequently on international law for *The Nation,* war had been regarded as "a temporary misfortune or disease, to be 'localized' as far as possible." The presumption was that wars with a diminishing number of barbarous peoples would continue as part of the civilizing process while relations among developed nations would grow ever more placid. But alas, Sedgwick noted ruefully, "for some reason, which philosophers have not yet fathomed, the world does not move on in a path of uninterrupted progress toward the millennium. What is won to-day is lost to-morrow." The wide gap between the brute facts of geopolitics and prospects for an irenic future occasioned a good deal of worried commentary during these years. But instead of being disheartened by the jungle of obstacles that stood between them and a peaceful world, cosmopolitan Americans kept their eyes fixed on a global path that bypassed the most treacherous terrain of contemporary international relations. In the end, they held fast to the belief that modern commercial and cultural forces making for global community would triumph over the time-honored but particularizing politics of force.[3]

A Warlike Modern Civilization

Liberals reflexively thought of war as an evil, but when it came to modern war the rapidity of change made it difficult to know precisely what one was talking about or to gauge its implications with confidence. From a strategic point of view, it was widely understood that standing armies were necessary because there was no longer sufficient time to mobilize forces following a dec-laration of war. That the Civil War experience, with its leisurely *levée en masse,* had been atypical was demonstrated by subsequent European wars that con-sumed less time than America would require for a full mobilization. "The fate of a campaign is now decided almost at its outset," one naval officer pointed out. Beyond that, the crystal ball very rapidly turned cloudy. New develop-ments in naval warfare had been so sweeping over the course of fifty years, ac-cording to *The Nation,* that "the old heroes of the quarter-deck . . . would not now, if recalled to earth, recognize their own profession." Technology was changing so rapidly that it was difficult even to form accurate assessments of comparative naval power. In part that was because the question of which new weapons technology would rise to dominance was still undetermined. The only surety was that the unpredictability of science had replaced the tradi-tions of seamanship. What remained was the certainty of uncertainty and the need to anticipate the unpredictable, which meant, in practical terms, that a nation had to be prepared for anything and everything.[4]

Many writers realized that the nineteenth century's advances were double-edged and that the distinction between war and peace was quite problematic. Although modern steam-powered transports were compressing distance, all-steel battleships with rifled cannons were their evil twin, reminders of the dangers of growing proximity. It was no secret that modern power was not measured primarily in population, fleets, or armies, but in industrial potential. The application of industrial resources to military applications was "changing the whole character of warfare, accelerating events, deciding the fate of battles, and the destiny of nations," said *The Galaxy.* Capitalists were as indispensable as military leaders, for steamships, railroads, and the telegraph had become as essential to triumph in war as they were to success in commerce. So inter-twined were the institutions of war and peace that the two were sometimes in-distinguishable. The positive features of modern civilization, acknowledged Julius Seelye, president of Amherst College, "may all be turned into deadly weapons of destruction." But this suggested that the machinery of war some-how commandeered and displaced the machinery of peace, when in fact the relationship was so tangled as to make them inseparable. Trying to explain this Janus-like mien of modern war, one writer suggested that "the details of the so-called 'operations of war' are in reality only the operations of peace greatly intensified and prosecuted under more difficult and exacting conditions."[5]

The standard script had the modern era bringing about an epochal reversal in which military power, formerly the key to increasing a state's wealth, would take a back seat to wealth-producing industry. As early as 1844, an extract from *Blackwood's* magazine had pointed out that "success, even in war, is to depend on the industry of peace; thus, in fact, providing a perpetual restriction on the belligerent propensities of nations." Viewed positively, might and right would be tightly connected because power would be concentrated in the most powerful, ergo the most civilized and righteous, states. But after the Civil War, the inherently peaceful bent of industrial civilization was increasingly open to question as aristocratic armies gave way to industrially based fighting forces like Germany's, which were controlled by traditional military elites. In war, as in politics, backward-looking groups had been able to shape modern industrial realities to their own purposes. As the peace reformer Elihu Burritt stated, "This armed-peace system is both the product and the parasite of modern civilization." But it was not simply atavistic groups who were responsible for the failure of modern commerce and communication to live up to their revolutionary billing: the evidence suggested that modern commercial imperatives were superseding the old dynastic and atavistic rationales for war. New causes, same results.[6]

For evidence of this double-stranded relationship, observers pointed to the pride of place assigned to military technologies at the international fairs. At the Paris Exposition of 1867, sited appropriately enough on the Champs de Mars, so many implements of warfare were on display that one observer imagined a "pitiless Aladdin . . . rubbing his lamp with no thought but to call into existence all things destructive to life." These exhibitions were intended as expressions, in the words of a Godkin editorial, of "the closing of the military stage in civilization, and the introduction of an era of competition in the arts of peace alone." But in the face of this overpowering emphasis on advanced weaponry, the notion that technology alone would bring about the millennium seemed just plain silly. By the end of this period, it was hardly surprising that honors and riches flowed to those individuals—Alfred Nobel and Hiram Maxim came instantly to mind—who were most adept at multiplying humankind's destructive powers. Small wonder, then, that the correspondence between civilization and peace could seem ridiculous to some. For doubters, the moral of the story was that progress itself was internally flawed and profoundly contradictory. "That nation is the most civilized which has the appliances to kill the most of another nation in the shortest time," observed Charles Dudley Warner. "This is the result of six thousand years of constant civilization." How progressive was civilization, actually? Not very, concluded *The Nation:* "We have not advanced so far beyond the savage state as outward appearances would indicate."[7]

The silver lining to this cloud of gloom, reassuring with regard to outcomes if not processes, was the Kantian hope that violence would beget peace, that the cacophony of strife would eventuate in a pacific harmony. "In the present condition of things it is not seen how war can be terminated except by war," said M. G. Upton, a frequent contributor to *The Overland Monthly*. In time, this contention became something of a cliché. Every new fearsome weapon, it was noted, was "apologized for on the ground that the way to terminate war is to render it so fearfully calamitous that nations, in mutual horror, will withhold from it." By this reasoning, the more powerful and destructive the new weapon, the more reason to cheer its emergence. In an early version of the doctrine of Mutually Assured Destruction, the international law expert (and mentor to Elihu Root) John Norton Pomeroy maintained that "if science should so far perfect the instruments of slaughter that every member of each opposing army would with absolute certainty be killed at a blow, then wars would cease." If people like this were correct, the world was at the doorstep of perpetual peace.[8]

These technological advances in the art of killing had additional blessings. One was that they deglamorized war by eliminating, as one writer put it, "the tempting chances for daring display and heroic self-devotion." Another benefit had to do with spiraling costs. "War, in these modern days, is too expensive a business to be entered upon for amusement," said a writer in *The Atlantic Monthly*. While capitalism had multiplied the destructive powers of war, it had also inflated its price tag to the point that nations would at some point have to think much longer and harder than formerly about entering into conflict. Anticipating the argument later made famous by Norman Angell in *The Great Illusion*, Sheldon Amos, a British professor of jurisprudence, argued that the costs of war "become matter of grave political consideration in the course of calculating the worth of the object to be attained, and the material or moral expensiveness of various competing means at hand for attaining it." The utility of war would henceforth be measured by the cold calculation of costs versus benefits. And why not? Over the centuries, religious denunciations of war had done little to stay those who believed they might profit from it. If war no longer paid, its enormous costs cried out for a better way.[9]

Despite all this talk of its destructiveness and expense, the effects of war were not all that clear, for a sizable body of opinion held that modern war might actually be more benign in the end. "The improvements in weapons of offensive warfare," argued Pomeroy, "the rifled guns, the, enormous shells, the dreaded torpedoes—are humane inventions, because they make wars on the whole less bloody." According to this train of thought, modern wars, though more violent and intense, were shorter in duration and hence less destructive overall. "As the conduct of war becomes more scientific, and the art becomes refined, and the implements more destructive," wrote Rear Admiral Stephen B. Luce, "the recurrence of war is lessened, the duration shortened, and the loss of human life diminished." Overall, John Fiske claimed, the damage caused by modern wars was "trifling" when compared with the carnage and bloodletting of premodern times. In other ways, too, war was becoming less destructive. The rejection of unnecessary killing, respect for property, reverence for works of art and public monuments, and better treatment of prisoners and noncombatants appeared to suggest that war's harshness was being softened. Developments in military medicine also pointed to the same consoling conclusion. Armies and wars also had their virtuous features, ranging from the socializing effects of military service to the noble sacrifices made in the cauldron of combat. Clearly, the twentieth-century concept of total war was far from people's minds. Perhaps war was not the ultimate evil.[10]

This sanguine appraisal of modern combat helps to explain why many liberals were more troubled by the *peacetime* consequences of militarization. To critics of the arms race like the mugwump reformer Edward Atkinson, nearly every conceivable pathology of European society, from poverty to anarchism and socialism, could be traced to the immense sums spent on armaments. The huge expenditure for war preparation since the 1840s, said *Appletons'*, was "something worse than madness." Although laissez-faire liberals ordinarily had few concrete proposals for alleviating poverty, reducing spending on armaments was one of them. Were those funds to be appropriated to education, necessary public works, and other uses, it was predicted that "pauperism and misery would rapidly disappear, and become memories of the past." *Scribner's* was astounded by "the waste of life, the waste of labor, the waste of the materials of life, the waste of the hoarded results of labor" produced by the arms race." Perhaps what was being spent on war was "enough to feed the poor of the world." Apart from the economic folly, one needed to factor in the drain on human capital, know-how that could be put to use in the production of goods and knowledge. Trying to measure the enormity of this loss, *The Nation* suggested that conscription was nothing less than "a draft on civilization itself." These shortcomings were amplified when one took into account the "danger to liberty" posed by large standing armies. Germans were living under "a harsh and impoverishing military despotism," and a regressive militarism was a principal cause of the French republic's troubles. Thus, when Pomeroy envisioned the possibility of military states dominating the continent, he saw "a triumph indeed, but not of civilization, not of humanity."[11]

In the end, such a heavily militarized civilization could not avoid warfare, however civilized its mode of conduct. The existence of enormous armies, argued the librarian James M. Hubbard, "only apparently hastens the time of the inevitable collision." The expenditures for armaments might have been justified had they produced the security that was their raison d'être, but here too they had failed miserably. Bismarckian Germany's quest for military invincibility had created a dynamic in which the French determination to match Germany measure for measure had generated even more insecurity within the *Kaiserreich*. Everyone claimed to desire peace, as was to be expected, but the psychological strain alone would prove to be too great. "The mere existence of these armaments must tend to bring on a collision," concluded *The Nation*. "The armies are there to be used," agreed Tuttle. Worse yet, even the end of this inescapable war would probably not bring true peace, for the cycle would begin all over again at an even higher level of investment. During these years, it was the Europeans who were from Mars and the Americans who were from Venus.[12]

The Democratic Culture of War

How to break the cycle? Technology alone could not do the job. The minister turned free thinker Moncure D. Conway, among others, argued that "mankind surely needs something less palpably material than a mechanical invention to heal its divisions, extinguish its jealousies, and knit its mass together in 'universal fraternity.'" Later generations would speak of institutional atavisms and cultural lag, but these concepts were already being anticipated during these years. Edward Atkinson located the source of the problem in the still dominant position of the aristocracies, "those whose present trade is war." Others attributed wars to "irresponsible power, the power of one or the few," which gave them the right to make "wars of pride, aggrandizement or dynastic interest." Lying deeper than the class or institutional roots were the cultural sources that nourished them. As *Appletons'* put it, "The development of our social machinery has proceeded much more rapidly than the development of the feelings which should correspond to it." A *Century* writer made much the same case: "Nowhere do ideas outlive their time so stubbornly as in the foreign policy of nations. . . . Nations have been embroiled in destructive wars by the mere ghosts of ideas—post-pliocene survivals that walked the earth as though they had a legitimate place in the existing order of things." Wars were to societies what dueling was to individuals: senseless survivals that nonetheless possessed extraordinary staying power. Custom was "still the tyrant of humanity," argued Edward Berwick, and custom continued to favor war as the preferred means for settling international disputes.[13]

On the assumption that war was a side effect of authoritarian modes of governance divorced from the desires of the people, the default position of liberals was that international conflict could be eradicated through democratization and the rule of public opinion. Peace and democracy went hand in hand. As one expounder of democratic peace theory *avant la lettre* put it, "the policy of disarmament can scarcely be expected to prevail until it is the people, those who bear the burdens and sacrifices and desolations of war, and not the kings and diplomatists, who decide the fiat of war or peace." The system would collapse only with "the vindication of the right of the individual to decide, each for himself, whether he will participate in his rulers' quarrels." Once representative regimes became the norm, interstate violence would become a thing of the past. Democratic discourse, "frank and free utterance" or what would later be called open diplomacy, would demystify jingoist fantasies—that and the publication of military budgets. With the quickening trend to constitutional government, public opinion had become increasingly important, and it was a far from negligible force even in autocracies. Overall, it was believed that publics were becoming less tolerant of war and "were every year less and less influenced by enthusiasm" and less susceptible to "traditional hates and prejudices." The optimistic interpretation was that jingoist ideas were "survivals of a time when war was a necessary agent in the progress of civilization."[14]

Nevertheless, more than a few thoughtful liberals believed that modern culture was becoming more warlike. Commerce and luxury may have enfeebled societies in the past, but respected critics like the British intellectual Walter Bagehot doubted that this was true of modern states. Godkin, in a piece for *The North American Review*, observed that highly civilized communities rushed into war "with an ardor that was unknown in antiquity, and sacrifice life in it with a prodigality which has certainly never been surpassed." The knee-jerk tendency to equate modern civilization with peace overlooked the fact that development had made some nations even more powerful, warlike, and fearsome, Germany being the most notable example. Although in many respects it was clearly the most enlightened nation on the continent, it was also "obviously the most dreaded and distrusted by its neighbors." Unfortunately, Great Britain and France, despite their representative governments, did not rank much lower on the bellicosity scale.[15]

The other side of the coin was that democratic public opinion in its current state was a chief source of present-day problems. "War is, in our time, essentially the people's work," believed Godkin. "All attempts to saddle emperors, kings, and nobles with the responsibility of it may as well be given up from this time forward." For the *Galaxy*, the chief threat to peace came from "patriotism, not professional soldiery." It was the people who clamored for war, whereas the princes seemed increasingly reluctant to stake their crowns in battle. Everyone was culpable, even women. Contrary to Fiske's view, public opinion had the effect of making the wars themselves more intense and "vastly more terrible," far more so than the often half-hearted demonstrations of princely prowess of centuries past. Instead of being fought over "frivolous points of etiquette and honor," modern wars represented "real and essential differences between peoples." This was only to be expected when nationalism was made an end in itself. Nationalism as an expression of the emancipatory spirit was progressive, but in more conservative dress it spoke powerfully "to local feelings, and therefore to what may be termed limited principles."[16]

Tory democracy in Great Britain, with its deliberate arousal of jingoism, was emblematic of this worrisome new turn in which the classes who had most feared democratic opinion had become the most adept in manipulating it for their own purposes. As an example, *The Nation* pointed to British misadventures in the Sudan, which likely would not have occurred in the absence of a rabid public egged on by an overwrought press. Without the continued prodding of the newspapers, "Chinese" Gordon, the general martyred at Khartoum, would likely have remained yet another anonymous British official in "a barbarous and remote African province." By dramatizing insignificant incidents, the newspapers were turning international relations into a form of theater and thereby playing on "the deepest-seated passions in the human heart." It was the ability and the willingness of leaders to exploit what *The Nation* called "the spectacular features of the government" that turned the stomachs of many liberals. In the United States, at least, inflammatory utterances by politicians, though far from uncommon, were comparatively harmless in the absence of a powerful army or navy to give them life.[17]

Because the press could only set on fire material that was combustible to begin with, structural democratization was not enough; also needed was a fundamental change in the popular attitude toward war. "So long as there is war in the heart and character of a people, there will be war in fact," concluded *Scribner's*. In the view of one writer, the susceptibility to hatred of other peoples remained "because the nightmare of obsolete ideas still rides the expression of public opinion." Unfortunately, the list of prejudices that gave rise to wars was quite long. When one looked for signs of the emergence of pacific public sentiment, all indicators continued to point in the opposite direction. Surprisingly little hope was invested in the work of peace advocates, who seemed addicted to "speeches and resolutions and conventions and theories and statistics." Although there was no shortage of peace reformers, the degree of public enthusiasm they aroused for their cause paled before the emotions mobilized by the jingoes. *The Nation,* commenting on the meager results of a peace congress held at Lausanne, was surprisingly pessimistic: "It is a moral revolution that is needed—in other words, a miracle."[18]

Insolvent Solutions: Arbitration, International Law, Neutrality

What was to be done? Leaving the future to laissez-faire had little appeal. Commenting impatiently on investing one's hopes in optimistic necessitarianism, *The Nation* sneered at the notion "that men must wait with their hands in their pockets and the faith in their hearts that all will turn out right in the end." In place of stale and fruitless discussions of the horrors of war and the joys of universal peace, there was a yearning for "practical methods." Unfortunately, the liberal alternatives to the war system most often mentioned—the growth of arbitration, the codification and acceptance of international law, and an enhanced role for neutrality—held little appeal during these years. Still in all, however disheartening the situation as Europe's military machines grew to fearsome proportions, liberals continued to hold out hope that legal progress would have an ameliorating impact.[19]

The high water mark of such hope was the 1871 Treaty of Washington and the successful arbitration of the *Alabama* claims. Upon its signing, *The Nation*, not normally given to panegyrics, acclaimed the treaty as "the greatest gain for civilization which our age has witnessed, the most solid victory which the great cause of Peace has ever won." But this euphoria was short-lived, as the way in which the treaty was negotiated and its disappointing coda left ample reasons to doubt its future significance. The continuing insistence on indirect damages—even during arguments before the Geneva arbitral commission—prompted Godkin to dismiss the experience as "a sorry farce." Although indirect damages had been useful as a stick to beat the British into agreeing to arbitrate, and although the demand played well to domestic audiences, the tactic was utterly lacking in the kind of seriousness that would be needed to make arbitration work in the future. As if to underscore the point, the idea of indirect damages returned in a counterfeit manner in the mid-1870s when the U.S. government began to consider the claims of insurers other than those who had suffered direct injury at the hands of the Confederate raider. Arthur Sedgwick was particularly incensed by this turn of events, sputtering that American behavior was making "making arbitration and the peaceful settlement of disputes a perpetual laughing-stock throughout the civilized world." Because arbitration had been used "as a cover for a monstrous act of fraud—and chicane," there was "no reason for sensible people feeling anything, but disgust at it."[20]

Quite apart from the deplorable way in which the United States had handled the affair, there was a widespread sense that the arbitration was an exception and not a path-breaking precedent. It was plain for all to see, as *Scribner's* pointed out, that no national interests were being sacrificed and that neither side stood to gain anything at all by going to war. It was precisely because war was not in the cards between the United States and Britain that the Treaty of Washington was unlikely to serve as a precedent for situations in which the possibility of war loomed larger. Arbitration presupposed a calculated willingness to arbitrate that was all too obviously absent in Europe. The minister and educator Samuel Ward Boardman dismissed the possibility that a continental Europe armed to the teeth would take the arbitral road. Could one seriously imagine an arbitration between Germany and France on a vital issue? Hardly. In addition, all the blather about Anglo-Saxonism undercut the universality of the precedent and limited its reach (though the inability to settle the perennial disputes with Canada over fishing rights suggested that even cultural ties had their limits). In sum, deep changes needed to take place in diplomatic practice and in governing institutions. "We cannot hope to see such a state of things in our generation," said *Appletons'*. *The Nation* observed in 1887 that "there has apparently never been a period in the world's history when . . . civilized nations seemed so little disposed to settle disputes by arbitration."[21]

Another liberal hobby horse was the advancement of international law, which, from an evolutionist point of view, seemed an inevitable accompaniment to the global spread of civilization. Ideally, according to Godkin, law would be "the only true controller of international relations." Political leaders like President Grant openly looked forward to the day when "a court, recognized by all nations, will settle international differences." This elevated American view of international law, according to one writer, took it to be "as binding upon nations as are the Ten Commandments upon individuals." True, it was generally understood that international law was a case of might making right through war, but whatever its shortcomings, at least the principles that had been agreed upon were treated with fidelity as the law. In the immediate aftermath of the Civil War, international law was thought to be advancing, at least in the long run. As an 1866 review of Henry Wheaton's popular textbook pointed out, "reason steadily gains ground; violence as steadily recedes." In his widely used compendium of international law, Theodore Dwight Woolsey pointed to the growing importance of international public opinion as a force promoting adherence to international law. "The Fejees or the Hottentots care little how the world regards them," he wrote, "but the opinion of civilized nations is highly valued by all those states which are now foremost in human affairs. Without such a value set on reputation, fear of censure could not exist, which is one of the ultimate bulwarks of international law." But this was a problematic formulation, at best, given the warlike temper of even democratic publics.[22]

With significant American participation, an *Institut de Droit International* was founded in 1873 in Ghent by European liberals eager to capitalize on the new technology of communication and international public opinion. But the optimism behind its founding had disappeared almost entirely by the 1880s as it became clear that international law was little influenced by international lawyers. In the absence of tribunals and institutions of enforcement, international law was a docile servant of powerful states. With a future conflict taken for granted, the powers were reluctant to concede points that might harm them in time of war. As a result, Sedgwick concluded, the work of codification and pushing forward the growth of international law was "more difficult and discouraging than it might have been a generation ago." This decline of faith in international law was part of what one historian has described as "the general decline of European liberalism" at the turn of the century. Indicative of the disdain felt by high officialdom was Prime Minister Lord Salisbury's curt dismissal of international law as something that reflected only "the prejudices of writers of text-books."[23]

It was a small consolation, but for some commentators advances in the law of neutrality appeared to provide a ray of light in an otherwise stygian darkness. International law generally was without an enforcement apparatus, but the law of neutrality compelled respect. As pointed out by John Norton Pomeroy, "the practical rules for the conduct of maritime warfare in form, in precision, in certainty, and in compulsive force, have, more than any others, the character and effect of true and positive law enforced by human sanctions, judicially applied." The cause of this advance, he suggested, was the worldwide spread of reverence for private property. A cynic would have been quick to add that the willingness of neutral nations to fight for their rights had something to do with it. Whatever its other shortcomings, the *Alabama* claims settlement at least appeared to have advanced principles applicable to the conduct of belligerents and neutrals. Thus *Scribner's* had initially hailed the treaty as "a great step towards checking war and the extension of war to neutral nations." But here, too, the Treaty of Washington promised far more than it delivered, for the so-called three rules of the Treaty of Washington, whose purpose was to limit the meddling of neutrals in belligerent affairs, badly misjudged the source of problems in the future, when the behavior of belligerent powers would be at issue. Hence it had no perceptible impact on subsequent developments in the law of neutrality.[24]

In retrospect, the year 1856, when at long last the British agreed to restrict seizures to contraband, had been the watershed year. Until that point, in *The*

Nation's view, clear progress had been made in neutral rights in which one could discern a process of "steady development" and perhaps an "irreversible movement." But the next two decades had demonstrated "a danger of a bar-barous reaction in an opposite direction." The European powers, increasingly preoccupied with preparing for war, were more concerned with augment-ing belligerent rights. Restricting seizures to contraband was an illusory ad-vance when the idea of "conditional contraband" was gaining ground. As a consequence of the industrialization of war, this meant that the list of contra-band items was likely to expand indefinitely. Crushing the enemy on land or on sea, by whatever means possible, was the paramount concern, neutrals be damned.[25]

Interpreting American Security in the Modern Era

By the 1880s, the lack of discernible progress toward a more peaceful world and the technologically supercharged arms race combined to precipitate a na-tional debate on preparedness in which, as historian Russell Weigley has ob-served, the military's concern for coastal defense became "almost obsessive." It was a peculiar debate, however. Unique among great nations, the United States had no enemies on its borders or in its immediate vicinity. Although advocates of preparedness failed to offer any convincing proof of the existence of a con-crete threat, it was precisely the absence of specifiable danger that fueled their arguments on behalf of rearmament. For example, Captain Eugene Griffin of the Army Corps of Engineers contended that "a thousand unforeseen incidents may at any moment involve us in diplomatic controversies which can only be settled by the sword." As this comment suggests, traditional fear was being re-placed by a diffuse modern anxiety.[26]

In the absence of facts and lessons drawn from experience, the discussion took the form of a debate about beliefs. Proponents of rearmament were forced to make the case for the certainty of war by combining two very different kinds of argument, traditional and modern. As one might expect, they maintained that war was in the nature of things. But they were equally likely to dwell on modern themes by pointing to the new and unforeseeable dangers posed by the revolution in military technology and by the interdependence of the shrinking modern world. This, too, was unsurprising, for it was the responsibility of mil-itary professionals to be well informed on technological developments in their field of expertise—peacetime generals are not always preoccupied with fighting the last war. War was normal, but the kinds of wars likely to be fought would be novel. What *was* surprising was the willingness of antimilitarist liberals to rely on traditional arguments about the irreducibly regional character of international politics. Although something of a role reversal was at work in this debate, each side accepted globalization as a fact, which it then proceeded to use for its own ideological purposes.

To begin with, nearly everyone agreed that the United States was militarily unprepared. Godkin readily granted that the obsolete remnants of the once-formidable Civil War navy were "almost useless for military purposes." "As far as available instruments are concerned, we are absolutely helpless," complained J. Russell Solely, a naval officer. "We have absolutely no means of defence," groused another navy man. "There has been no such spectacle in the previous history of the world, as this of a rich and pre-eminently powerful people inviting attack upon life and property . . . by leaving its coasts wholly undefended against the implements of war of the period." Critics took delight in enumerating the number and kinds of modern armored ships available to other powers, including Japan, China, and Chile and in suggesting the havoc that they could wreak. Every American seaport, argued *The North American Review,* was at the mercy of "a single hostile iron-clad ship." The same debility afflicted the dwarfish regular army, which, relegated to subduing all-but-defeated Indian tribes, was less a fighting force than "the custodian of what military knowledge exists in the country." This defenseless condition was even more disturbing if one accepted the view that modern wars were decided quickly. If conflict came, it stood to reason that the United States, even if not conquered, would surely be humiliated.[27]

Many of the arguments about the likelihood of war were based on traditional assumptions concerning human nature and the constancy of history. Most often these arguments were expressed in a Hobbesian idiom that pointed to anarchy as the central fact of international society. As Pomeroy put it, "The order of things as established by the Creator involves the existence of wars." Because wars were as much a feature of the international environment as ever, nearly everyone realized "the always possible chance of a contest with some civilized power." No nation achieved its objectives free of charge. To be fixated on the absence of threats in the present was not unlike someone predicting, on the basis of a perfectly cloudless sky, the absence of all storms in the future. If the issue was when, not whether a war would occur, it was obviously prudent to be prepared. Those who failed to grasp the nation's utter unpreparedness were "living in a fool's paradise."[28]

Yet the proponents of defense were not shy about using modern ideas about the collapsing of space and time to make their case. The implications of interdependence for national security made for scary reading. For the military-minded, technologically created proximity and the waning of geographic isolation made not for harmony, but for certain trouble. Eugene Griffin, rebutting those who continued to take comfort from America's geographic distance from Europe, insisted that "such ideas are fallacious." "Our geographical isolation is no longer a practical reality," he said. "The locomotive, the screw propeller and the submarine cable have annihilated space and time. Liverpool is now but six days from New York, and in war we measure distances by time, not miles." C. F. Goodrich, a naval engineer, pointed out that the modern conquest of distance had produced new threats from Spain, France, Germany, and Britain. It was common knowledge that Europe's economic storms traveled across the seas. Why not, then, military disturbances? The threat of European imperialism spreading to the Western Hemisphere occasioned comment as early as 1881 in an essay by the politician-diplomat John Kasson. This issue "touches every national interest," he wrote. Nevertheless, no one could point to a likely enemy in a manner sure to evoke the kind of fear that would make a *prima facie* case for preparedness.[29]

For most preparedness advocates, modern conditions only reinforced and amplified the ancient wisdom behind very traditional foreign policy outlooks. Civilization presented new dangers, but only in the form of a variation on old themes. Thus arguments about commercial rivalry tended to draw upon mercantilist traditions for their justification, in particular on the need for a strong navy to protect American commerce. Increased trade, said General McClellan, would create benefits, but he preferred to emphasize the negative side of interdependence, the many "causes of friction," that were bound to arise. Kasson warned of commercial rivalry in the hemisphere, claiming that "covetous eyes are cast on outlying islands and continental coasts of Central and South America." In the modern context, trade was simply one form of conflict between societies whose supreme expression was war. As Joseph Wharton of Bethlehem Steel and a high tariff advocate put it, trade was a "newer style of aggrandizement by winning the wealth of a neighbor through industrial assaults and trade invasions." "In this modern and highly civilized style of warfare," he continued, "the enemy's forces—his industrial population . . . are driven from their homes by starvation rather than by bullets in the field." This emphasis on the conflict-making side of trade was, of course, the inverse of the liberal contention that commerce and contact made for peace.[30]

Liberals tended in turn to stress the obsolete character of assumptions that were dear to friends of naval rearmament. *The Nation* ridiculed the notion, soon to be popularized by Mahan, that there was a necessary connection between a navy and the expansion of commerce. This might have been true "in a semi-barbarous age, when might makes right, and when commerce is in large part spoliation and piracy," it argued, "But it is not true in the present age of the world." Naval expansion, it insisted, would not guarantee "one ton more of foreign commerce than we now have." Navalist arguments for trade expansion were part of a package of "antiquated contrivances, such as bounties, or diplomatic tricks, or even war" that included everything except for the "natural and rational" remedy: free trade. On the need for force as a necessary complement to diplomacy, the journal could not recall a single instance from 1778 to 1889 when a major foreign power had "yielded anything to us on account of fear of our naval thunder." It was also far from certain that investments in naval power would bring a measurable increase in security because technological obsolescence came quickly in naval arms, which, after a few years, were "apt to be useless." The inevitable result would be to step onto the European-style treadmill.[31]

Besides responding with stock counterarguments, many liberals who normally spoke in a modern global register were quick to sing in a traditional key when it came to issues of national strategy. Take for example their deployment of the Monroe Doctrine to argue against an activist policy. The Doctrine, often ignored in the past, was by this time already beginning to take on the status of holy writ. But as it grew in sacredness, the need for Monrovian concern had declined in urgency. If the Monroe Doctrine was valid, the balance of power remained a purely European concern, which suggested the continuing need to steer clear of European interests and vice versa. In response to those who argued that enforcement of the Monroe Doctrine made necessary a sizable defense force, *The Century* insisted that because the United States was "clearly master of the situation . . . we can afford to talk less about the Monroe doctrine; for nowadays it enforces itself." *The Nation* agreed. Expansion across the continent had drastically diminished the chances for foreign intervention. "No nation on earth would dream of coming here to fight us," it said, "and it would require a very pressing irritation indeed to get an American army to go to Europe, even for a short summer war." American power was "universally recognized, and no intelligent European statesman would think for a moment of disputing its superiority on this continent."[32]

The tense situation in Europe was thus no reason to lose one's bearings. Theodore Dwight Woolsey, a declared "cosmopolite," argued that the idea of balance of power "means danger from abroad, from a neighbor, and there are no neighbors for us to fear." The separation of political systems imposed by the Atlantic Ocean and the Monroe Doctrine lessened the likelihood of European expansion into the hemisphere and precluded the emergence of a global balance of power. "There may therefore be a European, but there cannot at present, probably there never can be, an 'oecumenical' equilibrium," Woolsey insisted. He also doubted that the large European navies gave cause for American concern. Navies were useful for disrupting commerce, but for purposes of invasion they were an auxiliary force only. "No nation is much dreaded on account of its naval power," he argued. "By this arm of its power it can spread its operations over the world, but it cannot, by this arm alone, become a world-wide conqueror." For most liberals, then, when it came to defining national security, geographical factors of proximity, distance, and oceanic separation still mattered. In this mixed liberal view, modern technology had brought the world together commercially but not militarily. The oceans were simultaneously highways and impassable moats.[33]

A striking feature of these discussions was the virtual absence of social Darwinist rationales on a topic seemingly tailor-made to fit its arguments. It is true that Darwinian metaphors could be and were applied to virtually any human phenomenon of the day, but very little of this kind of talk was found in discussions of international relations. Exceptions were the occasional references, such as *The Nation*'s comment that "the fittest survive, even more surely among nations than among individuals," and this in a journal that was bitterly critical of military Darwinism. Luce appeared to take a Darwinian tack when he declared war to be "one of the great agencies by which human progress is effected." War, he said, was part of "the operation of the economic laws of nature for the government of the human family." But instead of the survival of the fittest, with its glorification of conflict, preparedness was advocated as a regret-table necessity in a quite traditional manner that would not have seemed out of place in the agonistic classical world of Rome and Athens, or even in Christian Rome for that matter. Thus, Luce could at the same time say that "insurance against war by preparation for it is, of all methods, the most business-like, the most humane, and the most in accordance with the teachings of the Christian religion."[34] *Si vis pacem, bellum para.*

Perhaps suspecting that Darwinian arguments would be unleashed, liberals launched preemptive attacks on the implicit contradictions of dog-eat-dog logic. *The Nation,* in an attempt at *reductio ad absurdum,* tracked Darwinian reasoning to the following conclusion: "The able-bodied go to war and fill the trenches; the weak remain at home and continue the family. In such case, can we accept the fact of survival as proof that the survivor was the fittest?" There was nothing scientific about this, it insisted. Rather, military Darwinism was the product of a "metaphysics of chauvinism" that rationalized war as a necessary good, "a mode of national self-affirmation" that confirmed superiority via military conquest. In this repulsive view, war was "nature's certificate of a people's fitness to live." Social Darwinism as a justification for extolling an international struggle for existence was a characteristic of European, especially German, thinking, in which the struggle for existence had become "the baptismal formula for the most cynical assertions of brute egoism." Far from being the instrument of progress, war was a reflection of "the brutal logic of contemporary European politics." It was an atavistic survival, "a relic of animalism," that in the modern context could drastically retard the progress of a people toward civilization. Darwinism also rejected the altruism and Christian ethics that many liberals prized as a central feature of modern civilization. In essence, it was no different from the godless Sophist arguments made by the Athenian emissaries to Melos that might made right.[35]

Although the discussion of threats to the United States was shrouded in ambiguity, one set of dangers could be reliably anticipated: the implications for the United States of a great war in Europe. The European balance of power was double-edged: beneficial to the United States in times of peace but harmful in times of war. Some commentators, Alfred Thayer Mahan being surprisingly among them, tended to minimize the consequences to America of a European war as "partial and indirect." But most of those who discussed the problem understood that in the past Europe had mattered immensely in practical terms because it had been the source of some deadly serious disputes centering on neutrality. Ironically, the American emphasis on neutral rights, a key component of isolationism since the achievement of independence, had also proven to be a potent force for involvement in intra-European conflicts. The neutrality doctrine had finally been codified in international law in the Treaty of Paris (1856), but subsequent developments made its application seem increasingly problematic. International backsliding on neutral rights, when combined with the growing likelihood of a European war, pointed unmistakably to the necessity of the United States participating in the arms race, for neutrality had always depended, in the last resort, on the willingness to employ credible military power.[36]

Whether or not a general European war would be good or bad for business was a matter of inconclusive debate. It was in any case irrelevant, for it seemed a foregone conclusion that the greater reliance of belligerents on the industrial manufactures and raw materials of neutral powers was likely to bring neutrals into their cross hairs. "This is an age in which neutrals have fallen on evil times," said *The Century*'s editorialist in 1889. The implications for the future were not very bright, for it was widely assumed that "in any future European war the United States will probably occupy its natural position as a neutral." J. Russell Soley predicted that the next European war would find the United States "something more than an interested spectator," which was "sure to find itself a mark for encroachments and aggressions." It was even conceivable, as John Kasson argued, that given the expanding European definitions of contraband, "War itself would become more fatal to neutral states than to belligerent interests." The handwriting was already on the wall during the Franco-Prussian War, at which time Godkin was "struck by the increasing difficulty of the position of neutrals in all wars. The close relations, as far as time and space are concerned, into which steam and the telegraph and commerce have now brought all civilized powers, make every armed struggle an object of intense interest to lookers-on, as well as to those actually engaged in it, and this interest, in turn, makes the belligerents increasingly sensitive and exacting." If war came, the United States, being the most powerful neutral, would not only follow its own interests but would likely become the custodian of neutral rights in general. This would be both dangerous and debasing because threatening to make war for the right to turn a profit from war would puncture the widespread impression that neutrality somehow corresponded with righteousness. Woolsey minced no words on this matter. "War now, to no small an extent, is carried on by neutrals and for neutrals," he wrote. "They are the capitalists in the workshop of death."[37]

Moreover, a completely impartial neutrality would be hard to pull off in such a war. It was a given that the nation would come under pressure from belligerents eager to mold neutral commerce to their strategic requirements. It did not take a soothsayer to predict great tension in relations with Great Britain. But what about other nations, and especially the land powers? *The Nation* pointed out the possibility, embedded in the Treaty of Washington, of conflicting neutral obligations in, say, a war between Russia and Britain. If the practical benefits were too one-sided, that would do violence to the impartiality that inhered in the very idea of neutrality. And if the economic stakes were great enough in such a situation, the pressure to enter the war on one side or the other would be enormous. Thus *The Century* wondered whether this concern for defending neutral rights "may not be made the means for transferring the once great neutral republic to the list of quasi-belligerents." In other words, the logic of neutrality might push irresistibly in the direction of unneutrality. Preparedness might put teeth in neutrality, but, as in the War of 1812, how to avoid putting the nation in the company of the great militarist powers at the same time was far from clear.[38]

In the final analysis, even though it was uncertain if modern conditions had increased or diminished the threats facing the United States from abroad, the concern with maintaining neutral rights left little choice but to proceed with naval rearmament. At a minimum, the United States would need an up-to-date navy to protect its interests in the event of a European war. Yet quite apart from the practical exigencies and notwithstanding its nationalist halo, neutral rights was an internationalist doctrine in at least two respects. First, it presumed economic interdependence, which was undoubtedly on the increase, thus making it necessary to worry about developments abroad. And second, it was a vital feature of international law. Thus a liberal journal like *The Nation*, which ordinarily opposed huge armaments spending, was forced to agree on the need for naval modernization. The existing situation, it admitted, was defensible "only by those who see no necessity for even the satirical semblance of a navy that we possess." Certainly, there were other reasons for building up the navy. A respectable fleet would be essential to securing the much-discussed interoceanic canal in Central America, though an American-built waterway was still far from a sure thing in 1890.[39] But a canal merely added to an already compelling rationale for building a modern navy.

America's Millennial Role in the World

These issues of war and peace, though momentous in themselves, raised the deeper question of America's historical role in the world. Few Americans would have disagreed with Herbert Spencer's prediction that "the Americans may reasonably look forward to a time when they will have produced a civilization grander than any the world has known." After the Civil War, recalled *The Atlantic Monthly,* Americans sensed "an entirely fresh force and feeling to our foreign relations." They smelled international greatness in the nation's future. "Nothing," proclaimed *The Nation,* "can ever now prevent us from playing a great part in the future of modern society, in influencing both its manners and ideas; and the larger the part we play, the more important will our diplomacy become." Speaking primarily about the United States' likely impact on the development of international law, one editorial predicted that by 1900 "no other government, or combination of governments, will be able to set up or impose any duty or doctrine which we have not sanctioned."[40]

Twenty-five years later, the world looked rather different. A telling example of the pessimism that had seeped into certain segments of liberal thought by the closing decade of the century was the gloomy view of the future contained in the sequel to Tennyson's famous poem "Locksley Hall." The first version, published in 1842, looked past human conflict to a future in which "the war-drum throbb'd no longer, and the battle-flags were furl'd In the Parliament of man, the Federation of the world." However, in "Locksley Hall: Sixty Years After," the sentiment had darkened quite a bit, as the poet now asked: "who can fancy warless men?" The elimination of war now seemed a distant fantasy:

Warless? war will die out late then. Will it ever? late or soon?
Can it, till this outworn earth be dead as yon dead world the moon?

The Yale literary scholar T. R. Lounsbury used the new Tennyson to question whether universal peace could ever be achieved in Europe. "Is, in truth, such a hope any longer cherished not as a remote probability but even as a remote possibility?" he asked rhetorically. Human beings seemed to be "mere helpless atoms floating on a stream of tendency the current of which we cannot control, and borne onward to a catastrophe we cannot foresee." Regarding earlier expectations of an era of universal peace, *The Nation* asked rhetorically, "Who believes it now?"[41]

The inescapable conclusion to be drawn from the trajectory of events was that Europe would remain Europe, with little prospect of being changed by the United States. The traditional universalist rationale for isolationism was that it would serve as a utopian example to the rest of the world. But the arms race then in progress showed only contempt for the American model that had been so widely touted at the end of the Civil War. Drawing a preparedness moral from the lesson, one writer noted that "all of the general increase of armament throughout the civilized world is in the face of the example set by this country of military and naval weakness and forbearance, and in spite of our professed devotion to the principles of arbitration." European militarism was here to stay for the foreseeable future and might even drag the United States into the Old World's quarrels. Isolationism in peace and neutral rights in war seemed to call for preparedness at a minimum and interventionism at the outside. How could an optimistic conclusion be derived from all this? How could American greatness find expression in the context of a civilization apparently bent on self-destruction?[42]

It was unthinkable to imagine a future in which the United States simply joined the ranks of the traditional great powers. Even proponents of armament realized that "to the great majority of the American people the experience of Europe is of no value as a guide." America was not like Europe; its international position was "entirely anomalous." In 1871, with the Civil War presumably having established once and for all the viability of the idea of republican confederation, Edward Everett Hale anticipated the imminent creation of a United States of Europe inspired by the American example, a hope that soon proved to be empty. A decade later, there seemed little prospect that Europe's political dynamics could be transformed by a bilateral relationship between republican exemplar and willing continental imitator. When viewed from a broader global framework, however, sunnier vistas opened up, for it was by that route that the European balance of power as an historically entrenched system could be bypassed. The solution, according to some prominent internationalists, was for the United States to play a central role in developing a global civilization rather than entering the lists as a traditional great power or resting content with the status of hemispheric hegemon. Because Europe on its own might never abandon war, it was in globality that the favorable prospects for civilization resided.[43]

The most prescient attempt to look into America's future by drawing connections with historical development on a global scale came from John Fiske, a well-known contributor of historical pieces to the higher-toned periodicals. Fiske's extraordinarily popular essay, "Manifest Destiny," which appeared in *Harper's* in 1884, has often been interpreted as a clarion call to empire. But empire was less on Fiske's mind than the desire to explain, from a Spencerian evolutionary framework, how a pacific America and a warlike Europe might come together in a peaceful global future. Like nearly everyone else, Fiske was upset by the course of developments on the continent. The challenge was to explain how military rivalry would be superseded by peaceful economic competition. (His master, Spencer, was not doing too well on this score.)[44]

At the outset, Fiske defined civilization as "primarily the gradual substitution of a state of peace for a state of war." One of the "seeming paradoxes" of world history was that peace could be maintained only through the constant readiness to make war. Readiness was all in earlier historical epochs when one saw "a few brilliant points of civilization surrounded on every side by a midnight blackness of barbarism." But now the struggle with barbarism was nearly at its historical terminus. "The only serious question," said Fiske, "is by what process of modification the barbarous races are to maintain their foot-hold upon the earth at all." Henceforth the central struggle would take place within civilization itself. The challenge of modern times was to assure the transfer of power from "the hands of the war-loving portion of the human race into the hands of the peace-loving portion—into the hands of the dollar-hunters."

The warriors would not surrender power willingly, nor could they be disarmed, which left external influences to do the job. Fiske imagined two historical processes running in parallel: the Anglo-Saxon/global and the European/local. Clearly, Americans had a huge role to play in fashioning the global future. "To have established such a system over one great continent is to have made a very good beginning toward establishing it over the world," said Fiske. Employing virtually the same idiom of global acculturation that would appear in Josiah Strong's best-seller, he predicted that "the work which the English race began when it colonized North America is destined to go on until every land on the earth's surface that is not already the seat of an old civilization shall become English in its language, in its religion, in its political habits and traditions, and to a predominant extent in the blood of its people." Like many others, he believed that English was destined to be the world's second language. "Whatever language any man may have learned in his infancy," said Fiske, "he will find it necessary sooner or later to learn to express his thoughts in English."

The global position of the United States would tell in the end. The "pacific pressure exerted upon Europe by America" was bound to have so great an impact that, "in due time," the continent would "find it worth while to adopt the lesson of federalism in order to do away with . . . useless warfare." If Europe hoped to "keep pace with America in the advance toward universal law and order," some sort of federal system would be necessary. Fiske knew that "linguistic and ethnological differences" threw up serious obstacles, but Europe had little choice in the matter. "The economic competition will become so keen," he predicted, "that European armies will have to be disbanded, the swords will have to be turned into ploughshares, and thus the victory of the industrial over the military type of civilization will at last become complete." Fiske concluded on a triumphant note: "Thus we may foresee in general how, by the gradual concentration of physical power into the hands of the most pacific communities, we may finally succeed in rendering warfare illegal all over the globe. As this process goes on, it may, after many more ages of political experience, become apparent that there is really no reason, in the nature of things, why the whole of mankind should not constitute politically one huge federation." Thus the emergence of a modern world system anchored by Anglo-Saxon cultures and political norms would force the collapse of the European structure. Once the Europeans realized that their model was bankrupt, the path enabling them to come together would finally be clear. It was in this way, as a review of Fiske's essay pointed out, that "the race which gained control of North America must become the dominant race of the world, and that its political ideas will assuredly prevail in the struggle for life."[45]

This blueprint was hardly unique to Fiske. If the future of the world could be derailed by developments within Europe, many Americans believed that it could be decided for the better outside of Europe on a global scale. A few years earlier, Godkin saw no chance that the United States could militarily force Europe to disarm, but nonmilitary means offered a more potent alternative. Thus he predicted that "before many years the steady offer of cheaper food than any heavily-taxed people can raise will make the maintenance of these enormous hosts unendurable." In 1886, a piece in *The Century* said much the same thing about the economic prospects of the European states. "Their natural development has been arrested," it argued. "Unless Bismarckism and Czarism and Chauvinism cease to control the peoples of Europe, they must lose even what they now have to the unencumbered American racer." Edward Atkinson put the issue this way: "In the great commerce of the world, what chance of success can there be on the part of states into the cost of whose product is charged the blood-tax of huge standing armies and of war-debts." And *The Nation*, in contemplating the creation of a European *Zollverein*, looked beyond Fiske to a period of peaceful Euro-American economic competition.[46]

As a political statement, Fiske's argument fit comfortably within the isolationist tradition. But it was also deeply internationalist, for the key to global progress and the vindication of America's historical role lay in the creation and maintenance of an open world environment in which liberal societies would have room to develop and ripen. Typically, civilization was conceived of as a process that expanded from core to periphery, but in this case the pressure for converting the core to full civilization would come from the outside, thanks to the New World's having taken the lead in creating a global society. Thus the general would transform the particular; the global periphery and the European center would exchange positions. Viewed in this light, globalization was not a mere outcome or resultant but a potent causal process in its own right. It was also a process that saved American internationalism from Eurocentrism or the fate of having to become like Europe. Unlike the thinking of some isolationists, in this formulation it was Europe and not the United States that existed outside the stream of time.[47]

Fiske's reaffirmation of America's redemptive mission appealed not only to Americans, but to non-American observers because his viewpoint was as much liberal and internationalist as it was American. The British internationalist James Anthony Froude agreed fully that the rejection of the European balance of power was prerequisite to stepping onto a new global stage on which the "drama of peace" could be played out. And continental leaders were not oblivious to the problem. A quotation attributed to the Italian premier Francesco Crispi affirmed the basic dynamics of Fiske's analysis, while withholding judgment on the final outcome. "I know it," said Crispi, "these armaments will end by ruining Europe for the benefit of America."[48]

Questions of preeminence aside, the global approach was also powerfully attractive to advocates of Anglo-Saxonism. George R. Parkin, the Canadian evangelist of imperial federation, tried to explain the global significance of Anglo-Saxon civilization to Americans by arguing that "any hindrance to the safe and free development of that civilization in either of its two great currents would be to the world's loss." This global context makes the appeal of Anglo-Saxonism more readily understandable. Insubstantial and ethereal from a purely bilateral perspective, Anglo-Saxonism offered a compelling global alternative to the European way of doing things. Since neither the United States nor Great Britain could hope to function effectively as a lone globalizer, it followed that a disaster to Great Britain could be viewed by an American "as a calamity to his own country and to the world." Even an American victory in a war against Great Britain would have a negative impact on "the interests of the civilized world at large." Some, like Thomas Wentworth Higginson, appeared to desire an alliance as the core of a greater federation, a "league of all honest and pacific nations against the turbulence of the ambitious and unruly." But it was less the survival of England as the makeweight in the European balance of power than England's role as an agent of globalization, Anglo-Saxon style, that mattered in the long run. An alliance between the two was out of the question, but if everything went as expected, there would be no need for Anglo-Saxonism to take an overtly political form.[49]

Fiske's view had a number of ingenious features. For one thing, it neatly resolved the tension between the need to remain isolated from Old World politics and the desire to be a "redeemer nation." It could satisfy both without compromising either. In addition, it frankly appreciated that liberalism was an embattled creed in the heartland of civilization while still managing to depict a triumphant liberal outcome. Fiske built a powerfully coherent historical case for optimism out of the otherwise dreamy American confidence that peace and prosperity were the natural destination of humanity. His argument grew out of the conviction that global developmental processes would, in the last analysis, exert an irresistible pressure on the parochial traditions of politics. There was nothing particularly original about this viewpoint, for he was simply applying a fundamental tenet of the liberal creed. "Vast mutual interests have developed in the consciousness, and are recognized in the foreign policy, of nations," argued the *Atlantic*. The pioneering political scientist Francis Lieber put it this way: "Formerly the process of nationalization was appearing as one of the novel things" going on; "now the process of internationalization is going on," a process that was governed by "the all-pervading law of interdependence." Fiske believed that the momentum of informal, non-governmental, commercial, and cultural processes ("soft power", in a more recent idiom) would be sufficient to drive nation-based power politics out of business.[50]

This was a huge and ultimately untenable assumption. In taking for granted the progress of globalization within an international system dominated by liberal powers, Fiske failed to anticipate the possibility that its ongoing development might become imperiled by states or coalitions hostile to liberal globalization. In retrospect, his solution took for granted as a natural condition the very process whose existence would soon be thrown into question. But various other shortcomings of Fiske's optimistic historical prophecy were readily apparent to critical readers of his day. A review in *Harper's* took him to task for ignoring human nature in his belief that the transition could take place without turbulence. "As the elements of time and space and diversity of tongue are being eliminated," wrote the reviewer, "there will be feuds, rivalries, ambitions, usurpations, conspiracies, rebellions, and conflicts of interest among men." War was still "a powerful stimulant," said one essay, while another wondered how the world could get along without it. This was all true enough. And as Mahan pointed out a few years later, the assumption that international relations outside Europe would be more peaceful was also open to question. Fiske himself was not unmindful of the obstacles to the fulfillment of his vision. A few years later, in an introduction to Harold Murdock's *The Reconstruction of Europe,* he admitted that "deep in the heart of mankind there still nestles the conviction that neither reason nor justice, but brute force, is the arbiter of human affairs." These criticisms would be amply borne out by a violent future in which America's global interventionism differed markedly from the peaceful role envisioned in Fiske's prophecy.[51]

Despite its many obvious predictive shortcomings, Fiske's prophetic essay managed to chart a course to the future that was strikingly prescient. For one thing, it was already apparent in his essay that Europe, the heartland of civilization, was beset by problems that it could not resolve alone. Fiske spoke for many other Americans who stayed abreast of international politics when he despaired at Europe's inability to cope with its own troubles, and he did so long before the calamities of the twentieth century would confirm the continent's penchant for self-destruction. Europe, it was already understood, could only be forced to change from the outside. Fiske's predictions about the United States' decisive impact on Europe's politics also proved to be correct, although he failed to anticipate that it would take an imperial form that would go a long way toward militarizing American society. Despite the unforeseen political and military intervention of the United States, in the course of which a new-found concern with power politics appeared at times to verge on obsession, the conviction that liberal commercial and cultural processes would play a huge and ultimately decisive role in shaping a benign world order would continue to exercise a powerful grip on the imaginations of American policy makers throughout the twentieth century and after. Although globalization had failed to save Europe from two wars, its potential for changing the political atmosphere was demonstrated after 1945 when the success of the liberal world economy did force the Soviet Union to abandon its principled opposition to capitalist democracy.

Most significant in the long run was the global perspective from which Fiske proceeded, whereby the problem would be solved by expanding it. In so doing, he was helping to lay the foundation for what would become the next century's realism. There was a circularity to this way of thinking, within which lurked interventionist implications yet unrecognized, that went something like this: The progress of civilization hinged on culture change; the civilizational forces that generated such internal change could only operate within an international system that actively promoted acculturating contact; that international system was maintained by the power of liberal nations that believed in civilization as culture change. The pattern of relationships resembles the game of rock, scissors, and paper in which no single alternative prevails at all times—civilization outranked particular cultures, but power trumped civilization, and culture, as the key resource of civilization, was more critical than naked power. Thus, although culture could not be transformed through power alone, power was hardly its antipode; on the contrary, power was essential to the functioning of the whole.

Another generation would pass before American liberals recognized that their understanding of global politics lacked a politics of globalization, but their ability to finally arrive at that recognition owed much to the foundation laid by people like Fiske. Although Fiske did not envision America intervening in Europe, his framework suggested that such an intervention, when the question did arise, would not be undertaken out of a concern with Europe alone. One of the principal legatees of nineteenth-century liberalism, President Woodrow Wilson, made this quite clear in December 1918 when he informed a British audience that the United States "is not interested in European politics. She is not interested merely in the peace of Europe, but in the peace of the world." This may seem like a strange statement coming from the lips of a statesman who had just plunged his nation into the greatest European war to date, but it makes perfect sense from a Fiskean global standpoint. While Fiske had been wrong about the extent of the United States' involvement in advancing its planetary agenda, Wilson's declaration was a reaffirmation of the nineteenth-century liberal belief in the primacy of the globalizing process.[52]

Thus, even after the unprecedented intervention of 1917, it was not Europe's political weather but the global climate that continued to attract the attention of American liberals. This meant that their worldview was neither Europeanist nor Eurocentric. Admittedly, Americans could not jump out of their Euro-Atlantic cultural skins, but once the necessary allowances are made, their recognition of the shaping power of the global environment and its seemingly autonomous social forces comes across as both remarkable and indispensable as a prerequisite to political globalism. There was nothing natural or self-evident about this outlook. Indeed, to those who did not share it, it seemed decidedly odd. European leaders and American Atlanticists would always have trouble understanding what they considered an eccentric obsession with relatively minor events on the periphery, hence their serious misgivings about the global preoccupations that characterized American foreign policy in the second half of the twentieth century.

For the German political theorist Carl Schmitt, enmity was the key to identity. "Tell me who your enemy is and I'll tell you who you are," was his formula. If asked to name an enemy, Americans of the nineteenth century would not have been able to identify an existentially alien Other.[53] Yet this did not mean that the United States as a liberal society lacked for either an identity or an enemy. Already during these years the belief in the fundamental unity of humankind was in process of creating a global identity for the nation. In due course, it would also be used in Schmitt's sense to define enemies who threatened to derail the liberal course of world history. Such nations and movements could take many forms: a *Kaiserreich*, a perceived global conspiracy of fascist gangster nations, or the Red colossus of communism. Those enemies would more often than not come from Europe, but, as relationships with Japan and Communist China would later illustrate, the West had exported and diffused civilization to the point that the periphery had become as important as the center. Americans of the late nineteenth century could not foresee any of these threats to the emergence of a liberal world society, but their view of history was dark enough to make for an overcast, even threatening, global dawn.[54]

Conclusion

Culture as Capability

Throughout the post-civil war period, a diverse assortment of writers and intellectuals explored the ways in which the seeming backwater of American isolation mingled with the main currents of globalization and international relations. This broad survey generated an understanding of the world that can be described as cultural in a number of respects. For one thing, the ideas out of which this appreciation was composed formed a loose but coherent network that lacked a center in one person or a single well-defined group of people. Just as no one can speak the entirety of the English language, no one individual was competent to elucidate the entire range of topics and opinions considered in this study, although a strategically situated intellectual like E.L Godkin enjoyed an unusually panoramic view of the liberal intellectual landscape. They were also cultural in content because so much of the conversation was devoted to cultural themes. This was true whether the particular topic of discussion was national identity, racial problems, the behavioral characteristics and social psychology of civilized nations, or the problems and prospects of non-Western civilizations. Finally, these discussions were cultural because they provided readers with a broad education about developments outside the United States. Because civilization was inherently universal, being modern required "cultivation," the acquisition of a cosmopolitan understanding of how the various dimensions of globalization fit together. For many, that meant becoming familiar with Europe, but for a growing number it meant indulging in a broader curiosity about the world. In this way, personal improvement, the cultivation of an internationalist way of being, or taking an international standpoint on the world meshed with planetary progress.[1]

How important were these ideas in their own day and in the long term? At the time, the political balance sheet was disappointing.[2] Taking a longer view, however, the legacy of liberal thought appears much more substantial. By the end of the twentieth century, the United States was nearly as firmly committed to free trade, both politically and academically, as it had once been addicted to protectionism; it had, by general acknowledgment, one of the most honest and efficient government bureaucracies in the world; the diplomatic and consular service had been professionalized; the nation was a staunch defender of international property rights in patents, trademarks, and copyrights; its art, science, literature, and university system were world-class; it was a major tourist destination as well as a leading supplier of visitors to other lands; war among the great powers had been rendered pretty much unthinkable, for a time, at least; and, in broad conformity to the predictions of people like John Fiske, something resembling a United States of Europe was being formed. Racism, though still present, had been thoroughly delegitimized, and so too had colonial-style imperialism. Moreover, to a far greater extent than in the nineteenth century, a global society was developing in which democracy was spreading throughout the world, even though in many places its roots were quite shallow. Although the reviews on economic performance were mixed, enough nations had been catapulted into industrial modernity to justify continuing hope for the global future of liberal developmentalism. As if to underscore these successes, the idea of civilization, reincarnated as "globalization," reemerged triumphant in the 1980s as a conceptual touchstone for intellectuals and for policy makers.[3]

Overall, then, although liberals were largely political failures in their own day, they were prescient. They were frequently overwhelmed by the crude political forces of Gilded Age democracy, but their outlook survived and eventually prospered to the point that the liberal agenda arguably had few remaining items of importance to pursue. Remarkably, some of the ideas that failed most miserably at the time and seemed least likely to succeed in the long term—most notably those having to do with racial equality—showed surprising staying power. The moral of the story is that in weighing the many shortcomings of nineteenth-century liberals, one needs to keep in mind that "the goal of an imagined liberal society was a more important force than the practice of liberalism."[4] Given their ability to put into effect many of their ideas, it may be missing the point to dwell on their early failures. They were marathoners, not sprinters.

But if many of their desires were realized in the next century, so too, beyond their worst imaginings, were their fears. Ever present as a prominent feature of the liberal temper was a disquieting sense that liberalism was a storm-tossed creed sailing into a turbulent future. In his modern classic, *The Consequences of Modernity*, Anthony Giddens described pioneering sociologists of modernization such as Weber and Durkheim as having been excessively optimistic, given their failure to anticipate the horrors of which modernity was capable. With the advantage of hindsight, more recent theorists of modernity have pointed to the built-in high consequence risks—ecological, nuclear, economic, genetic, to name the most obvious—that provoke deep worries about the future. Although nineteenth-century American liberals (like everyone else) failed to foresee the specific risks and dangers inherent in modernity, they did harbor deep doubts about the course of events, far more than one would expect from the stereotypical depictions of American liberalism as the optimistic ideology of progress in a congenitally "exceptionalist" nation. Central to this conflicted outlook was the idea that globalization and modernization, far from being inevitable processes, were deeply flawed and problematic in some fundamental respects. Nineteenth-century liberalism was no less diligent than Marxist analysis in noting contradictions: between past and present, culture and reason, pacific and belligerent tendencies, universalism and particularism, problematic present and enlightened future. Even the unflaggingly optimistic John Fiske acknowledged that progress "has been in an eminent degree contingent and partial."[5]

This ambivalence is understandable if one recalls that one aspect of the Enlightenment legacy was the understanding that enlightenment was not necessarily a permanent condition and that progress was not necessarily smooth and free of obstructions and setbacks. It came and it went. "It is our happiness," wrote E. B. Tylor, "to live in one of those eventful periods of intellectual and moral history, when the oft-closed gates of discovery and reform stand open at their widest. How long these days may last we cannot tell."[6] The existence of this Jekyll and Hyde sensibility suggests that our contemporary understanding of the two-edged nature of modernization is not at all new. To be sure, our appreciation of its negative features has been amplified by the brutalities of the twentieth century, but the multiple personality disorder of modern life was diagnosed long ago.[7]

Anxiety about the direction of history has been such a constant companion of liberal ideology that the two, though not formally joined together, enjoy an abiding common-law relationship. The ever-present uneasiness about an untimely demise, still visible today, suggests that liberalism has suffered from deep built-in insecurities about its historical stature. It has often been suggested that liberalism requires enemies, to the point of exaggerating them or even creating them where they do not exist. Maybe, and maybe not, but this sense of looming danger was clearly indispensable in at least one fundamental respect: in its absence, instead of becoming a fighting creed, that is, a full-fledged ideology, liberalism might have been content to depend on historical necessity to accomplish its ends, playing out a modern equivalent of fatalistically bowing before God's will. Because no ideology can continue to exist in a fantasy world of its own creation, a precondition of its survival is a realistic understanding of the obstacles to its realization. If a sense of threat is an essential feature of ideology, nineteenth-century liberalism was a proto-ideology imbued with the germs of that kind of awareness, which helps to explain how in the twentieth century it could become a full-blown belief system capable of organizing political action.

In inquiring into the origins of modern American internationalism, then, one answer is that it developed during these years of political isolation. These were years of cultural preparation in which a liberal elite received a broad grounding in the study of international relations in a rapidly globalizing world. Although liberal internationalism was only a minority point of view whose adherents often seemed to be talking to themselves, it had two things going for it: it was rooted in an intellectually coherent and morally powerful ideology, and it enjoyed the support of an influential segment of elite opinion. "'Best men' are indeed few," wrote Charles Eliot Norton, "but their influence is very strong on great numbers, and frames a temper which by degree becomes national."[8]

Actually, this trickle-down process of cultural transmission did not go nearly as smoothly as Norton suggested, inasmuch as succeeding generations of liberal globalists repeatedly expressed concern about the degree to which internationalism had been implanted into the nation's political culture. The never-ending demands for wider and deeper international education suggest that liberal cosmopolitanism never managed to seep into the rock-bottom strata of American culture and thereby become the background "social imaginary" on the basis of which an internationalist foreign policy became second nature, something taken for granted. In place of normalization, liberalism was an ideology that would have to settle for the consolation prize of rootedness in the culture. Put differently, liberals were "world disclosers" whose vision of the world would remain problematic and contested. Nevertheless, not even the continuing indifference, incomprehension, or hostility of the masses nor the opposition of isolationists could prevent their brand of internationalism from becoming indisputably the establishment view by the middle of the twentieth century and thereafter.[9]

Unfortunately, this explanation generates more questions than it answers. It is one thing to demonstrate the existence of a cosmopolitan international-ism in nineteenth-century culture; it is quite another to explain its ascen-dancy in the twentieth.[10] How, specifically, this body of ideas contributed to the emergence of a politically muscular globalism presents something of a problem. One can immediately see the resemblances among many of the ideas, which, when combined with temporal contiguity, might be sufficient to convince many historians, including this writer, that they are connected and hence important. But apart from the ever-present danger of mistaking prox-imity for causality,[11] this tells us nothing about why the ideas persisted and why they triumphed. Nor does it explain how they evolved and were trans-formed over time.[12] Moreover, temporal persistence is not the same as impor-tance, and to insist otherwise is mere suggestion, hand-waving avowal in place of reasoned argument and proof. Because success is never completely self-generated, the possibility remains that the success of internationalism can be traced to other, more potent causes.

And that's not all. Before culture's importance relative to other factors can be addressed, one needs an answer to the question of how, specifically, culture mattered. But that presumes that there is an answer to a prior, more abstract question: What does culture do? The most sweeping claim attributes a be-havioral determinism to culture that inverts the classic materialist base–superstructure relationship. Why, to take an obvious example, does the United States have so many deaths by gunshot? It's the gun culture, many would claim, an outlook that binds together street thugs, a media industry that feeds on the depiction of violence, a powerful grass-roots lobby, and constitutional strict constructionists. An extraordinarily clear statement of this strong causal position—the "culture is everything" approach in which reality is culturally constructed[13]—was given by Clifford Geertz in *The Interpretation of Cultures,* where he described the Parsonian view of cultures as symbol systems that "are to the process of social life as a computer's program is to its operations, the genic helix to the development of the organism, the blueprint to the construction of the bridge, the score to the performance of the symphony, or, to choose a humbler analogy, the recipe to the baking of the cake—so the symbol system is the information source that, to some measurable extent, gives shape, direction, particularity, and point to an ongoing flow of activity."[14]

In some ways, this top-down view of the power of culture is unquestionably true: Americans will continue to speak English, measure in inches and pounds, love baseball and football, eat to excess, commit murder at a rate far in excess of other developed countries, and be spatially mobile. They are also likely to develop newer and better instruments of warfare, further expand their propensity to consume, and continue to be among the most religious of developed nations, for these are the kinds of things that they tend to do—all "to some measurable extent." This is hardly revelatory, for if a culture could not do these kinds of things it would not have the ability to reproduce itself, to be a culture in the first place. Repetition, tradition, habit, behaviors learned through intergenerational transmission—as a human substitute for instinct these standard behaviors are among the first characteristics that come to mind when we think about culture.

In the late nineteenth century, only the politically isolationist U.S. posture toward Europe came close to being so deeply embedded. But these kinds of internalized, pre-reflective, naturalized behaviors are not typical of foreign relations, where the need to make agonizing and often highly nuanced choices is the norm. Moreover, in certain cases, conflicting traditions, or the emergence of challenges to an existing tradition, make it impossible to conduct policy on the basis of an unspoken background understanding in which routinized coping is the rule. Foreign policy traditions do exist, but foreign policymaking is not a product of cultural programming.[15]

In recent decades, the ability of culture to direct behavior has attracted a sizable following, especially among intellectuals attracted to the ideas of Michel Foucault, for whom culture is a form of power in which symbol systems or "discourses" create and legitimate hierarchies and inequalities and make people engage in quite specific institutional behaviors. Yet here one finds a tendency, often within the same text, to avoid strong causal language when discussing what culture does, as authors feel obliged to describe discourses as "contested" or "negotiated," and events as shaped, influenced, colored, filtered, informed by, or viewed through the lens of culture. If this

assertion of controlling influence while simultaneously fudging the corresponding ascription of causal power suggests some queasiness on their part
about making direct causal claims, it is understandable, for this perspective
can be deeply hostile to the scientific worldview. Small wonder, then, that
many advocates of harder social scientific disciplines tend to write off cultural
approaches as having little or no value in explaining a world governed by
cause and consequence. Even arguments on behalf of culture that are sympathetic to the enterprise of social science tend to get short shrift. According to
one noted scholar of the problem, "in every way 'culture' is the poor relation
of 'structure.'"[16]

For my purposes, it makes more sense to sidestep this issue by adopting an
expanded meaning of causality in which culture is not necessarily causal in
the commonly accepted instrumental understanding of the term. In fact, the
more modern and complex the culture, within which assorted ideologies are
sure to be contending for dominance, the greater the certainty that it is not.
With the full realization that the argument could get quite complicated very
quickly, I would like to restrict myself to making the very simple point that
culture "does" nothing in most instances because it is not a cause in the commonly understood scientific sense. Rather, it is the field of possibility for what
can and cannot be done. On the negative side, much of the emphasis in discussions of culture is on the restraints it imposes and barriers it erects, as in
"one doesn't do that sort of thing here." In America, eating dog or blowfish
testicles provokes revulsion, as does the idea of preserving the family's honor
by killing a sister who was raped. Culture also imposes limits on what can be
achieved at any time. In the absence of historical and cultural preconditions,
certain things are impossible of attainment, no matter how brilliant the people of the time. Thus Democritus could not have conceived of nuclear fusion
or Pythagoras the theory of relativity, Einstein could not have created string
theory, neither Greece nor Rome was capable of ending slavery, Mozart could
not have written "Jumpin' Jack Flash," Leonardo could not have invented the
I-Pod, and Henry Ford could not have contemplated manufacturing an SUV.
To imagine otherwise would not be counterfactual, but counter historical.

More positively, cultures are also storehouses or reservoirs of a range of be-
havioral capabilities, preferences, and creative possibilities whose embedded
skills, values, and aesthetic models provide the indispensable condition for
being able to do certain kinds of things. To some extent, cultures resemble

computer operating systems that are capable of accommodating, managing, and running a large but limited variety of software programs within their frameworks. Thus Americans can build nuclear weapons while the Yanomomi forest people cannot. Apart from the kinds of things Americans will continue to do or be debarred from doing in the future for cultural reasons, such as reverting to Stone Age behaviors, they might also become believers in collective security, begin to show greater concern for the global environment, rein in their appetite for fossil fuel consumption, return to a more secular kind of politics, or curb spending on military technology. All these possibilities and more exist because they are grounded in the culture. If, for instance, Americans had no shared background of environmental activism at all, any hope for organizing action to heal the global environment would be quite slender in view of their society's formidable history of rapacity toward nature. Even among the examples of the kinds of things Americans tend to do, one can conceive of the emergence of alternative, radically different behaviors. A useful way of thinking about culture in relation to history, then, might be to see it as enabling, but without having the power to determine a specific outcome in areas where human choice comes into play.[17]

Following this line of reasoning, my argument is that a body of internationalist thought elaborated in the late nineteenth century provided a cultural foundation for the emergence of imperialism and globalism. But many kinds of homes can be built on a platform or foundation, provided it is broad enough and capable of bearing the weight. Another metaphorical way of making the point is to talk of internationalism as having been nurtured in the cultural soil of the time. That is to say, American internationalism emerged historically; its adoption was possible only because it had roots in the past that allowed for future growth. But to talk about culture as a medium in which many different kinds of plants can grow while being inhospitable to others is very different from suggesting the cultural "roots" of something, which implies a determinate result based on laws of genetics. If one sees cultures as allowing for many different outcomes, it makes sense to speak of conflicting cultural currents or of the possibility of erecting a variety of structures on the same foundations or footings. To use an example from evolutionary theory, cultural potential is not unlike J. B. S. Haldane's famous peppered moths, which contained the genetic information that made possible the change in coloration of moth populations from predominantly white to black in response to higher industrial soot levels. Another way of putting the point would be to phrase it in terms of an older but still influential idiom that struck deep intellectual roots in the nineteenth century: If American internationalism is an ideology, it did not emerge as a reflex in the old Marxian sense from a material infrastructure. That would have been impossible, for it had to be embedded in a cultural milieu in the first place.[18] Or, in the language of Parsonian sociology, culture is an environment of action that, like any environment, is congenial to certain forms of life and hard on others.

There is nothing particularly new or original about any of this. The germ of the argument is present in Edmund Burke's idea that peoples cannot hope to enact ideas that depart radically from what their traditions have organically prepared and enabled them to put in place.[19] The point could just as well be made in a variety of other idioms that stress the importance of shared backgrounds as the precondition of specific forms of human activity. For my purposes, the importance of culture can best be fitted, albeit in only a very loose sense, within an Aristotelian taxonomy of causation (material, formal, efficient, and telic). One of the attractive features of the Aristotelian scheme is that it offers a broader perspective than the rather narrow billiard ball model of deterministic or high probability causation to which we unnecessarily tend to restrict ourselves. Aristotle's approach, as one scholar points out, provides a fruitful way of addressing issues of "inefficient causation" by offering a matrix of "becauses" that in combination answer the "why?" question so fully and satisfyingly that without them it would be hard to imagine the event in question having taken place. If I had to link culture to one of the items on this expanded Aristotelian menu of causality, as a believer in naturalism I would probably choose to describe it as a "material" cause, that is, as the raw material without which a thing cannot be brought into being, though I would concede the possibility of making a case for its being a formal or a telic cause—I'm not sure. But for my purposes it doesn't matter, for I am less interested in specifying the particular kind of causality than in expanding our willingness to go beyond physical or intentional definitions of cause and effect by including cultural fields as indispensable contexts of causal accounts. It is more important to accept culture as a necessary element of explanation than to view culture as necessity.[20]

The conversations of the late nineteenth century mattered, then, because they provided a cultural foundation on which a foreign policy structure was eventually built in the twentieth century. But although there was little doubt at the time that the United States was facing a destiny in which it would simultaneously shape and be shaped by the new global environment, it was far from clear how the story would play out. Nineteenth-century writers addressed the relationship between national policy and global process infrequently, if at all, with the result that they never challenged the core isolationist doctrine of political noninvolvement in European politics. Nevertheless the potential for such questioning was there because isolationism, far from being an end in itself, was clearly a subordinate element of a larger liberal worldview, a mere national policy tradition for which global civilization provided an encompassing conceptual framework.

One of the limits of liberal thought in the nineteenth century was that it was impossible for liberals to imagine the United States as a society alone, an eremitic nation existing outside a global environment congenial to the expansion of liberalism. But should the framework change, policy tradition would necessarily come into question. When the liberals' world picture was fundamentally challenged in the twentieth century, the choice between defending political isolation in an illiberal world and intervening to maintain an open world environment and a liberal course of history was not difficult to make. Of course, nineteenth-century liberals did not talk about this sort of thing, for it would have required them to seriously consider the possibility of historical turns of events that they could not yet imagine. Nevertheless, they were preparing the ground for taking seriously such challenges and for responding affirmatively to them.

I can still envision a skeptical reader accepting my broad argument while continuing to doubt that culture has anything substantial to offer by way of explanation. I would respond that, in the American case, at least, the role of culture as a storehouse of possibilities was of immense importance because internationalism was not likely to have been adopted on the basis of instrumental reason alone, for by that standard isolationism made much more sense. With internationalism, as with progress against racism, the problem is to explain its adoption in preference to behaviors that might be considered more realistic or more rational. As I see it, if one looks at the issue through the lens of rational choice theory, a commitment to internationalism is, or at least was, irrational. That is, there is a lack of incentive grounded in the self-interest of the individual (or state) to sacrifice for the creation of a public good. But it is one of the defining features of cultures that they happen to be historically rooted, which is to say, *pace* Hegel, that they themselves evolved not rationally but contingently. This in turn helps to explain why cultures differ from one another in ways that make foreign customs seem quite strange, if not bizarre. The particular form taken by a culture is not something that has to happen. To put it bluntly, the existence of internationalism as a stock element of America's cultural repertoire made possible the consideration and eventual adoption of policies that objective assessments of naked self-interest would have ruled out. Although internationalism is not exclusively American—by nature it cannot be—it has had a greater impact in the United States, and larger consequences for the world, than the liberal internationalist traditions of other nations.

That is a mouthful, to say the least, but it is put forward with modesty, for my concern in this book has been less with answering the question of how culture matters than to establish that it matters in the first place. Because there are cultural currents that run in all kinds of different directions, the job of tracing which flows merge eventually into the historical mainstream requires that the role of culture be related to other explanatory concepts or "factors" that, taken together, make up a widely assorted set of tools needed to assemble that complex artifact called historical understanding. If pursued with utmost seriousness, explaining the role of culture would require an explanation of historical explanation. It would take at least another book to discuss these factors and their snarled interrelationships, but any comprehensive account of a historical phenomenon would require, in addition to taking culture into consideration, a concurrent examination of other contributory factors such as material causation, ideology, decision making, historical accident, and new ways of thinking. Then these ingredients would need somehow to be gathered together and the results interpreted by the historian. If alliteration is any help, the entire bundle might be tied together with a string of C's: Culture, Causality, Credos, Choice, Contingency, Creativity, Complexity, and Construal.[21]

Within this scheme, I advance no claims for culture other than to insist on its indispensability as part of any explanatory framework that seeks to understand U.S. foreign relations. Nor would I assert that this is the only way in which culture matters. Other historians with different perspectives may well have different ways of making the case for its explanatory uses, which may or may not be reconcilable with my approach. But, for the purpose of answering the questions that most concerned me when I began this study—Why imperialism? Why internationalism in the twentieth century?—the existence of this vibrant body of ideas created an indispensable foundation of possibility for what came after, while for historians it provides an essential condition of intelligibility for understanding the history of American globalism. True, culture does not offer a comprehensive or conclusive explanation, but then no explanatory scheme can deliver on such a promise. For all its vagueness, conflicting crosscurrents, and indeterminacy, culture matters. Those are, in fact, the very qualities that make it so important.

Notes

Abbreviations

AM	*The Atlantic Monthly*
AmMiss	*The American Missionary*
Century	*The Century*
Galaxy	*The Galaxy*
Harper's	*Harper's New Monthly Magazine*
HW	*Harper's Weekly*
LA	*The Living Age*
M&B	*Manufacturer and Builder*
NAR	*The North American Review*
Nation	*The Nation*
NEM	*New England Magazine*
NEYR	*New Englander and Yale Review*
OM	*The Overland Monthly and Out West Magazine*
PR	*Princeton Review*
Putnam's	*Putnam's Monthly*
Scribner's	*Scribner's Magazine* and *Scribner's Monthly*
USDR	*The United States Democratic Review*

Introduction: Culture and Causality

1. Charles Taylor, *Sources of the Self: The Making of the Modern Identity* (Cambridge, MA, 1989), 393–394.

2. The attribution appears to be mistaken. The remark probably originated in a 1933 play, *Schlageter*, by Hanns Johst.

3. K. Anthony Appiah, "The Multiculturalist Misunderstanding," *The New York Review of Books* 44:15 (October 9, 1997), 30.

4. See, e.g., the essays in *Current Anthropology* 40, Supplement (February 1999), 51–52.

5. Eric Wolfe, "They Divide and Subdivide, and Call It Anthropology," *New York Times*, November 30, 1980, E9.

6. Leslie Butler, *Critical Americans: Victorian Intellectuals and Transatlantic Liberal Reform* (Chapel Hill, NC, 2007) is a fine study of a small group of such individuals.

7. For purposes of brevity, henceforth I will refer to these people as "Americans" or "liberal Americans" rather than as "readers of magazines who were interested in foreign relations and the world," or some such, but I do not want to stand accused of mistaking the part for the whole. For circulation figures, see Chapter 1 note 4.

8. For example, David D. Hall, "The Victorian Connection," in Daniel Walker Howe and Geoffrey Blodgett, eds., *Victorian America* (Philadelphia, 1976), 81, calls them "a limited but influential group of persons." One must have a satisfactory conception of what the middle class is before one can estimate its size, but alas, social scientists and historians have yet to come up with one. For some of the definitional difficulties, see Peter Stearns, "The Middle Class: Toward a Precise Definition," *Comparative Studies in Society and History* 21:3 (July 1979), 377–396. For "the elusive middle class," see Stuart Blumin, *The Emergence of the Middle Class: Social Experience in the American City, 1760–1900* (New York, 1989), 1–16; Linda Young, *Middle-Class Culture in the Nineteenth Century: America, Australia and Britain* (New York, 2003), 39–68. For hard data on wealth distribution, see Jeffrey G. Williamson and Peter H. Lindert, *American Inequality: A Macroeconomic History* (New York, 1980), 43–47.

9. Philip J. Powlick and Andrew Z. Katz, "Defining the American Public Opinion/Foreign Policy Nexus," *Mershon International Studies Review* 42 (May 1998), 28–61; Ole R. Holsti, *Public Opinion and American Foreign* Policy (Ann Arbor, MI, 2004), 99; Kenneth Weisbrode, "The State Department's Bureau of European Affairs and American Diplomacy, 1909–1989," Ph.D. dissertation, Harvard University, 2008, 3.

10. Lawrence E. Harrison, *The Central Liberal Truth: How Politics Can Change a Culture and Save It from Itself* (New York, 2006).

11. This is not to suggest that late nineteenth-century Americans were thinking in terms of the "soft power" popularized by Joseph S. Nye, Jr. in his *Soft Power: the Means to Success in World Politics* (New York, 2004). At this time, the thought that commercial and cultural flows could be harnessed to haul foreign policy cargo would have been quite alien to liberal Americans.

12. See, e.g., Melvyn Leffler, "Presidential Address: New Approaches, Old Interpretations, and Prospective Reconfigurations," *Diplomatic History* 19:2 (Spring 1995), 179–185; Thomas Alan Schwartz, "Explaining the Cultural Turn—or Detour?" *Diplomatic History* 31:1 (January 2007), 143–147; Bruce Nussbaum, "Capital, Not Culture," *Foreign Affairs* 76:2 (March/April 1997), 165. The skeptical references could be multiplied many times over.

13. On this point, I agree with Clifford Geertz: "In the human sciences, methodological discussions conducted in terms of general positions and abstracted principles are generally bootless. . . . The significant methodological works in both history and anthropology . . . tend at the same time to be significant empirical works." See his "History and Anthropology," in Ralph Cohen and Michael S. Roth, eds., *History and . . . Histories within the Human Sciences* (Charlottesville, VA, 1995), 251–252.

14. Nathaniel Shaler, *Nature and Man in America* (New York, 1891), 149.

15. A. G. Hopkins, ed., *Globalization in World History* (New York, 2002), 14, 124. For a discussion of the historical literature on globalization, see Duncan S. A. Bell, "Review Article: History and Globalization: Reflections on Temporality," *International Affairs* 79:4 (2003), 801–814.

16. John G. Sproat, *"The Best Men": Liberal Reformers in the Gilded Age* (New York, 1968), 275.

17. Robert Vitalis, "International Studies in America," Social Science Research Council Items & Issues 3/3-4 (Summer/Fall 2002), 2, 13–15 offers a capsule history of the field's development.

18. Without this enduring strain of thought, it would have been quixotic for Gunnar Myrdal to predict in his 1944 classic, *An American Dilemma,* that progress toward racial equality in the United States was not only possible but likely. Indeed, there would have been no dilemma to write about in the first place. Gunnar Myrdal, *An American Dilemma: The Negro Problem and American Democracy* (New York, 1944), xix, xlv–li, 1020.

19. For a discussion of pluralistic explanation in history, see Morton White, *A Philosophy of Culture: The Scope of Holistic Pragmatism* (Princeton, NJ, 2002), 89–106.

20. "Of the Life and History of Thucydides" in Richard Schlatter, ed., *Hobbes's Thucydides* (New Brunswick, NJ, 1975), 18.

21. Daniel C. Haskell, comp., *Nation, volumes 1–105, New York, 1865–1917: Indexes of Titles and Contributors* (New York, 1951–1953).

1. A Global Civilization

1. Paul Hirst and Graham Thompson, *Globalization in Question* (London, 1996); Paul Krugman, *Pop Internationalism* (Cambridge, MA, 1996), 207–212. Douglas A. Irwin, "The United States in a New Global Economy? A Century's Perspective," *The American Economic Review* 86 (May 1996), 41–46. Walter Russell Mead, "The American Foreign Policy Legacy," *Foreign Affairs* 81 (January/February 2002), 168 provides some interesting economic statistics. For example, from 1948 to 1957, U.S. foreign trade accounted, on average, for 7.3 percent of GNP, whereas from 1869 to 1893, its share was 13.4 percent.

2. Geographical atlases were still somewhat parochial, however. Susan Schulten, *The Geographical Imagination in America, 1880–1950* (Chicago, 2001), 29.

3. For the degree to which the consumption of international commodities and their cultural meanings had penetrated the American household, see Kristin Hoganson, "Cosmopolitan Domesticity: Importing the American Dream, 1865–1920," *American Historical Review* 107 (February 2002), 55–83.

4. Frank Luther Mott, *A History of American Magazines, 1885–1905,* 5 vols. (Cambridge, MA, 1957), III:34. Kenneth M. Price, "Charles Chesnutt, the *AM,* and the Intersection of African-American Fiction and Elite Culture," in Kenneth M. Price and Susan Belasco Smith, eds., *Periodical Literature in Nineteenth-Century America*

(Charlottesville, VA, 1995). Gerald D. Wolfe, *The House of Appleton* (Metuchen, NJ, 1981), 175–179; Mark A. DeWolfe Howe, *The Atlantic Monthly and Its Makers* (Boston, 1919); Henry Holt, *Garrulities of an Octogenarian Editor* (New York, 1923), 293; "Editor's Table," *Appletons'* 13 (January 2, 1875), 18; John Tebbel, *Between Covers: The Rise and Transformation of Book Publishing in America* (New York, 1987), 86–87. See also Mott, *A History of American Magazines,* II:493–515 and III:331–356. Edward E. Chielens, ed., *American Literary Magazines: The Eighteenth and Nineteenth Centuries* (Westport, CT, 1986); James Playsted Wood, *Magazines in the United States,* 3rd ed. (New York, 1971), 93–96; Robert E. Spiller, et al., *Literary History of the United States* (New York, 1963). Circulation figures had their ups and downs and vary from source to source, but overall the figures are small by later mass market standards. From about 6,000 in 1870, *The Nation's* numbers rose to a high of 12,000 in 1876; *The Atlantic* had a circulation of between 20,000 and 30,000 in the early 1870s, only to drop to 12,000 in 1881. *Harper's Monthly* stood at 100,000 in 1885, *The Century* at 200,000, while the influential *North American Review's* circulation, only 2,000 in 1871, reached 76,000 in 1891. John Gerow Gazley, *American Opinion of German Reunification 1848–1871* (New York, 1926), 566; Mott, *A History of American Magazines,* III:6, 31, 34, 375; II:493, for the much larger numbers at the turn of the century. Roland E. Wolseley, *Understanding Magazines,* 2nd ed. (Ames, IA, 1969), 32.

5. Henry Holt, "Some Practical Aspects of the Literary Life in the United States," *NEYR* 48–216 (March 1888), 108. William Cairns, "Later Magazines," *The Cambridge History of American Literature Part II: Later National Literature* (New York, 1921), 299–318, provides an overview of the landscape of magazine publishing for this period.

6. "*The Century's* First Year under Its New Name," *Century* 24 (1881), 938; *Nation* (July 6, 1865), 1; [George Walker], "Grant Duff's Miscellanies" (April 17, 1879), 270; "Beyond the Seas," *Scribner's* 1 (November 1870), 565; *Appletons'* 1 (April 3, 1869), ii; William B. Cairns, "Later Magazines," *Cambridge History,* 307; "Introductory," *Putnam's,* 1:1 (January 1853), 1–3.

7. Review of Paul Mougeolle, *Statique des XXX Civilsations, Nation* (February 7, 1884), 130; Right Hon. Lord Playfair, "Waste Products Made Useful," *North American Review* 155 (May 1892), 565; "Indexes to Civilization," *AM* 51 (January 1883), 138; "Literary Notes," *Appletons'* 5 (April 22, 1871), 475. These arguments were far from idiosyncratic. For a more recent scholarly discussion before the word "civilization" went out of vogue, see Robert Bierstadt, "Indices of Civilization," *American Journal of Sociology* 71:5 (March 1960), 483–490. The nineteenth-century discussion bears more than a passing resemblance to the vogue for classifying societies' level of development according to thermodynamic flows, that is, energy use, an approach championed by post–World War II anthropologists who adopted cultural ecology as their conceptual framework. For examples, see Leslie A. White, *The Concept of Cultural Systems: A Key to Understanding Tribes and Nations* (New York, 1975), 19.

8. See Anthony Giddens, *The Consequences of Modernity* (Stanford, CA, 1990), 17–21 and David Harvey, *The Condition of Postmodernity: An Enquiry into the Origins of Cultural Change* (Cambridge, MA, 1990), esp. 201–326.

9. Horatio Stebbins, "The Brahmo Somaj, or Protestantism in India," *OM* 3–2 (February 1884), 186; Lafcadio Hearn, "A Winter Journey to Japan," *Harper's* 81 (November 1890), 860; T. G. Appleton, "The Flowering of a Nation," *AM* 28 (September 1871), 316; Leonard Waldo, "Railroad Time and Public Time," *NAR* (December 1883), 608; Letter to the editor from W. F. Allen, "Standard Railway Time," *Century* 26 (September 1883), 796.

For the existence of local times, see Eviatar Zerubavel, "The Standardization of Time: A Sociohistorical Perspective," *American Journal of Sociology* 88 (July 1982), 1–23 and Clark Blaise, *Time Lord: Sir Sandford Fleming and the Creation of Standard Time* (New York, 2000), 30–46. Nevertheless, Francis Deak, "Computation of Time in International Law," *The American Journal of International Law* 20:3 (July 1926), 502–515 points out that this so-called standardization left much to be desired.

10. John Weiss, "A Letter about England," *AM* 15 (June 1865), 642; Henry M. Prentiss, "The North Pole and the South Pole," *OM* 16–92 (July 1990), 50; Michael Adas, *Machines as the Measure of Men: Science, Technology, and Ideologies of Western Dominance* (Ithaca, NY, 1989), 221–230; [W. E. Griffis], "Wilson's China," *Nation* (September 8, 1887), 196; William H. Burnham, "Economy in Intellectual Work," *Scribner's* 5 (March 1889), 306; Schele de Vere, "Around the World," *Appletons'* 2 (December 25, 1869), 594.

11. T. G. Appleton, "The Flowering of a Nation," *AM* 15 (September 1871), 316; E. L. Godkin, "The Prospects of the Political Art," *NAR* (April 1870), 412; Rev. C. N. Clark, "Historical Position of Modern Missions," *NEYR* 39 (September 1880), 580.

12. "The New Trials of the Roman Church," *NAR* 118 (April 1874), 29; "The United States and Europe," *AM* 8 (July 1861), 95; Erastus B. Bigelow, "On the Relations between Labor and Capital," *AM* 42 (October 1878), 483; G. M. Grant, "Time-Reckoning for the Twentieth Century," *Century* 33 (November 1886), 156; "The Railroad System," *NAR* 104 (July 1867), 483. This belief in evolutionary necessity experienced a revival in the late twentieth century. For one example, see Robert Wright, *Nonzero: The Logic of Human Destiny* (New York: Vintage, 2001).

13. "Languages and Dialects," *NAR* 104 (January 1867), 61; Rev. C. N. Clark, "Historical Position of Modern Missions," *NEYR* 39–154 (September 1880), 580; "Contemporary Sayings," *Appletons'* 11 (May 16, 1874), 639; M. Howland, "Literary Notes," *Appletons'* 9 (April 12, 1873), 508; Charles Sumner, "Prophetic Voices about America. A Monograph," *AM* 20 (September 1867), 282–283. See, e.g., the prediction of the hegemony of English in John Fiske, "The Theory of a Common Origin for all Languages," *AM* 48 (November 1881), 660. For a brief critical review of the literature, see Robert Phillipson, "English for Globalisation or for the World's People?" *International Review of Education* 47:3/4 (July 2001), 185–200. Richard W.

Bailey, *Images of English: A Cultural History of the Language* (Ann Arbor, MI, 1991), 59–117, surveys the spread of the language through the nineteenth century.

14. "Contemporary Sayings," *Appletons'* 11 (March 1874), 351 (quoting from an article in the *Pall Mall Gazette*); Rev. R. Donkersley, "The King's English," *The Ladies' Repository* 1–4 (April 1868), 300; "The Telegraph," *Harper's* 47 (1873), 360. For the analogy between language and other media, see Martin H. Geyer, "One Language for the World: The Metric System, International Coinage, Gold Standard, and the Rise of Internationalism, 1850–1900," in Martin H. Geyer and Johannes Paulmann, eds., *The Mechanics of Internationalism: Culture, Society, and Politics from the 1840s to the First World War* (London, 2001), 55–92.

15. Robert J. Antonio, *Marx and Modernity: Key Readings and Commentary* (Malden, MA, 2003). [W. D. Howells?], "Editorials," *Nation* (February 1, 1866), 133. To be sure, a similar kind of sensibility could be found at work prior to the Civil War. See "Ancient and Modern Civilization," *USDR* 24, Issue 131 (1849), 453.

16. C. C. Hazewell, "The Seventh Decade of the Nineteenth Century," *Harper's* 42 (1871), 277; Wade Hampton, "The Color-Line Question: What Is it?" *AmMiss* (July 1888), 179; Harry Cadman, "The Future of Industrialism," *OM* 15–90 (June 1890), 578.

17. N. C. Meeker, "Commerce and Human Progress," *Appletons'* 2 (September 18, 1869), 149; "Literary Notes," *Appletons'* 5 (April 22, 1871), 475; John Fiske, "The Laws of History," *NAR* 109 (July 1869), 199; "Celebrities of the Century," *Nation* (May 5, 1887), 393.

18. "The Highest Structure in the World," *AM* 63 (June 1889), 727; "International Bridge between France and England," *Appletons'* 2 (December 4, 1869), 487; John Short, "The Flooding of the Sahara," *Scribner's* 18 (1879), 441; "Table Talk," *Appletons'* 8 (August 17, 1872), 191; "Editor's Table," *Appletons'* 5–2 (August 1878), 186.

19. Hugh McCulloch, "Problems in American Politics," *Scribner's* 4 (1888), 423; Francis Parkman, "The Woman Question," *NAR* 129 (October 1879), 327.

20. Franklin Satterthwaite, "The Western Outlook for Sportsmen," *Harper's* 78 (1889), 874; "Overland Reminiscences," *OM* 1–1 (January 1883), 3; [E. L. Godkin], "England in Egypt," *Nation* (December 2, 1875), 353; "Notes," *Nation* (August 9, 1883), 119.

21. "Outcroppings," *OM* 2–11 (November 1883), 558; "International Travel," *Galaxy* 15 (1873), 843; Theodore Child, "Constantinople," *AM* 61 (January 1888), 78. Hans Magnus Enzenberger, "A Theory of Tourism," *New German Critique* 68 (Spring–Summer 1966), 25 locates the romantic yearning for the "pristine landscape and untouched history," but as I will argue below there is more to it than that. The review of the central ideas of the anthropology of tourism in L. L. Wynn, *Pyramids and Nightclubs* (Austin, TX, 2007), 12–22, makes clear that nineteenth-century writers anticipated much that was to come.

22. [E. L. Godkin], "The Russians and the English in Central Asia," *Nation* (October 15, 1868), 308; [Edmund Quincy], "Thibet," *Nation* (July 20, 1876), 43; "The Editor's

Easy Chair," *Harper's* 68 (1884), 479; [A. G. Sedgwick], "A Philadelphian Abroad," *Nation* (August 12, 1880), 116; W. T. Brigham, "An Uncommercial Republic," *Scribner's* 1 (1887), 714. Presumably, it was this flattening out of international life that led George Bernard Shaw to "dislike feeling at home when I'm abroad."

23. J. B. Drury, "Darwinism," *Scribner's* 1 (1875), 348; [Edmund Quincy], "Thibet," *Nation* (July 20, 1876), 43; "Strange Countries for to See," *AM* 4 (December 1859), 725; *LA* 59–755 (November 13, 1858), 549.

24. "Notes," *Nation* (November 12, 1885), 404; "The Week," *Nation* (October 12, 1871), 234; "Science and Human Brotherhood," *Nation* (October 26, 1871), 268; "Notes," *Nation* (August 9, 1883), 119. For bittersweet reflections on the arrival of cable service in Bermuda, see "Editor's Table," *Appletons'* 13 (May 1, 1875), 564; "Notes," *Nation* (August 21, 1884), 158. The quotation is from "The Task" (1785), a poem by William Cowper: "Oh for a lodge in some vast wilderness, Some boundless contiguity of shade, Where rumour of oppression and deceit, Of unsuccessful or successful war, Might never reach me more."

25. Charles Dudley Warner, "'Civilization,'" *Harper's* 78 (1889), 494; "Editor's Table," *Appletons'* 7–1 (July 1879), 88. On antimodernism in the fin-de-siècle period, see T. J. Jackson Lears, *No Place of Grace: Antimodernism and the Transformation of American Culture, 1880–1920* (Chicago, 1981).

26. John Fiske, "How America Came to Be Discovered," *Harper's* 64 (1881), 119. In 1867, the great naturalist Louis Agassiz announced that "the time for great discoveries is past." Quoted in Alan Rabinowitz, *Beyond the Last Village: A Journey of Discovery in Asia's Forbidden Wilderness* (Washington, DC, 2001), xv.

27. "Table-Talk," *Appletons'* 6 (October 28, 1871), 497; "The United States and Europe," *AM* 8 (1864), 95; "Between Europe and Asia," *AM* 15 (January 1865), 12; Fiske, "The Laws of History," 223. Robert Jervis, *System Effects: Complexity in Political and Social Life* (Princeton, NJ, 1997).

28. [George Walker], "Market Fluctuations," *Nation* (June 22, 1876), 398; Charles F. Dunbar, "Economic Science in America, 1776–1876," *NAR* 122 (January 1876), 128; Prof. Thorold Rogers, "Causes of Commercial Depression," *PR* 1 (1879), 212–213; "The Week," *Nation* (October 12, 1871), 234.

29. "The Poverty of England," *NAR* 109 (July 1869), 123; "Life Assurance," *AM* 18 (September 1866), 314. "Science and Human Brotherhood," *Nation* (October 26, 1871), 268.

30. "Short Cuts across the Globe," *Harper's* 1:1 (June 1850), 81; "What Are We Going to Make?" *AM* 2 (June 1858), 101; "East and West," *OM* 1–1 (January 1883), 105; "The Ideal Tendency," *AM* 1 (December 1858), 778.

31. "Oceanic Telegraphy," *Nation* (August 3, 1865), 144; Editorials (December 13, 1866), 473; "The Cable Newsmonger," *Nation* (May 16, 1867), 395; "The Week," *Nation* (August 16, 1866), 123; "Culture and Progress: The Difficulty to Americans of the Study of European Politics," *Scribner's* 8 (1874), 117; "The Week," *Nation* (July 3, 1884), 8.

32. "History by the Yard," *Nation* (November 23, 1865), 661; "The Week," *Nation* (February 20, 1879), 129; "Notes," *Nation* (June 22, 1876), 397; "International Travel," *Galaxy* 15 (1873), 843; "The Week," *Nation* (February 20, 1879), 129; G. Fredrick Wright, "Science and Life," *OM* 2–9 (September 1883), 281; "The Week," *Nation* (August 20, 1874), 115; William Matthews, "Civilization and Suicide," *NAR* 152 (April 1891), 481.

33. G. T. Ferris, "The Physical Dangers of Civilization," *NAR* 147 (September 1888), 352; "What Are We Going to Make?" *AM* 2 (June 1858), 96; W. H. Babcock, "The Future of Invention," *AM* 44 (August 1979), 139; "Notes," *Nation* (June 22, 1876), 397; Charles Dudley Warner, "Thoughts Suggested by Mr. Froude's Progress," *Scribner's* 7–1873 (January 1874), 352.

34. "Accidental Insurance," *Nation* (January 11, 1866), 44; [J. B. Hodgskin], "The Condition of Life Insurance among Us," *Nation* (January 26, 1871), 54; John M. Holcombe, "Life Insurance in the United States," *NAR* 150 (March 1890), 401. Anthony Giddens, *Modernity and Self-Identity Self and Society in the Late-Modern Age* (Stanford, CA, 1991), 132–133; Theodore M. Porter, *The Rise of Statistical Thinking 1820–1900* (Princeton, NJ, 1986), 71–90.

35. "The Week," *Nation* (September 16, 1886), 225; "The Outrages in Russia," *Century* 23 (1881), 948; "Science and Human Brotherhood," *Nation* (October 26, 1871), 268.

36. [W. H. Whitmore], "Thoms's Human Longetivity," *Nation* (August 7, 1873), 96; "Minor Mention," *Appletons'* 9 (1873), 634; Edward Jarvis, "The Increase of Human Life: II," *AM* 24 (November 1869), 581; "Notes," *Nation* (June 3, 1886), 471; "Editor's Table," *Appletons'* 13 (February 27, 1875), 278.

37. John S. Hittell, "The Spirit of the Age," *OM* 14–5 (May 1875), 425; "Editor's Table," *Appletons'* 13 (May 1, 1875), 564; John S. Hittell, "The Main Force of Culture," *OM* 12–3 (March 1874), 233; Edward Jarvis, "The Increase of Human Life: II," *AM* 24 (November 1869), 581; Fiske, "The Laws of History," 223; *Appletons'* 10 (September 27, 1873), 409; *Appletons'* 9 (1873), 634; [W. H. Whitmore], "Thoms's Human Longetivity," *Nation* (August 7, 1873), 96.

38. "Democracy and Moral Progress," *NAR* 137 (1883), 34. Daniel Rodgers in *Atlantic Crossings: Social Politics in a Progressive Age* (Cambridge, MA, 1998) has suggested that the United States was in some ways more internationalist prior to World War II, at least on the cultural level.

39. Joseph R. Hawley, "The Value of international Expositions," *NAR* 149 (September 1889), 317; "The Great Show at Paris," *Harper's* 35 (1867), 238; "Editor's Table," *Appletons'* 15 (February 12, 1876), 503; "Editor's Table," *Appletons'* 5–1 (July 1878), 88; [Earl Shinn], "The International Exhibition—XIII Italian Sculpture," *Nation* (August 17, 1876), 104. John E. Findling and Kimberly D. Pelle, eds., *Historical Dictionary of World's Fairs and Expositions: 1851–1898* (Westport, CT, 1990). On exhibitions, see Robert W. Rydell, *All the World's a Fair: Visions of Empire at American International Expositions, 1876–1916* (Chicago, 1984); Robert Rydell and

Nancy Gwinn, eds., *Fair Representations: World's Fairs and the Modern World* (Amsterdam, 1994).

40. "Drift-Wood; The Centenary," *Galaxy* 20 (1875), 118; "A Suggestion about the Centennial Exposition," *Nation* (June 19, 1873), 412; Joseph R. Hawley, "The Value of International Expositions," *NAR* 149 (September 1889), 316. For other international benefits of world's fairs, see William P. Blake, ed., *Reports of the United States Commissioners to the Paris Universal Exposition,* 1867 ed., Vol. I (Washington, DC, 1870), 3.

41. "Characteristics of the International Fair, VI" *AM* 39 (January 1877), 99; "Editor's Table," *Appletons'* 15 (May 20, 1876), 662; "Editor's Table," *Appletons'* 15 (January 1, 1876), 22.

42. Lt. Col. Thomas M. Anderson, U. S. A. "Have We a National Character?" *Galaxy* 21 (1876), 733; Murat Halstead, "Our National Conceits," *NAR* 149 (1889), 551; "Washington Society," *AM* 40 (December 1877), 655; [George Walker], "Grant Duff's Miscellanies," *Nation* (April 17, 1879), 270. For the Corliss engine, see John F. Kasson, *Civilizing the Machine: Technology and Republican Values in America, 1776–1900* (New York, 1976), 162. Merle Curti, "America at the World Fairs, 1851–1893," *The American Historical Review, 1851–1893* 55:4 (July 1950), 833–856. For nationalist emphasis, see Robert Rydell, John E. Findling, and Kimberly D. Pelle, *Fair America: World's Fairs in the United States* (Washington, DC, 2000).

43. [Auguste Laugel], "In Belgium," *Nation* (August 25, 1887), 150; Richard J. Hinton, "The Race for Commercial Supremacy in Asia," *Galaxy* 8 (1869), 181. David Engerman, "Research Agenda for the History of Tourism: Towards an International Social History," *American Studies International* 32 (October 1994), 3–31.

44. J. D. Phelan, "The Bent of International Intercourse," *OM* 6–32 (August 1885), 168; "Notes," *Nation* (February 19, 1885), 155; "The Record," *Appletons'* 11 (March 14, 1874), 352; [E. L. Godkin], "General Grant's Political Education Abroad," *Nation* (February 19, 1880), 130. (James Garfield also took a trip abroad in 1867, the journals for which were published posthumously); Edward Berwick, "The Great Want of All Civilized Nations," *OM* 14–79 (July 1889), 78; Felix L. Oswald, "The Coming Civilization," *NAR* 145 (1887), 661. Patricia Goldstone, *Making the World Safe for Tourism* (New Haven, CT, 2001), 9. For the years after 1890, see Christopher Endy, "Travel and World Power: Americans in Europe, 1890–1917," *Diplomatic History* 22 (Fall 1998), 565–594; the numbers are from Endy, 567. Maxine Feifer, *Tourism in History: from Imperial Rome to the Present* (New York, 1985), 164. See also the useful information on travel clubs in Kristin Hoganson, *Consumers' Imperium: The Global Production of American Domesticity 1865–1920* (Chapel Hill, NC, 2007), 258–278, the preponderance of which were formed toward the end of the century.

45. "Literature and Art," *Galaxy* 7 (1869), 137; [John A. Lewis], "Books on Spain," *Nation* (January 3, 1884), 16; "Our American Cousins," *Nation* (March 20, 1884), 263.

46. L. H. Hooper, "The Traveling American," *Appletons'* 12 (October 3, 1874), 425–426; "A New Kind of Scapegoat," *Nation* (April 8, 1875), 237; Lucy H. Hooper, "American Women Abroad," *Galaxy* 21 (1876), 818; [Godkin], "The Manners of

Americans in Europe," 97; [T. W. Higginson], "Memoir and Letters of Charles Sumner," *Nation* (December 13, 1877), 368. Mary Suzanne Schriber, *Writing Home: American Women Abroad 1830–1920* (Charlottesville, VA, 1997), 20–21; Feifer, *Tourism in History,* 270; William W. Stowe, *Going Abroad: European Travel in Nineteenth-Century American Culture* (Princeton, NJ, 1994), 41. *A Traveller's Companion: A Collection From Harper's Magazine* (New York, 1991), offers a compendium of facsimile articles from this period.

47. S. G. Young, "Foreign Modes of Living," *Galaxy* 14 (1872), 259; "Editor's Table," *Appletons'* 12 (November 14, 1874), 633; "Editor's Table," *Appletons'* 13 (May 15, 1875), 629; B. P. DeCosta, "Foreign Tips," *Harper's* 60 (1888), 334; Atmer W. Colgate, "Can the Trip to Europe Be Shortened?" *Galaxy* 20 (1875), 46. See Chapter 8 in this volume for a discussion of comparisons between civilizations.

48. Stowe, *Going Abroad,* 38; "How Not to Go Abroad," *Nation* (April 11, 1867), 299; "European Travel," *Scribner's* 18 (1879), 782; "The Mastery of Languages," *Nation* (April 9, 1868), 293; Charles W. Eliot, "What Is a Liberal Education?" *Century* 28 (1884), 206.

49. [Godkin], "The Manners of the Americans in Europe," 97; Samuel Williams, "Some Americans Who Travel," *OM* 2:5 (May 1869), 418; "Some Recent Books of Travel," *AM* 42 (November 1878), 580; "Editor's Table," *Appletons'* 10 (November 29, 1873), 697; "Field's *From Egypt to Japan,*" *AM* 41 (June 1878), 810; George E. Pond, "Driftwood," *Galaxy* 16 (September 1873), 413; "A Race With the Sun," *Nation* (March 6, 1890), 209; "The Week," *Nation* (August 15, 1889), 123; [William James], "Vacations," *Nation* (August 7, 1873), 90.

50. D. Jenkins, "Those Americans," *OM* 3–6 (December 1869), 534; "The Editor's Easy Chair," *Harper's* 79 (1889), 633.

51. "A Word for Our Wanderers," *Scribner's* 10 (September 1875), 638; Phelan, "International Intercourse," 165, 167, 169. "Why People Like to Live Abroad," *Nation* (July 16, 1874), 37; "Recent Literature: Harmon's Journey to Egypt," *AM* 31 (April 1873), 500.

52. Thomas W. Knox, "A Journey through Mongolia," *The Galaxy* 6 (August 1888), 160; J. D. Phelan, "International Intercourse," 167; "In Sunny Lands," *Nation* (October 8, 1885), 351. But [Rollo Ogden], "Tourists in Mexico," *Nation* (October 25, 1883), 357 saw value in encountering the gritty realities of everyday life in Mexico. As tourist accommodations in Mexico improved rapidly after 1880, travel to Latin America increased from 3.3. percent of American travelers in 1873 to 13.3 percent in 1890. See Matthew Simon, "The United States Balance of Payments, 1790–1860," *Trends in the American Economy in the Nineteenth Century* (Princeton, NJ, 1960), 664–672; Aida Mostkoff, "Foreign Visions and Images of Mexico: One Hundred Years of International Tourism, 1821–1921," Ph.D. dissertation, University of California, Los Angeles, 1999, 42–110.

53. "Going Abroad for an Education," *Century* 24 (1881), 795; Foster Rhea Dulles, *Americans Abroad: Two Centuries of European Travel* (Ann Arbor, MI, 1964), 43–140; "A Word for Our Wanderers," *Scribner's* 10 (September 1875), 638; "Going to

Europe," *Nation* (April 28, 1870), 270; "Short Trips to Europe," Harper's 43 (1871), 129; Jürgen Herbst, *The German School in American Scholarship: A Study in the Transfer of Culture* (Port Washington, NY, 1965), 1.

54. Hugh McCulloch, "Problems in American Politics," *Scribner's* 4 (1888), 423; Volker Barth, "The Twilight of Americanization—The United States at the Paris Universal Exhibition of 1867," unpublished paper delivered at the 3rd annual Conference on International history, (Cambridge, MA, 2003); [A. G. Sedgwick], "Egotism in Literature," *Nation* (May 29, 1884), 462.

55. Michael Adas, "From Settler Colony to Global Hegemon: Integrating the Exceptionalist Narrative of the American Experience into World History," *American Historical Review* 106:5 (December 2001), 1692–1720 discusses the concern of recent Americans to integrate America into the global narrative, but this concern was quite clearly present among nineteenth-century liberals.

2. Creating an International Identity: Culture, Commerce, and Diplomacy

1. "Recent Books on American History," *AM* 65 (February 1890), 274; Charles Bright and Michael Geyer, "Where in the World Is America?" in Thomas Bender, ed., *Rethinking American History in a Global Age* (Berkeley, CA, 2002), 71–73.

2. "A Carnival of Venice," *AM* 35 (February 1875), 176; Oliver Wendell Holmes, "The Americanized European," *AM* 35 (January 1875), 81; [W. A. Hammond], "The Humors of the Anthropologists," *Nation* (August 3, 1865), 143.

3. [Mrs. Thomas Vickers], Review of Frederick Rätzel, *Die Vereinigten Staaten von Nord-Amerika, Nation* (August 12, 1880), 120; Thomas Wentworth Higginson," A Plea for Culture," *AM* 19 (1867), 33; Frank Luther Mott, *A History of American Magazines, 1885–1905.* 5 vols. (Cambridge, MA, 1957), III: 335; "The Week," *Nation* (June 23, 1887), 522; James Bryce, *The American Commonwealth* (London and New York, 1888), 637; Titus Munson Coan, "A Nation without Neighbors," *Galaxy* 19 (February 1875), 171, 174.

4. "What Is an American?" *AM* 35 (May 1875), 566; Jane Grey Swisshelm, "The American Character," *Galaxy* 22 (November 1876), 618; Lt. Col. Thomas M. Anderson, U.S.A., "Have We a National Character?" *Galaxy* 21 (June 1876), 735. Small wonder that Richard Hildreth's 1849 *History of the United States,* which had portrayed the country as a collection of interest groups without a guiding national idea, had not been received enthusiastically. On this point see Ernst Breisach, *Historiography: Ancient, Medieval & Modern* (Chicago, 1994), 257–258.

5. J. R. Lowell, "On a certain Condescension in Foreigners," *AM* 23 (January 1869), 93; Lt. Col. Anderson, "Have We a National Character?" 735; Charles Dudley Warner, "What Is Your Culture to Me?" (August 1872), 478; H. D. Thoreau, "Life without Principle," *AM* 12 (September 1963), 493; O. B. Frothingham, "Democracy and Moral Progress," *NAR* 137 (July 1883), 28, quoting from Walt Whitman, *Specimen Days and Collect* (Philadelphia, 1882), 211.

6. Henry Holt, *Garrulities of an Octogenarian Editor* (New York, 1923), 96; J. C. Derby, *Fifty Years among Authors, Books, and Publishers* (New York, 1884), 187. The story is told in detail by Anthony J. Clark, *The Movement for International Copyright in Nineteenth Century America* (Westport, CT, 1973) and in summary, by Siva Vaidhyanathan, *Copyrights and Copywrongs: The Rise of Intellectual Property and How It Threatens Creativity* (New York, 2001), esp. 50–55. The international story is surveyed in Catherine Seville, *The Internationalisation of Copyright Law: Books, Buccaneers, and the Black Flag in the Nineteenth Century* (New York, 2006), esp. 180–252. The story of Mark Twain's starring role is told in Martin Thomson Buinicki, Jr., "Negotiating Copyright: Authorship and the Discourse of Literary Property Rights in Nineteenth-Century America," Ph.D. dissertation, University of Iowa, 2003, 233–290.

7. Letter to the editor from William Appleton, "Miscellany," *Appletons'* 6 (December 2, 1871), 640–641; "Culture and Progress Abroad," *Scribner's* 3 (January 1872), 375; "Notes," *Nation* (June 10, 1880), 437; Philip Quilibet [G. E. Pond], "Foreign Copyright," *Galaxy* 13 (January 1872), 122; "Editor's Table," *Appletons'* 11 (April 18, 1874), 505; [E. L. Godkin], "International Copyright," *Nation* (November 9, 1871), 301; J. Henry Harper, *The House of Harper: A Century of Publishing in Franklin Square* (New York, 1912), 110–115, provides a description of the courtesy of the trade.

8. Calvert Wilson, "International Copyright," *NEM*, 5–25 (November 1886), 8; D. Phelan, "The Bent of International Intercourse," *OM* 6–32 (August 1885), 166; "The Editor's Study," *Harper's* 76 (1888), 479; "Editor's Table," *Appletons'* 9 (March 15, 1873), 377; Herbert Ross Brown, "The Great American Novel," *American Literature* 7 (March 1935), 1–14.

Matthew Arnold published an essay in 1888 in which he contended that there was still not much worth reading produced in the United States, echoing the charge leveled sixty-eight years earlier in the *Edinburgh Review*. See Matthew Arnold, *Nineteenth Century* 23 (April 1888), 481–496; "Civilization in the United States," in Joanne Reitano, *The Tariff Question in the Gilded Age: The Great Debate of 1888* (University Park, PA, 1994), 119; Maurice Thompson, "Notes and Comments: Foreign Influence on American Fiction," *NAR* 149 (1889), 118; "International Copyright," *Scribner's* 10 (1875), 379; George Stuart Gordon, *Anglo-American Literary Relations* (New York, 1942), 94. French literary critics during these years were of the same opinion. See Jacques Portes, *The United States in French Opinion, 1870–1914*, trans. Elborg Forster (New York: Cambridge University Press, 2000), 426.

9. "American Authorship," *Scribner's* 11 (1875), 280, 281. "English and American Copyright," *Scribner's* 12 (1876), 900. [W. D. Howells], "One Branch of Native Industry That Needs Protection," *Nation* (December 21, 1865), 774–775; "Minor Mention," *Appletons'* 9 (March 1, 1873), 314.

Foreign authors could obtain American copyright but only under narrowly defined conditions that were subject to interpretation by the courts. If they were permanent residents of the United States, foreign authors could secure copyright. But everything boiled down to intent. Someone who stayed only a week in the country with the full intention of residing permanently might be eligible for copyright protection, whereas someone resident for, say ten years, who intended to return eventually to his native land was not. Securing copyright in Great Britain for an American author was possible, but only if publication took place in England, Scotland, Wales, or Ireland; if the book was published on the same day in the United States and Great Britain; and if the author was physically present within the British dominions at the time of publication. This was not an uncommon practice, and British publishers often used "copyright edition" in their advertisements of American books. Strangely enough, however, meeting these conditions did not guarantee copyright throughout the British Empire. In one notable case, Mark Twain, relying on poor legal advice, went to Canada, only to discover that his journey conferred no immunity from Canadian pirate publishers who were quick to print his work and market it in the United States. Through another set of complicated ruses, it was possible for an American author to secure copyright in France, and then in England, but with no guarantee that it would be worth the effort and expense.

Things worked rather differently in the theater, thanks to the widespread practice of putting on plays that, technically, had not yet been published. Because they existed only in manuscript form, they were considered to be the property of the author in common law. The irony was not lost on those who pointed out that by not taking advantage of copyright, playwrights enjoyed "the most absolute property-right known to the law." Under the common law doctrine of stage right as enforced in New York, playwrights resorted to the licensing of performance rights to their creations. On these various points, see E. S. Drone, "International Copyright," *Appletons'* 12 (November 21, 1874), 659; E. S. Drone, "Foreign Dramatists under American Laws," *Scribner's* 11 (1875), 90, 97; [A. G. Sedgwick], "Mark Twain's Visit to Canada," *Nation* (January 5, 1882), 7; "Notes," *Nation* (December 9, 1875), 372; "Notes," *Nation* (February 5, 1880), 97.

10. Henry Holt, "Some Practical Aspects of the Literary Life in the United States," *NEYR* 48 (March 1888), 172; "The Social Future as Foreshadowed by the French Elections," *Nation* (June 17, 1869), 469; "Editor's Table," *Appletons'* 9 (March 15, 1873), 377; Maurice Thompson, "Notes and Comments: Foreign Influence on American Fiction," *NAR* 149 (1889), 118.

11. "American Authorship," *Scribner's* 11 (1875), 280; "English and American Copyright," *Scribner's* 12 (1876), 900; "The Copyright Question," *Nation* (February 15, 1872), 101; "International Copyright," *Scribner's* 10 (1875), 379; "Authors' Rights," *Century* 23 (1881), 779. For a different take on American national literature in the 1880s, see Mark William Niemeyer, "American Literary Nationalism from 1850 to 1914: The Continuing Campaign," Ph.D. dissertation, University of Delaware, 1990, 329–377.

12. "Notes," *Nation* (December 20, 1888), 498; "American Authorship," *Scribner's* 11 (1875), 280. See also "The Copyright Negotiations," *Century* 23 (1881), 670; "Dr.

Appleton on Copyright," *Scribner's* 14 (1877), 108; [A. G. Sedgwick], "Drone on Copyright," *Nation* (May 1, 1879), 303; "The Copyright Question," *Nation* (February 15, 1872), 101; "Literary Property," *Appletons'* 6 (April 1879), 372. On copyright versus property rights, see "Minor Mention," *Appletons'* 9 (March 1, 1873), 314. In any case, copyright as a statutory concept worked "to resolve disputes under the statute, not to formulate guiding principles." See Lyman Ray Patterson, *Copyright in Historical Perspective* (Nashville, TN, 1968), 229.

13. Sedgwick, "Drone on Copyright," 303; "International Copyright," *Century* 23 (January 1882), 468; Murney Gerlach, *British Liberalism and the United States: Political and Social Thought in the Late Victorian Age* (New York, 2001), 142–145; Letter from O. W. Holmes on International Copyright, *Century* 30–3 (July 1885), 488; "International Copyright," *HW* 13 (February 1886), 98. See also [Thorvald Solberg], "The Copyright Bill and Protection," *Nation* (June 28, 1888), 522.

14. "The Dorsheimer Copyright Bill," *Century* 28 (1884), 144; [A. G. Sedgwick], "The Copyright Agitation," *Nation* (January 15, 1885), 50; [Thorvald Solberg], "The International Copyright Bill," *Nation* (January 19, 1888), 44; George Parsons Lathrop, "The Copyright Question," *Century* 30 (1885), 489.

15. "A Patriotic School-master," *AM* 36 (September 1875), 338–339. "American Literature, 1607–1885," *Nation* (February 24, 1887), 172; "International Copyright," *Century* 41 (1890), 150; Thomas Wentworth Higginson, "A Plea for Culture," *AM* 19 (1867), 33; "The Copyright Negotiations," *Century* 23 (1881), 671. On culture as high culture, see Lawrence W. Levine, *Highbrow/Lowbrow: The Emergence of Cultural Hierarchy in America* (Cambridge, MA, 1988), 223–225. For cultural monism, see George W. Stocking, Jr., *Race, Culture, and Evolution: Essays in the History of Anthropology* (Chicago, 1982), 72–85. The term most commonly used to express the particularity and uniqueness of people in the nineteenth century was not culture but "race." The issue is discussed in Chapter 5.

16. Phelan, "International Intercourse," 166; "Arnold's Mixed Essays," *AM* 44 (November 1879), 677–678; "Culture and Progress: Emerson's Fortune of the Republic," *Scribner's* 16 (1878), 903; John Fiske, "Athenian and American Life," *AM* 34 (November 1874), 559; "The Conditions of Art in America," *NAR* 102 (1866), 8; Edwin P. Whipple, "American Literature," *Harper's* 52 (1876), 401; Charles F. Dunbar, "Economic Science in America 1776–1876," *NAR* 122 (January 1876), 146; "Why We Have No Saturday Reviews," *Nation* (November 15, 1866), 393.

17. John S. Hittell, "The Main Force of Culture," *OM* 12–3 (March 1874), 230–235; "Editor's Table," *Appletons'* 13 (January 30, 1875), 149; "Table Talk," *Appletons'* 7 (March 9, 1872), 273; "Editor's Table," *Appletons'* 10 (December 6, 1873), 729; "Editor's Table," *Appletons'* 13 (January 30, 1875), 149.

18. Henry C. Carey, *Letters on International Copyright* (New York, 1868), 14, 15, 23, 33, 68, 69, 79, 80.

19. "The Copyright Treaty," *Nation* (September 22, 1881), 230; [W. F. Rae], "Special Correspondence: English Views of International Copyright," *Nation* (April 7, 1881),

236; "Open Letters on International Copyright," *Century* 3 (1885), 633; Washington Gladden, "The Ethics of Copyright," *Century* 36 (1888), 472; "The Copyright Negotiations," *Century* 23 (1881), 667; [A. G. Sedgwick], "The Author's Best Friend," *Nation* (September 7, 1882), 195.

20. [W. M. Griswold], "Mutations of the Book Trade in Germany," *Nation* (January 5, 1888), 9; Henry Holt, "Some Practical Aspects of the Literary Life in the United States," *NEYR* 48 (March 1888), 171; "What Americans Read," *NAR* 150 (1890), 533; "Dr. Appleton on Copyright," *Scribner's* 14 (1877), 108.

21. Holt quoted in Seville, *Internationalisation of Copyright Law*, 245; "Editorial on International Copyright," *Galaxy* 2 (1866), 291; [Thorvald Solberg], "The Copyright Bill and Protection," *Nation* (June 28, 1888), 522; [E. L. Godkin], "The Tax on Books," *Nation* (March 1, 1883), 184; Donald Marquand Dozer, "The Tariff on Books," *The Mississippi Valley Historical Review*, 36:1 (June 1949), 94.

22. "Editorials," *Nation* (February 21, 1867), 152; "Literary," *Nation* (July 12, 1866), 24; Charles Astor Bristed, "International Copyright," *Galaxy* 10 (1871), 811; [E. L. Godkin], "Twenty-Five Cents a Pound on Ideas," *Nation* (February 24, 1870), 118; Dozer, "The Tariff on Books," 73–96.

23. Holt, "Some Practical Aspects of the Literary Life in the United States," 186.

24. [E. L. Godkin], "Congressional Fostering of Art," *Nation* (April 19, 1883), 334; Dozer, "The Tariff on Books," 89; E. L. Godkin, *Unforeseen Tendencies in Democracy* (Freeport, NY, 1971 [1898]), 188. According to one historian, the tariff debates "reveal the basic political and economic assumptions of the political leaders of the Gilded Age." Tom E. Terrill, *The Tariff, Politics, and American Foreign Policy 1874–1901* (Westport, CT, 1973), 212. For the origins of the tariff, see Ida M. Tarbell, *The Tariff in Our Times* (New York, 1912), 10–14.

25. "The Week," *Nation* (September 12, 1867), 202. [E. L. Godkin], "The Tariff Controversy," *Nation* (March 3, 1870), 132; William G. Sumner, "The Argument against Protective Taxes," *PR* 1 (1881), 241; [E. L. Godkin], "The Proposed Protectionist Awakening," *Nation* (April 19, 1883), 334.

26. [E. L. Godkin], "The Tariff Controversy," 132; Charles F. Dunbar, "Economic Science in America, 1776–1876," *NAR* 122 (January 1876), 140; Paul Bairoch, *Economics and World History: Myths and Paradoxes* (Chicago, 1993), 23; "H. C. Carey's Principles of Social Science," *NAR* 103 (October 1866), 575; [Simon Newcomb], "Thompson's National Economy," *Nation* (May 13, 1875), 333. Ernst Teilhac, *Pioneers of American Economic Thought in the Nineteenth Century* (New York, 1936), 55–115 emphasizes Carey's opposition to the pessimistic doctrines of Malthus and Ricardo. For "the relative insularity of economic thought" during these years, Judith Goldstein, *Ideas, Interests, and American Trade Policy* (Ithaca, NY, 1993), 86. Richard C. Edwards, "Economic Sophistication in Nineteenth Century Congressional Tariff Debates," *The Journal of Economic History*, 30–34 (December 1970), 827, suggests that the problem of knowledge may have been more acute at the political level than at the level of economic theory.

27. David A. Wells, "The Creed of Free Trade," *AM* 36 (1875), 205, 207; [E. L. Godkin], "How Protection Affects Labor," *Nation* (May 25, 1871), 352; W. R. Fishback, "Communism and Protection," *NAR* 146 (1888), 227.

28. Abbott Kinney, "Protection," *OM* 12–68 (December 1888), 202; [E. L. Godkin], "The New German Political Economy," *Nation* (September 9, 1875), 161; "Bagehot's Economic Studies," *Nation* (March 18, 1880), 216; "The Origin of Protection," *Nation* (October 21, 1869), 333; [E. L. Godkin], "The Proposed Protectionist Awakening," *Nation* (April 19, 1883), 334; David A. Wells, "The First Century of the Republic," *Harper's* 50 (1875), 708; "Tariff Reactions," *NAR* 129 (1879), 498; "The Relation of Political Economy to the Labor Question," *Nation* (August 31, 1882), 184; J. M. Patterson, "Agriculture as a Force of Civilization," *Appletons'* 2 (December 18, 1869), 567.

29. John Bright, "Will England Return to Protection?" *NAR* 128 (June 1879), 696; Arthur Arnold, "A Plea for Free Trade," *PR* 1 (1879), 667; "The Week," *Nation* (July 12, 1866), 1; Kinney, "Protection," 202. Kinney was also the designer of the town of Venice, California.

30. [E. L. Godkin], "The English and French Tariff Troubles," *Nation* (June 16, 1881), 419; [E. L. Godkin], "The Real Obstacles to Free Trade," *Nation* (November 20, 1879), 338; "The Week," *Nation* (June 2, 1881), 381; [E. L. Godkin], "The Proposed Protectionist Awakening," 334.

31. Joseph Wharton, "National Self-Protection," *AM* 36 (September 1875), 300; David A. Wells, "Taxation in the United States," *NEYR* 43–181 (July 1884), 477, 469, 472; [E. L. Godkin], "The Tariff Controversy," 132; [A. V. Dicey], "Cobden," *Nation* (February 2, 1882), 104.

32. Wells, "The Creed of Free Trade," 216; "Tariff Reactions," *NAR* 129 (1879), 501, 508; D. Cady Eaton, "Thoughts about Protection and Centralization," *NEYR* 53–247 (October 1990), 375; "Cobden," *AM* 49 (March 1882), 416; [A. V. Dicey], "Cobden," 103–104.

33. Van Buren Denslow, "American Economics," *NAR* 139 (1884), 28; [D. M. Means], "The Gospel of Protection," *Nation* (September 20, 1888), 235; John Ball, Jr., "The Home and Foreign Markets," *NAR* 147 (1888), 231; "Notes," *Nation* (May 7, 1874), 299; John Ball, Jr., "The Chinese Wall," *NAR* 147 (1888), 106. Edward P. Crapol, *America for Americans: Economic Nationalism and Anglophobia in the Late Nineteenth Century* (Westport, CT, 1973).

34. "A Ready-made Foreign Market for American Goods," *Century* 29 (1884), 311–312; Edward F. Qualtrough, "Our Naval Necessities," *OM* 13 (April 1889), 423–429; Henry Hall, "The Future of American Shipping," *AM* 47 (February 1881), 166–176; David A. Wells, "How Shall the Nation Regain Prosperity? Part II" *NAR* 125 (September 1877), 287.

35. [E. L. Godkin], "The Revision of the Tariff," *Nation* (January 21, 1869), 44; "The Week," *Nation* (July 14, 1887), 23; " 'Fair Trade' in Great Britain," *Nation* (August 11, 1881), 109; Denslow, "American Economics," 12; "The Anglo-French Com-

mercial Treaty," *Nation* (September 8, 1881), 189; "Political Economy in Germany," *Nation* (November 4, 1875), 296; Otto Graf zu Stollberg Wernigerode, *Germany and the United States during the Era of Bismarck* (Reading, PA, 1937), 97. Some economic historians see the period 1870–1914 as a period of relatively open trade in Europe. See Phillip Anthony O'Hara, ed., *Encyclopedia of Political Economy* (London, 1999), I: 372. For tariff rates in Europe in 1875 and 1913, see Bairoch, *Economics and World History: Myths and Paradoxes,* 24, 26; Kevin O'Rourke and Jeffrey G. Williamson, *Globalization and History: The Evolution of a Nineteenth-Century Atlantic Economy* (Cambridge, MA, 1999), 93–118. For Italy, see Frank Coppa, "The Italian Tariff and the Conflict Between Agriculture and Industry: The Commercial Policy of Italy, 1860–1922," *The Journal of Economic History* 30 (December 1970), 45–49.

36. [E. L. Godkin], "Why Political Economy Has Not Been Cultivated in America," *Nation* (September 26, 1867), 255; Richard T. Ely, "The Past and the Present of Political Economy," *OM* 2–9 (September 1883), 234; [Godkin], "The New German Political Economy," 161; Herbert Tuttle, "Academic Socialism," *AM* 52 (July 1883), 204–205.

37. [Horace White], "The Proposed Wine Retaliation," *Nation* (January 17, 1884), 48; Abbott Kinney, "Protection," *OM* 12 (December 1888), 202; "The Week," *Nation* (January 24, 1884), 63; David A. Wells, "Tariff Revision: Its Necessity and Possible Methods," *PR* 2 (1882), 345, 352.

38. William Clarke, "William Ewart Gladstone," *NEM* 8 (April 1890), 127; "The Week," *Nation* (September 8, 1881), 185; W. E. Gladstone, "Free Trade or Protection," *NAR* 150 (1890), 25–26.

39. Gladstone, "Free Trade or Protection," 18, 28, 35; Justin S. Morrell, "Free Trade or Protection," *NAR* 150 (1890), 283.

40. Reitano, *The Tariff Question,* 99; William McKinley, "The Value of Protection," *NAR* 150 (1890), 744; Andrew Carnegie, "Summing Up the Tariff Discussion," *NAR* 151 (1890), 52, 72.

41. [Sidney Webster], "Mr. McKinley's Remarkable Bill," *Nation* (January 2, 1890), 4–5; "The Week," *Nation* (May 29, 1890), 423; "The Week," *Nation* (July 10, 1890), 22; "The Anglo-French Commercial treaty," *Nation* (September 8, 1881), 189; [Clarence Deming], "The Twilight of the Tariff," *Nation* (April 3, 1890), 272.

42. H. J. Philpott, "The Lesson of 1890," *OM* 16–96 (December 1890), 607–608; [E. L. Godkin], "The Blaine Explosion," *Nation* (September 11, 1890), 204; [E. L. Godkin], "Mr. Foster on International Trade," *Nation* (December 18, 1884), 518; "The Protectionist Revival in Europe," *Nation* (March 6, 1879), 161; "Recent Works on Trade and Finance," *NAR* 130 (1880), 410; "A Chapter in European Protection," *Nation* (August 2, 1888), 87.

43. "The 'Independents' in the Canvass," *NAR* 123 (October 1876), 461; "The Civil Service," *Scribner's* 12 (1876), 898; "Protectorates," *Nation* (January 21, 1869), 4; "The Week," *Nation* (August 22, 1872), 117; "A Reform in the Civil Service," *Scribner's* 15 (1877), 271.

44. "Civil Service of the United States," *NAR* 105 (1867), 478; "The Civil Service," 898; "Civil Service," *Scribner's* 5 (1872), 115; [C. C. Nott], "America's Colleges and Legislators," *Nation* (August 28, 1873), 142; Henry Brooks Adams, "Civil Service Reform," *NAR* 109 (1869), 472–473. Lodge is quoted in Michael Lind, *The Next American Nation: The New Nationalism and the American Revolution* (New York, 1995), 63

45. F. H. Morse, "Our Civil Service," *Harper's* 55 (1877), 298; [A. R. Macdonough], "Eaton's Civil Service in Great Britain," *Nation* (January 15, 1880), 46; Dorman B. Eaton, "Patronage Monopoly and the Pendleton Bill," *PR* 1 (1882), 90; Richard R. Ely, "The Prussian Civil Service," *OM* 1–5 (May 1883), 458; Richard H. Dana, "Points in American Politics," *NAR* 124 (January 1877), 18.

46. A. R. Macdonough, "Civil Service Reform," *Harper's* 40 (1870), 546; E. L. Godkin, "The Prospects of the Political Art," *NAR* 110 (April 1870), 412–413; "The Barbarism at St. Louis," *Nation* (November 25, 1875), 334; "The Week," *Nation* (January 10, 1867), 32.

47. George William Brown, "English Civil Service Reform," *AM* 43 (May 1879), 586; Charles O. Graves, "How It Was Done in Great Britain," *Scribner's* 14 (1877), 242; George M. Towle, "The British Civil Service," *Appletons'* 5 (March 4, 1871), 248–249; "Editor's Table," *Appletons'* 17 (August 7, 1875), 180; [Herbert Tuttle], "Lessons from the Prussian Civil Service," *Nation* (February 26, 1880), 150; "The History and Literature of Civil Service Reform," *PR* 42–1 (1870), 2; "Editor's Table," *Appletons'* 13 (May 22, 1875), 692. Mara Nacht Mayor, "Norton, Lowell and Godkin: A Study of American Attitudes toward England, 1865–1885," Ph.D. dissertation, Yale University, 1969, 260–265.

48. "*Staatsrecht, Wolkerrecht und Politik,*" *Nation* (April 28, 1870), 277; "The Week," *Nation* (December 28, 1871), 410; Theodore Roosevelt, "The Merit System Versus the Patronage System," *Century* 39 (1889), 633; E. L. Godkin, "The Civil Service Reform Controversy," *NAR* 134 (1882), 381; Henry Cabot Lodge, "Why Patronage in Offices Is Un-American," *Century* 40 (1890), 839.

49. "The Barbarism at St. Louis," *Nation* (November 25, 1875), 334; "The Week," *Nation* (April 12, 1877), 215; J. L. M. Curry, "Executive Patronage and Civil Service Reform," *Galaxy* 23 (June 1877), 829; A. R. Macdonough, "Civil Service Reform," *Harper's* 40 (1870), 549; "Competitive Examinations in China," *NAR* 111 (1870), 63; Lodge, "Why Patronage in Offices Is Un-American," 841; Justin McCarthy, "The Judgment of Paris," *Harper's* 40 (1870), 546.

50. [Sidney Webster], "Wanton Removal of Diplomatic Agents," *Nation* (May 23, 1889), 421; "The Week," *Nation* (February 16, 1871), 97–98; "Our Diplomatic Representatives," *Galaxy* 6 (1868), 132; [E. L. Godkin], "American Ministers Abroad," *Nation* (February 14, 1867), 132; "The Department of State and the Diplomatic Service," *Century* 35 (1887), 967; Dorman B. Eaton, "The Public Service and the Public," *AM* 41 (February 1878), 251. Robert Beisner, *From the Old Diplomacy to the New, 1865–1900* (Arlington Heights, IL, 1975), 30–32; Thomas M. Etzold, *Conduct of American Foreign Relations: The Other Side of Diplomacy* (New York, 1977), 19–23.

51. "Schuyler's American Diplomacy," *AM* 58 (September 1886), 417; "Our Foreign Legations," *Nation* (January 14, 1886), 27; Julius Bing, "Our Civil Service," *Putnam's* 12 (August 1868), 242–244.

52. "Solemn Trifling," *Nation* (March 28, 1867), 257–258; "Table-Talk," *Appletons'* 6 (September 23, 1871), 358; Albert Rhodes, "Our Diplomats and Consuls," *Scribner's* 13 (1876), 176.

53. "Foreign Legations," *Nation* (December 24, 1885), 524; "Table-Talk," *Appletons'* 6 (September 23, 1871), 358; Rhodes, "Our Diplomats and Consuls," 176; "The Moral of Mr. Schenk's case," *Nation* (December 9, 1875), 367.

54. "Editor's Table," *Appletons'* 15 (March 18, 1876), 377; "Our Foreign Legations," *Nation* (January 14, 1886), 26; "Foreign Legations," 524; George Makepeace Towle, "The American Consular Service," *NAR* 149 (889), 757; "One of the Questions Next in Order," *Nation* (November 19, 1868), 409; "The Poor Diplomats," *Appletons'* 3 (May 14, 1870), 551.

55. Dorman B. Eaton, "The Public Service and the Public," *AM* 41 (February 1878), 252; Charles Hale, "The Consular System of the United States," *NAR* 122 (1876), 327; C. Bates, "Life in the Cannibal Islands," *Scribner's* 1 (1870), 596; George M. Towle, "The British Civil Service," *Appletons'* 5 (March 4, 1871), 249.

56. [E. L. Godkin], "The Diplomatic and Consular Service Bill," *Nation* (December 17, 1868), 499; "The Editor's Easy Chair," *Harper's* 78 (1889), 815.

57. "The Week," *Nation* (May 21, 1885), 412; George M. Towle, "Our Consular Service," *AM* 29 (March 1872), 301; Editorial, *Galaxy* 3 (1867), 447; Edward Sylvester Morse, "Old Satsuma," *Harper's* 77 (1888), 523; "The Moral of Mr. Schenk's case," *Nation* (December 9, 1875), 367.

58. "A Modern Miracle," *Century* 25 (1882), 785. "The attempt on the President's life, along with other scandals, were not evidences of decadence, but rather the incidents of reform." Letter to the editor, *Century* 23 (1881), 146. Only 14,000 of 132,800 federal employees were originally covered by the Pendleton Act; by 1900, 40 percent were covered, with piecemeal additions made thereafter. See Patricia Wallace Ingraham, *The Foundation of Merit: Public Service in American Democracy* (Baltimore, MD, 1995), 30–54; Richard D. White, Jr., *Roosevelt the Reformer: Theodore Roosevelt as Civil Service Commissioner, 1889–1895* (Tuscaloosa, AL, 2003), 21–22.

59. [E. L. Godkin], "The Tariff Controversy," 132; "The Latest Protectionist Spook," *Nation* (October 11, 1888), 286; [A. V. Dicey], "Cobden," 104; Wells, "Taxation in the United States," 472.

3. Europe I: The Mirage of Republicanism

1. E. L. Godkin, "The Political Outlook," *Scribner's* 19 (1879), 620; "The Week," *Nation* (September 5, 1872), 146; "Editor's Table," *Appletons'* 155 (1876), 22; S. Rhett Roman, "American Chauvinism," *NAR* 155 (November 1892), 757.

2. Henry Carter Adams, "Democracy," *NEYR* 40 (November 1881), 769; "American Civilization," *AM* 9 (April 1862), 506; [Edward Dicey], "The European and American Order of Thought," *Nation* (October 12, 1865), 460.

3. "Motley's Historic Progress and American Democracy," *AM* 23 (April 1869), 519; [Henry Cabot Lodge], "Histoire des Etats Unis d'Amerique," *Nation* (March 20, 1879), 205; "Our Recent Foreign Relations" *AM* 14 (1864), 246; James Russell Lowell, "On a Certain Condescension in Foreigners," *AM* 23 (January 1869), 93; O. W. Holmes, "Our Progressive Independence," *AM* 13 (1864), 512; "Editor's Table," *Appletons'* 5 (September 1878), 280. For French views of American pretensions, see Pascal Ory, "From Baudelaire to Duhamel" in Denis Lacorne, Jacques Rupnik, and Marie-France Toinet, eds., *The Rise and Fall of Anti-Americanism: A Century of French Perception,* trans. Gerald Turner (London, 1990), 46. On the crippling impact of slavery on American idealism abroad, see Robert Kagan, *Dangerous Nation: America's Place in the World From Its Earliest Days to the Dawn of the Twentieth Century* (New York, 2006), 181–264.

4. Emilio Castelar, "The Republican Movement in Europe," *Harper's* 45 (872), 47; Castelar, "The Progress of Democracy in Europe," *NAR* 141 (1885), 415; "Ups and Downs of the Bonapartes and Bourbons," *AM* 27 (1871), 295; Robert L. Stanton, "The Political Outlook in France," *PR* 2 (1878), 546; Joseph F. Thompson, "The Drift of Europe, Christian and Social," *PR* 1 (1878), 735; Henry Carter Adams, "Democracy," *NEYR* 40 (November 1881), 765.

5. [E. L. Godkin], "Parliamentary Government," *Nation* (February 16, 1871), 101; Joseph F. Thompson, "The Drift of Europe, Christian and Social," *PR* 1 (January–June 1878), 735; "The Week," *Nation* (October 22, 1874), 261; "The Week," *Nation* (July 6, 1882), 2; "The Week," *Nation* (December 18, 1890), 473; Emilio Castelar, "The Best Sign of Our Times: Democratic Revolution and Evolution in Europe," *NAR* 152 (April 1891), 486; A Resident of Paris, "The Situation in France," *NAR* 125 (November 1877), 529. For the influence of American constitutionalism through the first half of the nineteenth century, see Bernard Bailyn, *To Begin the World Anew: The Genius and Ambiguities of the Founding Fathers* (New York, 2003), 131–149. Actually, the American Declaration of Independence appears to have been more widely copied. See David Armitage, *The Declaration of Independence: A Global History* (Cambridge, MA, 2007). For solid figures on democratization, see Tatu Vanhanen, *The Emergence of Democracy: A Comparative Study of 119 States, 1850–1979* (Helsinki, 1984), 70; percentages are found in Tatu Vanhanen, "A New Dataset for Measuring Democracy, 1810–1998," *Journal of Peace Research* 37 (2000), 259.

6. "Republicanism in Europe," *Scribner's* 1 (1870), 106; "Foreign Politics," *Nation* (April 15, 1869), 299; "Maine's Popular Government," *Nation* (March 25, 1886), 263; Henry Sumner Maine, *Popular Government: Four Essays* (London, 1885), x, 54. See also the conservative estimate by Titus Munson Coan, "American Timidity," in *Galaxy* 10 (1870), 182.

7. "Thomas Carlyle," *Nation* (September 5, 1867), 194.

8. "Notes," *Nation* (February 5, 1874), 92; "Some Impressions of the United States," *Nation* (June 7, 1883), 495.

9. "The United States and Europe," *AM* 8 (July 1861), 99; "Table-Talk," *Appletons'* 5 (March 18, 1871), 323; H. D. Jenkins, "My English Friends," *OM* 4–6 (June 1870), 571; Theodore Dwight Woolsey, "The Alabama Question," *NEYR* 28 (July 1869), 619; J. R. Lowell, "On a Certain Condescension in Foreigners," *AM* 23 (January 1869), 94; Pis G. Celozzi Baldelli, *Power Politics, Diplomacy, and the Avoidance of Hostilities between England and the United States in the Wake of the Civil War*, trans. Elena Bertozzi (Lewiston, NY, 1998), 47.

10. Letter to the editor, "Republican Propagandism," *Nation* (July 27, 1865), 108; Newman Hall, "An Address to the American People," *Harper's* 37 (1868), 234; "England and America," *AM* 14 (1864), 754.

11. "Four British Statesmen," *Galaxy* 2 (1866), 156; "Table-Talk," *Appletons'* 6 (December 23, 1871), 721; "Notes," *Nation* (September 19, 1872), 189; "The Political Future in England," *Nation* (August 15, 1867), 131; Carte Blanche [Percy Roberts], "England and the English," *De Bow's Review* 3 (March 1867), 236; "Table-Talk," *Appletons'* 7 (March 23, 1872), 329.

12. T. W. Reid, "Mr. Disraeli," *Appletons'* 7 (June 29, 1872), 714; "Disraeli in English Politics," [reprinted from the *Pall Mall Gazette*], *Appletons'* 6 (August 19, 1871), 216; [A. G. Sedgwick], "Brandes's 'Beaconsfield'," *Nation* (June 3, 1880), 421; "The Week," *Nation* (May 5, 1881), 309 [commenting on a proposed monument for Beaconsfield]; "Table-Talk," *Appletons'* 8 (November 30, 1872), 610; "Aristocracy," *NAR* 147 (November 1888), 594; "Editorials," *Nation* (December 13, 1866), 473.

13. D. W. Sion to Rollo Ogden, "26 March 1906," in Rollo Ogden, ed., *Life and Letters of Edwin Lawrence Godkin* (New York, 1907), 2:67; "Herbert Spencer in America," *Century* 24 (1881), 789; "Gladstone," *NAR* 136 (1883), 226; "The Week," *Nation* (December 7, 1882), 477; "The Week," *Nation* (September 6, 1883), 202; "Editor's Table," *Appletons'* 12 (December 26, 1874), 825; [E. L. Godkin], "Gladstone," *Nation* (January 19, 1888), 47; [E. L. Godkin], "Mr. Gladstone's Unpopularity," *Nation* (September 21, 1871), 191; William Clarke, "William Ewart Gladstone," *NEM* 8 (April 1880), 129; "Political Education of the People," *Century* 28 (1884), 784; T. H. S. Escott, "John Bright," *Century* 28 (1884), 439; "The Editor's Easy Chair," *Harper's* 79 (1889), 148–150. Murney Gerlach, *British Liberalism and the United States: Political and Social Thought in the Late Victorian Age* (New York, 2001).

14. "A Letter about England," *AM* 15 (1865), 642; George M. Towle, "English Elections," *Appletons'* 6 (September 30, 1871), 377; "Table-Talk," *Appletons'* 6 (August 12, 1871), 189; Justin McCarthy, "Joseph Arch and the New Emancipation," *Galaxy* 15 (1873), 453–460; [A. V. Dicey], "The Reform Bill in England," *Nation* (April 5, 1866), 424; Bernard Moses, "The Drift of Power in the English Government," *OM* 5 (March 1885), 239–247; "The Week," *Nation* (July 10, 1884), 23; Justin McCarthy, "The Liberal Triumvirate of England," *Galaxy* 7 (1869), 45; "The Week," *Nation* (September 24, 1885), 248; Emilio Castelar, "The Progress of Democracy in

Europe," *NAR* 141 (1885), 419; M. D. Conway, "John Stuart Mill," *Harper's* 47 (1873), 533. David Dimbleby and David Reynolds, *An Ocean Apart: The Relationship between Britain and America in the Twentieth Century* (London, 1988), 24.

15. "The New Republican Gospel," *Nation* (October 9, 1873), 237; "Editor's Table," *Appletons'* 12 (August 29, 1874), 281; Adam Badeau, "Our Relations with England," *Harper's* 40 (1870), 584; "The Change in English Politics," *Nation* (September 11, 1873), 173; "Notes," *Nation* (July 19, 1883), 55; Justin McCarthy, "Sir Charles Dilke and the English Republicans," *Galaxy* 13 (1872), 733; "The Week," *Nation* (August 26, 1869), 164.

16. Allen Thorndike Rice, "The Race for Primacy," *NAR* 145 (1887), 449; "Democracy in England," *Century* 32 (1886), 647; George M. Towle, "Reform and Revolution in England," *Galaxy* 2 (1866), 17; Goldwin Smith, "The Revolution in England," *NAR* 108 (1869), 248; Andrew Carnegie, "Democracy in England," *NAR* 142 (1886), 75. Technically, the Treason Felony Act of 1848 made it illegal to advocate ending the monarchy in favor of a republic.

17. William E. Gladstone, "Kin Beyond the Sea," *NAR* 127 (September–October 1878), 180, 183, 186, 197–198, 202.

18. A. V. Dicey, "What Are the Causes of the Conservative Reaction in England?," *Nation* (January 14, 1886), 30; [James Bryce], "Career of the Salisbury Ministry," *Nation* (February 18, 1886), 144; Journal entry, August 1, 1901, *Letters and Journals of Thomas Wentworth Higginson 1846–1906* (Boston, 1921), 319; Dimbleby and Reynolds, *An Ocean Apart*, 24; H. G. Nicholas, *The United States and Britain* (Chicago, 1975), 50.

19. Rice, "The Race for Primacy," 436–437; Albert Rhodes, "The English at Home," *Galaxy* 13 (1872), 777; "The American in England," *Appletons'* 7 (February 10, 1872), 155; Ernest Lambert, "Americanized Englishmen," *NAR* 147 (1888), 322.

20. "Table-Talk," *Appletons'* 8 (July 6, 1872), 24; The Editor, "Nebulae," *Galaxy* 16 (October 1873), 579–580; "Table-Talk," *Appletons'* 7 (January 27, 1872), 108; "Editor's Table," *Appletons'* 10 (October 11, 1873), 474 [referring to an article in *Galaxy*]; "Table-Talk," *Appletons'* 8 (September 7, 1872), 276; "The American in England," *Appletons'* 7 (February 10, 1872), 155; Henry Steele Commager, ed., *Britain through American Eyes* (London: The Bodley Head, 1974), 397; Richard Grant White, "English Women," *Galaxy* 23 (1877), 675; Richard Grant White, "English Traits," *Galaxy* 23 (1877), 520, 526.

21. Richard Grant White, "John Bull," *AM* 42 (August 1878), 228; Moncure D. Conway, "The Queen of England," *NAR* 145 (1887), 125; "An Opportunity for Anglomaniacs," *Nation* (July 14, 1881), 28; Cushing Strout, *The American Image of the Old World* (New York, 1963), 107–142; "The Week," *Nation* (July 20, 1882), 43; "Notes," *Nation* (August 9, 1883), 119; Henry Cabot Lodge, "Colonialism in the United States," *AM* 51 (May 1883), 625; Goldwin Smith, "The Hatred of England," *NAR* 150 (1890), 555; "The Week," *Nation* (August 17, 1882), 123. Indeed, until the late 1940s "twisting the lion's tail" would continue to be used by politicians as a way of winning votes. John E. Moser, *Twisting the Lion's Tail: American Anglophobia*

between the World Wars (New York, 1999), 3. Edward P. Crapol, *America for Americans: Economic Nationalism and Anglophobia in the Late Nineteenth Century* (Westport, CT, 1973), 13 argues that "anti-British nationalism reached its peak during the late nineteenth century."

22. "Politics" *AM* 31 (January 1873), 123.

23. "The Alabama Claims," *Galaxy* 5 (1868), 648; Philip Quilibet, "The 'Final and Amicable' Quarrel," *Galaxy* 13 (1872), 553.

24. "Charles Ingersoll's Fears for Democracy," *NAR* 121 (July 1875), 227; Philip Quilibet, "England and America," *Galaxy* 12 (July 1871), 112; [J. N. Pomeroy], "Gist of the Alabama Controversy," *Nation* (November 2, 1865), 549; Theodore Dwight Woolsey, "The Treaty of Washington in 1871," *NEYR* 32 (1873), 269; Quilibet, "The 'Final and Amicable' Quarrel," 553.

25. G. T. Ferris, "A Possible War and Its Probable Results," *NAR* 148 (1889), 32; "Morely's 'Life of Cobden,'" *Century* 24 (1881), 151; Thomas Wentworth Higginson, "Do Americans Hate England?" *NAR* 150 (1890), 752; Andrew Carnegie, "Do Americans Hate England?" *NAR* 150 (1890), 759; "Politics" *AM* 31 (January 1873), 129; Adam Badeau, "Our Relations with England," *Harper's* 40 (1870), 58; Murat Halstead, "Do Americans Hate England?" *NAR* 150 (1890), 763.

26. George R. Parkin, "The Reorganization of the British Empire," *Century* 37 (1888), 187; Josiah Strong, *Our Country: Its Possible Future and the Present Crisis* (New York, 1891), 208.

27. [A. V. Dicey], "Cobden," *Nation* (January 3, 1878), 13; D. H. Chamberlain, "Bryce's 'American Commonwealth,'" *NEYR* 50 (June 1889), 397; D. A. Wasson, "Mr. Buckle as a Thinker," *AM* 11 (January 11863), 40; "Foreign Politics," *Nation* (April 15, 1869), 200.

28. John C. Fleming, "Are We Anglo-Saxons?" *NAR* 153 (1891), 253, 255; Rice, "The Race for Primacy," 436–437; Herbert Tuttle, "Academic Socialism," *AM* 52 (August 1883), 210; J. D. Phelan, "The Bent of International Intercourse," *OM* 6–32 (August 1885), 166.

29. Alexander DeConde, *Ethnicity, Race, and American Foreign Policy* (Boston, 1992), 91–92; Alex Danchev, *On Specialness: Essays in Anglo-American Relations* (New York, 1998), 154; Mara Nacht Mayor, "Norton, Lowell and Godkin: A Study of American Attitudes Toward England, 1865–1885," Ph.D. dissertation, Yale University, 1969, 271–310, stresses, mistakenly, *The Nation*'s preoccupation with England.

30. [Henry James. Jr.], "Laugel's France Politique et Sociale," *Nation* (October 18, 1877), 245; Henry Blumenthal, *A Reappraisal of Franco-American Relations, 1830–1871* (Chapel Hill, NC, 1959).

31. *Nation* (July 6, 1865), 9; Elizabeth Brett White, *American Opinion of France: From Lafayette to Poincaré* (New York, 1927), 155, 173.

32. "The Political Prospect in Europe," *Nation* (January 23, 1868), 65; H. W. Homans, "France under the Second Empire," *NAR* 111 (1870), 411; Edward Stanwood, "Votes and Elections," *Appletons'* 9 (February 15, 1873), 236; Colin Bigelow, "Terms of Peace Proposed by the Great Powers," *Scribner's* 11 (1870), 297.

33. "Table-Talk," *Appletons'* 5 (January 28, 1871), 115; George M. Towle, "Imperial France: Past, Present, and future," *Galaxy* 3 (1867), 189; "Nebulae," *Galaxy* 1 (1866), 81; "Nebulae," *Galaxy* 1 (1866), 81; George M. Towle, "The Paris Markets," *Appletons'* 4 (September 24, 1870), 375; "Miscellany—Louis Napoleon," *Appletons'* 5 (May 6, 1871), 538.

34. "The Reforms in France," *Nation* (April 21, 1870), 251; "The Week," *Nation* (September 19, 1867), 222; "The Prospect in France," *Nation* (August 19, 1869), 146; "The Political prospect in Europe," *Nation* (January 23, 1868), 65; George M. Towle, "Emile Olivier," *Appletons'* 3 (March 5, 1870), 269.

35. "Scientific Notes: A Republic in France," *Appletons'* 4 (October 29, 1870), 531; "The Gains of the Year," *Nation* (January 5, 1871), 4; J. A., "Ups and Downs of the Bonapartes and Bourbons," *AM* 27 (1871), 295; "Table-Talk," *Appletons'* 4 (September 24, 1870), 382; White, *American Opinion of France,* 185; Gazley, *American Opinion of German Reunification 1848–1871* (New York, 1926), 382–392.

36. "Miscellany: French Character," *Appletons'* 5 (March 11, 1871), 299; "Guizot," *Galaxy* 11 (1871), 882; "The Week," *Nation* (September 15, 1870), 163.

37. "Table-Talk," *Appletons'* 4 (October 8, 1870), 437; "Republicanism in Europe," *Scribner's* 1 (1870), 106; [E. L. Godkin], "The French Republic," *Nation* (October 27, 1870), 272. In the language of later political science, liberals of this period tended to be "preconditionalists" rather than "universalists".

38. Washburne to Fish, May 31, 1871, *Franco-German War and Insurrection of the Commune: Correspondence of E. B. Washburne* (Washington, DC, 1878), 210; Edmond de Pressense, "Paris under the Commune," *PR* 1 (1872), 136; "The Week," *Nation* (May 25, 1871), 352; "The Week," *Nation* (July 27, 1871), 51. For prewar doubts about the French capacity for self-rule, see H. A. Delille, "The Extravagance of the French Court," *Galaxy* 2 (1866), 260; Eugene Benson, "Paris and the Parisians," *Galaxy* 4 (1867), 673; "The French Police," *Appletons'* 4 (July 30, 1870), 134.

39. "The Decadence of France," *Appletons'* 4 (December 3, 1870), 681; "The Week," *Nation* (May 15, 1873), 226; "Democracy and Monarchy in France," *Nation* (January 14, 1875), 29; "Things for All Republicans to Consider," *Nation* (September 28, 1871), 204; "Causes of French Failure," *Appletons'* 5 (January 21, 1871), 84; George M. Towle, "A Typical French Family," *Appletons'* 2 (December 18, 1869), 558; "French Character," *Appletons'* 5 (March 11, 1871), 298.

40. "Again thy star, 0 France—fair, lustrous star, In heavenly peace, clearer, more bright than ever, Shall rise immortal." Walt Whitman, "O Star of France!" *Galaxy* 11 (1871), 817.

41. "The Week," *Nation* (September 12, 1872), 163; "Notes," *Nation* (October 5, 1871), 230; Brander Matthews, "Notes on Parisian Newspaper," *Century* 35 (1887), 200; "The Week," *Nation* (October 5, 1882), 277; Albert Rhodes, "Views Abroad," *Galaxy* 17 (1874), 31–32; "The Week," *Nation* (May 30, 1872), 347.

42. Herbert Tuttle, "French Democracy," *AM* 29 (May 1872), 560, 564; "Editor's Table," *Appletons'* 3 (November 1877), 474; "Books of the Day," *Appletons'* 4 (June

1878), 581; "Table-Talk," *Appletons'* 6 (August 5, 1871), 152; "La Vie Publique en Angleterre," *Nation* (April 17, 1884), 350; "Recent French Books," *Nation* (January 21, 1886), 61.

43. Frank Preston Stearns, *Cambridge Sketches* (Philadelphia, 1905), 134; Lucy H. Hooper, "French Society and Parisianized Americans," *Appletons'* 12 (September 26, 1874), 395; Lucy H. Hooper, "The American Colony in Paris," *Appletons'* 11 (June 20, 1874), 779–781; "The Americans in Paris," *Appletons'* 8 (December 7, 1872), 645; Edward Dicey, "Paris after the Peace," *Appletons'* 5 (May 13, 1871), 553, 555; "Appearance of Paris," *Appletons'* 6 (December 16, 1871), 695; Eugene Benson, "Paris and the Parisians," *Galaxy* 4 (1867), 666; W. C. Brownell, "French Traits— Intelligence," *Scribner's* 3 (1888), 94; Albert Rhodes, "The Rag-Pickers of Paris," *Galaxy* 17 (1874), 200; Rhodes, "Foundlings of Paris," *Galaxy* 18 (November 1874), 668. Philip N. Katz, *From Appomattox to Montmartre: Americans and the Paris Commune* (Cambridge, MA, 1998), 26.

44. George M. Towle, "Modern French Clubs," *Galaxy* 5 (1868), 247; A Roving American [Edwin Lee Leon], "French Morals and Manners," *Appletons'* 1 (May 29, 1869), 115; Towle, "Typical French Family," 558; Albert Rhodes, "Woman's Occupations," *Galaxy* 21 (1876), 48; Rhodes, "Americans in Paris," *Galaxy* 17 (1874), 603; Hooper, "The American Colony in Paris," 779; Hooper, "French Society and Parisianized Americans," *Appletons'* 12 (September 26, 1874), 395–398.

45. George M. Towle, "Protestantism in France," *Appletons'* 6 (July 8, 1871), 38; George Merrill, "The French Republic," *Harper's* 62 (1881), 580; Edmond de Pressense, "The Religious Movement in France," *Harper's* 79 (1889), 540; "Decrease of Population in France," *Appletons'* 11 (April 4, 1874), 436.

46. Herbert Tuttle, "The Chauvinisme of the French," *AM* 30 (October 1872), 479–480; Albert Rhodes, "The French at Home," *Galaxy* 13 (1872), 448; [Charles A. Cutter], "A Frenchman on the American Constitution," *Nation* (August 21, 1884), 154; "Contributors' Club," *AM* 53 (March 1885), 428.

47. "Notes," *Nation* (January 26, 1888), 75; George Merrill, "The French Republic," *Harper's* 62 (1881), 581; "The Week," *Nation* (February 1, 1872), 67; "Notes," *Nation* (February 12, 1880), 119; Albert Rhodes, "The Forty Immortals," *Galaxy* 17 (1874), 748; Y. D., "The Forty Immortals," *Century* 27 (1883), 388–407; Theodore Child, "The Institute of France," *Harper's* 78 (1889), 520.

48. John Burroughs, "A Glimpse of France," *Appletons'* 9 (January 18, 1873), 107; H. A. Delille, "American Women and French Fashions," *Harper's* 35 (1867), 119; "Editor's Table," *Appletons'* 13 (April 17, 1875), 498; [E. L. Godkin], "Waiters and Waitresses," *Nation* (November 26, 1874), 346; L. H. Hooper, "The Cafes of Paris," *Appletons'* 12 (November 21, 1874), 650; [Frederick Sheldon], "The Theatres of Paris," *Nation* (April 22, 1880), 314.

49. "Editor's Table," *Appletons'* 3 (September 1877), 281; A Roving American, "French Morals and Manners," *Appletons'* 1 (April 24, 1869), 115; W. C. Brownell, "French Traits—Intelligence," *Scribner's* 3 (1888), 99; "Table-Talk," *Appletons'* 5

(February 11, 1871), 174; "Notes," _Nation_ (December 25, 1873), 425; "Editor's Table," _Appletons'_ 2 (1877), 188.

50. "A Republic Without Republicans," _Nation_ (August 20, 1874), 120–121; "The Week," _Nation_ (November 7, 1872), 291; "The Week," _Nation_ (February 16, 1871), 99; "French Politics," _Nation_ (June 18, 1874), 391; "French Character," _Appletons'_ 5 (March 11, 1871), 299; "The Sovereign of France," _Galaxy_ 16 (1873), 261; "The Great European Change," _Scribner's_ 2 (May 1871), 94.

51. Edward Stanwood, "Votes and Elections," _Appletons'_ 9 (February 15, 1873), 236; "Editor's Literary Record," _Harper's_ 71 (November 1885), 964; [A. V. Dicey], "Stephens's French Revolution," _Nation_ (February 24, 1887), 167; [A. V. Dicey], "Lessons of the French Revolution (I)," _Nation_ (November 6, 1873), 307; "Editor's Table," _Appletons'_ 4–4 (1878), 388; "The Situation in France," _Nation_ (January 25, 1872), 53.

52. Edwin De Leon, "The Count de Paris," _Appletons'_ 7 (February 3, 1872), 130; "The Probable Future of France," _Appletons'_ 7 (April 20, 1872), 429; John W. Dwinelle, "Napoléon III. Second Period, 1865 to 1872," _OM_ 10 (April 1873), 369; Emilio Castelar, "The Republican Movement in Europe," _Harper's_ 45 (1872), 48; "Table-Talk," _Appletons'_ 6 (July 1, 1871), 22.

53. "Editor's Table," _Appletons'_ 15 (March 11, 1876), 344; George M. Towle, "The Great French Tribune Gambetta," _Appletons'_ 5–6 (December 1878), 526; "The New Regime in France," _Nation_ (February 6, 1879), 97; "The Week," _Nation_ (January 13, 1881), 21; "Gambetta's Fall," _Nation_ (February 2, 1882), 94; "The Week," _Nation_ (October 19, 1882), 321; "End of French Imperialism," _Nation_ (June 26, 1879), 431; "The Week," _Nation_ (September 4, 1884), 189; Henry James, "Italy Revisited," _AM_ 41 (1878), 437.

54. [E. L. Godkin], "Affairs in France," _Nation_ (September 10, 1874), 166; [Henry James], "Laugel's France Politique et Sociale," _Nation_ (October 18, 1877), 245.

55. "Editor's Table," _Appletons'_ 13 (January 16, 1875), 85; "Notes," _Nation_ (December 7, 1882), 487; "The Week," _Nation_ (January 4, 1883), 1; "The Week," _Nation_ (October 19, 1882), 320; "The Week," _Nation_ (December 7, 1882), 477.

56. E. F. Noyes, "Progress of the French Republic," _NAR_ 134 (1882), 244; "Editor's Table," _NEM_ 5 (November 1886), 84; "The Unveiling of the Statue," _New York Times,_ October 29, 1886, 4; John Bodnar, "Immigrant America and Public History," _Journal of American History_ 73 (June 1986), 139–140; Portes, _Fascination and Misgivings: The United States in French Opinion_ (New York, 2000), 5.

57. "The Week," _Nation_ (January 25, 1883), 72; Anna Bicknell, "The Pretenders to the Throne of France," _Century_ 27 (1883), 251; "French Acceptance of Caesarism," _Nation_ (July 17, 1879), 37; "Editor's Table," _Appletons'_ 11 (March 14, 1874), 377; "The Week," _Nation_ (November 1, 1883), 363.

58. "The Week," _Nation_ (December 30, 1886), 533; "Exit Boulanger," _Nation_ (August 2, 1888), 87; "The French Scandal," _Nation_ (October 20, 1887), 308; Karl Blind, "The German Army," _NAR_ 149 (1889), 197.

59. [E. L. Godkin], "The Boulangist Episode," _Nation_ (October 9, 1890), 281; "The Week," _Nation_ (February 21, 1889), 151; "The Week," _Nation_ (May 2, 1889), 357;

"The Week," *Nation* (November 24, 1887), 407; [E. L. Godkin], "Boulanger Again," *Nation* (March 22, 1888), 231.

60. "The Week," *Nation* (May 9, 1889), 377; Mrs. Schuler van Rensellaer, "Impressions of the International Exhibition of 1889," *Century* 39 (1889), 316–317; William A. Clarke, "In Paris at the Centennial of the Revolution," *NEM* 1 (1889), 98; F. I. Vassault, "Are the French Capable of Self-Government?" *OM* 14 (November 1889), 521.

61. Marvin R. Zahnhiser, *Uncertain Friendship: American-French Diplomatic Relations through the Cold War* (New York, 1975), 159–160; Crane Brinton, *The Americans and the French* (Cambridge, MA, 1968), 59–61 passes over the period very quickly; Donald C. McKay, *The United States and France* (Cambridge, MA, 1951), 92; Philippe Roger, *The American Enemy: A Story of French Anti-Americanism*, trans. Sharon Bowman (Chicago, 2005), 97–128.

4. Europe II: Premodern Survivals

1. Francis Lieber, "Nationalism and Internationalism," *The Miscellaneous Writings of Francis Lieber* (Philadelphia, 1881), 243; Henry Carter Adams, "Democracy," *NEYR* 40 (November 1881), 758. On Lieber's internationalism, see Frank Freidel, *Francis Lieber, Nineteenth-Century Liberal* (Baton Rouge, LA, 1947), 387–417.

2. John S. Hittell, "Modern Civilization a Teutonic Product," *OM* 14 (March 1885), 253. The transformation itself is well known to historians. For a few accounts, see Jorg Nadler, "From Culture to Kultur: Changing American Perceptions of Imperial Germany, 1870–1914," in *Transatlantic Images and Perceptions: Germany and America Since 1776* (New York, 1997), 131–154; Detlef Junker, *The Manichean Trap* (Washington, DC, 1995), 17–18.

3. Henry M. Baird, "The French Conquest of Lorraine and Alsace," *Scribner's* 1 (1870), 367; [Auguste Laugel], "French and English Opinions on the Effects of the German War," *Nation* (September 13, 1866), 213; George Moritz Wahl, "Fürst Bismarck," *Harper's* 81 (1890), 90; "La Mornara's Revelation of the War of 1866," *NAR* 118 (1874), 175; W. H. Hemans, "Prussia and Germany," *NAR* 112 (1871), 156; Otto Graf zu Stollberg Wernigerode, *Germany and the United States During the Era of Bismarck* (Reading, PA, 1937), 97 and 86–107, which remains a good account of formal American views and actions during the war. See also John Gerow Gazley, *American Opinion of German Reunification 1848–1871* (New York, 1926), 383–424, which is based largely on newspapers as sources.

4. "Editor's Literary Record," *Harper's* 40 (1870), 928; George F. Pond, "Forces in European Politics," *Galaxy* 24 (1877), 240; "With Which Side Should We Sympathize?" *Nation* (July 21, 1870), 36; H. Villard, "Karl Otto von Bismarck-Schonhausen," *NAR* 108 (1869), 221.

5. "Table-Talk," *Appletons'* 4 (September 24, 1870), 382; John Fiske, "Athenian and American Life," *AM* 34 (November 1874), 567; J. K. Hosmer, "Giant in the Spiked Helmet," *AM* 27 (1871), 432; [E. L. Godkin], "Sympathy," *Nation* (July 28, 1870), 52; "Table Talk," *Appletons'* 4 (October 1, 1870), 411; Philip Dymond, "Some

Characteristics of Von Moltke," *AM* 63 (January 1889), 114; Richard R. Ely, "The Prussian Civil Service," *OM* 1 (May 1883), 451, 458; "The Week," *Nation* (February 26, 1874), 140; Theodore Child, "Impressions of Berlin," *Harper's* 81 (1890), 340; "Foreign Items," *Appletons'* 7 (May 11, 1872), 530; Kaye Wilson, "Berlin," *Appletons'* 7 (June 1, 1872), 509; William Wells, "On to Berlin," *Scribner's* 1 (1870), 172; "Miscellany," *Appletons'* 8 (November 23, 1872), 586; Robert Dale Owen, "A German Baron and English Reformers," *AM* 31 (June 1873), 31; R. E. B., "Wandering Thoughts about Germany," *Appletons'* 7 (August 1879), 118.

6. H. W. Hemans, "Prussia and Germany," *NAR* 112 (1871), 158; "Miscellany," *Appletons'* 4 (September 17, 1870), 355; C. C. Hazewell, "The Progress of Prussia," *AM* 18 (November 1866), 587; "Herder," *NAR* 115 (1872), 104; George Moritz Wahl, "Bismarck Fürst," *Harper's* 81 (1890), 90.

7. "Topics of the Time," *Scribner's* 2 (1871), 93; T. G. Appleton, "The Flowering of a Nation," *AM* 28 (September 1871), 317.

8. "Reviews," *Nation* (September 30, 1875), 218; [Charles Carroll], "Hart's German Universities," *Nation* (December 17, 1874), 400; Hjalmar Boyesen, "The University of Berlin," *Scribner's* 18 (1879), 211; Samuel Sheldon, "Why Our Students Go to Germany," *AM* 63 (April 1889), 467; "The Hohensteins," *Nation* (May 5, 1870), 292; "Notes for Readers," *Appletons'* 10 (February 1881), 190; "Notes," *Nation* (October 6, 1881), 275; [Horace White], "Technical Education," *Nation* (August 18, 1887), 130.

9. [Friedrich Kapp], "The Crisis in Prussia," *Nation,* (October 26, 1865), 519. "Talks with Bismarck," *Nation* (October 13, 1870), 233; "Bismarck in the House of Lords," *Nation* (April 4, 1872), 215; "King William of Prussia," *Appletons'* 4 (October 15, 1870), 467.

10. S. S. Conant, "Count Otto von Bismarck," *Harper's* 40 (1870), 661; William E. Hathaway, "The New German Empire," *The Ladies' Repository* 10 (October 1872), 289; Friedrich Kapp, "The Bombardment of Paris and the Expenses of War," *Nation* (November 3, 1870), 294; "Miscellany," *Appletons'* 5 (February 18, 1871), 204; W. H. Hemans, "Prussia and Germany," *NAR* 112 (1871), 158; "Bismarck and the Pope," *Nation* (June 6, 1872), 371.

11. "The Week," *Nation* (January 28, 1875), 51; F. Lichtenberger, "The Religious Movement in Germany," *Harper's* 79 (188), 438; "The Week," *Nation* (March 22, 1888), 229; "The Week," *Nation* (January 16, 1879), 42; [Carl Schurz], "Political Reaction in Germany," *Nation* (January 12, 1882), 27; "The Week," *Nation* (February 13, 1873), 107; [E. L. Godkin], "The Suppression of Socialism in Germany," *Nation* (October 3, 1878), 207; [F. W. Taussig], "The Socialistic Legislation in Germany," *Nation* (March 4, 1880), 169; [Herbert Tuttle], "The Economic Revolution in Germany," *Nation* (August 7, 1879), 92.

12. Richard Hudson, "The German Empire," *NEYR* 48 (May 1888), 316; Herbert Tuttle, "The Hohenzollerns," *Harper's* 68 (1884), 689; [Herbert Tuttle], "Reaction in Germany," *Nation* (June 5, 1879), 381; "The Week," *Nation* (January 20, 1887), 45;

"Germany and Rome," *Nation* (September 8, 1881), 190; [Friedrich Kapp], "The New German Elections," *Nation* (July 7, 1881), 8; [Herbert Tuttle], "The German Chancellor and the Diet," *Nation* (June 2, 1881), 383.

13. F. Lichtenberger, "The Religious Movement in Germany," *Harper's* 79 (188), 438; C. A. Eggert, "Does Prussia Love War?" *Century* 28 (1884), 156; Helen Zimmern, "Count von Moltke," *Century* 27 (1883), 689; Philip Dymond, "Some Characteristics of von Moltke," *AM* 63 (January 1889), 114–115.

14. Review of *Unser Reichskanzler, Nation* (March 20, 1884), 262; "Notes," *Nation* (February 5, 1885), 121; John A. Kasson, "Otto von Bismarck: Man and Minister," *NAR* 143 (1886), 118; [H. T. Finck], "Bismarck and Dr. Busch," *Nation* (January 30, 1879), 85; [F. W. Taussig], "The Socialistic Legislation in Germany," *Nation* (March 4, 1880), 169; "Bismarck," *Century* 35 (1878), 768; "Editor's Table," *Appletons'* 2 (1877), 572.

15. "Germany and Rome," *Nation* (September 8, 1881), 190; Herbert Tuttle, "The German Empire," *Harper's* 63 (1881), 602; "The Week," *Nation* (February 27, 1890), 169; [Carl Schurz], "Bismarck's Defeat," *Nation* (June 22, 1882), 517; [Tuttle], "The German Chancellorship," 55; [Herbert Tuttle], "Reaction in Germany," 381.

16. Zimmern, "von Moltke," 689. "The Week," *Nation* (February 27, 1890), 169; "The Week," *Nation* (November 17, 1887), 385; "The Week," *Nation* (September 13, 1888), 203; "The Week," *Nation* (October 20, 1887), 303; [Michael Heilprin], "Does Germany Anticipate War?" *Nation* (December 9, 1886), 471.

17. "The Week," *Nation* (April 17, 1890), 207; "The Week," *Nation* (September 13, 1888), 203; [E. L. Godkin], "The New Wine in the Old German Bottles," *Nation* (February 20, 1890), 147.

18. [E. L. Godkin], "The Effect of the Kaiser's Death," *Nation* (March 15, 1888), 210; [Auguste Laugel], "French Interest in Bismarck's Retirement," *Nation* (April 17, 1890), 311; "The Week," *Nation* (March 27, 1890), 251; George Moritz Wahl, "Fürst Bismarck," *Harper's* 81 (June 1890), 5; Harold Frederic, "An Empire's Young Chief," *New York Times*, August 17, 1890, 112; "The Week," *Nation* (March 20, 1890), 232.

19. George E. Pond, "Russian America," *Galaxy* 4 (1867), 108; William L. Kingsley, "Nihilism in Russia," *NEYR* 37 (1878), 572.

20. "Table-Talk," *Appletons'* 6 (December 30, 1871), 760; "Notes," *Nation* (September 18, 1873), 194; Karl Blind, "The Traditional Policy of Russia," *AM* 22 (November 1868), 585; "The Truth about Russia," *Nation* (October 22, 1868), 326–327; [A. V. Dicey], "Bryce's 'Transcaucasia and Ararat'," *Nation* (November 22, 1877), 320. On changing opinion of Russia during these years, Norman E. Saul, *Concord & Conflict: The United States and Russia 1867–1914* (Lawrence, KS, 1996), 189–200.

21. G. P. Huropatnik, "Russians in the United States: Social, Cultural, and Scientific Contacts in the 1870s," in Norman E. Saul and Richard D. McKinzie, eds., *Russian-American Dialogue on Cultural Relations 1776–1914* (Columbia, MO, 1997), 129–165; "Epic Russia," *AM* 58 (November 1886), 705; [Herbert Tuttle], "Russia as Viewed by Liberals and Tories," *Nation* (April 29, 1880), 321; "A Vital Question; or,

What Is to Be Done?," *Nation* (July 22, 1886), 78; Emilio Castelar, "The Republican Movement in Europe," *Harper's* 45 (November 1872), 849; "Current American Literature," *NAR* 145 (1887), 217.

22. Frank D. Millet, "Campaigning with the Cossacks," *Harper's* 74 (1887), 235; Ralph Meeker, "Through the Caucasus," *Harper's* 74 (1887), 715; W. S. Nelson, "On the Borders of Czardom," *NEM* 6 (October 1888), 541; Henry Lansdell, "The Sons of the Steppe," *Harper's* 75 (1887), 580.

23. George Carey Eggleston "Some Phases of Russian Life," *Appletons'* 2 (1877), 369; Eggleston, "Russian Dissent, Heresy, and Schism," *Appletons'* 2 (1877), 461; [Dicey], "Bryce's 'Transcaucasia and Ararat'," 320.

24. W. R. S. Ralston, "Russian Popular Legends, Part II," *Appletons'* 1 (May 8, 1869), 176; George B. McClellan, "The War in the East," *NAR* (125), 36; "The Week," *Nation* (April 13, 1882), 305; "Notes," *Nation* (November 8, 1888), 377; George Alfred Townsend, *The New World Compared with the Old* (New York, 1870), 616.

25. "The Week," *Nation* (June 9, 1881), 399; [W. P. Garrison], "An English Resident in Russia," *Nation* (September 27, 1866), 247; "Notes," *Nation* (August 31, 1876), 136; Thomas W. Knox, "The Imperial family of Russia," *Scribner's* 3 (1872), 218; Edna Dean Proctor, "Moscow and Southern Russia," *Scribner's* 5 (1872), 684; Robert L. Stanton, "The Political Outlook in France," *PR* 2 (1878), 577; McClellan, "War in the East," 36; John Fiske, "The Races of the Danube," *AM* 39 (April 1877), 402. For a brief survey of American views of the Russian peasantry and aristocracy during these years, see David C. Engerman, *Modernization from the Other Shore: American Intellectuals and the Romance of Russian Development* (Cambridge, MA, 2003), 28–46.

26. [Dicey], "Bryce's 'Transcaucasia and Ararat'," 320; Karl Blind, "The Traditional Policy of Russia," *AM* 22 (November 1868), 586; [Michael Heilprin], "The First Year of Alexander III," *Nation* (March 23, 1882), 244; [Michael Heilprin], "Russia and the Russians—II," *Nation* (June 1, 1882), 467; Marion Wilcox, "Mr. Eugene Schuyler's 'Peter the Great'," *NEYR* 43 (1884), 804; Karl Blind, "Conspiracies in Russia, Part III," *Appletons'* 7 (October 1879), 354.

27. "Editor's Table," *Appletons'* 12 (August 8, 1874), 186; "The Russian Storm-Cloud," *Nation* (July 8, 1886), 42.

28. [E. L. Godkin], "The Secret of Nihilism," *Nation* (March 11, 1880), 190; [Michael Heilprin], "Russia and the Russians—III," *Nation* (October 11, 1883), 316; Karl Blind, "Conspiracies in Russia," *Appletons'* 7 (July 1879), 57; Henry E. Bourne, "The Russian Church and Russian Dissent," *NEYR* 48 (April 1888), 244; A Russian Nihilist, "The Empire of the Discontented," *NAR* 128 (1879), 176; Albert F. Heard, "Justice and Law in Russia," *Harper's* 76 (1888), 928; "The Week," *Nation* (April 24, 1879), 277.

29. [Michael Heilprin], "Underground Russia," *Nation* (August 9, 1883), 123; Fritz Cunliffe-Owen, "Russian Nihilism, Chapters I and II," *Appletons'* 8 (March 1880), 219–231; Albert F. Heard, "Russia of To-day," *Harper's* 74 (1887), 583; "The Week," *Nation* (March 17, 1881), 177; "Affairs in Russia," *Nation* (June 5, 1884), 482;

Blind, "Conspiracies in Russia, Part III," 342; "The Danger of Delaying Reforms," *Century* 28 (October 1884), 945.

30. "Penal Servitude in Siberia," *Appletons'* 10 (June 1881), 543–552; H. Sutherland Edwards, "The Romanoffs," *Harper's* 67 (1883), 192; Anna Lauren Dawes, "George Kennan," *Century* 36 (1888), 231; "America Is not Russia," *Century* 35 (1887), 484; "Notes," *Nation* (January 12, 1888), 31; "The Week," *Nation* (April 17, 1890), 207.

31. Letter from George Kennan, "Is the Siberian Exile System to Be at Once Abolished?" *Century* 36 (1888), 794; "The Week," *Nation* (May 1, 1879), 295; Karl Blind, "Conspiracies in Russia, Part II," *Appletons'* 7 (September 1879), 274; "Editor's Table," *Appletons'* 14 (August 21, 1875), 246; "Editor's Table," *Appletons'* 13 (March 27, 1875), 406.

32. "Editor's Table," *Appletons'* 13 (March 27, 1875), 406; "The Week," *Nation* (June 9, 1881), 399; [Michael Heilprin], "The First Year of Alexander II," *Nation* (March 23, 1882), 244; Edwards, "The Romanoffs," 201.

33. Review of *Russia under the Tsars, Harper's* 71 (1885), 480; [Michael Heilprin], "The Czar and His people," *Nation* (October 28, 1886), 345; George B. McClellan, "The War in the East," *NAR* (125), 36; [Henry James], "Wallace's Russia," *Nation* (March 15, 1877), 165.

34. Charles Gates, "Poem: Spain," *Harper's* 38 (1869), 318.

35. "Spain," *Galaxy* 6 (1868), 712; [E. L. Godkin], "Economic Results of the Spanish Revolution," *Nation* (March 25, 1869), 227; [E. L. Godkin], "The Spanish Revolution," *Nation* (February 20, 1873), 129; [E. L. Godkin], "Federalism in Spain," *Nation* (April 17, 1873), 264; "The Week," *Nation* (April 16, 1874), 246.

36. Philip Quilibet [G. E. Pond], "The New-Born Republic," *Galaxy* 15 (1873), 561; Lyman Abbott, "The Spanish Revolution," *Harper's* 40 (1870), 273; [Godkin], "The Spanish Revolution," 130.

37. George M. Towle, "Castelar," *Appletons'* 9 (March 8, 1873), 335; Alvey Adee, "Reminiscences of Castelar," *Century* 31 (1885), 792; "Editor's Table," *Appletons'* 10 (July 12, 1873), 57.

38. "The Week," *Nation* (July 3, 1873), 4; "The Week," *Nation* (August 20, 1874), 115; "The Week," *Nation* (July 24, 1873), 51; "The Week," *Nation* (January 28, 1875), 51.

39. "The Week," *Nation* (January 7, 1875), 3; "The Week," *Nation* (February 4, 1875), 71; "The Week," *Nation* (April 15, 1875), 251; John Hay, *Castilian Days* (Boston, 1882), 370.

40. "The Week," *Nation* (March 14, 1872), 163; [E. L. Godkin], "Garibaldi," *Nation* (June 8, 1882), 477; John E. Curran, "Mazzini and the Italian Revolution," *NEYR* 38 (July 1879), 507; "The Week," *Nation* (March 14, 1872), 163; "Editor's Table," *Appletons'* 4 (1878), 290; William R. Thayer, "The Makers of New Italy," *AM* 62 (November 1888), 663, 668.

41. H. D. Jenkins, "Following the King," *OM* 2 (May 1869), 454; [W. P. Garrison], "The International Exhibition," *Nation* (November 9, 1876), 283; "The Week,"

Nation (June 23, 1881), 435; Lyman Abbott, "The City of the Saints," *Harper's* 45 (July 1872), 169.

42. [E. L. Godkin], "National Debt in Europe," *Nation* (April 9, 1868), 284; John E. Curran, "Prince Metternich in the Napoleonic Times," *NEYR* 39 (May 1880), 352; E. Gryzanovski, "The Regeneration of Italy," *NAR* 113 (1871), 274, 315; [G. P. Marsh], "Female Education in Italy," *Nation* (July 5, 1866), 5; "The Week," *Nation* (February 6, 1868), 103.

43. Thomas Bailey Aldrich, "From Ponkapog to Pesth," *AM* 39 (1877), 20, 29; Henry James, "Italy Revisited," *AM* 41 (1878), 438; "Table-Talk," *Appletons'* 7 (March 9, 1872), 273; [Henry James] "The After-Season at Rome," *Nation* (June 12, 1873), 399.

44. "Spain," *Galaxy* 6 (1868), 712; [E. Gryzanowski], "The Italian Problem," *Nation* (July 7, 1870), 5–7; Emilio Castelar, "The Republican Movement in Europe," *Harper's* 45 (1872), 372; [E. J. James], "State Ownership of Railways in Italy," *Nation* (August 24, 1882), 150; [Rollo Ogden], "Italian Emigration," *Nation* (May 30, 1889), 440; Review of "L'Italie qu'on Voit," *Nation* (April 26, 1883), 369; [Jessie W. Mario], "The Scrutin de Liste in Italy," *Nation* (March 2, 1882), 181.

45. "The Temporal Power of the Papacy," *Nation* (August 25, 1870), 124; William R. Thayer, "The Makers of New Italy," *AM* 62 (November 1888), 668; [E. L. Godkin], "The Papal Question," *Nation* (December 8, 1870), 381; "The Week," *Nation* (September 19, 1889), 224; George D. Watrous, "Guelf and Ghibelline in Italy To-day," *NEYR* 45 (May 1886), 403; E. Gryzanowski, "The New Trials of the Roman Church," *NAR* 118 (1874), 295; "Papa and the Dogma," *Scribner's* 1 (1870), 107.

46. "The Week," *Nation* (December 5, 1867), 447; J. M. Macdonald, "The Temporal Power of the Pope," *PR* 43 (1871), 138; [E. L. Godkin], "The Papal Question," *Nation* (December 8, 1870), 381; "Editor's Table," *Appletons'* 15 (January 28, 1876), 149.

47. [E. L. Godkin], "Some Considerations for Protestant Controversialists," *Nation* (April 7, 1870), 219; [G. P. Marsh], "The Catholic Church and Modern Civilization," *Nation* (September 19, 1867), 230–231; "The Ecumenical Council," *Appletons'* 3 (March 12, 1870), 299; [E. L. Godkin], "The Pope and the Catholic Nations," *Nation* (November 7, 1867), 376; [E. Gryzanowski], "The Roman Moth and the Roman Candle," *Nation* (March 17, 1870), 168; [E. L. Godkin], "The Church and the World," *Nation* (July 23, 1868), 67; Rev. Keatidge, "The Last Ecumenical Council," *Appletons'* 2 (December 11, 1869), 532; "Editor's Table," *Appletons'* 14 (November 20, 1875), 662.

48. "The Church Militant," *Nation* (June 18, 1868), 486; [E. L. Godkin], "Pius the Ninth," *Nation* (February 14, 1878), 108; "The Week," *Nation* (July 23, 1885), 63; "The Week," *Nation* (January 12, 1888), 223; "Modern Catholicism," *Century* 27 (1883), 625.

49. Luigi Monti, "Italy and the Pope," *Scribner's* 16 (1878), 357; "The Alarm about the Schools," *Nation* (December 16, 1875), 384; [E. L. Godkin], "The Pope's Inter-

ference in Germany," *Nation* (February 17, 1887), 137; "The Week," *Nation* (January 7, 1875), 3; "The Week," *Nation* (January 3, 1867), 3.

50. "The Crisis in the Catholic Church," *Nation* (March 7, 1872), 148; J. B. Chase, "A Chapter in the Religious History of Italy," *NEYR* 41 (November 1882), 778–791; "Modern Catholicism," *Century* 27 (1883), 625; [E. L. Godkin], "The Oecumenical Council and the Protestants," *Nation* (December 2, 1869), 476.

51. Henry James, "Italy Revisited," *AM* 41 (1878), 439; "The Latin Nations," *Scribner's* 5 (1872), 761; William L. Kingsley, "Victor Emmanuel: the First King of Italy," *NEYR* 37 (1878), 269; "Ten Years in Rome," *Galaxy* 9 (1870), 204; [Jessie W. Mario], "Italian Industrial Exposition," *Nation* (May 26, 1881), 369; E. Gryzanovski, "The Regeneration of Italy," *NAR* 113 (1871), 320–321.

52. "The Unifiers of Italy," *Nation* (June 26, 1890), 512.

53. [E. L. Godkin], "National Debt in Europe," *Nation* (April 9, 1868), 284; "The Situation in Bohemia," *Nation* (July 19, 1866), 51; Clemens Petersen, "A Visit to Vienna," *Galaxy* 16 (1873), 149; John Fiske, "The Races of the Danube," *AM* 39 (April 1877), 402.

54. Robert L. Stanton, "The Political Outlook in France," *PR* 2 (1878), 546, 576. "Table-Talk," *Appletons'* 6 (December 9, 1871), 665; [Michael Heilprin], "The Situation in Austria-Hungary," *Nation* (September 4, 1879), 153; [Michael Heilprin], "Croatia versus Hungary," *Nation* (September 6, 1883), 203; "The Week," *Nation* (September 22, 1887), 223; [Gustav Pollak], "Austrian Perplexities," *Nation* (September 11, 1890), 206.

55. George M. Towle, "Mementos of Mycenae," *Appletons'* 4 (1878), 152; Thomas D. Seymour, "Life and Travel in Modern Greece," *Scribner's* 4 (1888), 46; [L. R. Packard], "The Social State of Greece," *Nation* (February 4, 1869), 89; [E. L. Godkin], "The Resurrection of Greece," *Nation* (July 8, 1880), 25; "Editor's Table," *Appletons'* 12 (August 29, 1874), 282; "The Week," *Nation* (April 28, 1870), 266; "The Week," *Nation* (February 4, 1869), 83; "The Week," *Nation* (January 7, 1869), 2.

56. [A. V. Dicey], "Thirty Years of European History," *Nation* (October 23, 1890), 327; "Concerning Privilege," *Harper's* 79 (1889), 320.

57. George Makepeace Towle, "Spread of the Democratic Idea," *NAR* 150 (1890), 271; "Indications of Progress," *Scribner's* 15 (1877), 225.

58. "The Editor's Study," *Harper's* 76 (1888), 481; Edward Berwick, "The Great Want of All Civilized Nations," *OM* 14 (July 1889), 76.

5. The One and the Many: Race, Culture, and Civilization

1. Walt Whitman, "Democracy," *Galaxy* 4 (1867), 923; [Anonymous], "The Railroad System," *NAR* 104 (1867), 487; G. M. Grant, "Time-Reckoning for the Twentieth Century," *Century* 33 (November 1886), 156. On Whitman's cosmopolitanism, see Martin Thompson Buinicki, Jr., "Negotiating Copyright: Authorship and the Discourse of Literary Property Rights in Nineteenth-Century America," Ph.D. dissertation, University of Iowa, 2003, 169–174.

Had it fit within the time frame of this study, I would have inserted into the text the following marvelous extract. In 1851, an article in the *NEYR* described commerce as "creating intimate acquaintanceship and associated interests between people of the most diverse habits, languages, laws, and customs; which in short leads all to recognize in all others of whatever kindred, tribe or tongue, not anthropophagi, nor troglodytes, nor cyclops, nor pigmies, as the ancients did, but human beings, veritable men, with senses, dimensions, affections, passions like their own." "Physical Science and the Useful Arts in Their Relation to Christian Civilization," *NEYR* 9 (November 1851), 494.

2. [John Weiss], "A Letter about England," *AM* 15 (1865), 642; George Mooar, "Is Assimilation a Spent Force?" *OM* 16 (August 1890), 157; George Cary Eggleston, "Is the World Overcrowded?" *Appletons'* 14 (October 23, 1875), 531. According to Paul Seabright, in *The Company of Strangers: A Natural History of Economic Life* (Princeton, NJ, 2004), 234, the horizontal process of economic exchange depended on the "differences that make for a common interest among strangers."

3. George Fredrickson, *Racism: A Short History* (Princeton, NJ, 2002), 11; "Table Talk: Differences in Race," *Appletons'* 4 (December 24, 1870), 770. On the tension between the religious and secular bases of American political culture, see John Patrick Diggins, *The Lost Soul of American Politics: Virtue, Self-Interest, and the Foundations of Liberalism* (Chicago, 1986).

4. Henry N. Day, "The Chinese Migration," *NEYR* 29 (January 1870), 18; M. E. Strieby, "Caste in America," *AmMiss* 37 (December 1883), 376; Tayler Lewis, "The One Human race," *Scribner's* 3 (April 1872), 736; "Agassiz on Provinces of Creation, and the Unity of the Race," *PR* 41 (1869), 5; "Literary Notes: Christ in Modern Life," *Appletons'* 7 (May 11, 1872), 527. Historically, the conflict between science and religion has been the exception rather than the rule. The view of Stopford Brooke, a well-placed British cleric, who argued that Christ's ideas did not "contradict the ideas which direct scientific research, nor those which have been generalized from the results of that research," is much more representative of thoughtful religious opinion. See his *Christ in Modern Life* (London, 1872), iii.

5. Thomas F. Gossett, *Race: The History of an Idea in America* (Dallas, 1963), 244; Louis A. Cuddy and Clair M. Roche, *Evolution and Eugenics in American Literature and Culture, 1880–1940: Essays on Ideological Conflict and Complicity* (Lewisburg, PA, 2003), 18; Akira Iriye, *Cultural Internationalism and World Order* (Baltimore, MD, 1997), 43. For a particularly crude view, see Glenn C. Altschuler, *Race, Ethnicity, and Class in American Social Thought, 1865–1919* (Arlington Heights, IL, 1982), 2–3. Audrey Smedley, *Race in North America: Origin and Evolution of a Worldview* (Boulder, CO, 1993), 270–272, quotes and agrees with Mark Haller's view in *Eugenics: Hereditarian Attitudes in American Thought* that "between 1870 and 1900 educated Americans took giant strides toward a fairly wide acceptance of varying forms and degrees of racism." Even Myrdal, in *An American Dilemma: The Negro Problem and American Democracy,* (New York, 1944), 90, assumes the triumph of scientific racism.

6. Augustus Field Beard, *A Crusade of Brotherhood: A History of the American Missionary Association* (New York, 1972), 226–227; Roger Daniels and Harry H. L. Kitano, *American Racism: Exploration of the Nature of Prejudice* (Englewood Cliffs, NJ, 1970), 2.

7. Charles A. Gardiner, "The Future of the Negro," *NAR* 139 (1884), 80. Peter J. Bowler, *The Invention of Progress* (Cambridge, MA, 1989), 106–128, provides a brief summary of racialist trends in science during this period, while Stephen Jay Gould, *The Mismeasure of Man* (New York, 1996), 62–141, discusses the allure of craniometry. Reginald Horsman, *Race and Manifest Destiny: The Origins of American Racial Anglo-Saxonism* (Cambridge, MA, 1981), 156, argues that "by 1850 the natural inequality of the races was a scientific fact which was published widely." But once one gets past the obligatory references to Samuel Morton and Josiah Nott (pre-Civil War writers) and Louis Agassiz (a visceral racist), things get pretty thin, and their influence is presumed to have lasted for generations. See, e.g., Smedley, *Race in North America*, 236–242. However, early in our period, one writer chastises science—"the European theory of a single race"—for refusing to accept the common-sense conclusion that different races constituted different species. See "The American Races," *The Old Guard* 3 (March 1865), 131.

8. [F. V. Greene], "Turkish Life in War Time," *Nation* (May 12, 1881), 338; "The Week," *Nation* (January 10, 1867), 32; Chauncey Wright, "The Limits of Natural Selection," *NAR* 111 (1870), 282; "The Record," *Appletons' Journal* 12 (August 1, 1874), 160; [Kenyon Cox], "Art No Luxury," *Nation* (July 18, 1889), 46; "The Week," *Nation* (October 25, 1866), 323; "Thomson's Travels in Morocco," *Nation* (September 12, 1889), 216; Junius Henry Browne, "Types of American Beauty," *Galaxy* 11 (1871), 108; [Sir Leslie Stephen], "England," *Nation* (November 22, 1866), 414; "Race," *Appletons'* 5 (May 27, 1871), 625; John Fiske, "The Progress from Brute to Man," *NAR* 117 (1873), 255. The Oxford English Dictionary still provides as its lead definition: "A group of persons, animals, or plants, connected by common descent or origin." "The Anglican race" was a usage of Francis Lieber. See his *On Civil Liberty and Self-Government*, 3rd ed., revised, ed. Theodore D. Woolsey (Philadelphia, 1877), 295–296. Bradford Perkins, *The Great Rapprochement: England and the United States, 1895–1914* (New York, 1968), 79, points out the inconsistencies in the use of Anglo-Saxonism. On the various meanings of race, see Elazar Barkan, *The Retreat of Scientific Racism: Changing Concepts of Race in Britain and the United States between the World Wars* (Cambridge, UK, 1993), 2.

9. As quoted in James Surowiecki, *The Wisdom of Crowds* (New York, 2005), 169; Robert Merton, "The Matthew Effect in Science," *Science: New Series 129:* 3810 (January 1968), 59, for defining a scientific truth as something that is "a socially shared and socially validated body of knowledge"; Thomas Kuhn, *The Structure of Scientific Revolutions* (Chicago, 1962); Michael Banton, *Racial Consciousness* (London, 1988), 21; Franz Boas, Review of William Z. Ripley's *The Races of Europe* in *Race Language and Culture* (Chicago, 1940), 156. For an accurate characterization

of drawing implications from brain size as "mere inference," see Lillie Devereux Blake, "Dr. Hammond's Estimate of Women," *NAR* 137 (November 1883), 497.

10. "Topinard's Anthropology," *NAR* 126 (May 1878), 553; Stocking, *Race, Culture, and Evolution: Essays in the History of Anthropology* (New York, 1968), 165; "Essays on the Progress of Nations," *Nation* (February 11, 1869), 115. For an extreme example of environmentalism, see George M. Beard, "The Physical Future of the American People," *AM* 43 (June 1879), 719.

11. Ernest Renan, "What Is a Nation?" in Ernest Renan, *The Poetry of the Celtic Races, and Other Studies*, trans William G. Hutchison (Port Washington, NY, 1970), 74–75; Goldwin Smith, "The Greatness of the Romans," *The living Age* (June 15, 1878), 644; Ivan Hannaford, *Race: the History of an Idea in the West* (Washington, DC, 1996), 303. The assertion of a "scientific consensus" as found in Cathy Boeckmann, *A Question of Character: Scientific Racism and the Genres of American Fiction, 1892–1912* (Tuscaloosa, AL, 2000), 31, is quite common and thrown around rather too incautiously. Whether scientific racism made inroads after 1890 is, strictly speaking, not the concern of this book, but I would suggest the need to be careful in generalizing about this issue. If such a consensus did indeed exist, one wonders how opinions like the following, an example from the 1911 *Encyclopedia Brittanica* of what the sociologist E. A. Ross called the "equality fallacy," could be defended: "About the middle of the 19th century Dr Pritchard declared that many people debated whether it might not be permissible for the Australian settlers to shoot the natives as food for their dogs; some of the disputants arguing that savages were without the pale of human brotherhood. To-day the thesis that all mankind are one brotherhood needs no defence. The most primitive of existing aborigines are regarded merely as brethren who, through some defect or neglect of opportunity, have lagged behind in the race." See Hugh Chisholm, "Civilization," *Encyclopedia Brittanica*, (1911 edition), 408. At the same time, the entry for "Negro," written by Thomas Athol Joyce, reads as follows: "The mental constitution of the negro is very similar to that of a child, normally good-natured and cheerful, but subject to sudden fits of emotion and passion during which he is capable of performing acts of singular atrocity, impressionable, vain, but often exhibiting in the capacity of servant a doglike fidelity which has stood the supreme test." Meanwhile, the article on "Anthropology," written by E. B. Tylor (whose faculties were reportedly in decline), stated that "On the whole, it may be asserted that the doctrine of the unity of mankind stands on a firmer basis than in previous ages." On the need for caution in discussions of racism in the scientific climate of Victorian Britain, see Kenan Malik, *The Meaning of Race: Race, History and Culture in Western Society* (New York, 1996), 89–90.

12. G. Frederick Wright, "Uncertainties of Science," *OM* 2 (August 1883), 183; Josiah Royce, "The Freedom of Teaching," *OM* 2 (September 1883), 236; Richard Yeo, *Defining Science: William Whewell, Natural Knowledge, and Public Debate in Early Victorian Britain* (New York, 1993); Laura Snyder, *Reforming Philosophy: A Victorian Debate on Science and Society* (Chicago, 2006), esp. 33–155. On science as

organized skepticism, see Robert K. Merton, *The Sociology of Science* (Chicago, 1973), 277–278.

In some respects, the attitude toward racial science was not unlike our contemporary confusion and dissatisfaction with the constantly revised research findings about diet, in which the continual overturning of orthodoxies has bred public skepticism. The sense of frustration that is evident in the question asked by *Appletons'*—"Will any thing in the matters of diet or medicine ever become settled?"—has a distinctly contemporary ring to it. *The Nation* expressed a similar sense of confusion when trying to assess recommendations about physical health: "if we go behind the health books to the sources from which the authors extract their conclusions, we shall find that almost the only certain and unassailable rule of hygiene, which will bear universal application, is that pure air is good for the human animal, and that the more of it he has the better. All else is doubtful and disputed." "Books about Health," *Nation* (July 13, 1882), 271.

13. Robert G. Eccles, "The Relativity of Knowledge," in *Sociology: Popular Lectures and Discussions before the Brooklyn Ethical Association* (Boston, 1890); "The Editor's Study," *Harper's* 81 (1890), 966; "Lea's Superstition and Force," *NAR* 103 (1866), 594.

14. John C. Burnham, *How Superstition Won and Science Lost: Popularizing Science and Health in the United States* (New Brunswick, NJ, 1987), 151–152; Lewis Menand, *The Metaphysical Club* (New York, 2001), 144–145; [William James], "The Progress of Anthropology," *Nation* (February 6, 1868), 113. On the relationship between science and culture in Victorian England, see Douglas A. Lorimer, "Science and the Secularization of Victorian Images of Race," in Bernard Lightman, ed., *Victorian Science in Context* (Chicago, 1997), 212–235.

15. Charles Darwin, *The Descent of Man, and Selection in Relation to Sex* (London, 1871), 235. "Darwinism and Atheism," *M&B* 11 (May 1879), 110. Scholars disagree on what Darwin meant in the *Descent of Man*. For the argument that Darwin used race in this work as a way of providing a graded connection between man and other species, see Nancy Stepan, *The Idea of Race in Science: Great Britain, 1800–1960* (Hamden, CT, 1982), 47–66. Racial hierarchy also features prominently in Cuddy and Roche, *Evolution and Eugenics in American Literature and Culture*, 19. The thesis that Darwin was a racist and the first social Darwinist is developed in Edward S. Rayner, "Confusion and Cohesion in Emerging Sciences: Darwin, Wallace, and Social Darwinism," Ph.D. dissertation, University of Massachusetts, Amherst, September 1996. Adam Gopnik, *Angels and Ages: A Short Book About Darwin, Lincoln, and Modern Life* (New York, 2009), 155, dismisses this accusation as "simple misreading." For the nonracist implications of Darwinian evolution on the thought of Charles Loring Brace, see Mike Hawkins, *Social Darwinism in European and American Thought 1860–1945: Nature as Model and Nature as Threat* (New York, 1997), 61–64.

16. Stocking, *Race, Culture, and Evolution*, 74–81; Darwin, *The Descent of Man*, 184, 216, 226; Elazar Barkan, "Race and the Social Sciences," in Theodore M. Porter

and Dorothy Ross, eds., *Cambridge History of Science,* vol. 7, *The Modern Social Sciences* (New York, 2003), 697. However, as many authors have pointed out, the equality implied in a monogenetic view and the inegalitarianism suggested by a polygenetic stance were not necessarily borne out by a body of scientific opinion that was much more complex. Also, biological anthropologists today know that at various times there were several hominid species in existence.

17. Darwin, *The Descent of Man, 2ⁿᵈ ed.* (London, 1882), v; Chauncey Wright, "The Genesis of Species," *NAR* 113 (1871), 65. For a supporting interpretation, see Peter J. Richerson and Robert Boyd, *Not by Genes Alone: How Culture Transformed Human Evolution* (Chicago, 2005). But even if one conceded that modern men had larger brains than primordial savages, *The M&B* 10 (September 1878), 206, citing the Parisian craniologist Paul Broca no less, noted that the modern brain was "subjected to innumerable unconscious influences of education, which render it in some sense incommensurable with the brain of these yet half-brute creatures."

18. For the tangled meanings of race and culture, see George W. Stocking, Jr., *Victorian Anthropology* (New York: Free Press, 1987), 64, 142–143, 235. See Peter J. Bowler, *The Non-Darwinian Revolution: Reinterpreting a Historical Myth* (Baltimore, MD, 1988) for the extended argument that other influential strains of evolutionism operated independently of Darwinism.

19. R. W. Raymond, "National Characteristics," *OM* 3 (September 1869), 253; Chauncey Wright, "The Limits of Natural Selection," *NAR* 111 (1870), 290; Fiske, "The Progress from Brute to Man," 258–259; Fiske, *Outlines of Cosmic Philosophy,* II, (Boston, 1875), 311; Elvin Hatch, *Theories of Man & Culture* (New York, 1973), 32. Fiske elaborates on the importance of sociocultural explanations of progress in his *Outline of Cosmic Philosophy,* III, 281–329. On p. 311, he argues that the gulf between civilized humans and "the lowest contemporary races of humanity was for the most part established during an epoch at the very beginning of which we were zoologically the same that we are now." Elsewhere (II: 355–357), he expands on the Burkean nature of cultural change. E. Janet Browne, *Charles Darwin: The Power of Place* (New York, 2002), 253–254 briefly discusses the views of Wallace and Darwin on the respective places of biological and cultural evolution.

20. As *The Nation* acknowledged in 1884, the unity of the human race was "still a disputed point, and while, individually, we are disposed to accept it, yet we must in justice admit that there is a large and influential school of anthropologists who are not of this way of thinking." See "Indian Myths," *Nation* (September 11, 1884), 227.

21. "Notes," *Nation* (July 10, 1873), 24; E. L. Youmans, "The Civilization of Uses," *Appletons'* 2 (November 13, 1869), 409; E. L. Youmans, "Character of Herbert Spencer," *Appletons'* 2 (October 23, 1869), 310; "Law of Evolution," *Appletons'* 5 (June 17, 1871), 718; E. L. Youmans, "Spencer's Evolution Philosophy," *NAR* 129 (1879), 402. On Youmans's career, see Charles M. Haar, "E. L. Youmans: A Chapter in the Diffusion of Science in America," *Journal of the History of Ideas* 9:2 (April

1948), 193–213; Robert Young, "The Historiographic and Ideological Contexts of the Nineteenth-Century Debate about Man's Place in Nature," in Mikuláš Teich and Robert Young, eds., *Changing Perspectives in the History of Science: Essays in Honor of Joseph Needham* (Dordrecht, 1973), 348. For Youmans's attempts to internationalize popular science, see Andreas Daum, " 'The Next Great Task of Civilization': International Exchange in Science. The German-American Case, 1850–1900," in Martin H. Geyer and Johannes Paulmann, *The Mechanics of Internationalism: Culture, Society, and Politics from the 1840s to the First World War* (New York, 2001), 285–320. On Spencer, Darwinism, Victorian anthropology, and the importance of culture, see Mark Francis, *Herbert Spencer and the Invention of Modern Life* (Ithaca, NY, 2007), 295–301. Spencer has since become very much *passé*, but the same may not be true of his attempt to synthesize all types of knowledge.

22. Francis, *Herbert Spencer*, 322; "Herbert Spencer in America," *Century* 24 (1881), 789; Isaac L. Rice, "Herbert Spencer's Facts and Inferences," *NAR* 136 (1883), 557–567.

23. James, "The Progress of Anthropology," 113; Gossett, *Race*, 83.

24. Donald K. Grayson, *The Establishment of Human Antiquity* (New York, 1983), 210–220; "Editor's Literary Record," *Harper's* 49 (1874), 590; Review of E. B. Tylor's *Primitive Culture*, *NAR* 114 (1872), 231; Review of Gobineau's *Nouvelles Asiatiques*, *NAR* 125 (1876), 183; [F. W. Putnam], "The Stone Age of Great Britain," *Nation* (January 16, 1873), 44.

25. "Table-Talk," *Appletons'* 5 (June 17, 1871), 715; John Fiske, "The Primeval Ghost-World," *AM* 30 (November 1872), 584; Review of Tylor's *Primitive Culture*, 227; William Bender et al., "Darwinism and Christianity," *NEYR* 43 (1884), 181; E. B. Tylor, "On the Survival of Savage Thought in Modern Civilization," *Appletons'* 1 (July 31, 1869), 568; "Tylor's *Primitive Culture*" *AM* 34 (July 1874), 117. "The higher culture may be a further development of the lower, while the lower culture cannot be a degradation from the higher," said one review. See "Science," *AM* 29 (February 1872), 252.

26. Edward B. Tylor, *Researches into the Early History of Mankind* (New York, 1878), 372; [Garrick Mallery], "Army Sacrifices," *Nation* (May 1, 1879), 306; Tylor, *Primitive Culture* (New York, 1889), 6, 7. For a favorable review by the Swiss-American archaeologist A. F. Bandelier, see *Nation* (March 6, 1879), 170; Tylor, *Anthropology: An Introduction to the Study of Man and Civilization* (New York, 1881), 341; J. W. Burrow, *Evolution and Society: A Study in Victorian Social Theory* (Cambridge, UK, 1966), 248–249.

27. "Morgan's Ancient Society," *AM* 40 (September 1877), 375; Jerry D. Moore, *Visions of Culture* (Walnut Creek, CA, 1997), 35. For a racialist slant on proto-anthropologists like Brinton, Powell, Putnam, and Morgan, see Lee D. Baker, *From Savage to Negro: Anthropology and the Construction of Race, 1896–1954* (Berkeley, CA, 1998), 26–53. Morgan's belief in the universality of human potential is acknowledged by R. Carl Resek, *Lewis Henry Morgan: American Scholar* (Chicago, 1960),

137, 156. Adam Kuper, *The Invention of Primitive Society: Transformations of an Illusion* (London, 1988), 75 stresses the connection between British evolutionists and the relatively egalitarian German philologist Max Müller.

28. [A. V. Dicey], "Jowett's Thucydides—II," *Nation* (January 12, 1882), 40; "Notes," *Nation* (May 22, 1890), 415; Prof. J. W. Sewall, "Primitive Culture," *NEYR* 33 (1874), 224; "Editor's Study," *Harper's* 80 (1890), 966; G. Stanley Hall, "New Departures in Education," *NAR* 140 (1885), 148.

29. Tylor, *Primitive Culture*, 447; Stephen G. Alter, *Darwinism and the Linguistic Image: Language, Race and Natural Theology in the Nineteenth Century* (Baltimore, MD, 1999), 148; John Fiske, "The Laws of History," *NAR* 109 (1869), 230; Frederic H. Hedge, "The Method of History," *NAR* 111 (1870), 317; "Sayings and Doings at Home and Abroad," *Appletons'* 10 (July 12, 1873), 61. Maurice Olender, *The Languages of Paradise: Race, Religion, and Philology in the Nineteenth Century* (Cambridge, MA, 1992), 1–12.

30. Philip Quilibet, "International Science," *Galaxy* 14 (1872), 856; Edward A. Freeman, "The Unity of History," *Appletons'* 8 (August 17, 1872), 179; W. E. Gladstone, "Universitas Hominum; or, The Unity of History," *NAR* 145 (1887), 592.

31. "Editor's Literary Record," *Harper's* 42 (February 1871), 462; [A. V. Dicey], "Maine's Early History of Institutions," *Nation* (April 1, 1875), 225; "W. E. H. Lecky, Imagination in the Progress of Morals," *Appletons'* 1 (May 8, 1869), 183 "Editor's Table," *Appletons'* 93 (June 28, 1873), 861; [T. R. Lounsbury], "Taine's English Literature," *Nation* (January 4, 1872), 11. For Taine's emphasis on "blood," see Ivan Hannaford, *Race: The History of an Idea in the West* (Baltimore, MD, 1996), 250. For Maine's view of "race" as a matter of cultural development, see the introduction in Alan Diamond, ed., *The Victorian Achievement of Sir Henry Maine* (Cambridge, UK, 1991), 6.

32. Address of Rev. A. H. Bradford, *AmMiss* 44 (December 1890), 431; "The Human Race," *Nation* (November 28, 1872), 354; [A. V. Dicey], "Jowett's Thucydides—II," *Nation* (January 12, 1882), 40; "The Negro Race in Central Africa," *Nation* (October 17, 1889), 315. *Appletons'* agreed with Quatrefage's conclusions: "The argument for the unity of the human species (the author, it may be remarked, draws a radical line between race and species) is strong if not conclusive." See "Books of the Day," *Appletons'* 7 (October 1879), 383. On the *Popular Science Monthly*, see Charles R. Wilson, "Attitudes toward the American Indian as Expressed in Selected American Magazines, 1865–1900," M.A. thesis, University of Texas at El Paso, 1972.

33. "The Editor's Study," *Harper's* 81 (1890), 641; "A Japanese Boy," *NEYR* 52 (February 1990), 167; George W. Cable, "The Freedmen's Case in Equity," *Century* 29 (1884), 418; James Bryce, "England and Ireland," *Century* 26 (June 1883), 250. Douglas A. Lorimer, "Science and the Secularization of Victorian Images of Race," in Bernard Lightman, ed., *Victorian Science in Context* (Chicago, 1997), 215, suggests that two of the chief British racial determinists may have had far more readers in the late twentieth century than they did in the nineteenth.

34. R. W. Raymond, "National Characteristics," *OM* 3 (September 1869), 254; Tilden Edelstein, *Strange Enthusiasm: A Life of Thomas Wentworth Higginson* (New Haven, CT, 1968), 372; James Parton, "Antipathy to the Negro," *NAR* 127 (November–December 1878), 487; Nathaniel S. Shaler, "Race Prejudices," *AM* 58 (October 1886), 513. "Race," *Appletons'* 5 (May 27, 1871), 626; "Topics of the Time," *Scribner's* 2 (1871), 93; Prof. Lewis O. Brastow, "Christian Anthropology and Philanthropy," *NEYR* 45 (February 1886), 125; Fiske, "The Progress from Brute to Man," 274. For anthropologist Daniel G. Brinton's inconsistencies, see Thomas C. Patterson, *A Social History of Anthropology in the United States* (Berg, 2001), 43.

35. "The Savage Races," *Appletons'* 4 (1870), 121; [Horatio Hale], "The Negro Race in Central Africa," *Nation* (October 17, 1889), 315; "Notes: Critique of Nathaniel Shaler's Views," *Nation* (October 30, 1884), 378.

36. M. Howland, "Social Transformations," *Appletons'* 10 (July 12, 1873), 51.

37. John Manning, "The Maories," *OM* 7 (July 1881), 48.

38. Despite repeated efforts by anthropologists and many biologists to declare its death, the idea of cultural evolution not only survived but made a dramatic comeback by the close of the twentieth century. In an inversion of the Victorian-era tendency to subordinate Darwinism within a larger evolutionary context, recent thought has given pride of place to Darwinian adaptation through natural selection in the form of a theory of "dual inheritance" or "coevolution" in which selection proceeds along multiple tracks laid by biological and cultural processes. The chief inspiration for this move was Richard Dawkins's idea of "memes," originally proposed in *The Selfish Gene* (New York, 1976), as nongenetic replicators, the cultural component of a "Universal Darwinism" in which biological and cultural evolution are parts of a larger process of adaptation. Although the extent to which memes act independently of and sometimes contrary to genes as replicators is murky, nevertheless the emphasis on "cultural selection" as an aspect of an encompassing process of natural selection is clear. For instance, Daniel Dennett, in *Darwin's Dangerous Idea* (New York, 1995), 345, argues that cultural change is "not just a process that can be metaphorically described in these evolutionary idioms, but a phenomenon that obeys the laws of natural selection quite precisely." See also his *Consciousness Explained* (Boston, 1991), 199–210. Marion Blute argues that "the fundamental evolutionary concepts of transmission, innovation, selection, drift, migration, and so on are as applicable to a cultural as they are to a genetic subject matter"; see Blute, "Biologists on Sociocultural Evolution: A Critical Analysis," *Sociological Theory* 5:2 (Autumn 1987), 193. See also William H. Durham, "Advances in Evolutionary Culture Theory," *Annual Review of Anthropology* 19 (1990), 187–210. Peter J. Richerson and Robert Boyd, *Not by Genes Alone: How Culture Transformed Human Evolution* (Chicago, 2005), also link genetic and cultural evolution, as do Luigi Luca Cavalli Sforza and Marcus Feldman, *Cultural Transmission and Evolution: A Quantitative Approach* (Princeton, NJ, 1981). A complex evolutionary argument that makes room for the interaction of multiple elements, including Lamarckian learning, is made by

Eva Jablonka and Marion J. Lamb, *Evolution in Four Dimensions: Genetic, Epigenetic, Behavioral, and Symbolic Variation in the History of Life* (Cambridge, MA, 2005). For a survey of the rise, decline, and revival of cultural evolutionism, but without a tight connection to Darwinian biology, see Robert L. Carneiro, *Evolutionism in Cultural Anthropology* (Boulder, CO, 2003).

The matter is far from settled, however. For a more skeptical view that sees cultural evolution as a metaphor that cannot hope to match the depth and complexity offered by historical explanation, see Joseph Fracchia and R. C. Lewontin, "Does Culture Evolve?" *History and Theory* 38:4 Theme Issue 38: *The Return of Science: Evolutionary Ideas and History* (December 1999), 52–78, an essay that includes helpful bibliographical footnotes. See also the exchange between these two skeptics and W.G. Runciman in "Forum: Does Culture Evolve?" *History and Theory* 44 (February 2005), 1–41. Stephen Jay Gould has attacked a "Darwinian fundamentalism" that, in his view, Darwin himself would not have endorsed, a position that Niles Eldredge in *Reinventing Darwin: The Great Debate at the High Table of Evolutionary Theory* (New York, 1995) has referred to critically as "ultra-Darwinism." Gould's views are succinctly expressed in two essays in *The New York Review of Book,* "Darwinian Fundamentalism," *NYR* (June 12, 1997), 34–37, and "The Pleasures of Pluralism," *NYR* (June 26, 1997), 47–52, in which Gould maintains that "cultural change unfolds virtually in antithesis to Darwinian requirements." To be fair, there is an acknowledged element of doubt even in the mind of the theory's celebrated originator. See Dawkins, *The Extended Phenotype: The Gene as the Unit of Selection* (Oxford, 1982), 109–112. In addition, some researchers consider the neo-Darwinian synthesis, with its sharp separation of genes and culture, as the fundamentalist view. See Oren Harmon's review of Jablonka and Lamb, "The Evolution of Evolution," *The New Republic,* September 4, 2006, 27–33.

39. Carl Degler, *In Search of Human Nature: The Decline and Revival of Darwinism in American Thought* (New York, 1991), 1–12; "Christianity and Commerce," *Century* 23 (1881), 948; Chauncey Wright, "The Genesis of Species," *NAR* 113 (1871), 74. The long-standing affinity between social Darwinism and economics has been revived by Tyler Cowen, *Creative Destruction: How Globalization Is Changing the World's Cultures* (Princeton, NJ, 2002), who employs the "gains from trade" model as a way of understanding cultural exchange. From my perspective, this is a better way of looking at intercultural relations than cultural evolution, but, just as economics does not explain everything, the gains from trade metaphor misses a lot.

40. "Editor's Literary Record," *Harper's* 49 (1874), 590; George Ripley, "Darwinism," *Appletons'* 5 (March 25, 1871), 351; George Cary Eggleston, "Is the World Overcrowded?" *Appletons'* 14 (October 23, 1875), 531; Peter T. Austen, "Our Struggle for Existence," *NAR* 149 (1889), 250. The first reference to social Darwinism in the *New York Times* appears only in the 1920s. For other major newspapers with digitized historical databases, references begin to appear only in the 1950s and

1960s. Godfrey Hodgson, "Social Darwinism in Anglophone Academic Journals: A Contribution to the History of the Term," *Journal of Historical Sociology* 17 (December 2004), 428–463, dates academic usage to the 1940s.

41. William Hosea Ballou, "The Future American," *NAR* 145 (1887), 286, 289; E. W. Gilliam, "The African Problem," *NAR* 139 (1884), 425; T. T. Munger, "Immigration by Passport," *Century* 35 (1887), 792; "Table-Talk: Note on Race-Mixing," *Appletons'* 5 (January 14, 1871), 55. In his book, *Among the Guerrillas* (New York, 1866), 281–282, Edmund Kirke had predicted that, by current rates of miscegenation, "it will take six hundred years to reduce the remainder to the same tawny yellow, and eight hundred more years to give them the florid cuticle of the Anglo-Saxon."

42. "Indian Blood," *Nation* (August 17, 1865), 198; [E. L. Godkin], "The Intermarriage Bugbear," *Nation* (December 12, 1867), 482; "The Mixed Human Races," *Appletons'* 4 (December 3, 1870), 677; J. W. Powell, "From Savagery to Barbarism: Annual Address of the President," *Transactions of the Anthropological Society of Washington* 3 (1885), 173; N. C. Meeker, "Commerce and Human Progress," *Appletons'* 2–25 (September 18, 1869), 150; Canon George Rawlinson, "The Duties of Higher towards Lower Races in a Mixed Community," *PR* 2 (1878), 837. See Brian W. Dippie, *The Vanishing American: White Attitudes and Indian Policy* (Middletown, CT, 1982), 248–250 for the broader discussion of white–Indian miscegenation.

43. Ballou, "The Future American," 290; Rawlinson, "The Duties of Higher towards Lower Races in a Mixed Community," 846; A. J. Lawson, "National and Statistical: Money Value of Immigration," *Appletons'* 11 (January 3, 1874), 30; John C. Fleming, "Are We Anglo-Saxons?" *NAR* 153 (1891), 253.

44. George Mooar, "Is Assimilation a Spent Force?" *OM* 16 (August 1890), 158; J. P. Thompson, "How to Build a Nation," *NEYR* 28 (January 1869), 27; "Notes," *Nation* (February 26, 1885), 181.

45. "The Editor's Drawer," *Harper's* 77 (1888), 319; Mooar, "Is Assimilation a Spent Force?" 162; J. D. Phelan, "The Bent of International Intercourse," *OM* 6 (August 1885), 163. Horatio Seymour, "The Government of the United States," *NAR* 127, (1878), 375. Seymour would later concede the right of the American people to prohibit entirely the immigration of Chinese.

46. "The Editor's Easy Chair," *Harper's* 78 (1889), 660; Mooar, "Is Assimilation a Spent Force?" 158; Rev. E. S. Atwood, "Closing Words," *AmMiss* 38 (1884), 412; Rev. C. P. Osborne, "The Last Man," *AmMiss* 35 (1881), 197; Horace Buestead, "The Mutual Helpfulness of the Races as an Element in Missionary Work," *AmMiss* 39 (1885), 108; Address of Rev. A. H. Bradford," *AmMiss* 44 (December 1890), 435.

47. "The Cradle of the Human Race," *AM* 41 (February 1878), 157; Charles Gayarre, "The Southern Question," *NAR* 125 (November 1877), 479; [William James], "Herbert Spencer's Data on Ethics," *Nation* (September 11, 1879), 178; "Editor's Study," *Harper's* 80 (May 1890), 966; "Polynesian and Aryan," *Nation* (August 26, 1886), 181; John S. Hittell, "The Doom of the Californian Aborigines," *OM* 11 (June 1888), 610; Darwin, *Descent of Man.* See also Stuart C. Gilman, "Political Theory

and Degeneration," in J. Edward Chamberlin and Sander L. Gilman, eds., *Degenera-tion: The Dark Side of Progress* (New York, 1985), 179–191. Although the branching tree came to be widely used as a metaphor for evolution, the image of a coral reef, which also appeared in Darwin's notebooks, was superior in some ways because it emphasized both the evolution and the extinction of species.

48. Rev. Alexander Ranway, "Heroism and Statesmanship," *AmMiss* 34 (1880), 326; [Titus Munson Coan], "The Decay of the Polynesian," *Nation* (July 24, 1879), 54; [J. M. Hubbard], "The Australian Aborigines," *Nation* (February 6, 1890), 115; D. McGregor Means, "Chinese Immigration and Political Economy," *NEYR* 36 (January 1877), 9; John Fiske, "Are We Celts or Teutons?" *Appletons'* 2 (October 9, 1869), 243. Patrick Brantlinger, *Dark Vanishings*, 12, cites Zygmunt Bauman's *Modernity and the Holocaust* to the effect that "modernization or 'social development' as such is genocidal." Brantlinger also quotes *The Communist Manifesto*'s verdict that all nations "on pain of extinction" are compelled to adopt the bourgeois mode of production. The problem with this view, thanks to its conflation of biological and cultural extinction, is that it turns much if not all of history, in which cultures come and go, into a genocidal process. On cultural genocide as a useful concept, see George E. Tinker, *Missionary Conquest: The Gospel and Native American Cultural Genocide* (Minneapolis, 1993), esp. 5–8. For the greater influence of racist social Darwinism in Germany, see Richard Weikart, "Progress through Racial Extermination: Social Darwinism, Eugenics, and Pacifism in Germany, 1860–1918," *German Studies Review* 26/2 (2003), 273–294.

49. E. B. Tylor, "On the Survival of Savage Thought in Modern Civilization, Part II," *Appletons'* 1 (August 7, 1869), 99; "Fornander's Polynesian race," *Nation* (January 26, 1882), 82; T. B.[Thomas Bangs] Thorpe, "Glimpses of Indian Life," *Appletons'* 4 (August 13, 1870), 177.

50. Rawlinson, "The Duties of Higher towards Lower Races in a Mixed Community," 847; H. D. Thoreau, "Life without Principle," *AM* 12 (September 1863), 491.

51. "Critique of Nathaniel Shaler's Views," *Nation* (October 30, 1884), 378; "The Week," *Nation* (May 6, 1869), 357; "Address of the Rev. Geo. M. Boynton," *AmMiss* 36 (1882), 261; "Table-Talk," *Appletons'* 7 (May 4, 1872), 499; "Table-Talk," *Appletons'* 7 (March 9, 1872), 273; W. D. Whitney, "Language and Education," *NAR* 113 (1871), 348.

52. John S. Hittell, "Modern Civilization a Teutonic Product," *OM* 14 (March 1875), 255; "Table-Talk: Difference in Races," *Appletons'* 4 (December 24, 1870), 770. For example, Michael Adas, *Machines as the Measure of Men* (Ithaca, NY, 1990), 271–342, argues that race does not explain everything and that there was in fact much talk of lifting premodern societies out of backwardness.

53. This is the message that I take from a reading of Ronald I. Takaki, *Iron Cages; Race and Culture in Nineteenth Century America* (New York, 1979), though I am stressing the positive side of the picture that is implied, but left unstated, in his argument and though I cannot accept the neo-Marxist perspective that makes ideol-

ogy and cultural superstructural epiphenomena (which perhaps help to explain why race is treated as such a plastic phenomenon). For an explanation of Takaki's positive side, the review by Robert Brent Toplin, "Minorities and Materialism," *Reviews in American History* 9:2 (June 1981), 190–193, is far more informative. Writing from a Marxist perspective, in a work that ends with the Civil War, Herbert Aptheker, *Anti-Racism in U.S. History: The First Two Hundred Years* (Westport, CT, 1992), xiv, stresses working-class antiracism.

54. Race as a scientific construct is not dead, however. It matters in the diagnosis and treatment of diseases and is an important tool in forensic anthropology. For a contemporary summation of the connection between race and science, see Armand Marie Leroi, "A Family Tree in Every Gene," *New York Times*, March 14, 2005. (See the articles in *Nature Genetics* on which this op ed piece is based.) Gunnar Myrdal, *An American Dilemma: The Negro Problem and Modern Democracy*. Even a pioneering antiracist anthropologist like Anténor Firmin, in *The Equality of the Human Races (Positivist Anthropology)*, trans. Asselin Charles (New York, 2000), 444, acknowledged that certain races rely on "favorable evolutionary circumstances to achieve a level of development and acquire certain aptitudes not yet attained by others."

55. John Stuart Mill, *On Liberty* (London, 1921), 3.

6. The Promise of Local Equality: Assimilating African Americans, Chinese, and Native Americans

1. "Inter-Blending of Missionary Work," *AmMiss* 42 (1888), 243.

2. For one such individual, see Mark Elliott, *Color-Blind Justice: Albion Tourgee and the Quest for Racial Equality from the Civil War to Plessy v. Ferguson* (New York, 2006). Herbert Aptheker, "Anti-Racism in the United States: 1865–1890," in Benjamin P. Bowser, ed., *Racism and Anti-Racism in World Perspective* (Thousand Oaks, CA, 1995), 67–80, provides a brief compendium of antiracist thought among whites during these years. That it was a mixed picture comes across when one considers the rise in the number of state laws prohibiting racially mixed marriages during this period. On the growth of legal strictures against race-mixing, see James R. Browning, "Anti-Miscegenation Laws in the United States," *Duke Bar Journal* 1 (March 1951), 26–41. But while there was an increase in the total number of states prohibiting racially mixed marriages between 1865 and 1890, seven northern states repealed such legislation during these years. See Joseph R. Washington. Jr., *Marriage in Black and White* (Boston, 1971). Interestingly, none of the racial reformers mentioned by Ralph E. Luker, *The Social Gospel in Black and White* (Chapel Hill, NC, 1991), 230, correspond to the egalitarians whose views are discussed in this study. With a few exceptions, the same holds true for the protagonists of James M. McPherson's *The Abolitionist Legacy: from Reconstruction to the NAACP* (Princeton, NJ, 1975).

3. [W. G. Sumner], "Seward's Chinese Immigration," *Nation* (February 24, 1881), 134. For a discussion of some varieties of racism, see Kwame Anthony Appiah, *In My Father's House: Africa in the Philosophy of Culture* (New York, 1992), 13–15.

4. Thomas F. Gossett, *Race: The History of an Idea in America* (Dallas, TX, 1963), 286; Nathaniel Southgate Shaler, "Science and the African Problem," *AM* 66 (July 1890), 36–45; on Shaler, see Joel Williamson, *The Crucible of Race: Black-White Relations in the American South Since Emancipation* (New York, 1984), 119–121. George Fredrickson, *The Black Image in the White Mind: The Debate on Afro-American Character and Destiny, 1817–1914* (New York, 1971), 321, sees racism accepted by "all but a tiny (and often uncertain) minority of white spokesmen." The currents running counter to the main drift of racial ideology and politics are covered by Luker, *The Social Gospel in Black and White*; McPherson, *Abolitionist Legacy*; Elliott, *Color-Blind Justice*, and Leslie Butler, *Critical Americans: Vixtorian Intellectuals and Transatlantic Liberal reform* (Chapel Hill, NC, 2007), while Williamson, *Crucible of Race*, 85–108, discusses the small body of southern liberals on race in the postbellum period.

5. "Is the Negro Dying Out?" *AmMiss* 32 (1878), 39; Edward A. Pollard, "The Romance of the Negro," *Galaxy*, 12 (1871), 470; "The Distribution of the Blacks," *Nation* (June 10, 1880), 431; Charles A. Gardiner "The Future of the Negro," *NAR* 139 (1884), 81; John T. Morgan, *ibid.*, 84; [E. L. Godkin], "The Negro Problem," *Nation* (January 23, 1890), 64; "A Permanent Necessity," *AmMiss* 37 (1883), 67; A. J. Biddle, "A Blind Samson," *AmMiss* 36 (1882), 77. For post–Civil War expectations of the disappearance of the Negro, see Nancy Stepan, "Biology and Degeneration, Races and Proper Places," in J. Edwaard Chamberlin and Sander L. Gilman, eds., *Degeneration: The Dark Aide of Progress* (New York, 1985), 101–102.

6. Daniel H. Chamberlain, "The Race Problem at the South," *NEYR* 52 (June 1890), 511; "The Week," *Nation* (June 4, 1885), 451; "The Week," *Nation* (June 25, 1885), 512; [Godkin], "The Negro Problem," 64; D. H. Chamberlain, "Reconstruction and the Negro," *NAR* 128 (1879), 162; James Parton, "Antipathy to the Negro," *NAR* 127 (1878), 491; [E. P. Clark], "The Poor Negro," *Nation* (August 12, 1886), 131; Henry Watterson, "The 'Solid South'," *NAR* 128 (January 1879), 55. By 1904 Chamberlain would become a convert to racism.

7. [E. L. Godkin], "The Negro's Claim to Office," *Nation* (August 1, 1867), 90; [Godkin], "The Negro Problem," 64; Rev. M. E. Strieby, "The Political Progress of the Freedmen," *AmMiss* 3 (January 1879), 5; "Southern Society," *Nation* (February 4, 1875), 73; "The Week," *Nation* (January 23, 1890), 61.

8. "The South," *AmMiss* 39 (1885), 356; "Mixed Schools," *AmMiss* 35 (1881), 69; "The Remedy—But Who Is to Furnish It?" *AmMiss* 43 (1889), 91; "A History of the Negro Race in America," *Harper's* 67 (1883), 960; Booker T. Washington, "Education Will Solve the Race Problem, A Reply," *NAR* 171 (August 1900), 222; Gail Hamilton, "Race Prejudice," *NAR* 141 (1885), 477. Some black spokespeople, notably Frederick Douglass, agreed fully. "The increase or diminution of the negro's

political and social power will depend entirely upon himself." See "The Future of the Negro," *NAR* 139 (July 1884), 85.

9. J. T. L. Preston, "Religious Education of the Colored People of the South," *NEYR* 37 (September 1878), 680–698; "General Survey," *AmMiss* 33 (1879), 376; "Effect on the Negro of a Divided White Vote," *Nation* (September 6, 1877), 147; Joel Chandler Harris, "The Future of the Negro," *NAR* 139 (July 1884), 85. For the argument that the very same ideology of free labor that played such a large role in ending slavery was in large measure responsible for ruling out of bounds any discussion of governmental affirmative action in economic or social policy, see Heather Cox Richardson, *The Death of Reconstruction: Race, Labor, and Politics in the Post-Civil War North 1865–1901* (Cambridge, MA, 2001).

10. James Parton, "Antipathy to the Negro," *NAR* 127 (November–December 1878), 488; M. E. Striebey, "The Political Progress of the Freedmen," *AmMiss* 33 (1879), 5; Samuel Chapman Armstrong, "The Future of the Negro," *NAR* 139 (July 1884), 96; Edmund Kirke, "How Shall the Negro Be Educated?" *NAR* 143 (1886), 426; Rev. C.H Richards, "Protection by Development," *AmMiss* 32 (1878), 19; "Humanity," *Nation* (January 7, 1869), 6; E. W. Gilliam, "The African Problem," *NAR* 139 (1884), 417.

11. T. U. Dudley, "How Shall We Help the Negro?" *Century* 30 (1885), 277; G. W. Cable, "The Silent South," *Century* 30 (1885), 677, 691; Hamilton, "Race Prejudice," 477; "The Future of the Negro," *NAR* 139 (1884), 97; Edmund Kirke, "How Shall the Negro Be Educated?" *NAR* 143 (1886), 422; W. H. Ruffner, "The Co-education of the White and Colored Races," *Scribner's* 8 (1874), 86. For Cable's racial views, see John Cleman, *George Washington Cable Revisited* (New York, 1996), 116–130. See also Ronald T. Takaki, *Iron Cages: Race and Culture in Nineteenth-Century America* (New York, 1982), 205–211.

12. "The Freedman's Case in Equity," *Century* 29 (1884), 409.

13. Oliver Johnson, "The Future of the Negro, *NAR* 139 (1884), 93; "The Problematic South," *Nation* (May 15, 1890), 398; William Mathews, "The Negro Intellect," *NAR* 149 (1889), 92; J. T. L. Preston, "Religious Education of the Colored People of the South," *NEYR* 37 (September 1878), 683; C. C. Painter, "The Negro for His Place," *AmMiss* 35 (1881), 166; A. H. Bradford, "The Time Factor in the Southern Problem," *AmMiss* 42 (1888), 125.

14. Chamberlain, "The Race Problem," 516; William C. Blackwood, "The Future of the Republic," *OM* 4 (December 1884), 634; "The Week," *Nation* (March 8, 1888), 289; "The Week," *Nation* (January 23, 1890), 61; Mathews, "The Negro Intellect," 98; "Prejudice and Progress," *Century* 30 (1885), 965; Fredrickson, *The Black Image in the White Mind*, 242–243; James Bryce, "Thoughts on the Negro problem," *NAR* 153 (December 1891), 658–659. For the racial thinking of the *Century*'s editors at this time, Richard Watson Gilder and Robert Underwood Johnson, see J. Scott-Childress Reynolds, "Cultural Reconstruction: Nation, Race, and the Invention of the American Magazine, 1830–1915," 388–389. On the appeal to time, see Luker, *The Social Gospel in Black and White*, 117–122.

15. "In Plain Black and White," *AmMiss* 39 (1885), 135. Stephan and Abigal Thernstrom, *America in Black and White: One Nation Indivisible* (New York, 1997), reads like a historical vindication of the liberal emphasis on work and slow cultural change.

16. "Emigration and Immigration," *Nation* (April 10, 1890), 302. For anti-Chinese racism as a counterpart to hatred of blacks, at least on the west coast, see Alexander Saxton, *The Indispensable Enemy: Labor and the Anti-Chinese Movement in California* (Berkeley, CA, 1871), 44–45, though the emphasis is overwhelmingly economic.

17. H. Shewin, "Observations on the Chinese Laborer," *OM* 7 (January 1886), 96; George F. Seward, "Mongolian Immigration," *NAR* 134 (June 1882), 573; Raphael Pumpelly, "Our Impending Chinese Problem," *Galaxy* (July 1869), 31; "The Editor's Table," *Appletons'* 10 (July 5, 1873), 26.

18. R. W. Raymond, "National Characteristics," *OM* 3 (September 1969), 256; A. W. Loomis, "The Six Chinese Companies," *OM* 1 (1868), 226–227; A. W. Loomis, "What Our Chinamen Read," *OM* 1 (December 1868), 530; A. W. Loomis, "Our Heathen Temples," *OM* 1 (November 1868), 461.

19. "Music and the Drama," *Appletons'* 12 (September 19, 1874), 282; H. F. Krehbiel, "Chinese Music," *Century* 41 (1890), 449; George H. Fitch, "In a Chinese Theater," *Century* 24 (1881), 192; Henry Burden McDowell, "The Chinese Theater," *Century* 29 (1884), 30; N. B. Dennys, "Chinese Theaters," *Appletons'* 4 (September 24, 1870), 373.

20. C. C. Coffin, "China in Our Kitchens," *AM* 23 (June 1869), 749; Alexander Young, "Chinese Gamblers," *Appletons'* 5 (January 7, 1871), 8; A. W. Loomis, "The Chinese as Agriculturalists," *OM* 4 (June 1870), 526–532; "The Chinamen," *Appletons'* 4 (December 24, 1870), 774; William F. G. Shanks, "Chinese Skilled Labor," *Scribner's* 2 (1871), 499; [A. G. Sedgwick], "The New Standard of Emigration," *Nation* (January 3, 1884), 6.

21. M. J. Dee, "Chinese Immigration," *NAR* 126 (May 1878), 525; N. S. Dodge, "John Chinaman," *Appletons'* 3 (January 15, 1870), 75; Albert S. Evans, "From the Orient Direct," *AM* 24 (November 1869), 546; A. W. Loomis, "How Our Chinamen Are Employed," *OM* 2 (March 1869), 238; An American Housewife, "A Plea for Chinese Labor," *Scribner's* 2 (1871), 286, 289; "The Week," *Nation* (October 22, 1868), 323.

22. "The Week," *Nation* (May 4, 1882), 370; "Table-Talk," *Appletons'* 5 (April 8, 1871), 415; Loomis, "How Our Chinamen Are Employed," 239; Frank H. Norton, "Our Labor System and the Chinese," *Scribner's* 2 (1871), 62; "The Week," *Nation* (August 19, 1869), 143; [E. L. Godkin], "The Coming of the Barbarian," *Nation* (July 15, 1869), 45; "The Editor's Table," *Appletons'* 10 (July 5, 1873), 26.

23. Edward R. Burlingame, "An Asiatic Invasion," *Scribner's* 13 (1876), 692; "A Shoemaker's Contribution to the Chinese Discussion," *OM* 7 (April 1886), 415; A. B. Stout, "The Commerce of Asia and Oceania," *OM* 8 (February 1872), 175.

24. J. H. Twichell, "The United States and China—The Situation," *AmMiss* 33 (1879), 406; "The Week," *Nation* (July 25, 1878), 48; "The Week," *Nation* (August 23, 1883), 153; "The Week," *Nation* (March 9, 1882), 196; "The Chinese in California," *Scribner's* 13 (1876), 414–415; "The Week," *Nation* (May 18, 1876), 315; "The Week," *Nation* (May 11, 1882), 390.

25. "The Week," *Nation* (October 22, 1885), 332; "The Two Parties and the Chinese," *AmMiss* 34 (1880), 262; J. P. Widney, "The Chinese Question," *OM* 2 (December 1883), 627–631; "The Week," *Nation* (June 16, 1887), 500.

26. A. A. Sargent, "The Wyoming Anti-Chinese Riot," *OM* 67 (November 1885), 507; Letter to the editor on the Chinese question, *Nation* (May 8, 1879), 317; M. J. Dee, "Chinese Immigration," *NAR* 126 (May 1878), 508; "Notes," *Nation* (July 17, 1879), 43; "The Chinese Debate," *Nation* (February 20, 1879), 130; Thomas J. Vivian, "John Chinaman in San Francisco," *Scribner's* 12 (1876), 866, 871; H. Latham, "Chinese Slavery," *OM* 3 (February 1884), 175.

27. J. P. Widney, "The Chinese Question," *OM* 2 (December 1883), 629; E. W. Gilliam, "Chinese Immigration," *NAR* 143 (1886), 33; Abbott Kinney, "Under the Shadow of the Dragon," *OM* 2 (November 1883), 459; A. A. Sargent, "The Wyoming Anti-Chinese Riot," *OM* 67 (November 1885), 510; H. Latham, "Chinese Slavery," *OM* 3 (February 1884), 175; John F. Miller, "Certain Phases of the Chinese Question," *OM* 7 (April 1886), 429; "The Week," *Nation* (August 15, 1878), 89; "Shall Immigration Be Restricted," *Century* 34 (1887), 954; John Durst, "The Exclusion of the Chinese," *NAR* 139 (1884), 257; Silas B. Dutcher, "Manifest Destiny," *Appletons'* 3 (March 19, 1870), 353.

28. Theodore D. Woolsey, "The Experiment of the Union with Its Preparations," *Harper's* 51 (1875), 682; A. A. Sargent, "The Wyoming Anti-Chinese Riot—Again," *OM* 7 (1886), 56; Gilliam, "The African Problem," 429; Henry N. Day, "The Chinese Migration," *NEYR* 29 (January 1870), 14; Catherine Baldwin, "The Chinese in San Francisco—The Sixth Year of Qwong See," *Harper's* 62 (1881), 70.

29. John F. Miller, "Certain Phases of the Chinese Question," *OM* 7 (April 1886), 434; "The Chinese Debate," *Nation* (February 20, 1879), 130; John Durst, "The Exclusion of the Chinese," *NAR* 139 (1884), 261; M. J. Dee, "Chinese Immigration," *NAR* 126 (May 1878), 524; Gilliam, "Chinese Immigration," 79.

30. William James, "Rationality, Activity and Faith," *PR* 2 (1882), 78; Pumpelly, "Our Impending Chinese Problem," 23; "The Week," *Nation* (May 4, 1882), 371.

31. "Address of Sen. Geo. F. Hoar, *AmMiss* 35 (1881), 370; [E. L. Godkin], "The Republican Party and the Chinese Bill," *Nation* (March 16, 1882), 222; Day, "The Chinese Migration," 3; "The Week," *Nation* (June 10, 1886), 479; "A Shoemaker's Contribution to the Chinese Discussion," *OM* 7 (April 1886), 415; "Notes and Comments: Poem, 'A Plea,' " *NAR* 146 (February 1888), 220; "The Week," *Nation* (April 6, 1882), 283.

32. J., "The Wyoming Anti-Chinese Riot—Another View," *OM* 6 (December 1885), 575; Pumpelly, "Our Impending Chinese Problem," 23; James L. Bowen, "The

Celestials in Sunday School," *Scribner's* 1 (1870), 558; George Mooar, "Is Assimilation a Spent Force?" *OM* 16 (August 1890), 160.

33. N. S. Dodge, "John Chinaman," *Appletons'* 3 (January 15, 1870), 75; [W. H. Bishop], "Inglis's Australia," *Nation* (August 26, 1880), 155; Lyman Abbott, "The Two Methods," *AmMiss* 34 (1880), 374; "What Shall We Do with the Chinese," *AmMiss* 39 (1885), 193; George F. Seward, "Mongolian Immigration," *NAR* 134 (June 1882), 567.

34. Day, "The Chinese Migration," 1; J. H. Twichell, "The United States and China—The Situation," *AmMiss* 33 (1879), 409; "The Chinese Debate," *Nation* (February 20, 1879), 130; "The Week," *Nation* (September 27, 1888), 239; "Chinese Indemnity Bill," *AmMiss* 41 (1887), 101; "The Week," *Nation* (November 19, 1885), 414; [E. L. Godkin], "A Strange Doctrine Indeed," *Nation* (March 11, 1886), 206–207. For the unfolding of restrictionist attitudes and legislation elsewhere, see R. A. Huttenback, "The British Empire as a 'White Man's Country'—Racial Attitudes and Immigration Legislation in the Colonies of White Settlement," *The Journal of British Studies* 13 (November 1973), 108–137.

35. "The Chinese Treaty," *Nation* (September 6, 1888), 184; "The Week," *Nation* (March 4, 1886), 179; Rev. Joseph E. Roy, "Report on Chinese Work," *AmMiss* 44 (December 1890), 392; George F. Seward, "Mongolian Immigration," *NAR* 134 (June 1882), 576.

36. Andrew Gyory, *Closing the Gate: Race, Politics, and the Chinese Exclusion Act* (Chapel Hill, NC, 1998). For the differential views of Californians on Indians and blacks, see Luther W. Spoehr, "Sambo and the Heathen Chinee: Californians' Racial Stereotypes in the Late 1870s," in Michael L. Krenn, ed., *Race and Foreign Policy in the Ages of Territorial and Market Expansion, 1840 to 1900* (New York, 1998), 149–168.

37. Francis Paul Prucha, *The Indians in American Society: From the Revolutionary War to the Present* (Berkeley, CA, 1985), 5–10; Sherry L. Smith, *Reimagining Indians: Native Americans through Anglo Eyes, 1880–1940* (New York, 2000), 217. On the multiple possibilities of social Darwinism in the United States based on some representative figures, see Hawkins, *Social Darwinism in European and American Thought, 1890–1945: Nature as Model and Nature as Threat* (New York, 1997), 104–122.

38. Nelson A. Miles, "The Indian Problem," *NAR* 128 (1879), 304; "Indian Wars," *AmMiss* 32 (1878), 293. For a recent scholarly evaluation, see Robert M. Utley, "Total War on the American Indian Frontier," in Manfred F. Boemeke, Roger Chickering, and Stig Förster, eds., *Anticipating Total War: The German and American Experiences, 1871–1914* (New York, 1999), 399–414.

39. [J. D. Cox], "A Century of Dishonor," *Nation* (March 3, 1881), 152; "The Week," *Nation* (June 6, 1867), 445; "The Week," *Nation* (November 26, 1868), 430; [F. A. Walker], "The Indian Problem," *Nation* (June 16, 1870), 389; "Massacres of the Mountains," *Nation* (June 17, 1886), 513; Herbert Welsh, "The Past and Present Indian Question," *NEM* 9 (October 1990), 260.

40. Carl Schurz, "Present Aspects of the Indian Problem," *NAR* 133 (July 1881), 1; Helen Hunt Jackson, *A Century of Dishonor: The Early Crusade for Indian Reform* (New York, 1965), 341–342; [A. F. Bandelier], "Removal of the Apaches from Arizona," *Nation* (September 9, 1886), 208; "The Week," *Nation* (June 16, 1870), 375; Robert Patterson, "Our Indian Policy," *OM* 11 (September 1873), 210; H. H. [Helen Hunt Jackson?], "The Wards of the United States Government," *Scribner's* 19 (1879), 777–778; M. E. Strieby, "The Look Forward," *AmMiss* 39 (1885), 353; [A. A. Woodhull], "The Plains of the Great West," *Nation* (February 8, 1877), 91. Jackson was not making a case for preservation of the Indian way of life. She advocated only the fulfillment of treaty commitments and a scrupulous regard for Indian property rights, a solution that most reformers considered nearly as unsatisfactory as the existing system. She seemed more interested in white peace of mind than in doing something substantive about the problem of the Indian in white civilization.

41. [G. E. Pond], "The New Indian Hostilities," *Nation* (January 17, 1867), 52; [Cox], "A Century of Dishonor," 152; Herbert Welsh, "The Past and Present Indian Question," *NEM* 9 (October 1990), 258; "The Two Indian Policies," *AmMiss* 32 (1878), 102; [J. N. Pomeroy], "The Recent Change in the Indian Bureau," *Nation* (August 17, 1871), 100; Thomas Williamson, "The Indian Question," *PR* 50 (October 1876), 628; George E. Tinker, *Missionary Conquest: The Gospel and Native American Cultural Genocide* (Minneapolis, 1993), 126n.

42. [Joseph Anderson], "Red Cloud Seen through Friendly Eyes," *Nation* (July 28, 1870), 62; Vincent Colyer, "Shall the Red-Men Be Exterminated?" *Putnam's* 14 (September 1869), 367–374; Joel Pfister, *Individuality Incorporated: Indians and the Multicultural Modern* (Durham, NC, 2004), 70; "The Week," *Nation* (June 16, 1870), 375; L. Edwin Dudley, "How to Treat the Indians," *Scribner's* 10 (1875), 484; [Joseph Anderson], "The Indian in Literature," *Nation* (November 20, 1873), 342; J. Elliot, "Our Indians and the Duty of the Presbyterian Church to Them," *PR* 5 (1876), 77; John S. Hittell, "The Doom of the Californian Aborigines," *OM* 11 (June 1888), 614.

43. See the figures in "Indian Notes," *AmMiss* 32 (1878), 41; [Garrick Mallery], "Lessons of the Bannock War," *Nation* (July 25, 1878), 51–52; Carl Schurz, "Aspects of the Indian Problem," *AmMiss* 37 (1883), 106; Carl Schurz, "Present Aspects of the Indian Problem," *NAR* 133 (1881), 6; [J. D. Cox], "The Army and the Indians," *Nation* (April 15, 1880), 292. Brian W. Dippie, *The Vanishing American: White Attitudes and U.S. Indian Policy* (Middletown, CT, 1982), 122–129. The population figures would continue to decline until they reached their nadir in the census of 1900. On the eighteenth century, see Joseph S. Lucas, "Civilization or Extinction: Citizens and Indians in the Early United States," *The Journal of the Historical Society* 6:2 (2006), 235–249.

44. H. H., "The Wards of the United States Government," *Scribner's* 19 (1879), 782; "The Week," *Nation* (July 16, 1874), 34.

45. "The Native Races of America," *Galaxy* 19 (1875), 76; J. C. Cremony, "The Apache Race," *OM* 1 (September 1868), 201; "Among the Sioux of Dakota," *Nation*

(October 20, 1881), 320; Dudley, "How to Treat the Indians," 485; "Army Sacrifices," *Nation* (May 1, 1879), 306.

46. "The Week," *Nation* (April 17, 1873), 261; Frank H. Head, "Our Ishmaelites," *OM* 4 (February 1870), 105; [E. L. Godkin], "Our Indian Wards," *Nation* (July 13, 1876), 21. For Indians as savages, see "Memoranda; the Noble Red Man," *Galaxy* 10 (1871), 427–428; "Turk and Indian," *Galaxy* 24 (1877), 695. Prucha, *The Indians in American Society,* emphasizes religiously oriented humanitarian reformers. For Morgan, see Frederick E. Hoxie, *A Final Promise: The Campaign to Assimilate the Indians 1880–1920* (Lincoln, NE, 1984), 18–20.

47. "The Week," *Nation* (October 18, 1877), 234; Francis A. Walker, *The Indian Question* (Boston, 1874), 15; Elaine Goodale, "Plain Words on the Indian Question," *NEM* 8 (April 1880), 146; "Address of Gen. S. C. Armstrong," *AmMiss* 35 (1881), 404; Eugene V. Smalley, "A New Solution of the Indian Question," *Century* 30 (1885), 813; Anna Lamoens Dawes, "An Unknown Nation," *Harper's* 76 (1888), 604.

48. Rev. John C. Lowrie, "Our Indian Affairs," *PR* 3 (1874), 13; Samuel Chapman Armstrong, "The Indians," *AmMiss* 37 (1883), 19; H. H., "The Wards of the United States Government," *Scribner's* 19 (1879), 775; [E. L. Godkin], "The Indian Difficulty," *Nation* (December 31, 1868), 545; Vincent Colyer, "Shall the Red-Men be Exterminated?" *Putnam's* 14 (September 1869), 368–369; C. T. Hopkins, "Thoughts toward Revising the Federal Constitution," *OM* 6 (October 1885), 396; *New York Tribune,* February 13, 1880, 4, in Hoxie, *Final Promise,* 15; "Paragraphs," *AmMiss* 40 (1886), 186; T. B. Thorpe, "Glimpses of Indian Life," *Appletons'* 4 (August 13, 1870), 177; Open Letters, H. O. Ladd, "Indian Education in the South-West," *Century* 33 (1886), 653–655.

49. Roy Harvey Pearce, *The Savages of America: A Study of the Indian and the Idea of Civilization,* rev. ed. (Baltimore, MD, 1965); Rev. Addison P. Foster, "The Indian Conference at Lake Mohonk," *AmMiss* 38 (1884), 324; "The Indians' Last Stand," *Nation* (January 7, 1886), 7; Frank H. Head, "Our Ishmaelites," *OM* 4 (February 1870), 106–107.

50. J. Elliot, "Our Indians and the Duty of the Presbyterian Church to Them," *PR* 5 (1876), 77; Address of Rev. Thomas L. Riggs, *AmMiss* 43 (1889), 386; Benson J. Lossing, "Our Barbarian Brethren," *Harper's* 40 (1870), 811; [A. L. Riggs], "What Shall We Do with the Indian?" *Nation* (October 31, 1867), 356.

51. Prucha, *Americanizing the American Indians: Writings by 'Friends' of the Indian 1880–1900* (Lincoln, NE, 1973), 7–8; Rev. Charles W. Shelton, "The Indians from a Christian Standpoint," *AmMiss* 39 (1885), 371; E. L. Huggins, "A Suggestion on the Indian Problem," *OM* 6 (December 1885), 571; Carl Schurz, "Aspects of the Indian Problem," *AmMiss* 37 (1883), 106; [A. G. Sedgwick], "The Indian Bureau Transfer," *Nation* (January 2, 1879), 7; "Notes," *Nation* (February 26, 1880), 155; Gail Hamilton, "The Lion's Side of the Lion Question," *NAR* 146 (March 1888), 294.

52. "The Mixed Human Races," *Appletons'* 4 (1870), 677; Philip C. Garrett, "Indian Citizenship," Proceedings of the Fourth Annual Mohonk Conference (1886) in

Prucha, *Americanizing the American Indians*, 61; [Garrick Mallery], "Otis's Indian Question," *Nation* (July 4, 1878), 13. For census data, see Campbell Gibson and Kay Jung, "Historical Statistics on Population Totals by Race, 1790 to 1990," Working Paper Series No. 56 (Washington, DC, September 2002). For a work that emphasizes the role of racial science in defining the image of the Indian in racial terms, see Robert E. Berkhofer, Jr., *The White Man's Indian* (New York, 1978), 55–61.

53. "Notes," *Nation* (March 17, 1881), 185; Helen W. Ludlow, "Indian Education at Hampton and Carlisle," *Harper's* 62 (1881), 659; E. L. Huggins, "A Suggestion on the Indian Question," *OM* 6 (December 1885), 570–571; [A. A. Woodhull], "One of the Indian Outbreaks," *Nation* (August 6, 1874), 85; "Can the Indian Be Educated?" *AmMiss* 40 (1886), 96.

54. Elaine Goodale, "How to Americanize the Indian," *NEYR* 53 (May 1890), 452; Thomas Williamson, "The Indian Question," *PR* 5 (October 1876), 627; Sherman Day, "Civilizing the Indians of California," *OM* 2 (December 1883), 578; M. E. Strieby, "The Vernacular in Indian Schools," *AmMiss* 42 (1888), 119; "The Government and the Indians," *AmMiss* 43 (1889), 127; Letter to the editor by Lewis Henry, *Nation* (July 20, 1876), 41.

55. James C. Welling, "Race Education," *NAR* 136 (1883), 359, 363; George S. Wilson, "How Shall the American Savage Be Civilized?" *AM* 50 (November 1882), 598.

56. Frederic Remington, "On the Indian Reservations," *NEM* 38 (1889), 539; Sherman Day, "Civilizing the Indians of California," *OM* 2 (December 1883), 575.

57. "The Week," *Nation* (June 29, 1882), 532; "Report on Indian Work," *AmMiss* 42 (1888), 355; James B. Thayer, "The Dawes Bill and the Indians," *AM* 61 (March 1888), 316.

58. Willard Beatty, "The Goal of Indian Assimilation," *The Canadian Journal of Economics and Political Science* 12 (August 1946), 396.

59. Hoxie, *Final Promise*, 187; [W. A. Linn], "The Brutality of Civilization," *Nation* (May 30, 1889), 439.

60. Hoxie, *Final Promise*, 33, 39.

61. Adam Smith, *The Theory of Moral Sentiments* (Philadelphia, 1817), III: 215–217.

7. Beyond Orientalism: Explaining Other Worlds

1. Edward Jarvis, "The Increase of Human Life," *AM* 24 (December 1869), 716; John Fiske, "The Laws of History," *NAR* 109 (1869), 204; Richard J. Hinton, "The Race for Commercial Supremacy in Asia," *Galaxy* 8 (1869), 184.

2. [Fitzedward Hall], "The Gist of the Koran," *Nation* (November 20, 1879), 352; George B. McClellan, "The War in Egypt," *Century* 24 (1881), 784; [Fitzedward Hall], "Hindu Literature," *Nation* (May 23, 1878), 344.

3. Walter B. Scaife, "Moslem Influence on the Renaissance," *OM* 3 (April 1884), 373; "Literary," *Appletons'* 13 (April 24, 1875), 533; S. P. Scott, "The Moslem Empire

in Spain," *OM* 15 (August 1875), 178; Charles Dudley Warner, "Saunterings about Constantinople," *Scribner's* 13 (1876), 245; Edward E. Salisbury, "On Some of the Relations between Islam and Christianity," *NEYR* 35 (October 1876), 752–772.

4. Rev. Edward Hungerford, "The Intellectual Mission of the Saracens," *AM* 58 (December 1886), 823; [E. L. Godkin], "The Disappointment in Egypt," *Nation* (September 28, 1882), 257; [W. M. Ferris], "The Caliph Haroun Alraschid," *Nation* (June 9, 1881), 412; Charles Dudley Warner, "Across Africa," *AM* 50 (August 1882), 174; James Freeman Clarke, "Mohammed and His Place in Universal History," *AM* 24 (November 1869), 626.

5. "The Week," *Nation* (December 1, 1887), 427; [Fitzedward Hall], "Hindu Literature," *Nation* (May 23, 1878), 344; "Freese's Tour through Palestine and Syria," *Nation* (July 8, 1869), 32; Lester I. Vogel, *To See a Promised Land: Americans and the Holy Land in the Nineteenth Century* (University Park, PA, 1993), 69–76; Charles Dudley Warner, "At the Gates of the East," *AM* 36 (November 1875), 529; "Thomson's Travels in Morocco," *Nation* (September 12, 1889), 216; Albert Rhodes, "Life among the Beduins," *Galaxy* 22 (1876), 45; [Michael Heilprin], "Wilson's Outlines of History," *Nation* (November 9, 1865), 596; Albert Rhodes, "The Arabs at Home," *Galaxy* 13 (1872), 610; Charles S. Robinson, "Ajellak Allah; or, The Women of the Arabs," *Scribner's* 7 (1873), 564; [Hall], "Hindu Literature," 344; "Cruelty toward Animals in Damascus," *Appletons'* 14 (August 7, 1875), 177.

6. "Recent Literature: Farley's Modern Turkey," *AM* 31 (April 1973), 500; Clarke, "Mohammed," 626; "The Week," *Nation* (January 17, 1867), 43.

7. Laurence Oliphant, "Christian Policy in Turkey," *NAR* 124 (1877), 196; "Arabia," *PR* 37 (1865), 350; [Michael Heilprin], "Wilson's Outlines of History," *Nation* (November 9, 1865), 596; McClellan, "The War in Egypt," 784; E. D. C. Prime, "Civil and Religious Liberty in Turkey," *PR* 4 (1875), 608; "A Turkish Effendi on Christendom and Islam," *Appletons'* 8 (March 1880), 267.

8. [W. J. Stillman], "Crete," *Nation* (April 18, 1867), 319; [E. L. Godkin], "The Right and Wrong of the Egyptian Question," *Nation* (July 20, 1882), 46; S. G. W. Benjamin, "From Brusa to Constantinople," *Harper's* 55 (1877), 731; Warner, "Saunterings about Constantinople," 239; George F. Herrick, "The Site of Constantinople," *Galaxy* 22 (1876), 772; C. H. Jones, "An Englishman in Turkey," *Appletons'* 3 (January 1877), 79; "Editor's Table," *Appletons'* 2 (December 1877), 569; "Editor's Table," *Appletons'* 15 (June 17, 1876), 796.

9. A. H. Guernsey, "Syria under the Last Five Turkish Sultans," *Appletons'* 1–6 (1876), 519; Henry O. Dwight, "The Family Life of the Turks," *Harper's* 62 (1881), 605; "A Terrible Indictment," *Appletons'* 15 (February 26, 1876), 271; "The Prospect of a General War in Europe," *Nation* (May 4, 1876), 288; [E. L. Godkin], "American Opinion on the War in the East," *Nation* (May 3, 1877), 260; Michael B. Oren, *Power, Faith, and Fantasy: America in the Middle East 1776 to the Present* (New York, 2006), 247, 285, argues that modernization was very much on the minds of Americans who were familiar with the region.

10. The Roving American, "The Egyptian Gentleman at Home," *Appletons'* 5 (January 14, 1871), 45; "Editor's Table," *Appletons'* 15 (May 27, 1876), 695; [E. L. Godkin], "The Imbroglio in Central Asia," *Nation* (February 13, 1873), 110; John William De Forest, "The Russians on the Bosphorus," *AM* 41 (April 1878), 510.

11. [E. L. Godkin], "What Will Mr. Gladstone Do with Egypt?" *Nation* (September 21, 1882), 236; "The Week," *Nation* (July 7, 1881), 3.

12. "The Week," *Nation* (September 7, 1876), 113; "The Week," *Nation* (February 15, 1877), 97; Edwin De Leon, "The Khedive of Egypt," *Appletons'* 5 (June 3, 1871), 646; "Editor's Table," *Appletons'* 15 (May 27, 1876), 69; A. H. Guernsey, "The Eastern Question," *Galaxy* 23 (1877), 36.

13. [R. D. Osborn], "The Future of Islam," *Nation* (July 27, 1882), 78; E. L. Godkin, "The Eastern Question," *NAR* 124 (1877), 125; "The Arabs and the African Problem," *Harper's* Weekly 2 (1889), 94; [Fitzedward Hall], "The Gist of the Koran," *Nation* (November 20, 1879), 352; [Fitzedward Hall], "Muhammedanism," *Nation* (April 18, 1878), 262; Edward Hungerford, "The Intellectual Mission of the Saracens," *AM* 58 (December 1886), 829; [E. L. Godkin], "The Part of Religion in the Turkish problem," *Nation* (September 21, 1876), 176; "Christian Work in Egypt," *PR* 40 (1868), 567–568.

14. Richard J. Hinton, "The Race for Commercial Supremacy in Asia," *Galaxy* 8 (1869), 185; "Africa: Extracts from the Journal of H. M. Ladd," *AmMiss* 36 (1882), 19; George B. McClellan, "The War in Egypt," 784; Edward E. Salisbury, "On Some of the Relations between Islam and Christianity," *NEYR* 35 (October 1876), 753; "The French Troubles in Africa," *Nation* (July 21, 1881), 46; E. D. C. Prime, "Civil and Religious Liberty in Turkey," *PR* 4 (1875), 627–628; "The Week," *Nation* (November 7, 1867), 367; "Herzegovina and the Late Uprising," *Nation* (March 8, 1877), 151.

15. "The Week," *Nation* (January 3, 1884), 3; "The French in North Africa," *Nation* (September 22, 1881), 228; "The Week," *Nation* (December 20, 1883), 501; "The Week," *Nation* (April 3, 1884), 287; [Godkin], "The Imbroglio in Central Asia," 110; J. Augustus Johnson, "The Colonization of Palestine," *Century* 24 (1881), 293, 296, recounts details of some failed colonization schemes.

16. *"Arabia,"* *PR* 37 (1865), 372; S. Wells Williams, "Afghanistan and the English," *NEYR* 38 (1879), 112–113; [Eugene Schuyler], "Americans in Turkey," *Nation* (March 7, 1878), 170; "Notes," *Nation* (December 13, 1888), 479; [Godkin], "The Imbroglio in Central Asia," 111; "Culture and Progress: Mohammed and Mohammedanism," *Scribner's* 11 (1875), 133. For the fascinating story of an early missionary attempt, see Ussama Makdisi, *Artillery of Heaven: American Missionaries and the Failed Conversion of the Middle East* (Ithaca, NY, 2008).

17. Charles Stuart Welles, "The Tour of the Nile," *Scribner's* 11 (1875), 156; [E. L. Godkin], "The Part of Religion in the Turkish Problem," *Nation* (September 21, 1876), 176; Henry O. Dwight, "Some Peculiarities of Turkish Politics," *Harper's* 61 (1880), 749–750; "Freese's Tour through Palestine and Syria," *Nation* (July 8, 1869), 32; "Into Morocco," *Nation* (May 15, 1890), 400; "Farley's Turkey," *AM* 31 (April 1873), 499.

18. [Samuel Beal], "Johnson's Religion of China," *Nation* (August 7, 1879), 97.

19. A. A. Hayes, "China and the United States," *AM* 59 (May 1887), 587; "China," *Nation* (September 6, 1883), 197; John Bonner, "An Empire in Ruin," *OM* 15 (February 1890), 173; "Notes," *Nation* (May 24, 1877), 309–310; John Addison Porter, "Some Race-Problems in China: Dr. S. Wells Williams' 'Middle Kingdom,'" *NEYR* 43 (January 1884), 81; "Gems of Chinese Literature," *Nation* (January 24, 1884), 81; Isaac Bassett Choate, "A Bit of Old China," *The New England* 5 (March 1887), 418; [E. S. Holden], "A Chinese Translation of the Constitution of the United States," *Nation* (January 12, 1882), 29; Porter, "Some Race-Problems in China," 91.

20. Porter, "Some Race-Problems in China," 82; Bonner, "An Empire in Ruin," 173; James Freeman Clarke, "Confucius and the Chinese, or the Prose of Asia," *AM* 24 (1869), 338; Percival Lowell, "The Soul of the Far East," *AM* 60 (September 1887), 407; H. Krehbiel, "Chinese Music," *Century* 41 (1890), 449.

21. Stephen Powers, "The Language of Confucius," *OM* 7 (October 1871), 353; [S. W. Williams], "A Woman's Account of Canton," *Nation* (March 11, 1880), 197; "Review of Pumpelly's across America and Asia," *Harper's* 40 (1870), 462. Powers was characterized by Alfred Kroeber as having "an astoundingly quick and vivid sympathy," in Alfred Kroeber, *Handbook of the Indians of California* (Washington, DC, 1925), ix. For a contemporaneous survey of the kind of scholarly work then being done, see Henri Cordier, *Half a Decade of Chinese Studies* (Leyden, 1892).

22. "Notes," *Nation* (September 1, 1887), 174; [Addison Van Name], "Legge's Chinese Classics," *Nation* (September 15, 1870), 176; [E. L. Godkin], "The Chinese Treaty," *Nation* (September 10, 1868), 206; "Notes," *Nation* (July 4, 1872), 12; William Speer, "Democracy of the Chinese," *Harper's* 37 (1868), 842; Walter A. Rose, "A Chinese Dinner," *Appletons'* 7 (January 27, 1872), 95; J. S. Sewall, "A Study in Chinese History," *NEYR* 31 (1872), 76.

23. "Notes," *Nation* (April 2, 1885), 282; "Sayings and Doings at Home and Abroad," *Appletons'* 10 (August 2, 1873), 159; Karl Bismark, "The Marriage of the Emperor of China," *Galaxy* 19 (1875), 188; "Miscellany," *Appletons'* 7 (May 11, 1872), 529; Thomas W. Knox, "The Chinese Embassy to the Foreign Powers," *Harper's* 37 (1868), 592; "More Light on the Chinese Question," *Nation* (October 14, 1869), 309; James Harrison Wilson, *China* (New York, 1901), 160.

24. Spencer C. Browne, "Queer Sights and Ways in Pekin," *OM* 7 (September 1871), 242; S. Wells Williams, "The Perpetuity of Chinese Institutions," *NAR* 131 (1880), 208; Porter, "Some Race-Problems in China," 86; R. H. Graves, "Chinese Triennial Examinations," *OM* 8 (March 1872), 263; Bonner, "An Empire in Ruin," 179; Mill, *Considerations on Representative Government* (New York, 1875), 51; "The Week," *Nation* (September 23, 1869), 244; Raphael Pumpelly, "Western Policy in China," *NAR* 106 (1868), 502. Peggy Champlin, *Raphael Pumpelly: Gentleman Geologist of the Gilded Age* (Tuscaloosa, AL, 1994), 75, 131–133.

25. "Foreign Lands: Williams's The Middle Kingdom," *AM* 52 (December 1881), 832; "Miscellany," *Appletons'* 9 (March 22, 1873), 404; "China, J. H. Wilson," *NAR* 145

(October 1887), 463; Wilson, *China,* 84; "Western Policy in China," *NAR* 106 (1868), 600, 609; Raphael Pumpelly, "Our Impending Chinese problem," *Galaxy* (July 1869), 27; "The Middle Kingdom," *Nation* (November 8, 1883), 399.

26. "The *North American Review* for July," *Nation* (July 16, 1874), 44; W. A. P. Martin, *"The Renaissance in China,"* *NEYR* 28 (January 1869), 47; Richard J. Hinton, "The Race for Commercial Supremacy in Asia," *Galaxy* 8 (1869), 192; [S. W. Williams], "Martin's 'The Chinese,'" *Nation* (April 7, 1881), 245.

27. W. L. Kingsley, "The Missionary Invasion of China," *NEYR* 52 (January 1990), 47, 63; Porter, "Some Race-Problems in China," 93, 94; Hinton, "The Race for Commercial Supremacy in Asia," 180; [W. E. Griffis], "Wilson's China," *Nation* (September 8, 1887), 196; "China, J. H. Wilson," 462–464.

28. George B. Davis, *Outlines of International Law* (New York, 1887), 215; "More Light on the Chinese Question," *Nation* (October 14, 1869), 224; Thomas Knox, "John Comprador," *Harper's* 57 (1878), 434; "The Week," *Nation* (September 26, 1872), 195. For a brief biography of Knox, see Stephen Fiske, *Off-Hand Portraits of Prominent New Yorkers* (New York, 1884), 222–228.

29. "The Chinese Embassy to Christendom," *Nation* (February 20, 1868), 146; John Russell Young, "American Influence in China," *NAR* 151 (1890), 197; "Editor's Table," *Appletons'* 15 (January 22, 1876), 120; M. Howland, "Social Transformations," *Appletons'* 10 (July 12, 1873), 51.

30. P. B. Simmons, "Five Years in Japan," *Galaxy* 5 (1868), 606; Noah Brooks, "Awakened Japan," *Scribner's* 3 (April 1872), 669; "Ourselves as the Heathens See Us," *Nation* (July 18, 1872), 45; Asa S. Colton, "Japan," *Princeton* 1 (1872), 748; E. H. House, "The Present and Future of Japan," *Harper's* 46 (1873), 858; "Young Japan," *Nation* (April 19, 1883), 347; P. B. Simmons, "Five Years in Japan," *Galaxy* 5 (1868), 606; [R. J. Cross, A .G. Sedgwick, and Arnold Tanzer], "Three Books of Travel," *Nation* (March 7, 1889), 209. American writing on Japan during these years is surveyed by Inazo Nitobe, *The Intercourse between the United States and Japan: An Historical Sketch* (Baltimore, MD, 1891), 141–150.

31. "Miscellany," *Appletons'* 8 (July 20, 1872), 82; "Art in Japan," *Appletons'* 8 (August 10, 1872), 166, quoted from James Brooks, *Seven Months' Run, Up, and Down, and Around the* World (New York, 1872); Theodore Wores, "An American Artist in Japan," *Century* 38 (1889), 670; Noah Brooks, "Japan, Some Pictures," *Scribner's* 11 (1875), 180; [Russell Sturgis], "The Fine Arts of Japan," *Nation* (July 16, 1868), 56; "Dresser's Japan," *Nation* (March 1, 1883), 193.

32. William Elliot Griffis, "Japanese Art Symbols," *Scribner's* 5 (1889), 88; "Characteristics of the International Fair, I," *AM* 38 (July 1876), 91; "The Art and Industries of Japan," *Nation* (May 30, 1889), 44; W. E. McArthur, "Some Japanese Interiors," *OM* 6 (January 1875), 18; "Dresser's Japan," *Nation* (March 1, 1883), 93; "Japanese Lyrical Odes," *Nation* (May 16, 1867), 391.

33. "Editor's Table," *Appletons'* 10 (August 30, 1873), 281; "New Books," *Appletons' New Books* 1 (1876), 479; Gilman P. Briggs, "An Adventure in Japan," *Scribner's* 2

(1871), 513; Lyman Abbott, "Pictures of the Japanese," *Harper's* 39 (1869), 322; "Japanese Women," *Appletons'* 8 (July 6, 1872), 25; W. Henry Winslow, "Japanese Popular Art and Sketch Books," *NEM* 9 (November 1990), 348; [W. E. Griffis], "Miss Bird's Japan," *Nation* (December 30, 1880), 467.

34. *Nation* (July 18, 1872), 45; "Japanese Lyrical Odes," *Nation* (May 16, 1867), 391; Thomas W. Knox, "European Influences in Asia," *NAR* 141 (1885), 91; Rikizo Nakashima, "Mr. Percival Lowell's Misconception of the Character of the Japanese," *NEYR* 50 (February 1889), 97; P. B. Simmons, "Five Years in Japan," *Galaxy* 5 (1868), 615; William E. Griffis, "Household Superstitions in Japan," *Appletons'* 15 (January 15, 1876), 85; Leon De Rosny, "The Literature, History, and Civilization of the Japanese," *PR* 1 (1872), 321; "Japan," *AM* 5 (1860), 722.

35. "Progress in China and Japan," *Appletons'* 8 (October 19, 1872), 443; "Notes," *Nation* (February 8, 1877), 89; "From a Correspondent in Japan," *Appletons'* 3 (May 7, 1870), 522; "Gleanings from Japan," *Nation* (August 29, 1889), 179; William Elliott Griffis, "Nature and People in Japan," *Century* 39 (1889), 231; Jas. Harris, "Japanese Holy Places," *OM* 1 (1868), 240; "Japanese Advance in Civilization," *Appletons'* 8 (September 28, 1872), 360; "Culture and Progress: A New Language Wanted," *Scribner's* 5 (1872), 770–771; "Literary Notes," *Appletons'* 9 (April 12, 1873), 508.

36. *Nation* (July 18, 1872), 45; M. Howland, "Social Transformations," *Appletons'* 10 (July 12, 1873), 51; [Raphael Pumpelly], "The Mikado's Empire," *Nation* (November 23, 1876), 316; "Young Japan," *Appletons'* 88 (November 16, 1872), 545; "The Week," *Nation* (September 11, 1873), 171; J. S. Sewall, "The Invincible Armada," *NEYR* (September 1890), 201.

37. William Elliott Griffis, "Japanese Art, Artists, and Artisans," *Scribner's* 3 (1888), 122; Brooks, "Awakened Japan," 671; Richard Williamson, Jr., "The Japanese Stage," *Galaxy* 21 (1876), 82; "Editor's Table," *Appletons'* 10 (August 30, 1873), 281; "Things Japanese," *Nation* (September 4, 1890), 199. On the romantic jeremiad, see Joseph M. Henning, *Outposts of Civilization: Race, Religion, and the Formative Years of American-Japanese Relations* (New York, 2000), 103–108.

38. "Winsor's Narrative and Critical History of America, Vol. I," *AM* 63 (1889), 120–121; Brooks, "Awakened Japan," 669; "Notes," *Nation* (March 28, 1872), 206; "Leading Men of Japan," *Nation* (March 8, 1883), 217.

39. "The Industrial Transition in Japan," *Nation* (June 12, 1890), 476; "Notes," *Nation* (September 1, 1887), 174; Leon De Rosny, "The Literature, History, and Civilization of the Japanese," *Princeton* 1 (1872), 309.

40. "Hubner's Ramble Round the World," *AM* 35 (February 1875), 239; W. E. Griffis, "A Modernized Japanese City," *Appletons'* 13 (March 20, 1875), 369; Alfred H. Guernsey, "The Mikado's Empire," *Harper's* 53 (1876), 496, quoting from the conclusion of a book by Griffis. William Elliott Griffis, "The Recent Revolutions in Japan," *NAR* 120 (1875), 314. William Elliott Griffis, "Nature and People in Japan," *Century* 39 (1889), 231.

41. "Table Talk: Japanese Advance in Civilization," *Appletons'* 8 (September 28, 1872), 360; [Raphael Pumpelly], "Progressive Japan," *Nation* (August 7, 1879), 100; "Notes," *Nation* (June 5, 1890), 453; [W. E. Griffis], "Coercion in Japan," *Nation* (February 16, 1888), 129; "The Constitution of Japan," *Nation* (March 21, 1889), 240. For the official view, see K. Kaneko, "An Outline of the Japanese Constitution," *AM* 65 (February 1890), 187–192; [E. W. Clement], "A Japanese State Legislature," *Nation* (February 27, 1890), 174.

42. "Gleanings from Japan," *Nation* (August 29, 1889), 179; Thomas W. Knox, "European Influences in Asia," *NAR* 141 (1885), 91; W. E. Griffis, "A Modernized Japanese City," *Appletons'* 13 (March 20, 1875), 369; Guernsey, "The Mikado's Empire," 496; William Elliott Griffis, "Nature and People in Japan," *Century* 39 (1889), 231; E. H. House, "The Present and Future of Japan," *Harper's* 46 (1873), 864; Brooks, "Awakened Japan," 671. On this point, see Frank Ninkovich, "History and Memory in Postwar U.S.-Japanese Relations," in Marc Gallicchio, ed., *The Unpredictability of the Past: Memories of the Asia-Pacific War in U.S.-East Asian Relations* (Durham, NC, 2007), 85–120.

43. George R. Parkin, "The Workingman in Australia," *Century* 41 (1890), 607; [W. H. Bishop], "Inglis's Australia," *Nation* (August 26, 1880), 156; "Souvenirs of Some Continents," *Nation* (November 5, 1885), 385.

44. John Hayes, "Australia," *OM* 4–2 (February 1870), 121; "Miscellany," *Appletons'* 9 (March 29, 1873), 436; [J. M. Hubbard], "The Australian Aborigines," *Nation* (February 6, 1890), 115; "Editor's Study," *Harper's* 80 (1890), 966.

45. G. M. Clarke, "Resources of New Zealand," *OM* 6 (March 1871), 252; John Manning, "The Maories," *OM* 7 (July 1871), 49; Sir Julius Vogel, "The Islands of the Pacific, New Zealand, and Australia," *PR* 1 (1879), 437.

46. William Churchill, "Domestic Poisons of the Sub-Papuans," *NEYR* 53 (July 1890), 32–33; [J. D. Hague], "Among the Cannibals," *Nation* (April 10, 1884), 322; "The South Sea Islands, Part I," *Appletons' Journal* 15 (April 22, 1876), 515; "Notes," *Nation* (May 9, 1889), 388; Therese Yelverton, "Borneo Cinnabar Mines," *OM* 10 (May 1873), 434; S. S. Boynton, "Life in Samoa," *OM* 13 (May 1889), 538.

47. William H. Rideing, "The South Sea Islands, Part I," *Appletons'* 15 (April 22, 1876), 515; "The World's Paradises," *Appletons'* 8–2 (February 1880), 183; W. T. Pritchard, "Consulate amongst the Fijis," *OM* 2 (April 1869), 333.

48. Lieut. J. D. J. Keiley, "Tahiti," *Galaxy* 21 (1876), 367; [J. D. Hague], "The Wanderer in the South Seas," *Nation* (November 29, 1883), 457; [Hague], "Among the Cannibals," 323; "Polynesian and Aryan," *Nation* (August 26, 1886), 181.

49. [W. M. Ferriss], "The Melanesian Languages," *Nation* (September 23, 1886), 256; "Social Life in the Tropics," *OM* 1 (December 1868), 569; [Titus Munson Coan], "Honolulu," *Nation* (March 17, 1881), 193; [William Thompson] Bacon, "Missionary Work in Hawaii," *NEYR* 31 (1872), 495–496; George B. Merrill, "Hawaiian Civilization," *OM* 1 (July 1868), 69–81.

50. "Social Life in the Tropics," *OM* 1 (December 1868), 564; [Titus Munson Coan], "The Decay of the Polynesian," *Nation* (July 24, 1879), 54; [Titus Munson Coan], "Honolulu," *Nation* (March 17, 1881), 193; [Titus Munson Coan], "The Peopling of Hawaii," *Nation* (September 11, 1879), 171; "The Week," *Nation* (December 3, 1874), 359.

51. [Titus Munson Coan], "The Decay of the Polynesian," 54; George B. Merrill, "Hawaiian Civilization," *OM* 1 (July 1868), 78; Bacon, "Missionary Work in Hawaii," 641; Charles Nordhoff, "Hawaii-nei," *Harper's* 47 (1873), 546.

52. "Recent Literature: Anderson's History of the Missions of the American Board of Commissioners for Foreign Missions," *AM* 40 (November 1877), 628; "Life in Hawaii," *Nation* (May 25, 1882), 449.

53. Rufus Anderson, "The Hawaiian Islands: Their Progress and Condition under Missionary Labors," *NEYR* 24 (1865), 368; Paul William Harris, *Nothing But Christ: Rufus Anderson and the Ideology of Protestant Foreign Missions* (New York, 1999); "Recent Literature: Anderson's History of the Missions," 628; F. L. Clarke, "The Political Revolution in the Hawaiian Islands," *OM* 11 (March 1888), 304; Agnes M. Manning, "Among the Islands," *OM* 4 (March 1870), 217.

54. Charles Dudley Warner, "At the Gates of the East," *AM* 36 (November 1875), 524; Theodore Child, "Constantinople," *AM* 61 (January 1888), 78, 79.

55. Edward Jarvis, "The Increase of Human Life," *AM* 24 (October 1869), 495; Washington Gladden, "Christianity and Wealth," *Century* 28 (1884), 903, 904; Moncure D. Conway, "The Great Show at Paris," *Harper's* 35 (1867), 243; [Auguste Laugel], "Barbarian Sights at the Exposition. Paris," *Nation* (September 26, 1889), 249.

56. Rev. L. L. Paine, "Christianity in Its Progressive Relations," *NEYR* 30 (October 1871), 585; Bacon, "Missionary Work in Hawaii," 541; "Notes and Comments: Why Am I a Missionary?" *NAR* 148 (1889), 264; W. L. Kingsley, "The Missionary Invasion of China," *NEYR* 52 (January 1890), 47; Gladden, "Christianity and Wealth," 904.

57. Gail Hamilton, "Heathendom and Christendom under Test," *NAR* 143 (1886), 539; Letter from Joseph Hews, "Are the Heathen Our Inferiors?" *NAR* 144 (1887), 110; [G. W. Warren], "From Egypt to Japan," *Nation* (August 22, 1878), 120; W. A. P. Martin, *The Chinese: Their Education, Philosophy, and Letters* (New York, 1881), 277; [Samuel Wells Williams], "Martin's 'The Chinese'," *Nation* (April 7, 1881), 245; Henry Field, *From Egypt to Japan* (New York, 1877), 257, 259.

58. [R. D. Osborn and W. E. Griffis], "An India and a China Missionary," *Nation* (March 14, 1889), 229; "The Week," *Nation* (November 1, 1888), 347; "Notes," *Nation* (February 23, 1888), 156, 157. See also Todd M. Johnson, *Countdown to 1900: World Evangelism at the End of the Nineteenth Century* (Birmingham, AL, 1988), Chapter 14. Andrew N. Porter, *Religion Versus Empire?: British Protestant Missionaries and Overseas Expansion, 1700–1914* (New York, 2004), sees a growing tension not only between missionaries and empire, but also between missionaries and the civilizing mission.

59. Rev. M. E. Dwight, "The Contest as It Is To-Day," *NEYR* 43 (1884), 580; "An Open Letter by Rev. Noah Porter," *NEYR* 46 February (1887), 173; [G. W. Warren], "From Egypt to Japan," *Nation* (August 22, 1878), 120; Maria L. Child, "The Intermingling of Religions" *AM* 28 (October 1871), 394–395; "Religion and Progress," *Nation* (March 22, 1883), 259; "Der Buddhismus in seiner Psychologie," *Nation* (May 10, 1883), 410.

60. George Frederic Parsons, "The Growth of Materialism," *AM* 60 (August 1887), 160–161; Hon. Henry C. Robinson, "Edwin Arnold's Light of Asia," *NEYR* 39 (1880), 711; Edward Hungerford, "Buddhism and Christianity," *NEYR* 33 (1874), 282, 284; "Der Buddhismus in seiner Psychologie," *Nation* (May 10, 1883), 410; C. W. Clapp, "The Historic Religions of India: Buddhism," *NEYR* 41 (1882), 623; "Lectures on the Science of Religion," *Nation* (February 15, 1872), 11; Mrs. Fannie Roper Feudge, "The Mammoth Religion of the World," *Galaxy* 16–3 (September 1873), 354.

61. For the subsequent transformation of the missionary sensibility, see Lian Xi, *The Conversion of Missionaries: Liberalism in American Protestant Missions in China, 1907–1932* (University Park, PA, 1997).

62. Edward Said, *Orientalism* (New York, 1978) makes the classic argument for a naturalized sense of superiority, with nary a word to say about the potential for equality in Western views. A detailed response to Said that emphasizes the West's commitment to rationalism, universalism, objectivity, and self-criticism can be found in Ibn Warraq, *Defending the West: A Critique of Edward Said's Orientalism* (Amherst, NY, 2007), esp. 57–83. For what it's worth, concepts of fixed social hierarchy have been more characteristic of oriental worldviews, which were themselves not exclusively oriental but part of "the general tendencies of societies," as Louis Dumont has pointed out in *Homo Hierarchicus* (Chicago, 1970), 20.

8. Empire and Civilization

1. Ernest May, in his classic *American Imperialism: A Speculative Essay* (New York, 1968), attributes the source of imperialism's popularity in 1898 to changing intellectual fashions in Europe that were picked up by the American opinion elite. My research suggests otherwise. The reviews of European writers on imperialism were infrequent and insufficiently laudatory, whereas home-grown writing on the topic was of large quantity and recognizably American in tone and emphasis. More important than this disagreement is that May, in thinking to pose the question of the origins of this enthusiasm, was the first historian to understand that there must have been some historical and cultural foundation for it. The present book owes a great deal to this insight. In the absence of the right questions, answers are impossible.

2. "The Colonial Policy of France," *Nation* (November 22, 1888), 409; "Foreign Lands, A Review of Samuel Wells Williams, *The Middle Kingdom*," *AM* 52 (December

1883), 831; Maximilian Schele de Vere, "Around the World," *Appletons'* 2 (December 25, 1869), 596; Rev. C. N. Clark, "Historical Position of Modern Missions," *NEYR* 39 (1880), 570–571. This emphasis on the transformational role of commerce is explored in Mona Domosh, *American Commodities in an Age of Empire* (New York, 2006).

3. Thomas W. Knox, "A Journey through Mongolia," *Galaxy* 6 (August 1868), 161; Richard J. Hinton, "The Race for Commercial Supremacy in Asia," *Galaxy* 8 (1869), 194.

4. Mill, *Considerations on Representative Government* (New York, 1875), 346–347. For an essay that emphasizes Mill's belief in deracination, see David Theo Goldberg, "Liberalism's Limits: Carlyle and Mill on 'The Negro Question,'" in Julie K. Ward and Tommy L. Lott, eds., *Philosophers on Race: Critical Essays* (Oxford, 2002), 195–204. Sankar Muthra, *Enlightenment against Empire* (Princeton, NJ, 2003), 279–281 considers some of the differences between eighteenth- and nineteenth-century thinkers. Jennifer Pitts, *A Turn to Empire: The Rise of Imperial Liberalism in Britain and France* (Princeton, NJ, 2005), 138–162, 254–256.

5. "India and Its Native Princes," *Scribner's* 11 (1875), 65; George M. Towle, "The Peoples of India, Part I," *Appletons'* 15 (June 10, 1876), 737–742; "The Dawn of British Trade to the East Indies," *Nation* (April 21,1887), 348; "Relations of India with Greece and Rome," *PR* 38 (1866), 394; Horatio Stebbins, "The Brahmo Somaj, or Protestantism in India," *OM* 3 (February 1884), 186. On the work of Indian orientalists, see Ibn Warraq, *Defending the West: A Critique of Edward Said's Orientalism* (Amherst, NY, 2007), 212–214.

6. Horatio Stebbins, "The Brahmo Somaj, or Protestantism in India," *OM* 3 (February 1884), 186; James Freeman Clarke, "A New Chapter of Christian Evidences," *AM* 23 (1869), 310; [Fitzedward Hall and John Avery], "Dowson's Guide to Hindu Mythology," *Nation* (October 30, 1879), 295; John Avery, "European Writers on India," *NEYR* 35 (July 1876), 431, 440; [Fitzedward Hall], "Hindu Literature," *Nation* (May 23, 1878), 344; "Indian and Its Native Princes," 65; [R. D. Osborn], "British Power in India," *Nation* (June 30, 1887), 556.

7. Goldwin Smith, "The Hatred of England," *NAR* 150 (1890), 558; Henry Field, *From Egypt to Japan* (New York, 1877), 239–240; [R. D. Osborn], "Seeley's Expansion of England," *Nation* (December 6, 1883), 473–475; "Abuses of Victory—British Morals in India," *USDR* 42 (October 1858), 310; Allen Thorndike Rice, "The Race for Primacy," *NAR* 145 (1887), 448; [Fitzedward Hall], "Muhammedanism," *Nation* (April 18, 1878), 262.

8. [R. J. Cross], "England and Her Colonies," *Nation* (June 12, 1890), 473; [R. J. Cross, A. G. Sedgwick, and Arnold Tanzer], "Three Books of Travel," *Nation* (March 7, 1889), 209; Thomas W. Knox, "European Influences in Asia," *NAR* 141 (1885), 86; Knox, "The English in India," *Harper's* 58 (March 1879), 574.

9. [R. D. Osborn], "Christianity in India," *Nation* (February 26, 1885), 185; "The Northeast Frontier of India," *Nation* (September 17, 1885), 242; [R. D. Osborn], "The Last War in Afghanistan," *Nation* (May 2, 1889), 371; [E. L. Godkin], "The Tory

Prospects in England," *Nation* (April 7, 1881), 235; [R. D. Osborn and W. E. Griffis], "An India and a China Missionary," *Nation* (March 14, 1889), 229; [R. D. Osborn], "A Soldier's Life," *Nation* (April 28, 1881), 299.

10. [R. D. Osborn], "The Afghan Frontier of British India," *Nation* (November 22, 1888), 419; [Osborn], "Christianity in India," 185; A. H. Guernsey, "The English in India," *Harper's* 25 (October 1862), 688; Knox, "The English in India," 575; [R. D. Osborn], "Lord Lawrence," *Nation* (April 5, 1883), 299; [Osborn], "The Afghan Frontier of British India," 419; "Men and Events of My Time in India," *Nation* (May 11, 1882), 407.

11. Edward E. Hale, "Cotton from First to Last," *NEM* 9 (September 1890), 127; [F. H. Hill], "The Indian Empire," *Nation* (August 26, 1886), 180; [A. V. Dicey], "Wheeler's Short History of India," *Nation* (September 30, 1880), 240.

12. Knox, "The English in India," 574; [R. D. Osborn], "Child-life by the Ganges," *AM* 1 (1857), 625; "British Power in India," *Nation* (June 30, 1887), 557.

13. [A. C. Sellar], "The Indian Famine," *Nation* (October 4, 1877), 210; Smith, "The Hatred of England," 558; "The Week," *Nation* (February 8, 1877), 82; "Notes," *Nation* (September 27, 1877), 197; [R. D. Osborn], "The Economic Revolution in India," *Nation* (October 4, 1883), 298; "Editor's Table," *Appletons'* 11 (June 20, 1874), 249. India's population remained fairly static during the 19th century, though it did rise significantly toward the end. On British Malthusians and laissez-faire, see S. Ambirajan, "Malthusian Population Theory and Indian Famine Policy in the Nineteenth Century," *Population Studies*, 30 (March 1976), 5–14. Amartya Sen, in Development as Freedom (New York, 2000), 175, asserts that "the sense of distance between the ruler and the ruled—between 'us' and 'them'—is a crucial feature of famines."

14. Charles Dudley Warner, "England," *Century* 25 (November 1882), 137, 139; Henry George, *Progress and Poverty* (San Francisco, 1879), 50; Amrita Lal Roy, "British Rule in India," *NAR* (April 1886), 361; "Men and Events of My Time in India," *Nation* (May 11, 1882), 407; Goldwin Smith, "The Prospect of a Moral Interregnum," *AM* 44 (1879), 638–640; "Notes," *Nation* (September 27, 1877), 197; Knox, "European Influences in Asia," 86. For synopses of British famine responses, see Mike Davis, *Late Victorian Holocausts: El Niño Famines and the Making of the Third World* (New York, 2001), 311–314 and Willam A. Dando, *The Geography of Famine* (New York, 1980), 137–140.

15. "New India; or, India in Transition," *Nation* (February 4, 1886), 109; [Rollo Ogden], "Native Life in India," *Nation* (May 16, 1889), 411; John C. Sundberg, "The Ram Movement," *OM* 12 (November 1888), 540; Sir Edwin Arnold, "The Duty and Destiny of England in India," *NAR* 154 (1891), 168.

16. Smith, "The Hatred of England," 558; [W. D. Whitney], "Johnson's Oriental Religions," *Nation* (November 21, 1872), 338; [Ogden], "Native Life in India," 411; George M. Towle, "The Peoples of India, Part II," *Appletons'* 15 (June 17, 1876), 771–772.

17. "Notes," *Nation* (June 19, 1873), 418; [M. D. Conway], "A Vice-Queen of India," *Nation* (February 27, 1890), 181; "Editors Table," *Appletons'* 15 (April 1, 1876),

438. Generally, essayists tended to credit sociological reasons, such as self-protection of husbands from their wives, rather than those that stressed "undying attachment" to the husband as the cause." See "Foreign Items," *Appletons'* 5 (June 24, 1871), 745.

18. "The Week," *Nation* (November 12, 1868), 383; Knox, "European Influences in Asia," 86.

19. [R. D. Osborn], "Sketches of Indian Life," *Nation* (July 26, 1888), 78; George M. Towle, "The Peoples of India, Part III," *Appletons'* 15 (1876), 804–805; John F. Hurst, "A Native Publishing House in India," *Harper's* 75 (1887), 356; "The Week," *Nation* (August 16, 1883), 129; "The Week," *Nation* (December 13, 1888), 467.

20. [E. L. Godkin], "The Negro's Claim to Office," *Nation* (August 1, 1867), 90; "Questions of British Policy in India," *Nation* (August 30, 1883), 176; "The Week," *Nation* (December 13, 1888), 467.

21. [W. D. Whitney], "A Hindu Traveller in India," *Nation* (July 15, 1869), 52; [Osborn], "Sketches of Indian Life," 78; Amrita Lal Roy, as quoted by Richard Danzig, "The Announcement of August 20, 1917," *The Journal of Asian Studies* 28 (November 1968), 33; Smith, "The Hatred of England," 558; [Osborn], "The Afghan Frontier of British India," 419.

22. "The Indian Revolt," *AM* 1 (1857), 220, 223; Murat Halstead, "Do Americans Hate England?" *NAR* 150 (1890), 562; "Lives of Indian Officers," *Nation* (October 24, 1867), 330; [E. L. Godkin], "The Last Invasion of Afghanistan," *Nation* (January 16, 1879), 44; "Hunter's Rural Bengal," *Nation* (January 28, 1869), 71; "Address of Professor Graham Taylor," *AmMiss* 43 (1889), 375–376; [N. D. Davis], "Proconsulship under the British Empire," *Nation* (July 17, 1890), 53; "The Week," *Nation* (September 2, 1875), 144.

23. [F. H. Hill], "The Indian Empire," *Nation* (August 26, 1886), 180; "The Week," *Nation* (September 2, 1875), 143; "The Week," *Nation* (September 18, 1884), 233; [Dicey], "Wheeler's Short History of India," 240, 241; "New India; or, India in Transition," *Nation* (February 4, 1886), 109; [R. D. Osborn], "Great Britain and Her Colonies," *Nation* (November 22, 1883), 432; Canon George Rawlinson, "The Position of England in the East," *PR* 2 (1880), 8.

24. Amrita Lal Roy, "English Rule in India," *NAR* 142 (1886), 355, 363, 369; Scriman Madhwa-Charyar, "A Plea for the Pagan Hindoo," *NAR* 145 (1887), 325–326; Raj Coomar Roy, "Child Marriage in India," *NAR* 147 (1888), 415–424. In the end, Roy casts his lot with the workingmen and "the western proletariat" and ends with a paean to internationalism.

25. A. H. Guernsey, "The Prince of Wales in India," *Appletons'* 3 (1877), 1–15; [A. V. Dicey], "Green's History of the English People," *Nation* (September 9, 1880), 188.

26. "Christian Work in Egypt," *PR* 40 (1868), 547; Oliver Ritt, "Egypt and the Isthmus of Suez," *Appletons'* 2 (December 11, 1869), 534; "Editors Table," *Appletons'* 12 (September 12, 1874), 344; Professor Schele de Vere, "Egypt," *Appletons'* 3 (January 22, 1870), 99.

27. C. H. Woodman, "New Egypt," *Appletons'* 2 (December 1877), 543; Charles Stuart Welles, "The Tour of the Nile," *Scribner's* 11 (1875), 48; Albert Rhodes, "The Egyptians at Home," *Galaxy* 14 (1872), 150; Edward L. Wilson, "The Modern Nile," *Scribner's* 2 (1887), 282; "The Pomp of Egypt," *Appletons'* 10 (October 25, 1873), 530.

28. The Roving American, "The Egyptian Gentleman at Home," *Appletons'* 5 (January 7, 1871), 14; George B. McClellan, "A Winter on the Nile," *Scribner's* 13 (1876), 372; Edwin De Leon, "The New Egypt of Khédive Ismaïl," *Appletons'* 14 (August 14, 1875), 207.

29. Welles, "The Tour of the Nile," 156; "Christian Work in Egypt," *PR* 40 (1868), 547; "Editors Table," *Appletons'* 12 (December 19, 1874), 793.

30. Professor Schele de Vere, "Egypt," *Appletons'* 3 (January 22, 1870), 99; P. H. Morgan, "The Suez Canal: A History," *Appletons'* 8 (April 1880), 309; "The Week," *Nation* (April 20, 1876), 257; "The Week," *Nation* (April 27, 1876), 271; Albert Rhodes, "The Egyptians at Home," *Galaxy* 14 (1872), 157.

31. [E. L. Godkin], "England in Egypt," *Nation* (December 2, 1875), 353; Henry Mitchell, "The Coast of Egypt and the Suez Canal," *NAR* 109 (1869), 509; McClellan, "A Winter on the Nile," 372; "The Week," *Nation* (August 24, 1882), 145.

32. "The Week," *Nation* (July 13, 1882), 22; "The Week," *Nation* (September 14, 1882), 211; George B. McClellan, "The War in Egypt," *Century* 24 (1881), 784; Fanny Stone, "Diary of an American Girl in Cairo, during the War of 1882," *Century* 28 (1884), 291; [E. L. Godkin], "What Will Mr. Gladstone Do with Egypt?" *Nation* (September 21, 1882), 236.

33. "The Week," *Nation* (October 12, 1882), 207; "The Week," *Nation* (September 14, 1882), 211; Halstead, "Do Americans Hate England?" 562; [E. L. Godkin], "The Right and Wrong of the Egyptian Question," *Nation* (July 20, 1882), 46; "Summary of the Week's News," *Nation* (August 17, 1882), 125; "The Week," *Nation* (August 16, 1883), 129. On American ambivalence, see Michael B. Oren, *Power, Faith, and Fantasy: America in the Middle East 1776 to the Present* (New York: Norton, 2006), 257–261.

34. [Michael Heilprin], "Wallace's Egypt," *Nation* (January 10, 1884), 39; "The Week," *Nation* (October 19, 1882), 321; "The Week," *Nation* (August 16, 1883), 129; "The Egyptian Campaigns, 1882 to 1885," *Nation* (June 16, 1887), 516; "L'Instruction Publique en Egypte," *Nation* (May 1, 1890), 361.

35. "Notes," *Nation* (August 1, 1889), 96; [E. L. Godkin], "The Week: French Colonization," *Nation* (December 21, 1882), 525; C. C. Hazewell, "The Progress of Prussia," *AM* 18 (November 1866), 581; "France in Africa," *Nation* (October 20, 1870), 164; [Michael Heilprin], "France as a Colonizer," *Nation* (June 25, 1885), 518; "The Week," *Nation* (November 1, 1883), 363; [E. Gryzanowski], "International Ignorance," *Nation* (October 6, 1870), 217. For an opposing view on French colonizing capabilities, see Andrew McFarland Davis, "The French as Colonists," *OM* 5 (March 1885), 225.

36. [Ogden], "The Colonial Policy of France," 409; [Michael Heilprin], "The French Expedition to Tonquin," *Nation* (May 31, 1883), 462; [E. L. Godkin], "French Expansion in Africa," *Nation* (May 26, 1881), 363; G. Reynolds, "The French Struggle for Naval and Colonial Power," *AM* 12 (November 1863), 626; [E. L. Godkin], "Wars and Rumors of Wars," *Nation* (September 4, 1884), 193.

37. F. Reclus, "Marshal MacMahon, Duke of Magenta, President of the French Republic," *Galaxy* 18 (1874), 354; [Godkin], "French Expansion in Africa," 363; "The French in North Africa," *Nation* (September 22, 1881), 228; "The Week," *Nation* (October 6, 1881), 263; "The Week," *Nation* (December 16, 1886), 489; "Notes: Colonial France," *Nation* (December 16, 1886), 498; "The Week," *Nation* (July 28, 1881), 63.

38. G. Reynolds, "The French Struggle for Naval and Colonial Power," *AM* 12 (November 1863), 631; [Godkin], "French Expansion in Africa," 363; [R. D. Osborn], "The Scourge of Christendom," *Nation* (May 8, 1884), 411; "France in Africa," *Nation* (October 20, 1870), 164; "The Week," *Nation* (August 6, 1885), 103.

39. "The Week," *Nation* (November 1, 1883), 363; [W. D. Griffis], "Across Chryse," *Nation* (July 12, 1883), 37; "The Week," *Nation* (December 20, 1883), 501; [R. D. Osborn], "France in Tonquin," *Nation* (October 23, 1884), 356, 357; Augustine Heard, "France and Indo-China," *Century* 32 (1886), 420; [Ogden], "The Colonial Policy of France," 409. For the complex relationship between the Catholic missionary enterprise and the colonial ambitions of the republic, see J.P. Daughton, *An Empire Divided: Religion, Republicanism, and the Making of French Colonialism, 1880-1914* (New York, 2006).

40. "The Chinese in Central Asia," *Nation* (August 14, 1879), 113; Rev. Selah Merrill, "Central Asia," *NEYR* 34 (January 1875), 1; [E. L. Godkin], "The Imbroglio in Central Asia," *Nation* (February 13, 1873), 110; [E. L. Godkin], "The Mussulman Bugbear," *Nation* (March 5, 1885), 195.

41. "The Week," *Nation* (January 27, 1870), 51; *Nation* (November 7, 1878), 281; [E. L. Godkin], "The Russians and the English in Central Asia," *Nation* (October 15, 1868), 308; Rev. Selah Merrill, "Central Asia," *NEYR* 34 (January 1875), 20; "Some Recent Books of Travel," *AM* 42 (November 1878), 583; W. H. Ray, "Russia in Asia," *AM* 59 (April 1887), 477; William Simpson, "With the Afghan Boundary Commission," *Harper's* 72 (March 1886), 601; "Bonvalot's Heart of Asia," *Nation* (June 13, 1889), 493; "Some Recent Books of Travel," *AM* 42 (November 1878), 584.

42. S. Wells Williams, "Afghanistan and the English," *NEYR* 38 (1879), 110; William Simpson, "With the Afghan Boundary Commission," *AM* 59 (March 1886), 601; "An American in Turkistan," *Scribner's* 13 (1876), 223; Thomas W. Knox, "Russian Policy in Asia," *Harper's* 47 (1873), 219; [Godkin], "The Imbroglio in Central Asia," 110.

43. George B. McClellan, "The War in the East," *NAR* 125 (July 1877), 36; [R. D. Osborn], "Among the Mongols," *Nation* (January 3, 1884), 18.

44. George M. Towle, "Turkistan and Its People," *Appletons'* 2–1 (1877), 59; "Culture and Progress," *Scribner's* 13 (1876), 572; "An American in Turkistan," 223; *Nation* (February 1, 1877), 77; "Table-Talk," *Appletons'* 7 (March 2, 1872), 246.

45. Americus, "The Annexation of San Domingo," *Galaxy* 11 (1871), 410–413; John Ball, Jr., "The Home and Foreign Markets," *NAR* 147 (1888), 231.

46. [J. D. Cox], "Mr. Seward's Diplomacy," *Nation* (November 29, 1883), 453; "The Week," *Nation* (June 16, 1870), 375; [Gustav Koerner], "What Will the San Domingo Commission Do?" *Nation* (February 2, 1871), 68; "The Week," *Nation* (March 2, 1871), 133; [E. L. Godkin], "The St. Domingo Row," *Nation* (December 29, 1870), 432; "Notes," *Nation* (July 24, 1873), 59. Love, *Race over Empire*, 39–77.

47. George H. Bates, "Some Aspects of the Samoan Question," *Century* 37 (1888), 947–948; Guy Powles, in a review of Paul M. Kennedy, "The Samoan Tangle," *Pacific Historical Review* 48 (Summer 1975), 299; "The Week," *Nation* (October 20, 1887), 302; "The Week," *Nation* (January 31, 1889), 81; "The Week," *Nation* (April 4, 1889), 276; "The Week," *Nation* (January 30, 1890), 83.

48. "The Danish Muddle," *Nation* (April 1, 1869), 249; "Protectorates," *Nation* (January 21, 1869), 4; "The Annexation Fever," *Nation* (April 15, 1869), 289; "The Week," *Nation* (December 19, 1867), 493; [A. G. Sedgwick], "The St. Domingo Bargain," *Nation* (February 3, 1870), 68; [E. L. Godkin], "The New San Domingo Scheme," *Nation* (January 23, 1873), 52; "The Week," *Nation* (March 2, 1871), 133.

49. "The Earth-Hunger," *Nation* (January 2, 1868), 5; [Sedgwick], "The St. Domingo Bargain," 68; [E. L. Godkin], "The St. Domingo Row," *Nation* (December 29, 1870), 432; "The Week," *Nation* (December 19, 1867), 493; "The Week," *Nation* (September 10, 1885), 207.

50. [Godkin], "The New San Domingo Scheme," 52; Goldwin Smith, "Is Universal Suffrage a Failure?" *AM* 43 (January 1879), 74; "Ghosts in Our Foreign Policy," *Century* 23 (1881), 778; Charles Sumner, "Prophetic Voices about America. A Monograph," *AM* 20 (September 1867), 306; "The Earth-Hunger," *Nation* (January 2, 1868), 4.

51. Richard J. Hinton, "The Race for Commercial Supremacy with Asia," *Galaxy* 8 (1869), 194; D. D. Porter, "National Prospects and Resources," *Galaxy* 6 (1868), 63; [William James], "Herbert Spencer's Data on Ethics," *Nation* (September 11, 1879), 178.

52. "Foreign Lands," *AM* 52 (December 1883), 831. On terminology, see Helen Tiffin, Gareth Griffiths, and Bill Ashcroft, eds., *Post-Colonial Studies: The Key Concepts* (New York, 2007), 204–206.

53. George R. Parkin, "The Reorganization of the British Empire," *Century* 37 (1888), 187, 189; J. E. [Joseph Edward?] Chamberlain, "A Dream of Anglo-Saxondom," *Galaxy* 24 (1877), 790.

54. John Fiske, "The Overthrow of French Power in the New World," *Harper's* 65 (1882), 99; [E. L. Godkin], "An English Dream of 'Americanization,'" *Nation* (April

5, 1883), 290; "Foreign Lands," *AM* 52 (December 1883), 831. Richard Hofstadter, *Social Darwinism in American Thought* (Boston, 1992), 171–172, grossly misidentified Anglo-Saxonism as "the dominant abstract rationale of American imperialism" by the mid-1880s.

55. [R. D. Osborn], "Seeley's Expansion of England," *Nation* (December 6, 1883), 473–475; "Annexation, or Federation," *Century* 37 (1888), 471; William Clarke, "An English Imperialist Bubble," *NAR* 141 (1885), 65.

56. "Oceana; or, England and Her Colonies," *Nation* (February 18, 1886), 155; [N. D. Davis], "Proconsulship under the British Empire," *Nation* (July 17, 1890), 53; [R. J. Cross], "England and Her Colonies," *Nation* (June 12, 1890), 473; [R. D. Osborn], "Great Britain and Her Colonies," *Nation* (November 22, 1883), 433–434; John Fiske, "The Overthrow of French Power in the New World," *Harper's* 65 (1882), 112; "Zincke's Plough and the Dollar," *AM* 53 (February 1884), 279; Andrew Carnegie, "Democracy in England," *NAR* 142 (1886), 77.

57. Dorothea R. Muller, "Josiah Strong and American Nationalism: A Reconsideration," *Journal of American History* 53 (December 1966), 487–503. As one historian has noted, Strong is "one of the most quoted but least understood figures in American religious history." See James Eldin Reed, "American Foreign Policy, The Politics of Missions and Josiah Strong, 1890–1900," *Church History* 41/2 (June 1972), 232. Fiske's geopolitical argument will be taken up in Chapter 10.

58. Address of Rev. Josiah Strong, *AmMiss* 49 (December 1895), 424. Strong appeared to be referring to Aryan mixtures in *Our Country,* but a few years later, in an address before the American Missionary Association, when discussing the place of Negroes, Indians, and Chinese, he made clear the more expansive diameter of his melting pot. "Three races?" he asked, "No; all one family, all blood relatives." Address of Rev. Josiah Strong, *AmMiss* 49 (December 1895), 424.

59. For a different view of Strong, see Thomas F. Gossett, "Imperialism and the Anglo-Saxon," in Michael L. Krenn, *Race and Foreign Policy in the Ages of Territorial and Market Expansion, 1840 to 1900* (New York, 1998), 336–337.

60. Muller, "Josiah Strong and American Nationalism," 495. He would advocate staying in Cuba and the Philippines, but only for altruistic reasons.

61. Strong, *Our Country* (1891 edition), 263; Muller, "Josiah Strong and American Nationalism," 495; Muller, "The Social Philosophy of Josiah Strong," *Church History* 282 (1959), 192–193.

9. International Politics

1. [Auguste Laugel], "The Unsettled State of Europe," *Nation* (December 7, 1865), 17. A year later it reported that "the dogs of war are not yet loosed but they seem to be getting impatient and restless. "M. Laboulaye's' Election," *Nation* (April 26, 1866), 525; Whitelaw Reid, "The Memoirs of Talleyrand," *Century* 41 (January 1891), 368.

2. William Seward, "Oration, The Destiny of America," in George E. Baker, ed., *The Life of William H. Seward with Selections from His Works* (New York, 1855), 331.

3. "Development of Nationalities," *Catholic World* 4 (November 1866), 247; "The Uses of the Geneva Arbitration," *Nation* (August 29, 1872), 134–135; [E. L. Godkin], "Sympathy," *Nation* (July 28, 1870), 52; "The Transfer of Power in Europe," *Nation* (August 25, 1870), 118; [E. L. Godkin], "National Debt in Europe," *Nation* (April 9, 1868), 284; "European Prospects," *Nation* (September 5, 1867), 193.

4. "The Week," *Nation* (February 11, 1869), 103; [Auguste Laugel], "France and Prussia," *Nation* (October 4, 1866), 274; [Auguste Laugel], "Napoleon's Miscalculations," *Nation* (August 23, 1866), 154; "European Prospects," *Nation* (September 5, 1867), 193.

5. "Table Talk," *Appletons'* 4 (September 24, 1870), 382; "The Struggle on the Rhine," *Galaxy* 10 (1871), 416; [E. L. Godkin], "The Terms of Peace," *Nation* (September 15, 1870), 164; Hermann von Holst, "The Causes of the French-German War," *NEYR* 30 (1871), 102; "Politics," *Nation* (September 29, 1870), 201; [C. I Barnard], "The Military Resources of Russia and France," *Nation* (October 13, 1870), 239.

6. [E. L. Godkin], "The Papal Question," *Nation* (December 8, 1870), 381; "Papa and the Dogma," *Scribner's* 1 (1870), 107; "The Pope in Extremity," *Appletons'* 4 (November 26, 1870), 654; "The European Outlook," *Scribner's* 1 (1870), 341; George E. Pond, "The Fate of Small European States," *Galaxy* 19 (1875), 266.

7. George E. Pond, "The Fate of Small European States," *Galaxy* 19 (1875), 266; "The Results of the War," *Nation* (March 2, 1871), 237; "The Week," *Nation* (October 6, 1870), 214; "The Recent Events in France," *Catholic World* 4 (December 1871), 290; Philip Quilibet, "The War of 1870," *Galaxy* 10 (1871), 709–710; "War Notes: The Decadence of France," *Appletons'* 4 (December 3, 1870), 681.

8. [E. L. Godkin], "The New War Cloud in Europe," *Nation* (September 14, 1871), 173; "The Last Rumor of War," *Nation* (May 27, 1875), 536; "The Next Crisis in Europe," *Nation* (October 7, 1875), 226; George F. Pond, "Forces in European Politics," *Galaxy* 24 (1877), 241; "War Notes," *Appletons'* 4 (December 3, 1870), 680.

9. "The Next Crisis in Europe," 226; "The Last Rumor of War," 536; "Editor's Table," *Appletons'* 10 (December 27, 1873), 825.

10. Pond, "Forces in European Politics," 229.

11. J. S. C. Abbott, "The Eastern Question," *Putnam's* 13 (April 1869), 464; Charles Dudley Warner, "Saunterings about Constantinople," *Scribner's* 13 (1876), 244; "The Week," *Nation* (October 14, 1875), 239.

12. [E. L. Godkin], "The Turkish Collapse," *Nation* (January 24, 1878), 53; George F. Herrick, "The Site of Constantinople," *Galaxy* 22 (1876), 774; "The Prospect of a General War in Europe," *Nation* (May 4, 1876), 288.

13. [E. L. Godkin], "The Effect of the Russian Reverses on Western Politics," *Nation* (September 27, 1877), 191; "Literary, Scientific, and Statistical Items," *The Ladies' Repository* 27 (March 1867), 185; [Godkin], "The Turkish Collapse," 54.

14. "The Russians on the Bosphorus," *AM* 41 (April 1878), 503; John Fiske, "The Races of the Danube," *AM* 39 (April 1877), 402; Daniel S. Gregory, "The Eastern Problem," *PR* 1 (1878), 50; "The Week," *Nation* (January 17, 1867), 43.

15. [E. L. Godkin], "The Turkish Crisis," *Nation* (September 30, 1880), 234; [E. L. Godkin], "The Turkish Crisis," *Nation* (October 26, 1876), 252; "Editor's Table," *Appletons'* 3–3 (September 1877), 283; [E. L. Godkin], "The Turkish Revolution," *Nation* (June 8, 1876), 361; [E. L. Godkin], "Pius the Ninth" *Nation* (February 14, 1878), 108; "The Art of Politics," *Nation* (February 7, 1878), 89.

The intertwined emphases on race, religion, and civilization were well articulated in a poem, "The Burden of Istamboul," by the novelist and essayist J. W. DeForest in "The Burden of Istamboul," *Appletons'* 3–2 (1877), 138.

16. "The Struggle in the Orient," *Galaxy* 24 (1877), 694; [E. L. Godkin], "Baker's Turkey," *Nation* (June 7, 1877), 340; [E. L. Godkin], "American Opinion on the War in the East," *Nation* (May 3, 1877), 260; [E. L. Godkin], "The Turco-Russian Campaign," *Nation* (August 23, 1877), 115; William L. Kingsley, "Why Should We Give Our Sympathy to Russia in the Present War?" *NEYR* 37 (January 1878), 115–116; "The Defeat of the Turk," *Scribner's* 16 (1878), 143.

17. "Editor's Table," *Appletons'* 15 (June 17, 1876), 796; J. W. De Forest, "A Turko-Russian War," *Harper's* 56 (1878), 261; George M. Towle, "The Defenses of Constantinople," *Appletons'* 2–3 (1877), 266; [Michael Heilprin], "The Races of European Turkey," *Nation* (January 2, 1879), 17; George B. McClellan, "The War in Egypt," *Century* 24 (1881), 784.

18. [Michael Heilprin], "The Czar and His People," *Nation* (October 28, 1886), 345; "Editor's Table," *Appletons'* 2–3 (1877), 285; Thomas L. Anderson, "The Irrepressible Conflict in the East," *Galaxy* 24 (November 1877), 694; Laurence Oliphant, "Christian Policy in Turkey," *NAR* 124 (1877), 212.

19. [Michael Heilprin], "Pan-Slavism," *Nation* (May 14, 1868), 388; "Russia," *Appletons'* 7 (February 3, 1872), 135; Daniel S. Gregory, "The Eastern Problem," *PR* 1 (1878), 91; Abbott, "The Eastern Question," 456; Anonymous, "The Monroe Doctrine and the Isthmian Canal," *NAR* 130 (1879), 500; Cyrus Hamlin, "The Dream of Russia," *AM* 58 (December 1886), 772.

20. Pond, "Forces in European Politics," 241; Abbott, "The Eastern Question," 462; Book Reviews, *OM* 12 (October 1888), 446; "Literary, Scientific, and Statistical Items," 185.

21. E. L. Godkin, "The Eastern Question," *NAR* 124 (1877), 125; [Herbert Tuttle], "Russia as Viewed by Liberals and Tories," *Nation* (April 29, 1880), 321; "Editor's Table," *Appletons'* 2–3 (1877), 377; E. W. Stoughton, "Popular Fallacies about Russia," *NAR* 130 (June 1880), 35; "The Week," *Nation* (April 18, 1878), 256; [E. L. Godkin], "The Turco-Russian Complication," *Nation* (April 19, 1877), 232.

22. [E. L. Godkin], "The Mussulman Bugbear," *Nation* (March 5, 1885), 195; Allan B. Magruder, "The Will of Peter the Great and the Eastern Question," *AM* 42 (1878), 35; William L. Kingsley, "Why Should We Give Our Sympathy to Russia in

the Present War?" *NEYR* 37 (January 1878), 129–130; [E. L. Godkin], "The Change in the Estimate of Russian Power," *Nation* (January 18, 1877), 36; "The German-Austrian Alliance," *Nation* (October 23, 1879), 270; Eugene Schuyler, "United Bulgaria," *NAR* 141 (1885), 470.

23. Herbert P. Tuttle, "The New Eastern Question," *AM* 49 (1882), 808; Robert L. Stanton, "The Political Outlook in France," *PR* 2 (1878), 546, 577; Edward A. Freeman, "Fulfillment of the Berlin Treaty," *PR* 1 (1880), 62; "The German-Austrian Alliance," *Nation* (October 23, 1879), 269; Old Diplomatist, "The Congress of Berlin and Its Consequences," *NAR* 127 (December 1878), 394, 397; Hecker, "The Russian Chancellor," *Catholic World* 24 (March 1877), 730; "The Week," *Nation* (February 26, 1880), 147.

24. [Michael Heilprin], "The Three Emperors' Meeting," *Nation* (October 9, 1884), 304; "Notes," *Nation* (November 12, 1885), 405; "The Week," *Nation* (September 2, 1886), 187; "Notes," *Nation* (June 30, 1887), 554; [Michael Heilprin], "The Panbulgarian Revolution," *Nation* (September 24, 1885), 253; George Rawlinson, "The Future of Turkey," *PR* 2 (1882), 134.

25. "The Week," *Nation* (December 21, 1882), 521; [Michael Heilprin], "Bismarck's Coalition," *Nation* (September 27, 1883), 268; [Michael Heilprin], "Does Germany Anticipate War?" *Nation* (December 9, 1886), 471; [Herbert Tuttle], "Germany and Russia," *Nation* (April 1, 1880), 248; [Michael Heilprin], "The Bulgarian Revolution," *Nation* (August 26, 1886), 173; "The Week," *Nation* (December 30, 1886), 533; [Michael Heilprin], "Rumania in the Eastern Conflict," *Nation* (November 11, 1886), 388; [E. L. Godkin], "What Will Russia Do?" *Nation* (February 9, 1888), 108.

26. "The Week," *Nation* (April 8, 1886), 289; "Summary of the Week's News," *Nation* (February 3, 1887), 91; "The Week," *Nation* (February 10, 1887), 109; "The Week," *Nation* (January 5, 1888), 3; "The Week," *Nation* (October 17, 1889), 303.

27. [Auguste Laugel], "Leroy-Beaulieu on the State of Europe," *Nation* (March 22, 1888), 233; "The Week," *Nation* (December 16, 1886), 489; "The Week," *Nation* (September 15, 1887), 201; "The Week," *Nation* (March 1, 1888), 167; "Politics and the Exposition," *Nation* (June 27, 1889), 522.

28. [E. L. Godkin], "The European Prospect," *Nation* (December 13, 1888), 471; [Auguste Laugel], "The Diplomatic Situation in Europe," *Nation* (June 24, 1875), 422; [Michael Heilprin], "The Approaching German Elections," *Nation* (October 2, 1884), 282; John A Kasson, "The Hohenzollern Kaiser," *NAR* 146 (April 1888), 378; James M. Hubbard, "Warlike Europe," *NAR* 151 (1890), 125; "Life in Russia, First Paper," *Appletons'* 13 (March 20, 1875), 366.

29. [Heilprin], "The Panbulgarian Revolution," 253; George M. Towle, "Turkistan and Its People," *Appletons'* 2–1 (1877), 56; "Editor's Table," *Appletons'* 12 (August 8, 1874), 186; An Old Diplomatist, "The Congress of Berlin and Its Consequences," *NAR* 127 (December 1878), 402.

30. "The Russians at the Gates of Herat," *Nation* (April 23, 1885), 345; "England, Russia, and India," *AM* 56 (1885), 119; [E. L. Godkin], "The Afghan War," *Nation*

(April 16, 1885), 317; [Eugene Schuyler], "The Progress of Russia in Asia," *Nation* (April 19, 1866), 488; W. H. Ray, "Russia in Asia," *AM* 59 (April 1887), 480; Sir Edwin Arnold, "The Duty and Destiny of England in India," *NAR* 154 (1891), 169.

31. Rev. Selah Merrill, "Central Asia," *NEYR* 34 (January 1875), 21; [E. L. Godkin], "The Work for Peace Societies," *Nation* (November 7, 1878), 281; "The Week," *Nation* (March 18, 1869), 203.

32. Towle, "Turkistan and Its People," 56, 57; "An American in Turkistan," *Scribner's* 13 (1876), 211–224; [Raphael Pumpelly], "Turkestan," *Nation* (February 1, 1877), 77.

33. W. L. Fawcett, "The Gate of India," *Century* 30 (1885), 408; Stoughton, "Popular Fallacies about Russia," 528; William L. Kingsley, "Why Should We Give Our Sympathy to Russia in the Present War?" *NEYR* 37 (January 1878), 129–130; Thomas W. Knox, "Russian Policy in Asia," *Harper's* 47 (1873), 219; "England, Russia, and India," *AM* 56 (1885), 119; "Editor's Table," *Appletons'* 9 (May 31, 1873), 730; "Bonvalot's Heart of Asia," *Nation* (June 13, 1889), 493; Selah Merrill, "Central Asia," *NEYR* 34 (January 1875), 28.

34. S. Wells Williams, "Afghanistan and the English," *NEYR* 38 (1879), 95, 98; Zadel B. Gustafson, "Afghanistan," *Harper's* 58 (1878), 618; [R. D. Osborn], "The Last War in Afghanistan," *Nation* (May 2, 1889), 371; [E. L. Godkin], "The English Disaster in Afghanistan," *Nation* (August 5, 1880), 89; [E. L. Godkin], "The Rumor of War," *Nation* (March 19, 1885), 235; "The Week," *Nation* (October 7, 1880), 247; "The Troubles in Afghanistan," *Nation* (September 1, 1881), 168.

35. [R. D. Osborn], "The Merv Oasis," *Nation* (December 21, 1882), 534; "The Russian Menace and the Defence of India," *Nation* (April 30, 1885), 358; "Landsell's Russian Central Asia," *AM* 56 (September 1885), 425; [R. D. Osborn], "Central Asia," *Nation* (June 2, 1887), 475; [R. D. Osborn], "India in 1857," *Nation* (March 19, 1885), 245.

36. "The Revolt in Kabul," *Nation* (September 11, 1879), 169; [E. L. Godkin], "England in Egypt," *Nation* (December 2, 1875), 353; [E. L. Godkin], "The Sudan News," *Nation* (February 26, 1885), 174.

37. [James Bryce], "Clive," *Nation* (October 16, 1890), 307; E. H. House, "The Martyrdom of an Empire," *AM* 47 (May 1881), 619; [Horace White], "English and German Colonies," *Nation* (January 1, 1885), 8.

38. [E. L. Godkin], "The Conservative Succession in England," *Nation* (May 12, 1881), 329–330; "The Political Prospect in England," *Nation* (March 18, 1880), 207; [E. L. Godkin], "England and Russia," *Nation* (August 1, 1878), 65; [James Bryce], "The Condition of Mr. Gladstone's Ministry," *Nation* (September 13, 1883), 220; "The Political Future in England," *Nation* (August 15, 1867), 131; [Alfred Webb], "The British War Spirit and Its Effects upon Character," *Nation* (March 12, 1885), 216; "The Coming Democracy," *Nation* (October 26, 1882), 362.

39. W. S. Stead, "Chinese Gordon," *Century* 28 (1884), 562; "The Week," *Nation* (September 24, 1885), 248; [E. L. Godkin], "The Mussulman Bugbear," *Nation* (March 5, 1885), 195; "General Gordon at Khartum," *Nation* (August 6, 1885), 118; "The

Week," *Nation* (February 12, 1885), 127; "The Week," *Nation* (August 8, 1889), 103; "The Week," *Nation* (December 11, 1890), 453; [E. L. Godkin], "The Sudan News," *Nation* (December 20, 1888), 493.

40. William Clarke, "An English Imperialist Bubble," *NAR* 141 (1885), 65; [E. L. Godkin], "The Capture of Khartum," *Nation* (February 12, 1885), 132; "The Revolt in Kabul," *Nation* (September 11, 1879), 170; [E. L. Godkin], "The English Navy Scare," *Nation* (October 2, 1884), 282; "Notes," *Nation* (February 19, 1885), 155; [Gamaliel Bradford], "Triumphant Democracy," *Nation* (June 3, 1886), 473.

41. [Michael Heilprin], "Bismarck's Coalition," *Nation* (September 27, 1883), 267; "The Week," *Nation* (September 11, 1884), 211; "The French in North Africa," *Nation* (September 22, 1881), 228; "Japan and the Pacific," *Nation* (September 25, 1890), 255.

42. "The Week," *Nation* (February 3, 1887), 89; Theodore Woolsey, "The European Equilibrium," *PR* 2 (1878), 735–736; "The Week," *Nation* (January 15, 1885), 45; [E. L. Godkin], "Wars and Rumors of War," *Nation* (September 4, 1884), 193.

43. "The Week," *Nation* (July 20, 1882), 43; Thomas W. Knox, "The English in India," *Harper's* 58 (1878), 575; "Oriental Experience," *Nation* (May 29, 1884), 471; Theodore Bacon, "Contemporary England," *NEYR* 25 (1866), 634; "The Week," *Nation* (June 2, 1870), 345; "Editor's Table," *Appletons'* 14 (July 31, 1875), 149.

44. [W. P. Garrison], "Perry of Japan," *Nation* (December 1, 1887), 442; William Elliot Griffis, "Nature and People in Japan," *Century* 39 (1889), 239; J. H. Twichell, "The United States and China—The Situation," *AmMiss* 33 (1879), 403; A. A. Hayes Jr., "China and the United States," *AM* 59 (May 1887), 587.

45. Gerrit W. Gong, *The Standard of 'Civilization' in International Society* (Oxford: Clarendon Press, 1984), 10–15. The emergence of American consular courts is discussed in Jeffrey T. Gayton, "From Here to Extraterritoriality: American Sovereignty Within and Beyond Borders," Ph.D. dissertation, University of Wisconsin-Madison, 2003, 58–110 and Eileen P. Scully, *Bargaining with the State from Afar: American Citizenship in Treaty Port China, 1844–1912* (New York, 2001), 21–48.

46. "The Chinese Question," *Nation* (September 9, 1869), 205; "The Week," *Nation* (May 6, 1869), 347; John Addison Porter, "Some Race-Problems in China," *NEYR* 43 (January 1884), 96; John Bonner, "An Empire in Ruin," *OM* 15 (February 1890), 180.

47. S. S. Kim, "Burlingame and the Inauguration of the Co-operative Policy," *Modern Asian Studies* 5 (1971), 351; W. A. P. Martin, "The Renaissance in China," *NEYR* 28 (January 1869), 67–68; [Samuel Wells Williams], "Martin's 'The Chinese'," *Nation* (April 7, 1881), 245.

48. Porter, "Some Race-Problems in China," 96; Richard J. Hinton, "A Talk with Mr. Burlingame about China," *Galaxy* 6 (1868), 614; "The Week," *Nation* (July 23, 1868), 63.

49. "China and the Chinese," *Nation* (May 6, 1869), 358; William Speer, "Democracy of the Chinese," *Harper's* 37 (1868), 839, 850; "Editor's Drawer," *Harper's* 37 (September 1868), 564; Hinton, "A Talk with Mr. Burlingame about China," 613.

50. [W. E. Griffis], "Reed's Japan," *Nation* (April 21, 1881), 281; Rikizo Nakashimam, "Mr. Percival Lowell's Misconception of the Character of the Japanese," *NEYR* 50 (February 1889), 97; "Notes," *Nation* (December 1, 1887), 440; "Notes," *Nation* (March 15, 1888), 217.

51. [E. L. Godkin], "The Chinese Treaty," *Nation* (September 10, 1868), 206; "The New Turn of Affairs in China," *Nation* (September 2, 1869), 185; [John Norton Pomeroy], "Our Duty as Regards China," *Nation* (August 17, 1871), 101.

52. Raphael Pumpelly, "Western Policy in China," *NAR* 106 (1868), 597–598; Pomeroy, "Our Duty as Regards China," 101; "More Light on the Chinese Question," *Nation* (October 14, 1869), 224.

53. "Foreign Lands," *AM* 52 (December 1883), 831; "Chinese Progress," *Nation* (May 13, 1869), 370; Henry Hall, "The Future of American Shipping," *AM* 47 (February 1881), 171; Raphael Pumpelly, *My Reminiscences* (New York, 1918) II: 474; Irwin McDowell, "The Future Influence of China," *OM* 7 (April 1886), 422–428.

54. John Russell Young, "American Influence in China," *NAR* 151 (1890), 193; [W. E. Griffis], "Wilson's China," *Nation* (September 8, 1887), 196.

55. "The Record," *Appletons'* 10 (August 9, 1873), 192; "Editor's Table," *Appletons'* 14 (October 16, 1875), 503; "The Week," *Nation* (November 29, 1883), 440; "The Week," *Nation* (September 6, 1883), 197; "The Chinese in Central Asia," *Nation* (August 14, 1879), 113.

56. "China Speaks for Herself," *AM* 56 (July 1885), 84; Pomeroy, "Our Duty as Regards China," 101; [Henry James, Jr.], "Thomson's Indo-China and China," *Nation* (April 22, 1875), 280; [R. D. Osborn], "A Dilapidated Empire," *Nation* (September 27, 1888), 256; W. A. P. Martin, "The Renaissance in China," *NEYR* 28 (January 1869), 47.

57. "Japanese Treaty Revision," *Nation* (March 29, 1888), 254; S. Wells Williams, "Miss Bird's Japan and Yezo," *NEYR* 40 (1881), 210–211; E. H. House, "The Martyrdom of an Empire," *AM* 47 (May 1881), 619; [Raphael Pumpelly], "The Mikado's Empire," *Nation* (November 23, 1876), 316. In addition to China and Japan, Americans enjoyed extraterritorial rights throughout Egypt and the Ottoman Empire. On Egypt, see P. H. Morgan, "The International Tribunals of Egypt, Part II," *Appletons'* 9 (October 1880), 315; and Nathan J. Brown, "Retrospective: Law and Imperialism: Egypt in Comparative Perspective," *Law & Society Review* 29:1 (1995), 103–126.

58. "The Week," *Nation* (September 27, 1888), 239; A. A. Hayes, "China and the United States," *AM* 59 (May 1887), 591; [E. L. Godkin], "A Strange Doctrine, Indeed," *Nation* (March 11, 1886), 207; J. H. Twichell, "The United States and China— The Situation," *AmMiss* 33 (1879), 403; "China and the United States," *Harper's Weekly* 28 (September 1889), 771.

59. Porter, "Some Race-Problems in China," 96; Thomas W. Knox, "European Influences in Asia," *NAR* 141 (1885), 91–92; "Notes," *Nation* (September 3, 1885), 197.

10. The Future of International Relations

1. Francis Lieber, "An Ode to the Sub-Atlantic Telegraph," *LA* 52 (March 7, 1857), 606; Goldwin Smith, "The Study of History," *AM* 25 (1870), 48; Leigh Mann, "Intellectual Basis of Civilized Peace," *OM* 10 (March 1873), 219; Harry Cadman, "The Future of Industrialism," *OM* 15 (June 1890), 580; Emilio Castelar, "The Republican Movement in Europe," *Harper's* 45 (1872), 384; "An International Panacea," *Nation* (August 9, 1866), 111; Fiske, *Outlines of Cosmic Philosophy* (Boston, 1875), II: 266. Interdependence, wrote Nathaniel Shaler in *Nature and Man,* 150, increased the "sympathetic motives."

2. Edward Self, "Why They Come," *NAR* 134 (1882), 866; [E. L. Godkin], "The Pope's Interference in Germany," *Nation* (February 17, 1887), 137; "Harold Murdock: The Reconstruction of Europe," *AM* 65 (February 1890), 271–272; "The Week," *Nation* (July 21, 1887), 43; "The Plate-Armor and Big-Gun Farce in Europe," *Nation* (November 21, 1872), 330; "The Week," *Nation* (February 19, 1885), 149; "The Prospect of Another European War," *Nation* (May 2, 1872), 285; [A. G. Sedgwick], "[Herbert Spencer's] The Development of Ceremony," *Nation* (August 5, 1880), 98. For some figures on army sizes, see Singer, J. David, Stuart Brenner, and John Stuckey, in Bruce Russett, ed., *Peace, War, and Numbers* (Beverly Hills, 1972), 19–48. By one count the period 1840–1880 witnessed 177 "war-like confrontations." On the explosion of international violence in the period 1840–1880, see Michael Geyer and Charles Bright, "Global Violence and Nationalizing Wars in Eurasia and America: The Geopolitics of War in the Mid-nineteenth Century," *Comparative Studies in History and Society* 38–4 (October 1996), 621–623. On Spencer's prescriptive optimism and descriptive pessimism, see Casper Sylvest, "War, Evolution and Internationalism: The International Thought of Herbert Spencer," paper prepared for the 46th Annual ISA Convention, 1–5 March 2005, Honolulu, Hawaii.

3. "The Week," *Nation* (February 16, 1888), 127; [A. V. Dicey], "Thirty Years of European History," *Nation* (October 23, 1890), 327; Arthur G. Sedgwick, "Unforeseen Results of the *Alabama* Dispute," *AM* 41 (June 1878), 776; "Commerce Versus Glory," *LA* 10 (September 19, 1846), 581.

4. General George W. Wingate, "Comment on Colonel Rice's Paper," *Century* 36 (1888), 943; Gen. Wesley Merritt, "The Standing Army of the United States," *Harper's* 80 (1890), 508; Open letters, C. F. Goodrich, "Our National Defenses, A Suggestion," *Century* 30 (1885), 172; "The Mechanics of Modern Naval Warfare," *NAR* 103 (1866), 185; [C. H. Davis], "Modern Navies," *Nation* (September 23, 1880), 225; Isaac Newton, "Has the Day of Great Navies Passed?" *Galaxy* 24 (1877), 293; C. Sleeman, "The Development of Machine Guns," *NAR* 139 (1884), 365; Woods Pasha, "Naval Tactics of the Future," *NAR* 141 (1885), 269; David D. Porter, "Naval Wars of the Future," *NAR* 148 (1889), 3.

5. "War Versus Civilization," *Appletons'* 5 (March 11, 1871), 298; "The Rehabilitation of Spain," *AM* 9 (March 1862), 361; "Table-Talk," *Appletons'* 6 (December 9,

1871), 665; "Use of Electricity in War," *M&B* 10 (January 1878), 9; Julius Seelye, "Dynamite as a Factor in Civilization," *NAR* 137 (1883), 6; John Millis, "Electricity in War. II. In Land Warfare," *Scribner's* 6 (1889), 425.

6. "Novel Appliances of War," *LA* 5 (May 3, 1845), 226; "The British Fleet," [from Blackwood's Magazine], *LA* 1 (May 25, 1844), 80; "The Week," *Nation* (October 11, 1883), 302; [E. L. Godkin], "The European Armaments," *Nation* (July 1, 1875), 5; Elihu Burritt, "The Two Burdens of War," The *Galaxy* 12 (August 1871), 211.

7. "War Material at the Exposition," *Nation* (January 7, 1869), 14; [E. L. Godkin], "The Prospects of the Centennial Exposition," *Nation* (February 19, 1874), 118; Stephen B. Luce, "The Benefits of War," *NAR* 153 (1891), 681; "Editor's Table," *Appletons'* 14 (October 23, 1875), 535; "War," *The Complete Writings of Charles Dudley Warner* (Hartford, CT, 1904), 113; "The Week," *Nation* (April 18, 1889), 316.

8. M. G. Upton, "Fluctuations in Defensive Warfare," *OM* M. G. Upton 6 (June 1871), 541; "Table-Talk," *Appletons'* 4 (August 30, 1870), 199; John Norton Pomeroy, "The Law of Maritime Warfare as It Affects the Belligerents," *NAR* 114 (1872), 403; Sir Edward J. Reed, "The Navies of the Continent," *Harper's* 74 (1887), 381.

9. Mann, "Intellectual Basis of Civilized Peace," 217; Allan D. Brown, "Torpedoes and Torpedo Boats," *Harper's* 65 (1882), 47. See also Brown's "Naval Architecture, Past and Present," *Harper's* 44 (March 1872), 514–523; Sheldon Amos, "The Laws of War in Their Bearing on Peace," *PR* 2 (1879), 373; David A. Wells, "Are Titles and Debts Property?" *AM* 40 (September 1877), 847; G. Reynolds, "Abyssinia and King Theodore," *AM* 21 (1868), 717.

10. Pomeroy, "The Law of Maritime Warfare," 403; Millis, "Electricity in War," 425; John Fiske, "Manifest Destiny," *Harper's* 70 (March 1885), 585; [E. L. Godkin], "The Spectacular View of War," *Nation* (December 22, 1870), 416; "War Notes," *Appletons'* 4 (October 22, 1870), 501; [Godkin], "The European Armaments," 298. John Whiteclay Chambers, "The American Debate over Modern War, 1871–1914," in *Anticipating Total War*, 241–280, though he has little to say about these years, does make clear the uncertainty that characterized thinking about the future of warfare.

11. "The Week," *Nation* (January 16, 1868), 43; "The Week," *Nation* (November 15, 1883), 405; Edward Atkinson, "The Food Question in America and Europe," *Century* 33 (1886), 247; "A New Danger," *Appletons'* 3 (May 14, 1870), 558; "The Week," *Nation* (March 6, 1890), 193; "Tax for Barbarism," *Scribner's* 14 (1877), 561; "The Week," *Nation* (January 1, 1880), 5; "The Week," *Nation* (October 11, 1883), 302; Joseph F. Thompson, "The Drift of Europe, Christian and Social," *PR* 1 (1878), 758; "Belgium and the Belgians," *AmMiss* 65 (April 1890), 482; Pomeroy, "The Law of Maritime Warfare," 407.

12. James M. Hubbard, "Warlike Europe," *NAR* 151 (1890), 125; [E. L. Godkin], "The French Crisis," *Nation* (May 26, 1887), 444; "The Week," *Nation* (February 19, 1880), 129; Herbert P. Tuttle, "The New Eastern Question," *AM* 49 (1882), 812.

13. M. D. Conway, "More of the Great Show at Paris," *Harper's* 35 (November 1877), 792; Edward Atkinson, "The Relative Strength and Weakness of Nations," *Century* 33 (February 1887), 614; "Editor's Table," *Appletons'* 11 (June 20, 1874), 825; "War versus Civilization," *Appletons'* 5 (March 11, 1871), 298; "Ghosts in Our Foreign Policy," *Century* 23 (1882), 778; "The Week," *Nation* (July 6, 1871), 3; Edward Berwick, "The Great Want of All Civilized Nations," *OM* 14 (July 1889), 79.

14. William Clarke, "In Paris at the Centennial of the Revolution," *NEM* 7 (1889), 104, 106; "Editor's Table," *Appletons'* 13 (June 19, 1875), 787; "New Books," *Appletons'* 2–6 (1877), 575; Andrew Carnegie, "Democracy in England," *NAR* 142 (1886), 79; Henry T. Tuckerman, "American Diplomacy," *AM* 22 (September 1868), 348; "The European Uneasiness," *Nation* (October 8, 1868), 285; Joseph F. Thompson, "The Drift of Europe, Christian and Social," *PR* 1 (1878), 735; "The Close of the 'Entente Cordiale' with Russia," *Nation* (January 18, 1872), 38; T. J. Lawrence, *Essays on Some Disputed Questions of International Law* (Cambridge, MA, 1885), 164.

15. "Passages from Walter Bagehot's 'Physics and Politics,'" *Appletons'* 9 (January 1, 1873), 21; E. L. Godkin, "Commercial Immorality and Political Corruption," *NAR* 107 (1868), 260; "Editor's Table," *Appletons'* 11 (April 11, 1874), 473.

16. [E. L. Godkin], "Peace," *Nation* (December 29, 1870), 433; George E. Pond, "Driftwood: And on Earth, Peace," *Galaxy* 19 (1875), 123; "Editor's Table," *Appletons'* 2–6 (1877), 571; "Table-Talk," *Appletons'* 4 (December 31, 1870), 794; "New Books," *Appletons'* 2–6 (1877), 575; [A. V. Dicey], "Seeley's Life and Times of Stein," *Nation* (September 11, 1879), 180.

17. "How the Sudan Got into English politics," *Nation* (February 28, 1884), 183; "The Week," *Nation* (July 3, 1884), 8; *Nation* (December 29, 1870), 433; "The Conservative Succession in England," *Nation* (May 12, 1881), 328; "The Week," *Nation* (February 10, 1887), 109.

18. [Godkin], "The European Armaments," 5; "National Strength and National Weakness," *Century* 33 (1887), 650; [E. L. Godkin], "Peace," 433; [E. L. Godkin], "The Meetings at the Hague," *Nation* (October 14, 1875), 242; "The Washington Treaty and the Peace Reformers," *Scribner's* 3 (1872), 232; [C. E. Norton], "The Congress of the Peace and Liberty in Lausanne," *Nation* (October 21, 1869), 336.

19. "Notes," *Nation* (April 24, 1879), 286; Clarke, "In Paris at the Centennial of the Revolution," 104, 106; [Godkin], "The Spectacular Theory of War," 416.

20. "The Week," *Nation* (May 25, 1871), 349; "The Week," *Nation* (July 4, 1872), 3; [E. L. Godkin], "The Treaty Muddle," *Nation* (May 16, 1872), 317; Philip Quilibet, "The 'Final and Amicable' Quarrel," *Galaxy* 13 (1872), 553; [A. G. Sedgwick], "The Alabama Job," *Nation* (April 6, 1876), 225; [A. G. Sedgwick and E. L. Godkin], "The Geneva Bill," *Nation* (July 27, 1876), 54.

21. "The Washington Treaty and the Peace Reformers," *Scribner's* 3 (1872), 232; "Editor's Table," *Appletons'* 11 (June 20, 1874), 825; Philip Quilibet, "Arbitration," *Galaxy* 18 (August 1874), 264; S. W. Boardman, "Arbitration as a Substitute for War," *Princeton* 3 (1874), 310; "The Week," *Nation* (July 21, 1887), 43; Henry Cabot

Lodge, "The Fisheries Question," *NAR* 146 (1888), 121; "The Week," *Nation* (July 21, 1887), 43; "The Plate-Armor and Big-Gun Farce in Europe," *Nation* (November 21, 1872), 330. Writers on international law, noting the growing number of arbitration clauses in treaties, tended to be more optimistic.

22. Charles B. Elliott, "The Behring Sea Question," *AM* 64 (February 1890), 184; [Auguste Laugel], "The Unsettled State of Europe," *Nation* (December 7, 1865), 717; "International Arbitration," *NAR* 102 (1866), 502; "Europe's Future," *Catholic World* 13 (April 1871), 80; "What Is the Use of International Law?" *Nation* (May 13, 1869), 36; "The Present Aspect of International Law," *NAR* 103 (1866), 466; Theodore Dwight Woolsey, *Introduction to the Study of International Law*, 2d ed., rev. and enl. (New York, 1864), 33. See also John M. Raymond and Barbara Frischholz, "Lawyers Who Established International Law," *The American Journal of International Law* 76 (October 1982), 816–818. For Woolsey's influence, see George A. King, *Theodore Dwight Woolsey, His Political and Social Ideas* (Chicago, 1956), 78–116.

23. [A. G. Sedgwick], "International Law-Making," *Nation* (October 4, 1883), 289; Martti Koskenniemi, *The Gentle Civilizer of Nations: The Rise and Fall of International Law, 1870–1960* (New York, 2002), 63, 34, 36–38. Koskenniemi further argues (p. 63) that in the United States, as in Europe, "Liberal cosmopolitanism was increasingly limited to the outlook of bourgeois and aristocratic classes." But given the role of the American middle class, the stature of liberal cosmopolitanism remained quite high in the United States even as it was on the defensive in fin-de-siécle Europe. For some prominent Americans involved in creation of the Institut, see Kurt H. Nadelmann, "The Institut de Droit International and American Private International Law: For a Story Society," *The American Journal of Comparative Law* 5:4 (Autumn 1956), 617.

24. Pomeroy, "The Law of Maritime Warfare," 379; "The Treaty of Washington," *Scribner's* 2 (1871), 546; Sedgwick, "International Law-Making," 289; "Belligerents and Neutrals," *Nation* (August 3, 1876), 70.

25. "Belligerents and Neutrals," 69, 70; [A. G. Sedgwick], "A Reaction in International Law," *Nation* (May 6, 1875), 310; J. Russell Soley, "The Effect on American Commerce of an Anglo-Continental War," *Scribner's* 6 (1889), 547; [E. L. Godkin], "Neutrals and Contraband," *Nation* (September 15, 1870), 165; Sedgwick, "International Law-Making," 289.

26. Russell Weigley, *Towards an American Army* (New York, 1962), 284; "An Urgent Measure of National Defense and Our Naval Necessities or Is our Nation Defenceless?" *Century* 34 (1887), 630–631; Eugene Griffin, "Our Sea-Coast Defenses," *NAR* 147 (1888), 69.

27. [E. L. Godkin], "How Should We Fight Spain?" *Nation* (December 4, 1873), 364; Soley, "The Effect on American Commerce of an Anglo-Continental War," 551; F. V. Greene, "Our Defenceless Coasts," *Scribner's* 1 (1887), 57; August V. Kautz, "Our National Military System," *Century* 36 (1888), 938; General George W.

Wingate, "Comment on Colonel Rice's Paper," *Century* 36 (1888), 943; Henry Hall, "The Future of American Shipping," *AM* 47 (February 1881), 174.

28. Pomeroy, "The Law of Maritime Warfare as It Affects the Belligerents," 402; Eugene Griffin, "Our Sea-Coast Defenses," *NAR* 147 (1888), 69; [John William De Forest], "Our Military Past and Future," *AM* 44 (1879), 562; Henry P. Wells, "The Defense of Our Sea-Ports," *Harper's* 71 (1885), 927; Edward F. Qualtrough, "Our Naval Necessities," *OM* 13 (April 1889), 423; Tomas F. Edmands, "Is Our Nation Defenceless?" *NAR* 152 (1891), 381.

29. "Table-Talk," *Appletons'* 6 (September 23, 1871), 357; Griffin, "Our Sea-Coast Defenses," 69; "Open Letters: Our National Defenses. A Suggestion," *NEM* 30 (1885), 173–174; Thorold Rogers, "Causes of Commercial Depression," *PR* 1 (1879), 235; John A. Kasson, "The Monroe Doctrine in 1881," *NAR* 133 (1882), 529.

30. George B. McClellan, "The Army and the Militia," *Harper's* 72 (1886), 295; Kasson, "The Monroe Doctrine in 1881," 525; Joseph Wharton, "National Self-Protection," *AM* 36 (September 1875), 300.

31. "The Week," *Nation* (April 18, 1889), 316; [Carl Schurz], "Mr. Blaine's Manifesto," *Nation* (February 9, 1882), 114; "Our Diplomacy," *Nation* (July 11, 1889), 24; "The Week," *Nation* (February 23, 1882), 156.

32. Anonymous, "The Monroe Doctrine and the Isthmian Canal," *NAR* 130 (1879), 500; "Ghosts in Our Foreign Policy," *Century* 23 (1882), 778; "The Week," *Nation* (November 15, 1883), 403; [Carl Schurz], "A Spirited Foreign Policy," *Nation* (March 9, 1882), 200.

33. Theodore S. Woolsey, *Theodore Dwight Woolsey: His Early Years* (New Haven, 1912), 56, Theodore Woolsey, "The European Equilibrium," *PR* 2 (1878), 735–736; Editorial, *Galaxy* 2 (1866), 581. This was an interesting way of looking at things, for civil liberty, to the extent that it depended on the absence of close and menacing neighbors, was defined at least in part as a spatial phenomenon. M. G. Upton, "Fluctuations in Defensive Warfare," *OM* 6–6 (June 1871), 538.

34. "The Week," *Nation* (July 20, 1882), 43; Luce, "The Benefits of War," 672, 683; Peter T. Austen, "Our Struggle for Existence," *NAR* 149 (1889), 250.

35. "Chapters on Evolution," *Nation* (May 17, 1883), 432; [William James], "Herbert Spencer's Data on Ethics," *Nation* (September 11, 1879), 178; [Calvin Thomas], "The Metaphysics of Chauvinism," *Nation* (July 8, 1886), 28; "Notes," *Nation* (September 20, 1883), 252. For the general absence of social Darwinism in the discourse of this period, see the pathbreaking Robert C. Bannister, *Social Darwinism: Science and Myth in Anglo-American Social Thought* (Philadelphia: Temple University Press, 1979), esp. 226–242.

36. "Skinner's Issues of American Politics," *NAR* 117 (1873), 231; Alfred Thayer Mahan, "The United States Looking Outward," *AM* 66 (December 1890), 817–818.

37. "The Week," *Nation* (April 2, 1885), 271; "Why the War Has Not Been More Disastrous to Trade," *Nation* (September 22, 1870), 185; "The Coast and the Navy," *Century* 37 (April 1889), 952; "The Week," *Nation* (June 1, 1882), 451; Soley, "The

Effect on American Commerce of an Anglo-Continental War," 550, 539, 545; [Godkin], "Neutrals and Contraband," 165; "Belligerents and Neutrals," *Nation* (August 3, 1876), 70; Theodore Woolsey, "The Alabama Question," *NEYR* 28 (July 1869), 619. Given the situation, Godkin at one point suggested quick intervention on behalf of one side or the other as a way of resolving the otherwise intolerable problems posed by neutrality. See [Godkin], "Neutrals and Contraband," 165.

38. [A. G. Sedgwick], "Our Position in Case of a War," *Nation* (April 25, 1878), 271; "The Coast and the Navy," *Century* 37 (April 1889), 952; [Horace White], "The Uses of a Navy," *Nation* (April 18, 1889), 319; "Miscellany," *Appleton's* 13 (January 30, 1875), 159.

39. S. W. Boardman, "Arbitration as a Substitute for War," *Princeton* 30 (1874), 315; "The Week," *Nation* (February 5, 1880), 88; "The Week," *Nation* (August 24, 1882), 145.

40. Henry Cabot Lodge, "Colonialism in the United States," *AM* 51 (May 1883), 626; "American Diplomacy," *AM* 22 (1868), 348; "The American Diplomatic Service," *Nation* (February 27, 1868), 166; [E. L. Godkin], "Something More about Our 'Case'," *Nation* (March 21, 1872), 181.

41. T. R. Lounsbury, "The Two Locksley Halls," *Scribner's* 6 (1889), 252, 253; "The Man Versus the State," *Nation* (July 9, 1885), 40.

42. [E. L. Godkin], "What the United States Does for Europe," *Nation* (January 6, 1881), 4; Charles H. Stockton, "The Reconstruction of the U.S. Navy," *OM* 16 (October 1990), 382.

43. Edward Everett Hale, "The United States of Europe," *Old and New*, III (March 1867), 260–267, reprinted in *The Great Design of Henry IV and the United States of Europe* (Boston, 1909), 77–91; F. V. Greene, "Our Defenceless Coasts," *Scribner's* 1 (1887), 51; "The French Arms Investigation," *Nation* (April 4, 1872), 212.

44. John Fiske, "Manifest Destiny," *Harper's* (March 1885), 578–590. On p. 581 Fiske, fearing the loss of republican purity, appeared to be leaning against an imperialist future for the United States.

45. "Editor's Easy Chair," *Harper's* 70 (1885), 972.

46. [E. L. Godkin], "What the United States Do for Europe," *Nation* (January 6, 1881), 5; "National Strength and National Weakness," *Century* 33 (February 1887), 650; Atkinson, "The Relative Strength and Weakness of Nations," 430; Mann, "Intellectual Basis of Civilized Peace," 219; [W. C. Ford], "A European Zollverein," *Nation* (June 30, 1887), 547.

47. I am thinking here of David Noble's *The End of American History: Democracy, Capitalism, and the Metaphor of Two Worlds in Anglo-American Historical Writing 1880–1980* (Minneapolis, 1985), which argues that Americans "have thought and written as if the United States was absolutely independent, standing apart in its uniqueness from the rest of human experience" (p. 7).

48. James Anthony Froude, "England and Her Colonies," *PR* 1 (1878), 918; "The Week," *Nation* (October 16, 1890), 299.

49. George R. Parkin, "The Reorganization of the British Empire," *Century* 37 (1888), 191–192; Soley, "The Effect on American Commerce of an Anglo-Continental

War," 545; G. T. Ferris, "A Possible War and Its Probable Results," *NAR* 148 (1889), 133; "Culture and Progress," *Scribner's* 10 (1875), 521. This Americocentric view of Anglo-Saxondom was expressed at about the same time by the historian George Bancroft, who saw the United States as the new center of the English-speaking world. See his annual address delivered in New York, April 27, 1886, *Papers of the American Historical Association* II (1887), 7–13.

50. Ernest Lee Tuveson, *Redeemer Nation: The Idea of America's Millennial Role* (Chicago, 1968), 173; Henry T. Tuckerman, "American Diplomacy," *AM* 22 (September 1868), 351; Francis Lieber, "Nationalism and Internationalism," *The Miscellaneous Writings of Francis Lieber* (Philadelphia, 1881), 241; N. C. Meeker, "Commerce and Human Progress," *Appletons'* 2 (September 18, 1869), 150. See Reginald Horsman, *Race and Manifest Destiny: The Origins of American Racial Anglo-Saxonism* (Cambridge, MA, 1981), 293–297 for some antebellum expressions of this outlook.

51. "Editor's Easy Chair," *Harper's* 70 (1885), 972; "New Reasons for Peace," *Century* 24 (1882), 151; Alfred Thayer Mahan, "The United States Looking Outward," *AM* 66 (December 1890), 818; "The Reconstruction of Europe. Harold Murdock," *AM* 65 (February 1890), 272. However, Fiske's introduction to the 1895 edition of Murdock's book expressed optimism: "He who is inclined to take optimistic views of human history must contemplate the course of events during the past forty years with genuine satisfaction" (p. xxiii).

52. Address at Free Trade Hall, Manchester, December 30, 1918, in Arthur Link, ed., *The Papers of Woodrow Wilson* (Princeton, NJ, 1996–1994), 5:352.

53. The first war plan was written in 1896 in anticipation of a confrontation with Spain over the Cuban crisis. The color-coded contingency plans for war with specific countries only began to appear after the formation of a Joint Army Navy Planning Board in 1904.

54. Mark Lilla, *The Reckless Mind: The Intellectual in Politics* (New York, 2001), 57.

Conclusion: Culture as Capability

1. Leslie Butler, *Critical Americans: Victorian Intellectuals and Transatlantic Liberal Reform* (Chapel Hill, NC, 2007), 7–8.

2. John G. Sproat, *"The Best Men": Liberal Reformers in the Gilded Age* (New York, 1968), 275, describes mugwump reformism as "a pathetic failure."

3. For a brief history of the uses of "globalization," see Nayan Chanda, *Bound Together: How Traders, Preachers, Adventurers, and Warriors Shaped Globalization* (New Haven, 2007), 245–270.

4. C. A. Bayly, *The Birth of the Modern World 1780–1914* (Malden, MA, 2004), 306.

5. Giddens, *The Consequences of Modernity* (Stanford, CA, 1990), 8–10; Fiske, *Cosmic Philosophy, III,* (Boston, 1875), 285–286; Ulrich Beck, *Risk Society: Towards a New Modernity,* trans. Mark Ritter (London, 1992); Charles Perrow, *Normal Accidents: Living with High-Risk Technologies* (Princeton, NJ, 1999).

6. Tylor, *Primitive Culture* (New York, 1889), 452.

7. To some extent—but only some—American liberalism paralleled the trajectory of European intellectual trends, where, as one historian puts it, "pessimism began to colonize liberalism in increasingly powerful and sustained ways." See Daniel Pick, *Faces of Degeneration: A European Disorder, c.1848–c.1918* (New York, 1989), 57.

8. Charles Eliot Norton to Chauncey Wright, September 13, 1870, *Letters of Charles Eliot Norton* (Boston, 1913), I: 200 73. This emphasis on elites would also carry over into American conceptions of how an "international mind" could be created in the twentieth century. The emergence of a global culture is inherently problematic, but the ambition of nurturing the formation of powerful liberal cosmopolitan elites capable of influencing policies within their own nations has to a large extent been realized. This idea would eventually become the core of the U.S. government's programs in cultural relations.

9. In speaking of the transforming impact of feminism, for example, Charles Spinosa, Fernando Flores, and Hubert L. Dreyfus, in *Disclosing New Worlds* (Cambridge, MA, 1997), 2, describe it as having "changed the way we see women prior to our reflective judgments." However, except for the minority of internationalists who took this view of the world for granted, liberal internationalism has yet to achieve this kind of transformation in our way of being. It remains very much a contested ideology, or, to revert to Kuhnian language, it is pre-paradigmatic in cultural terms. On the importance of "imaginaries," see Charles Taylor, *Modern Social Imaginaries* (Durham, NC, 2004), 23–30. Perhaps the issue is best conceptualized in terms of culture and ideology. For a splendid discussion of how ideologies are naturalized into an unstable cultural hegemony, see Jean Comaroff and John Comaroff, *Of Revelation and Revolutions: Christianity and Consciousness in South Africa* (Chicago, 1991), 23–27. On the whole, as my closing paragraphs suggest, I would argue that the ideas of Heidegger/Gadamer, Foucault, and Bourdieu, with their emphasis on automatic reproduction, are too narrow and circumscribed to describe what goes on in the modern world.

10. It is another matter entirely to explain how and why liberal international came to have such an outsized influence in the United States. For the purposes of this book, it was enough to treat it as being "there." But any serious attempt at a causal explanation would have to take into account, in addition to religion and commerce, such factors as geography, dislike of European politics, the extent of American involvement in the world, American universalism, and the acculturative power of the melting pot. The account would need to be comparative, too. And then everything would have to be put together along the complex lines of what I suggest in the penultimate paragraph.

11. R.C. Lewontin and Joseph Fracchia, "Does Culture Evolve?" *History and Theory* 38:4 Theme Issue 38: *The Return of Science: Evolutionary Ideas and History* (December 1999), 78.

12. For instance, Robert David Johnson's *The Peace Progressives and American Foreign Relations* (Cambridge, MA, 1995) traces a path in which ideological heirs of the Mugwumps and abolitionists end up as isolationists in the 1930s.

13. Roy D'Andrade, "Culture Is Not Everything," in E. L. Cerroni-Long, ed., *Anthropological Theory in North America* (Westport, CT, 1999), 85–104.

14. Clifford Geertz, *The Interpretation of Cultures* (New York, 1973), 250. This statement of the importance and functioning of culture is open to serious question, as Geertz himself goes on to point out. Geertz's own view is essentially semiotic, focusing on the meaning of culture and its interpretation.

15. See Glen Fisher, *Mindsets: The Role of Culture and Perception in International Relations* (Yarmouth, ME, 1988), 47, for a concise version of the cultural programming argument.

16. On Foucault and culture, see J. M. Balkan, *Cultural Software: A Theory of Ideology* (New Haven, CT: Yale, 1998), 26–27 and Hubert Dreyfus, *Michel Foucault: Beyond Structuralism and Hermeneutics* (Chicago: University of Chicago Press, 1983), xxxvii. For the status of cultural explanations more generally, see Mario Bunge, *The Sociology-Philosophy Connection* (New Brunswick, NJ, 1999), 145–146; Margaret Archer, *Culture and Agency: The Place of Culture in Social Theory* (New York, 1988), 1. For a sympathetic reading of Foucault's understanding of science, see Ian Hacking, "Foucault's Immature science," *Noûs* 13:1 (March 1979), 39–51. For a work that situates Foucault's thought within a French tradition of historical thinking about science, see Gary Gutting, *Michel Foucault's Archaeology of Scientific Reason* (New York, 1989).

17. David J. Elkins and Richard E. B. Simeon, "A Cause in Search of Its Effect, or What Does Culture Explain?" *Comparative Politics* 11:2 (January 1979), 133: "The causal status of any [cultural] assumption is permissive rather than deterministic."

18. Paul Ricoeur, *Lectures on Ideology and Utopia* (New York, 1986), 128: "the independence, autonomy, and consistency of ideologies presuppose another framework than that of superstructure and infrastructure."

19. Without "ancient opinions and rules of life," said Burke, societies "have no compass to govern us, nor can we know distinctly to what port we steer." *Reflections on the Revolution in France* (New Haven, CT, 2003), 67.

20. Julia Annas, "Aristotle on Inefficient Causation," *The Philosophical Quarterly* 32 (October 1982), 319; A. L. Kroeber, "White's View of Culture," *American Anthropologist* 50 (July–September 1948), 410–412; David Bidney, "On the Concept of Culture and Some Cultural Fallacies," *American Anthropologist* 46:1 (January–March 1944), 41; David Bidney, "On the Philosophy of Culture in the Social Sciences," *The Journal of Philosophy* 39:17 (August 1942), 453–454; Margaret Mooney Marini and Burton Singer, "Causality in the Social Sciences," *Sociological Methodology* 18 (1988), 353–354.

21. On cultural crosscurrents, contradictions, and the "myth of cultural integration," see Lawrence E. Harrison, *The Central Liberal Truth: How Politics Can Change*

a Culture and Save it From Itself (New York, 2006), 38; Archer, *Culture and Agency,*
1–21. My original intention was to elaborate on these explanatory factors in an ap-
pendix to this volume, but after a futile effort to provide distilled commentaries on
each, I came to realize, because of the sheer intricacy of the explanatory mechanism,
that it would be better not to discuss them at all rather than to give a thin and anemic
account of what is a vital and full-blooded organon. It was not only the complexity
of the individual elements that proved daunting, but also the tangled connections between them. The relationship between culture and ideology alone could have filled at
least another chapter or book, as could perennial problems of structure and agency
and many other conundrums about which I have either not thought sufficiently or
which I do not have the skill to sort out.

Index

Harvard University Press is a member of Green Press Initiative (greenpressinitiative.org), a nonprofit organization working to help publishers and printers increase their use of recycled paper and decrease their use of fiber derived from endangered forests. This book was printed on 100% recycled paper containing 50% post-consumer waste and processed chlorine free.